NEW YORK REVIEW COMICS

VOICES IN THE DARK

ULLI LUST's acclaimed graphic memoir *Today Is the Last Day of the Rest of Your Life* was called a "sprawling, meditative graphic novel [that] ripples with exuberance" by *The New York Times*. Her published work includes pieces of comics journalism as well as erotic-mythological poems, and she runs the online publishing company www.electrocomics.com. She was born in Vienna and lives and works in Berlin.

MARCEL BEYER is an award-winning German novelist and poet. His 1995 novel *Flughunde*, upon which Ulli Lust's graphic novel is based, was translated in 1997 as *The Karnau Tapes*. He is a visiting professor at the European Graduate School in Saas-Fee, Switzerland.

JOHN BROWNJOHN has translated over 160 books, including works by Willy Brandt, Hans Hellmut Kirst, and Walter Moers.

NIKA KNIGHT is a writer and translator of German literature, most recently Svenja Leiber's novel *The Last Country* (2015).

THIS IS A NEW YORK REVIEW COMIC
PUBLISHED BY THE NEW YORK REVIEW OF BOOKS
435 Hudson Street, New York, NY 10014
www.nyrb.com

The work *Flughunde* by Marcel Beyer was first published in 1995 by Suhrkamp Verlag Frankfurt am Main.
The graphic novel *Flughunde* by Marcel Beyer and Ulli Lust was first published in 2013 by Suhrkamp Verlag Berlin.

First published as *The Karnau Tapes* by Secker & Warburg, an imprint of Vintage. Vintage is part of the Penguin Random House group companies.
The translator has asserted his right to be identified as the translator of the work.

Library of Congress Cataloging-in-Publication Data

Names: Lust, Ulli, 1967- author, artist. | Brownjohn, John, translator. | Knight, Nika, translator. | Graphic novelization of (work): Beyer, Marcel, 1965-. Flughunde.
Title: Voices in the dark / Ulli Lust ; translated by John Brownjohn ; translation adapted by Nika Knight.
Other titles: Flughunde. English.
Description: New York : New York Review Comics, 2017. | Graphic novel based on Flughunde by Marcel Beyer. | Translated from the German. | Description based on print version record and CIP data provided by publisher; resource not viewed.
Identifiers: LCCN 2017008611 (print) | LCCN 2017011495 (ebook) | ISBN 9781681371061 (epub) | ISBN 9781681371054 (paperback)
Subjects: LCSH: Lust, Ulli, 1967---Comic books, strips, etc. | Comic books, strips, etc.--Germany--Translations into English. | National Socialism--Comic books, strips, etc. | World War, 1939-1945--Comic books, strips, etc. | Graphic novels. | BISAC: COMICS & GRAPHIC NOVELS / Literary.
Classification: LCC PN6790.A93 (ebook) | LCC PN6790.A93 L873713 2017 (print) | DDC 741.5/9436--dc23
LC record available at https://lccn.loc.gov/2017008611

ISBN 978-1-68137-105-4
Available as an electronic book; ISBN 978-1-68137-106-1

Printed in Italy
10 9 8 7 6 5 4 3 2 1

VOICES IN THE DARK

BY

ULLI LUST

BASED ON A NOVEL BY

MARCEL BEYER

TRANSLATED BY
JOHN BROWNJOHN

TRANSLATION ADAPTED BY
NIKA KNIGHT

ENGLISH LETTERING BY
KEVIN CANNON

NEW YORK REVIEW COMICS · *New York*

VOICES IN THE DARK

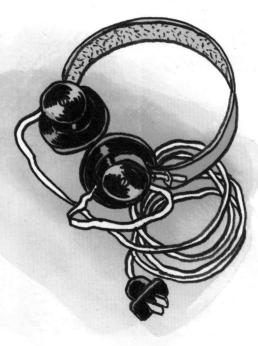

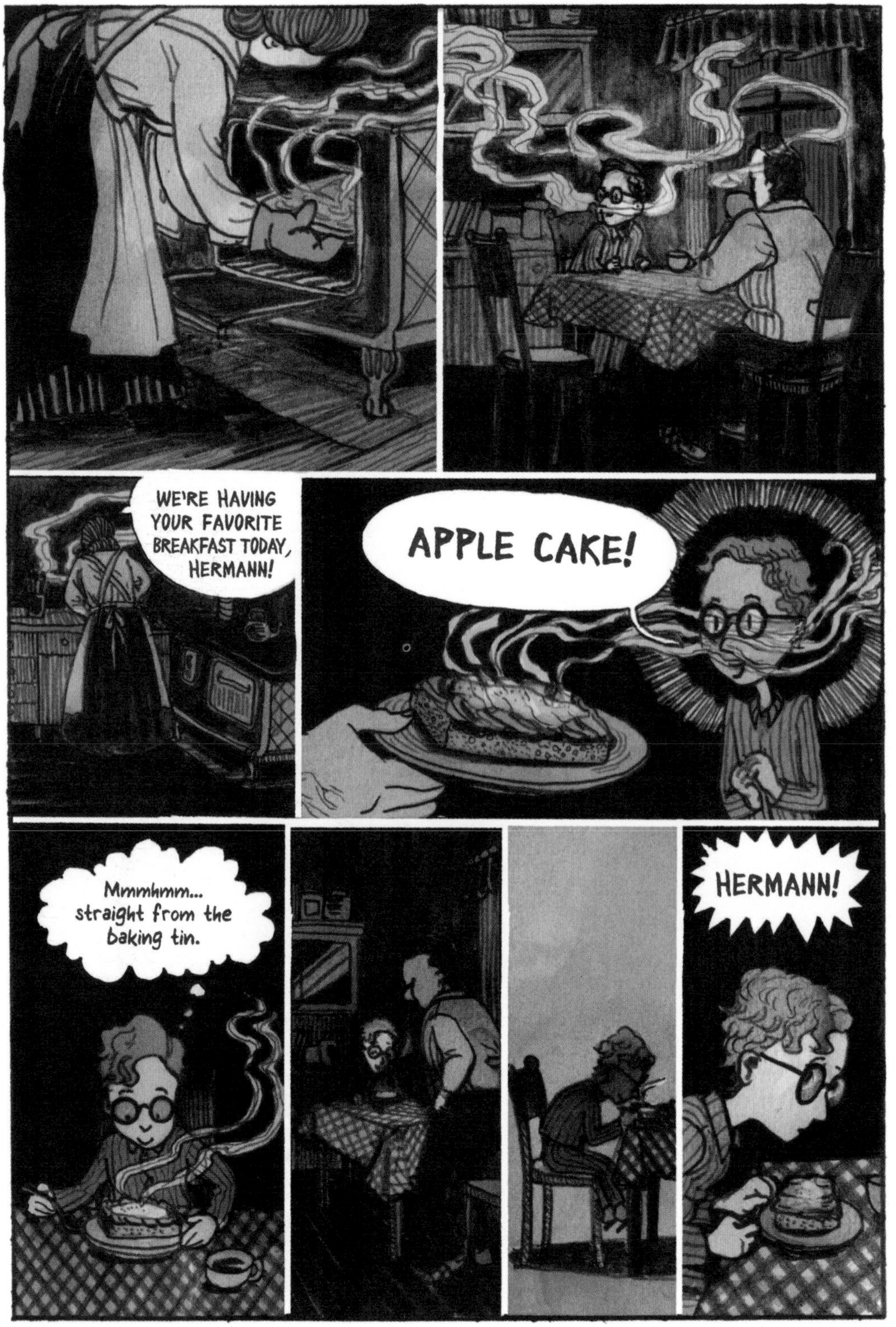
WE'RE HAVING YOUR FAVORITE BREAKFAST TODAY, HERMANN!
APPLE CAKE!
Mmmhmm... straight from the baking tin.
HERMANN!

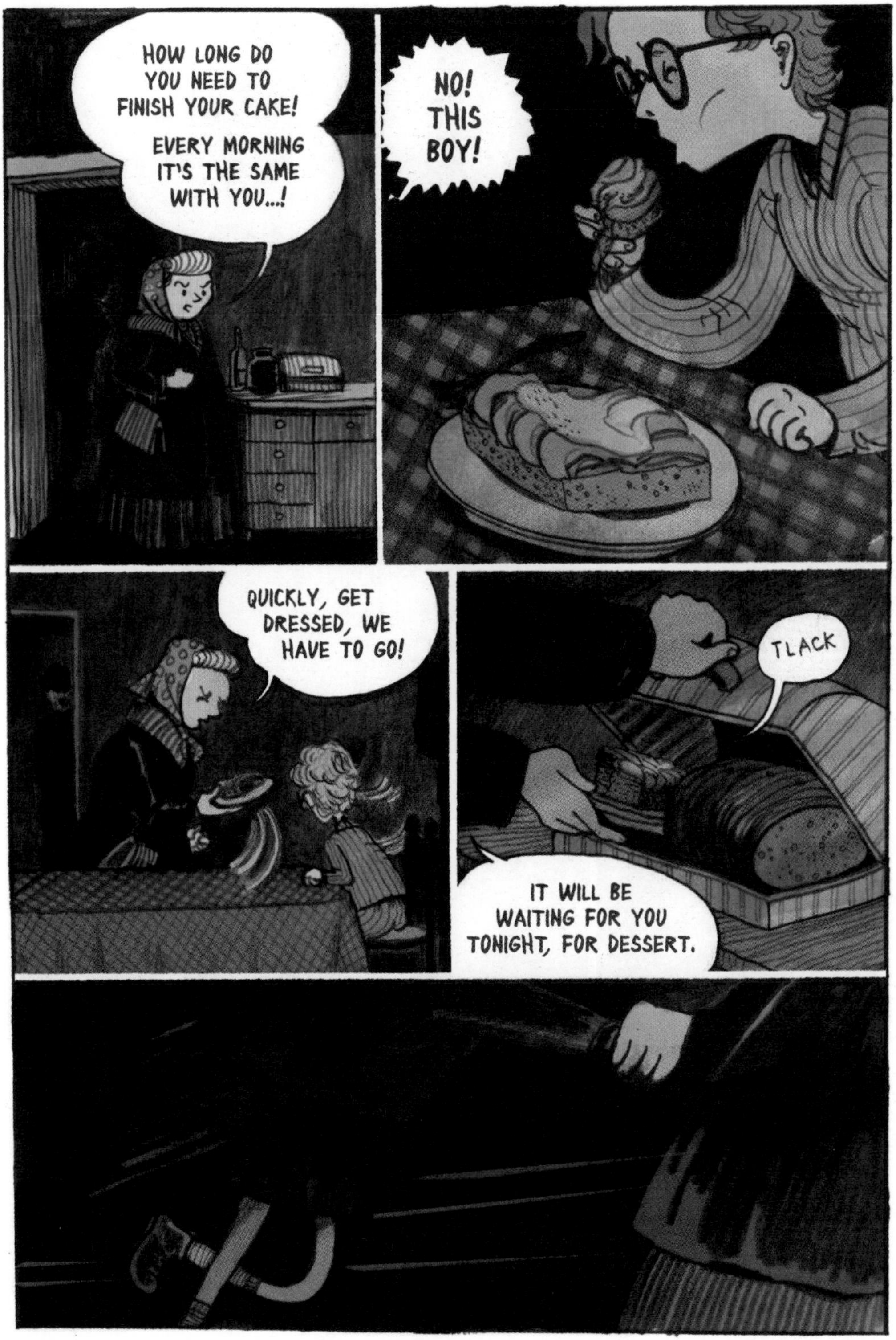
HOW LONG DO YOU NEED TO FINISH YOUR CAKE!
EVERY MORNING IT'S THE SAME WITH YOU...!
NO! THIS BOY!
QUICKLY, GET DRESSED, WE HAVE TO GO!
TLACK
IT WILL BE WAITING FOR YOU TONIGHT, FOR DESSERT.

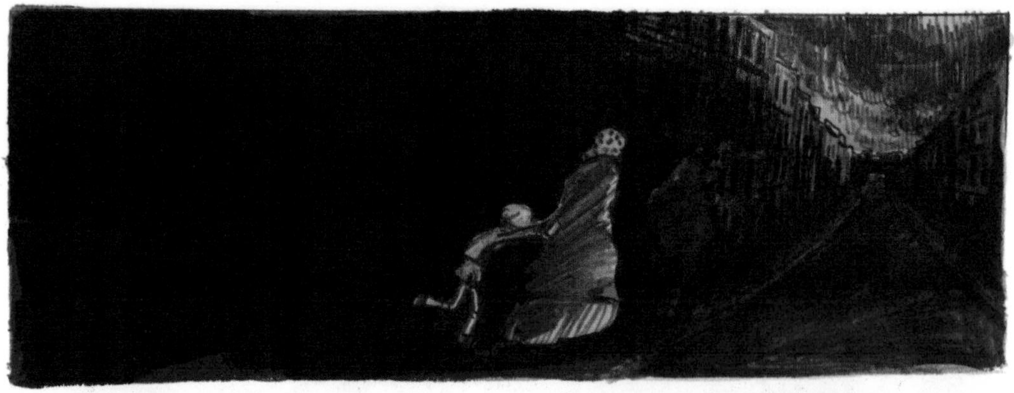

It wasn't within my power to prolong the darkness and make strangers' voices sleep on while a parental hand continued to tow me ...

... through the residue of the night that would inevitably, menacingly, transmute itself into the world of imperious voices, of clamor and commotion.

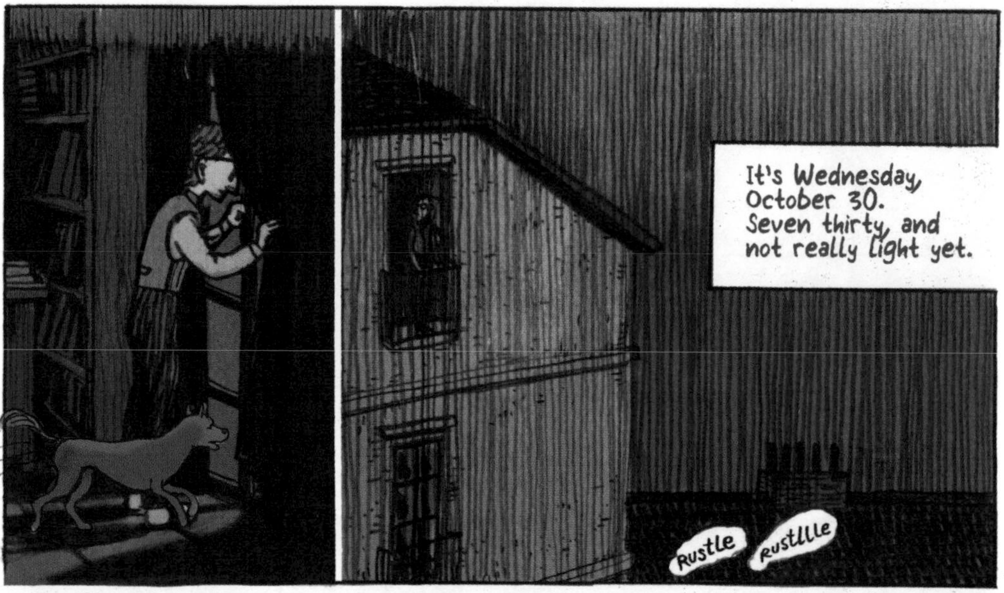

It's Wednesday, October 30. Seven thirty, and not really light yet.
Rustle
rustllle

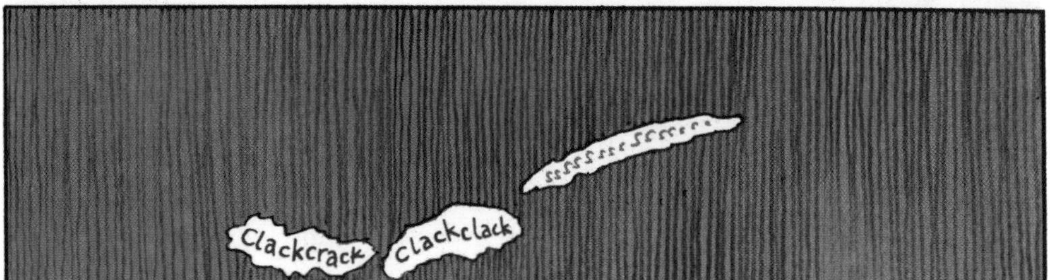

Clackcrack
clackclack

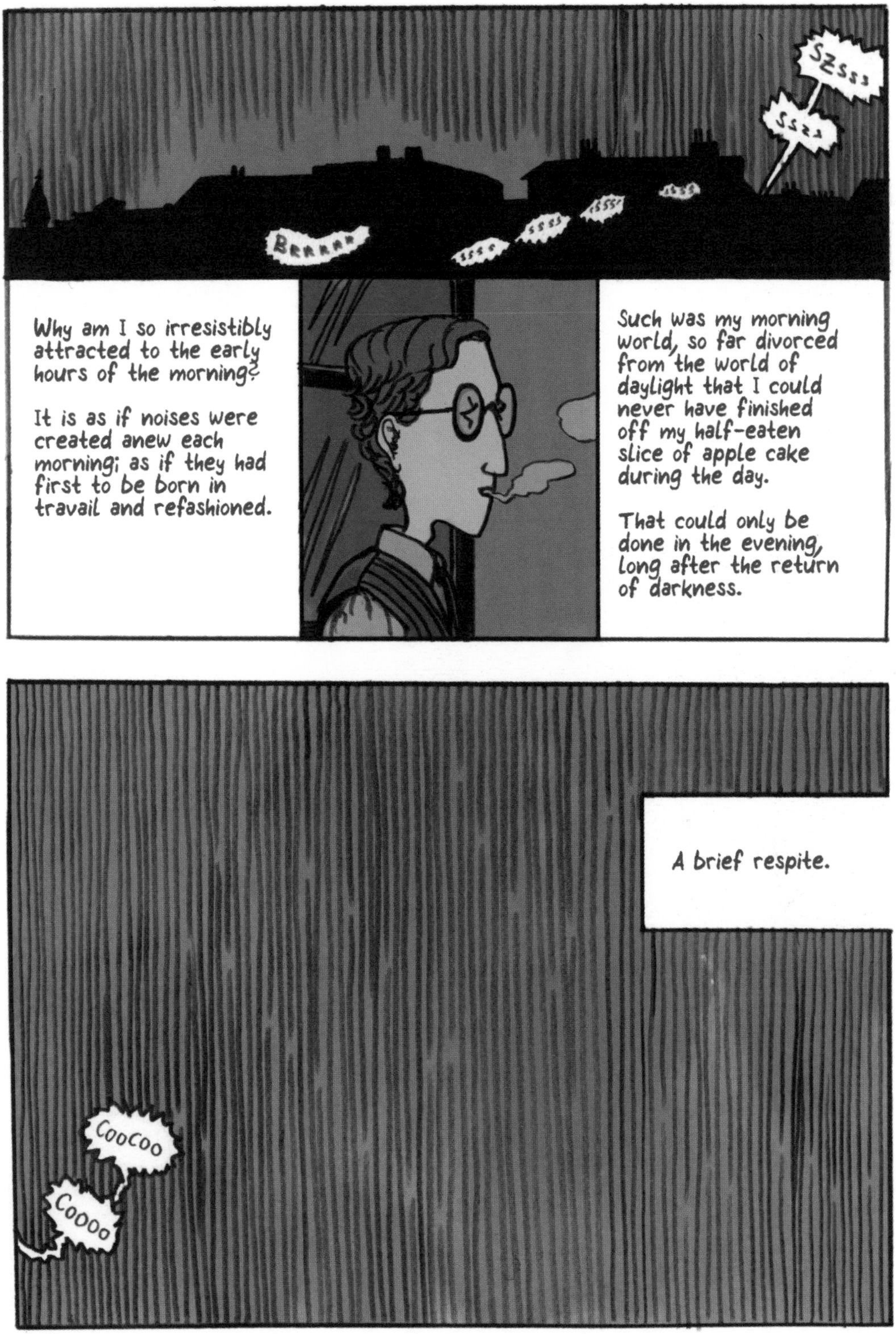
Brrrrr
Why am I so irresistibly attracted to the early hours of the morning?
It is as if noises were created anew each morning; as if they had first to be born in travail and refashioned.
Such was my morning world, so far divorced from the world of daylight that I could never have finished off my half-eaten slice of apple cake during the day.
That could only be done in the evening, long after the return of darkness.
A brief respite.
Coocoo
Coooo

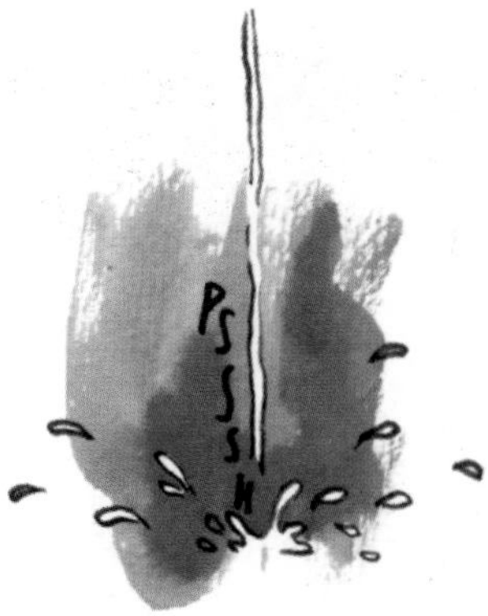
PSSSH

I.

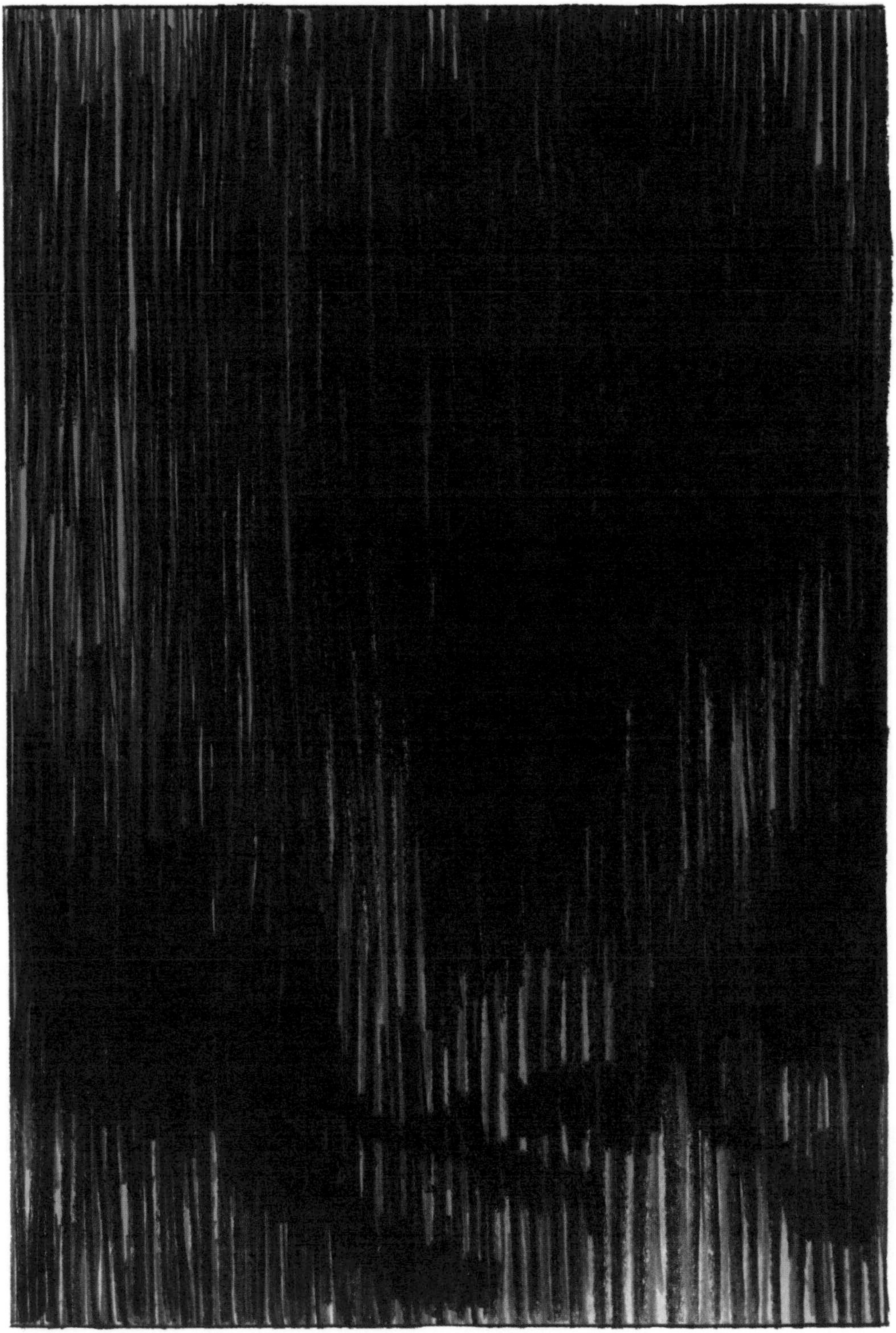

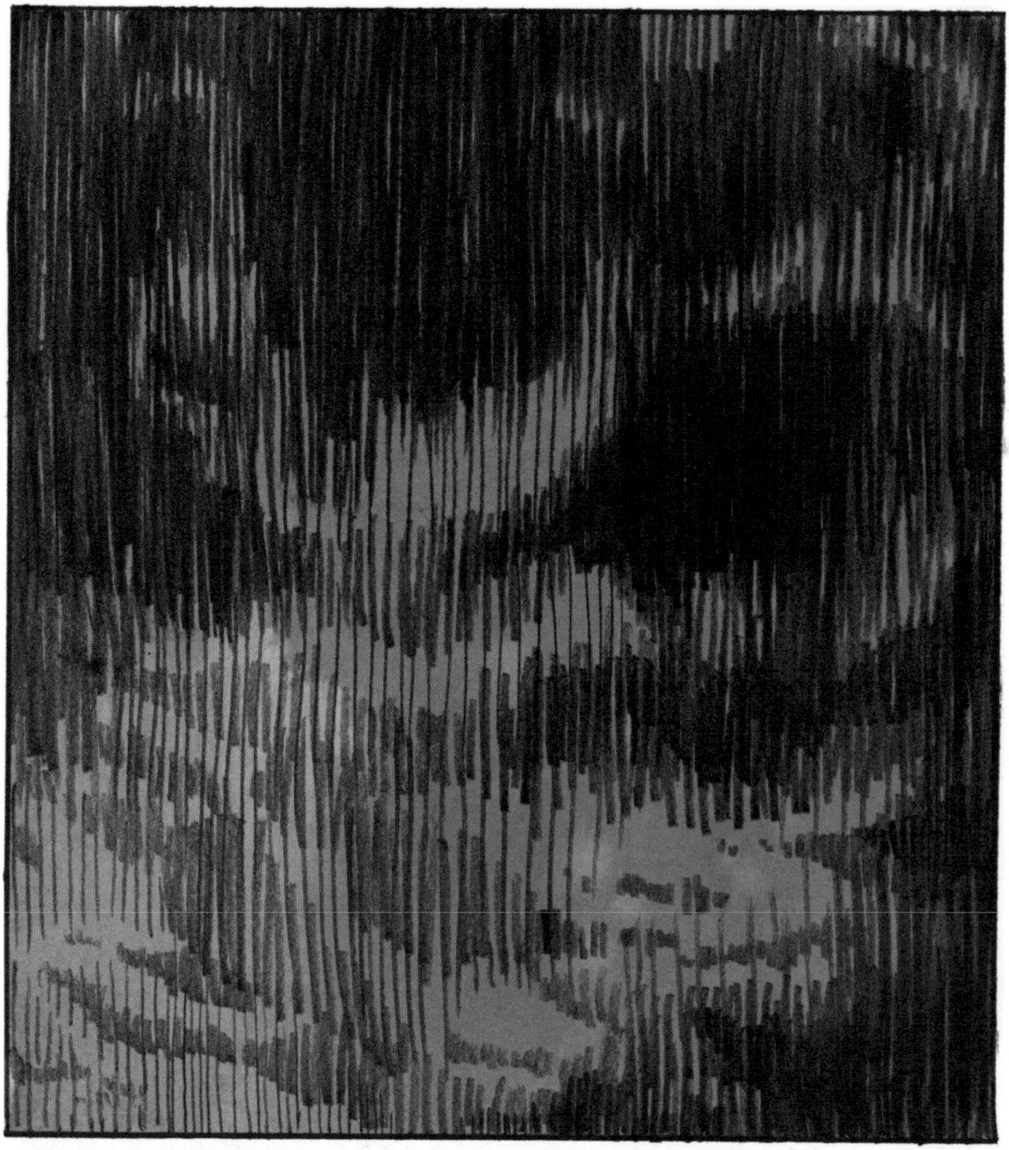

A voice punctures
the dawn stillness.

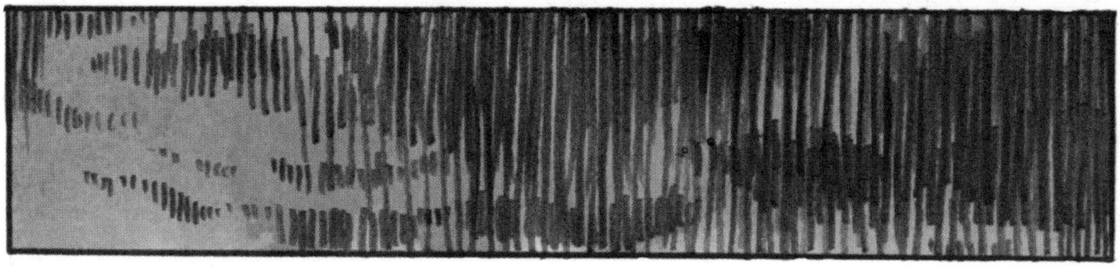

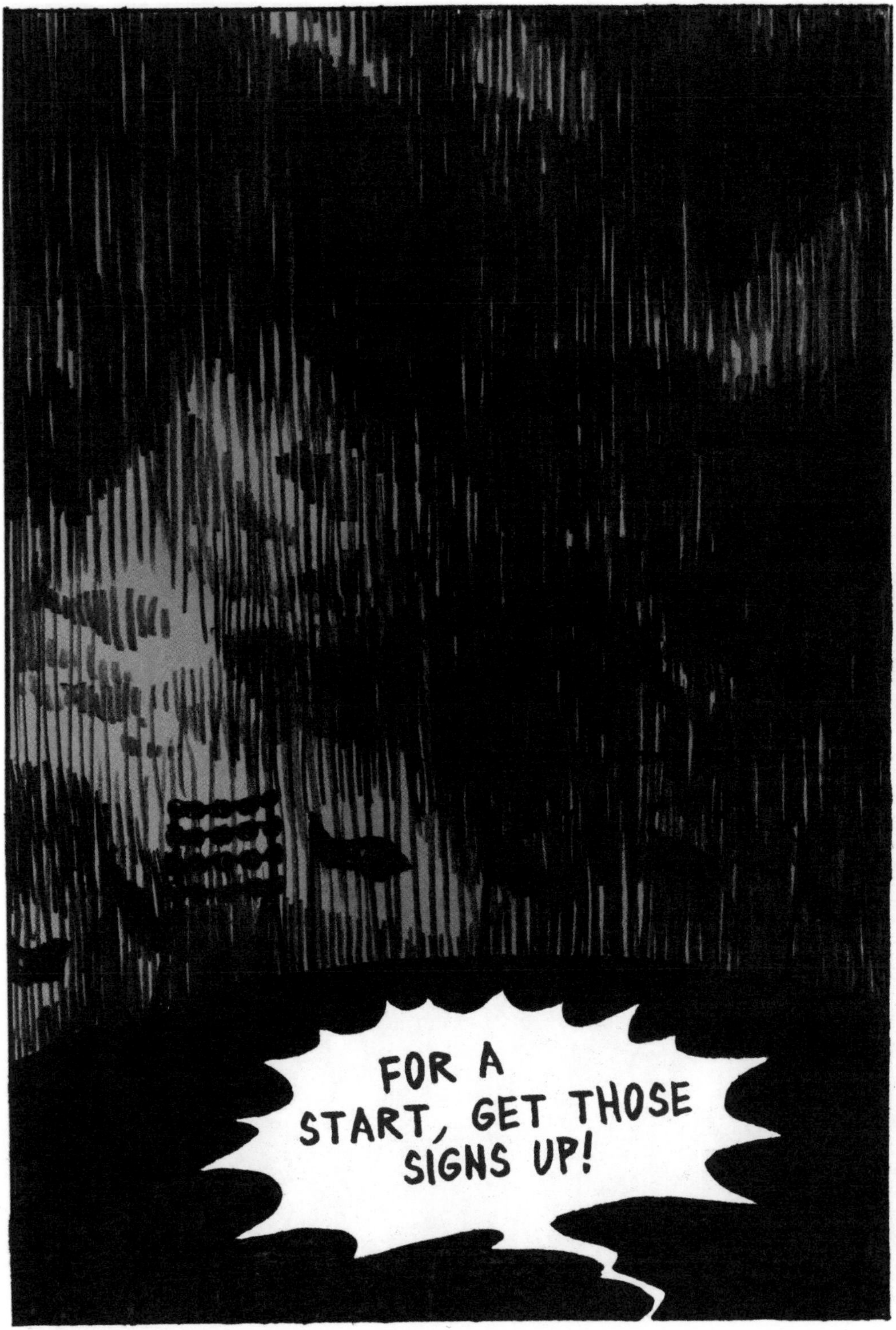
FOR A START, GET THOSE SIGNS UP!

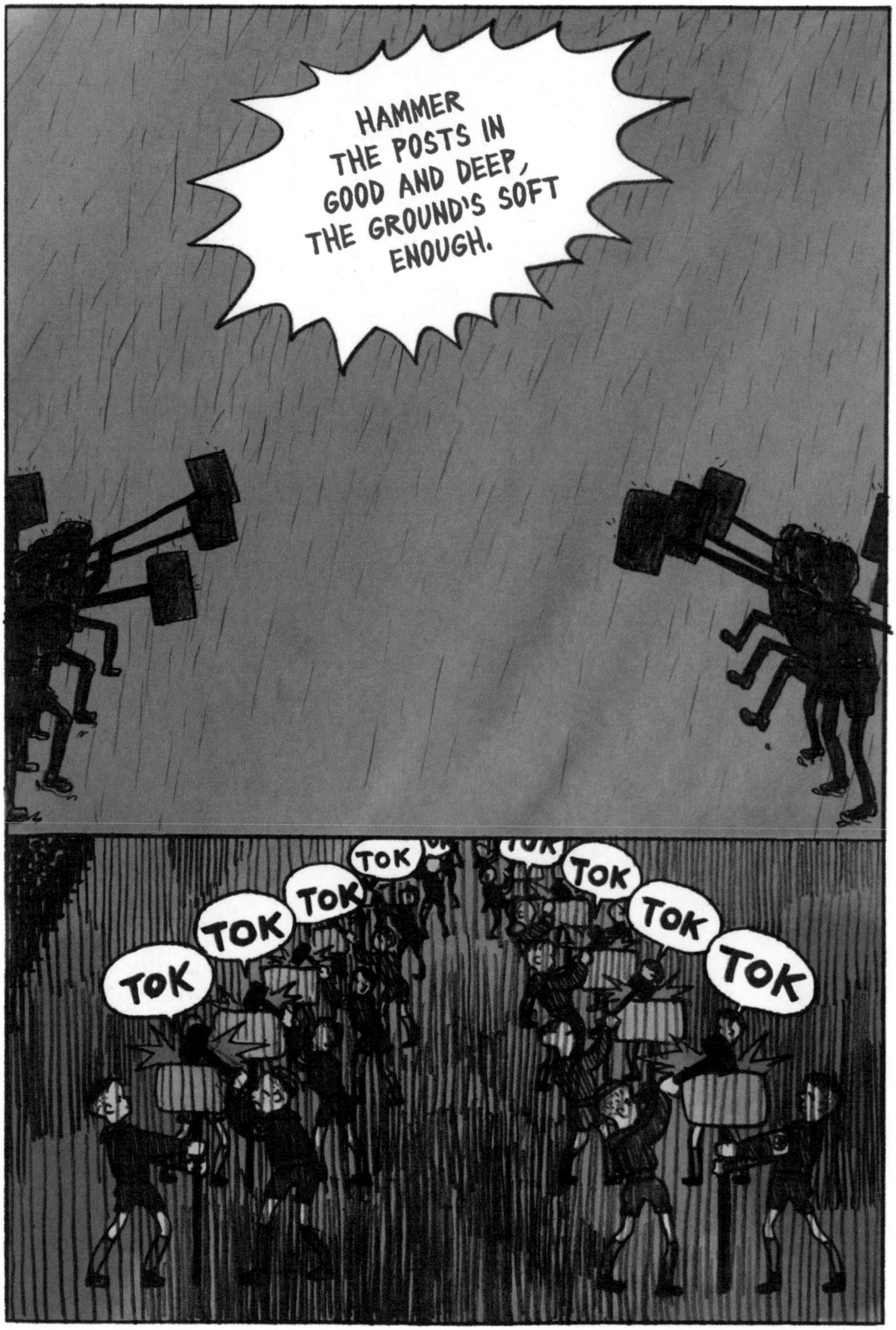
HAMMER THE POSTS IN GOOD AND DEEP, THE GROUND'S SOFT ENOUGH.
TOK
TOK
TOK
TOK
TOK
TOK
TOK

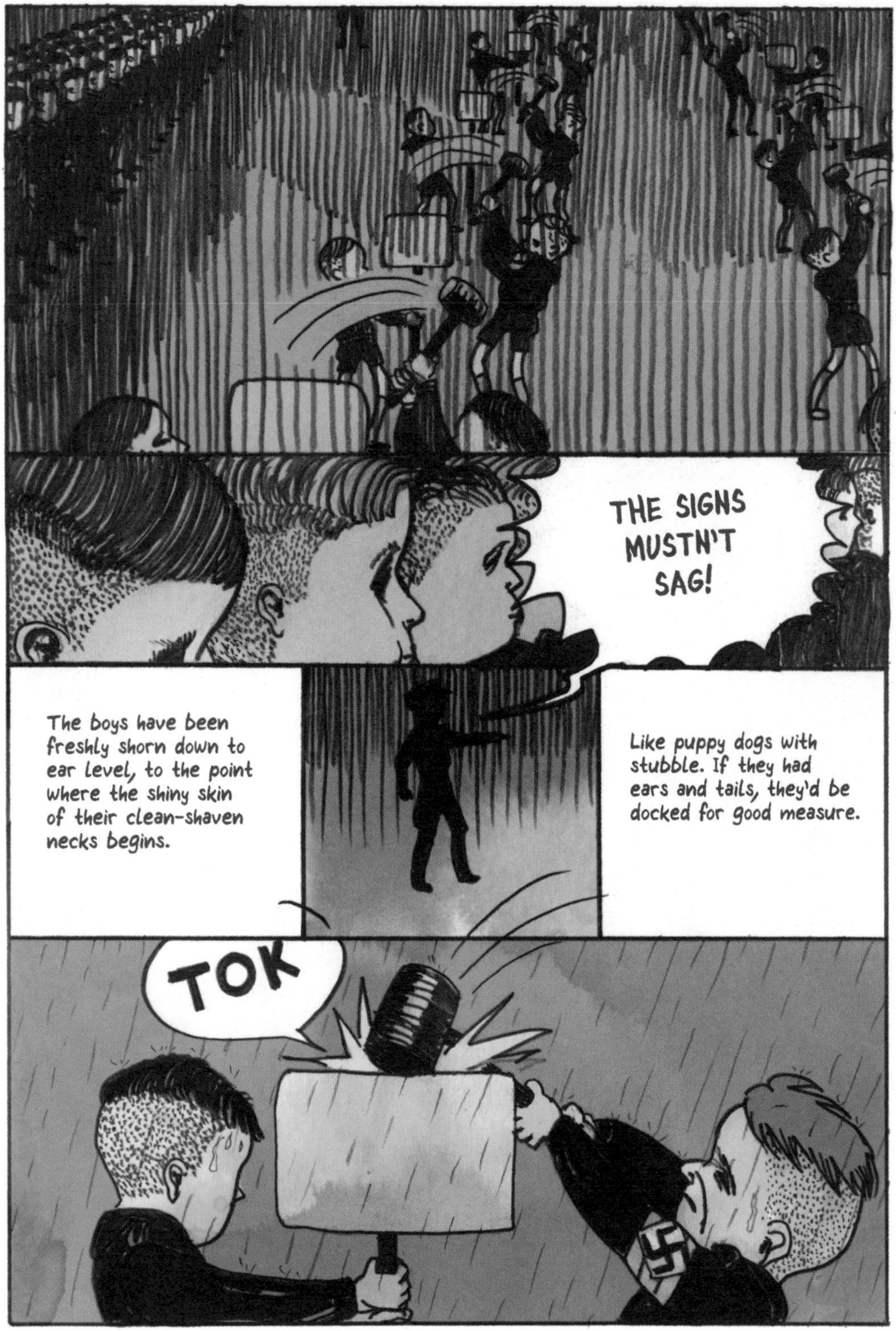
THE SIGNS MUSTN'T SAG!
The boys have been freshly shorn down to ear level, to the point where the shiny skin of their clean-shaven necks begins.
Like puppy dogs with stubble. If they had ears and tails, they'd be docked for good measure.
TOK

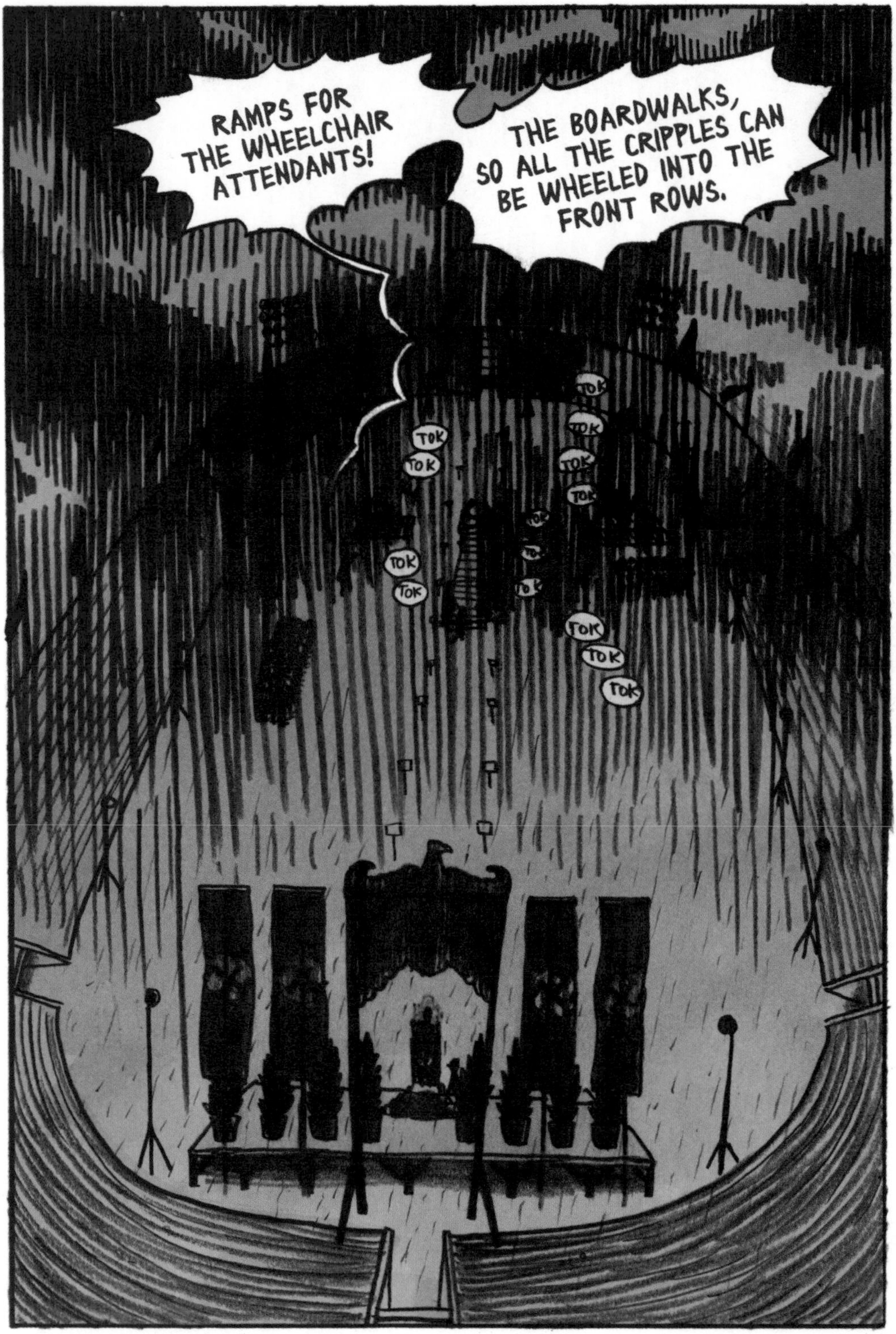
RAMPS FOR THE WHEELCHAIR ATTENDANTS!
THE BOARDWALKS, SO ALL THE CRIPPLES CAN BE WHEELED INTO THE FRONT ROWS.
TOK
TOK
TOK
TOK
TOK
TOK
TOK
TOK
TOK
TOK
TOK
TOK
TOK
TOK
TOK

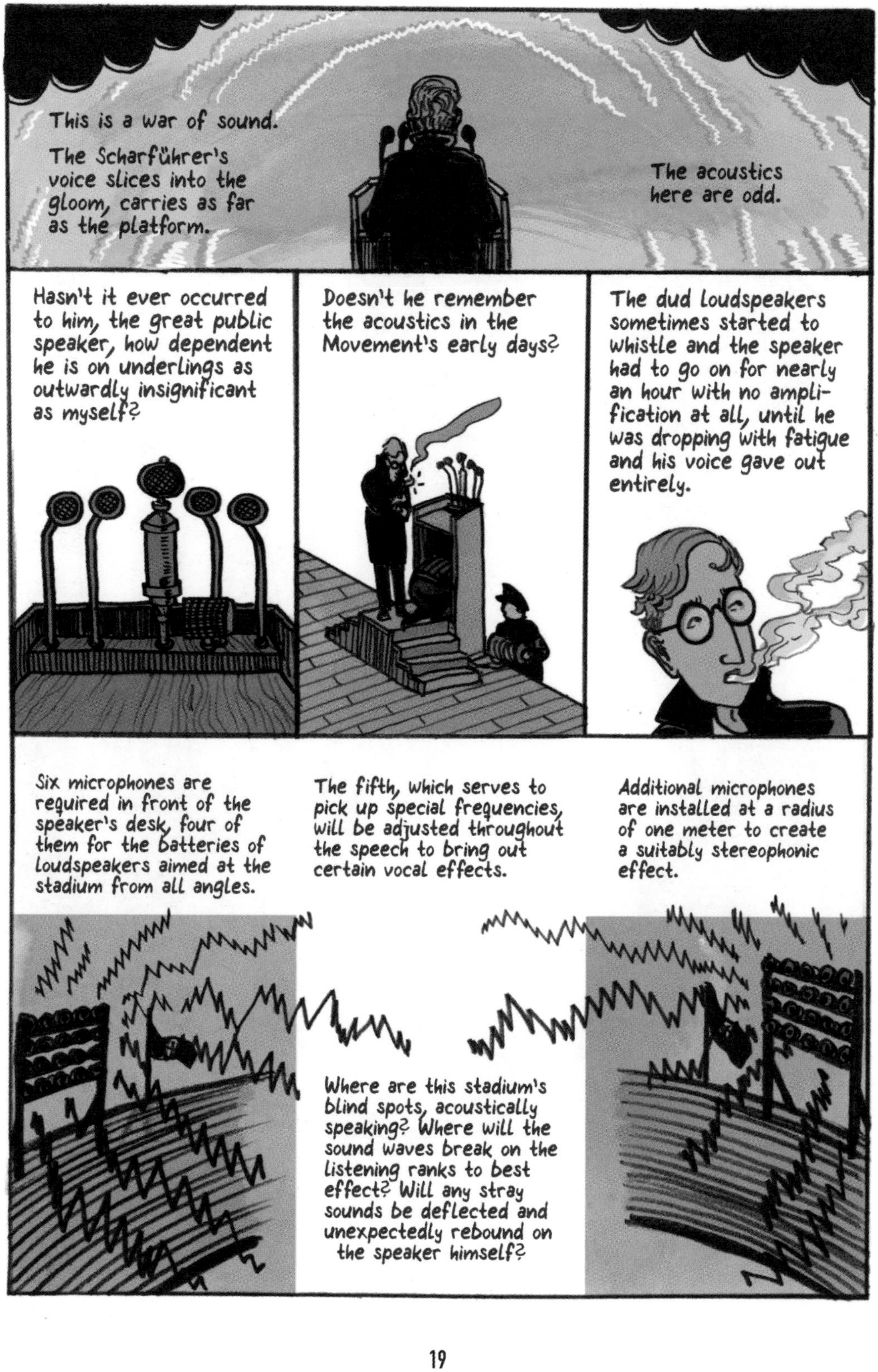
This is a war of sound.
The Scharführer's voice slices into the gloom, carries as far as the platform.
The acoustics here are odd.
Hasn't it ever occurred to him, the great public speaker, how dependent he is on underlings as outwardly insignificant as myself?
Doesn't he remember the acoustics in the Movement's early days?
The dud loudspeakers sometimes started to whistle and the speaker had to go on for nearly an hour with no amplification at all, until he was dropping with fatigue and his voice gave out entirely.
Six microphones are required in front of the speaker's desk, four of them for the batteries of loudspeakers aimed at the stadium from all angles.
The fifth, which serves to pick up special frequencies, will be adjusted throughout the speech to bring out certain vocal effects.
Additional microphones are installed at a radius of one meter to create a suitably stereophonic effect.
Where are this stadium's blind spots, acoustically speaking? Where will the sound waves break on the listening ranks to best effect? Will any stray sounds be deflected and unexpectedly rebound on the speaker himself?

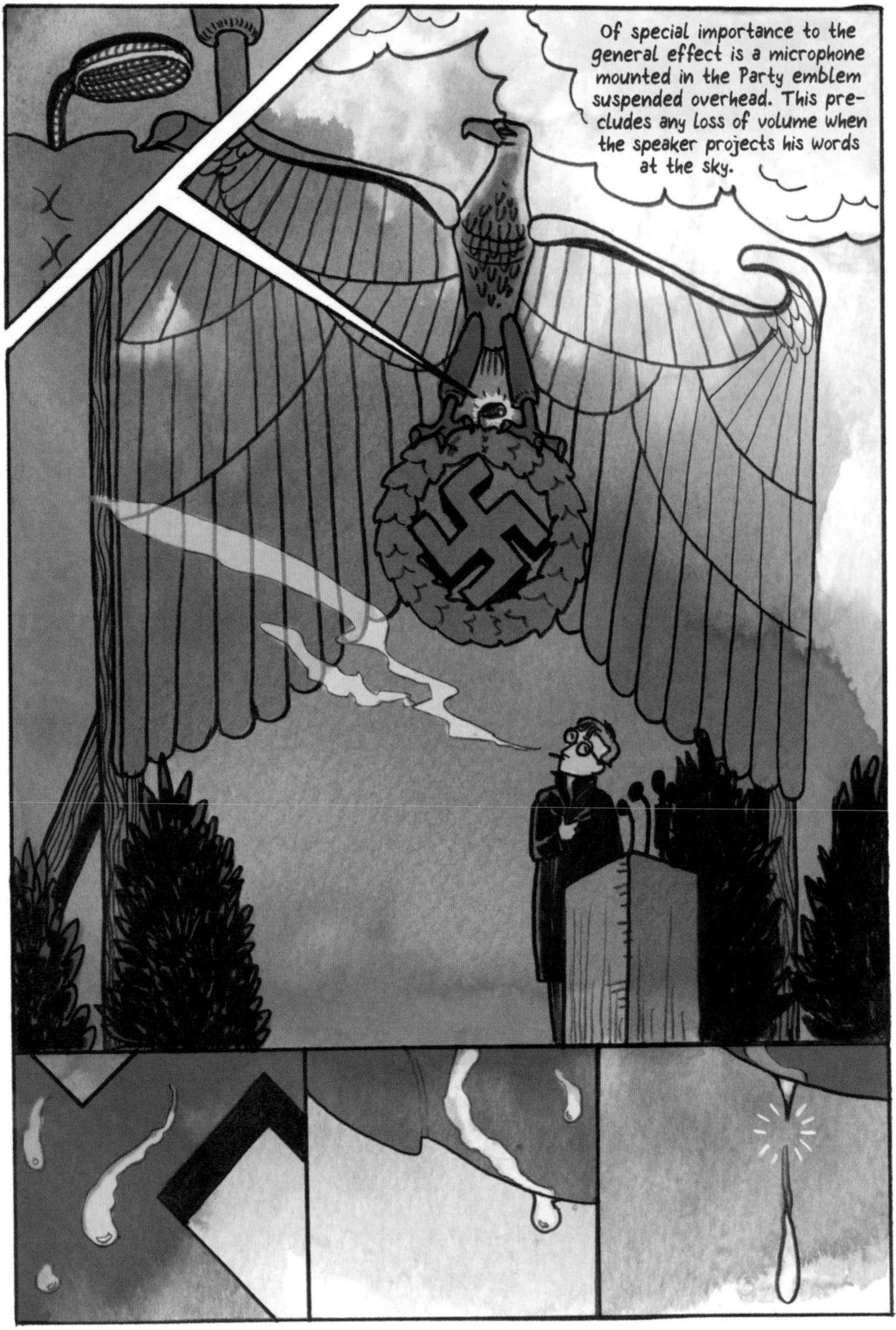
Of special importance to the general effect is a microphone mounted in the Party emblem suspended overhead. This precludes any loss of volume when the speaker projects his words at the sky.

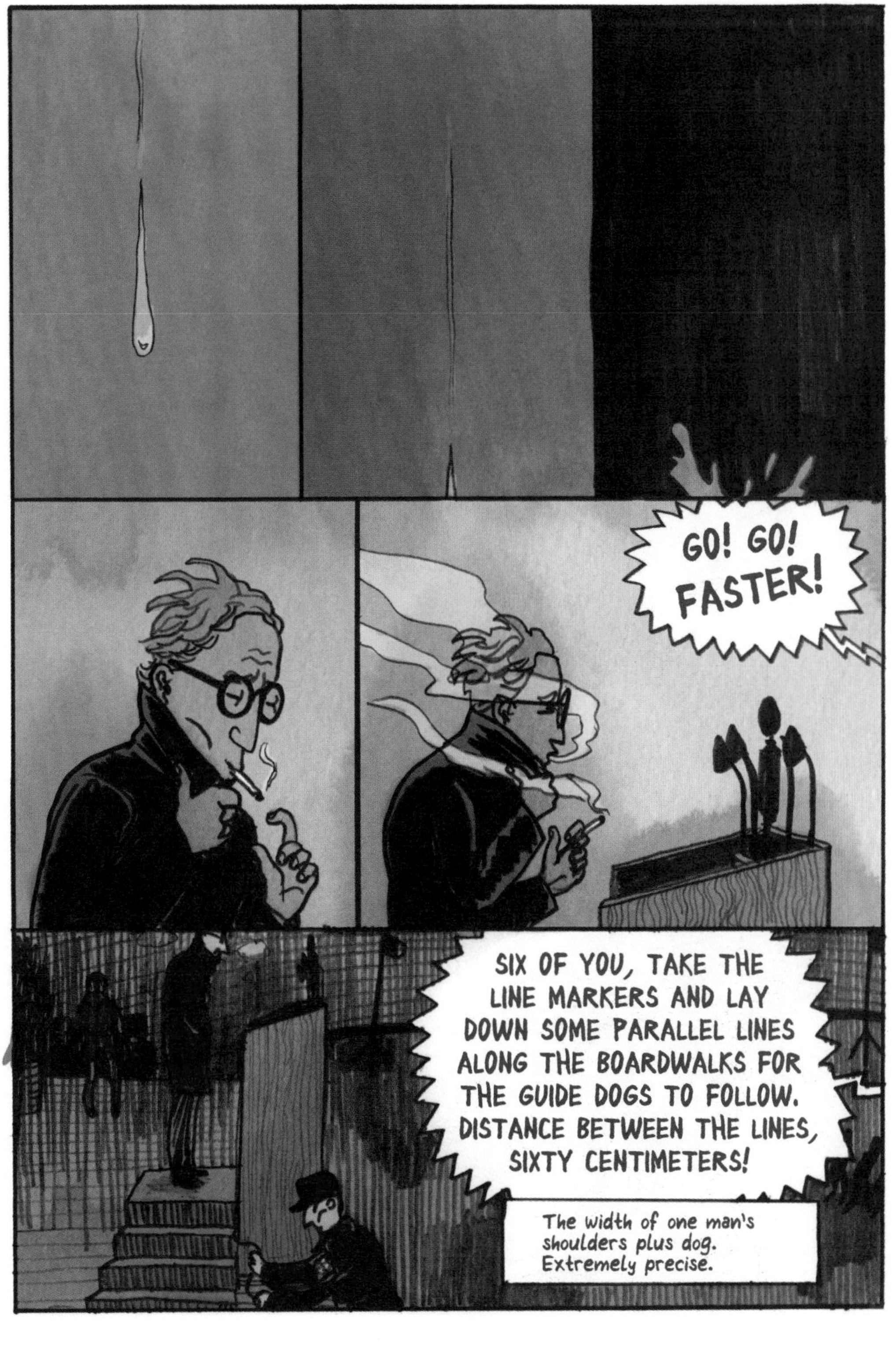
GO! GO! FASTER!
SIX OF YOU, TAKE THE LINE MARKERS AND LAY DOWN SOME PARALLEL LINES ALONG THE BOARDWALKS FOR THE GUIDE DOGS TO FOLLOW. DISTANCE BETWEEN THE LINES, SIXTY CENTIMETERS!
The width of one man's shoulders plus dog. Extremely precise.

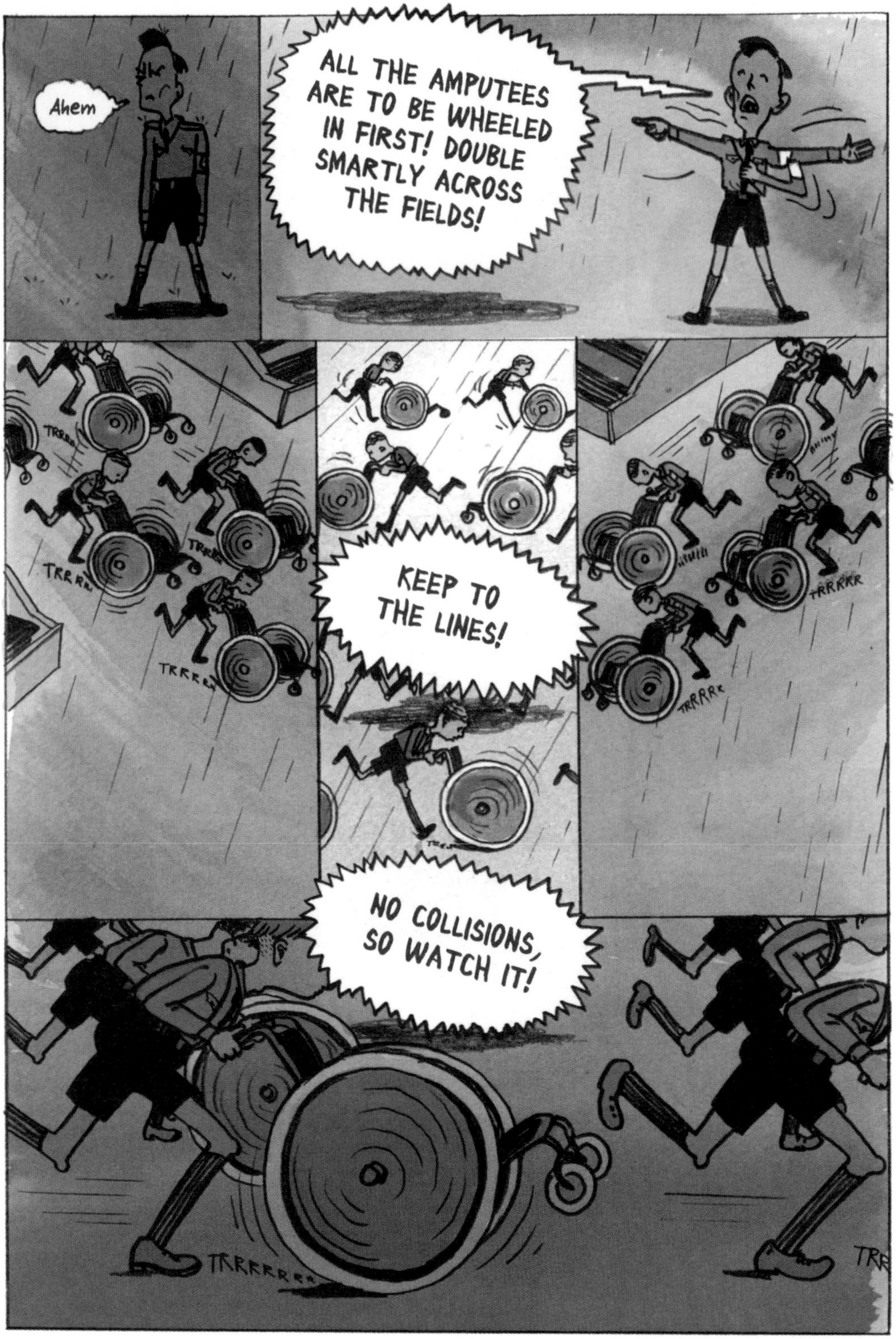
Ahem
ALL THE AMPUTEES ARE TO BE WHEELED IN FIRST! DOUBLE SMARTLY ACROSS THE FIELDS!
TRRRR
TRRRR
TRRRR
TRRRR
KEEP TO THE LINES!
TRRRRR
TRRRRR
NO COLLISIONS, SO WATCH IT!
TRRRRRRRR
TRR

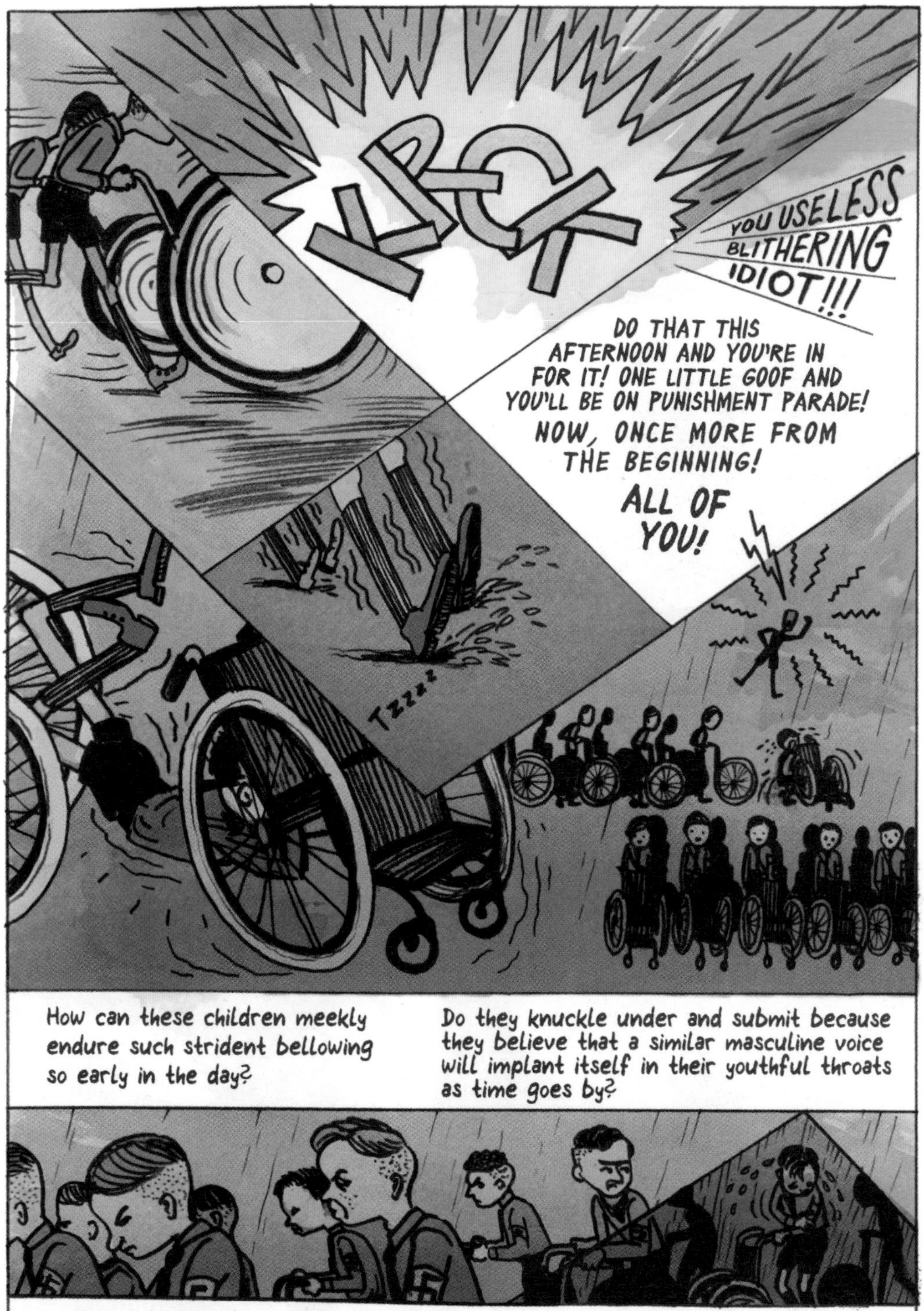
KRCK
YOU USELESS BLITHERING IDIOT!!!
DO THAT THIS AFTERNOON AND YOU'RE IN FOR IT! ONE LITTLE GOOF AND YOU'LL BE ON PUNISHMENT PARADE!
NOW, ONCE MORE FROM THE BEGINNING!
ALL OF YOU!
Tzzzz
How can these children meekly endure such strident bellowing so early in the day?
Do they knuckle under and submit because they believe that a similar masculine voice will implant itself in their youthful throats as time goes by?
The whole procedure will be rehearsed several times more before noon to ensure that the WWI cripples and other disabled veterans are paraded without a hitch.

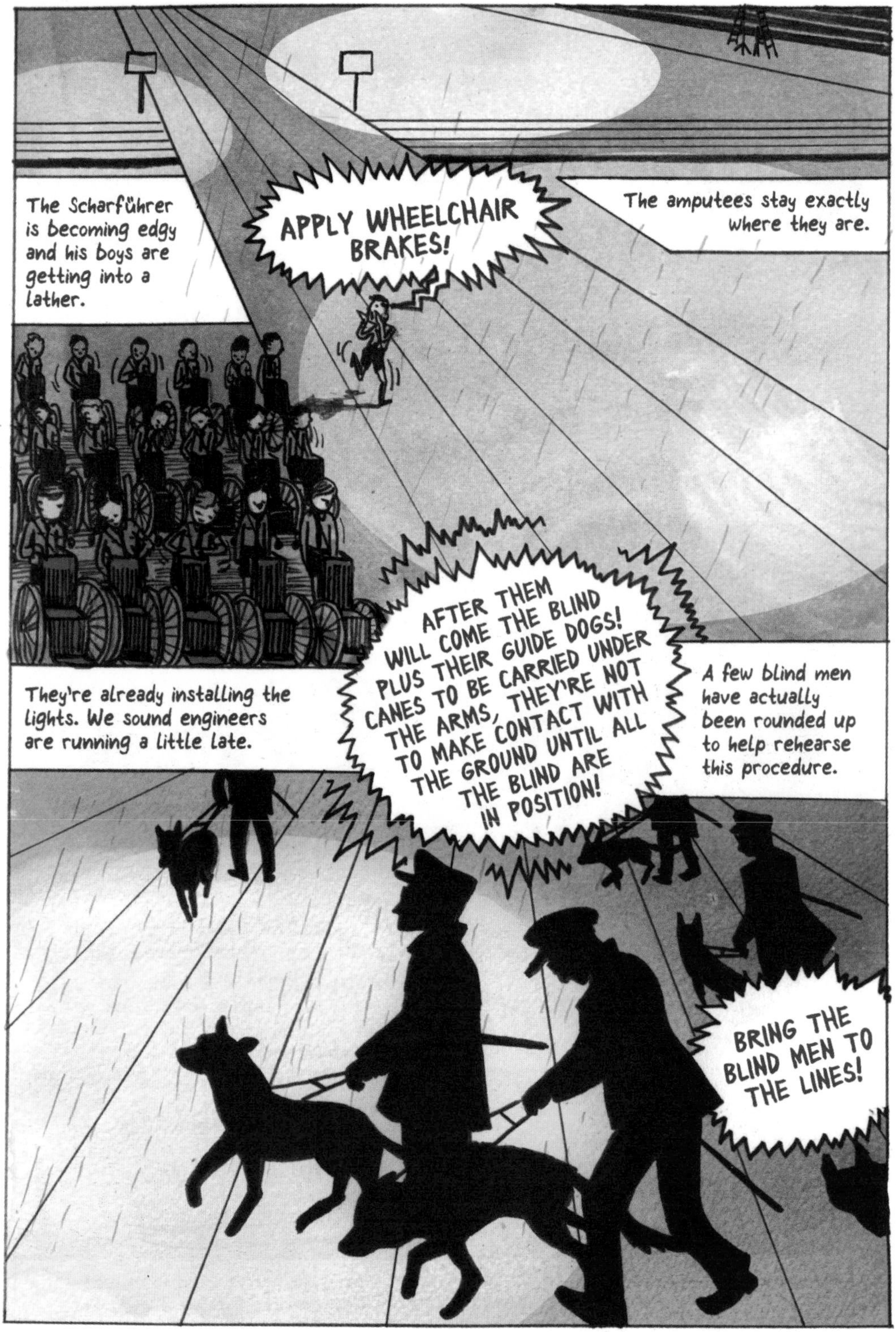
The Scharführer is becoming edgy and his boys are getting into a lather.
APPLY WHEELCHAIR BRAKES!
The amputees stay exactly where they are.
They're already installing the lights. We sound engineers are running a little late.
AFTER THEM WILL COME THE BLIND PLUS THEIR GUIDE DOGS! CANES TO BE CARRIED UNDER THE ARMS, THEY'RE NOT TO MAKE CONTACT WITH THE GROUND UNTIL ALL THE BLIND ARE IN POSITION!
A few blind men have actually been rounded up to help rehearse this procedure.
BRING THE BLIND MEN TO THE LINES!

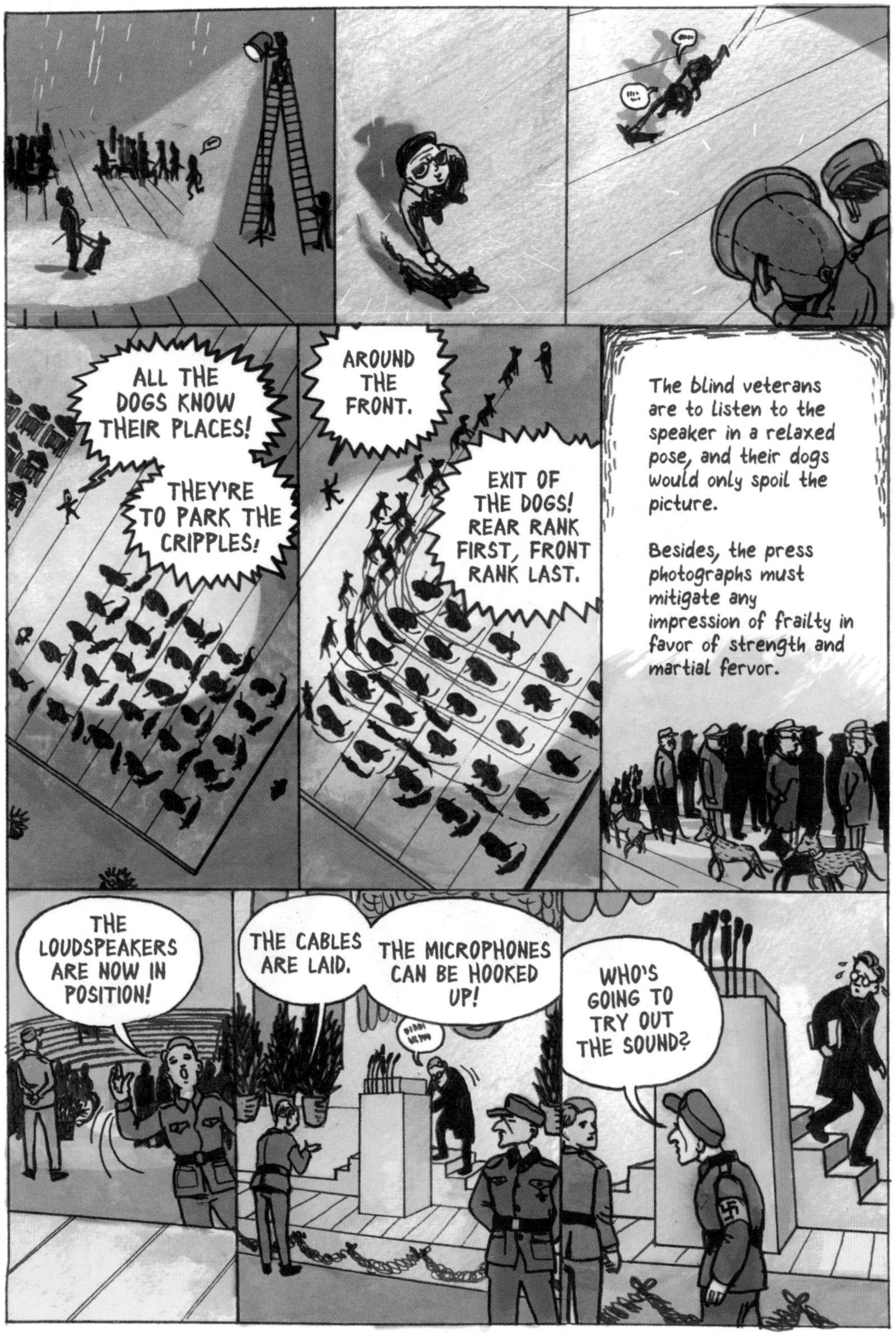
ALL THE DOGS KNOW THEIR PLACES!
THEY'RE TO PARK THE CRIPPLES!
AROUND THE FRONT.
EXIT OF THE DOGS! REAR RANK FIRST, FRONT RANK LAST.
The blind veterans are to listen to the speaker in a relaxed pose, and their dogs would only spoil the picture.
Besides, the press photographs must mitigate any impression of frailty in favor of strength and martial fervor.
THE LOUDSPEAKERS ARE NOW IN POSITION!
THE CABLES ARE LAID.
THE MICROPHONES CAN BE HOOKED UP!
WHO'S GOING TO TRY OUT THE SOUND?

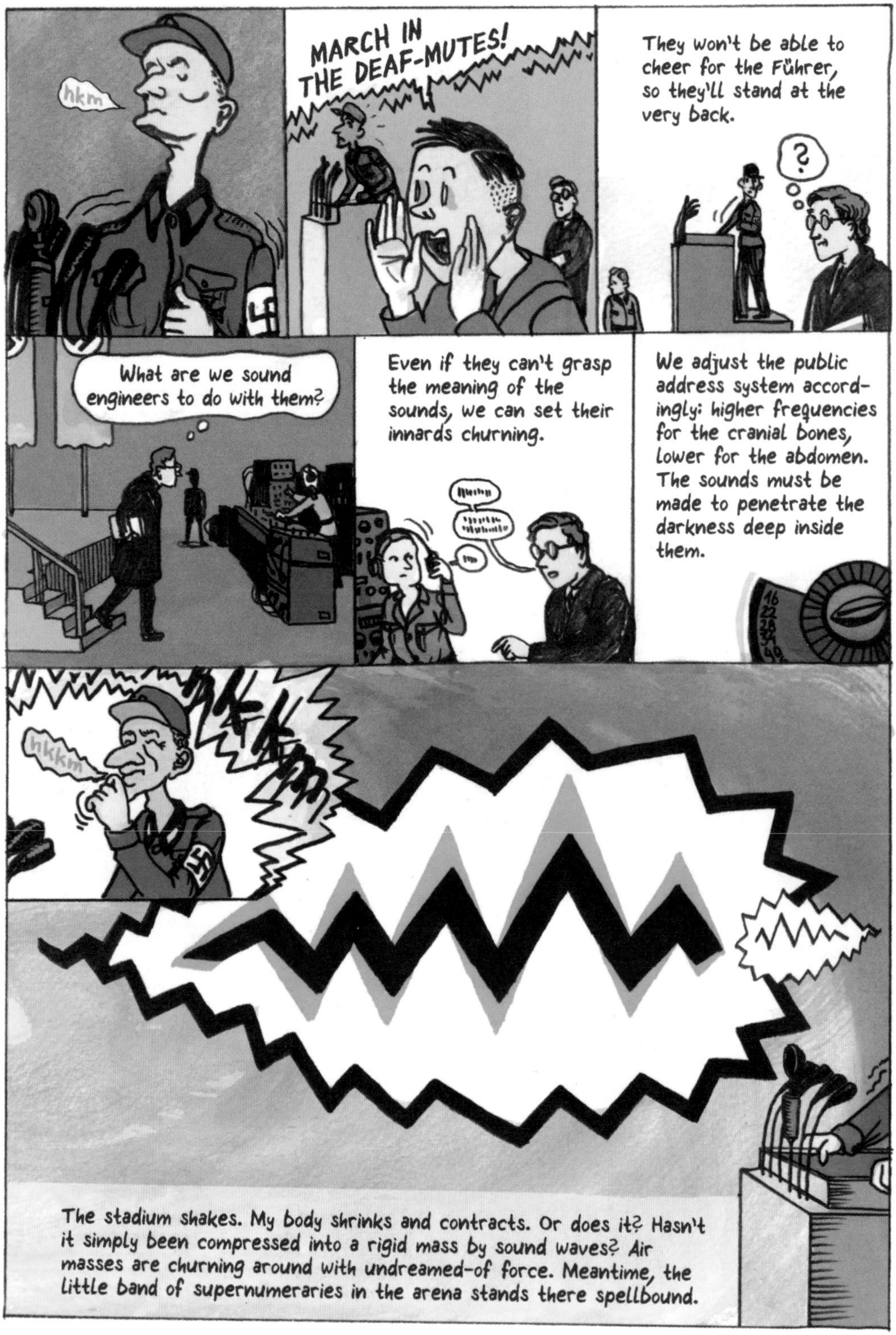
hkm
MARCH IN THE DEAF-MUTES!
They won't be able to cheer for the Führer, so they'll stand at the very back.
?
What are we sound engineers to do with them?
Even if they can't grasp the meaning of the sounds, we can set their innards churning.
We adjust the public address system accordingly: higher frequencies for the cranial bones, lower for the abdomen. The sounds must be made to penetrate the darkness deep inside them.
hkkm
The stadium shakes. My body shrinks and contracts. Or does it? Hasn't it simply been compressed into a rigid mass by sound waves? Air masses are churning around with undreamed-of force. Meantime, the little band of supernumeraries in the arena stands there spellbound.

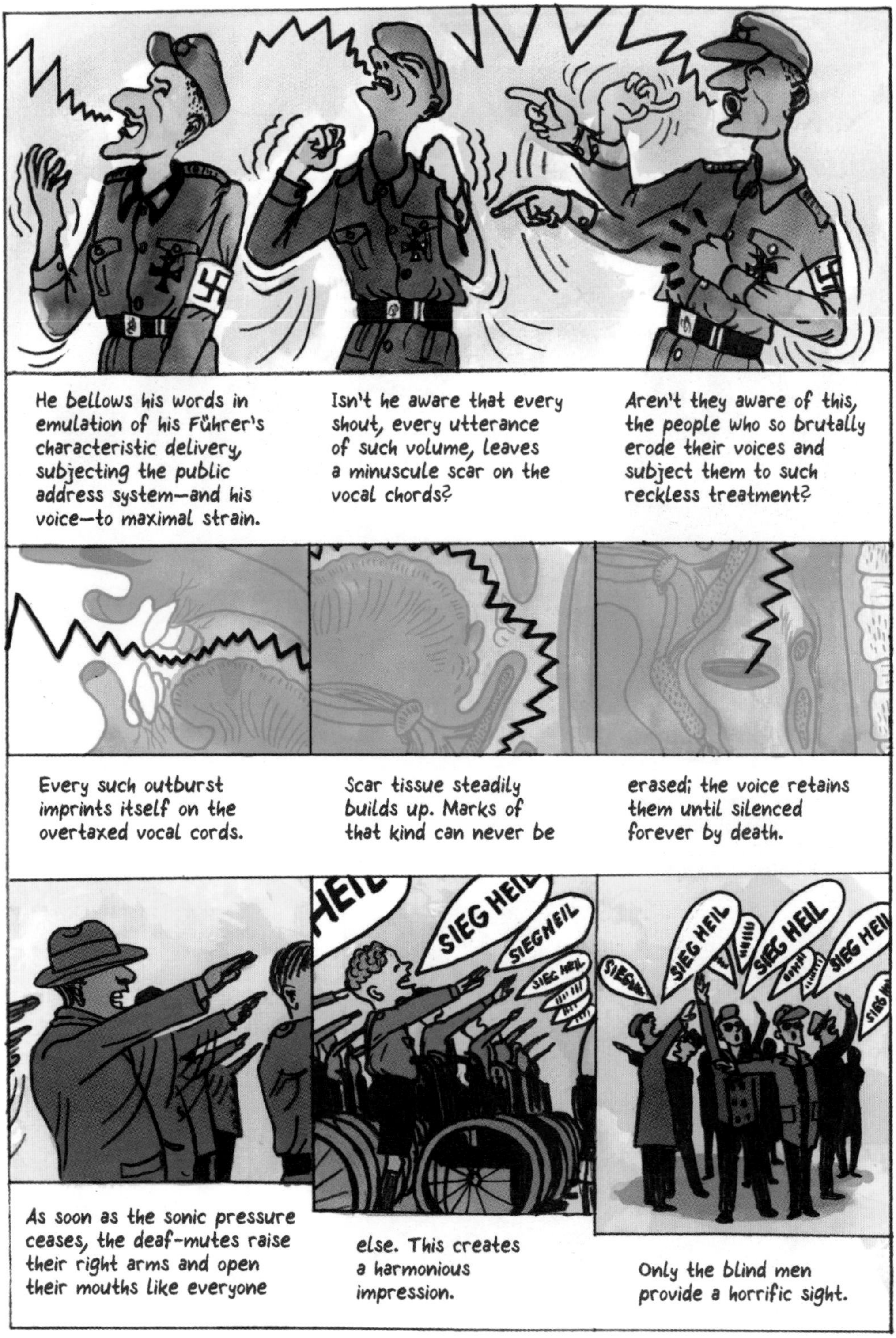
He bellows his words in emulation of his Führer's characteristic delivery, subjecting the public address system—and his voice—to maximal strain.
Isn't he aware that every shout, every utterance of such volume, leaves a minuscule scar on the vocal chords?
Aren't they aware of this, the people who so brutally erode their voices and subject them to such reckless treatment?
Every such outburst imprints itself on the overtaxed vocal cords.
Scar tissue steadily builds up. Marks of that kind can never be
erased; the voice retains them until silenced forever by death.
As soon as the sonic pressure ceases, the deaf-mutes raise their right arms and open their mouths like everyone
HEIL
SIEG HEIL
SIEGHEIL
SIEG HEIL
else. This creates a harmonious impression.
SIEG HEIL
SIEG HEIL
SIEG HEIL
Only the blind men provide a horrific sight.

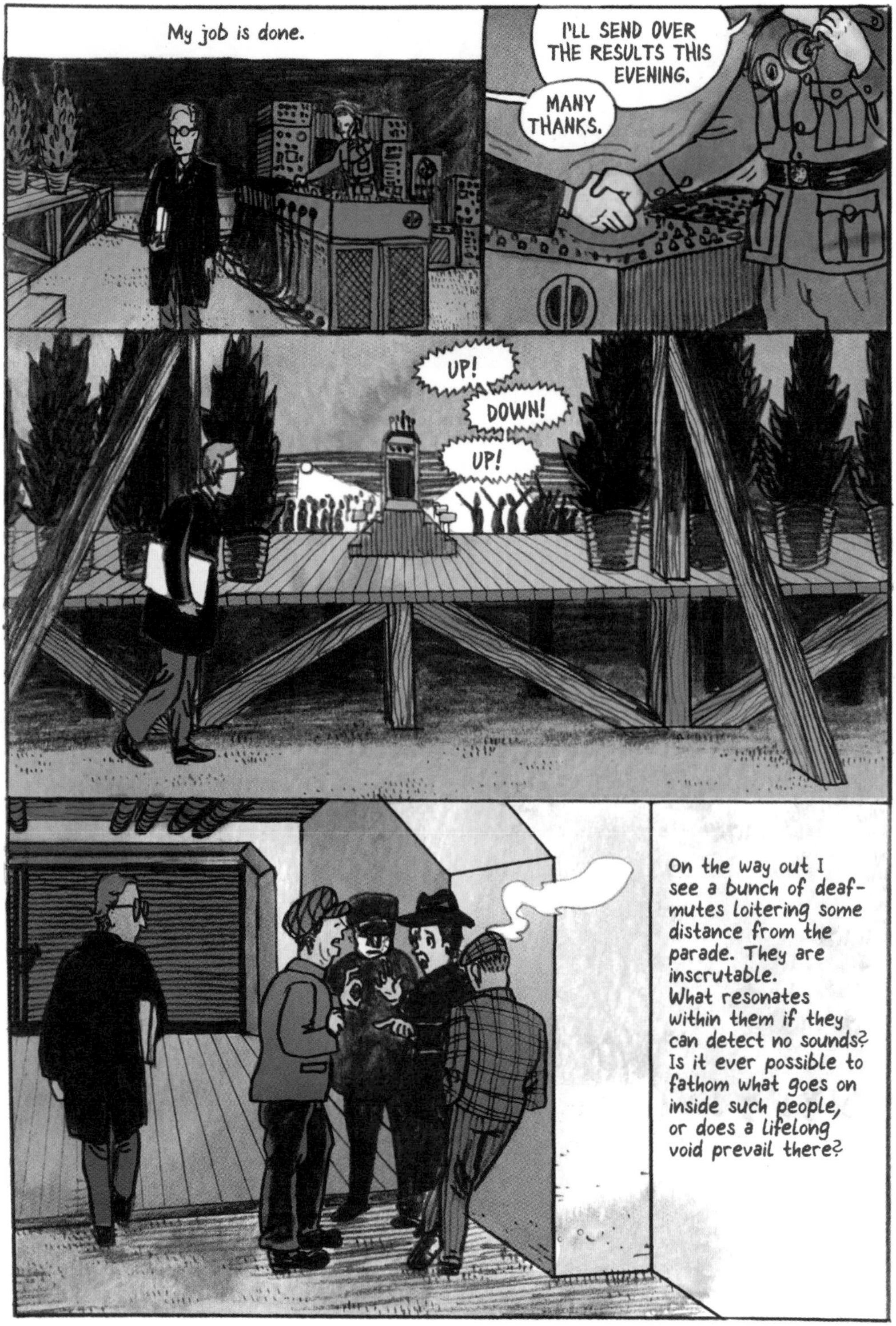
My job is done.
I'LL SEND OVER THE RESULTS THIS EVENING.
MANY THANKS.
UP!
DOWN!
UP!
On the way out I see a bunch of deaf-mutes loitering some distance from the parade. They are inscrutable.
What resonates within them if they can detect no sounds? Is it ever possible to fathom what goes on inside such people, or does a lifelong void prevail there?

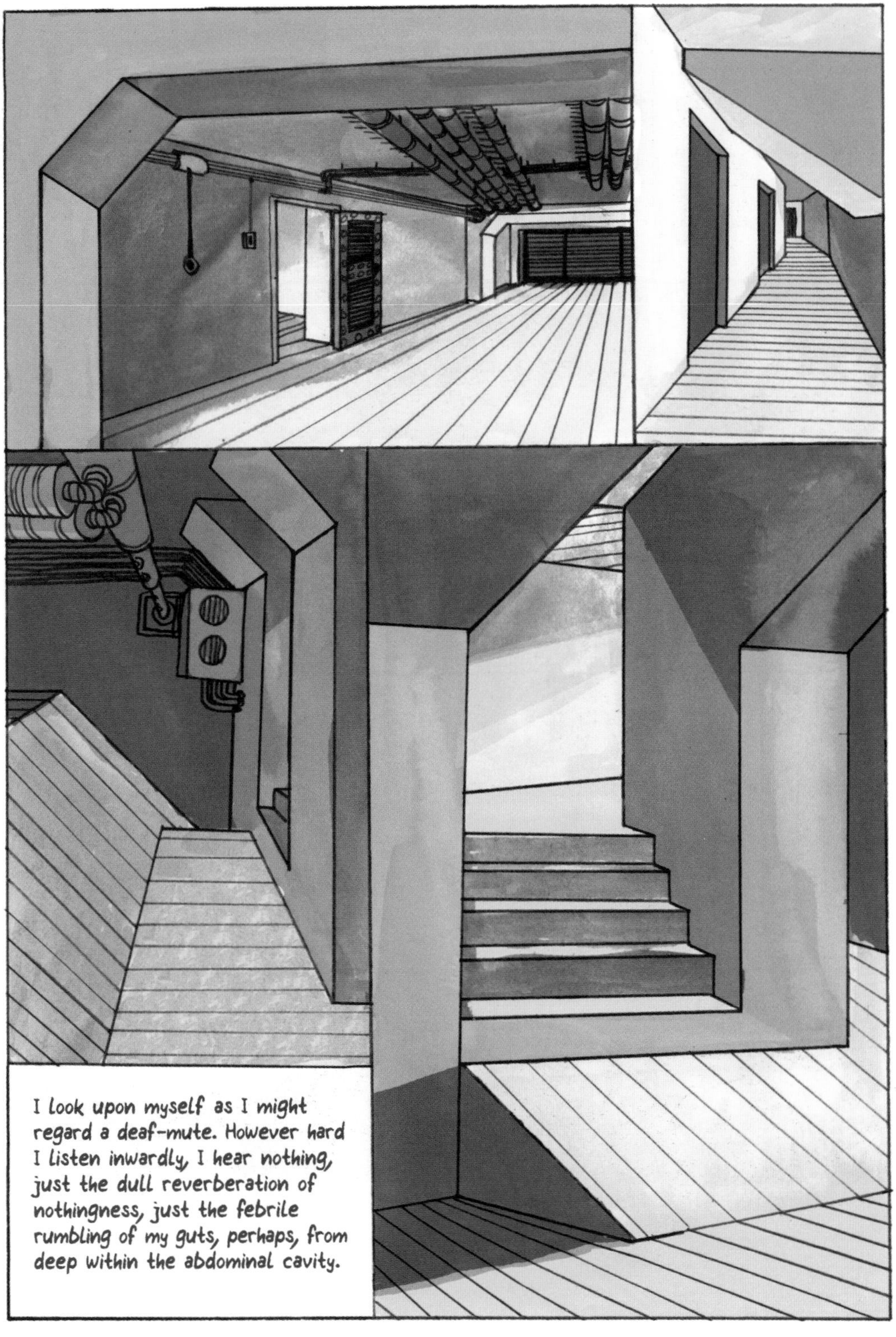
I look upon myself as I might regard a deaf-mute. However hard I listen inwardly, I hear nothing, just the dull reverberation of nothingness, just the febrile rumbling of my guts, perhaps, from deep within the abdominal cavity.

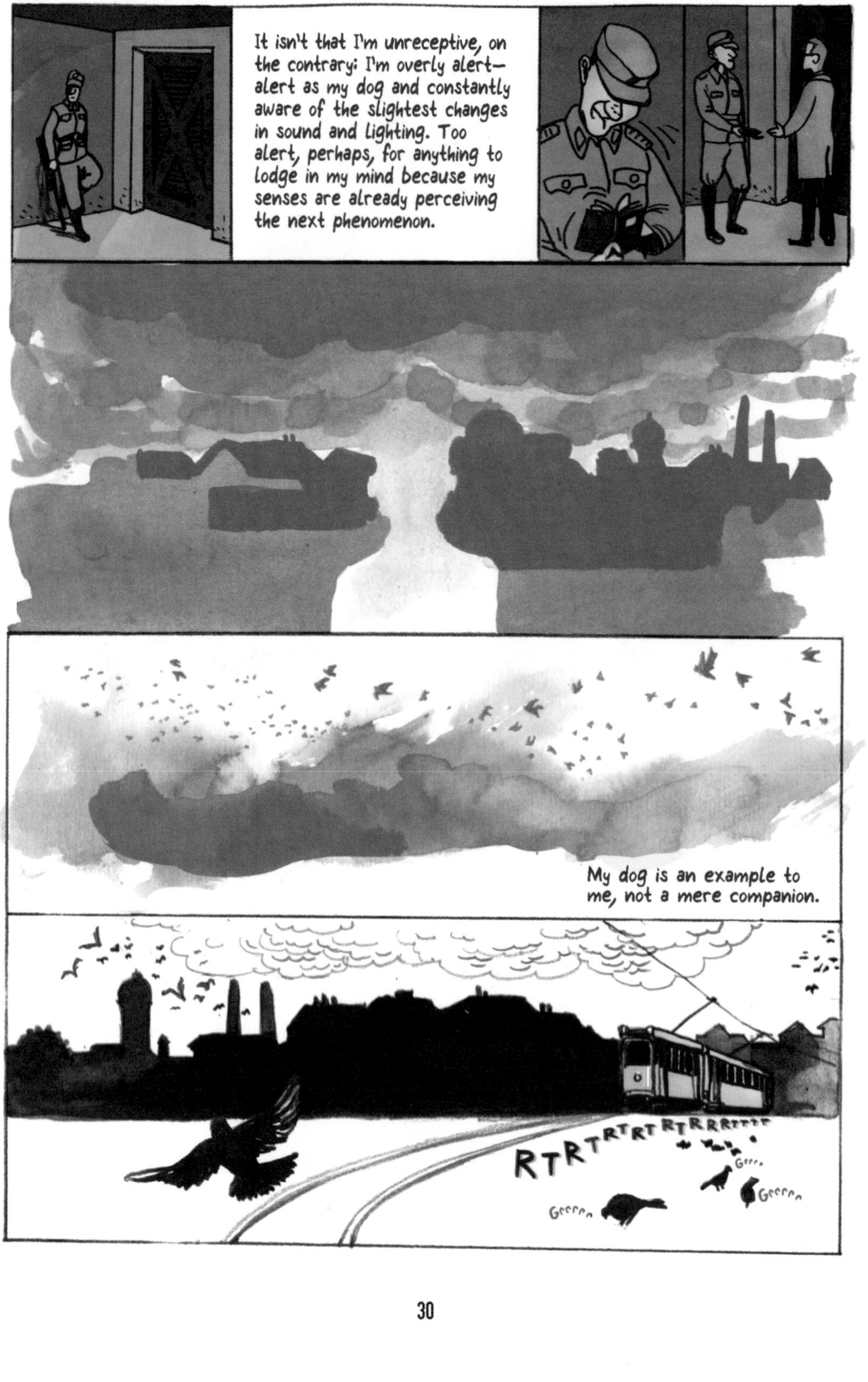

It isn't that I'm unreceptive, on the contrary: I'm overly alert—alert as my dog and constantly aware of the slightest changes in sound and lighting. Too alert, perhaps, for anything to lodge in my mind because my senses are already perceiving the next phenomenon.
My dog is an example to me, not a mere companion.
RTRTRTRTRTRTRRRrrrr
Grrrr
Grrrr
Grrrrr

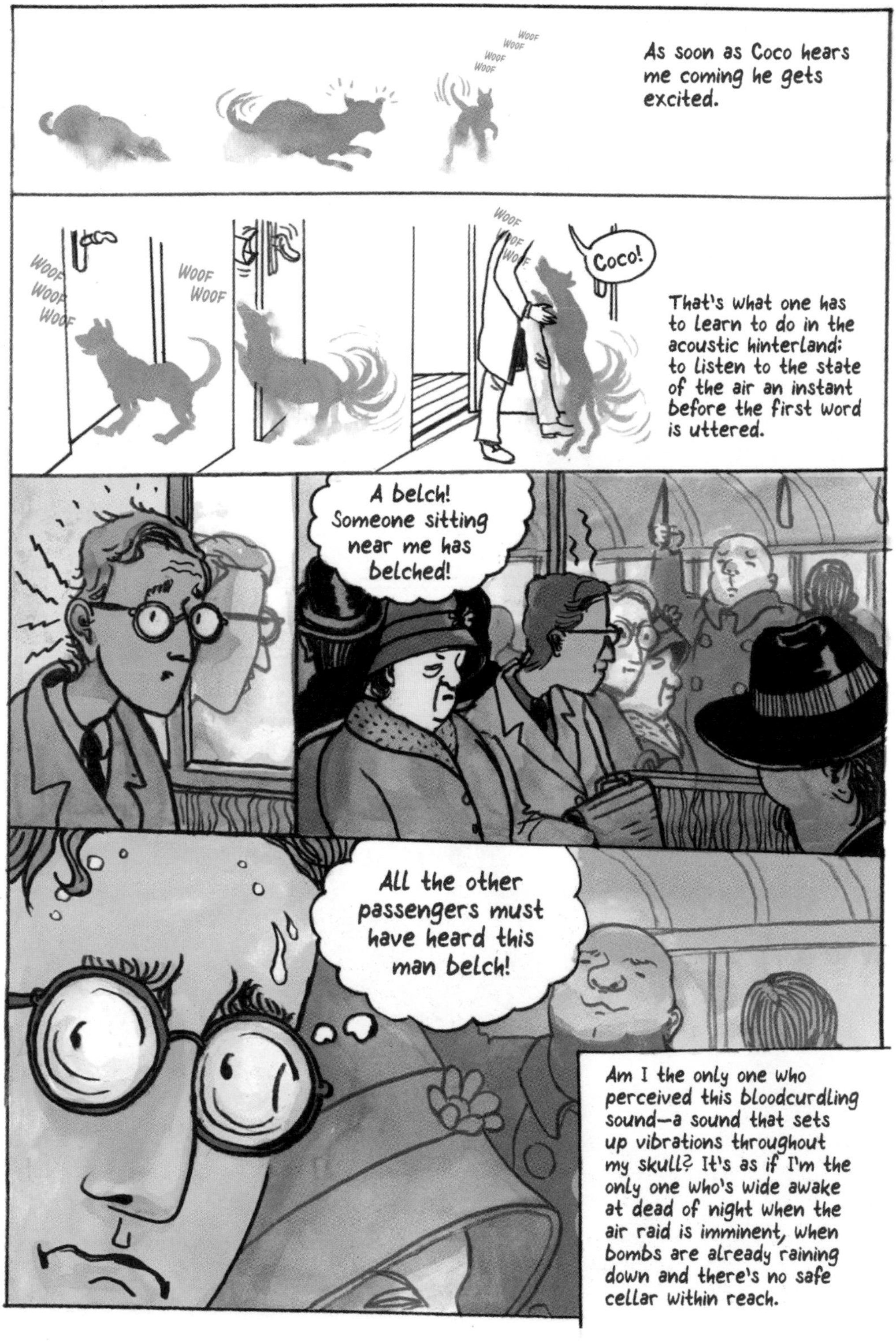
WOOF
WOOF
WOOF
WOOF
As soon as Coco hears me coming he gets excited.
WOOF
WOOF
WOOF
WOOF
WOOF
WOOF
WOOF
WOOF
Coco!
That's what one has to learn to do in the acoustic hinterland: to listen to the state of the air an instant before the first word is uttered.
A belch! Someone sitting near me has belched!
All the other passengers must have heard this man belch!
Am I the only one who perceived this bloodcurdling sound—a sound that sets up vibrations throughout my skull? It's as if I'm the only one who's wide awake at dead of night when the air raid is imminent, when bombs are already raining down and there's no safe cellar within reach.

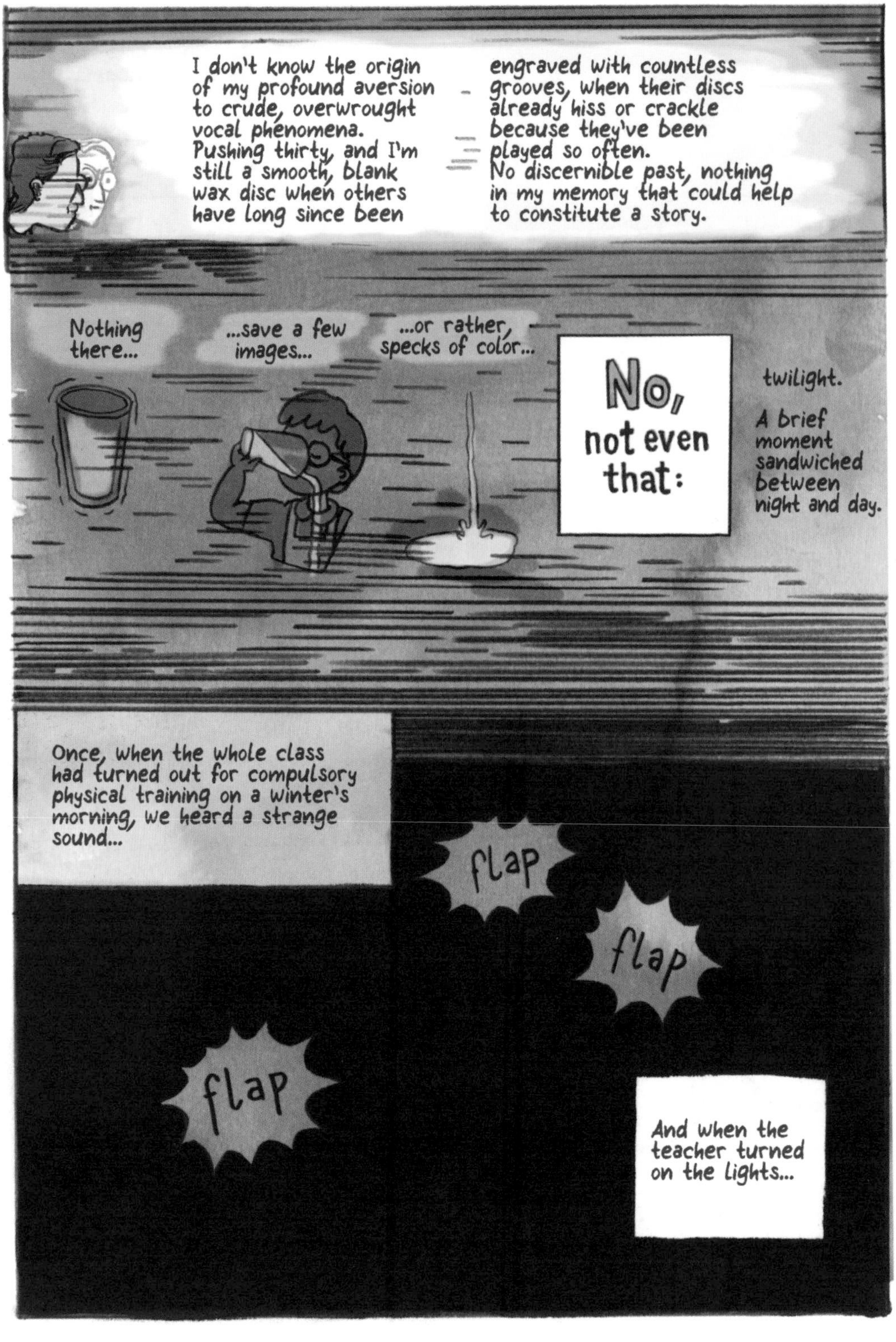
I don't know the origin of my profound aversion to crude, overwrought vocal phenomena. Pushing thirty, and I'm still a smooth, blank wax disc when others have long since been
engraved with countless grooves, when their discs already hiss or crackle because they've been played so often. No discernible past, nothing in my memory that could help to constitute a story.
Nothing there...
...save a few images...
...or rather, specks of color...
No, not even that:
twilight.
A brief moment sandwiched between night and day.
Once, when the whole class had turned out for compulsory physical training on a winter's morning, we heard a strange sound...
flap
flap
flap
And when the teacher turned on the lights...

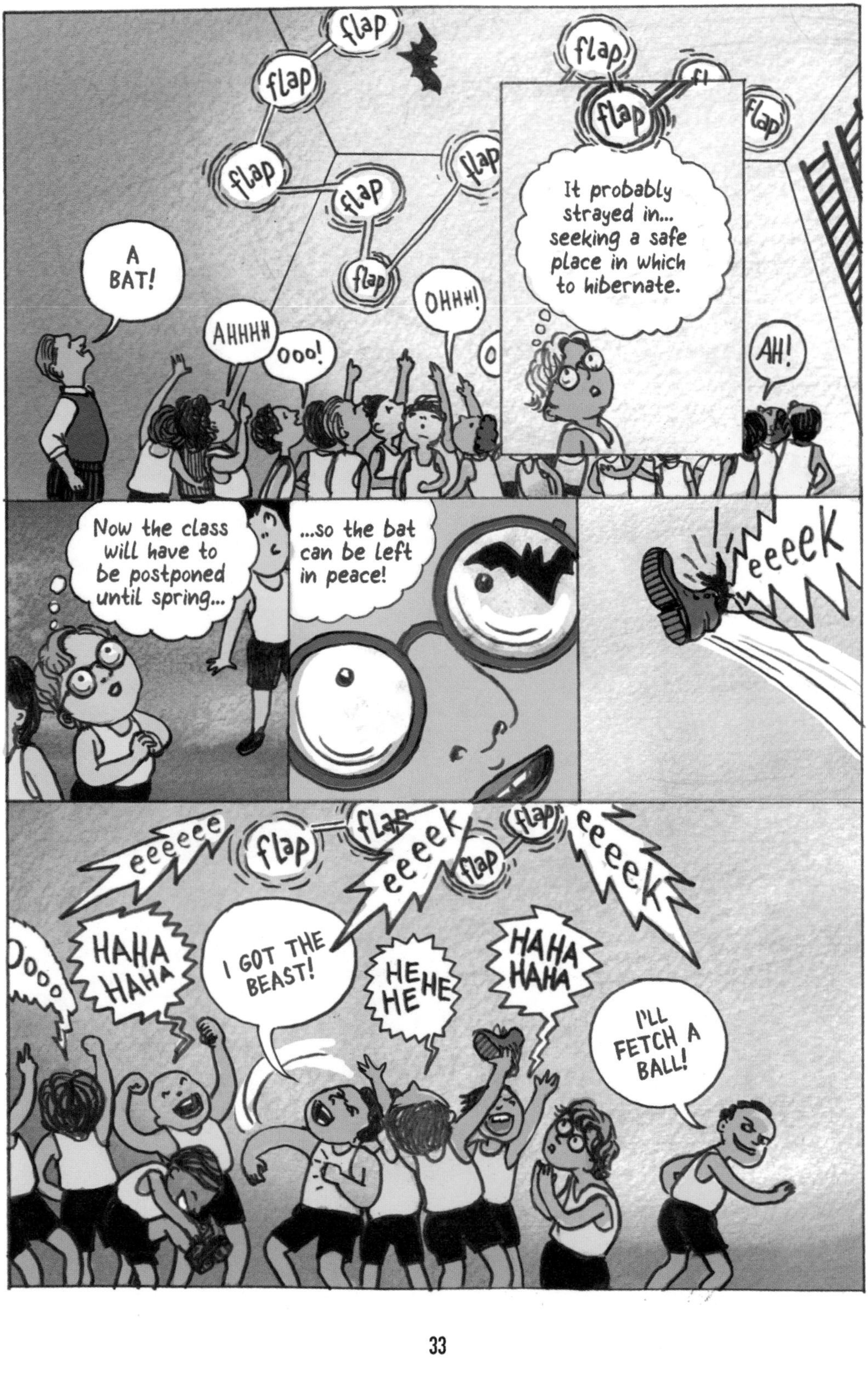
flap
flap
flap
flap
flap
flap
flap
flap
flap
A BAT!
AHHHH
Ooo!
OHHH!
It probably strayed in... seeking a safe place in which to hibernate.
AH!
Now the class will have to be postponed until spring...
...so the bat can be left in peace!
eeeek
eeeeee
flap
flap
eeeek
flap
flap
eeeek
HAHA HAHA
I GOT THE BEAST!
HE HE HE
HAHA HAHA
I'LL FETCH A BALL!

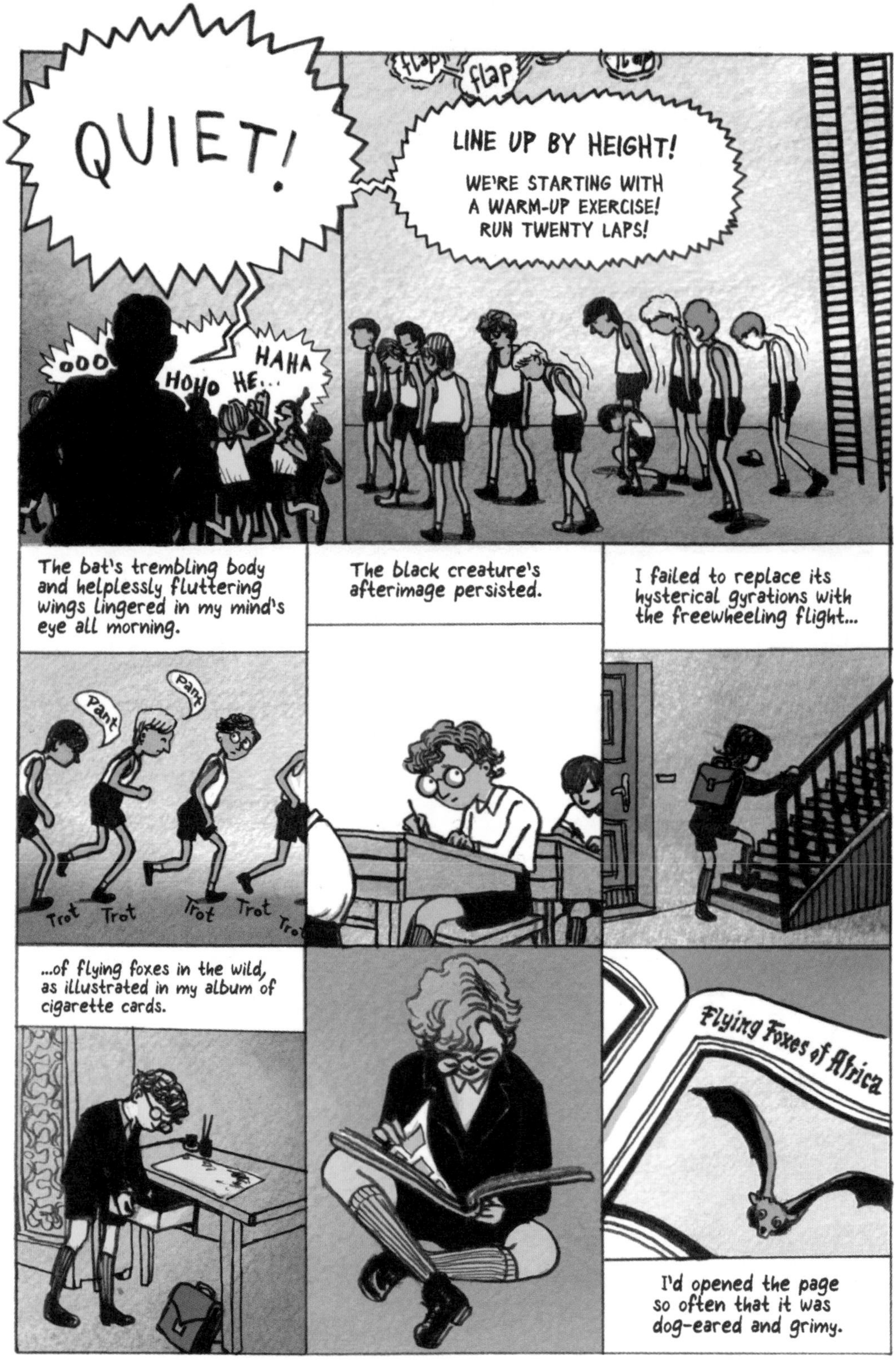
QUIET!
OOO
HOHO
HE...
HAHA
flap
flap
flap
LINE UP BY HEIGHT!
WE'RE STARTING WITH A WARM-UP EXERCISE! RUN TWENTY LAPS!
The bat's trembling body and helplessly fluttering wings lingered in my mind's eye all morning.
Pant
Pant
Trot
Trot
Trot
Trot
The black creature's afterimage persisted.
I failed to replace its hysterical gyrations with the freewheeling flight...
...of flying foxes in the wild, as illustrated in my album of cigarette cards.
Flying Foxes of Africa
I'd opened the page so often that it was dog-eared and grimy.

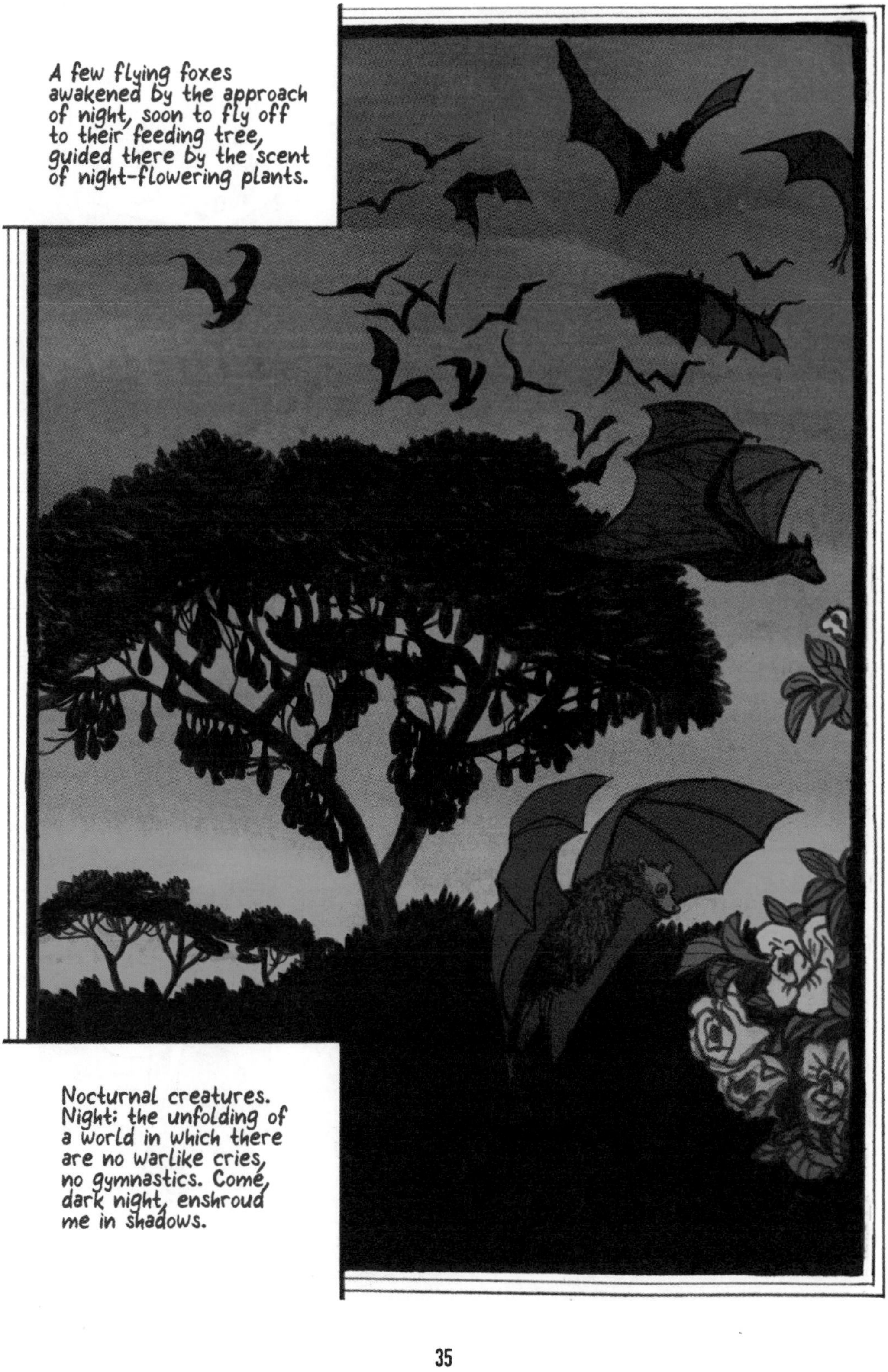
A few flying foxes awakened by the approach of night, soon to fly off to their feeding tree, guided there by the scent of night-flowering plants.
Nocturnal creatures. Night: the unfolding of a world in which there are no warlike cries, no gymnastics. Come, dark night, enshroud me in shadows.

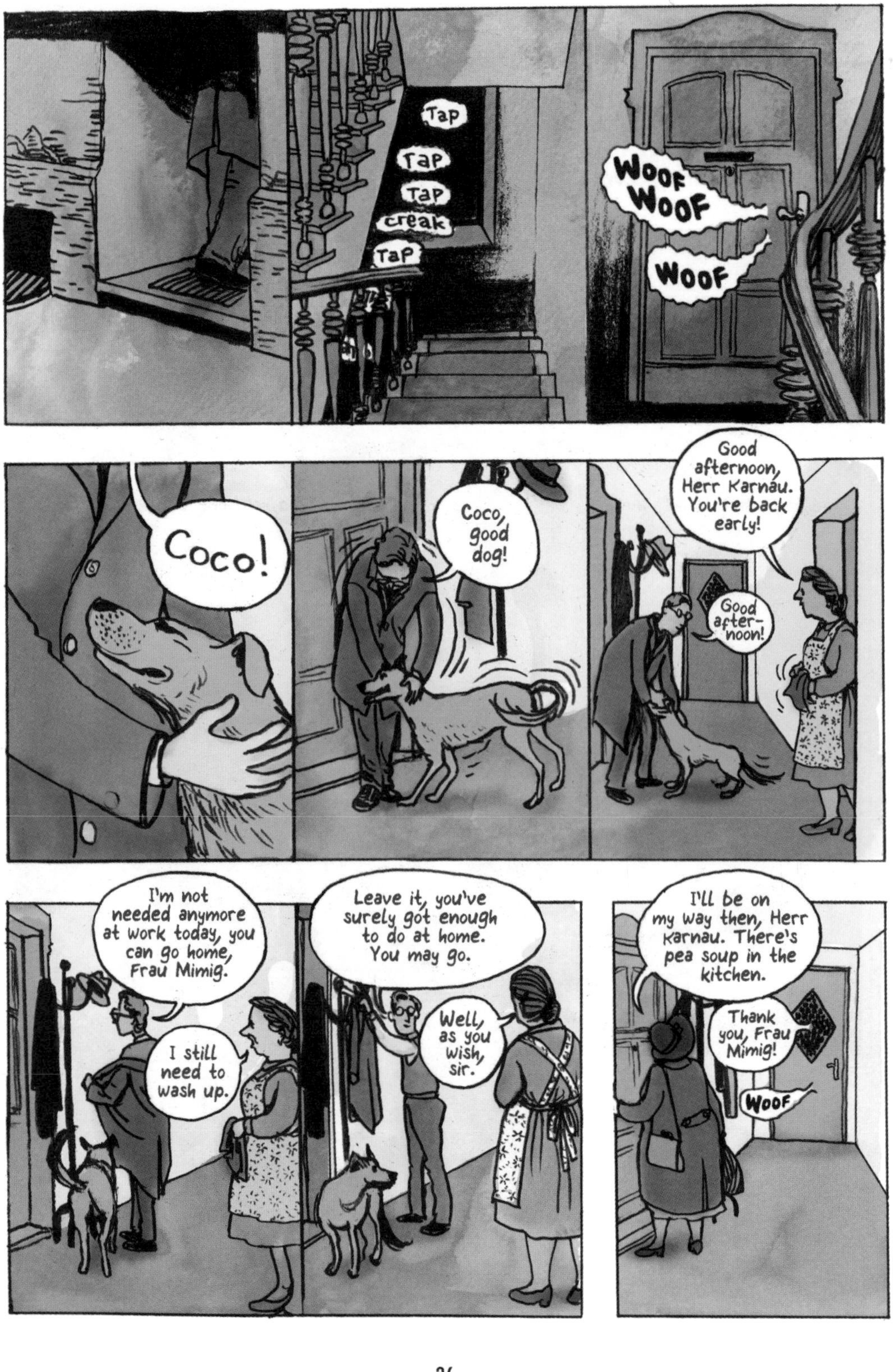
Tap
Tap
Tap
creak
Tap
WOOF
WOOF
WOOF
Coco!
Coco, good dog!
Good afternoon, Herr Karnau. You're back early!
Good after-noon!
I'm not needed anymore at work today, you can go home, Frau Mimig.
I still need to wash up.
Leave it, you've surely got enough to do at home. You may go.
Well, as you wish, sir.
I'll be on my way then, Herr Karnau. There's pea soup in the kitchen.
Thank you, Frau Mimig!
WOOF

Why do I feel so infinitely serene when I sit down beside my gramophone...

...and hold one of these black shellac discs in my hands?

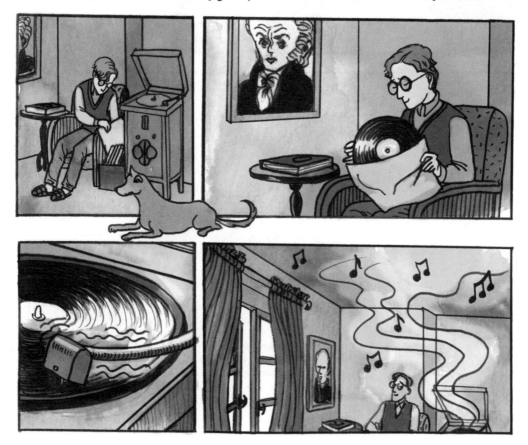

Every playing of the record erodes a
little of its substance, an amalgam
of resin, soot, and the waxy
deposits of the lac insect.
Living creatures made their
contribution to the disc.
Their secretions were
compressed so that sound
could become matter,
just as the sounds
engraved on the
disc are themselves
secretions and vital
signs of human origin.

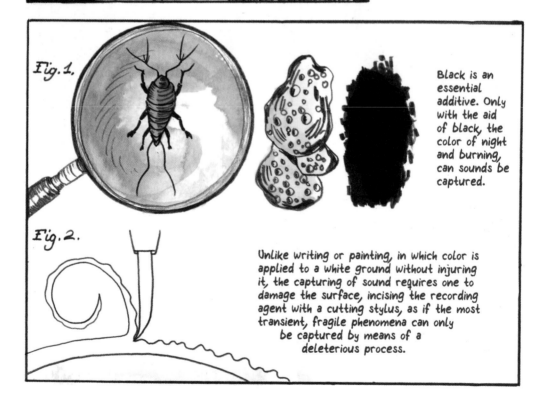

Fig. 1.

Black is an
essential
additive. Only
with the aid
of black, the
color of night
and burning,
can sounds be
captured.

Fig. 2.

Unlike writing or painting, in which color is
applied to a white ground without injuring
it, the capturing of sound requires one to
damage the surface, incising the recording
agent with a cutting stylus, as if the most
transient, fragile phenomena can only
be captured by means of a
deleterious process.

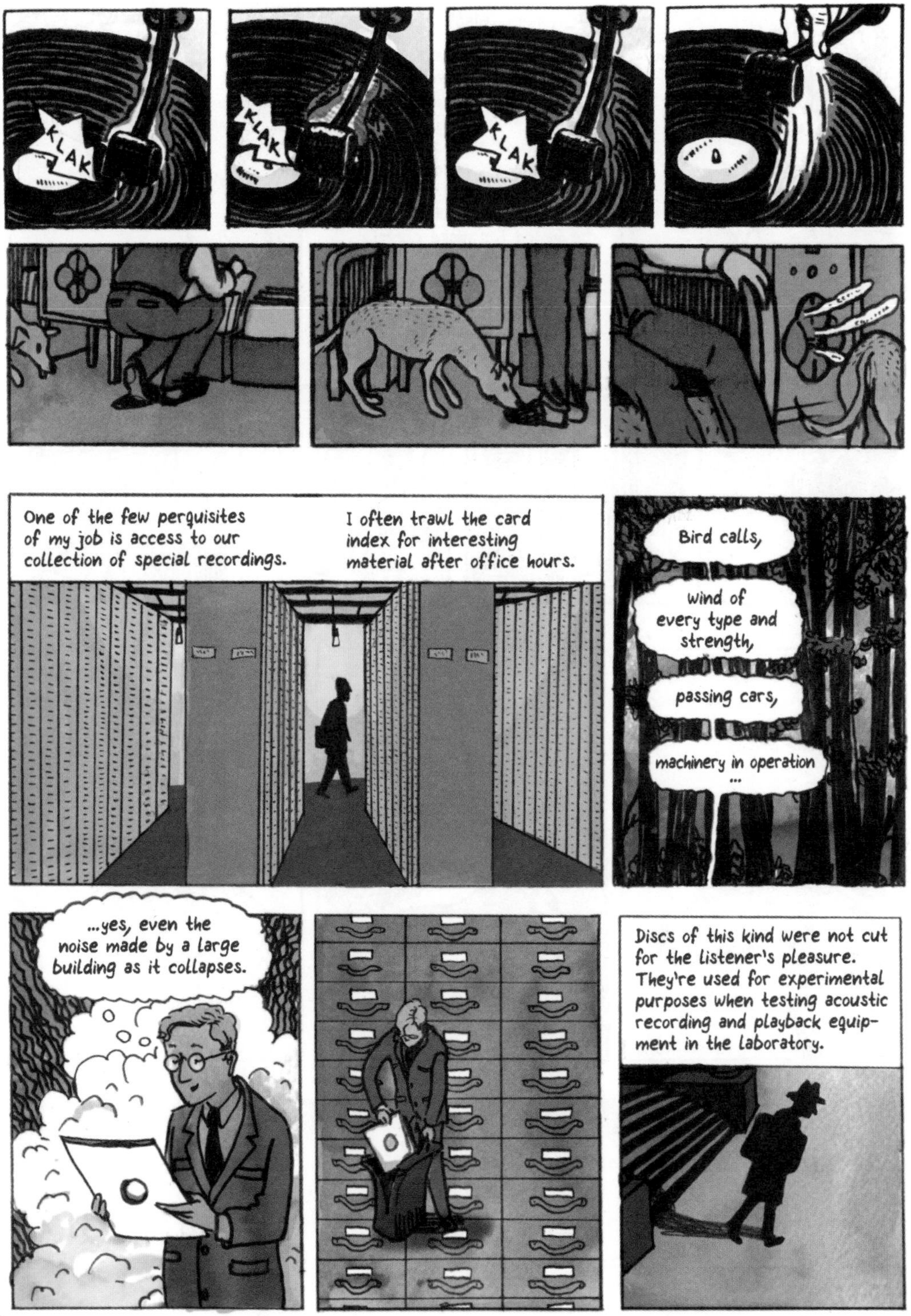
KLAK
KLAK
KLAK
One of the few perquisites of my job is access to our collection of special recordings.
I often trawl the card index for interesting material after office hours.
Bird calls,
wind of every type and strength,
passing cars,
machinery in operation ...
...yes, even the noise made by a large building as it collapses.
Discs of this kind were not cut for the listener's pleasure. They're used for experimental purposes when testing acoustic recording and playback equipment in the laboratory.

YEAHHH! mmhmm

I've brought home some recordings of speech, but also some unusual sounds of human origin. I'm even fonder of the voice alone than of singing with instrumental accompaniment. The quivering glottis and the operation of the tongue can be heard far more clearly when the organ lies naked and exposed to the ear.

mmhmmmmm

Where is his sense of hearing located? Where is the capacity for generating sounds rooted in his canine brain?

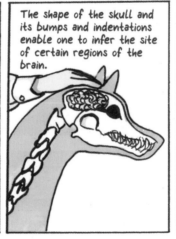

The shape of the skull and its bumps and indentations enable one to infer the site of certain regions of the brain.

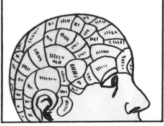

Professor Gall discovered this at the end of the eighteenth century. To Gall, every head was a cerebral map; his observations filled whole phrenological atlases.

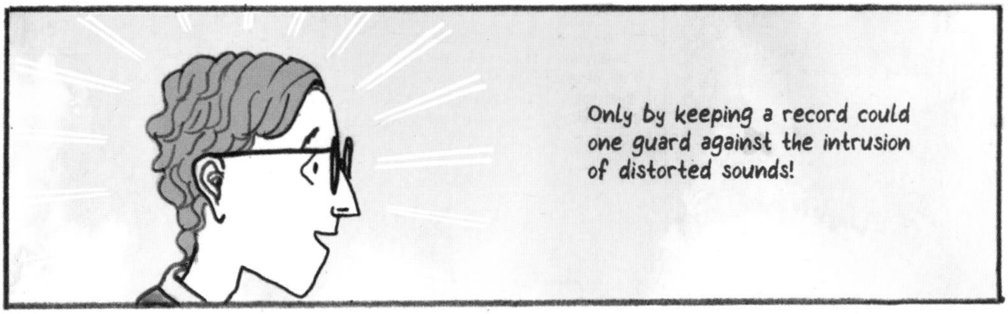
Only by keeping a record could one guard against the intrusion of distorted sounds!

The nature of the human voice is such, however, that this record would merely be the rudiments, perhaps, of a map that defines the hearers' location, a map on which the bottom left corner, at most, displays a few faint lines devoid of an established scale.

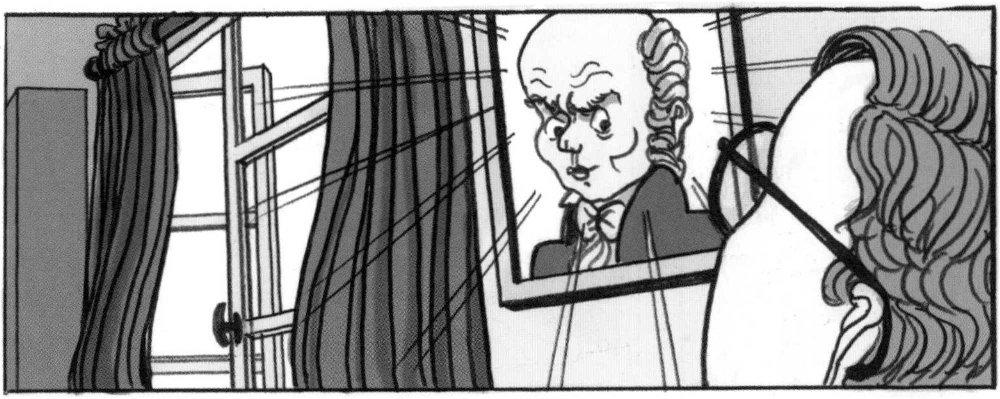

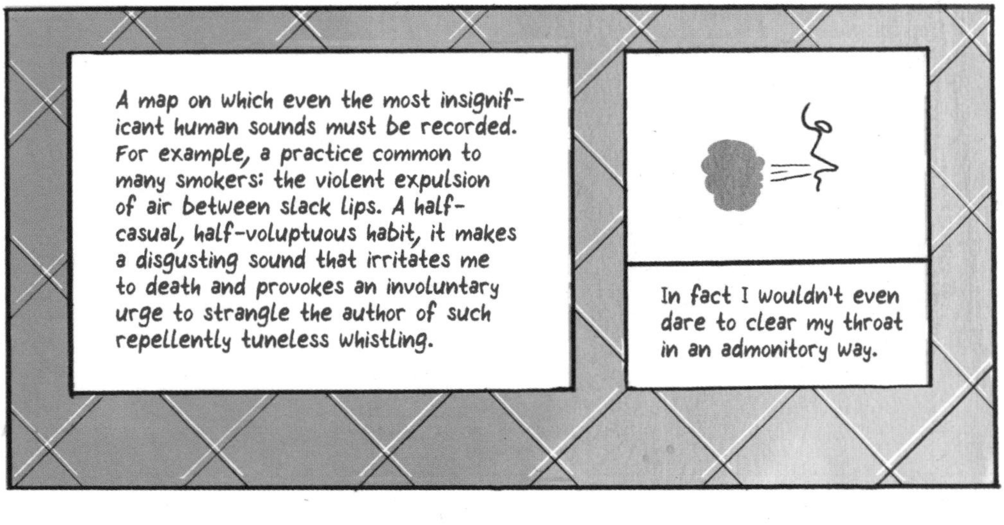
A map on which even the most insignificant human sounds must be recorded. For example, a practice common to many smokers: the violent expulsion of air between slack lips. A half-casual, half-voluptuous habit, it makes a disgusting sound that irritates me to death and provokes an involuntary urge to strangle the author of such repellently tuneless whistling.
In fact I wouldn't even dare to clear my throat in an admonitory way.

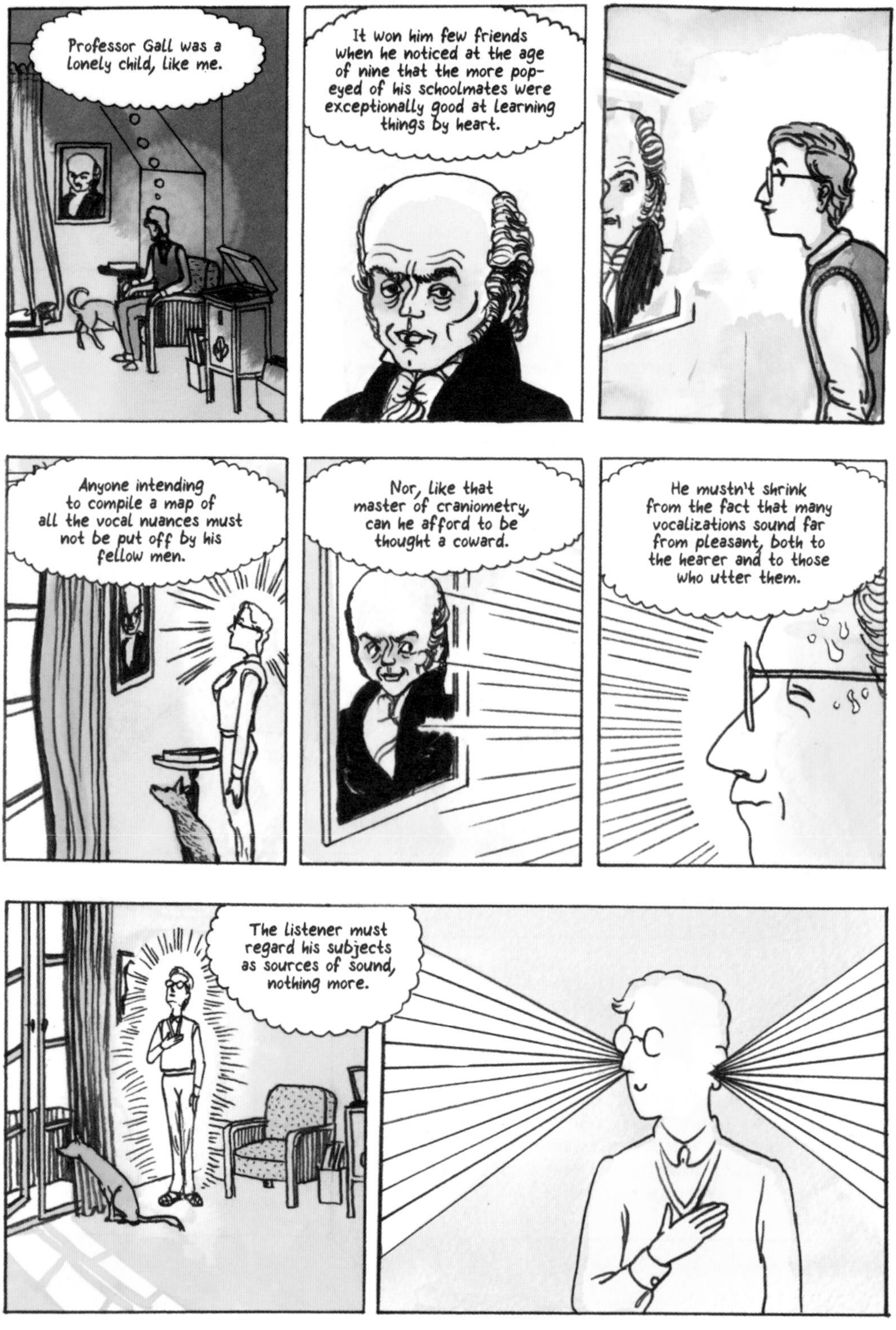
Professor Gall was a lonely child, like me.
It won him few friends when he noticed at the age of nine that the more pop-eyed of his schoolmates were exceptionally good at learning things by heart.
Anyone intending to compile a map of all the vocal nuances must not be put off by his fellow men.
Nor, like that master of craniometry, can he afford to be thought a coward.
He mustn't shrink from the fact that many vocalizations sound far from pleasant, both to the hearer and to those who utter them.
The listener must regard his subjects as sources of sound, nothing more.

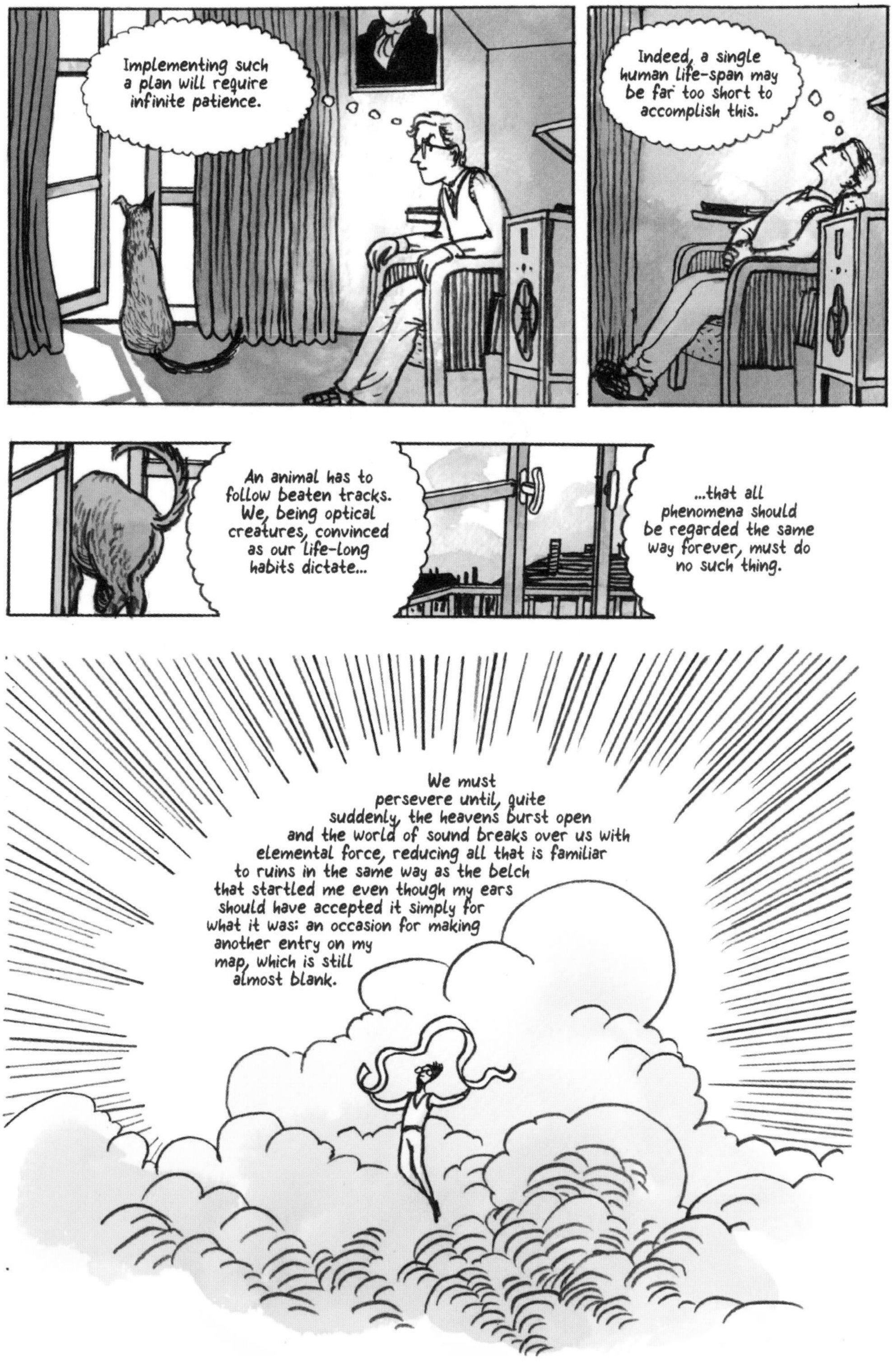
Implementing such a plan will require infinite patience.
Indeed, a single human life-span may be far too short to accomplish this.
An animal has to follow beaten tracks. We, being optical creatures, convinced as our life-long habits dictate...
...that all phenomena should be regarded the same way forever, must do no such thing.
We must persevere until, quite suddenly, the heavens burst open and the world of sound breaks over us with elemental force, reducing all that is familiar to ruins in the same way as the belch that startled me even though my ears should have accepted it simply for what it was: an occasion for making another entry on my map, which is still almost blank.

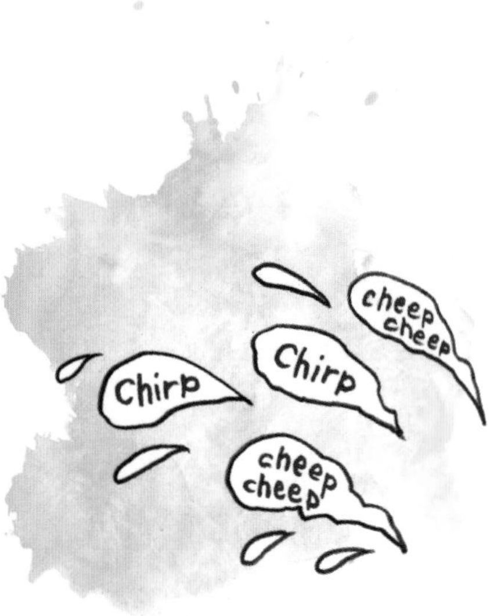
cheep cheep
Chirp
Chirp
cheep cheep

II.

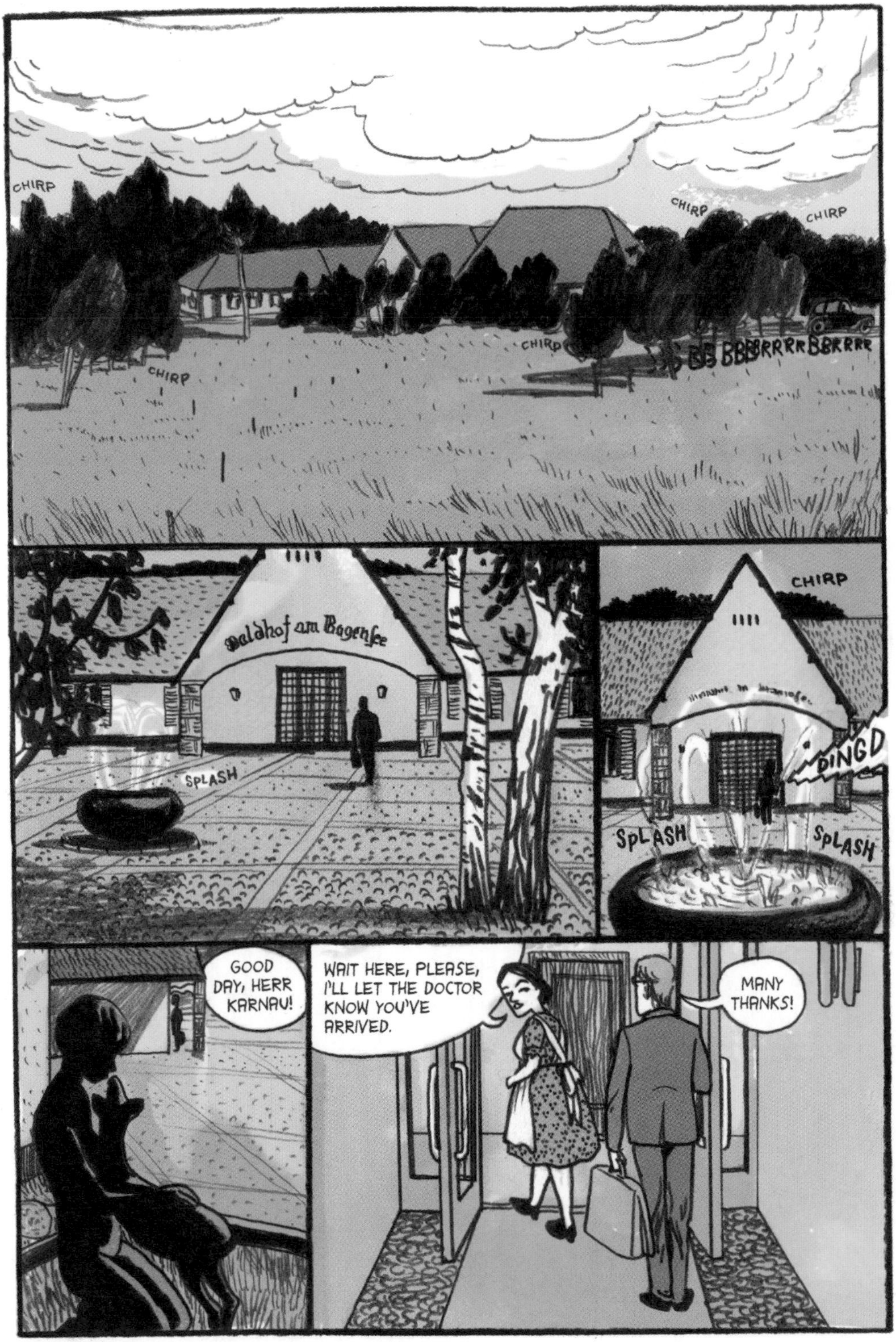
CHIRP
CHIRP
CHIRP
CHIRP
CHIRP
BBBBBRRRRRBRRRRR
Waldhof am Bogensee
SPLASH
CHIRP
DINGD
SPLASH
SPLASH
GOOD DAY, HERR KARNAU!
WAIT HERE, PLEASE, I'LL LET THE DOCTOR KNOW YOU'VE ARRIVED.
MANY THANKS!

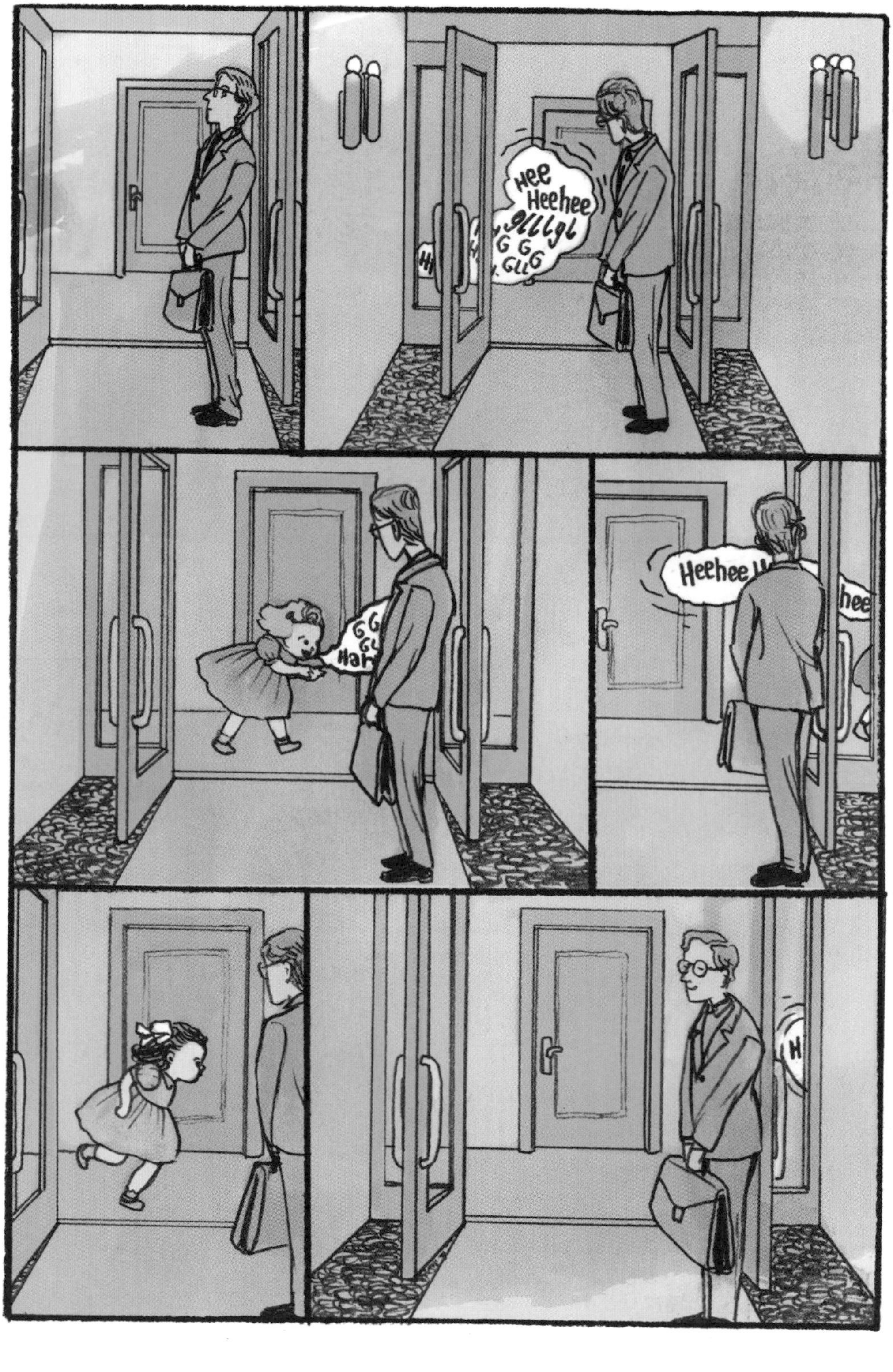
Hee
Heehee
gllllgl
G G
GLLG
G G
GL
Har
Heehee
hee

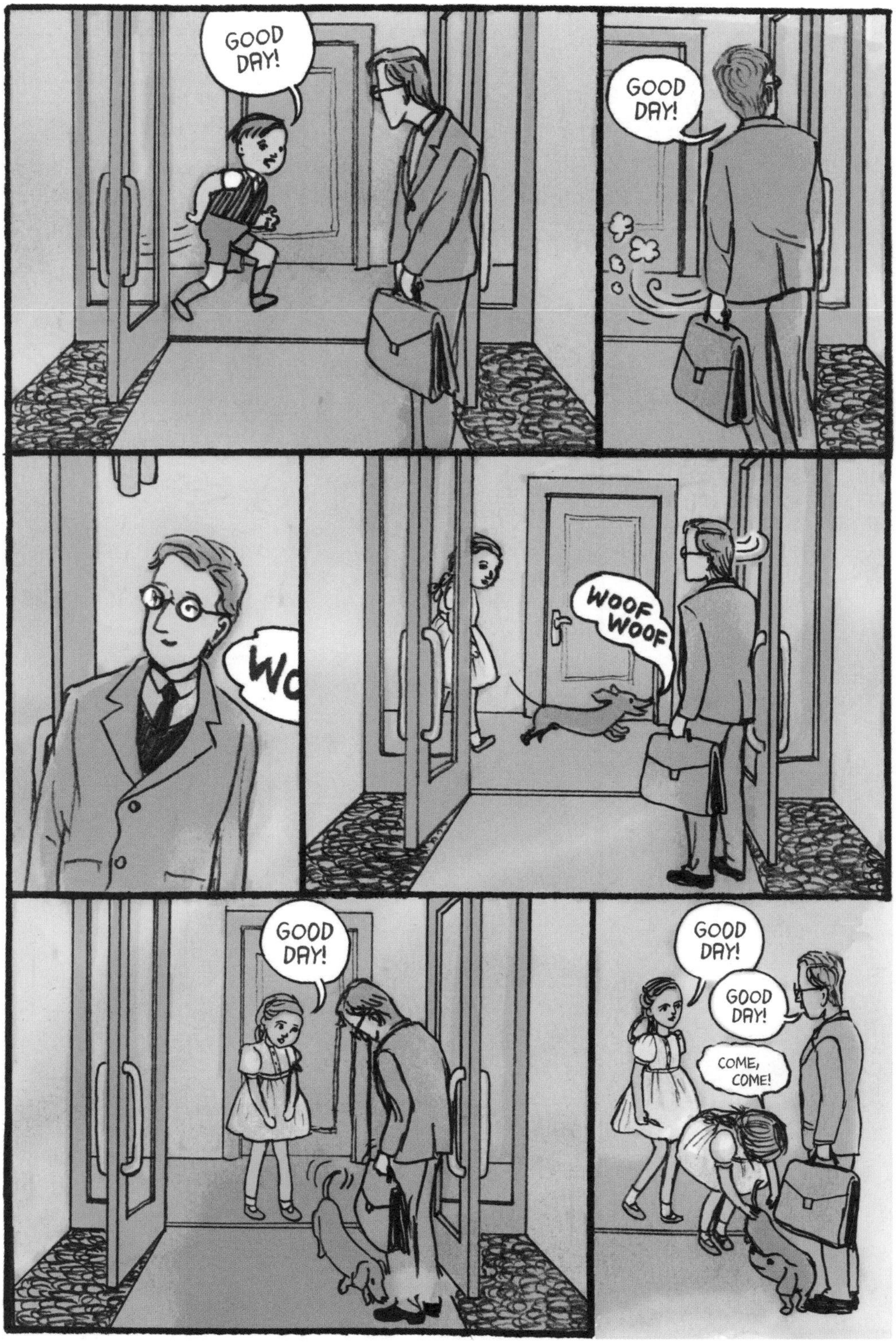
GOOD DAY!
GOOD DAY!
WO
WOOF WOOF
GOOD DAY!
GOOD DAY!
GOOD DAY!
COME, COME!

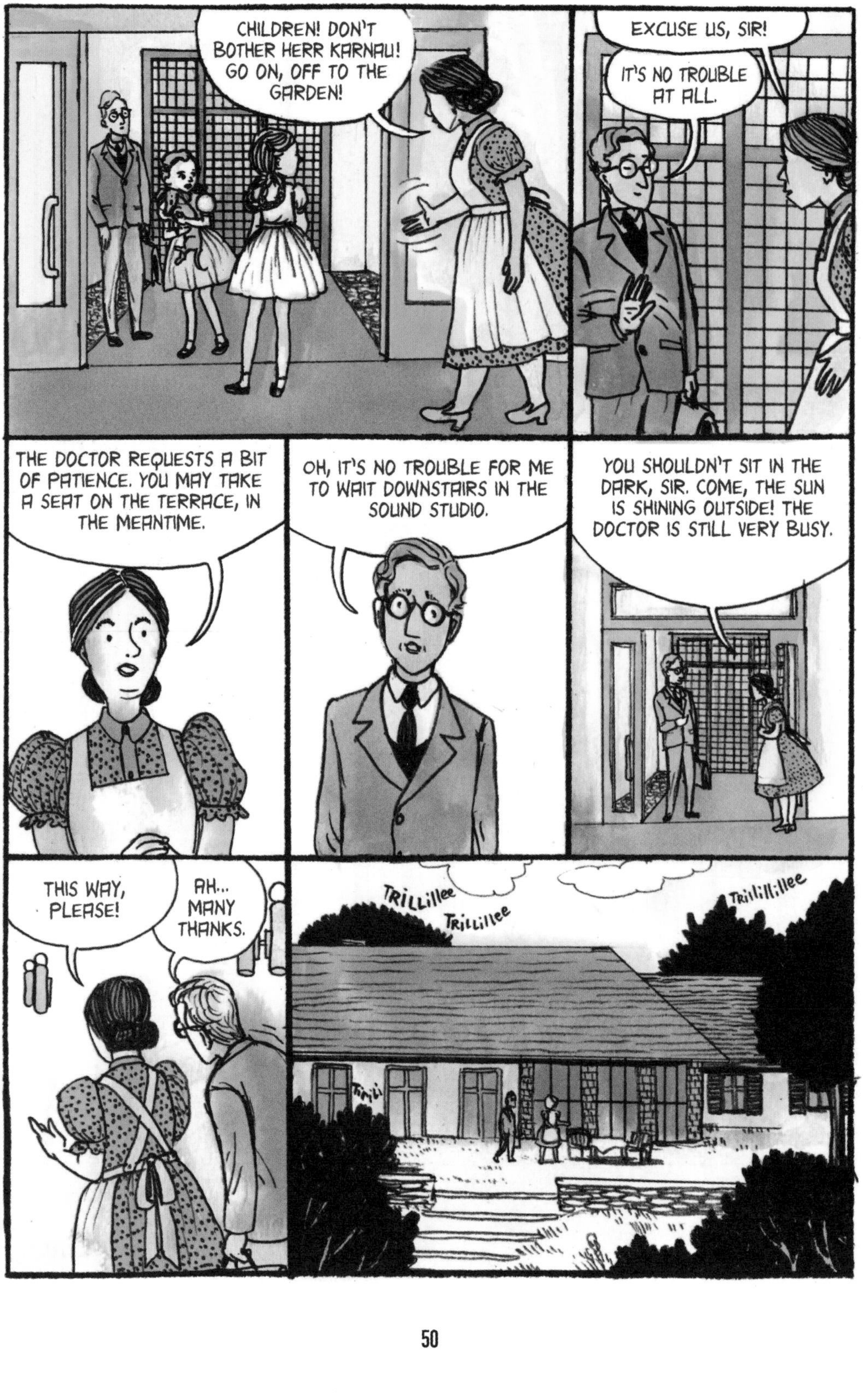
CHILDREN! DON'T BOTHER HERR KARNAU! GO ON, OFF TO THE GARDEN!
EXCUSE US, SIR!
IT'S NO TROUBLE AT ALL.
THE DOCTOR REQUESTS A BIT OF PATIENCE. YOU MAY TAKE A SEAT ON THE TERRACE, IN THE MEANTIME.
OH, IT'S NO TROUBLE FOR ME TO WAIT DOWNSTAIRS IN THE SOUND STUDIO.
YOU SHOULDN'T SIT IN THE DARK, SIR. COME, THE SUN IS SHINING OUTSIDE! THE DOCTOR IS STILL VERY BUSY.
THIS WAY, PLEASE!
AH... MANY THANKS.
TRILLillee
TRILLillee
Trillillillee
Trili

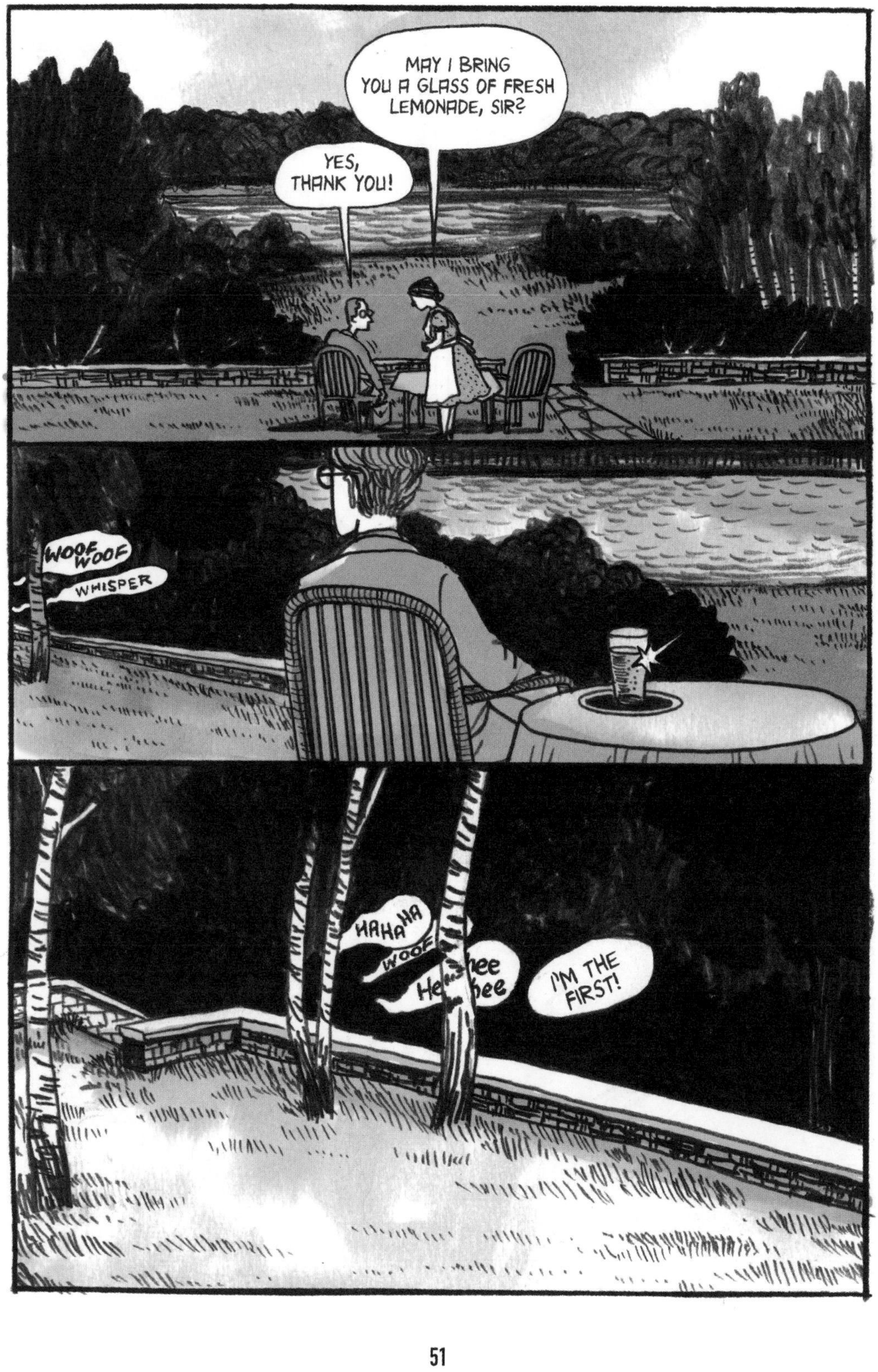
MAY I BRING YOU A GLASS OF FRESH LEMONADE, SIR?
YES, THANK YOU!
WOOF WOOF
WHISPER
HAHAHA
WOOF
hee
hee
I'M THE FIRST!

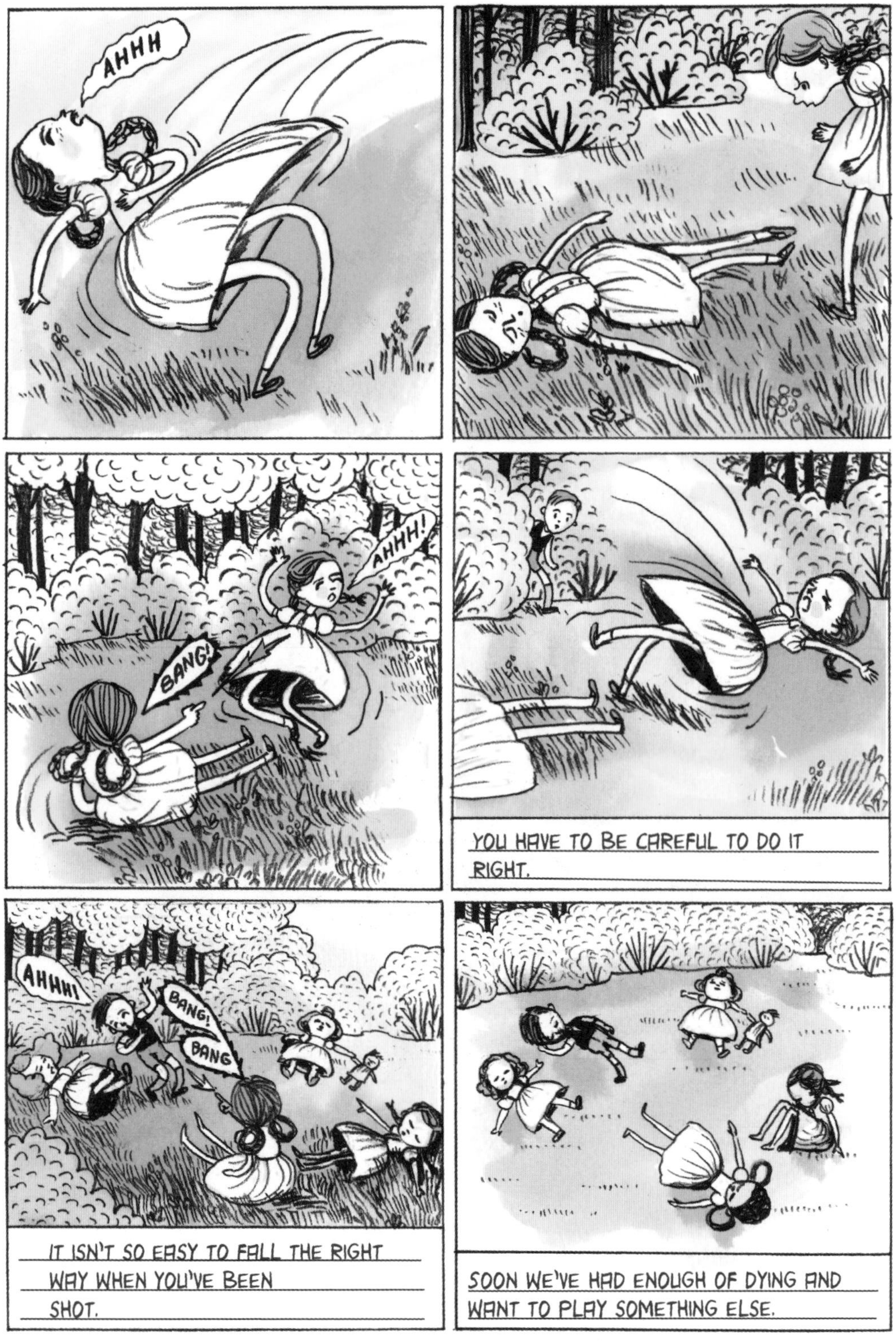
AHHH
AHHH!
BANG!
YOU HAVE TO BE CAREFUL TO DO IT RIGHT.
AHHH!
BANG!
BANG
IT ISN'T SO EASY TO FALL THE RIGHT WAY WHEN YOU'VE BEEN SHOT.
SOON WE'VE HAD ENOUGH OF DYING AND WANT TO PLAY SOMETHING ELSE.

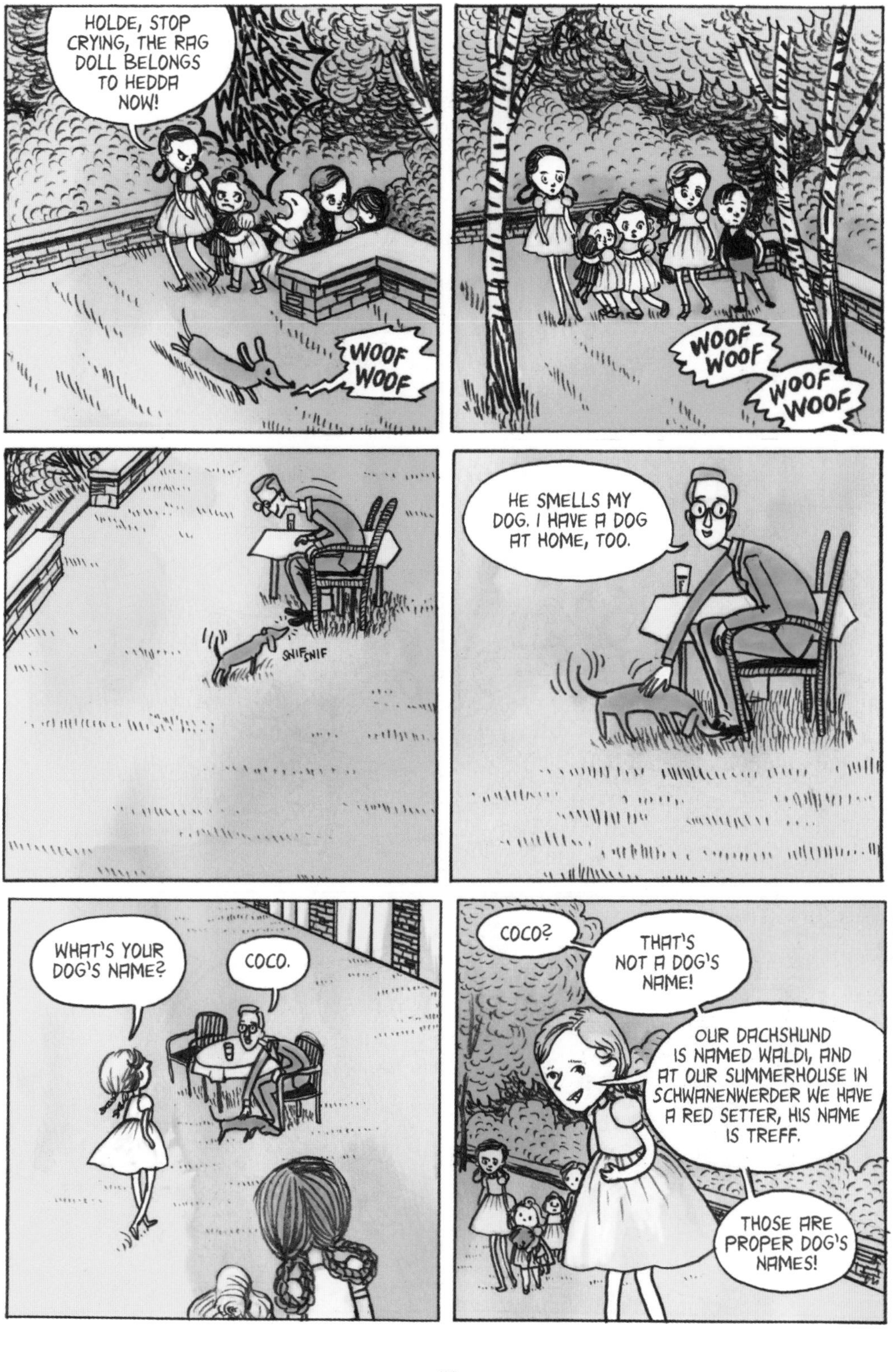
HOLDE, STOP CRYING, THE RAG DOLL BELONGS TO HEDDA NOW!
WOOF WOOF
WOOF WOOF
WOOF WOOF
SNIF SNIF
HE SMELLS MY DOG. I HAVE A DOG AT HOME, TOO.
WHAT'S YOUR DOG'S NAME?
COCO.
COCO?
THAT'S NOT A DOG'S NAME!
OUR DACHSHUND IS NAMED WALDI, AND AT OUR SUMMERHOUSE IN SCHWANENWERDER WE HAVE A RED SETTER, HIS NAME IS TREFF.
THOSE ARE PROPER DOG'S NAMES!

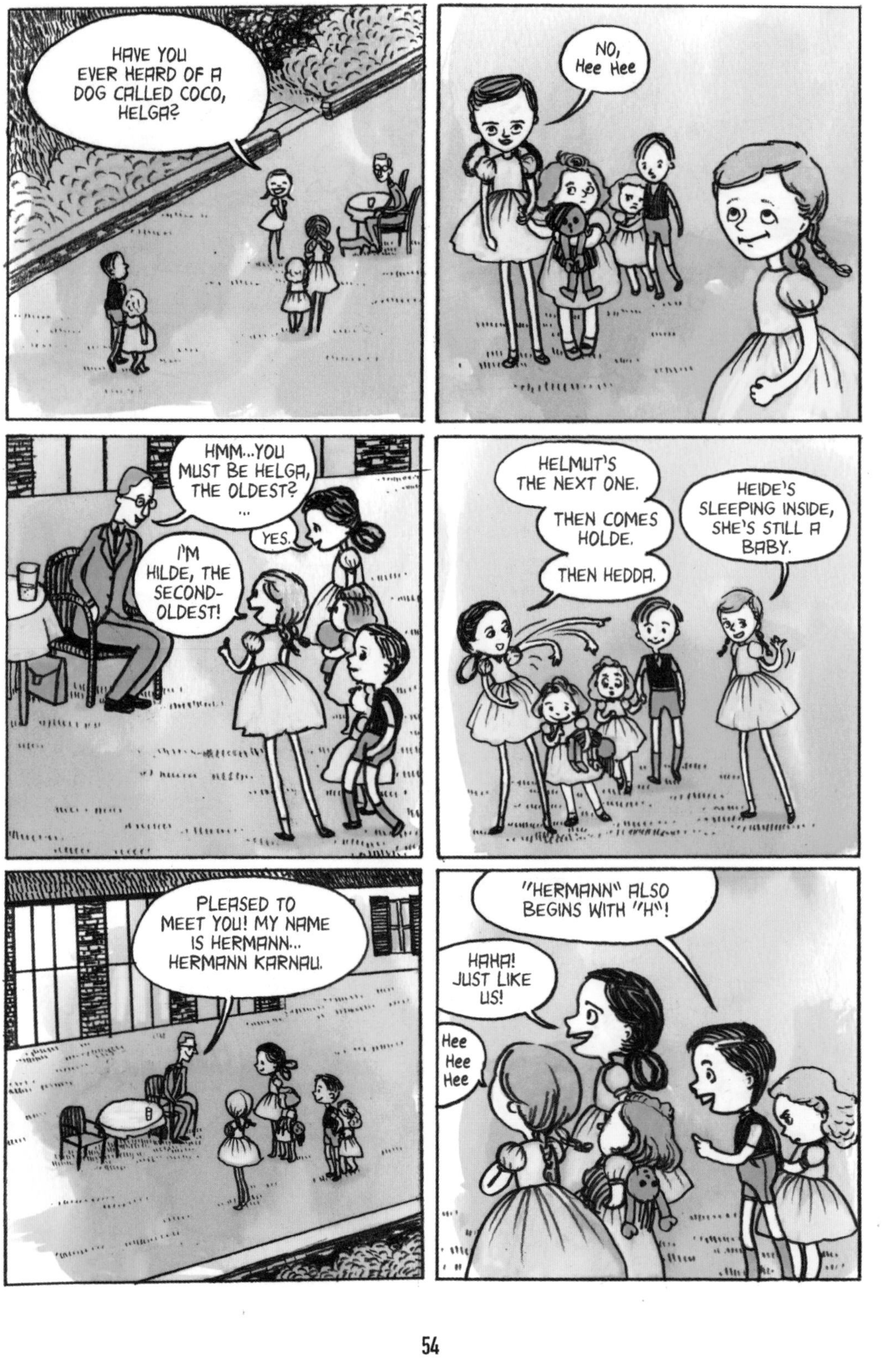
HAVE YOU EVER HEARD OF A DOG CALLED COCO, HELGA?
NO, Hee Hee
HMM...YOU MUST BE HELGA, THE OLDEST? ...
YES.
I'M HILDE, THE SECOND-OLDEST!
HELMUT'S THE NEXT ONE.
THEN COMES HOLDE.
THEN HEDDA.
HEIDE'S SLEEPING INSIDE, SHE'S STILL A BABY.
PLEASED TO MEET YOU! MY NAME IS HERMANN... HERMANN KARNAU.
"HERMANN" ALSO BEGINS WITH "H"!
HAHA! JUST LIKE US!
Hee Hee Hee

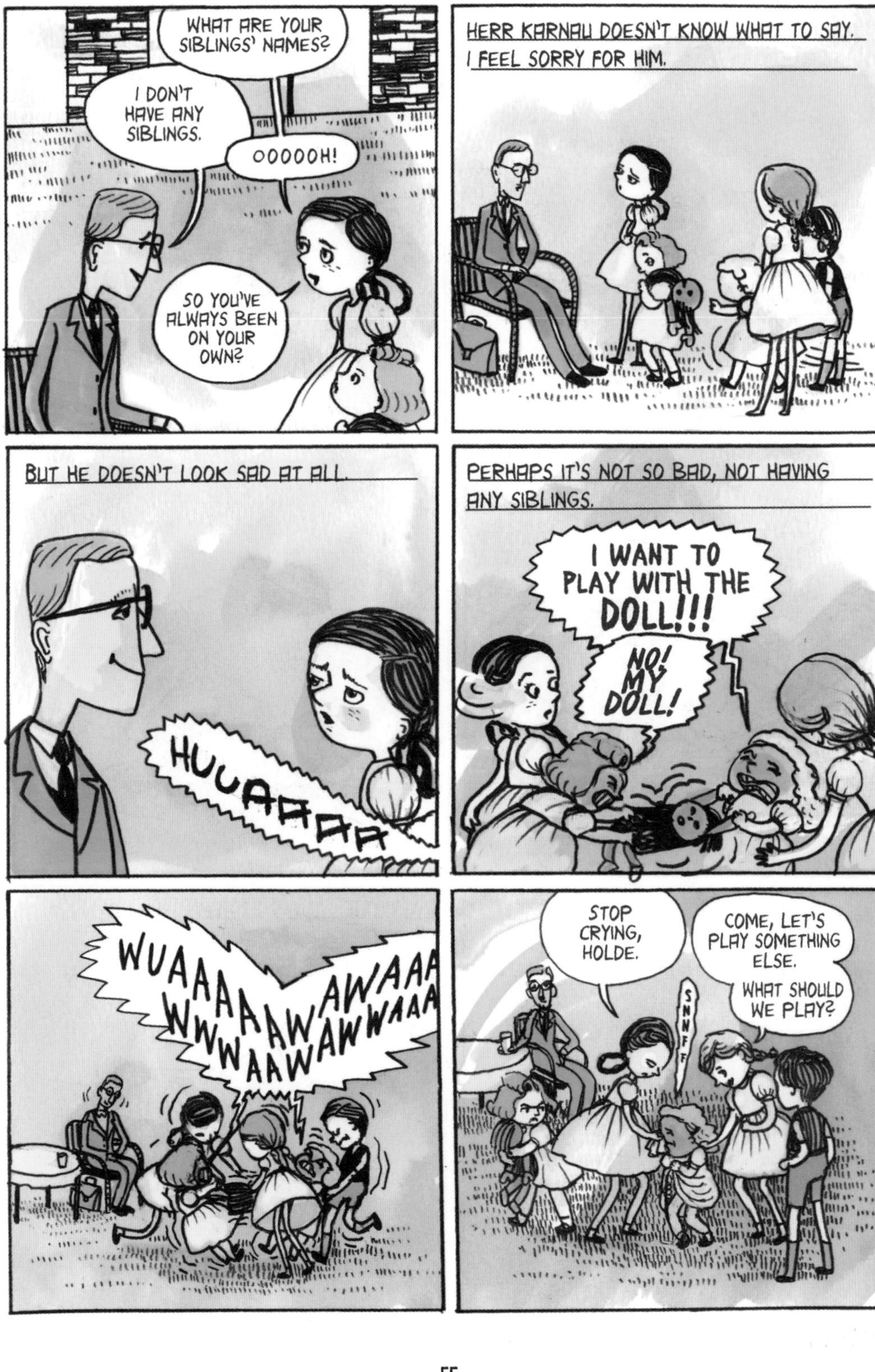
WHAT ARE YOUR SIBLINGS' NAMES?
I DON'T HAVE ANY SIBLINGS.
OOOOOH!
SO YOU'VE ALWAYS BEEN ON YOUR OWN?
HERR KARNAU DOESN'T KNOW WHAT TO SAY. I FEEL SORRY FOR HIM.
BUT HE DOESN'T LOOK SAD AT ALL.
HUUAAAA
PERHAPS IT'S NOT SO BAD, NOT HAVING ANY SIBLINGS.
I WANT TO PLAY WITH THE DOLL!!!
NO! MY DOLL!
WUAAAAAAWAAA
WWWAAWAWAWWAAA
STOP CRYING, HOLDE.
SNNFF
COME, LET'S PLAY SOMETHING ELSE.
WHAT SHOULD WE PLAY?

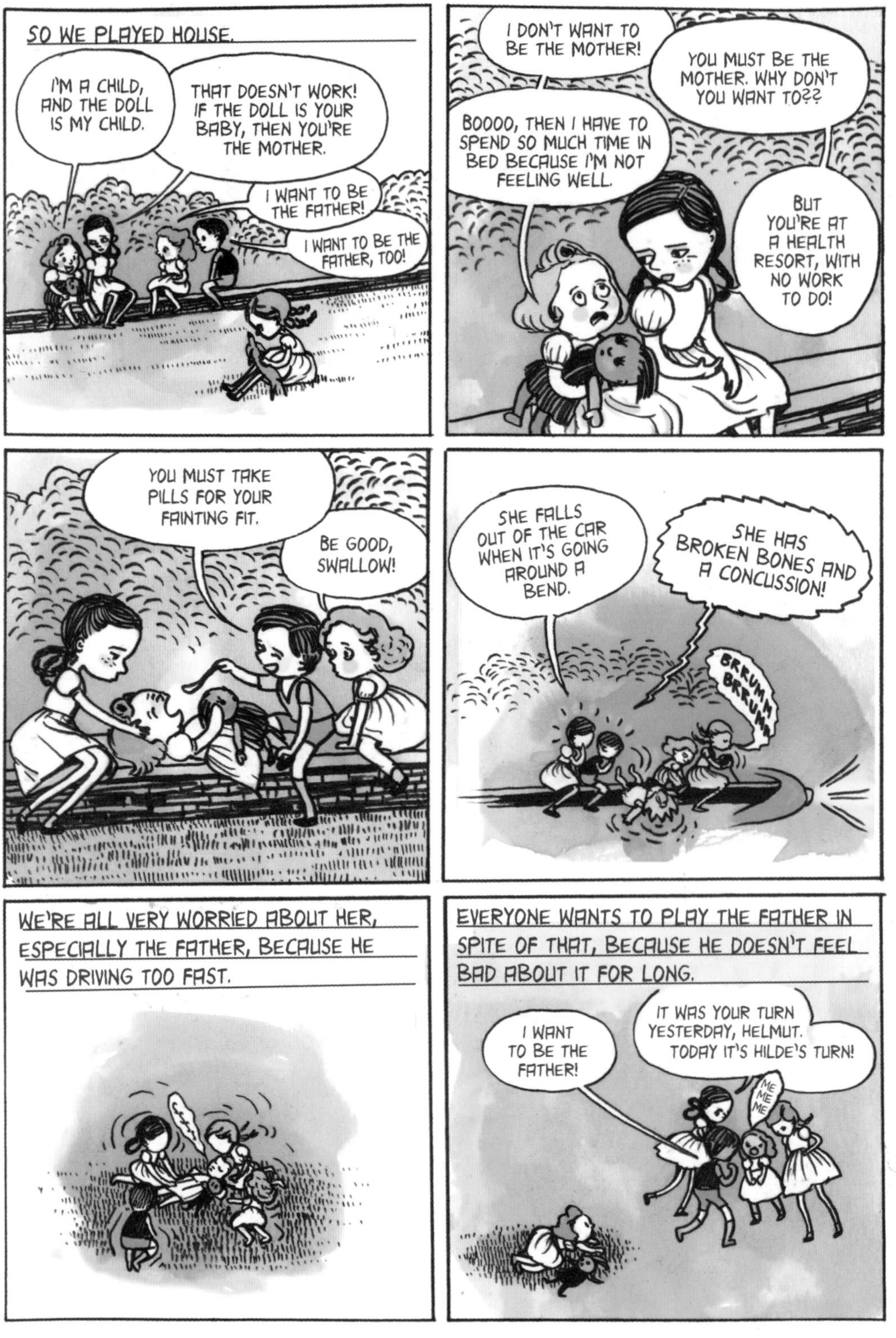

SO WE PLAYED HOUSE.
I'M A CHILD, AND THE DOLL IS MY CHILD.
THAT DOESN'T WORK! IF THE DOLL IS YOUR BABY, THEN YOU'RE THE MOTHER.
I WANT TO BE THE FATHER!
I WANT TO BE THE FATHER, TOO!
I DON'T WANT TO BE THE MOTHER!
YOU MUST BE THE MOTHER. WHY DON'T YOU WANT TO??
BOOOO, THEN I HAVE TO SPEND SO MUCH TIME IN BED BECAUSE I'M NOT FEELING WELL.
BUT YOU'RE AT A HEALTH RESORT, WITH NO WORK TO DO!
YOU MUST TAKE PILLS FOR YOUR FAINTING FIT.
BE GOOD, SWALLOW!
SHE FALLS OUT OF THE CAR WHEN IT'S GOING AROUND A BEND.
SHE HAS BROKEN BONES AND A CONCUSSION!
BRRUMM BRRUMM
WE'RE ALL VERY WORRIED ABOUT HER, ESPECIALLY THE FATHER, BECAUSE HE WAS DRIVING TOO FAST.
EVERYONE WANTS TO PLAY THE FATHER IN SPITE OF THAT, BECAUSE HE DOESN'T FEEL BAD ABOUT IT FOR LONG.
I WANT TO BE THE FATHER!
IT WAS YOUR TURN YESTERDAY, HELMUT. TODAY IT'S HILDE'S TURN!
ME ME ME

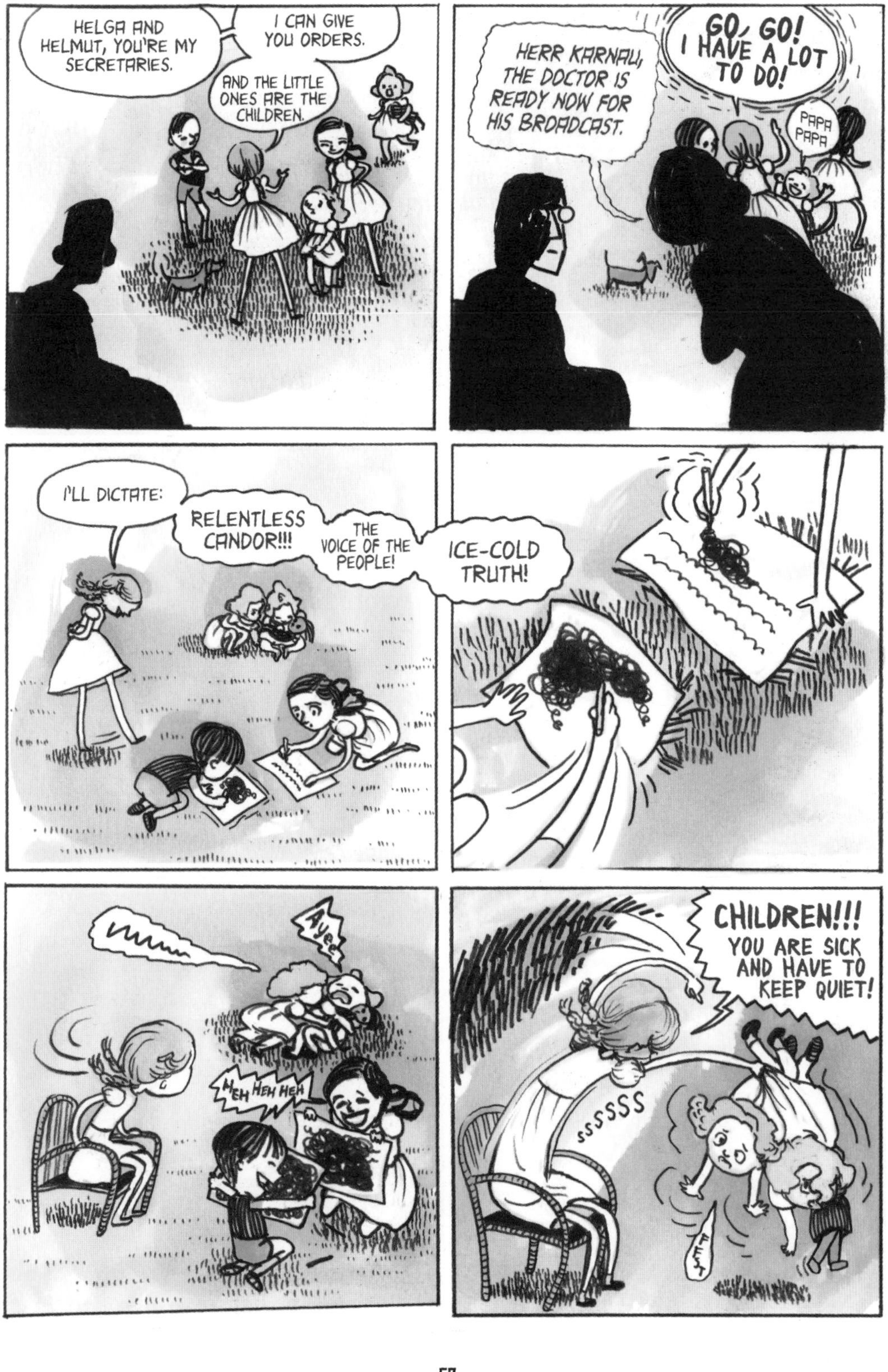
HELGA AND HELMUT, YOU'RE MY SECRETARIES.
I CAN GIVE YOU ORDERS.
AND THE LITTLE ONES ARE THE CHILDREN.
HERR KARNAU, THE DOCTOR IS READY NOW FOR HIS BROADCAST.
GO, GO! I HAVE A LOT TO DO!
PAPA PAPA
I'LL DICTATE:
RELENTLESS CANDOR!!!
THE VOICE OF THE PEOPLE!
ICE-COLD TRUTH!
AYEE
HEH HEH HEH
CHILDREN!!! YOU ARE SICK AND HAVE TO KEEP QUIET!
SSSSSS
PFFT

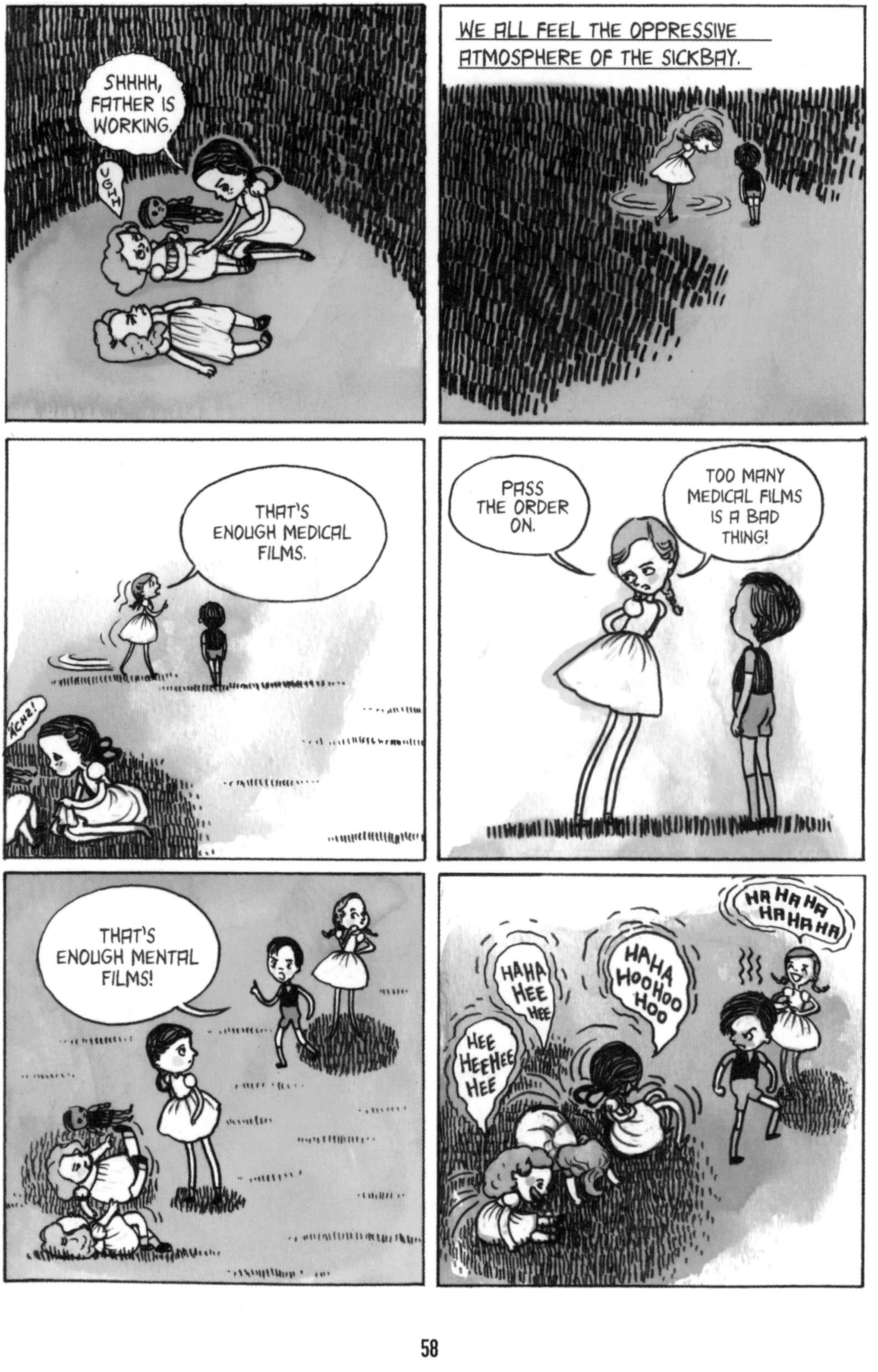
SHHHH, FATHER IS WORKING.
UGHH
WE ALL FEEL THE OPPRESSIVE ATMOSPHERE OF THE SICKBAY.
THAT'S ENOUGH MEDICAL FILMS.
PASS THE ORDER ON.
TOO MANY MEDICAL FILMS IS A BAD THING!
THAT'S ENOUGH MENTAL FILMS!
HEE HEEHEE HEE
HAHA HEE HEE
HAHA HOO HOO HOO
HA HA HA HA HA HA

WE CALL HELMUT TRAN, FROM TRAN AND HELLE, THE TWO FILM CHARACTERS INVENTED BY THE FATHER HIMSELF.

HA HA HA, YOU'RE TRAN.

I DON'T WANT TO PLAY ANYMORE!

HA HA TRAN AND HELLE!

HEE HEE HEE HEE HEE HOO HOO

WHAT'S GOING ON BACK THERE?!

MMPF.

NO ONE LAUGHS IN THE SICKBAY!

...!

BOOOO WE ALWAYS HAVE TO BE STILL!

WE WANT TO PLAY TOO!

MMPF.

NOW THE CHILDREN CAN PLAY TOO!

YOU'RE ALLOWED TO BE PRESENT AT THE SCREENINGS.

FINALLY!

YEEHEE

YOOHOO

THERE ARE MOUNTAINEERING FILMS, NEWSREELS, AND CHILDREN'S FILMS, WHICH EVEN THE FATHER FINDS AMUSING.

THAT IS A FILM WITH MICKEY MOUSE. MICKEY MOUSE RUNS AND RUNS AND...

...SUDDENLY THERE'S A CLIFF, THE FLOOR'S GONE, AND MICKEY MOUSE STILL KEEPS ON RUNNING.

HOW COME?

HE DOESN'T FALL?

NO.

FINALLY THE FATHER SAYS, "STOP THE PROJECTOR. THIS FILM IS BANNED."

59

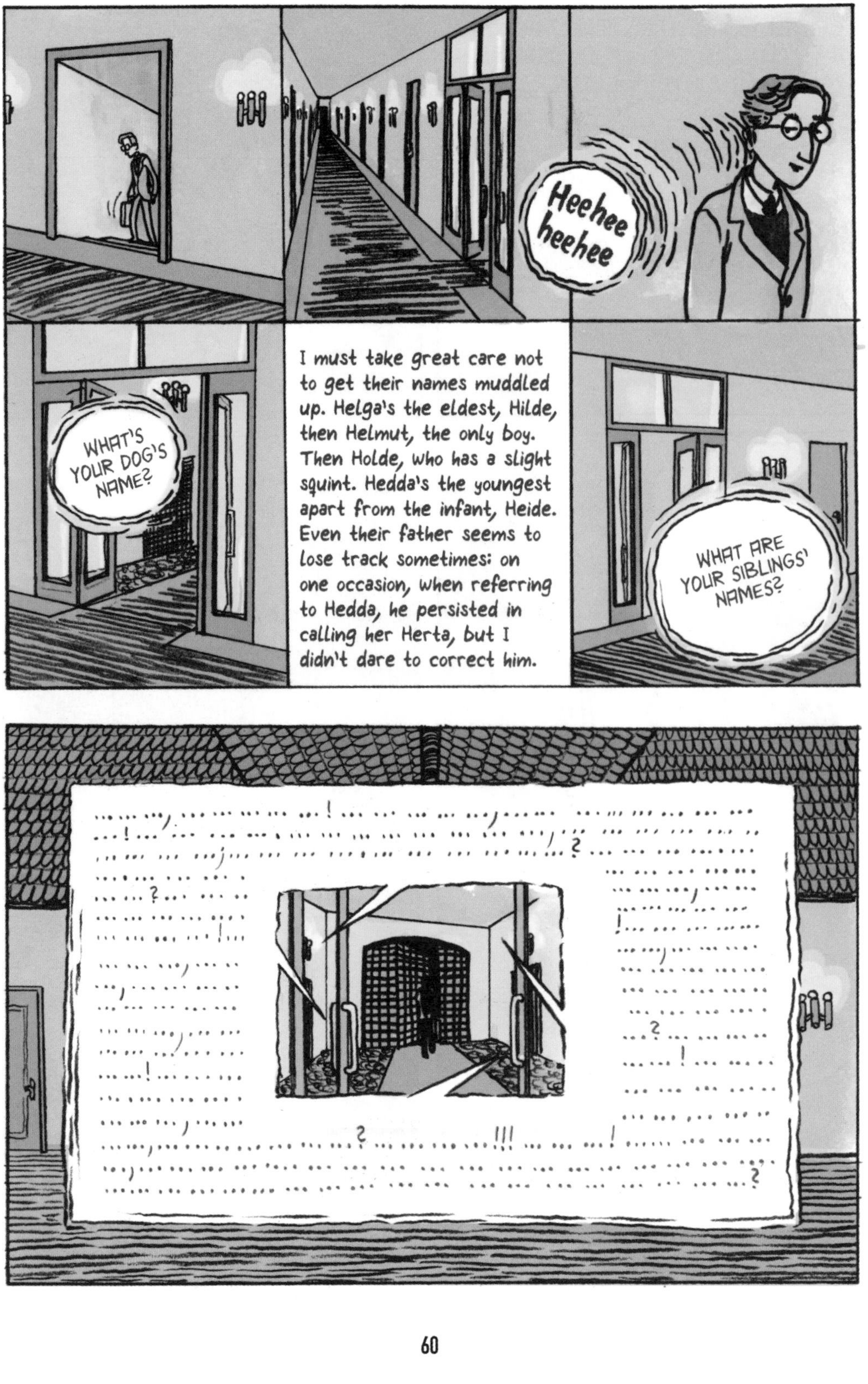
Heehee heehee
WHAT'S YOUR DOG'S NAME?
I must take great care not to get their names muddled up. Helga's the eldest, Hilde, then Helmut, the only boy. Then Holde, who has a slight squint. Hedda's the youngest apart from the infant, Heide. Even their father seems to lose track sometimes: on one occasion, when referring to Hedda, he persisted in calling her Herta, but I didn't dare to correct him.
WHAT ARE YOUR SIBLINGS' NAMES?

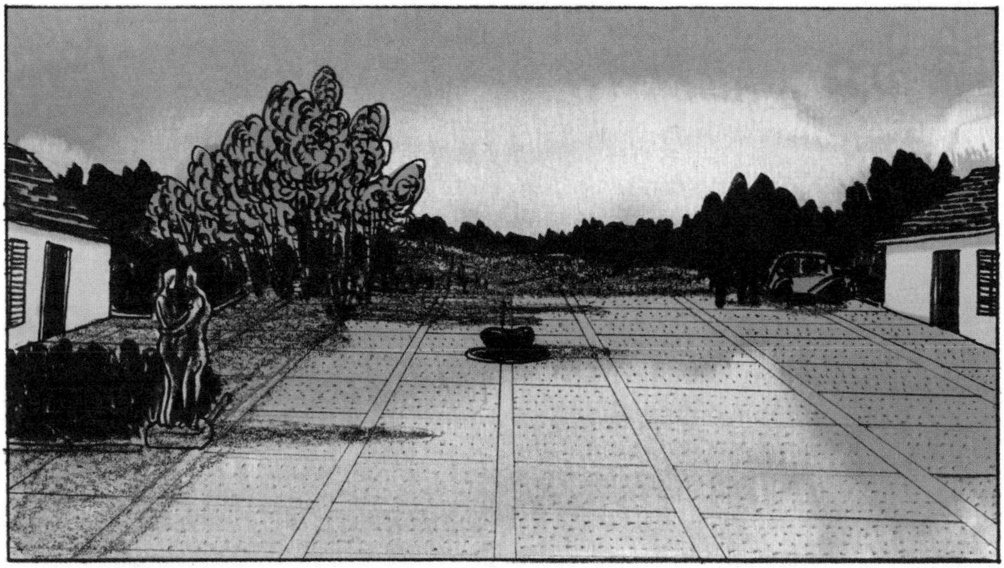

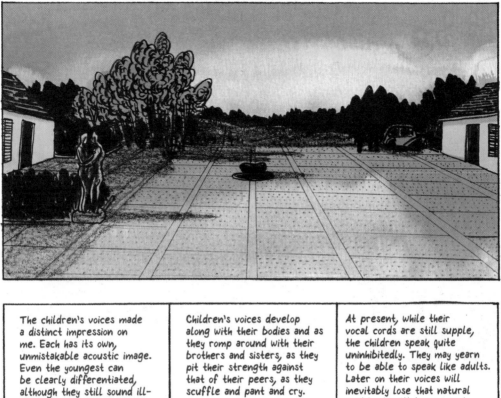

The children's voices made a distinct impression on me. Each has its own, unmistakable acoustic image. Even the youngest can be clearly differentiated, although they still sound ill-defined and will only develop fully as the years go by.

Children's voices develop along with their bodies and as they romp around with their brothers and sisters, as they pit their strength against that of their peers, as they scuffle and pant and cry.

At present, while their vocal cords are still supple, the children speak quite uninhibitedly. They may yearn to be able to speak like adults. Later on their voices will inevitably lose that natural quality, they'll learn how to cough, to emit polite little coughs behind an upraised hand.

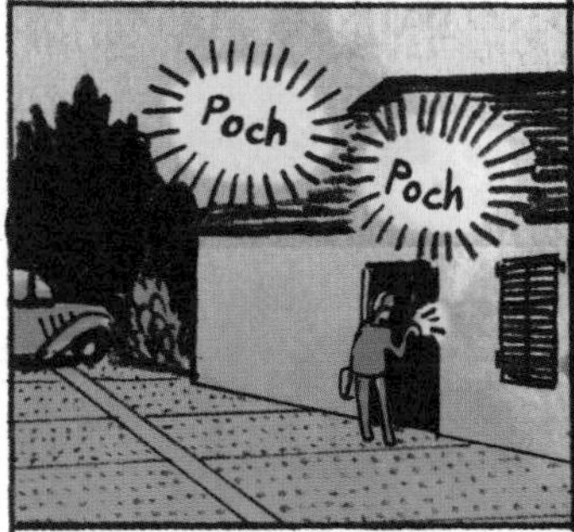
Poch
Poch

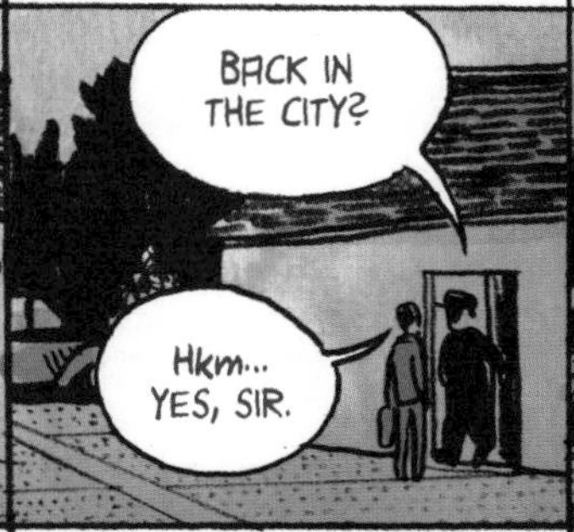
BACK IN THE CITY?
Hkm... YES, SIR.

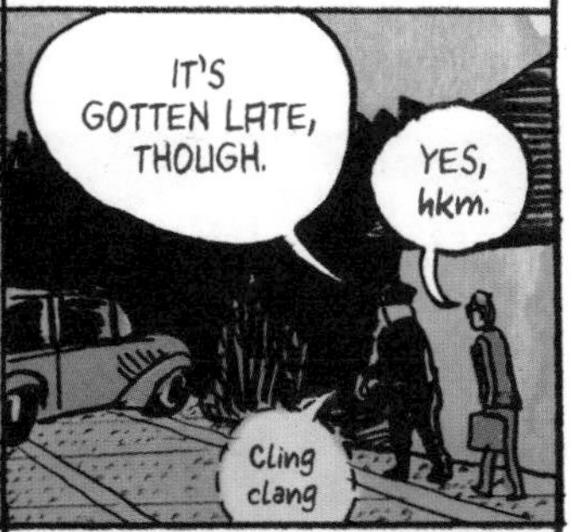
IT'S GOTTEN LATE, THOUGH.
YES, hkm.
Cling clang

All the polite fillers, the "reallys" and "you-don't-says" that dissuade people from tearing each other limb from limb at the slightest conversational tiff. The voice is steadily abraded by prescribed patterns of speech until death supervenes, by which time it has become a strangled sound located at the base of the tongue.

It will dawn on the children, sooner or later, that they no longer enjoy free use of their voices. Helmut will attain this painful realization as soon as his voice starts to break. The larynx suddenly refuses to obey and becomes a sore point, an ever open wound in the throat.

The vocal cords are strained and distorted, and the tongue, too, weakens because all it can articulate are fragmentary sounds that fluctuate in pitch. And Helmut will be alarmed to find that his voice is slipping from his grasp. Like everything else.

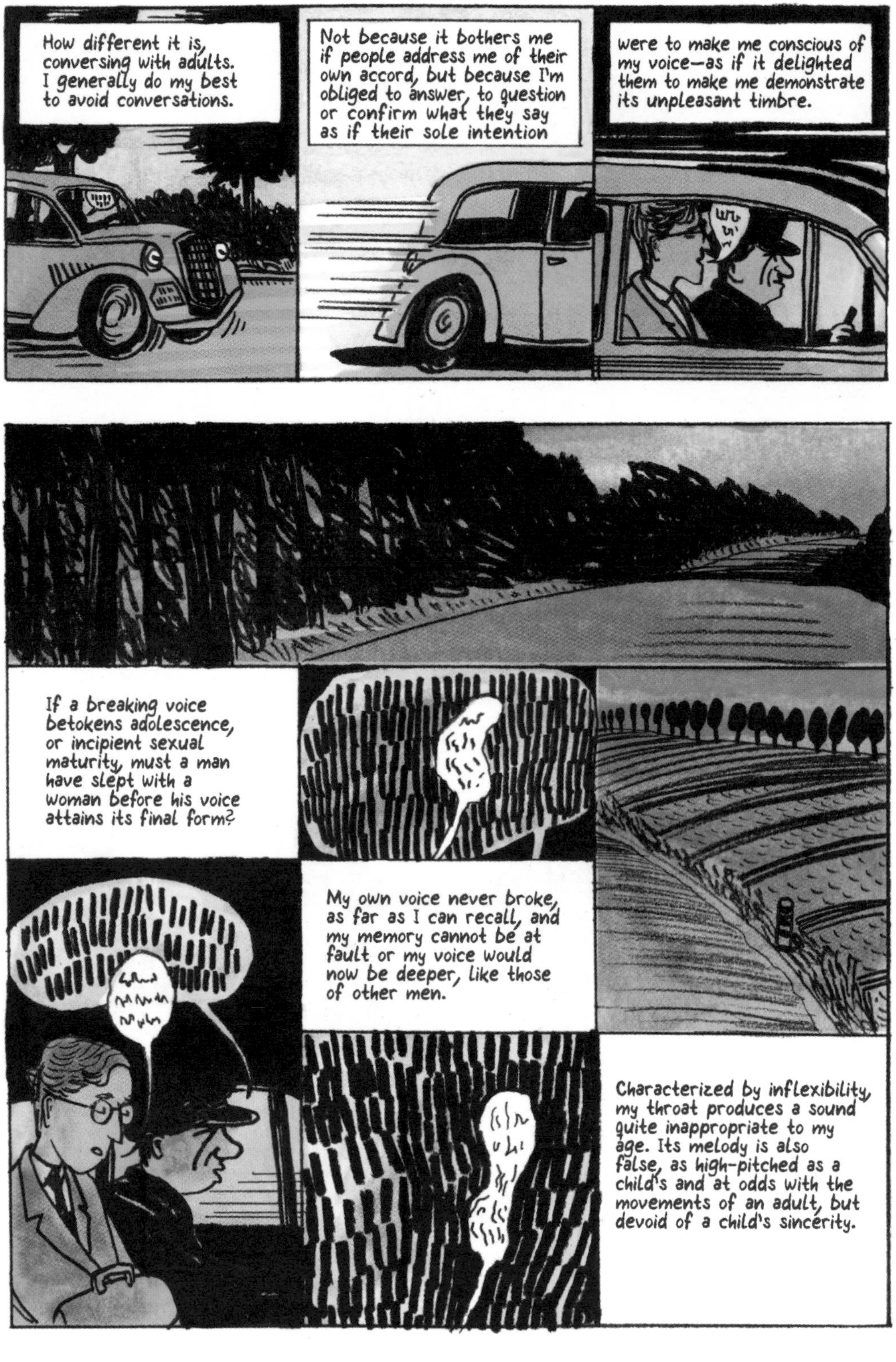
How different it is, conversing with adults. I generally do my best to avoid conversations.
Not because it bothers me if people address me of their own accord, but because I'm obliged to answer, to question or confirm what they say as if their sole intention
were to make me conscious of my voice—as if it delighted them to make me demonstrate its unpleasant timbre.
If a breaking voice betokens adolescence, or incipient sexual maturity, must a man have slept with a woman before his voice attains its final form?
My own voice never broke, as far as I can recall, and my memory cannot be at fault or my voice would now be deeper, like those of other men.
Characterized by inflexibility, my throat produces a sound quite inappropriate to my age. Its melody is also false, as high-pitched as a child's and at odds with the movements of an adult, but devoid of a child's sincerity.

Might it be worth devoting the half-hour before supper to my work?

My collection of sounds is steadily growing: I've already managed to compile about a hundred examples of the strangest utterances. Some are everyday noises, throat-clearings, little coughs and sniffs that are heedlessly emitted by the sound source but mercilessly recorded on disc. My collection includes some genuine treasures, including this recording of a brothel — given to me by an acquaintance. People must be monitored even when making love. Soon after it was recorded, the brothel was closed down for fear of disease. According to my friend, it even employed the services of dogs trained to copulate with the aid of soiled underclothes.

WOOF WOOF WOOF WOOF

GRRRRRRR

Is there anything I would not record?

WOOF WOOF

Very few voices are free from scars and simply coated with a soft, delicate network of veins. Small wonder that the impalpable something called the soul—the molded breath of life that constitutes the human being—is thought to reside in the human voice.

Hee hee! Hee hee!

WOOF WOOF WOOF WOOF

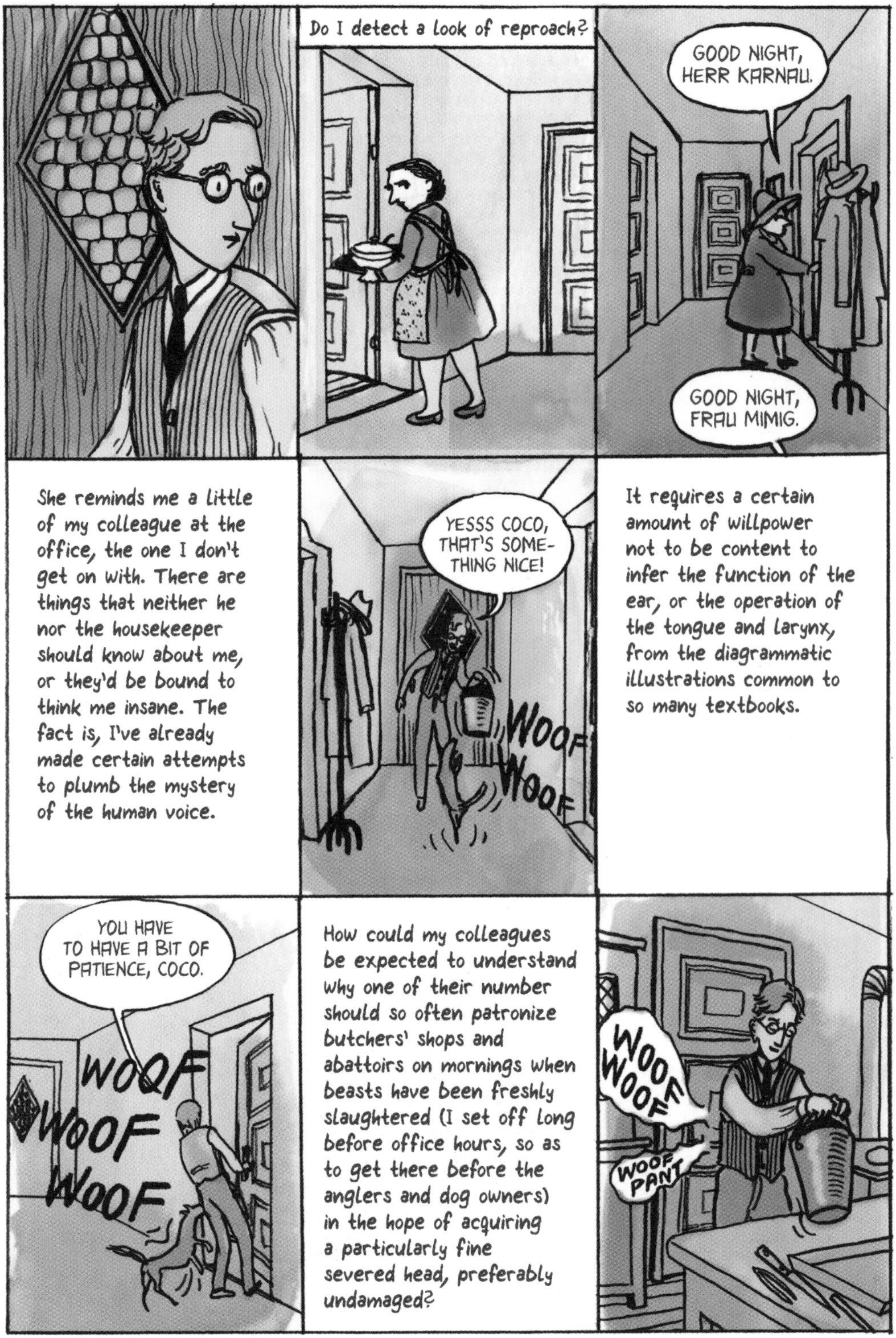
Do I detect a look of reproach?
GOOD NIGHT, HERR KARNAU.
GOOD NIGHT, FRAU MIMIG.
She reminds me a little of my colleague at the office, the one I don't get on with. There are things that neither he nor the housekeeper should know about me, or they'd be bound to think me insane. The fact is, I've already made certain attempts to plumb the mystery of the human voice.
YESSS COCO, THAT'S SOMETHING NICE!
WOOF WOOF
It requires a certain amount of willpower not to be content to infer the function of the ear, or the operation of the tongue and larynx, from the diagrammatic illustrations common to so many textbooks.
YOU HAVE TO HAVE A BIT OF PATIENCE, COCO.
WOOF WOOF WOOF
How could my colleagues be expected to understand why one of their number should so often patronize butchers' shops and abattoirs on mornings when beasts have been freshly slaughtered (I set off long before office hours, so as to get there before the anglers and dog owners) in the hope of acquiring a particularly fine severed head, preferably undamaged?
WOOF WOOF
WOOF PANT

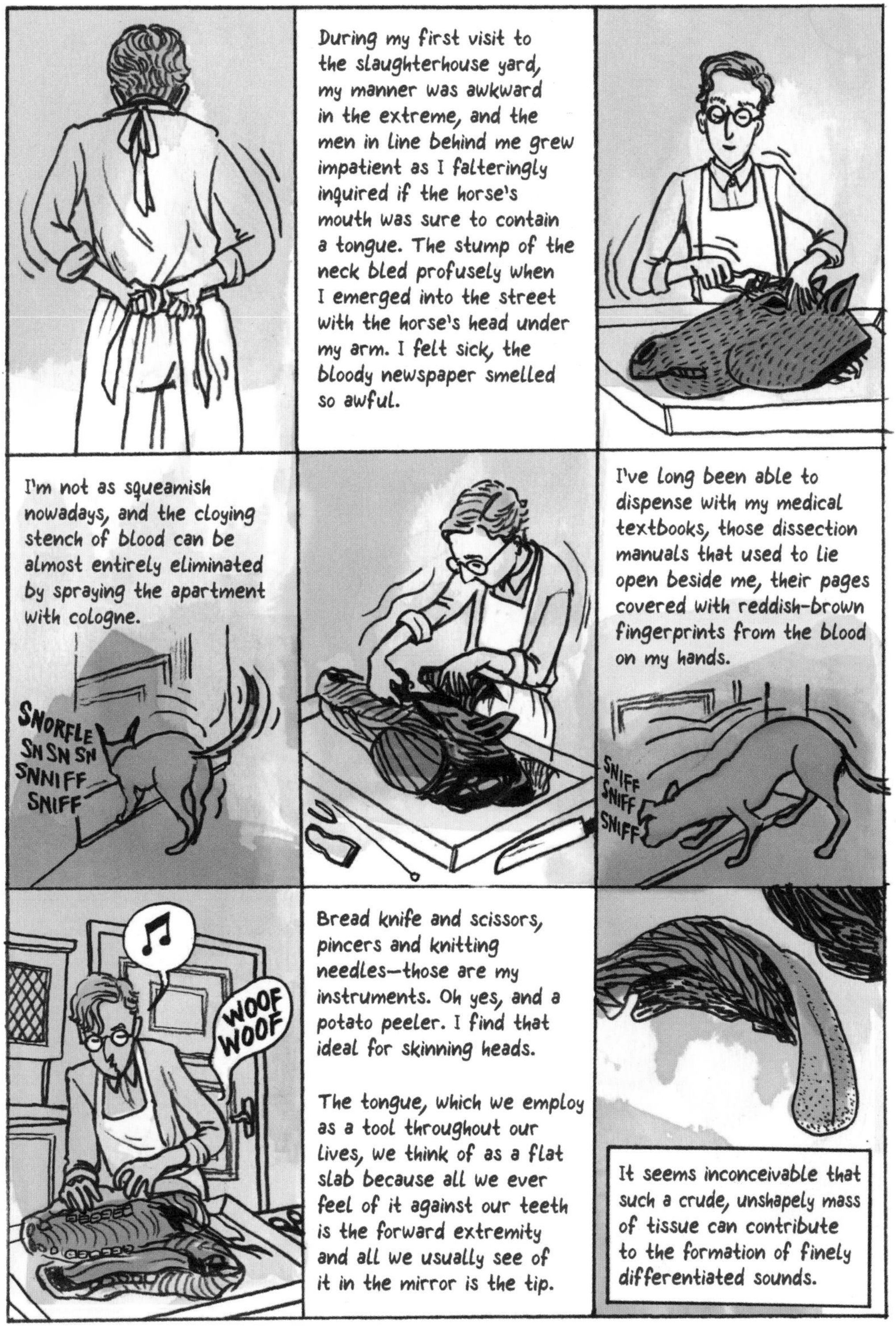
During my first visit to the slaughterhouse yard, my manner was awkward in the extreme, and the men in line behind me grew impatient as I falteringly inquired if the horse's mouth was sure to contain a tongue. The stump of the neck bled profusely when I emerged into the street with the horse's head under my arm. I felt sick, the bloody newspaper smelled so awful.
I'm not as squeamish nowadays, and the cloying stench of blood can be almost entirely eliminated by spraying the apartment with cologne.
SNORFLE SN SN SN SNNIFF SNIFF
I've long been able to dispense with my medical textbooks, those dissection manuals that used to lie open beside me, their pages covered with reddish-brown fingerprints from the blood on my hands.
SNIFF SNIFF SNIFF
WOOF WOOF
Bread knife and scissors, pincers and knitting needles—those are my instruments. Oh yes, and a potato peeler. I find that ideal for skinning heads.
The tongue, which we employ as a tool throughout our lives, we think of as a flat slab because all we ever feel of it against our teeth is the forward extremity and all we usually see of it in the mirror is the tip.
It seems inconceivable that such a crude, unshapely mass of tissue can contribute to the formation of finely differentiated sounds.

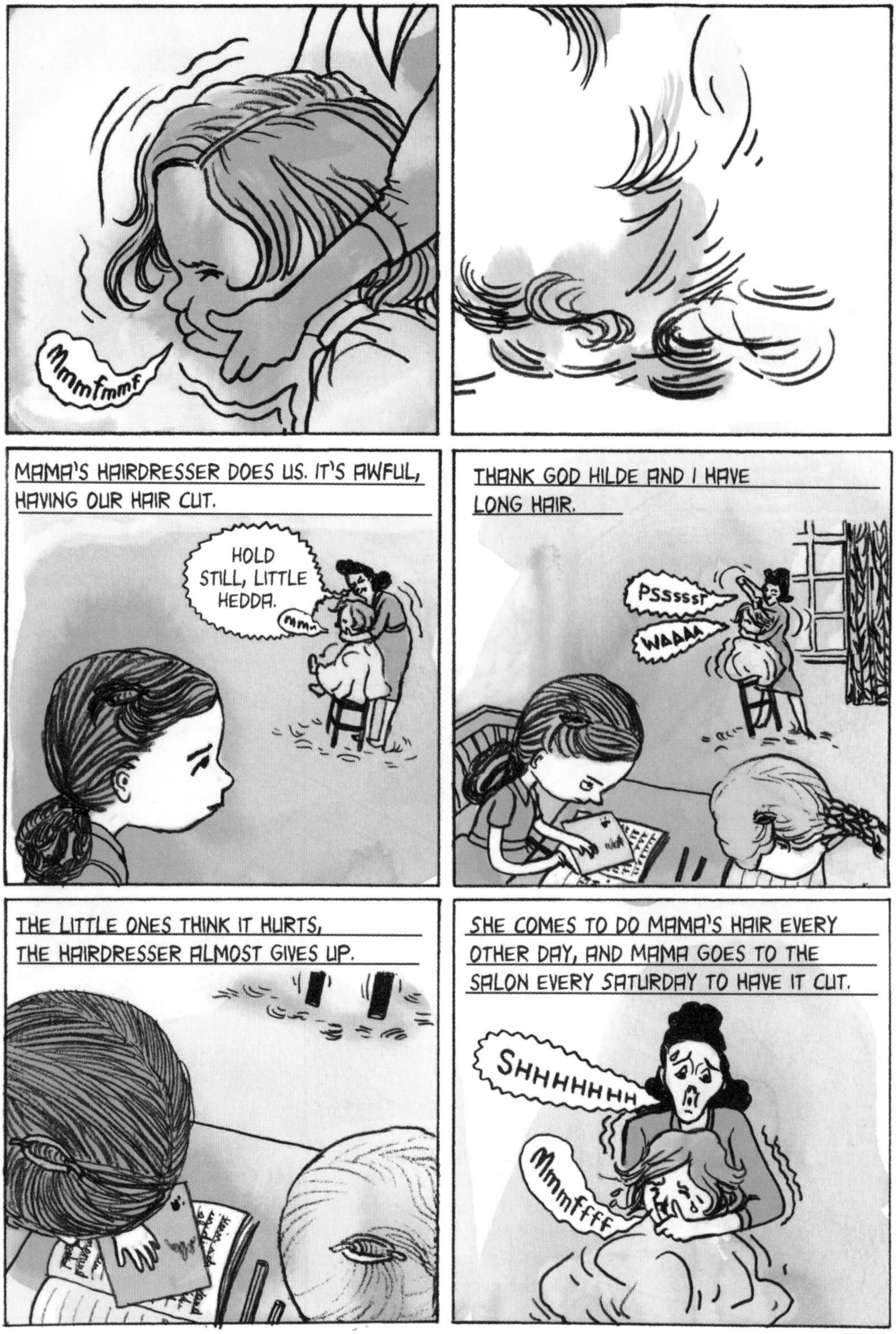
Mmmfmmf
MAMA'S HAIRDRESSER DOES US. IT'S AWFUL, HAVING OUR HAIR CUT.
HOLD STILL, LITTLE HEDDA.
THANK GOD HILDE AND I HAVE LONG HAIR.
PSSSSST
WAAAA
THE LITTLE ONES THINK IT HURTS, THE HAIRDRESSER ALMOST GIVES UP.
SHE COMES TO DO MAMA'S HAIR EVERY OTHER DAY, AND MAMA GOES TO THE SALON EVERY SATURDAY TO HAVE IT CUT.
SHHHHHHH
Mmmffff

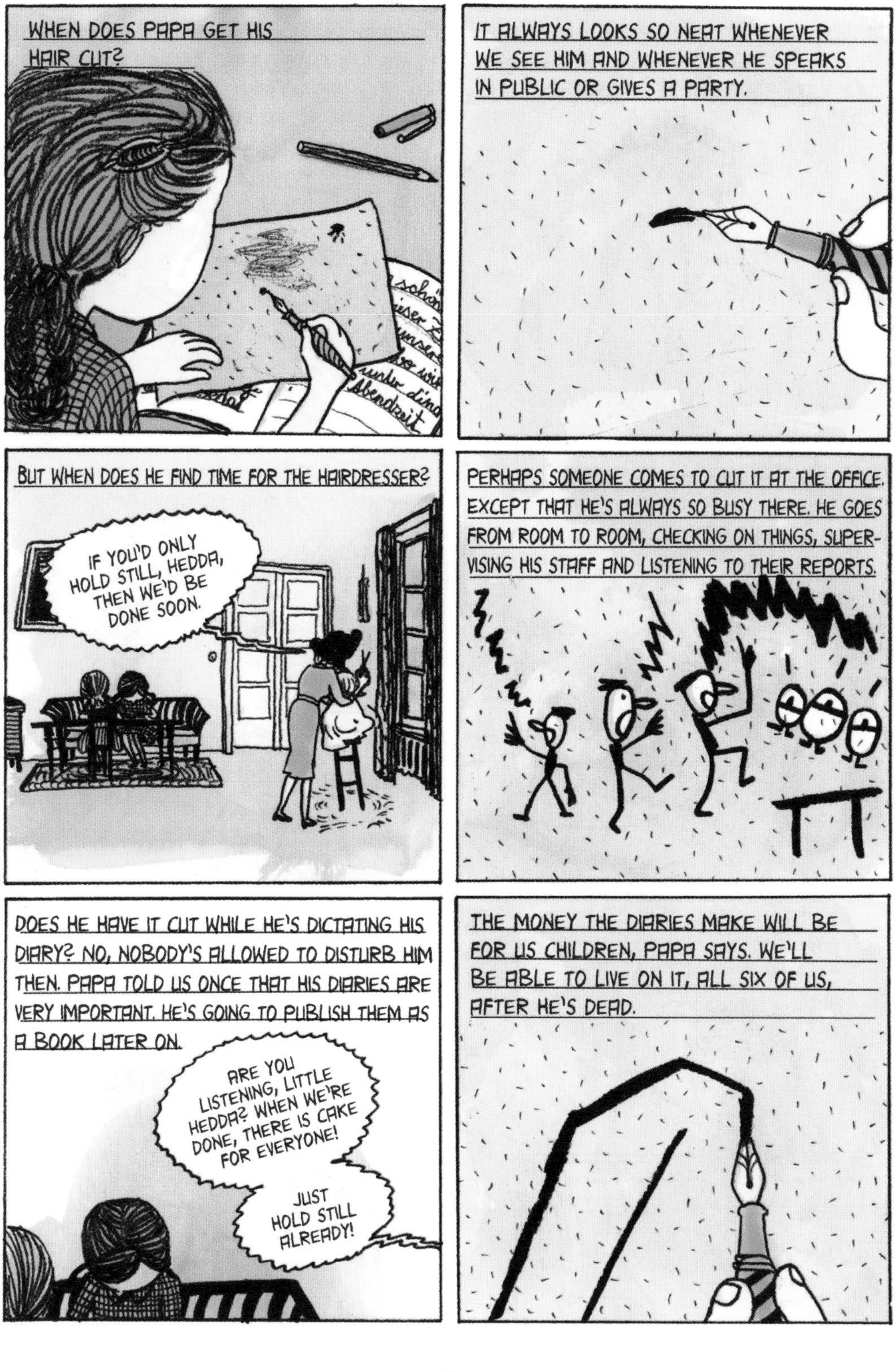
WHEN DOES PAPA GET HIS HAIR CUT?
IT ALWAYS LOOKS SO NEAT WHENEVER WE SEE HIM AND WHENEVER HE SPEAKS IN PUBLIC OR GIVES A PARTY.
BUT WHEN DOES HE FIND TIME FOR THE HAIRDRESSER?
IF YOU'D ONLY HOLD STILL, HEDDA, THEN WE'D BE DONE SOON.
PERHAPS SOMEONE COMES TO CUT IT AT THE OFFICE. EXCEPT THAT HE'S ALWAYS SO BUSY THERE. HE GOES FROM ROOM TO ROOM, CHECKING ON THINGS, SUPER-VISING HIS STAFF AND LISTENING TO THEIR REPORTS.
DOES HE HAVE IT CUT WHILE HE'S DICTATING HIS DIARY? NO, NOBODY'S ALLOWED TO DISTURB HIM THEN. PAPA TOLD US ONCE THAT HIS DIARIES ARE VERY IMPORTANT. HE'S GOING TO PUBLISH THEM AS A BOOK LATER ON.
ARE YOU LISTENING, LITTLE HEDDA? WHEN WE'RE DONE, THERE IS CAKE FOR EVERYONE!
JUST HOLD STILL ALREADY!
THE MONEY THE DIARIES MAKE WILL BE FOR US CHILDREN, PAPA SAYS. WE'LL BE ABLE TO LIVE ON IT, ALL SIX OF US, AFTER HE'S DEAD.

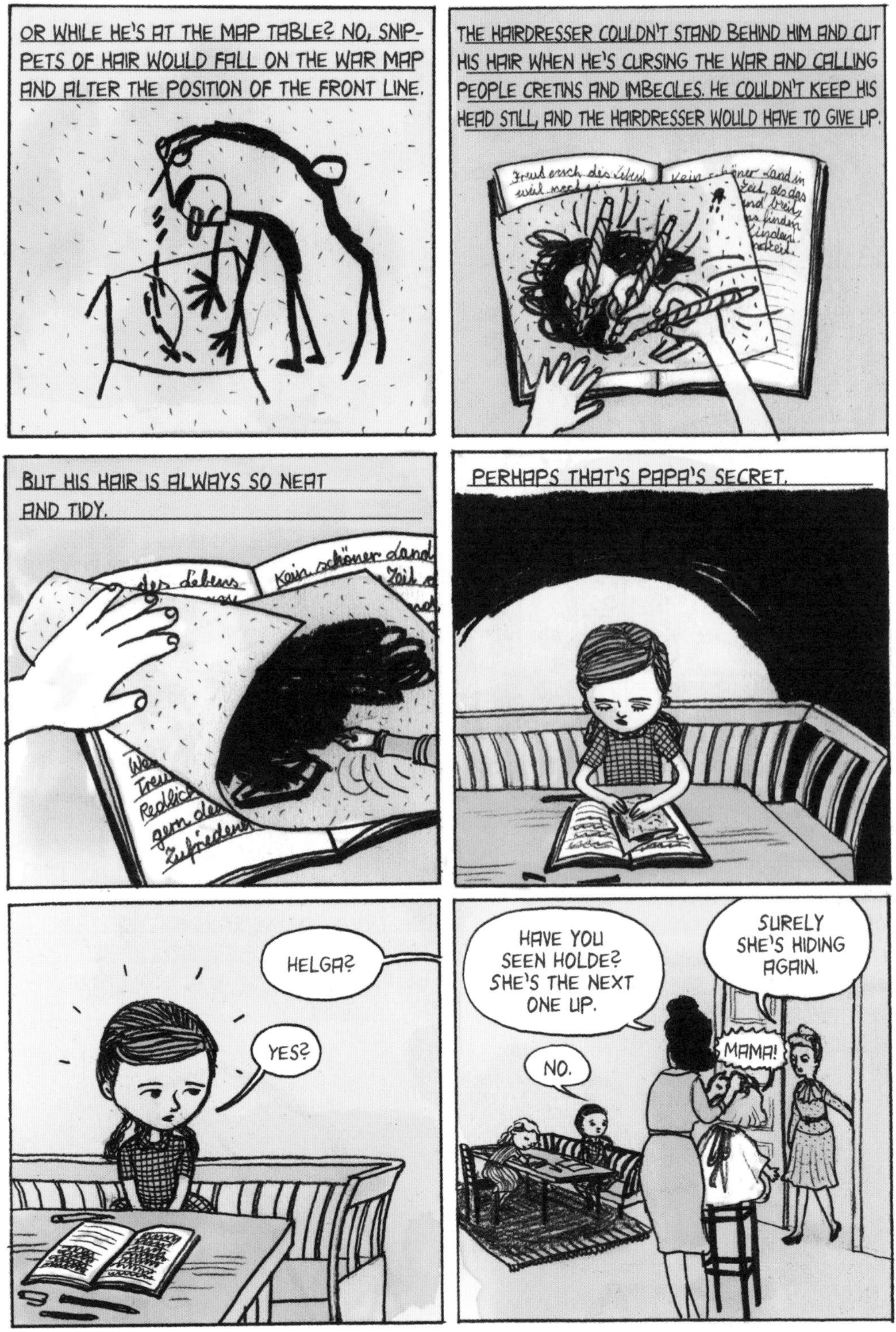

OR WHILE HE'S AT THE MAP TABLE? NO, SNIPPETS OF HAIR WOULD FALL ON THE WAR MAP AND ALTER THE POSITION OF THE FRONT LINE.
THE HAIRDRESSER COULDN'T STAND BEHIND HIM AND CUT HIS HAIR WHEN HE'S CURSING THE WAR AND CALLING PEOPLE CRETINS AND IMBECILES. HE COULDN'T KEEP HIS HEAD STILL, AND THE HAIRDRESSER WOULD HAVE TO GIVE UP.
BUT HIS HAIR IS ALWAYS SO NEAT AND TIDY.
PERHAPS THAT'S PAPA'S SECRET.
HELGA?
YES?
HAVE YOU SEEN HOLDE? SHE'S THE NEXT ONE UP.
SURELY SHE'S HIDING AGAIN.
MAMA!
NO.

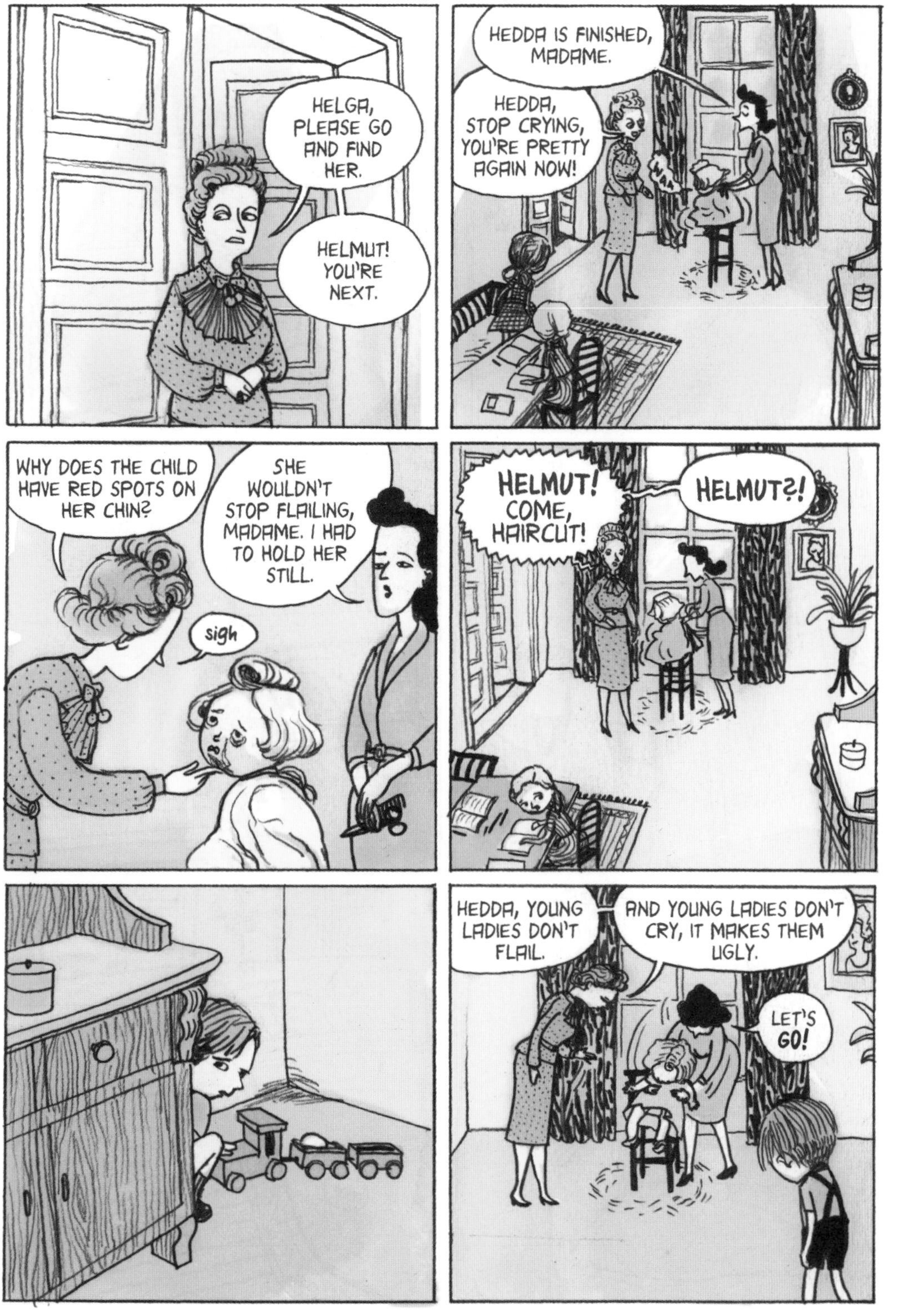
HELGA, PLEASE GO AND FIND HER.
HELMUT! YOU'RE NEXT.
HEDDA IS FINISHED, MADAME.
HEDDA, STOP CRYING, YOU'RE PRETTY AGAIN NOW!
WAA
WHY DOES THE CHILD HAVE RED SPOTS ON HER CHIN?
SHE WOULDN'T STOP FLAILING, MADAME. I HAD TO HOLD HER STILL.
sigh
HELMUT! COME, HAIRCUT!
HELMUT?!
HEDDA, YOUNG LADIES DON'T FLAIL.
AND YOUNG LADIES DON'T CRY, IT MAKES THEM UGLY.
LET'S GO!

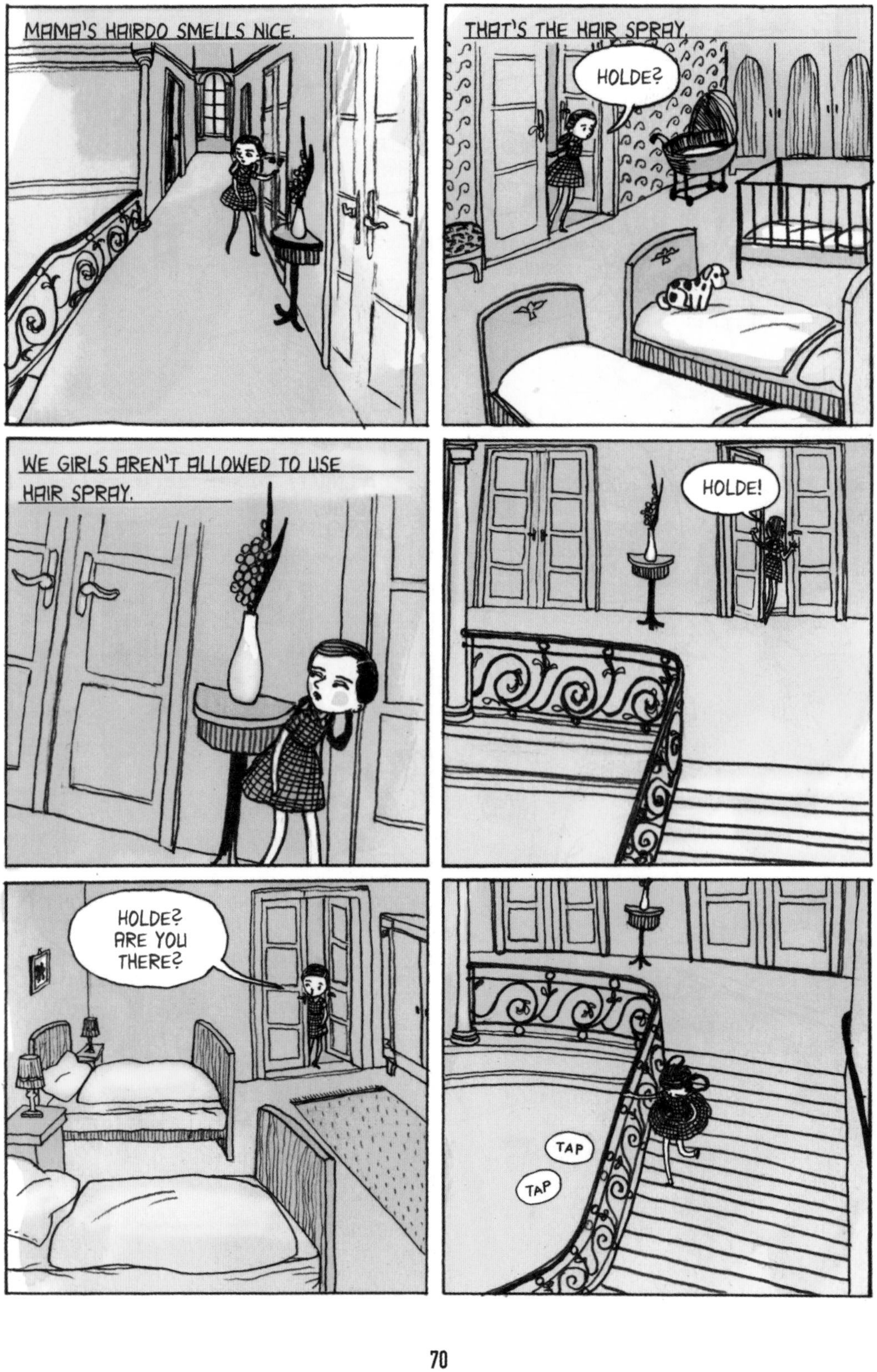
MAMA'S HAIRDO SMELLS NICE.
THAT'S THE HAIR SPRAY.
HOLDE?
WE GIRLS AREN'T ALLOWED TO USE HAIR SPRAY.
HOLDE!
HOLDE? ARE YOU THERE?
TAP
TAP

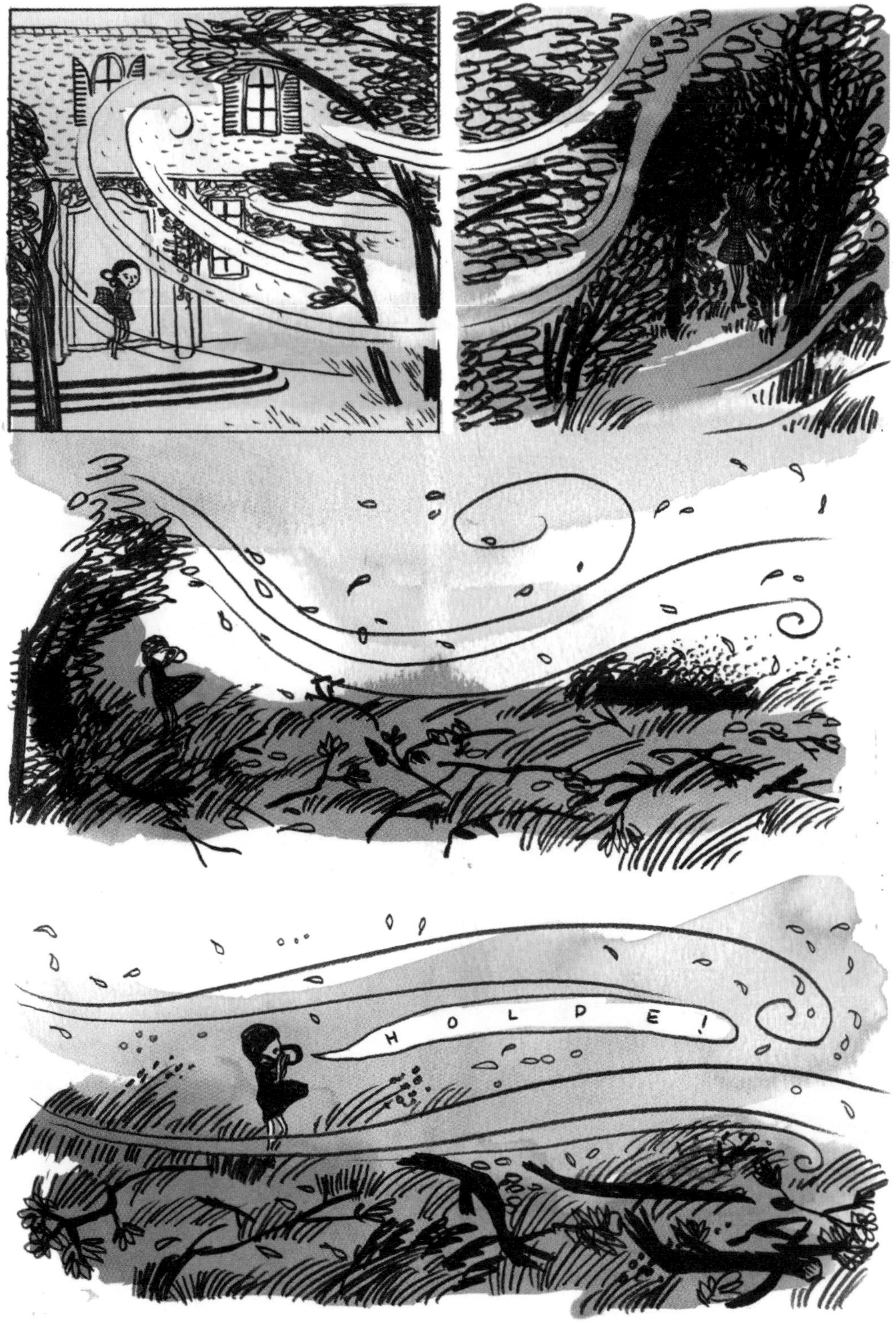
HOLDE!

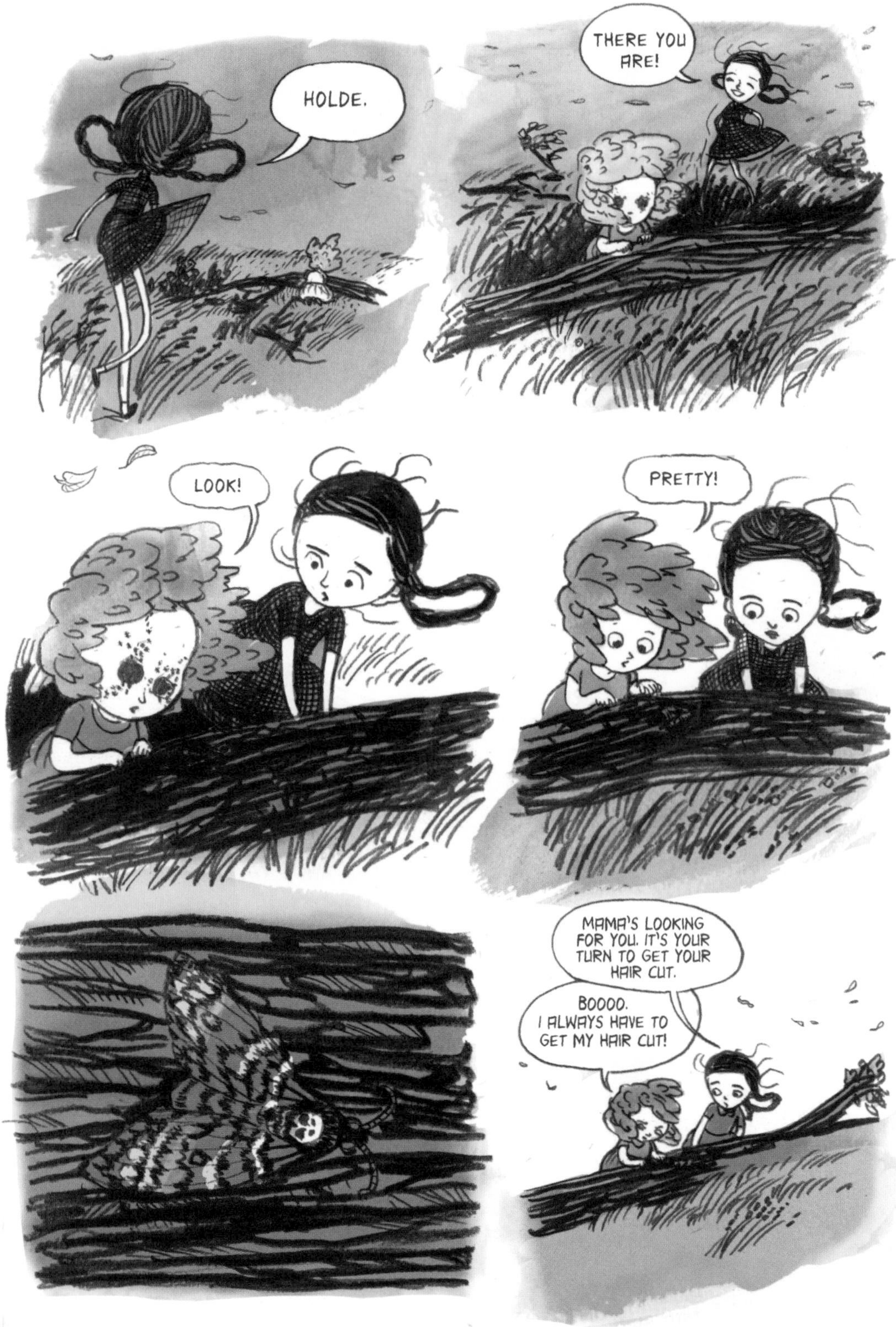
HOLDE.
THERE YOU ARE!
LOOK!
PRETTY!
MAMA'S LOOKING FOR YOU. IT'S YOUR TURN TO GET YOUR HAIR CUT.
BOOOO. I ALWAYS HAVE TO GET MY HAIR CUT!

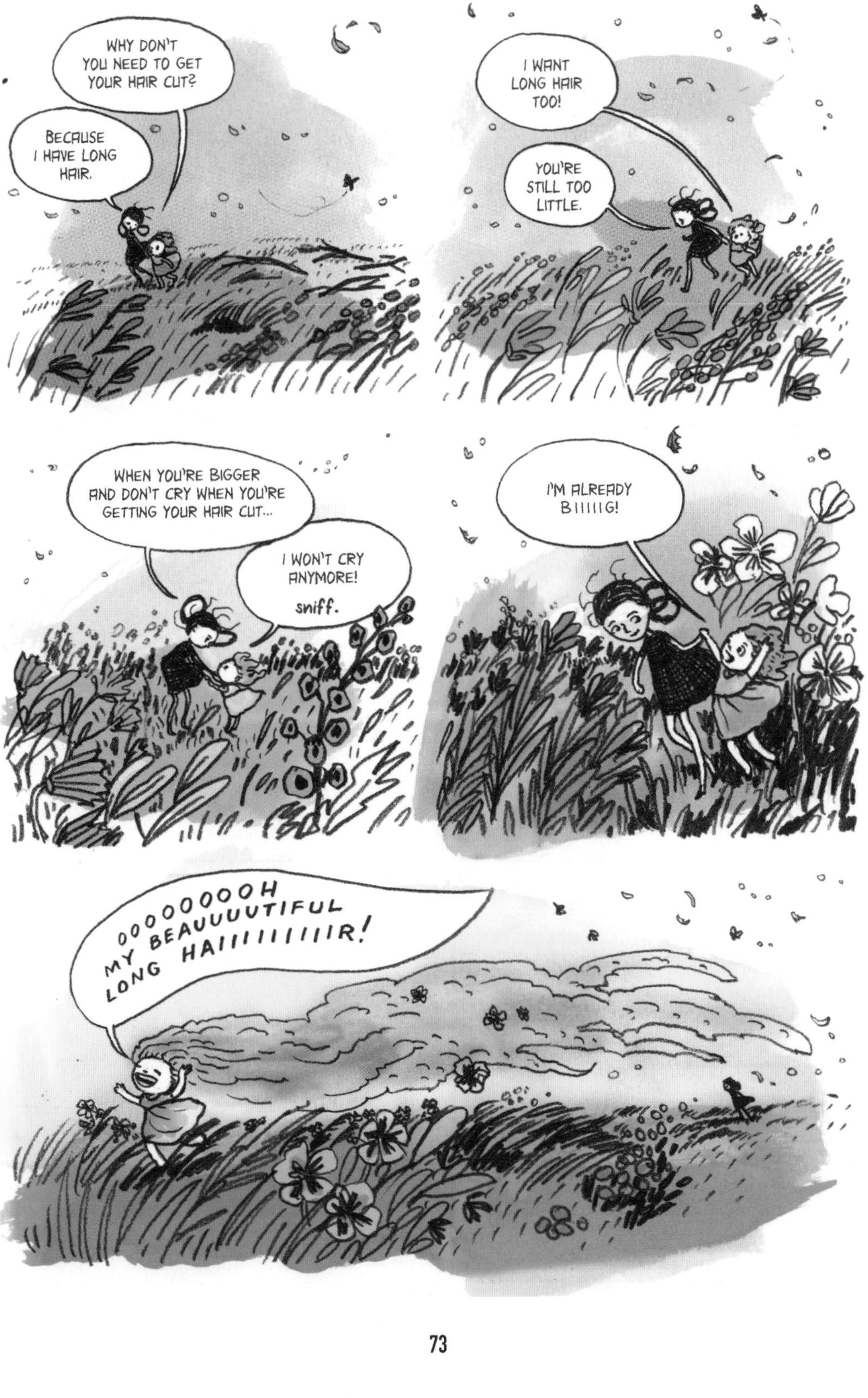
WHY DON'T YOU NEED TO GET YOUR HAIR CUT?
BECAUSE I HAVE LONG HAIR.
I WANT LONG HAIR TOO!
YOU'RE STILL TOO LITTLE.
WHEN YOU'RE BIGGER AND DON'T CRY WHEN YOU'RE GETTING YOUR HAIR CUT...
I WON'T CRY ANYMORE!
sniff.
I'M ALREADY BIIIIIG!
OOOOOOOOH MY BEAUUUUTIFUL LONG HAIIIIIIIIR!

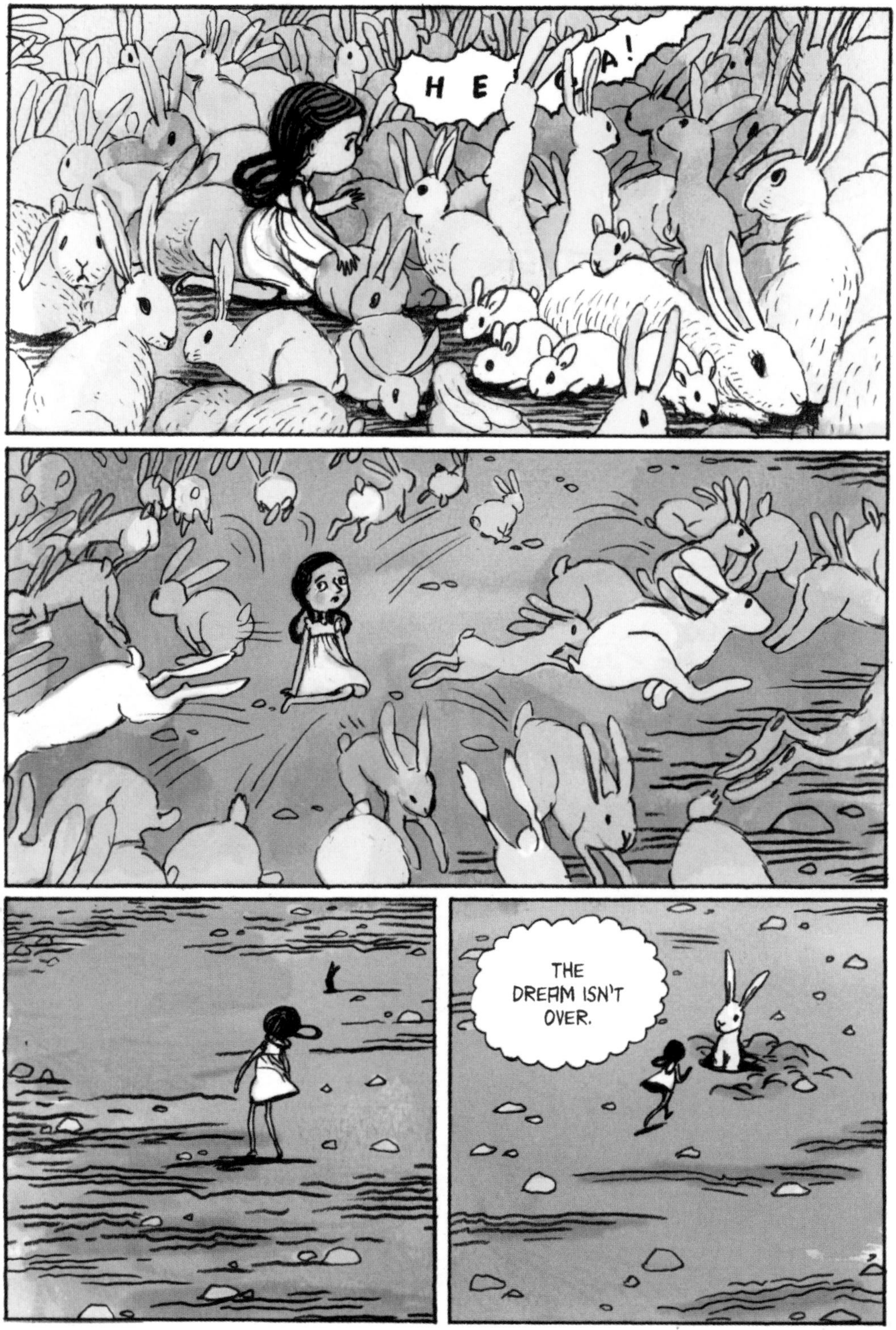
H E A!
THE DREAM ISN'T OVER.

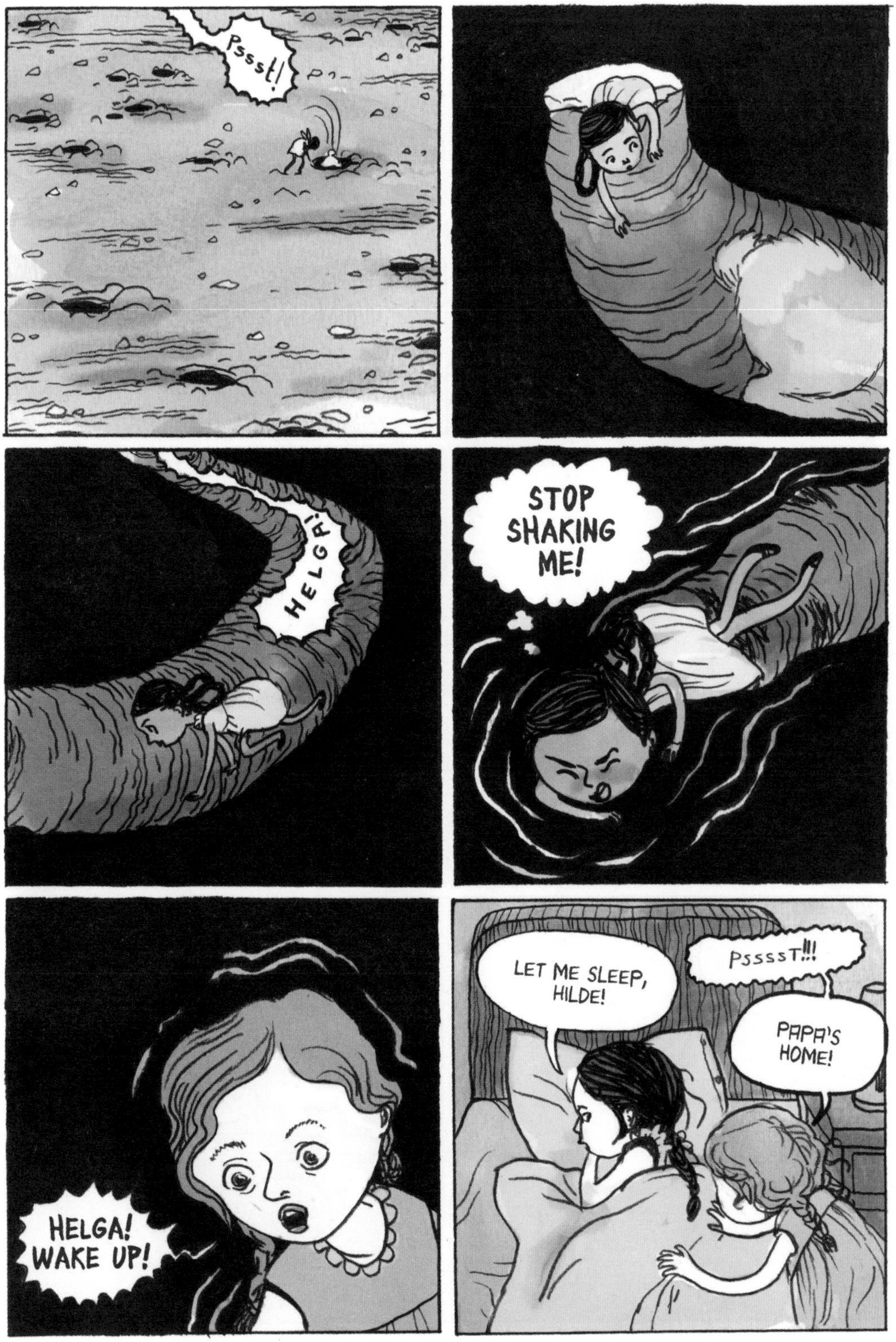
Pssst!
HELGA!
STOP SHAKING ME!
HELGA! WAKE UP!
LET ME SLEEP, HILDE!
PSSSST!!!
PAPA'S HOME!

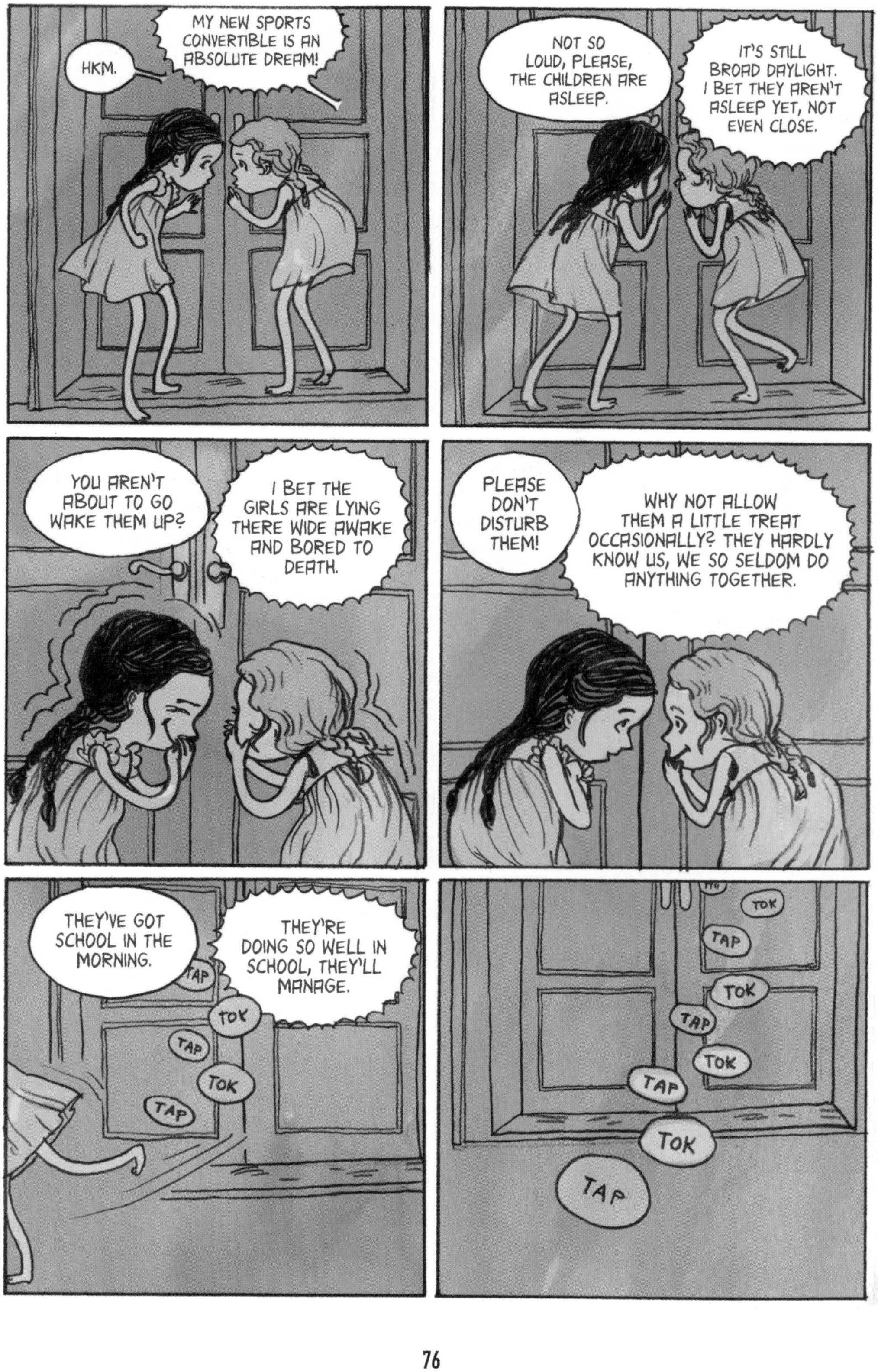

HKM.
MY NEW SPORTS CONVERTIBLE IS AN ABSOLUTE DREAM!
NOT SO LOUD, PLEASE, THE CHILDREN ARE ASLEEP.
IT'S STILL BROAD DAYLIGHT. I BET THEY AREN'T ASLEEP YET, NOT EVEN CLOSE.
YOU AREN'T ABOUT TO GO WAKE THEM UP?
I BET THE GIRLS ARE LYING THERE WIDE AWAKE AND BORED TO DEATH.
PLEASE DON'T DISTURB THEM!
WHY NOT ALLOW THEM A LITTLE TREAT OCCASIONALLY? THEY HARDLY KNOW US, WE SO SELDOM DO ANYTHING TOGETHER.
THEY'VE GOT SCHOOL IN THE MORNING.
THEY'RE DOING SO WELL IN SCHOOL, THEY'LL MANAGE.
TAP
TOK
TAP
TOK
TAP
TOK
TAP
TOK
TAP
TOK
TAP
TOK
TAP

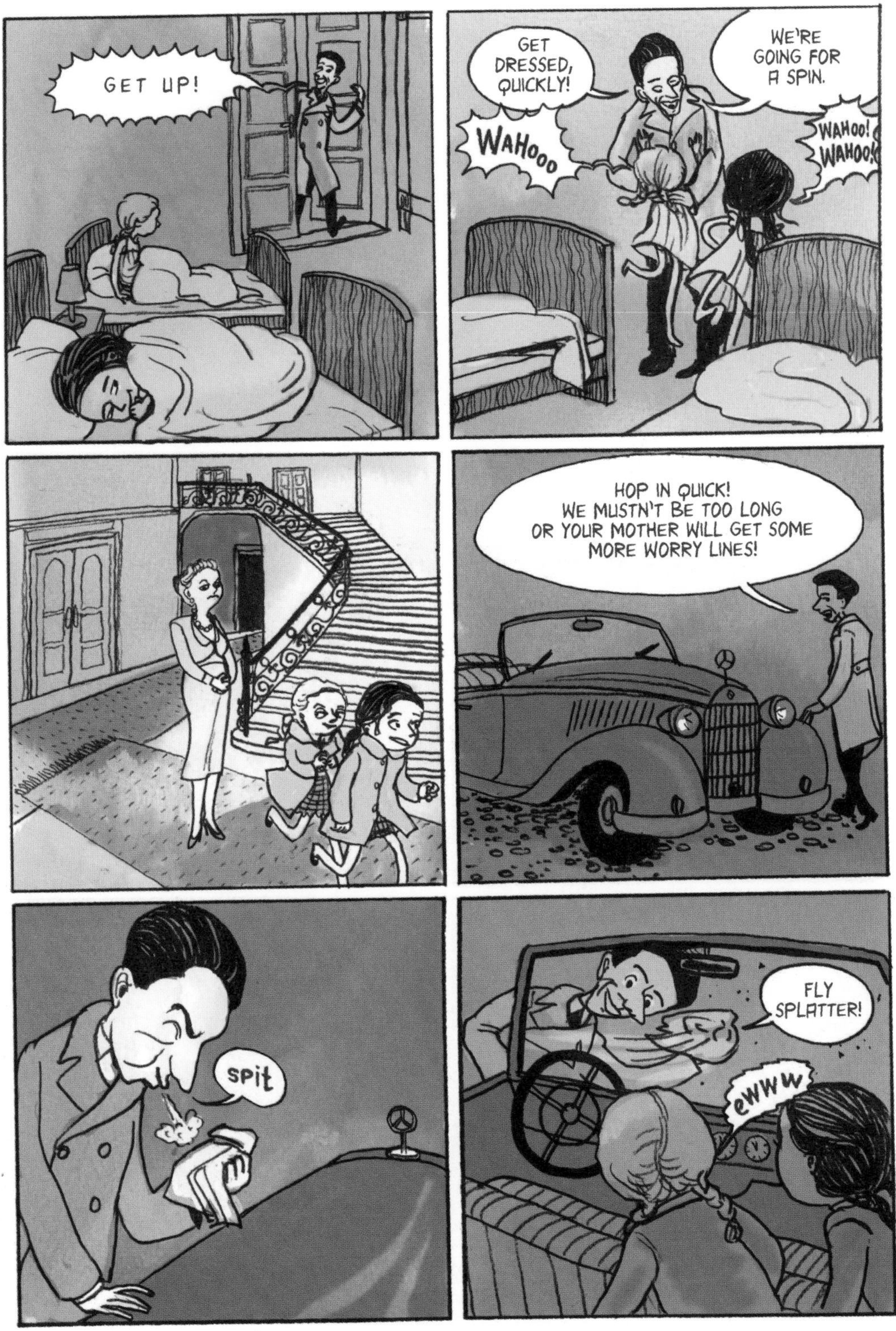
GET UP!
GET DRESSED, QUICKLY!
WE'RE GOING FOR A SPIN.
WAHooo
WAHOO! WAHOO!
HOP IN QUICK! WE MUSTN'T BE TOO LONG OR YOUR MOTHER WILL GET SOME MORE WORRY LINES!
spit
FLY SPLATTER!
eWWW

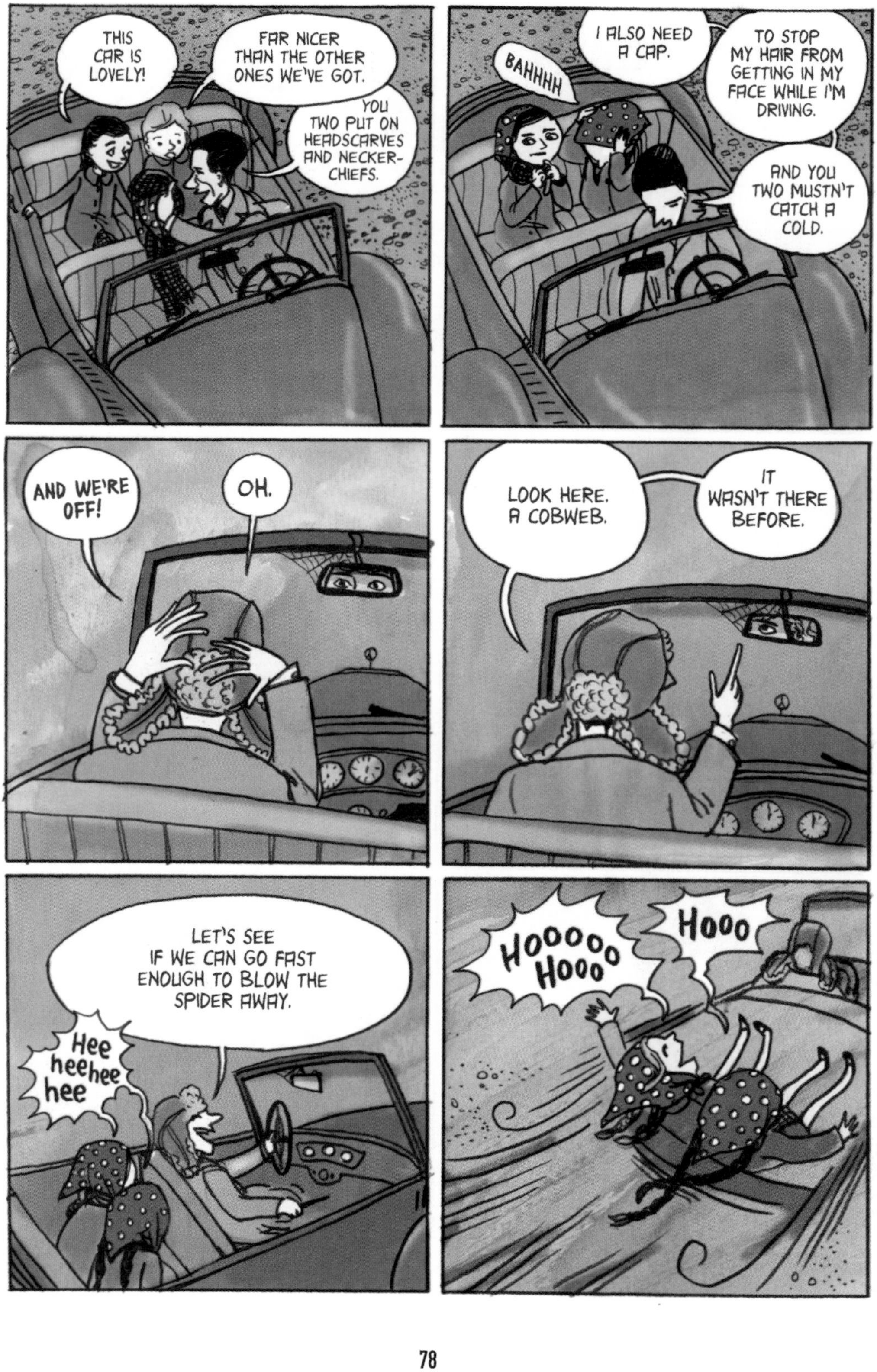
THIS CAR IS LOVELY!
FAR NICER THAN THE OTHER ONES WE'VE GOT.
YOU TWO PUT ON HEADSCARVES AND NECKER-CHIEFS.
BAHHHH
I ALSO NEED A CAP.
TO STOP MY HAIR FROM GETTING IN MY FACE WHILE I'M DRIVING.
AND YOU TWO MUSTN'T CATCH A COLD.
AND WE'RE OFF!
OH.
LOOK HERE. A COBWEB.
IT WASN'T THERE BEFORE.
LET'S SEE IF WE CAN GO FAST ENOUGH TO BLOW THE SPIDER AWAY.
Hee heehee hee
Hooooo Hoooo
Hooo

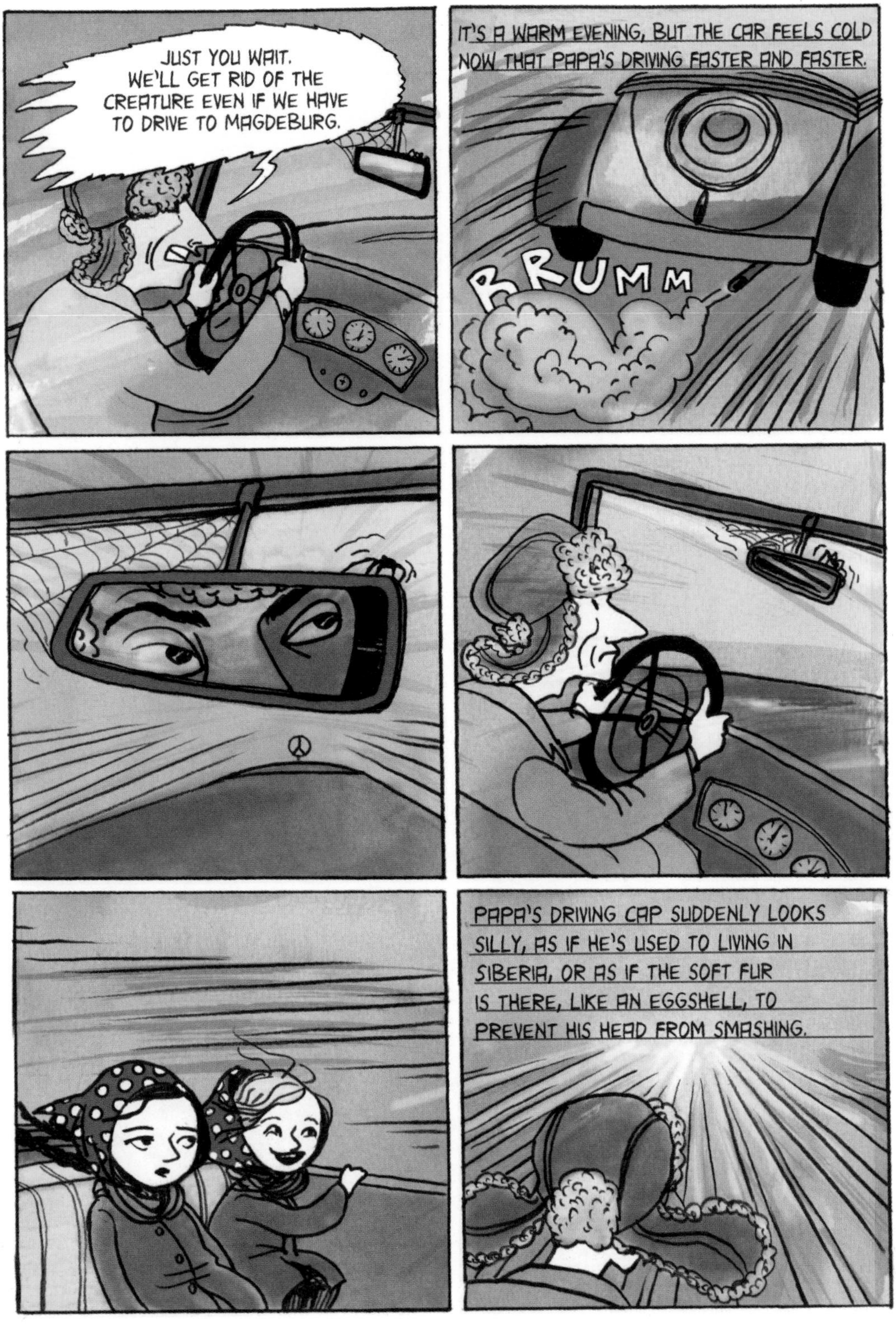
JUST YOU WAIT. WE'LL GET RID OF THE CREATURE EVEN IF WE HAVE TO DRIVE TO MAGDEBURG.
IT'S A WARM EVENING, BUT THE CAR FEELS COLD NOW THAT PAPA'S DRIVING FASTER AND FASTER.
BRUMM
PAPA'S DRIVING CAP SUDDENLY LOOKS SILLY, AS IF HE'S USED TO LIVING IN SIBERIA, OR AS IF THE SOFT FUR IS THERE, LIKE AN EGGSHELL, TO PREVENT HIS HEAD FROM SMASHING.

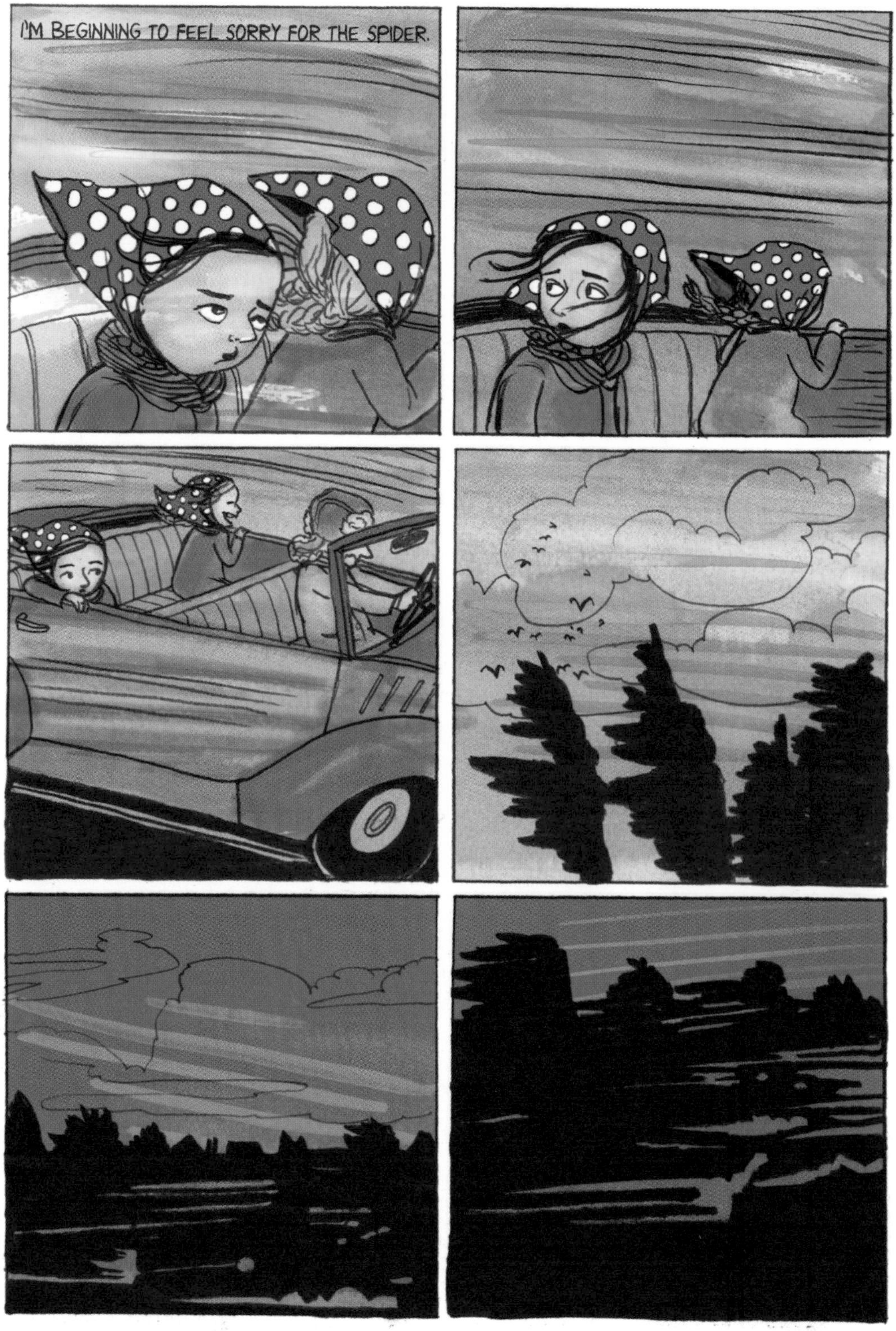
I'M BEGINNING TO FEEL SORRY FOR THE SPIDER.

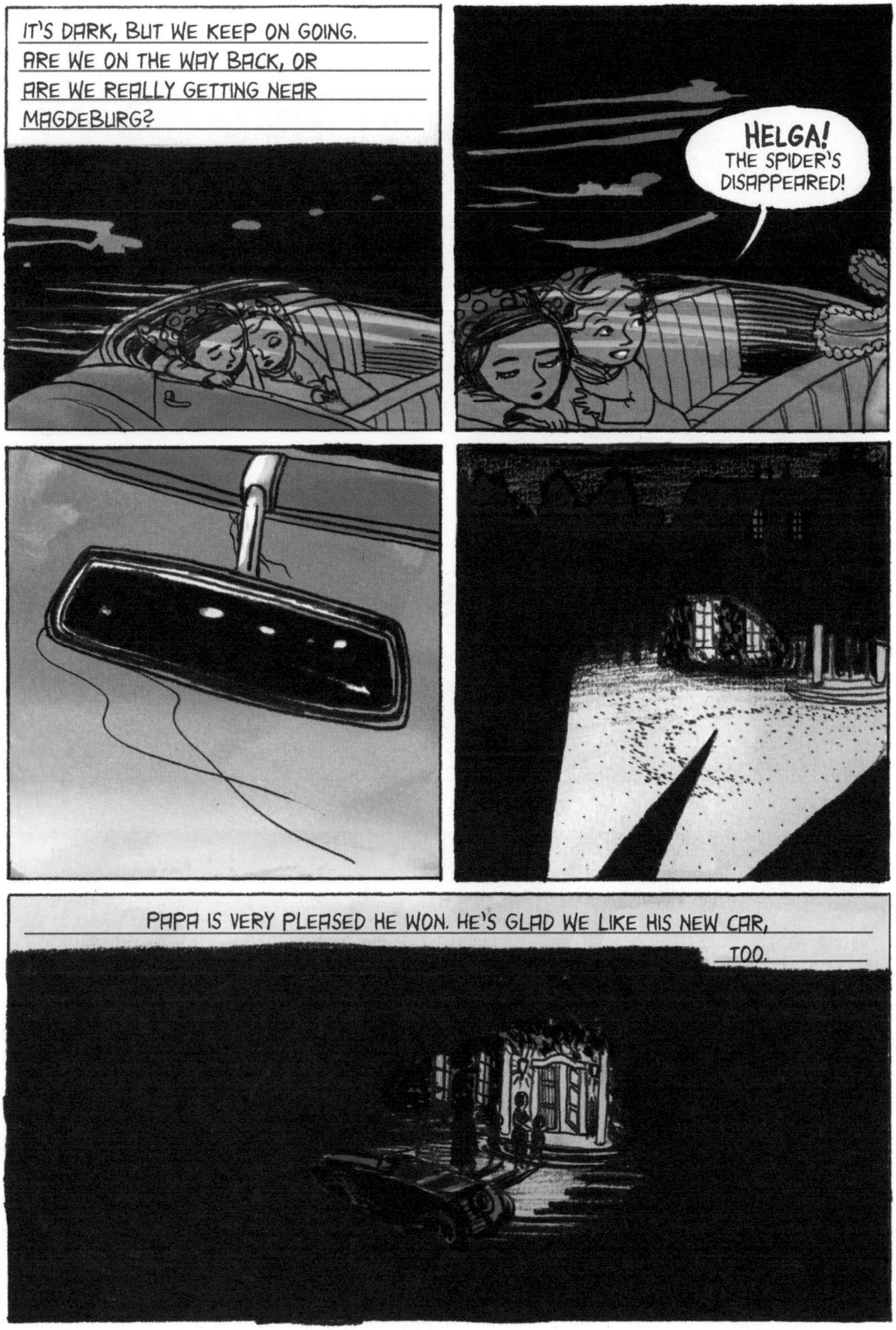
IT'S DARK, BUT WE KEEP ON GOING. ARE WE ON THE WAY BACK, OR ARE WE REALLY GETTING NEAR MAGDEBURG?
HELGA! THE SPIDER'S DISAPPEARED!
PAPA IS VERY PLEASED HE WON. HE'S GLAD WE LIKE HIS NEW CAR, TOO.

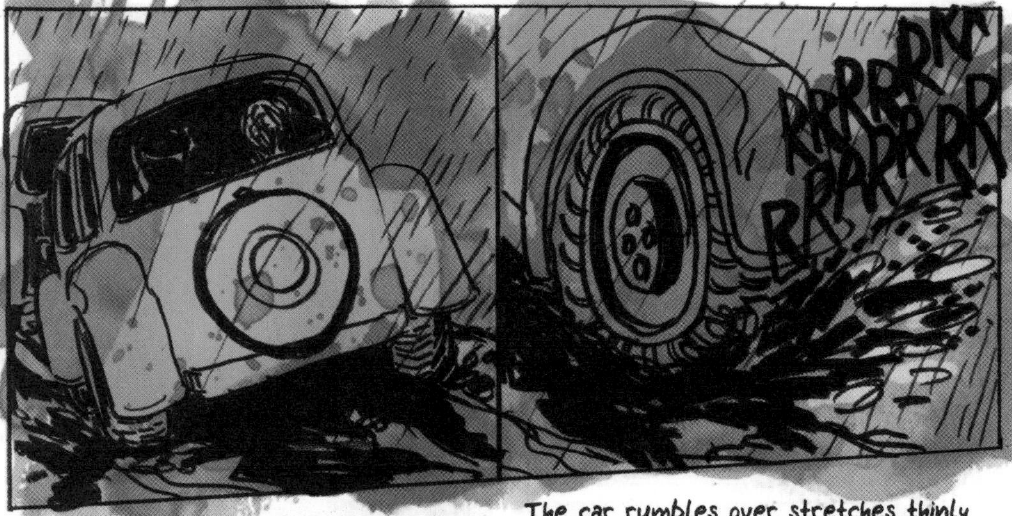

Air buffets the windows with every detonation. The earth moves too, and the gray-brown, rain-swept dusk is tremulous with gunsmoke.

The car rumbles over stretches thinly coated with gravel and toils through slushy mud as it steadily, inexorably follows the rutted tracks of the supply route deep into enemy territory.

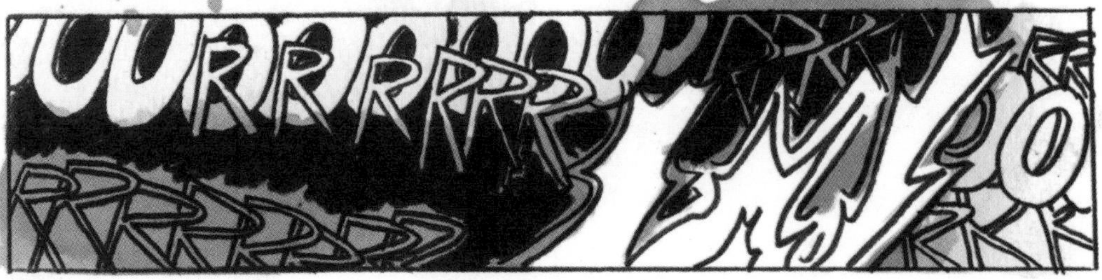

We wait for a convoy to pass.

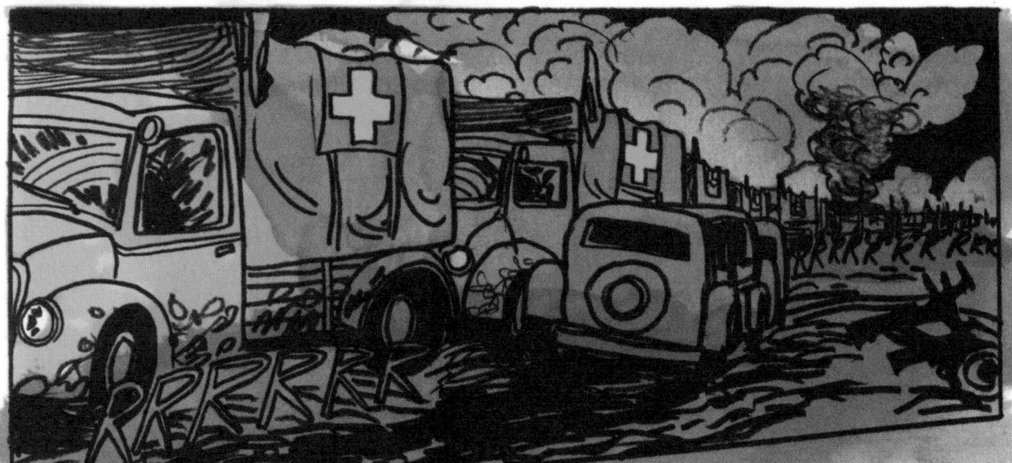

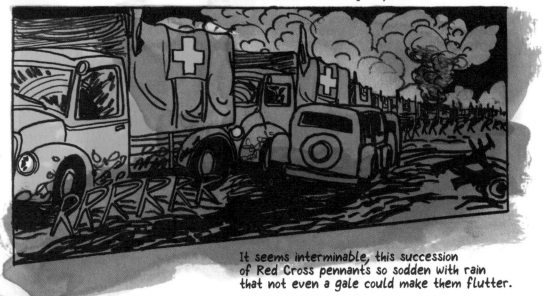

It seems interminable, this succession of Red Cross pennants so sodden with rain that not even a gale could make them flutter.

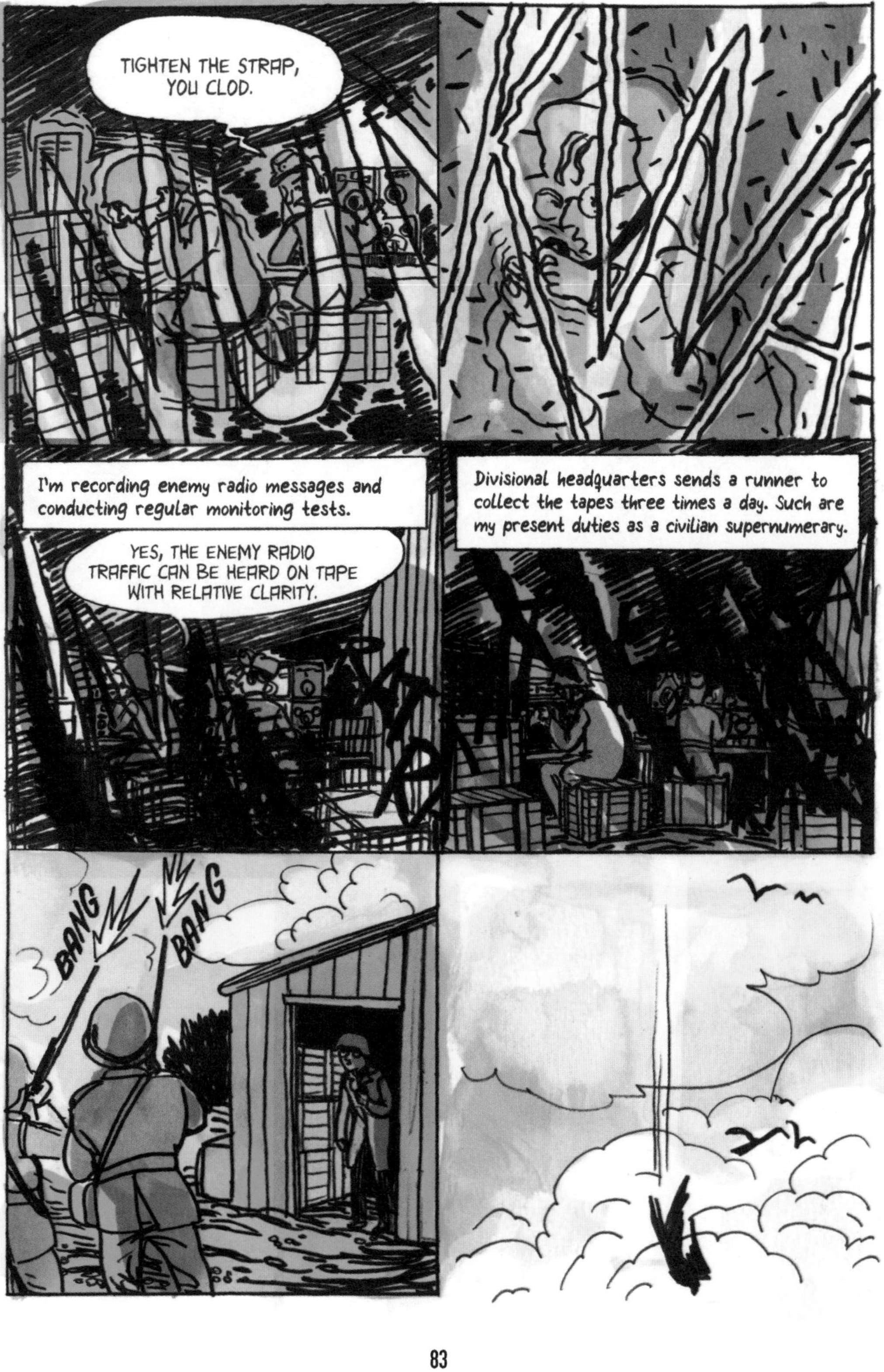
TIGHTEN THE STRAP, YOU CLOD.
I'm recording enemy radio messages and conducting regular monitoring tests.
YES, THE ENEMY RADIO TRAFFIC CAN BE HEARD ON TAPE WITH RELATIVE CLARITY.
Divisional headquarters sends a runner to collect the tapes three times a day. Such are my present duties as a civilian supernumerary.
BANG
BANG

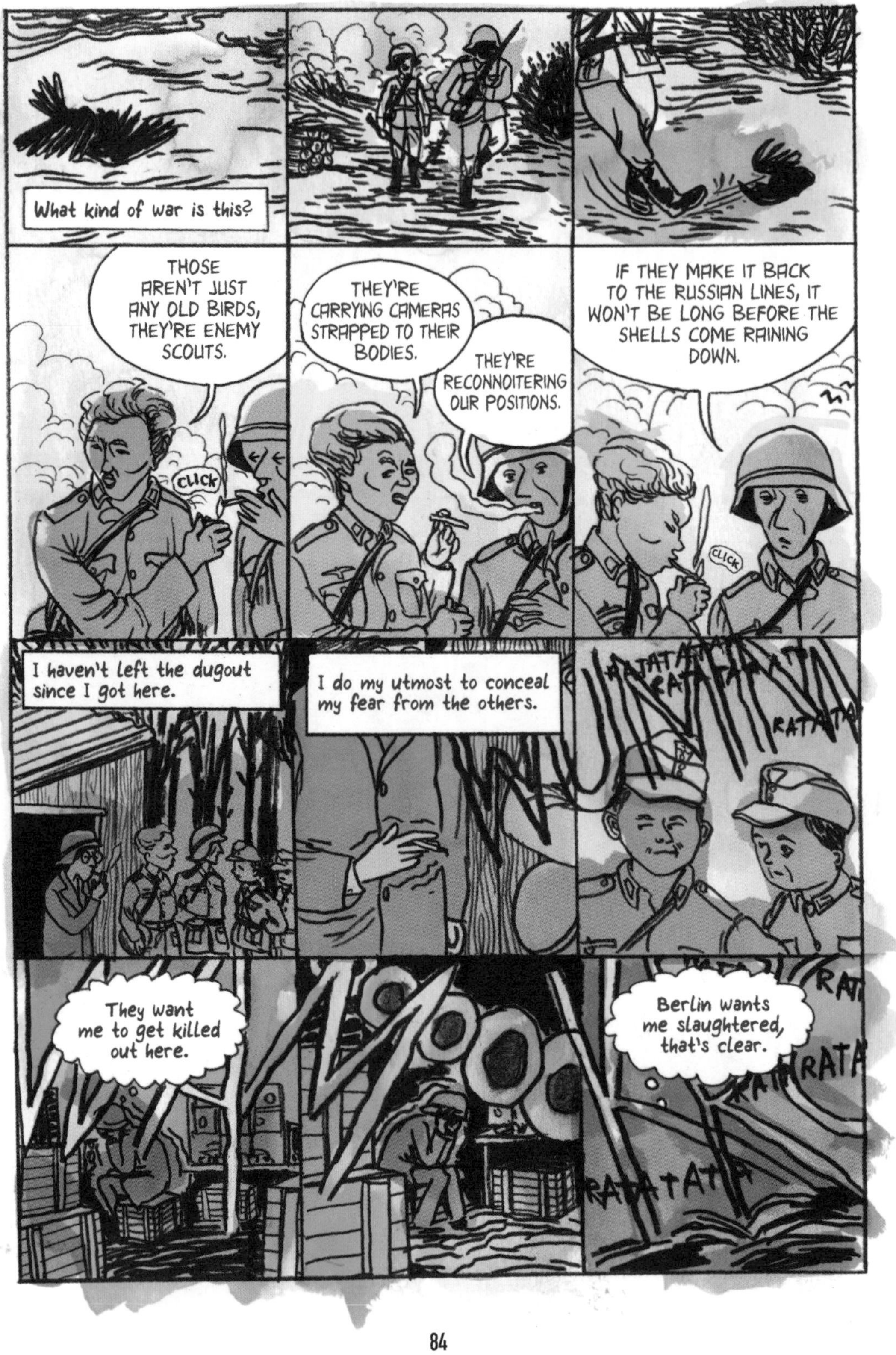
What kind of war is this?
THOSE AREN'T JUST ANY OLD BIRDS, THEY'RE ENEMY SCOUTS.
CLICK
THEY'RE CARRYING CAMERAS STRAPPED TO THEIR BODIES.
THEY'RE RECONNOITERING OUR POSITIONS.
IF THEY MAKE IT BACK TO THE RUSSIAN LINES, IT WON'T BE LONG BEFORE THE SHELLS COME RAINING DOWN.
CLICK
I haven't left the dugout since I got here.
I do my utmost to conceal my fear from the others.
RATATA
RATATA
They want me to get killed out here.
Berlin wants me slaughtered, that's clear.
RATA
RATATATA

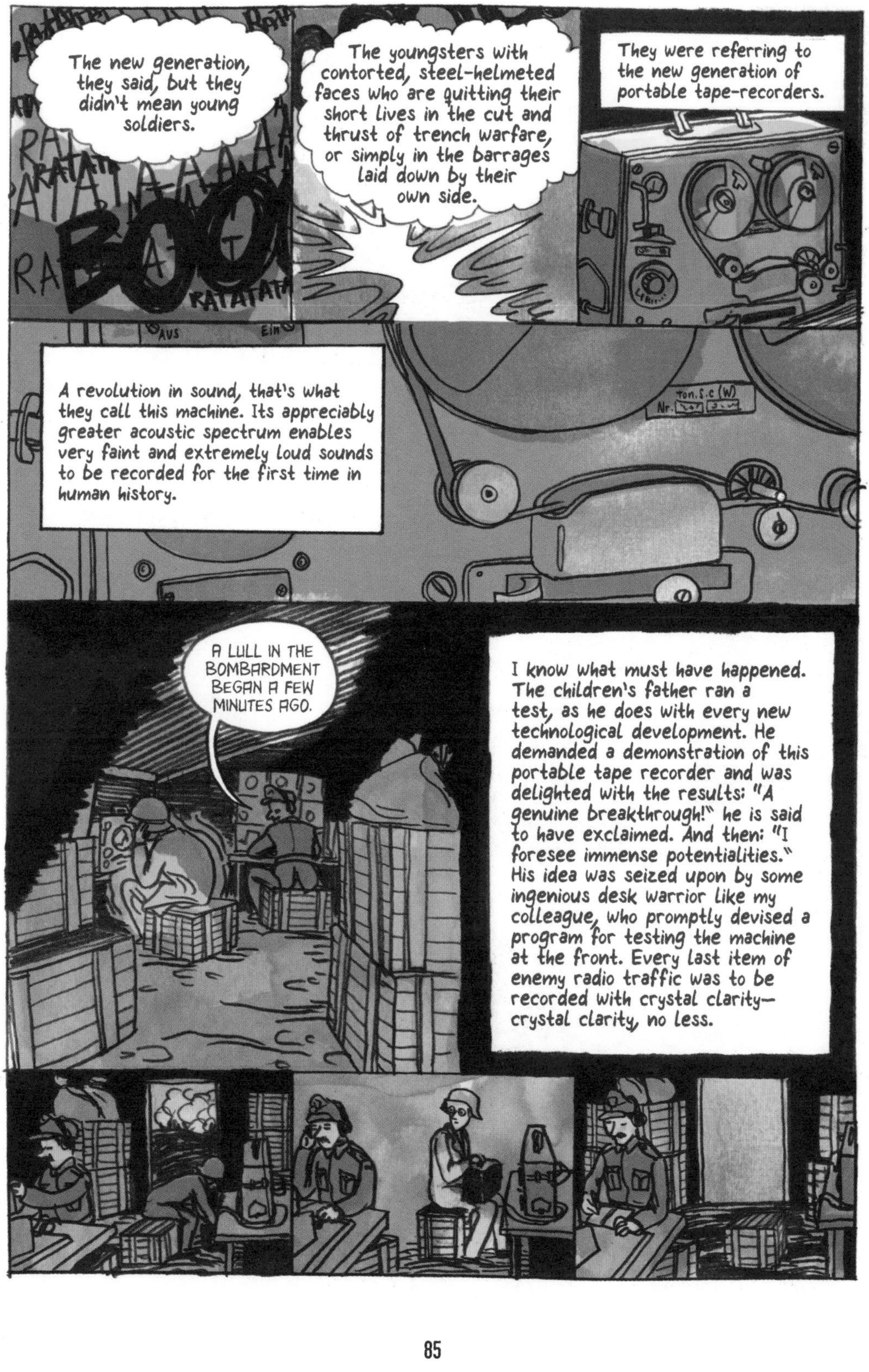
The new generation, they said, but they didn't mean young soldiers.
The youngsters with contorted, steel-helmeted faces who are quitting their short lives in the cut and thrust of trench warfare, or simply in the barrages laid down by their own side.
They were referring to the new generation of portable tape-recorders.
A revolution in sound, that's what they call this machine. Its appreciably greater acoustic spectrum enables very faint and extremely loud sounds to be recorded for the first time in human history.
A LULL IN THE BOMBARDMENT BEGAN A FEW MINUTES AGO.
I know what must have happened. The children's father ran a test, as he does with every new technological development. He demanded a demonstration of this portable tape recorder and was delighted with the results: "A genuine breakthrough!" he is said to have exclaimed. And then: "I foresee immense potentialities." His idea was seized upon by some ingenious desk warrior like my colleague, who promptly devised a program for testing the machine at the front. Every last item of enemy radio traffic was to be recorded with crystal clarity—crystal clarity, no less.

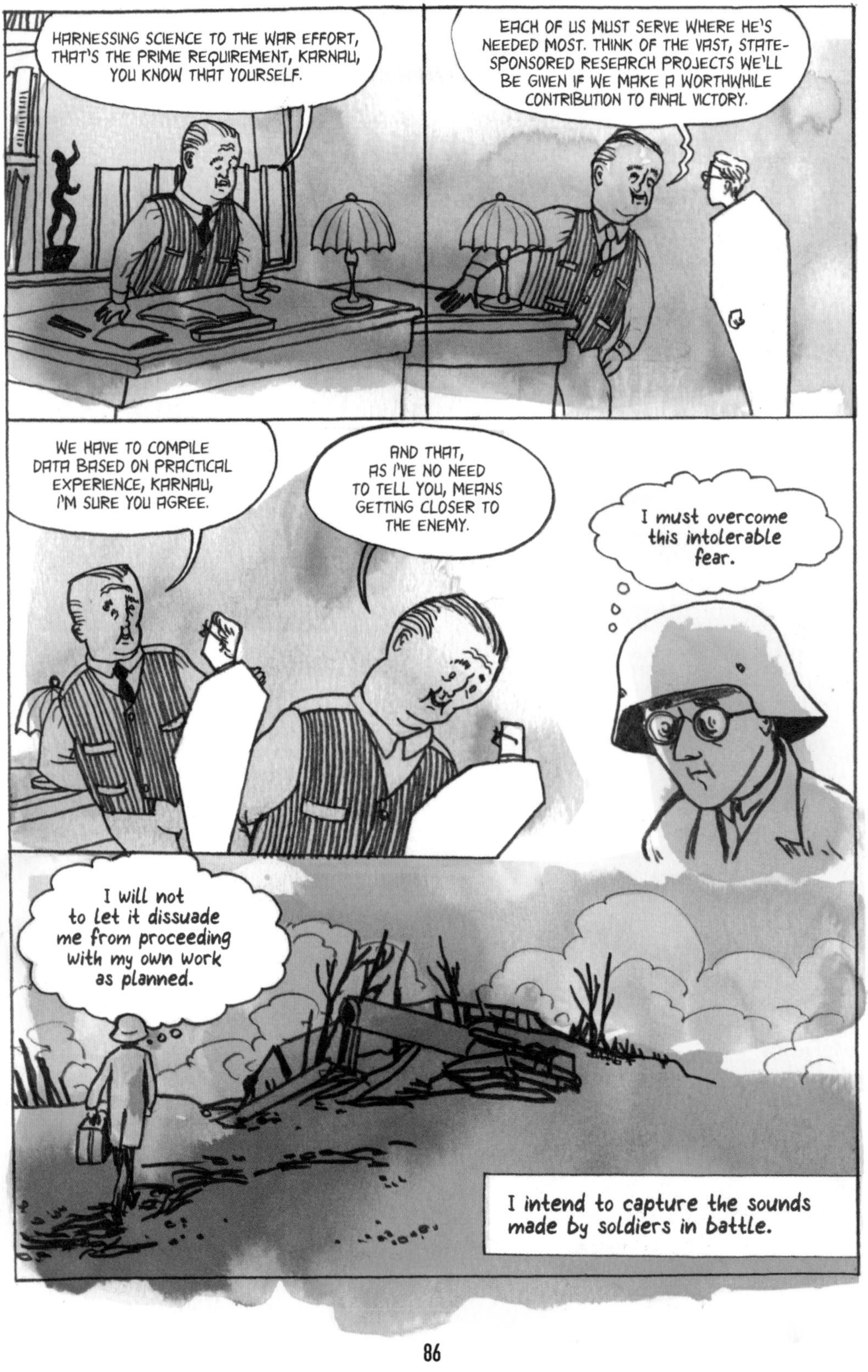
HARNESSING SCIENCE TO THE WAR EFFORT, THAT'S THE PRIME REQUIREMENT, KARNAU, YOU KNOW THAT YOURSELF.
EACH OF US MUST SERVE WHERE HE'S NEEDED MOST. THINK OF THE VAST, STATE-SPONSORED RESEARCH PROJECTS WE'LL BE GIVEN IF WE MAKE A WORTHWHILE CONTRIBUTION TO FINAL VICTORY.
WE HAVE TO COMPILE DATA BASED ON PRACTICAL EXPERIENCE, KARNAU, I'M SURE YOU AGREE.
AND THAT, AS I'VE NO NEED TO TELL YOU, MEANS GETTING CLOSER TO THE ENEMY.
I must overcome this intolerable fear.
I will not to let it dissuade me from proceeding with my own work as planned.
I intend to capture the sounds made by soldiers in battle.

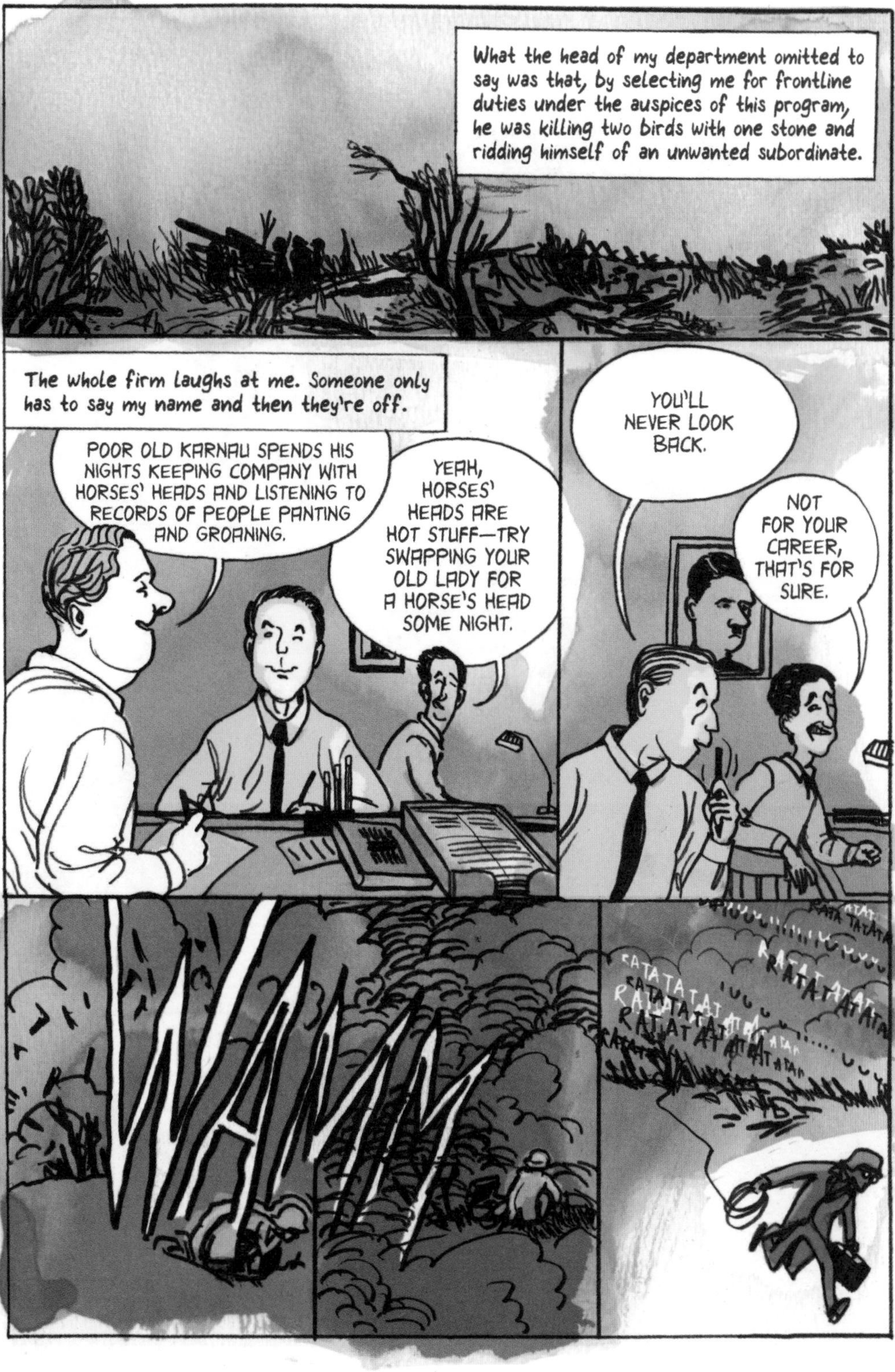

What the head of my department omitted to say was that, by selecting me for frontline duties under the auspices of this program, he was killing two birds with one stone and ridding himself of an unwanted subordinate.
The whole firm laughs at me. Someone only has to say my name and then they're off.
POOR OLD KARNAU SPENDS HIS NIGHTS KEEPING COMPANY WITH HORSES' HEADS AND LISTENING TO RECORDS OF PEOPLE PANTING AND GROANING.
YEAH, HORSES' HEADS ARE HOT STUFF—TRY SWAPPING YOUR OLD LADY FOR A HORSE'S HEAD SOME NIGHT.
YOU'LL NEVER LOOK BACK.
NOT FOR YOUR CAREER, THAT'S FOR SURE.
WAMM
RATATATAT

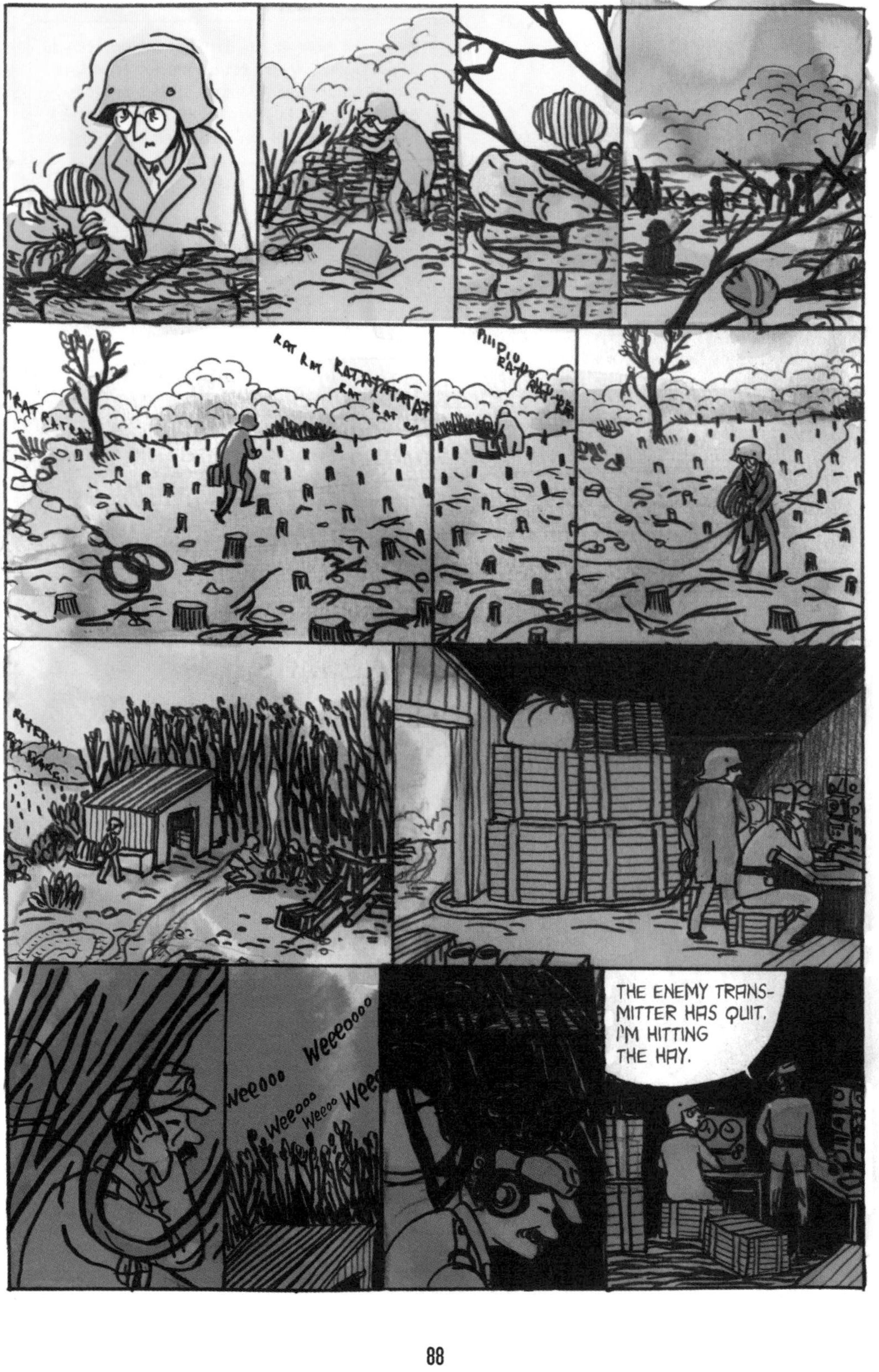
RAT RAT RATATATATAT
RAT RAT
RATATAT
Weeoooo
Weeooo
Weeooo
Weeoo
THE ENEMY TRANS-
MITTER HAS QUIT.
I'M HITTING
THE HAY.

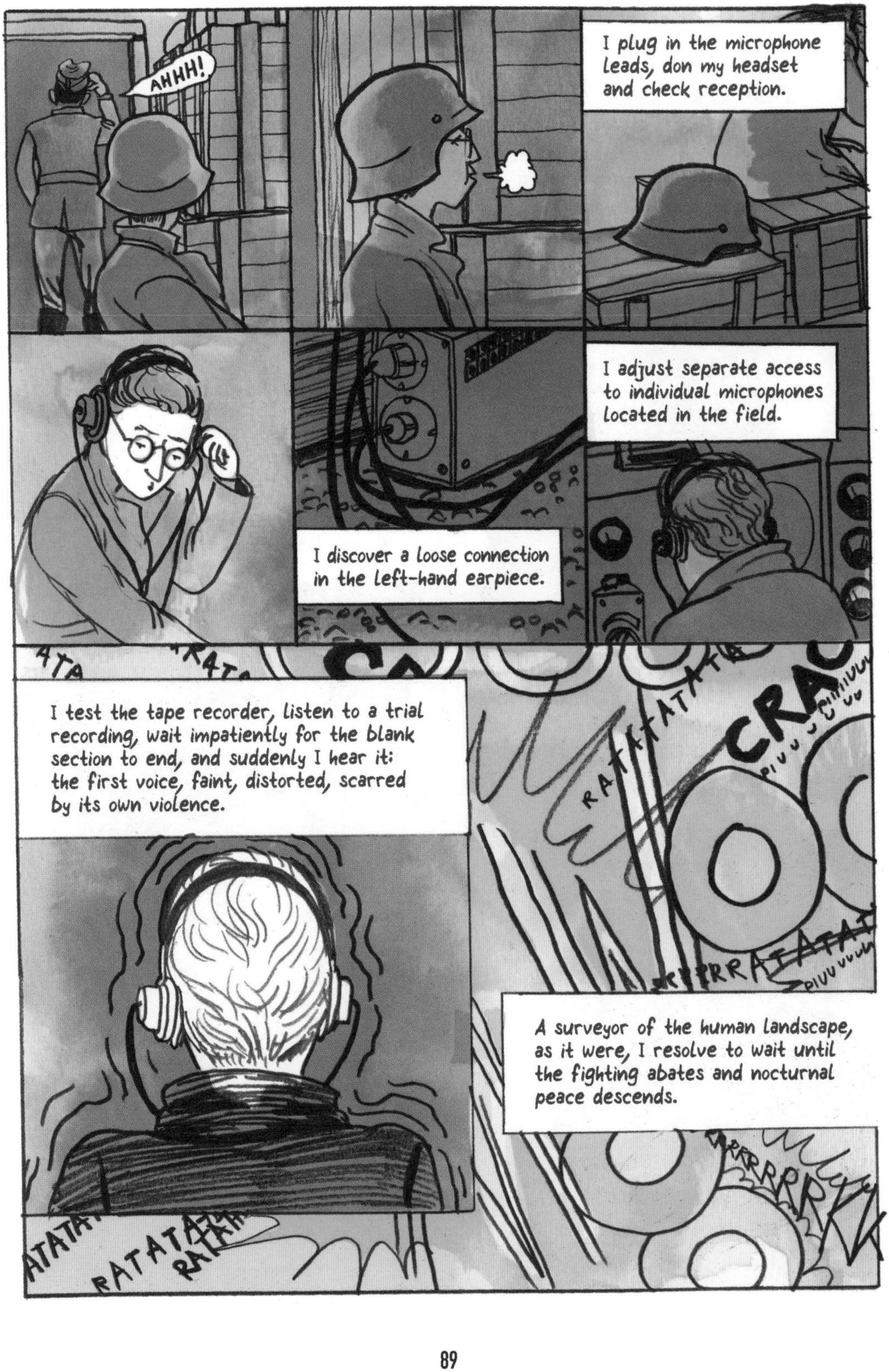
AHHH!
I plug in the microphone leads, don my headset and check reception.
I adjust separate access to individual microphones located in the field.
I discover a loose connection in the left-hand earpiece.
I test the tape recorder, listen to a trial recording, wait impatiently for the blank section to end, and suddenly I hear it: the first voice, faint, distorted, scarred by its own violence.
RATATATATA
CRA
PIUUUUU
A surveyor of the human landscape, as it were, I resolve to wait until the fighting abates and nocturnal peace descends.
RATATA
RATATA

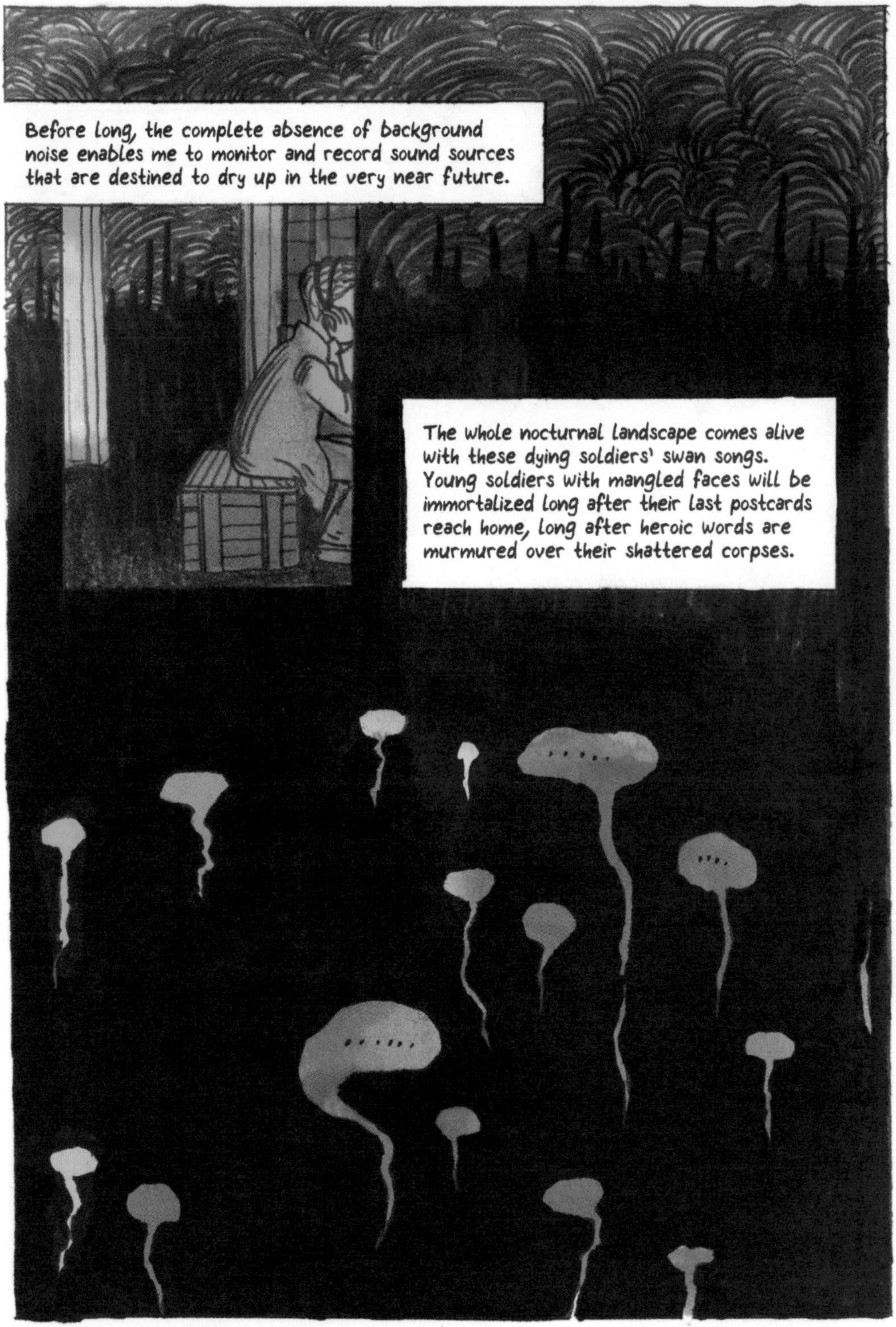
Before long, the complete absence of background noise enables me to monitor and record sound sources that are destined to dry up in the very near future.
The whole nocturnal landscape comes alive with these dying soldiers' swan songs. Young soldiers with mangled faces will be immortalized long after their last postcards reach home, long after heroic words are murmured over their shattered corpses.
......
....
.....

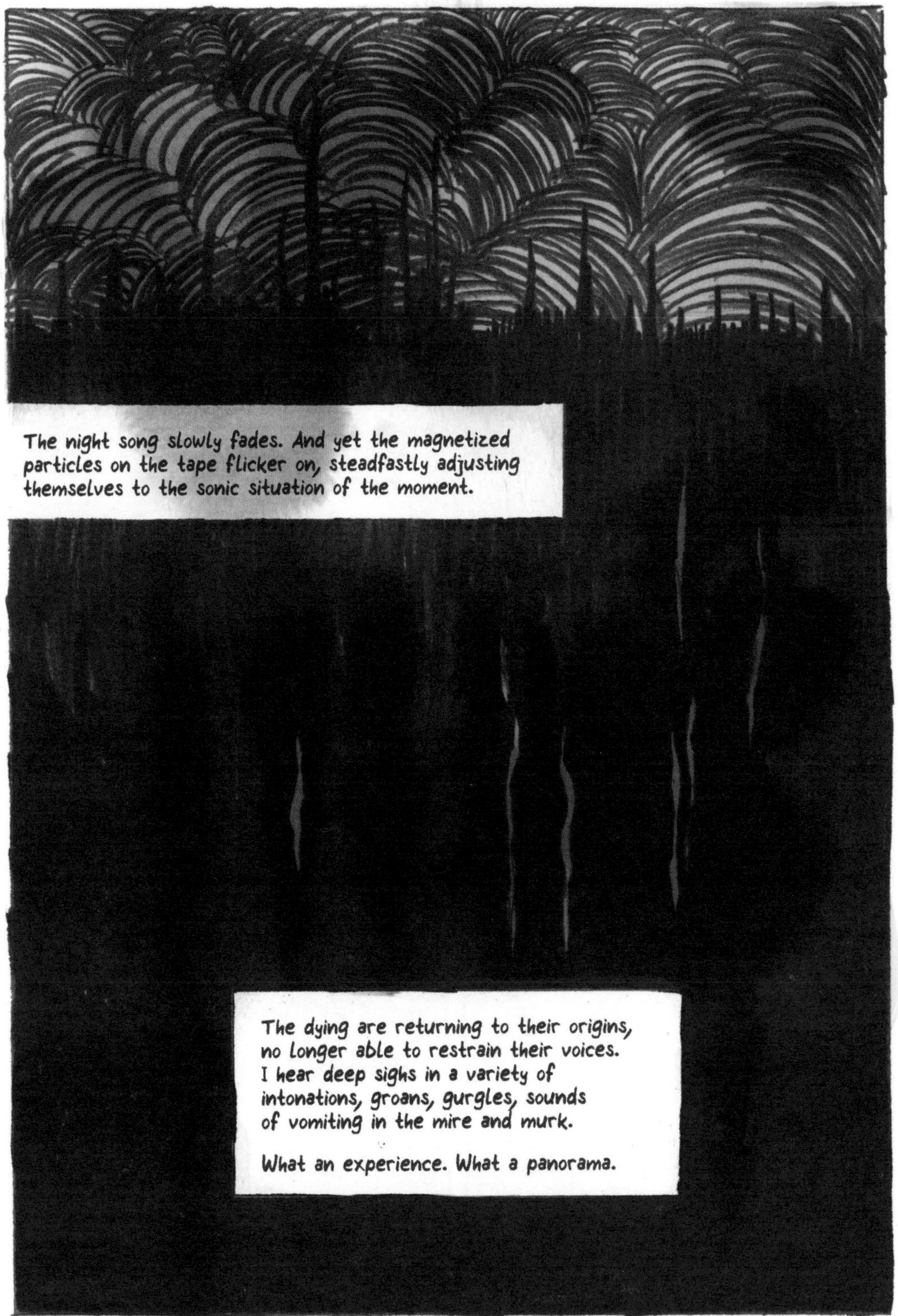
The night song slowly fades. And yet the magnetized particles on the tape flicker on, steadfastly adjusting themselves to the sonic situation of the moment.
The dying are returning to their origins, no longer able to restrain their voices. I hear deep sighs in a variety of intonations, groans, gurgles, sounds of vomiting in the mire and murk.
What an experience. What a panorama.

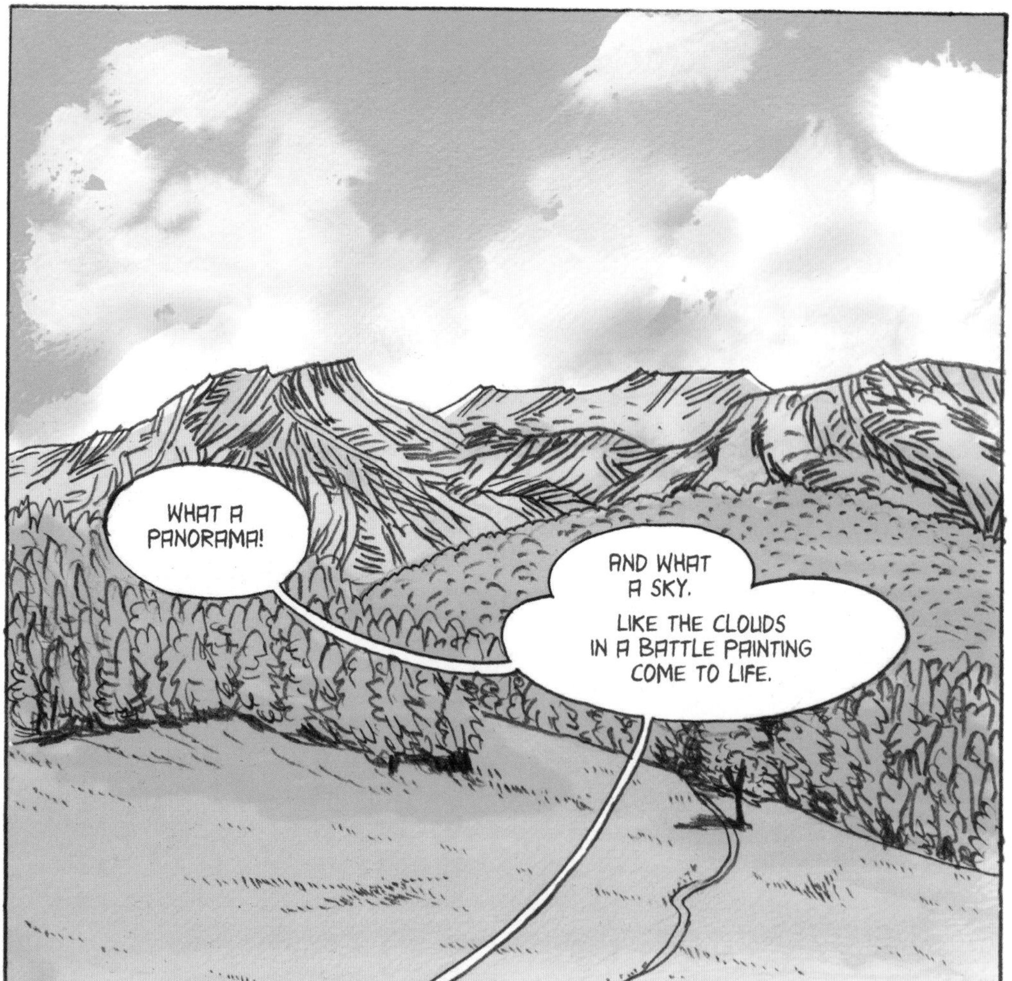
WHAT A PANORAMA!
AND WHAT A SKY.
LIKE THE CLOUDS IN A BATTLE PAINTING COME TO LIFE.

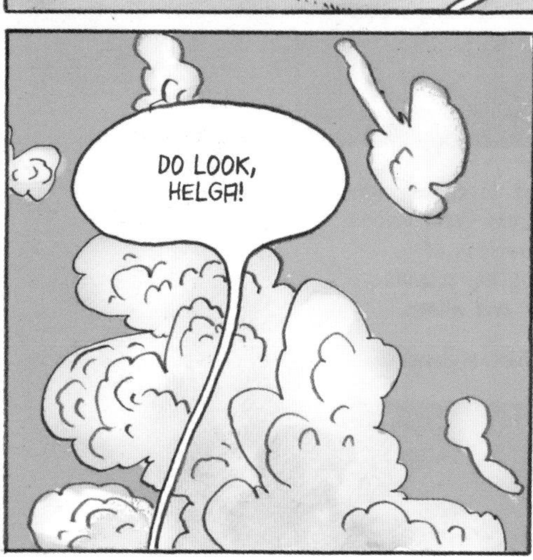
DO LOOK, HELGA!

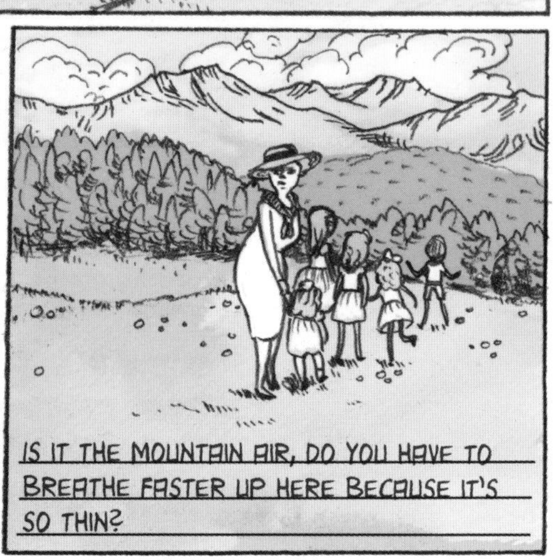
IS IT THE MOUNTAIN AIR, DO YOU HAVE TO BREATHE FASTER UP HERE BECAUSE IT'S SO THIN?

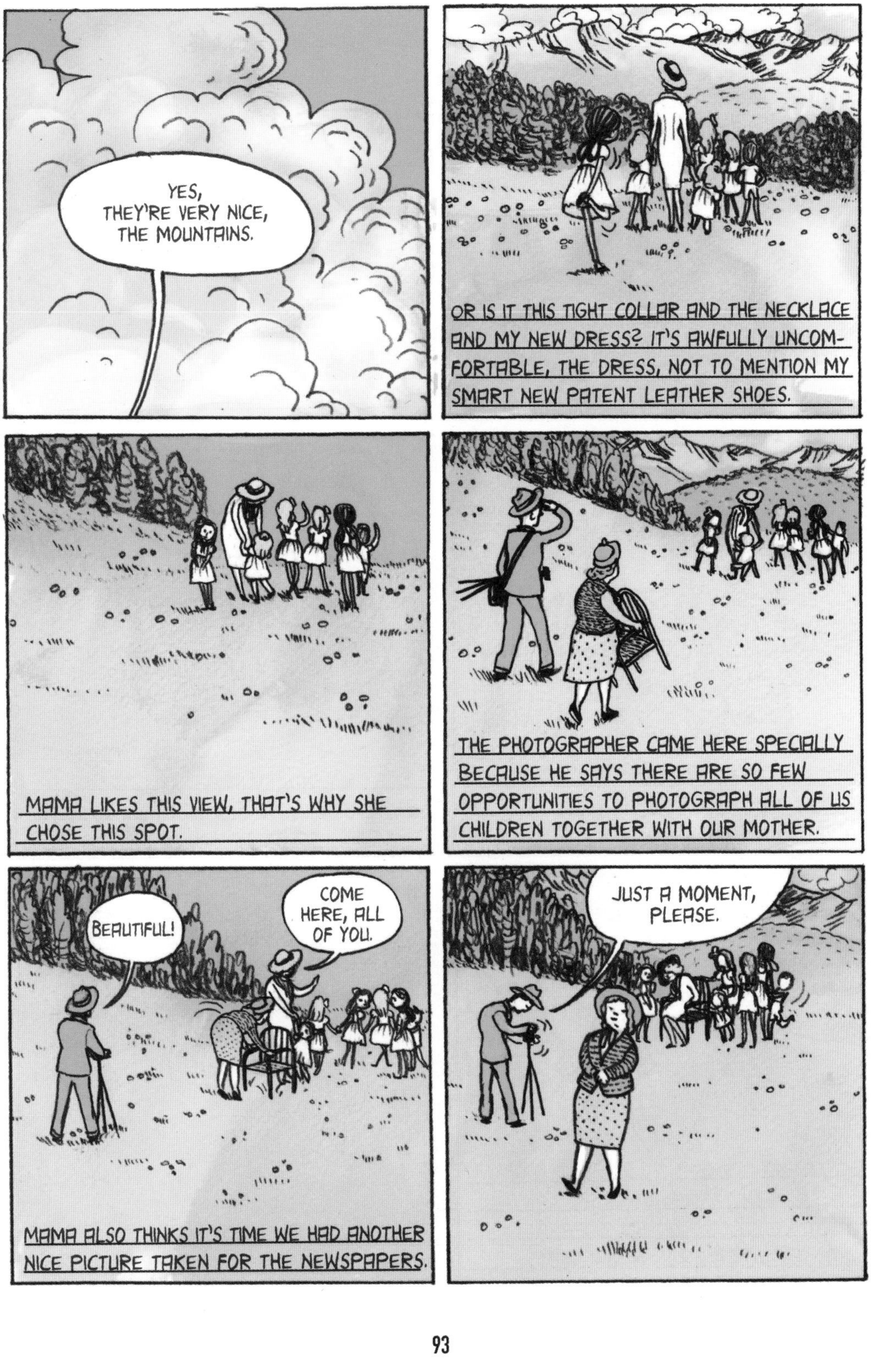
YES, THEY'RE VERY NICE, THE MOUNTAINS.
OR IS IT THIS TIGHT COLLAR AND THE NECKLACE AND MY NEW DRESS? IT'S AWFULLY UNCOMFORTABLE, THE DRESS, NOT TO MENTION MY SMART NEW PATENT LEATHER SHOES.
MAMA LIKES THIS VIEW, THAT'S WHY SHE CHOSE THIS SPOT.
THE PHOTOGRAPHER CAME HERE SPECIALLY BECAUSE HE SAYS THERE ARE SO FEW OPPORTUNITIES TO PHOTOGRAPH ALL OF US CHILDREN TOGETHER WITH OUR MOTHER.
BEAUTIFUL!
COME HERE, ALL OF YOU.
MAMA ALSO THINKS IT'S TIME WE HAD ANOTHER NICE PICTURE TAKEN FOR THE NEWSPAPERS.
JUST A MOMENT, PLEASE.

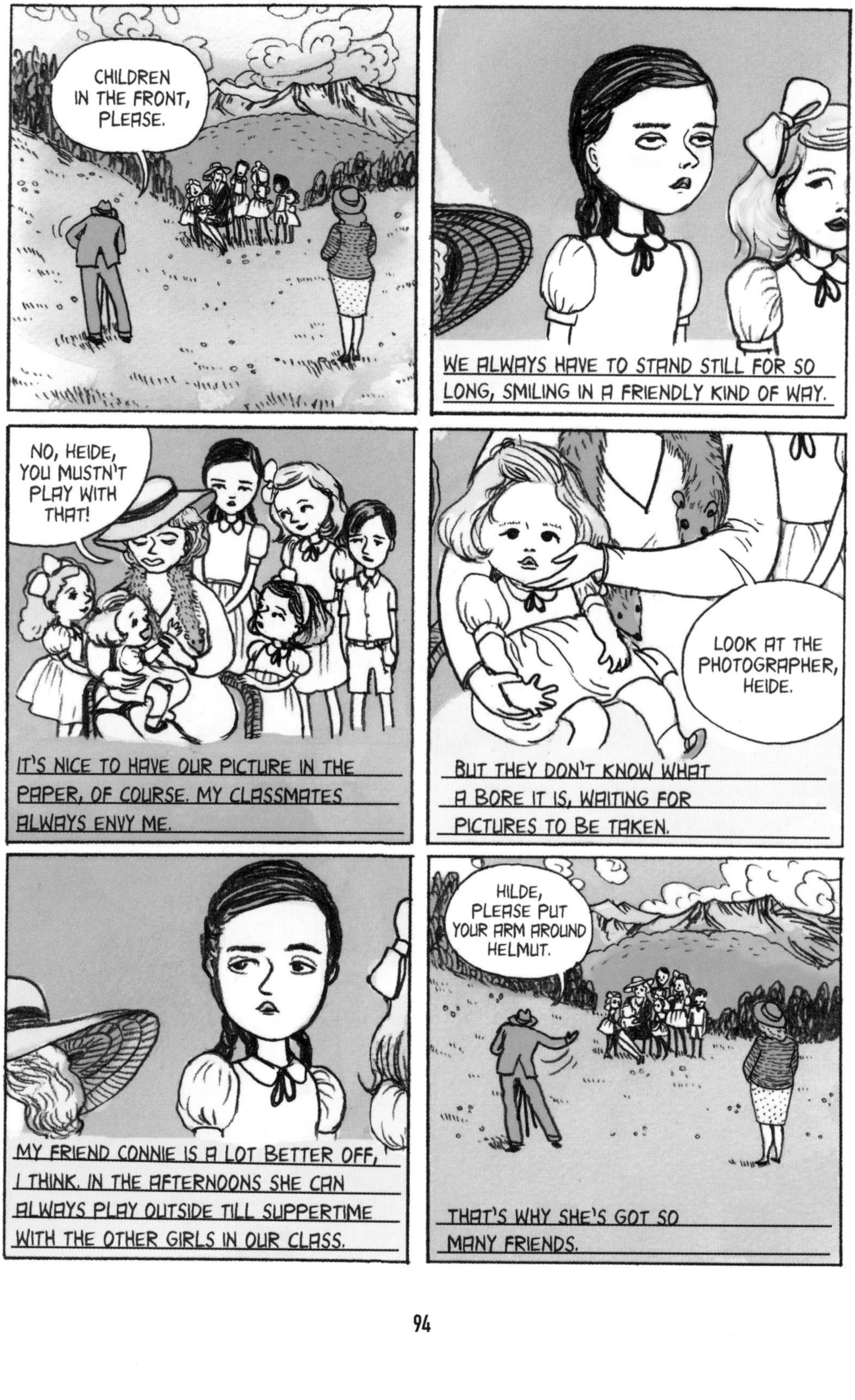
CHILDREN IN THE FRONT, PLEASE.
WE ALWAYS HAVE TO STAND STILL FOR SO LONG, SMILING IN A FRIENDLY KIND OF WAY.
NO, HEIDE, YOU MUSTN'T PLAY WITH THAT!
IT'S NICE TO HAVE OUR PICTURE IN THE PAPER, OF COURSE. MY CLASSMATES ALWAYS ENVY ME.
LOOK AT THE PHOTOGRAPHER, HEIDE.
BUT THEY DON'T KNOW WHAT A BORE IT IS, WAITING FOR PICTURES TO BE TAKEN.
MY FRIEND CONNIE IS A LOT BETTER OFF, I THINK. IN THE AFTERNOONS SHE CAN ALWAYS PLAY OUTSIDE TILL SUPPERTIME WITH THE OTHER GIRLS IN OUR CLASS.
HILDE, PLEASE PUT YOUR ARM AROUND HELMUT.
THAT'S WHY SHE'S GOT SO MANY FRIENDS.

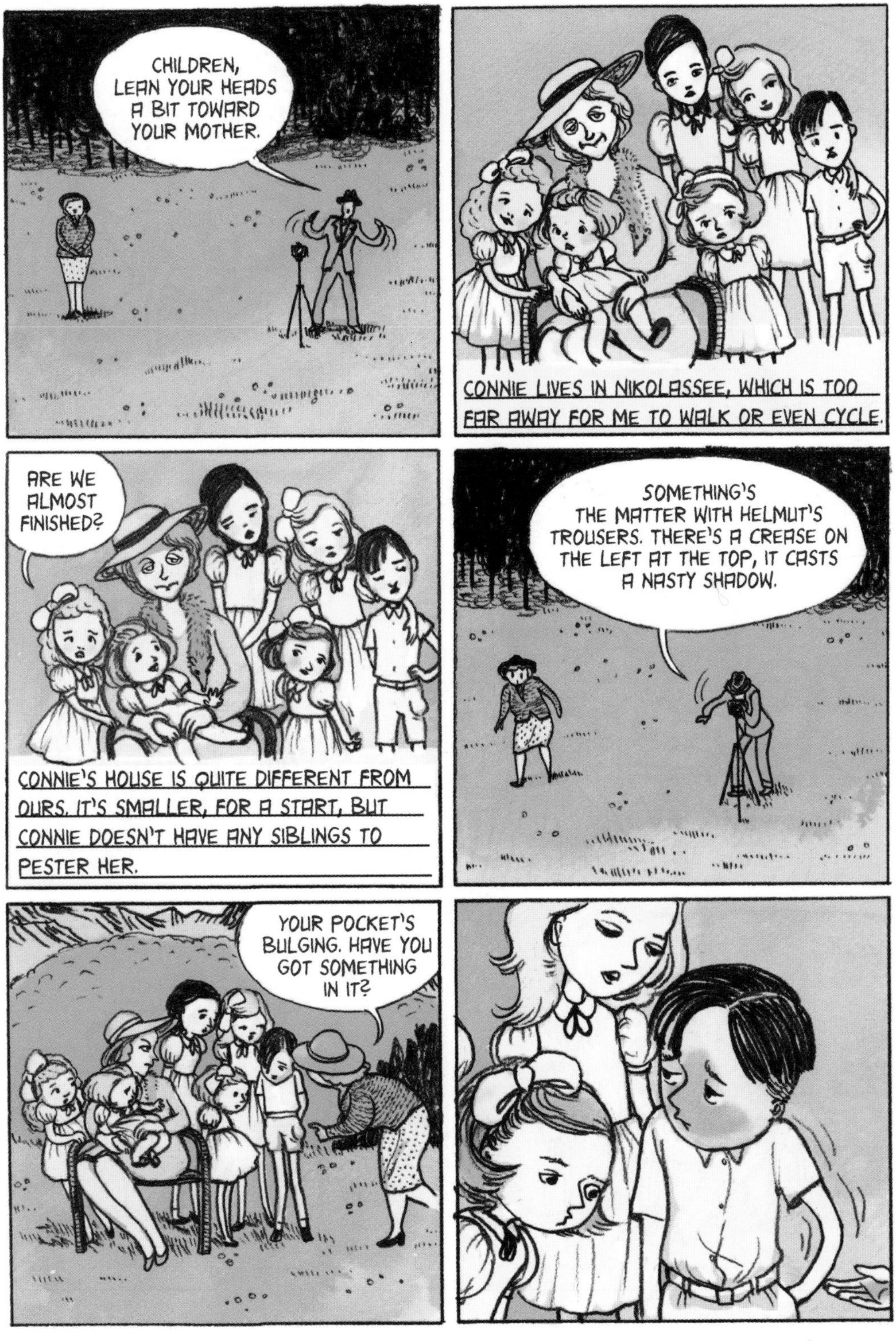
CHILDREN, LEAN YOUR HEADS A BIT TOWARD YOUR MOTHER.
CONNIE LIVES IN NIKOLASSEE, WHICH IS TOO FAR AWAY FOR ME TO WALK OR EVEN CYCLE.
ARE WE ALMOST FINISHED?
CONNIE'S HOUSE IS QUITE DIFFERENT FROM OURS. IT'S SMALLER, FOR A START, BUT CONNIE DOESN'T HAVE ANY SIBLINGS TO PESTER HER.
SOMETHING'S THE MATTER WITH HELMUT'S TROUSERS. THERE'S A CREASE ON THE LEFT AT THE TOP, IT CASTS A NASTY SHADOW.
YOUR POCKET'S BULGING. HAVE YOU GOT SOMETHING IN IT?

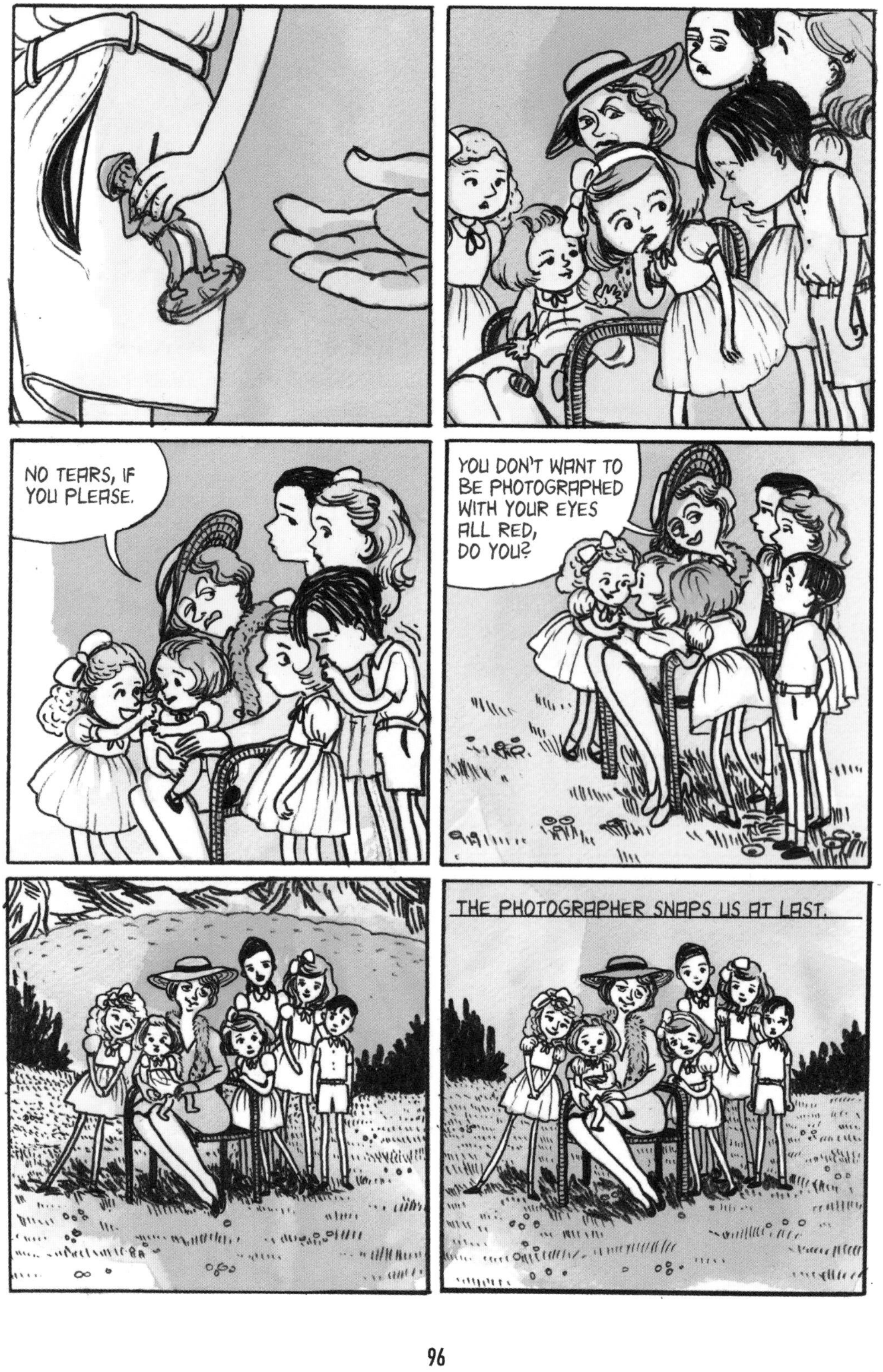
NO TEARS, IF YOU PLEASE.
YOU DON'T WANT TO BE PHOTOGRAPHED WITH YOUR EYES ALL RED, DO YOU?
THE PHOTOGRAPHER SNAPS US AT LAST.

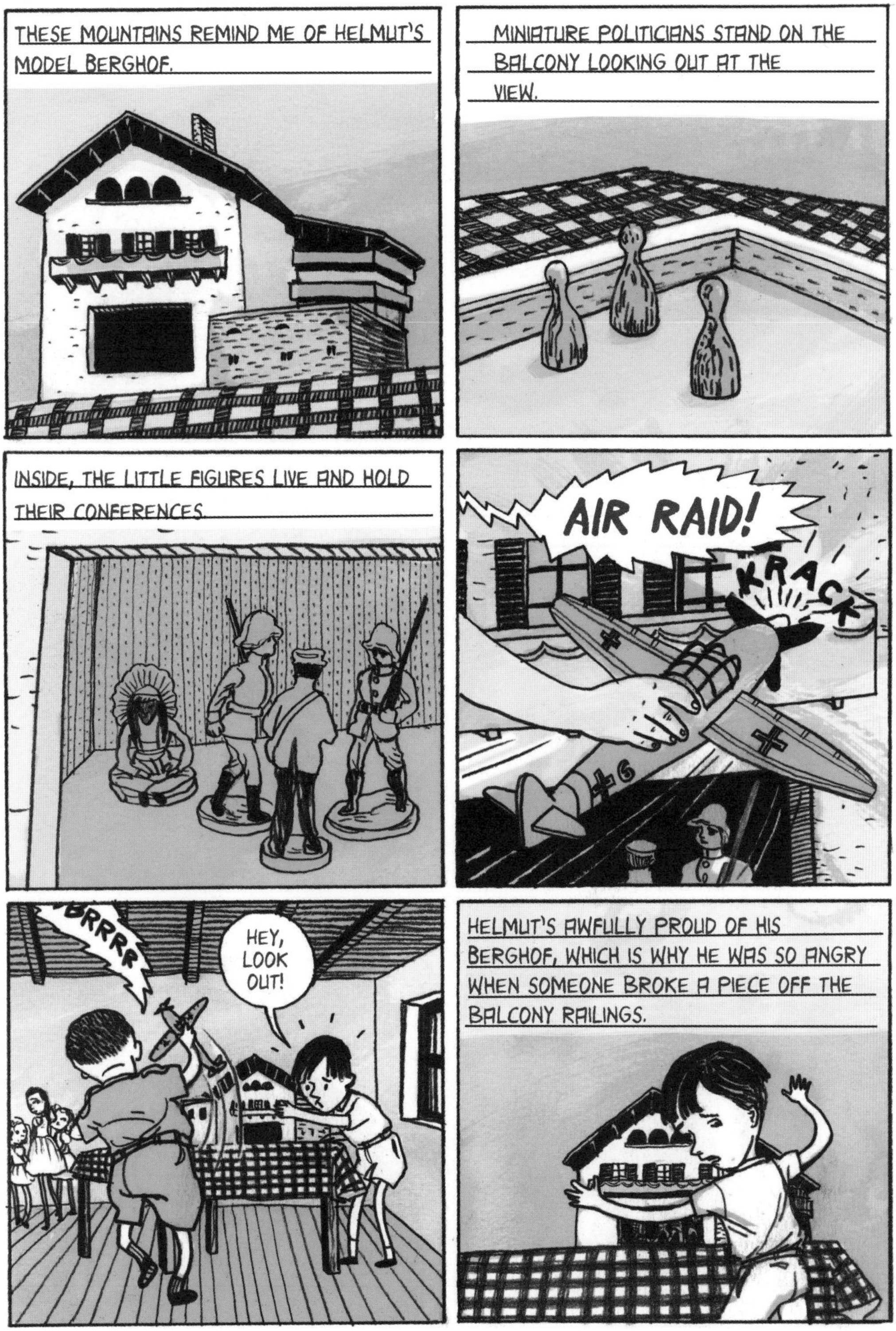
THESE MOUNTAINS REMIND ME OF HELMUT'S MODEL BERGHOF.
MINIATURE POLITICIANS STAND ON THE BALCONY LOOKING OUT AT THE VIEW.
INSIDE, THE LITTLE FIGURES LIVE AND HOLD THEIR CONFERENCES.
AIR RAID!
KRACK
BRRRR
HEY, LOOK OUT!
HELMUT'S AWFULLY PROUD OF HIS BERGHOF, WHICH IS WHY HE WAS SO ANGRY WHEN SOMEONE BROKE A PIECE OFF THE BALCONY RAILINGS.

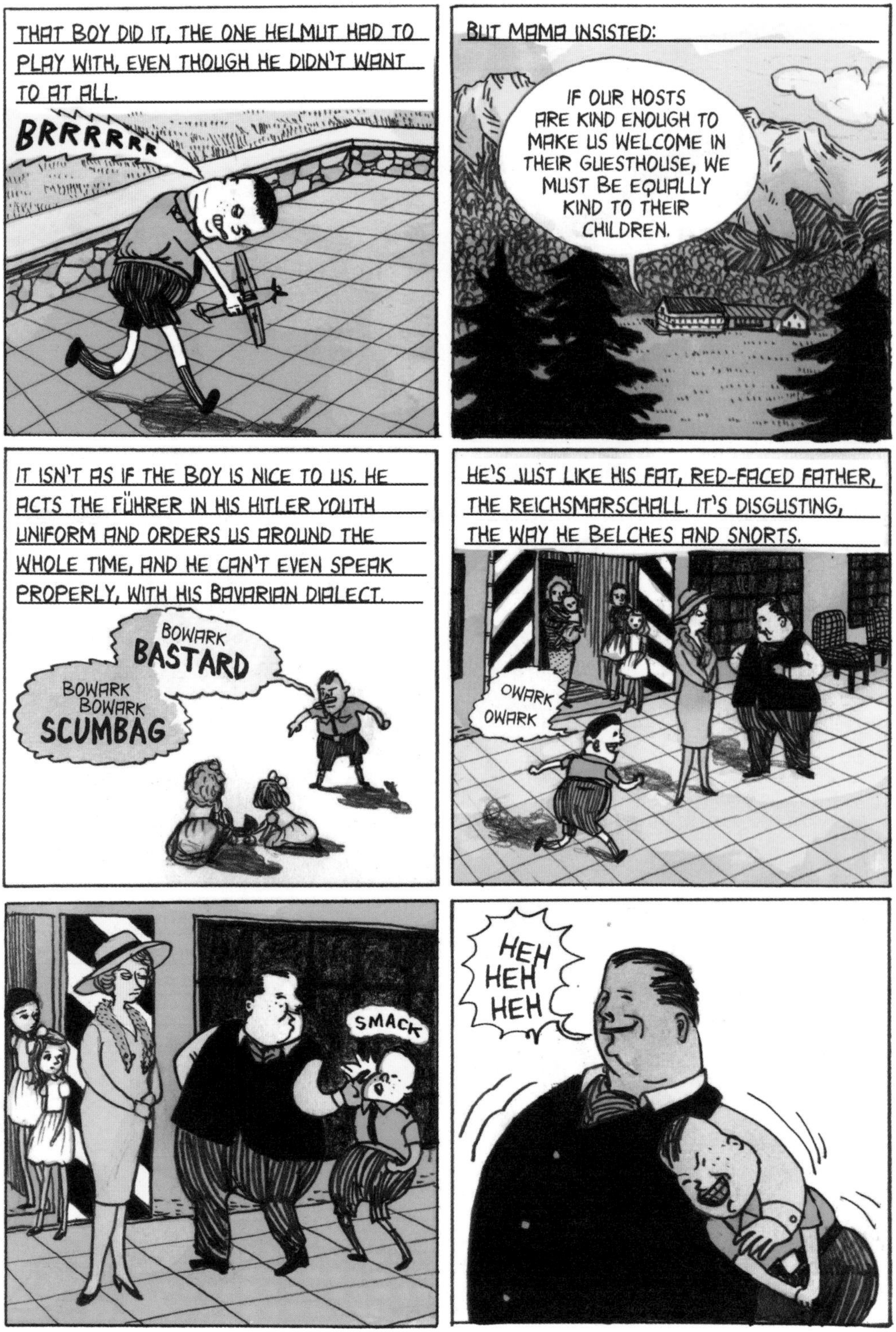
THAT BOY DID IT, THE ONE HELMUT HAD TO PLAY WITH, EVEN THOUGH HE DIDN'T WANT TO AT ALL.
BRRRRRRR
BUT MAMA INSISTED:
IF OUR HOSTS ARE KIND ENOUGH TO MAKE US WELCOME IN THEIR GUESTHOUSE, WE MUST BE EQUALLY KIND TO THEIR CHILDREN.
IT ISN'T AS IF THE BOY IS NICE TO US. HE ACTS THE FÜHRER IN HIS HITLER YOUTH UNIFORM AND ORDERS US AROUND THE WHOLE TIME, AND HE CAN'T EVEN SPEAK PROPERLY, WITH HIS BAVARIAN DIALECT.
BOWARK BASTARD
BOWARK BOWARK SCUMBAG
HE'S JUST LIKE HIS FAT, RED-FACED FATHER, THE REICHSMARSCHALL. IT'S DISGUSTING, THE WAY HE BELCHES AND SNORTS.
OWARK OWARK
SMACK
HEH HEH HEH

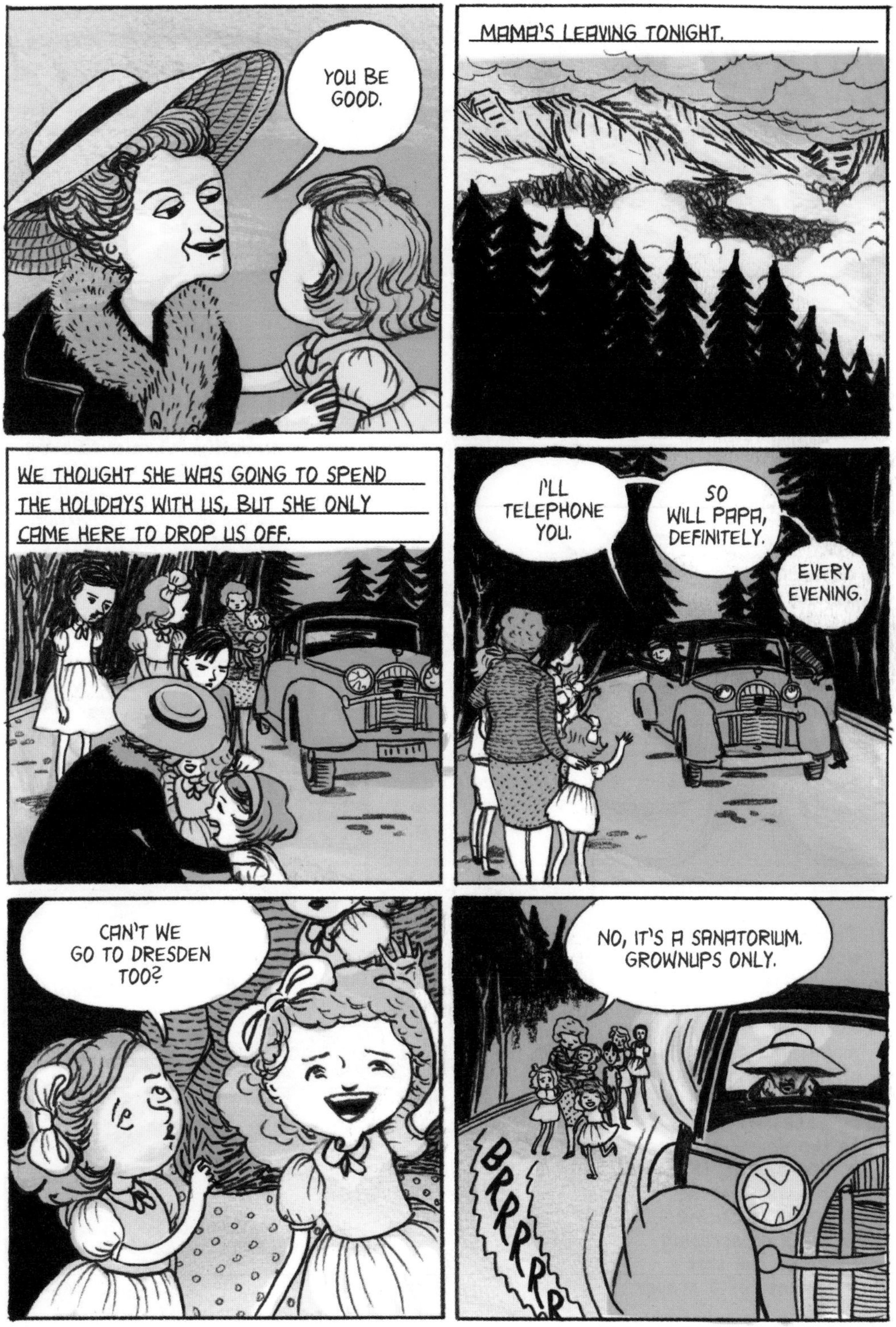
YOU BE GOOD.
MAMA'S LEAVING TONIGHT.
WE THOUGHT SHE WAS GOING TO SPEND THE HOLIDAYS WITH US, BUT SHE ONLY CAME HERE TO DROP US OFF.
I'LL TELEPHONE YOU.
SO WILL PAPA, DEFINITELY.
EVERY EVENING.
CAN'T WE GO TO DRESDEN TOO?
NO, IT'S A SANATORIUM. GROWNUPS ONLY.
BRRRRRR

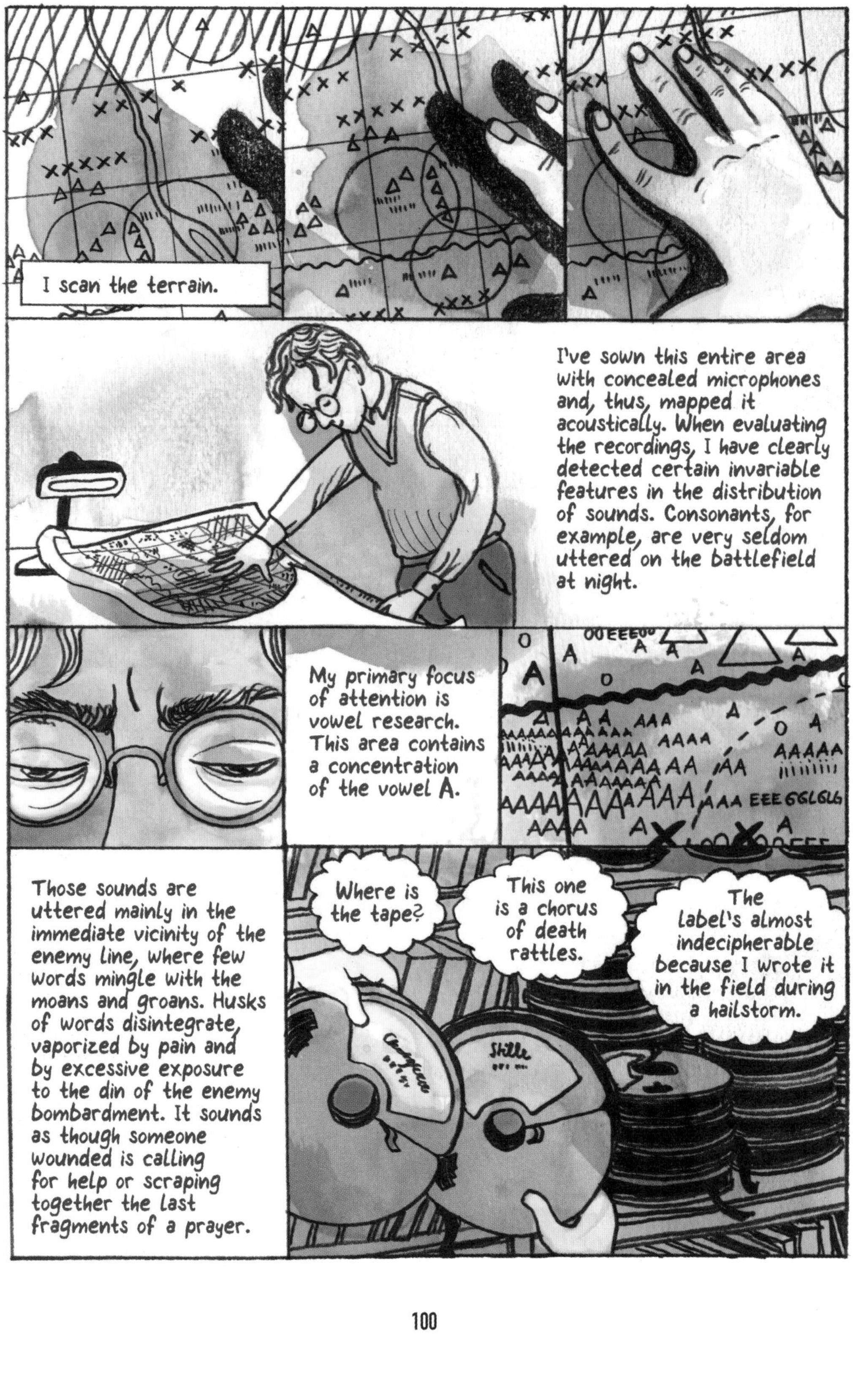
I scan the terrain.
I've sown this entire area with concealed microphones and, thus, mapped it acoustically. When evaluating the recordings, I have clearly detected certain invariable features in the distribution of sounds. Consonants, for example, are very seldom uttered on the battlefield at night.
My primary focus of attention is vowel research. This area contains a concentration of the vowel A.
Those sounds are uttered mainly in the immediate vicinity of the enemy line, where few words mingle with the moans and groans. Husks of words disintegrate, vaporized by pain and by excessive exposure to the din of the enemy bombardment. It sounds as though someone wounded is calling for help or scraping together the last fragments of a prayer.
Where is the tape?
This one is a chorus of death rattles.
The label's almost indecipherable because I wrote it in the field during a hailstorm.
Stille

This one's of silence.

A whole tapeful of silence recorded afterwards, when nothing—vocally speaking—was stirring.

THUMP

And this here, open vowels impinging on gutturals, is a youngster in his death throes losing all vocal control. An unimaginable screech, that was.

Off   On

I have become a voice thief. With these tapes, I can reach into any man's depths without his knowledge. I can extract anything from those depths and take possession of it, anything and everything down to the last, intimate breath exhaled by a dying man.

SSTSSSSTSSSSSSSSTS

And listen, almost there, quiet, just listen.

SSTSSS

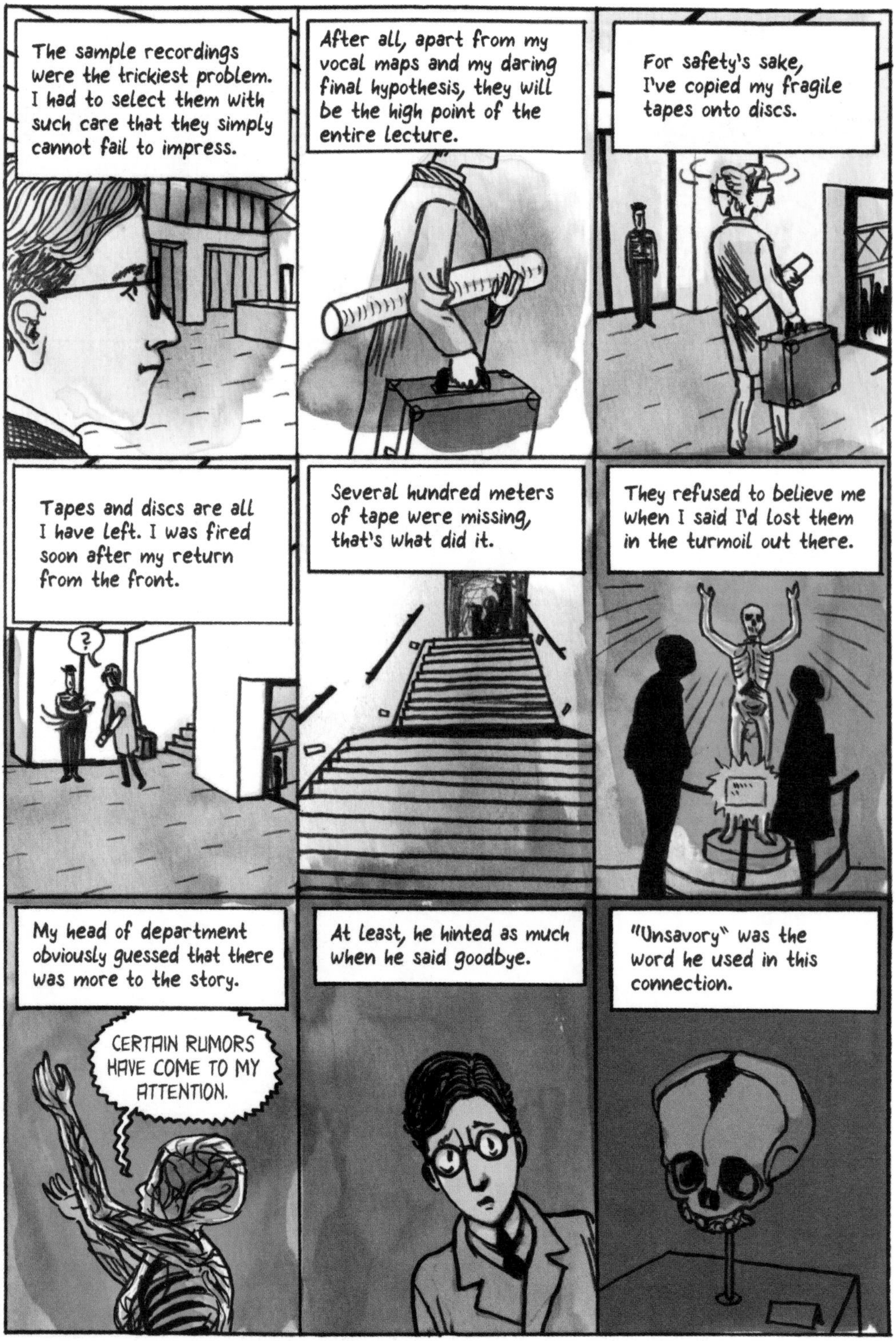
The sample recordings were the trickiest problem. I had to select them with such care that they simply cannot fail to impress.
After all, apart from my vocal maps and my daring final hypothesis, they will be the high point of the entire lecture.
For safety's sake, I've copied my fragile tapes onto discs.
Tapes and discs are all I have left. I was fired soon after my return from the front.
?
Several hundred meters of tape were missing, that's what did it.
They refused to believe me when I said I'd lost them in the turmoil out there.
My head of department obviously guessed that there was more to the story.
CERTAIN RUMORS HAVE COME TO MY ATTENTION.
At least, he hinted as much when he said goodbye.
"Unsavory" was the word he used in this connection.

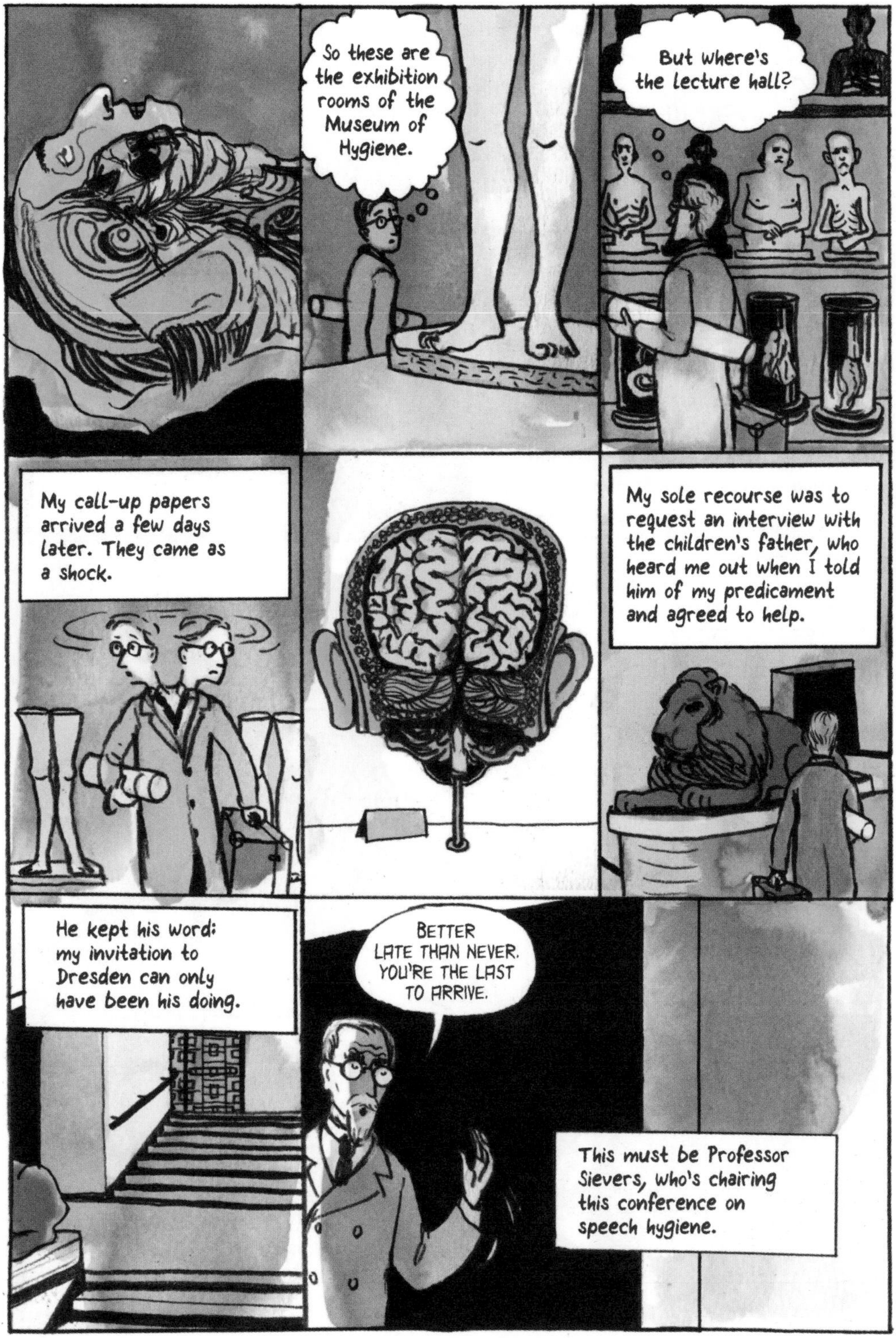

So these are the exhibition rooms of the Museum of Hygiene.
But where's the lecture hall?
My call-up papers arrived a few days later. They came as a shock.
My sole recourse was to request an interview with the children's father, who heard me out when I told him of my predicament and agreed to help.
He kept his word: my invitation to Dresden can only have been his doing.
BETTER LATE THAN NEVER. YOU'RE THE LAST TO ARRIVE.
This must be Professor Sievers, who's chairing this conference on speech hygiene.

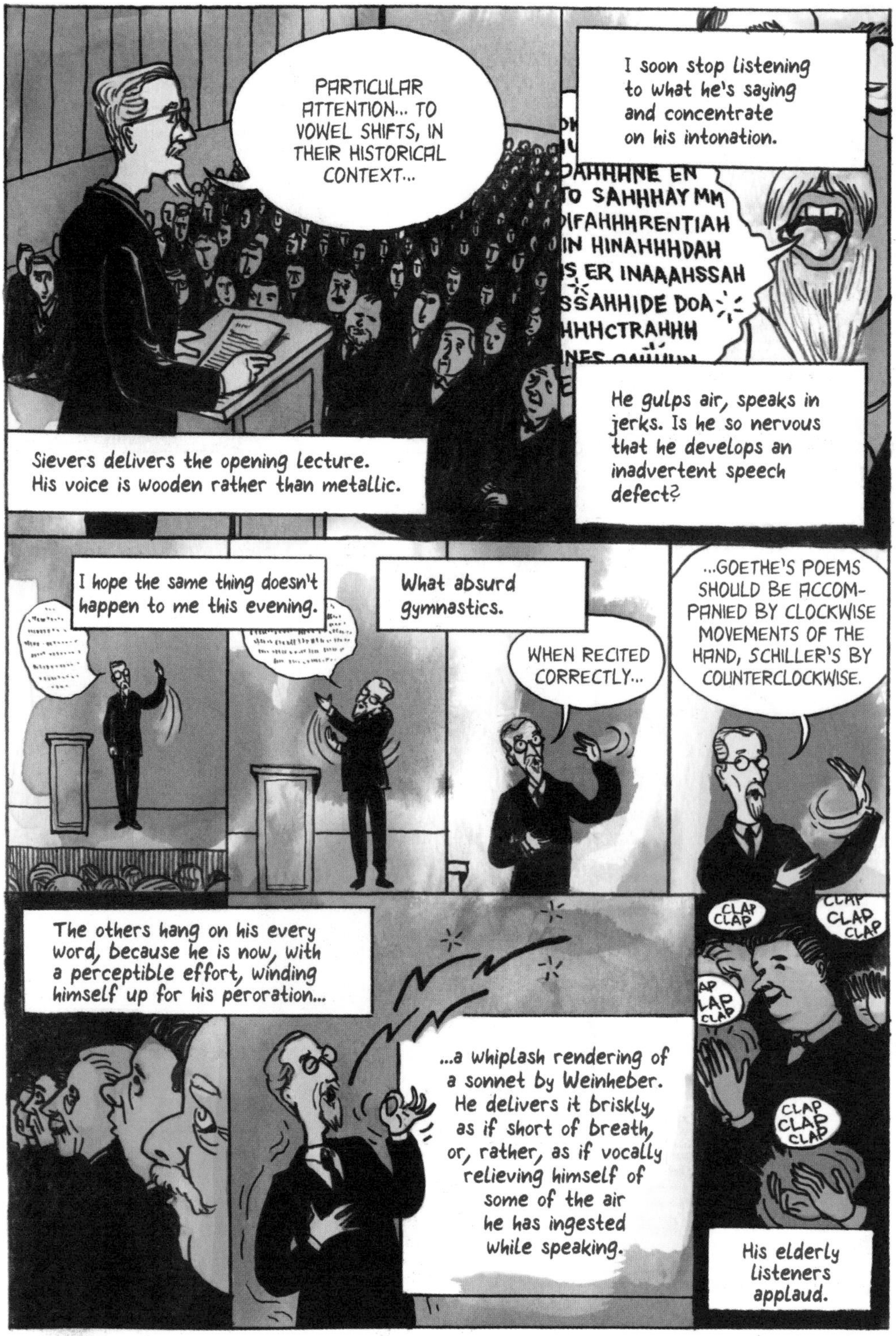
PARTICULAR ATTENTION... TO VOWEL SHIFTS, IN THEIR HISTORICAL CONTEXT...
Sievers delivers the opening lecture. His voice is wooden rather than metallic.
I soon stop listening to what he's saying and concentrate on his intonation.
DAHHHNE EN
TO SAHHHAY MM
IFAHHHRENTIAH
IN HINAHHHDAH
S ER INAAAHSSAH
SSAHHIDE DOA
HHHCTRAHHH
He gulps air, speaks in jerks. Is he so nervous that he develops an inadvertent speech defect?
I hope the same thing doesn't happen to me this evening.
What absurd gymnastics.
WHEN RECITED CORRECTLY...
...GOETHE'S POEMS SHOULD BE ACCOMPANIED BY CLOCKWISE MOVEMENTS OF THE HAND, SCHILLER'S BY COUNTERCLOCKWISE.
The others hang on his every word, because he is now, with a perceptible effort, winding himself up for his peroration...
...a whiplash rendering of a sonnet by Weinheber. He delivers it briskly, as if short of breath, or, rather, as if vocally relieving himself of some of the air he has ingested while speaking.
CLAP CLAP
CLAP CLAP CLAP
CLAP CLAP CLAP
CLAP CLAP CLAP
His elderly listeners applaud.

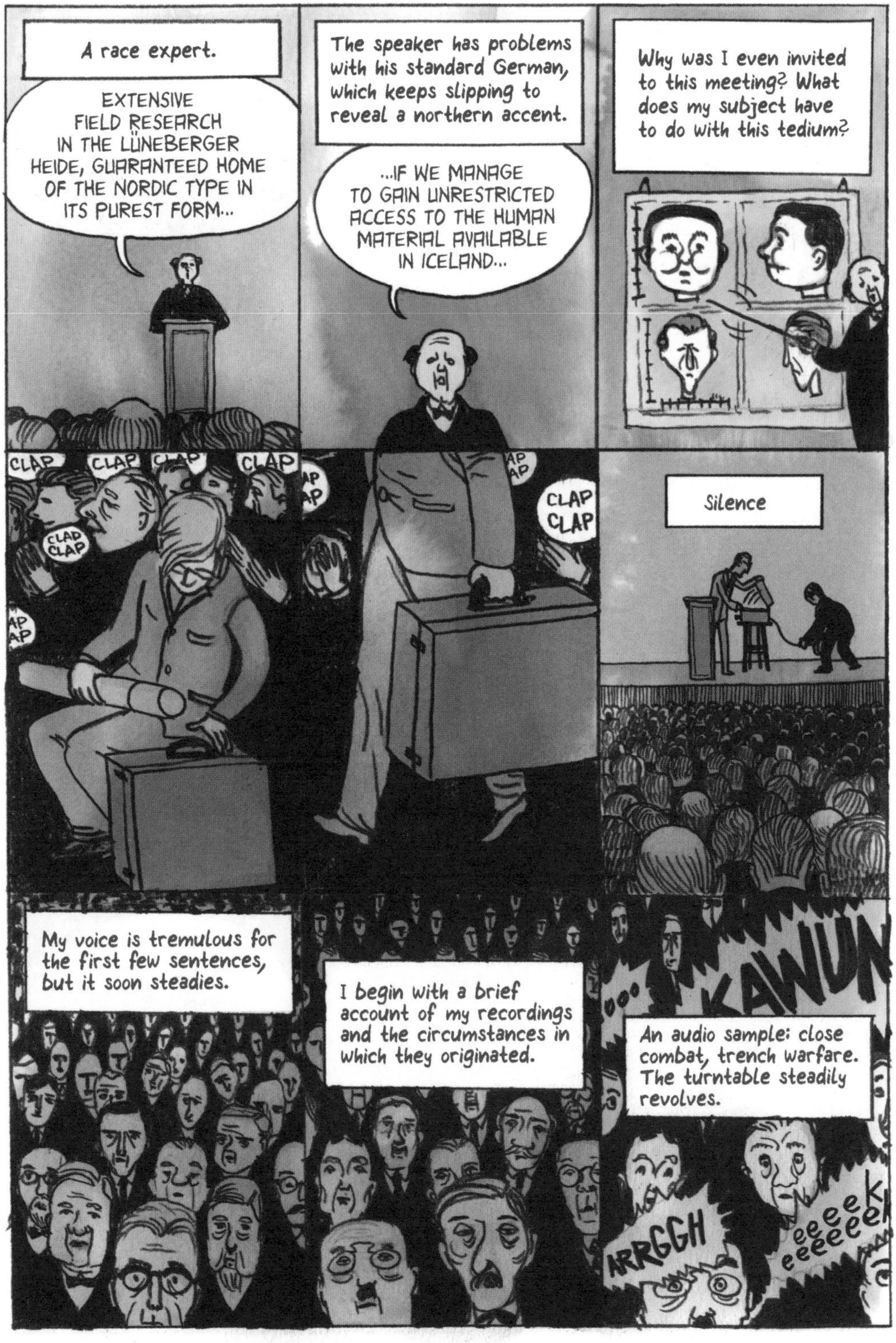
A race expert.
EXTENSIVE FIELD RESEARCH IN THE LÜNEBERGER HEIDE, GUARANTEED HOME OF THE NORDIC TYPE IN ITS PUREST FORM...
The speaker has problems with his standard German, which keeps slipping to reveal a northern accent.
...IF WE MANAGE TO GAIN UNRESTRICTED ACCESS TO THE HUMAN MATERIAL AVAILABLE IN ICELAND...
Why was I even invited to this meeting? What does my subject have to do with this tedium?
CLAP
CLAP
CLAP
CLAD CLAP
CLAP CLAP
Silence
My voice is tremulous for the first few sentences, but it soon steadies.
I begin with a brief account of my recordings and the circumstances in which they originated.
KAWUN
An audio sample: close combat, trench warfare. The turntable steadily revolves.
ARRGGH
eeeeek eeeeeee

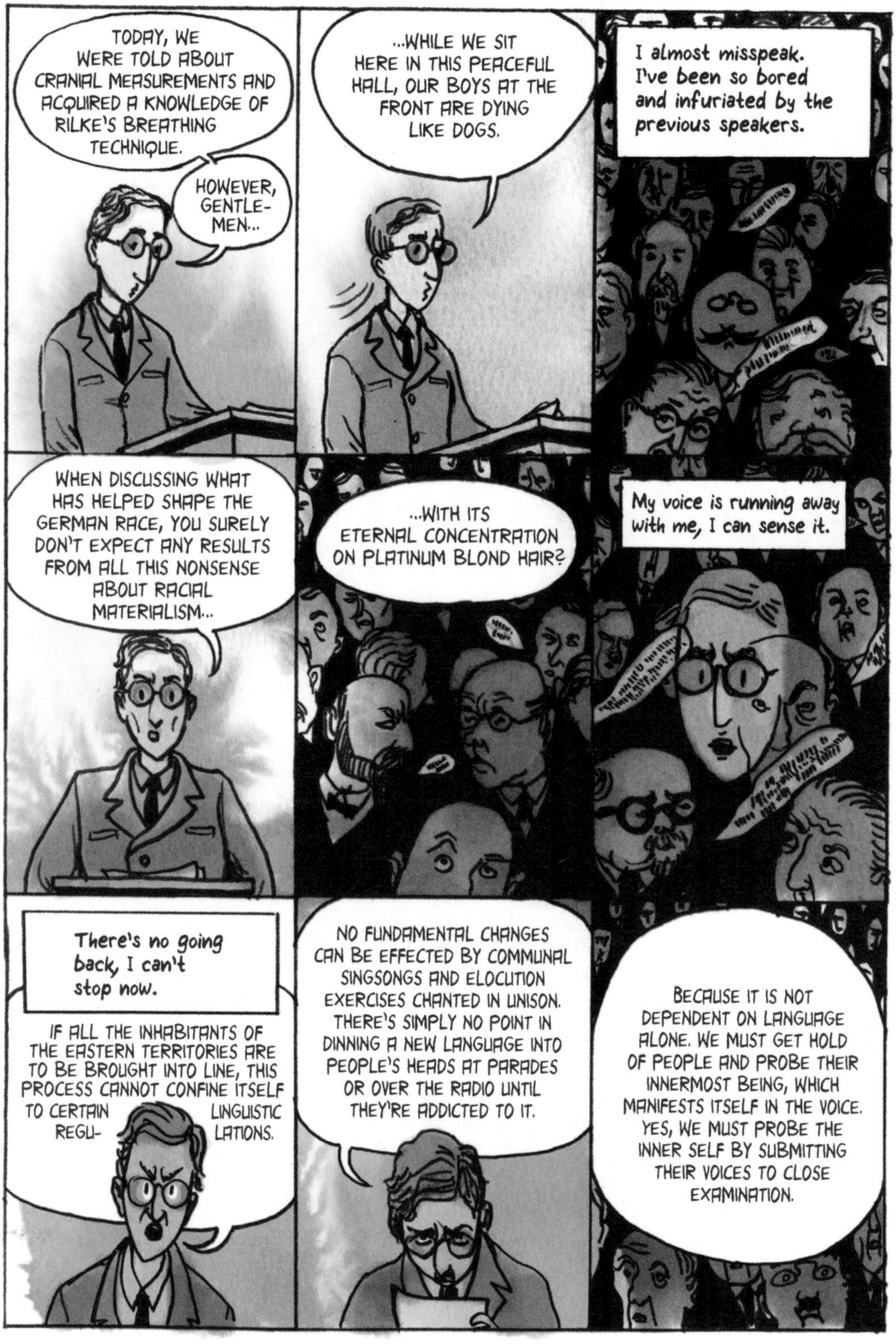
TODAY, WE WERE TOLD ABOUT CRANIAL MEASUREMENTS AND ACQUIRED A KNOWLEDGE OF RILKE'S BREATHING TECHNIQUE.
HOWEVER, GENTLE-MEN...
...WHILE WE SIT HERE IN THIS PEACEFUL HALL, OUR BOYS AT THE FRONT ARE DYING LIKE DOGS.
I almost misspeak. I've been so bored and infuriated by the previous speakers.
WHEN DISCUSSING WHAT HAS HELPED SHAPE THE GERMAN RACE, YOU SURELY DON'T EXPECT ANY RESULTS FROM ALL THIS NONSENSE ABOUT RACIAL MATERIALISM...
...WITH ITS ETERNAL CONCENTRATION ON PLATINUM BLOND HAIR?
My voice is running away with me, I can sense it.
There's no going back, I can't stop now.
IF ALL THE INHABITANTS OF THE EASTERN TERRITORIES ARE TO BE BROUGHT INTO LINE, THIS PROCESS CANNOT CONFINE ITSELF TO CERTAIN LINGUISTIC REGU-LATIONS.
NO FUNDAMENTAL CHANGES CAN BE EFFECTED BY COMMUNAL SINGSONGS AND ELOCUTION EXERCISES CHANTED IN UNISON. THERE'S SIMPLY NO POINT IN DINNING A NEW LANGUAGE INTO PEOPLE'S HEADS AT PARADES OR OVER THE RADIO UNTIL THEY'RE ADDICTED TO IT.
BECAUSE IT IS NOT DEPENDENT ON LANGUAGE ALONE. WE MUST GET HOLD OF PEOPLE AND PROBE THEIR INNERMOST BEING, WHICH MANIFESTS ITSELF IN THE VOICE. YES, WE MUST PROBE THE INNER SELF BY SUBMITTING THEIR VOICES TO CLOSE EXAMINATION.

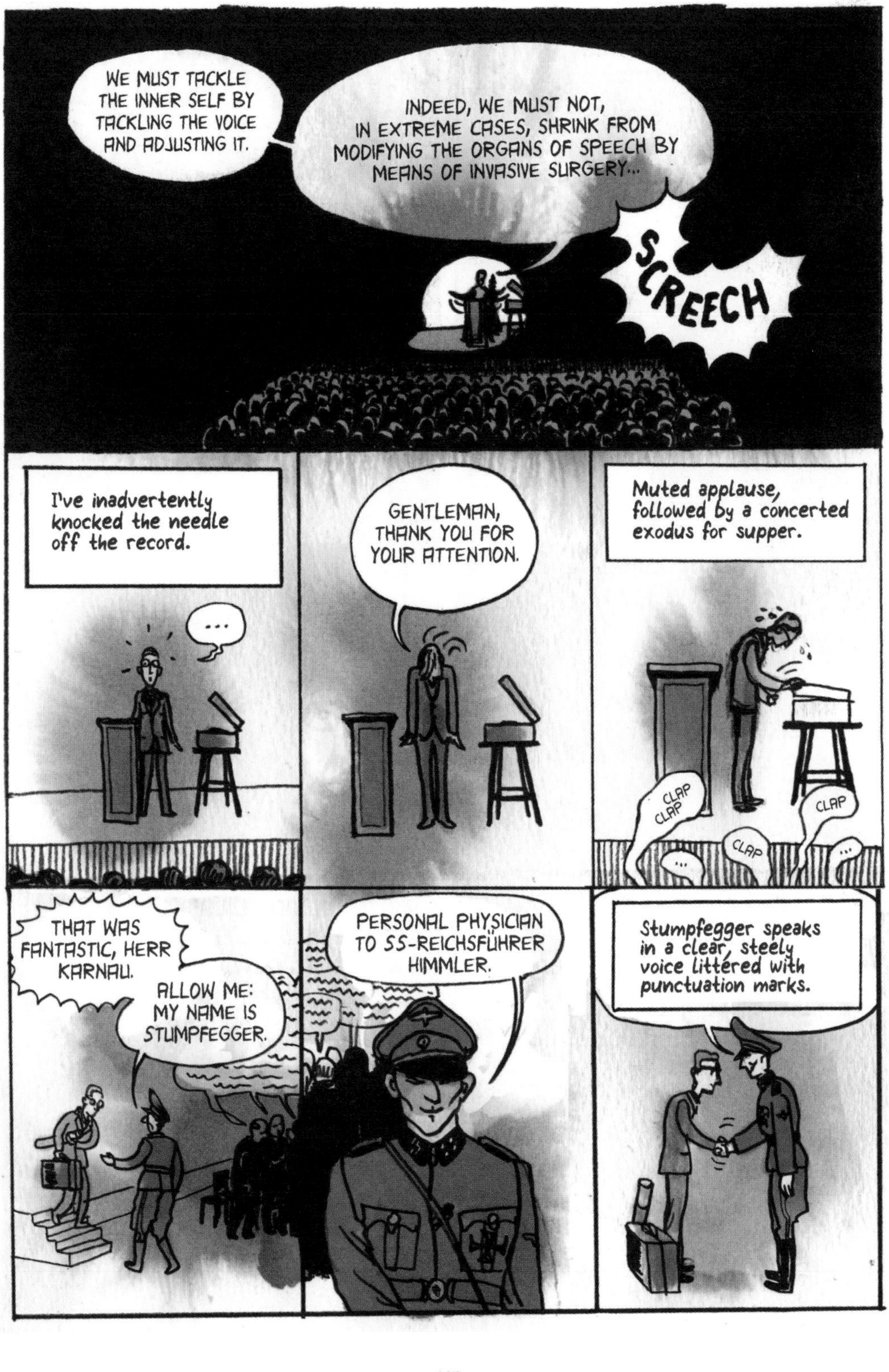
WE MUST TACKLE THE INNER SELF BY TACKLING THE VOICE AND ADJUSTING IT.
INDEED, WE MUST NOT, IN EXTREME CASES, SHRINK FROM MODIFYING THE ORGANS OF SPEECH BY MEANS OF INVASIVE SURGERY...
SCREECH
I've inadvertently knocked the needle off the record.
...
GENTLEMAN, THANK YOU FOR YOUR ATTENTION.
Muted applause, followed by a concerted exodus for supper.
CLAP CLAP
CLAP
CLAP
...
...
THAT WAS FANTASTIC, HERR KARNAU.
ALLOW ME: MY NAME IS STUMPFEGGER.
PERSONAL PHYSICIAN TO SS-REICHSFÜHRER HIMMLER.
Stumpfegger speaks in a clear, steely voice littered with punctuation marks.

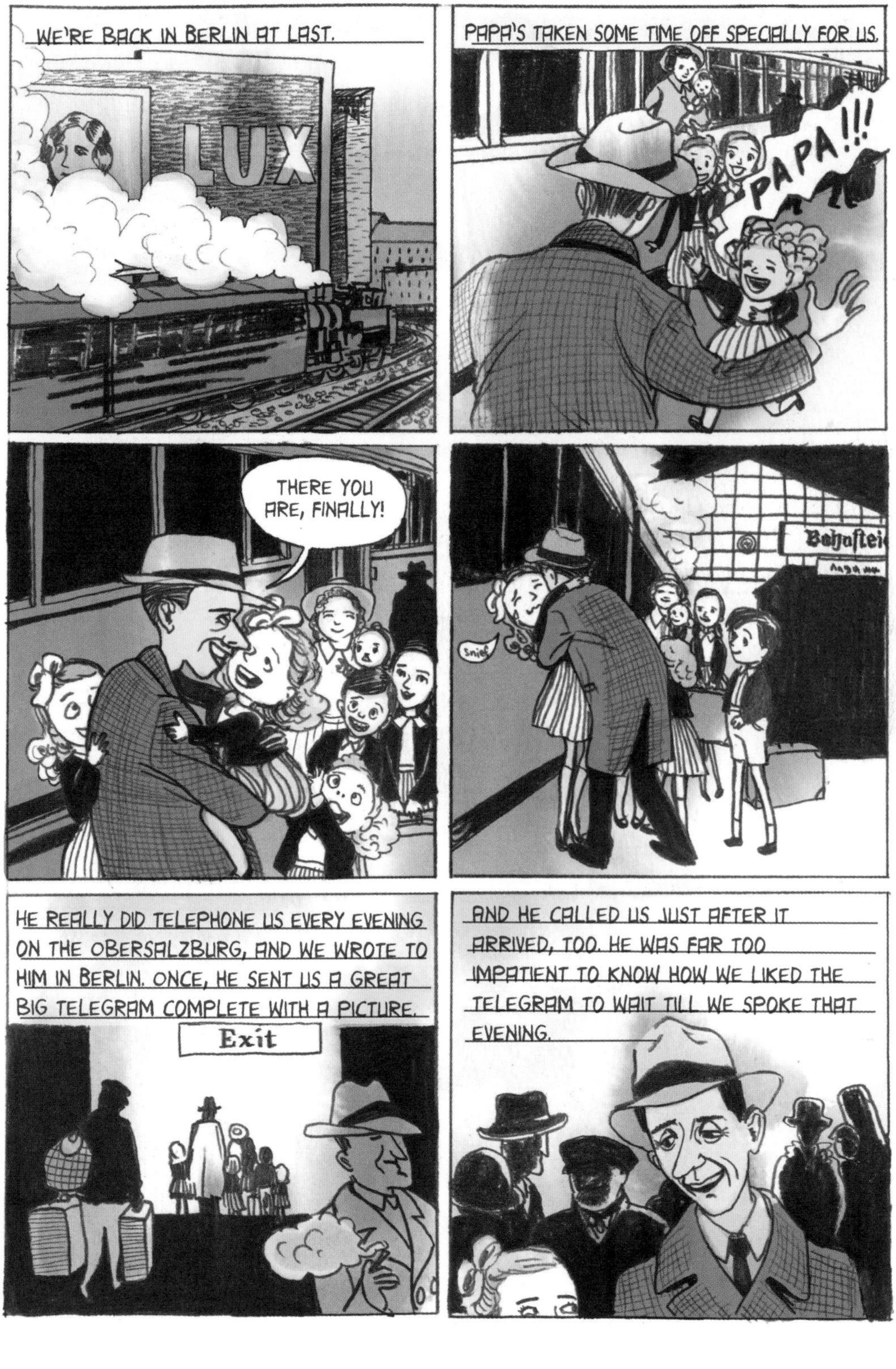
WE'RE BACK IN BERLIN AT LAST.
LUX
PAPA'S TAKEN SOME TIME OFF SPECIALLY FOR US.
PAPA!!!
THERE YOU ARE, FINALLY!
HE REALLY DID TELEPHONE US EVERY EVENING ON THE OBERSALZBURG, AND WE WROTE TO HIM IN BERLIN. ONCE, HE SENT US A GREAT BIG TELEGRAM COMPLETE WITH A PICTURE.
Exit
AND HE CALLED US JUST AFTER IT ARRIVED, TOO. HE WAS FAR TOO IMPATIENT TO KNOW HOW WE LIKED THE TELEGRAM TO WAIT TILL WE SPOKE THAT EVENING.

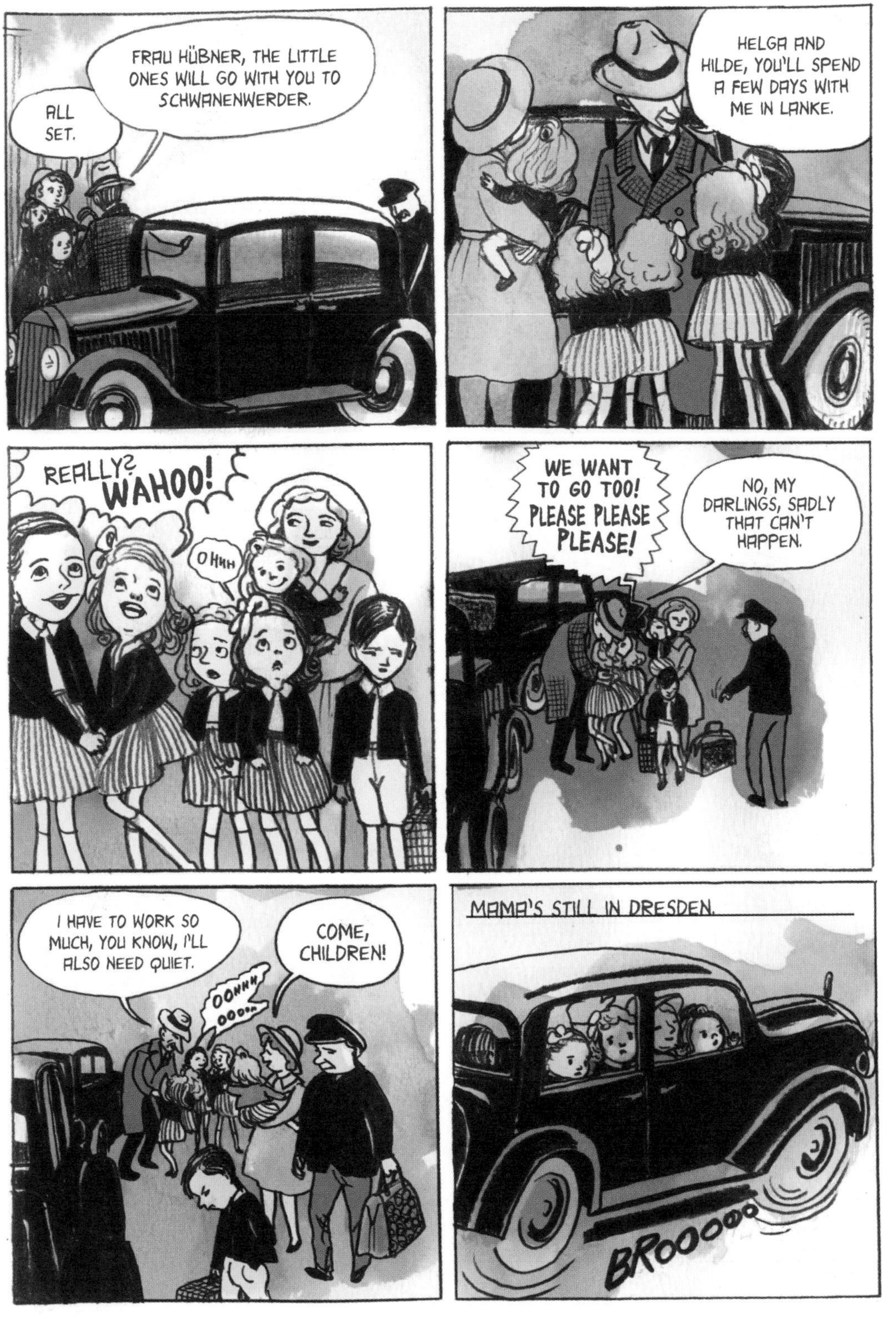
FRAU HÜBNER, THE LITTLE ONES WILL GO WITH YOU TO SCHWANENWERDER.
ALL SET.
HELGA AND HILDE, YOU'LL SPEND A FEW DAYS WITH ME IN LANKE.
REALLY? WAHOO!
OHHH
WE WANT TO GO TOO! PLEASE PLEASE PLEASE!
NO, MY DARLINGS, SADLY THAT CAN'T HAPPEN.
I HAVE TO WORK SO MUCH, YOU KNOW, I'LL ALSO NEED QUIET.
COME, CHILDREN!
OOHHH, OOO...
MAMA'S STILL IN DRESDEN.
BROOOOO

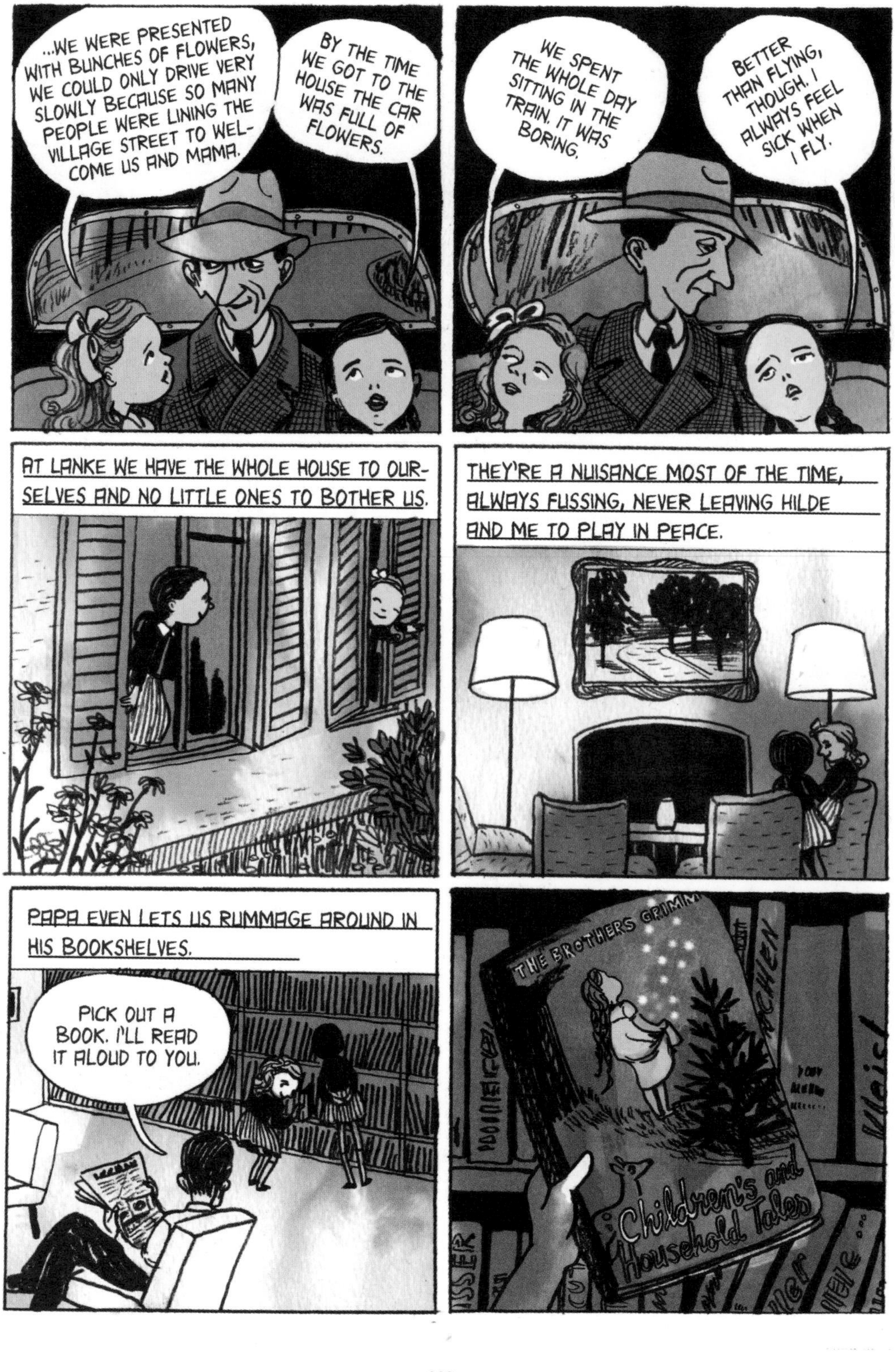
...WE WERE PRESENTED WITH BUNCHES OF FLOWERS, WE COULD ONLY DRIVE VERY SLOWLY BECAUSE SO MANY PEOPLE WERE LINING THE VILLAGE STREET TO WEL-COME US AND MAMA.
BY THE TIME WE GOT TO THE HOUSE THE CAR WAS FULL OF FLOWERS.
WE SPENT THE WHOLE DAY SITTING IN THE TRAIN. IT WAS BORING.
BETTER THAN FLYING, THOUGH. I ALWAYS FEEL SICK WHEN I FLY.
AT LANKE WE HAVE THE WHOLE HOUSE TO OUR-SELVES AND NO LITTLE ONES TO BOTHER US.
THEY'RE A NUISANCE MOST OF THE TIME, ALWAYS FUSSING, NEVER LEAVING HILDE AND ME TO PLAY IN PEACE.
PAPA EVEN LETS US RUMMAGE AROUND IN HIS BOOKSHELVES.
PICK OUT A BOOK. I'LL READ IT ALOUD TO YOU.
THE BROTHERS GRIMM
Children's and Household Tales

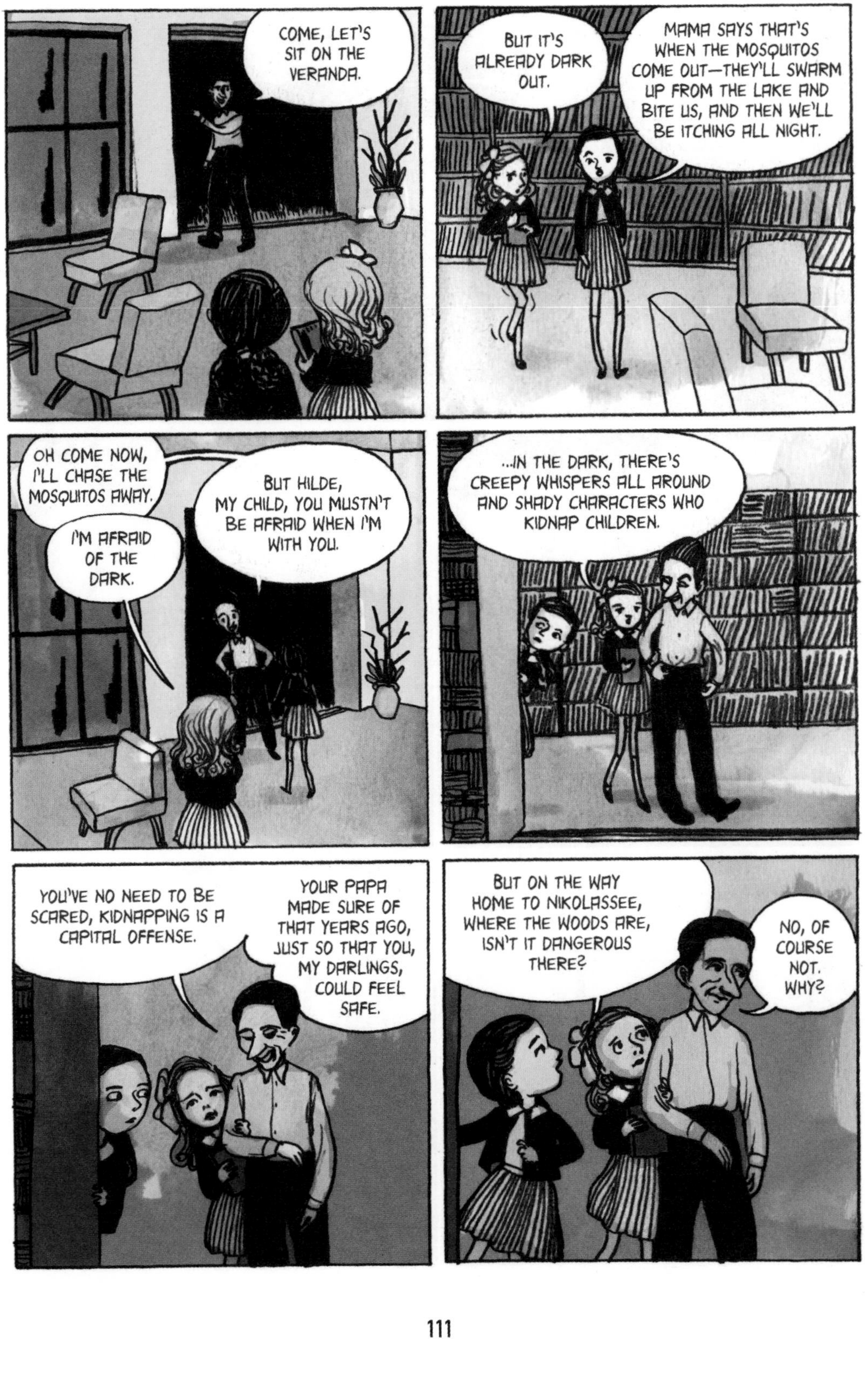
COME, LET'S SIT ON THE VERANDA.
BUT IT'S ALREADY DARK OUT.
MAMA SAYS THAT'S WHEN THE MOSQUITOS COME OUT—THEY'LL SWARM UP FROM THE LAKE AND BITE US, AND THEN WE'LL BE ITCHING ALL NIGHT.
OH COME NOW, I'LL CHASE THE MOSQUITOS AWAY.
I'M AFRAID OF THE DARK.
BUT HILDE, MY CHILD, YOU MUSTN'T BE AFRAID WHEN I'M WITH YOU.
...IN THE DARK, THERE'S CREEPY WHISPERS ALL AROUND AND SHADY CHARACTERS WHO KIDNAP CHILDREN.
YOU'VE NO NEED TO BE SCARED, KIDNAPPING IS A CAPITAL OFFENSE.
YOUR PAPA MADE SURE OF THAT YEARS AGO, JUST SO THAT YOU, MY DARLINGS, COULD FEEL SAFE.
BUT ON THE WAY HOME TO NIKOLASSEE, WHERE THE WOODS ARE, ISN'T IT DANGEROUS THERE?
NO, OF COURSE NOT. WHY?

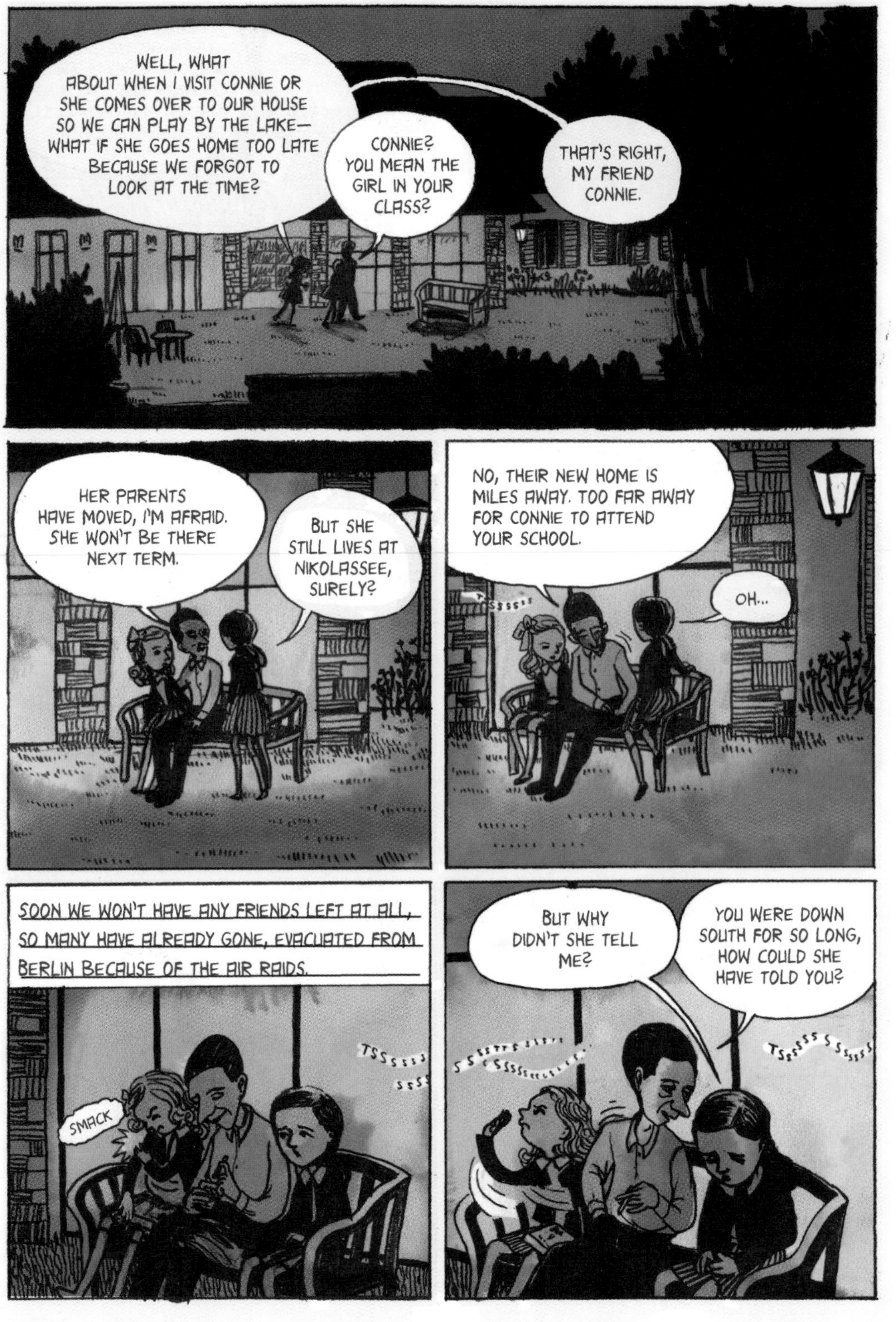
WELL, WHAT ABOUT WHEN I VISIT CONNIE OR SHE COMES OVER TO OUR HOUSE SO WE CAN PLAY BY THE LAKE— WHAT IF SHE GOES HOME TOO LATE BECAUSE WE FORGOT TO LOOK AT THE TIME?
CONNIE? YOU MEAN THE GIRL IN YOUR CLASS?
THAT'S RIGHT, MY FRIEND CONNIE.
HER PARENTS HAVE MOVED, I'M AFRAID. SHE WON'T BE THERE NEXT TERM.
BUT SHE STILL LIVES AT NIKOLASSEE, SURELY?
NO, THEIR NEW HOME IS MILES AWAY. TOO FAR AWAY FOR CONNIE TO ATTEND YOUR SCHOOL.
OH...
SOON WE WON'T HAVE ANY FRIENDS LEFT AT ALL, SO MANY HAVE ALREADY GONE, EVACUATED FROM BERLIN BECAUSE OF THE AIR RAIDS.
SMACK
BUT WHY DIDN'T SHE TELL ME?
YOU WERE DOWN SOUTH FOR SO LONG, HOW COULD SHE HAVE TOLD YOU?

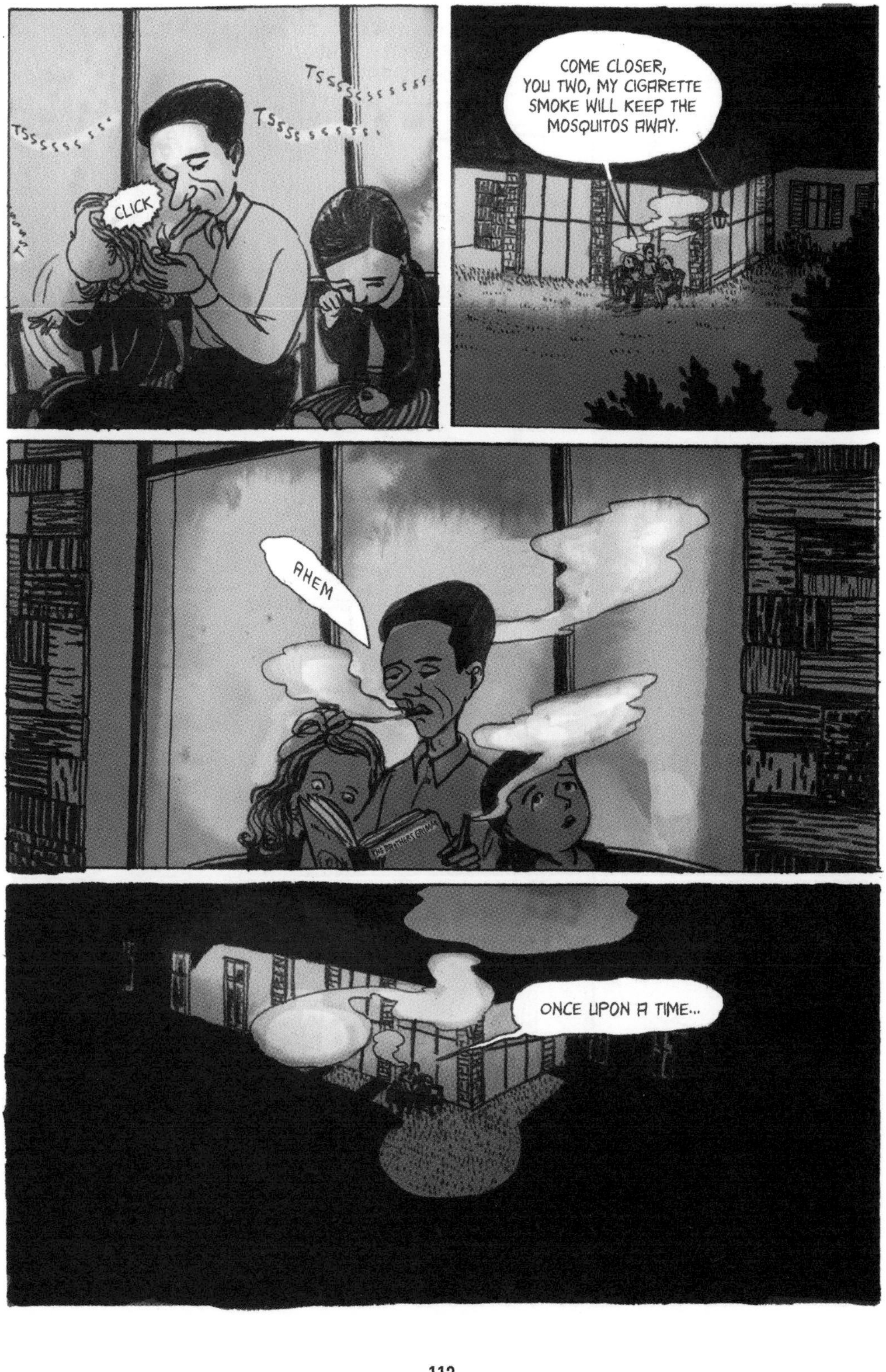
TSSSSSSSSSSSSS
TSSSSSSSSSS
TSSSSSSSSS
CLICK
COME CLOSER, YOU TWO, MY CIGARETTE SMOKE WILL KEEP THE MOSQUITOS AWAY.
AHEM
THE BROTHERS GRIMM
ONCE UPON A TIME...

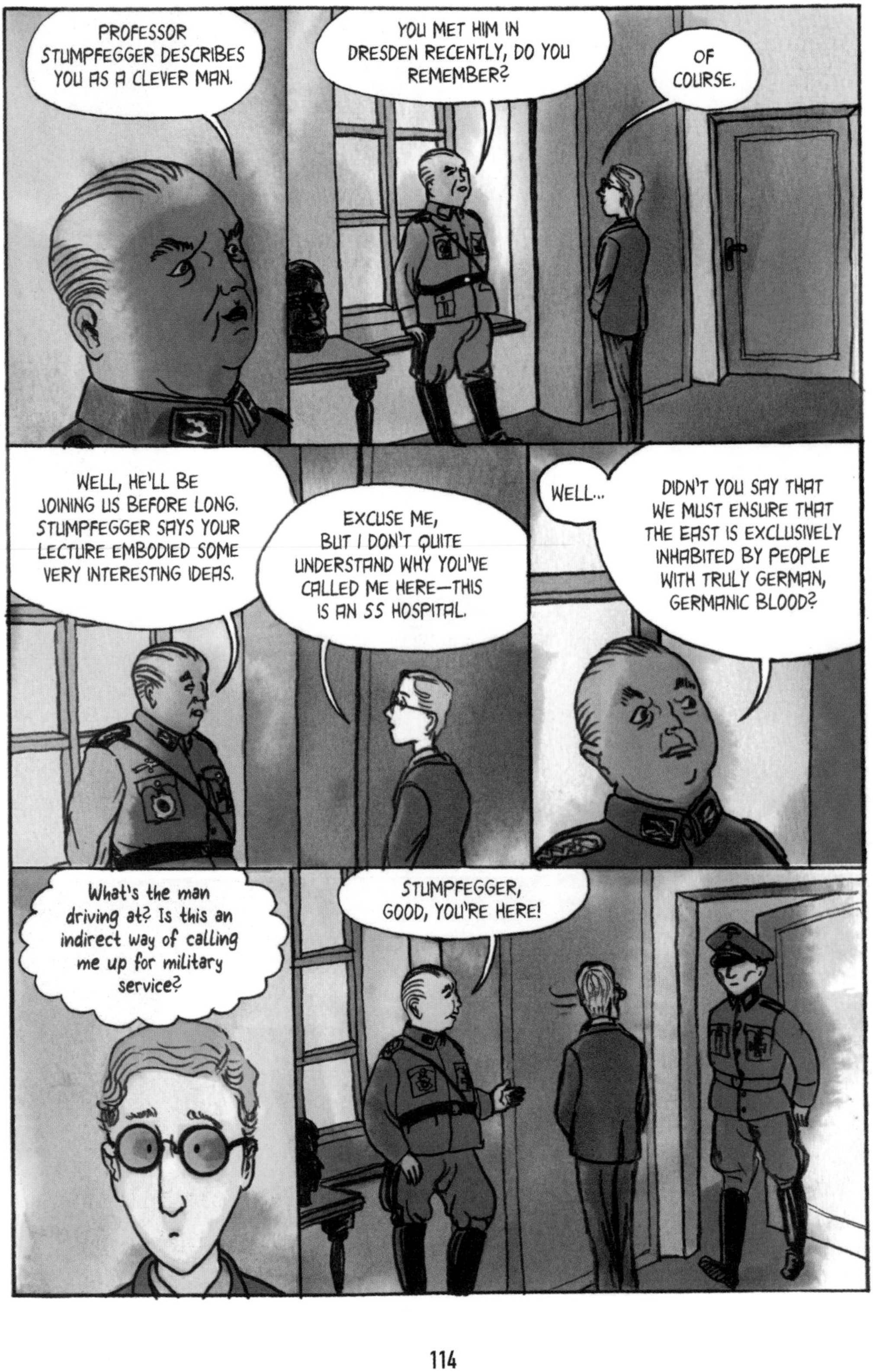
PROFESSOR STUMPFEGGER DESCRIBES YOU AS A CLEVER MAN.
YOU MET HIM IN DRESDEN RECENTLY, DO YOU REMEMBER?
OF COURSE.
WELL, HE'LL BE JOINING US BEFORE LONG. STUMPFEGGER SAYS YOUR LECTURE EMBODIED SOME VERY INTERESTING IDEAS.
EXCUSE ME, BUT I DON'T QUITE UNDERSTAND WHY YOU'VE CALLED ME HERE—THIS IS AN SS HOSPITAL.
WELL...
DIDN'T YOU SAY THAT WE MUST ENSURE THAT THE EAST IS EXCLUSIVELY INHABITED BY PEOPLE WITH TRULY GERMAN, GERMANIC BLOOD?
What's the man driving at? Is this an indirect way of calling me up for military service?
STUMPFEGGER, GOOD, YOU'RE HERE!

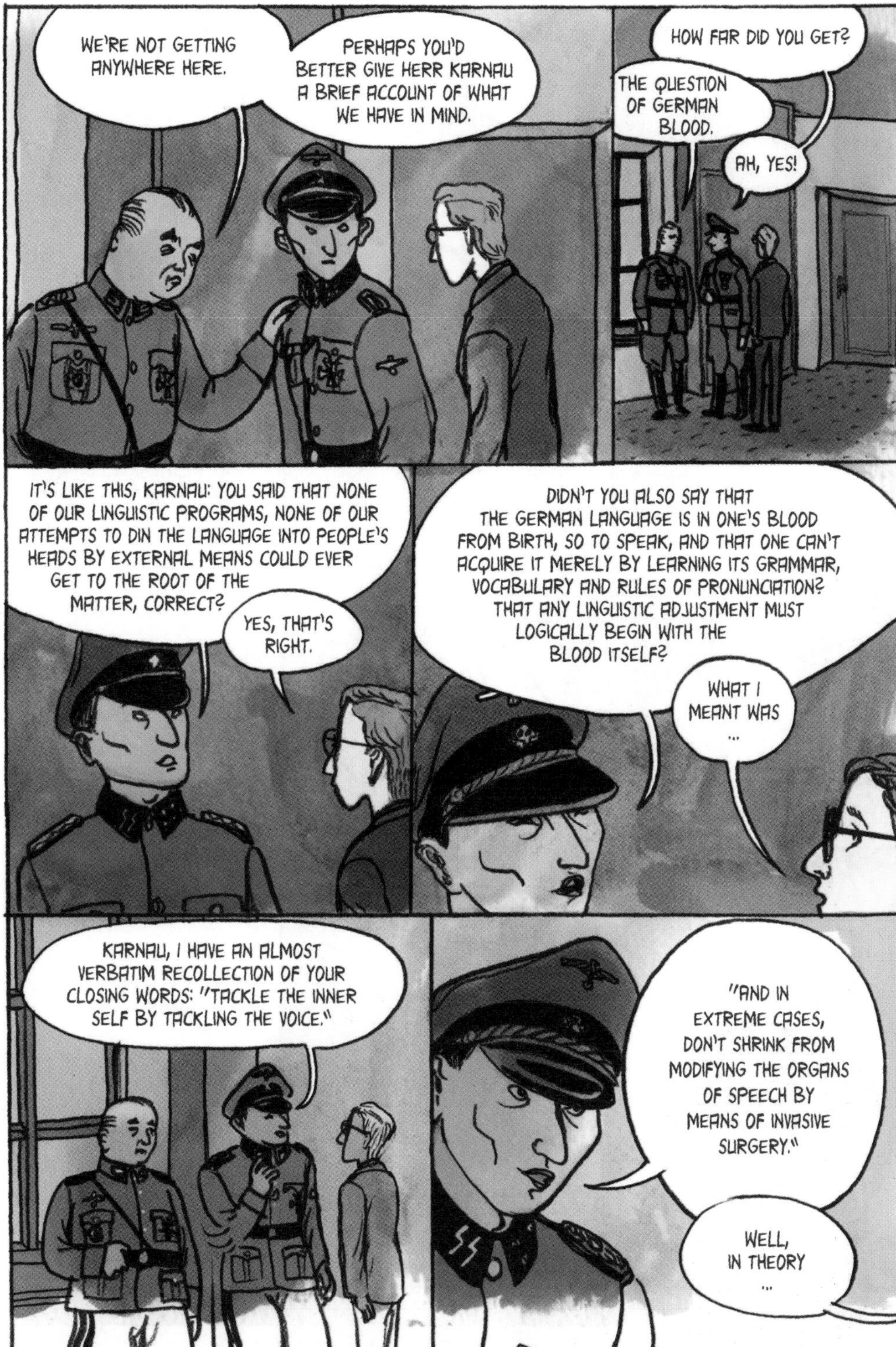
WE'RE NOT GETTING ANYWHERE HERE.
PERHAPS YOU'D BETTER GIVE HERR KARNAU A BRIEF ACCOUNT OF WHAT WE HAVE IN MIND.
HOW FAR DID YOU GET?
THE QUESTION OF GERMAN BLOOD.
AH, YES!
IT'S LIKE THIS, KARNAU: YOU SAID THAT NONE OF OUR LINGUISTIC PROGRAMS, NONE OF OUR ATTEMPTS TO DIN THE LANGUAGE INTO PEOPLE'S HEADS BY EXTERNAL MEANS COULD EVER GET TO THE ROOT OF THE MATTER, CORRECT?
YES, THAT'S RIGHT.
DIDN'T YOU ALSO SAY THAT THE GERMAN LANGUAGE IS IN ONE'S BLOOD FROM BIRTH, SO TO SPEAK, AND THAT ONE CAN'T ACQUIRE IT MERELY BY LEARNING ITS GRAMMAR, VOCABULARY AND RULES OF PRONUNCIATION? THAT ANY LINGUISTIC ADJUSTMENT MUST LOGICALLY BEGIN WITH THE BLOOD ITSELF?
WHAT I MEANT WAS ...
KARNAU, I HAVE AN ALMOST VERBATIM RECOLLECTION OF YOUR CLOSING WORDS: "TACKLE THE INNER SELF BY TACKLING THE VOICE."
"AND IN EXTREME CASES, DON'T SHRINK FROM MODIFYING THE ORGANS OF SPEECH BY MEANS OF INVASIVE SURGERY."
WELL, IN THEORY ...

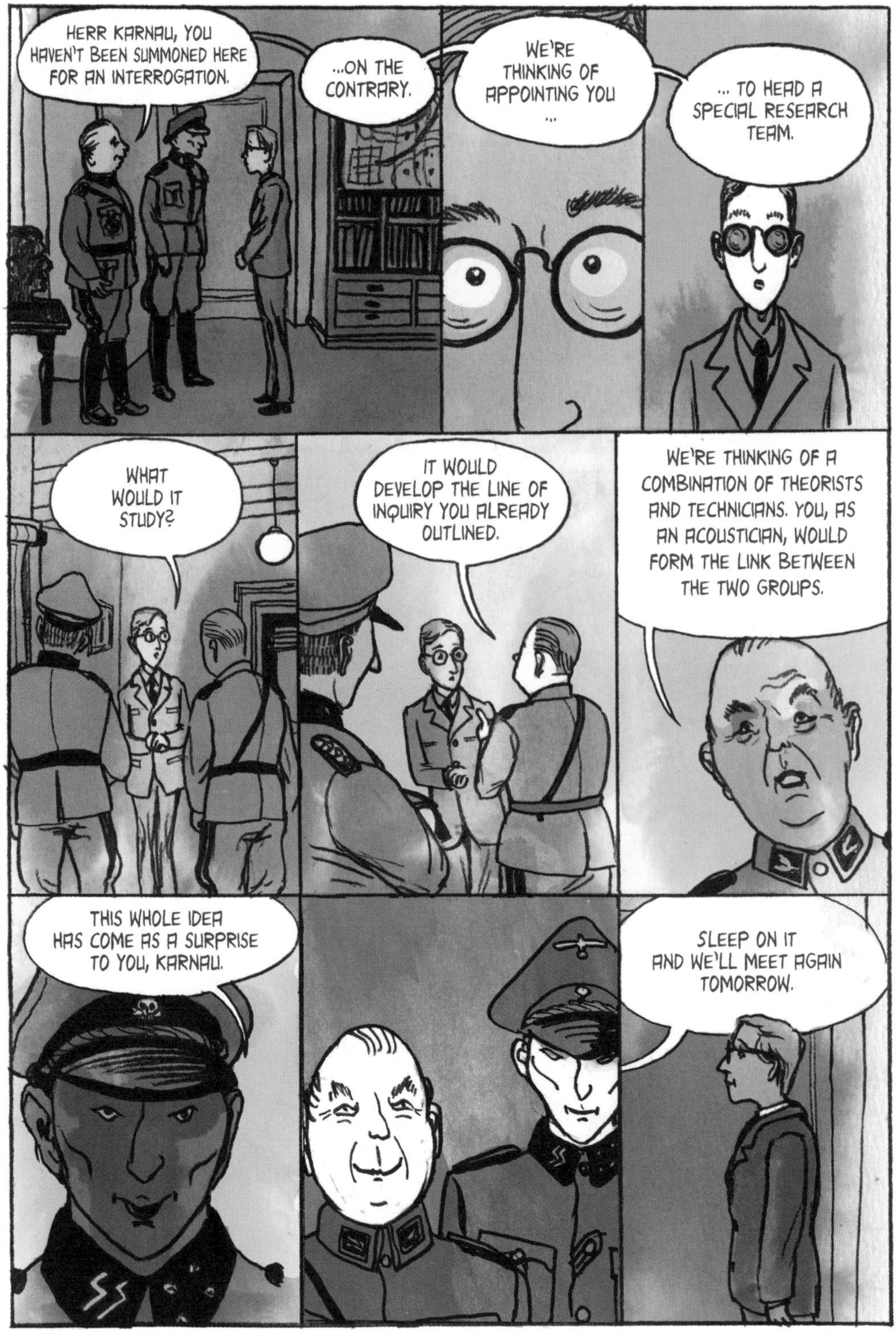
HERR KARNAU, YOU HAVEN'T BEEN SUMMONED HERE FOR AN INTERROGATION.
...ON THE CONTRARY.
WE'RE THINKING OF APPOINTING YOU ...
... TO HEAD A SPECIAL RESEARCH TEAM.
WHAT WOULD IT STUDY?
IT WOULD DEVELOP THE LINE OF INQUIRY YOU ALREADY OUTLINED.
WE'RE THINKING OF A COMBINATION OF THEORISTS AND TECHNICIANS. YOU, AS AN ACOUSTICIAN, WOULD FORM THE LINK BETWEEN THE TWO GROUPS.
THIS WHOLE IDEA HAS COME AS A SURPRISE TO YOU, KARNAU.
SLEEP ON IT AND WE'LL MEET AGAIN TOMORROW.

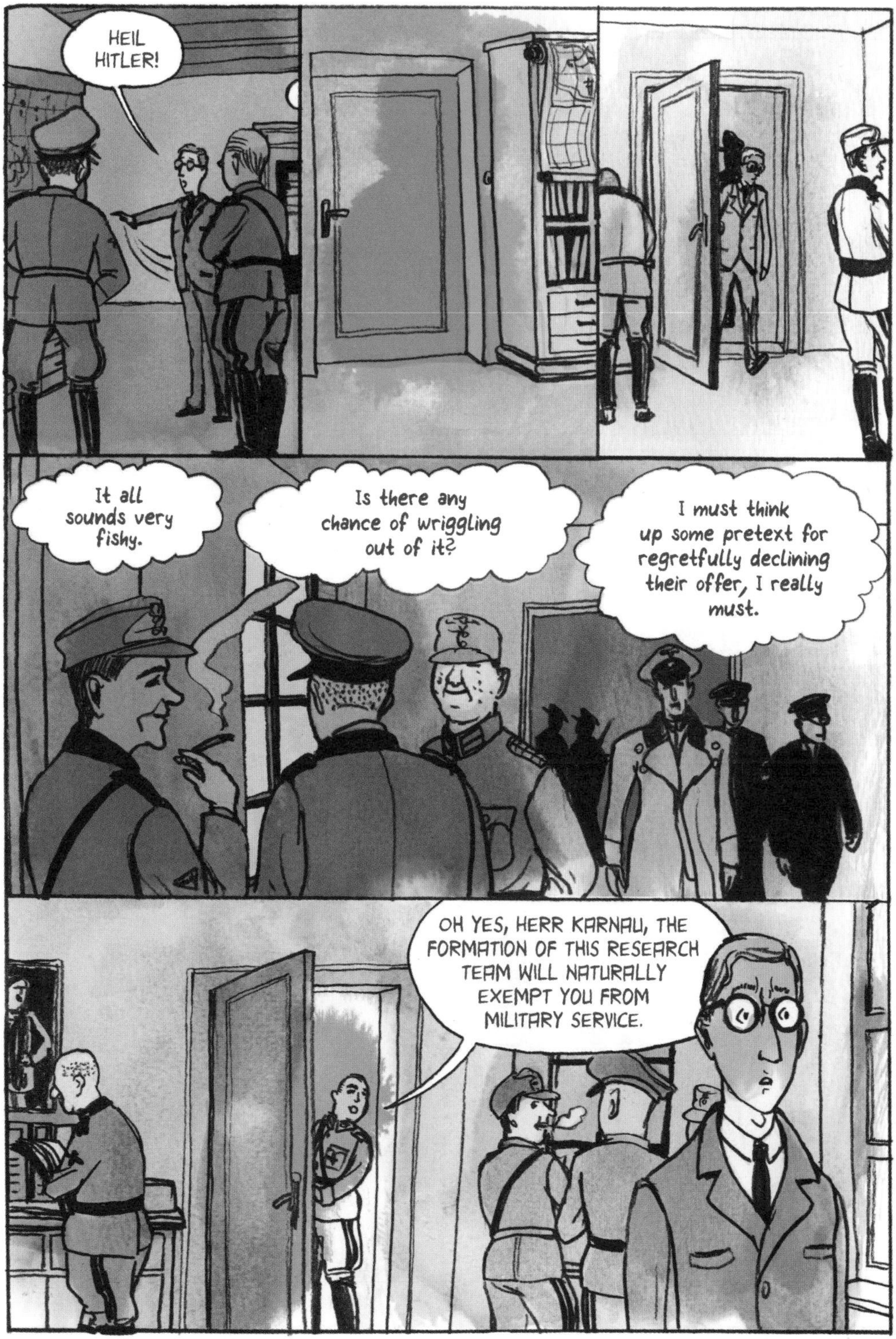
HEIL HITLER!
It all sounds very fishy.
Is there any chance of wriggling out of it?
I must think up some pretext for regretfully declining their offer, I really must.
OH YES, HERR KARNAU, THE FORMATION OF THIS RESEARCH TEAM WILL NATURALLY EXEMPT YOU FROM MILITARY SERVICE.

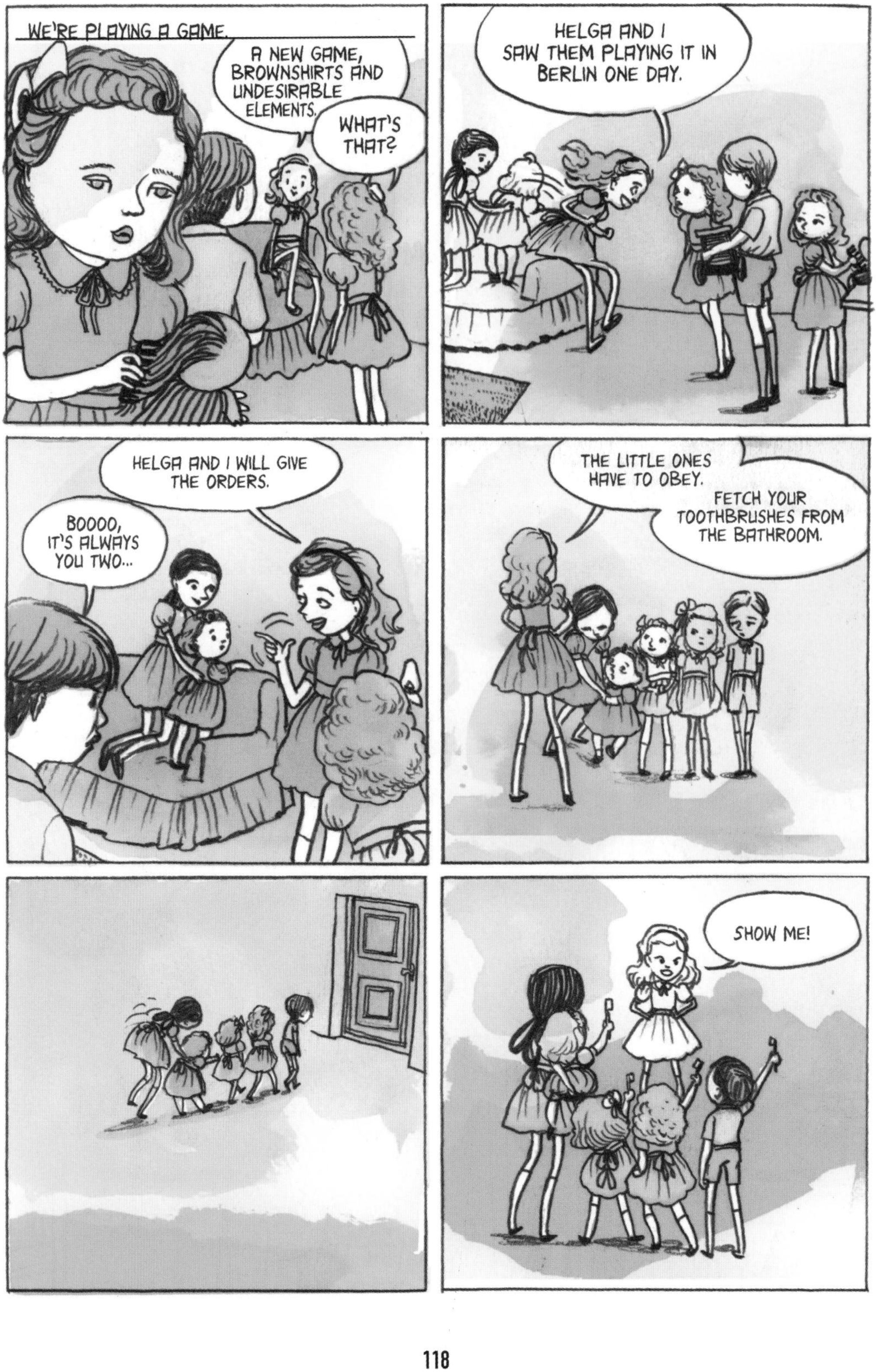
WE'RE PLAYING A GAME.
A NEW GAME, BROWNSHIRTS AND UNDESIRABLE ELEMENTS.
WHAT'S THAT?
HELGA AND I SAW THEM PLAYING IT IN BERLIN ONE DAY.
HELGA AND I WILL GIVE THE ORDERS.
BOOOO, IT'S ALWAYS YOU TWO...
THE LITTLE ONES HAVE TO OBEY.
FETCH YOUR TOOTHBRUSHES FROM THE BATHROOM.
SHOW ME!

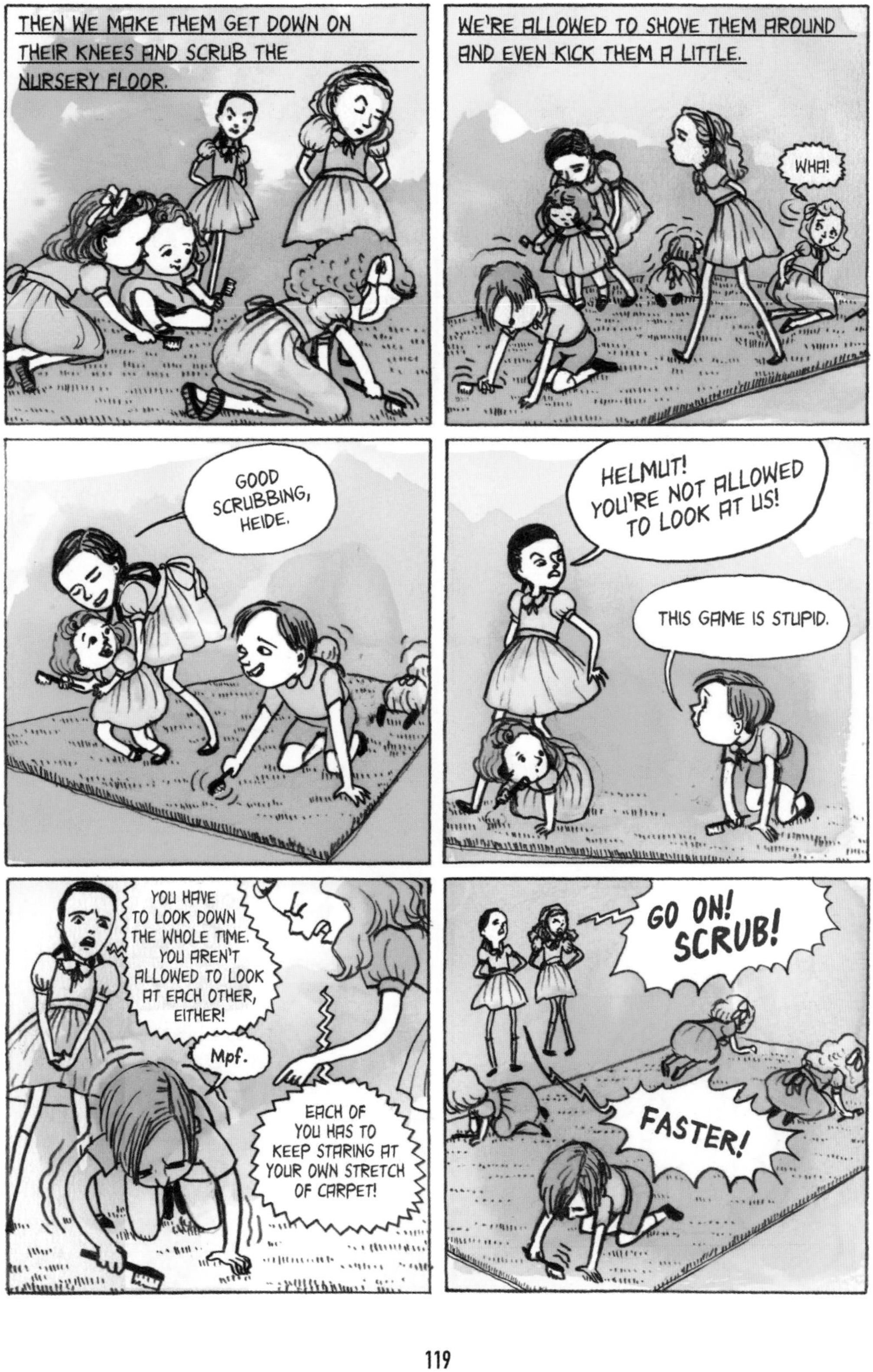
THEN WE MAKE THEM GET DOWN ON THEIR KNEES AND SCRUB THE NURSERY FLOOR.
WE'RE ALLOWED TO SHOVE THEM AROUND AND EVEN KICK THEM A LITTLE.
WHA!
GOOD SCRUBBING, HEIDE.
HELMUT! YOU'RE NOT ALLOWED TO LOOK AT US!
THIS GAME IS STUPID.
YOU HAVE TO LOOK DOWN THE WHOLE TIME. YOU AREN'T ALLOWED TO LOOK AT EACH OTHER, EITHER!
Mpf.
EACH OF YOU HAS TO KEEP STARING AT YOUR OWN STRETCH OF CARPET!
GO ON! SCRUB!
FASTER!

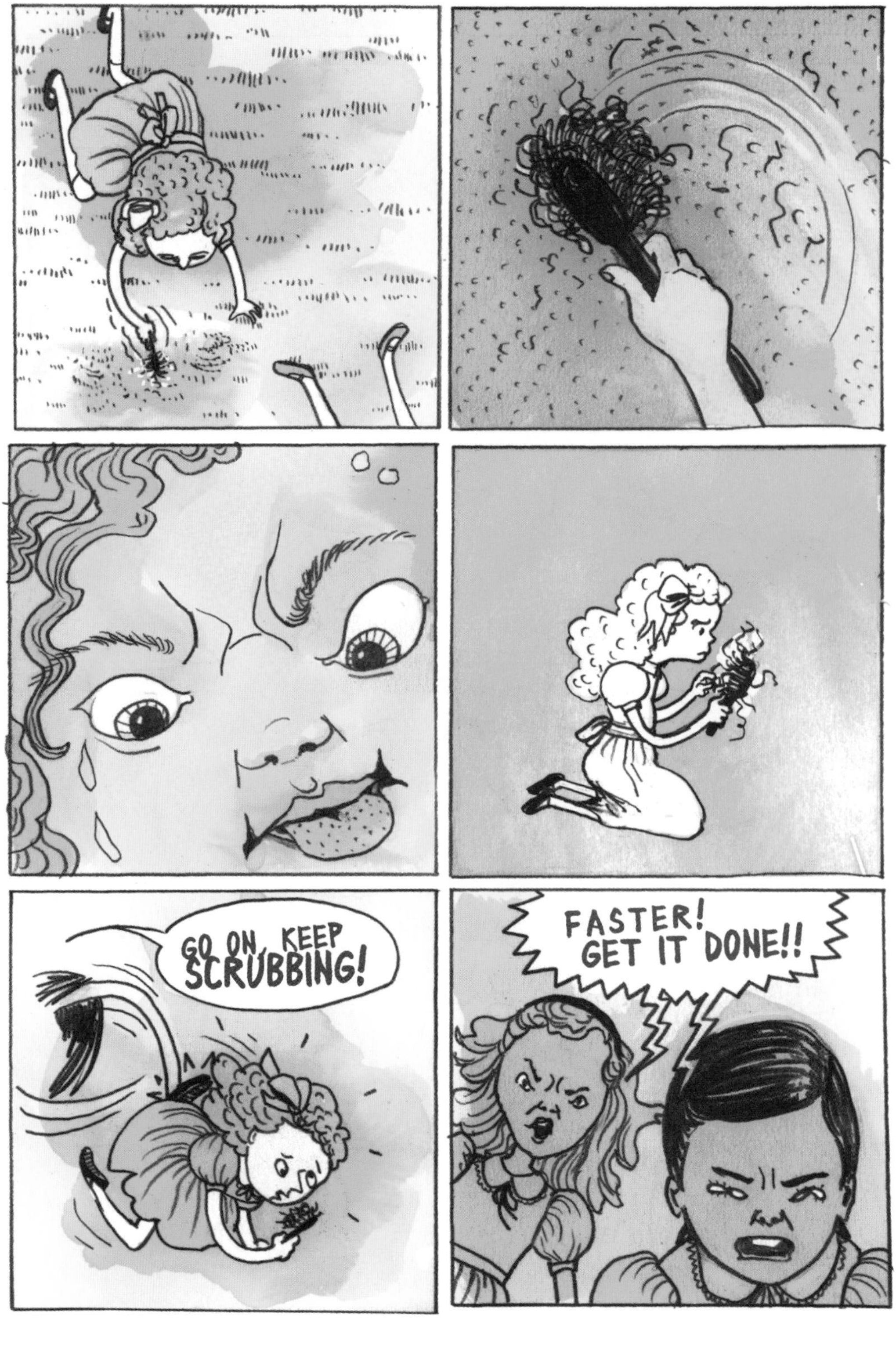
GO ON, KEEP SCRUBBING!
FASTER! GET IT DONE!!

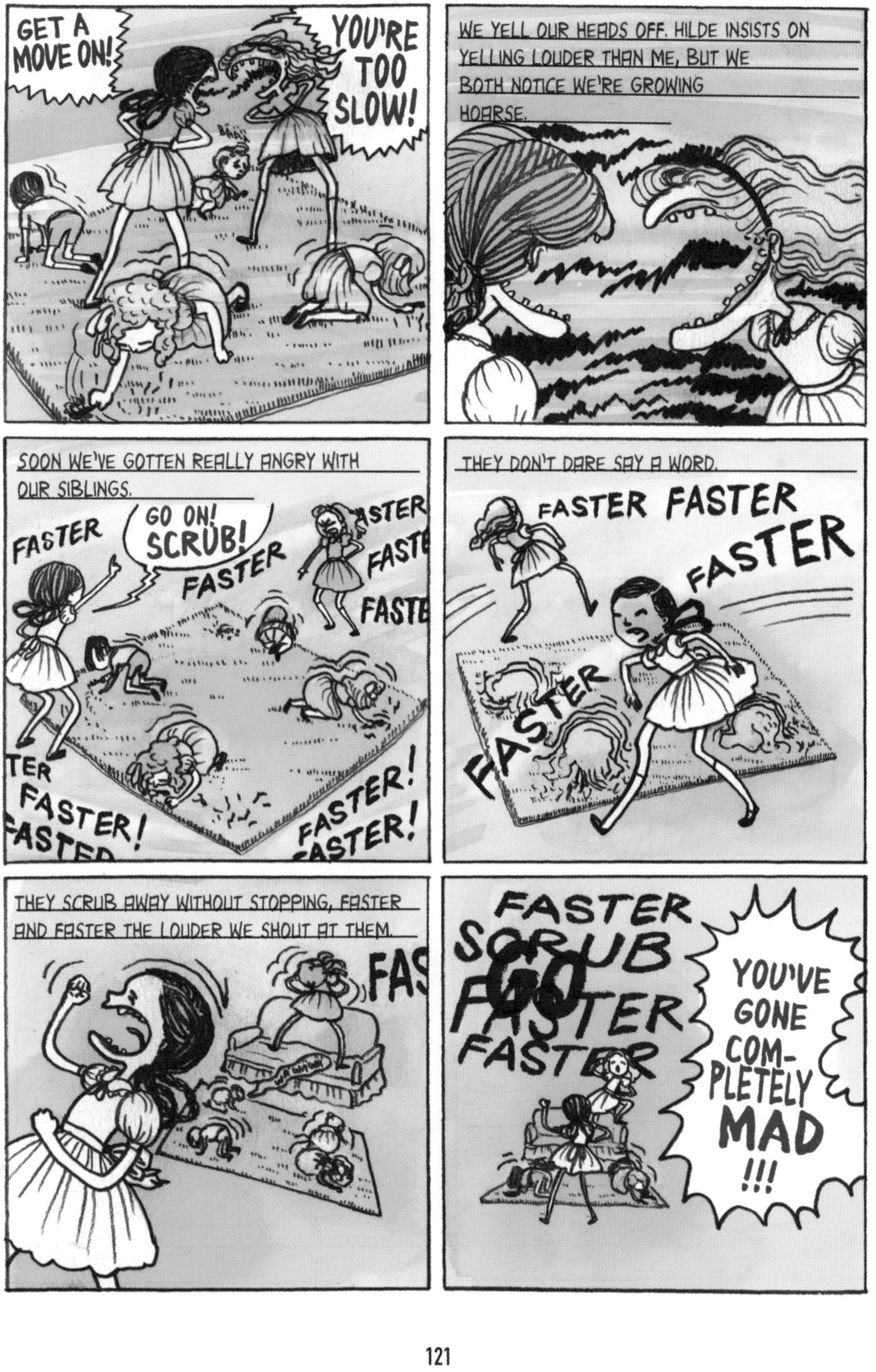

GET A MOVE ON!
YOU'RE TOO SLOW!
WE YELL OUR HEADS OFF. HILDE INSISTS ON YELLING LOUDER THAN ME, BUT WE BOTH NOTICE WE'RE GROWING HOARSE.
SOON WE'VE GOTTEN REALLY ANGRY WITH OUR SIBLINGS.
FASTER
GO ON! SCRUB!
FASTER
ASTER
FASTE
FASTE
TER
FASTER!
FASTER!
ASTER!
THEY DON'T DARE SAY A WORD.
FASTER FASTER
FASTER
FASTER
FASTER
THEY SCRUB AWAY WITHOUT STOPPING, FASTER AND FASTER THE LOUDER WE SHOUT AT THEM.
FAS
FASTER
SCRUB
GO
FASTER
FASTER
YOU'VE GONE COM-PLETELY MAD !!!

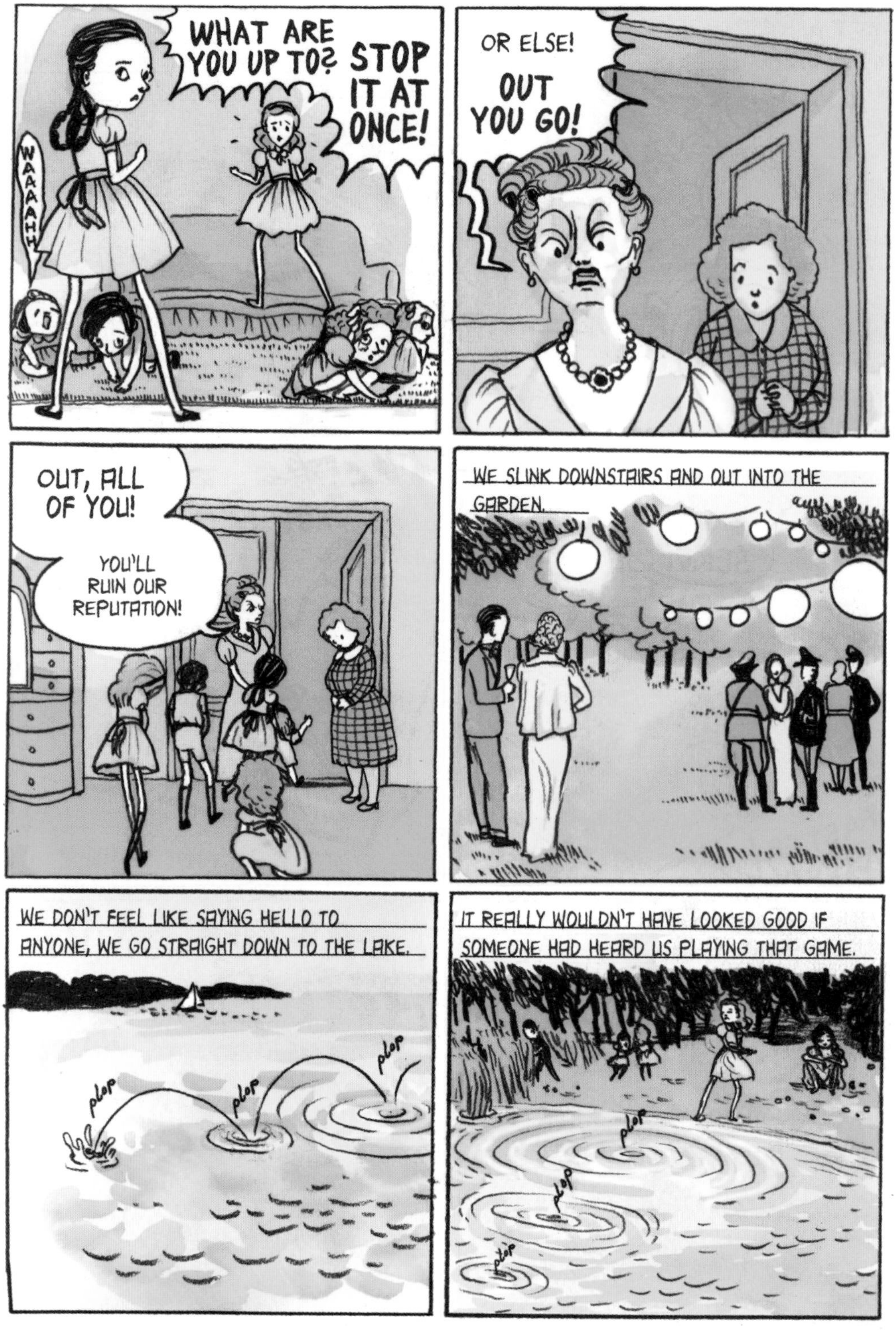
WHAT ARE YOU UP TO?
STOP IT AT ONCE!
WAAAAAHH
OR ELSE!
OUT YOU GO!
OUT, ALL OF YOU!
YOU'LL RUIN OUR REPUTATION!
WE SLINK DOWNSTAIRS AND OUT INTO THE GARDEN.
WE DON'T FEEL LIKE SAYING HELLO TO ANYONE, WE GO STRAIGHT DOWN TO THE LAKE.
plop
plop
plop
IT REALLY WOULDN'T HAVE LOOKED GOOD IF SOMEONE HAD HEARD US PLAYING THAT GAME.
plop
plop
plop

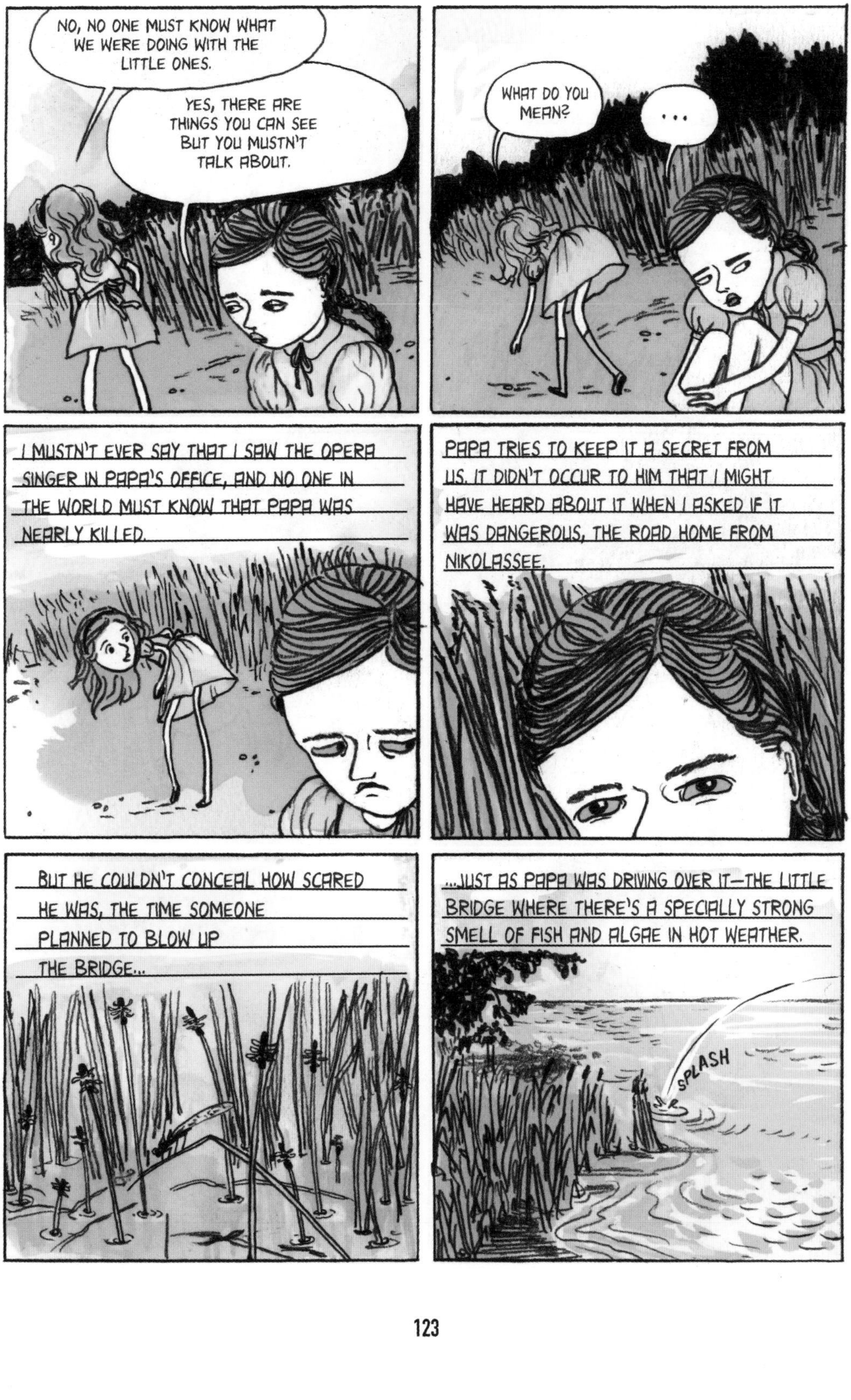
NO, NO ONE MUST KNOW WHAT WE WERE DOING WITH THE LITTLE ONES.
YES, THERE ARE THINGS YOU CAN SEE BUT YOU MUSTN'T TALK ABOUT.
WHAT DO YOU MEAN?
. . .
I MUSTN'T EVER SAY THAT I SAW THE OPERA SINGER IN PAPA'S OFFICE, AND NO ONE IN THE WORLD MUST KNOW THAT PAPA WAS NEARLY KILLED.
PAPA TRIES TO KEEP IT A SECRET FROM US. IT DIDN'T OCCUR TO HIM THAT I MIGHT HAVE HEARD ABOUT IT WHEN I ASKED IF IT WAS DANGEROUS, THE ROAD HOME FROM NIKOLASSEE.
BUT HE COULDN'T CONCEAL HOW SCARED HE WAS, THE TIME SOMEONE PLANNED TO BLOW UP THE BRIDGE...
...JUST AS PAPA WAS DRIVING OVER IT—THE LITTLE BRIDGE WHERE THERE'S A SPECIALLY STRONG SMELL OF FISH AND ALGAE IN HOT WEATHER.
SPLASH

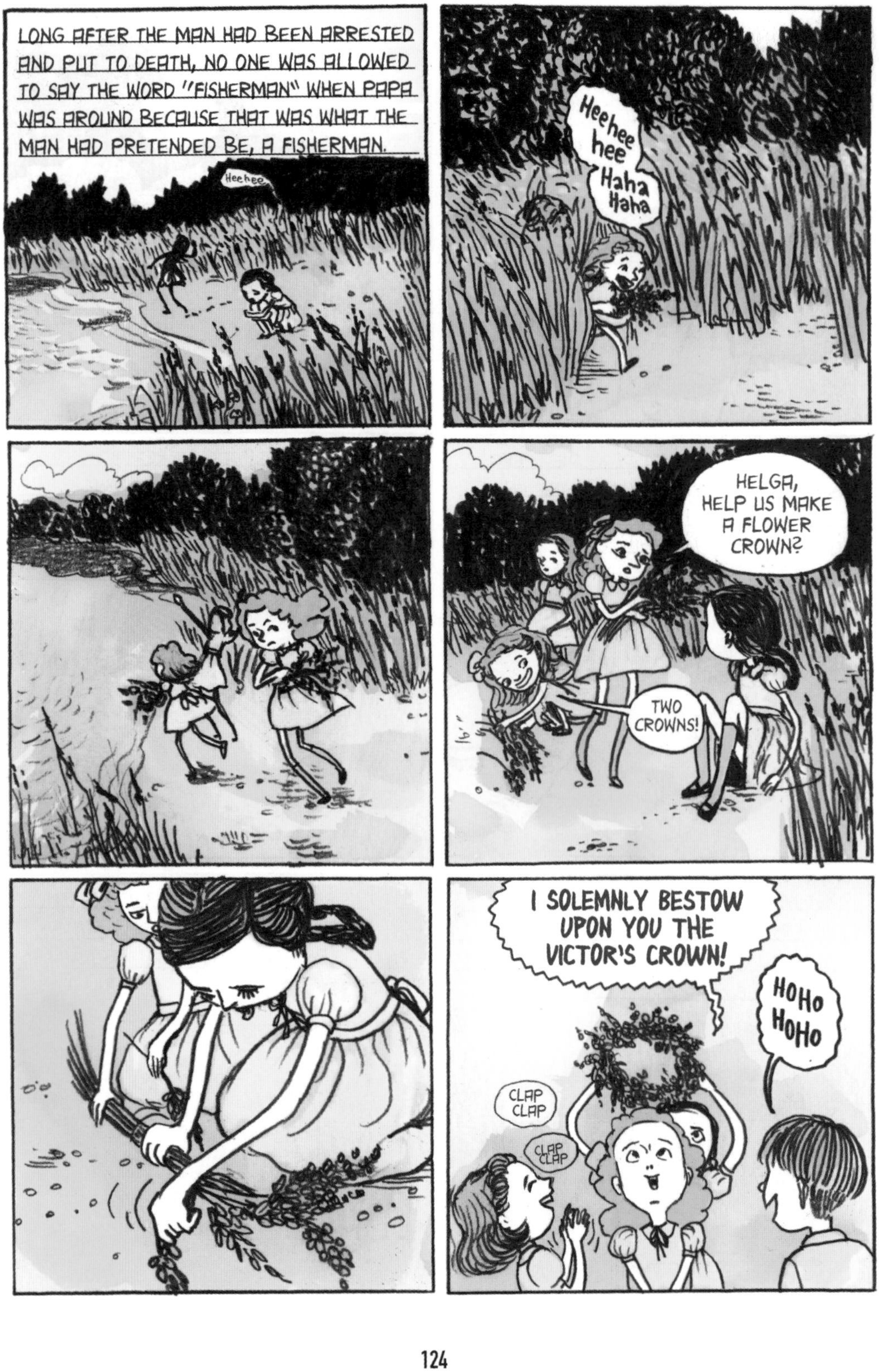
LONG AFTER THE MAN HAD BEEN ARRESTED AND PUT TO DEATH, NO ONE WAS ALLOWED TO SAY THE WORD "FISHERMAN" WHEN PAPA WAS AROUND BECAUSE THAT WAS WHAT THE MAN HAD PRETENDED BE, A FISHERMAN.
Heehee
Heehee hee
Haha Haha
HELGA, HELP US MAKE A FLOWER CROWN?
TWO CROWNS!
I SOLEMNLY BESTOW UPON YOU THE VICTOR'S CROWN!
HoHo HoHo
CLAP CLAP
CLAP CLAP

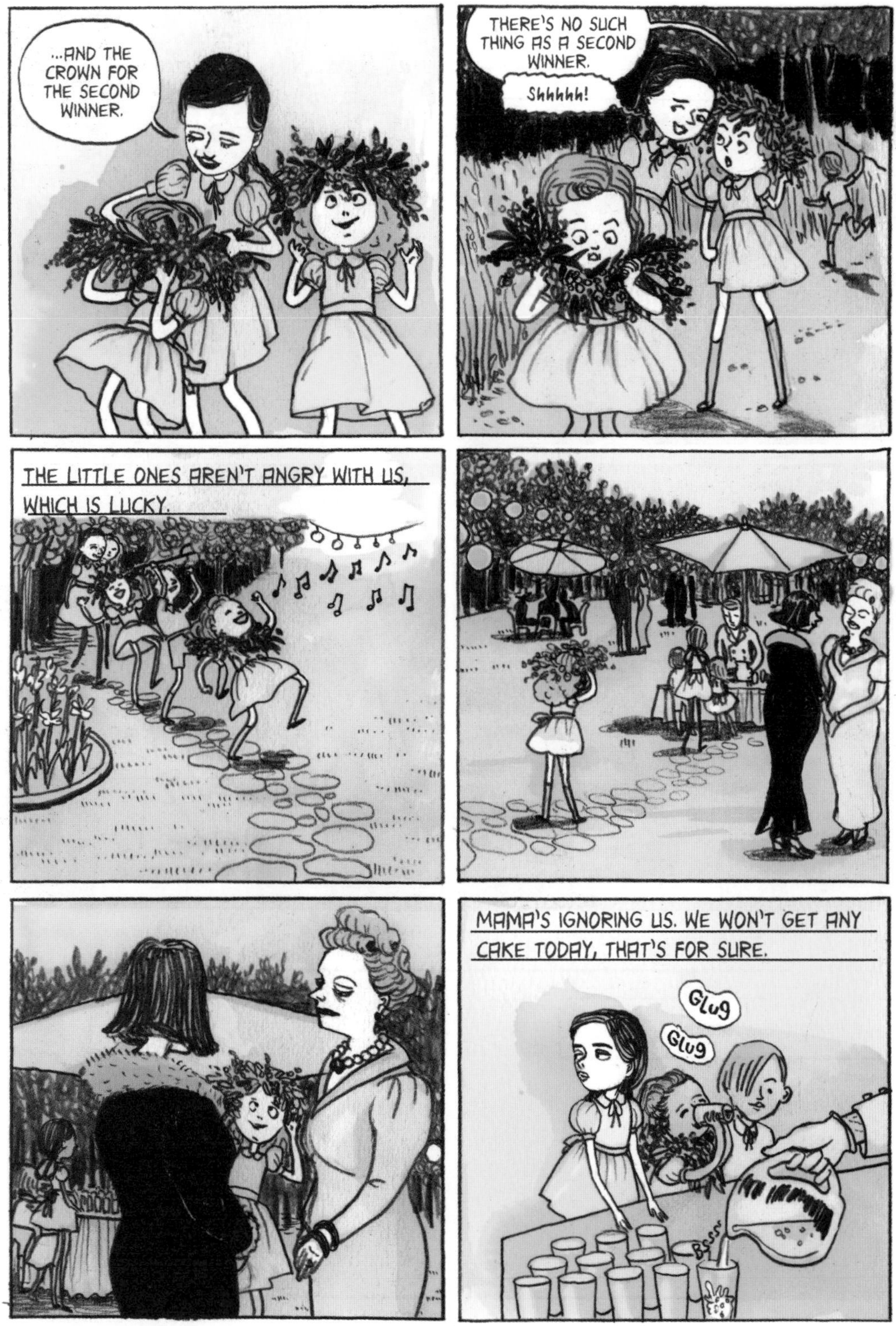
...AND THE CROWN FOR THE SECOND WINNER.
THERE'S NO SUCH THING AS A SECOND WINNER.
Shhhhh!
THE LITTLE ONES AREN'T ANGRY WITH US, WHICH IS LUCKY.
MAMA'S IGNORING US. WE WON'T GET ANY CAKE TODAY, THAT'S FOR SURE.
Glug
Glug

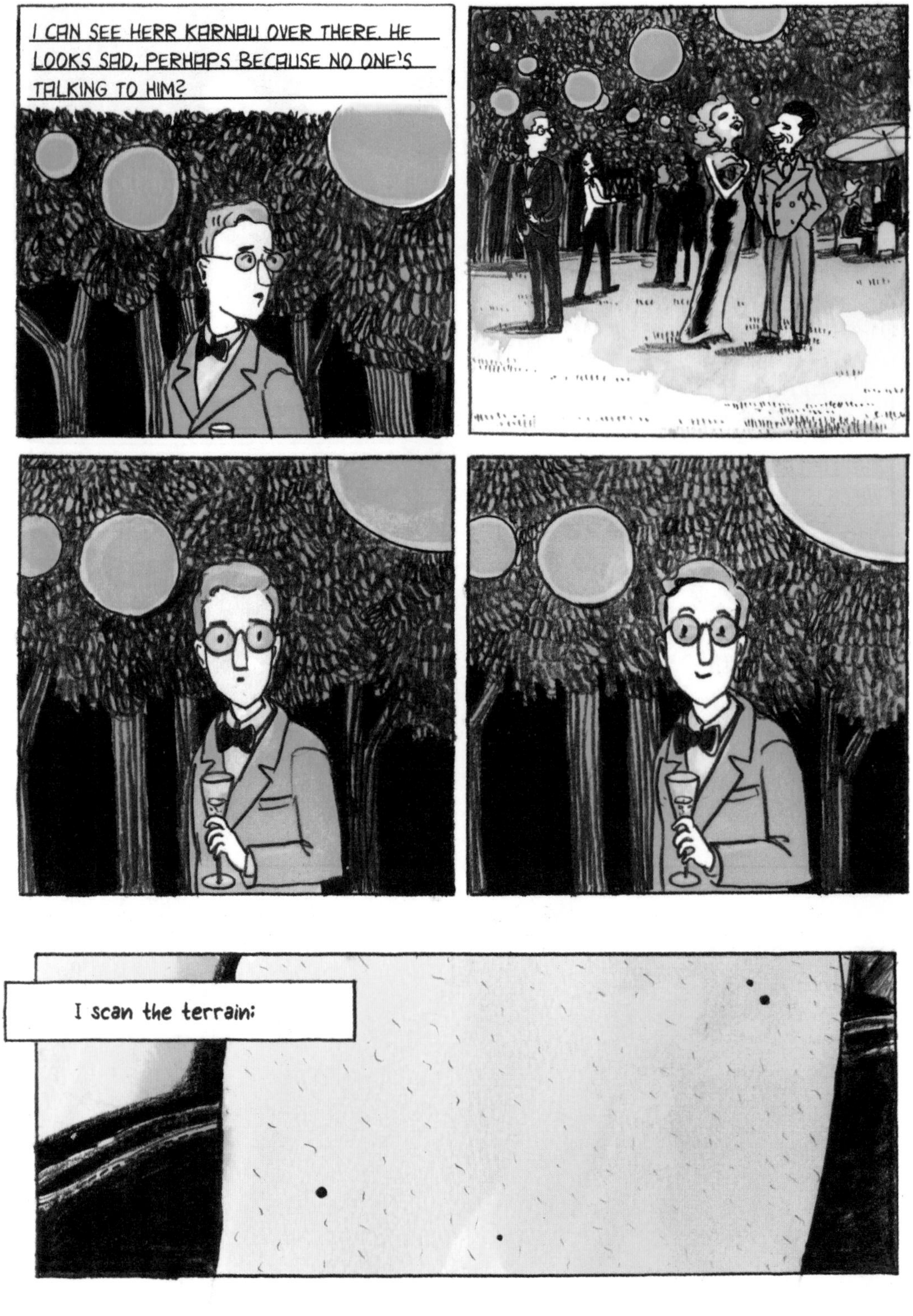
I CAN SEE HERR KARNAU OVER THERE. HE LOOKS SAD, PERHAPS BECAUSE NO ONE'S TALKING TO HIM?
I scan the terrain:

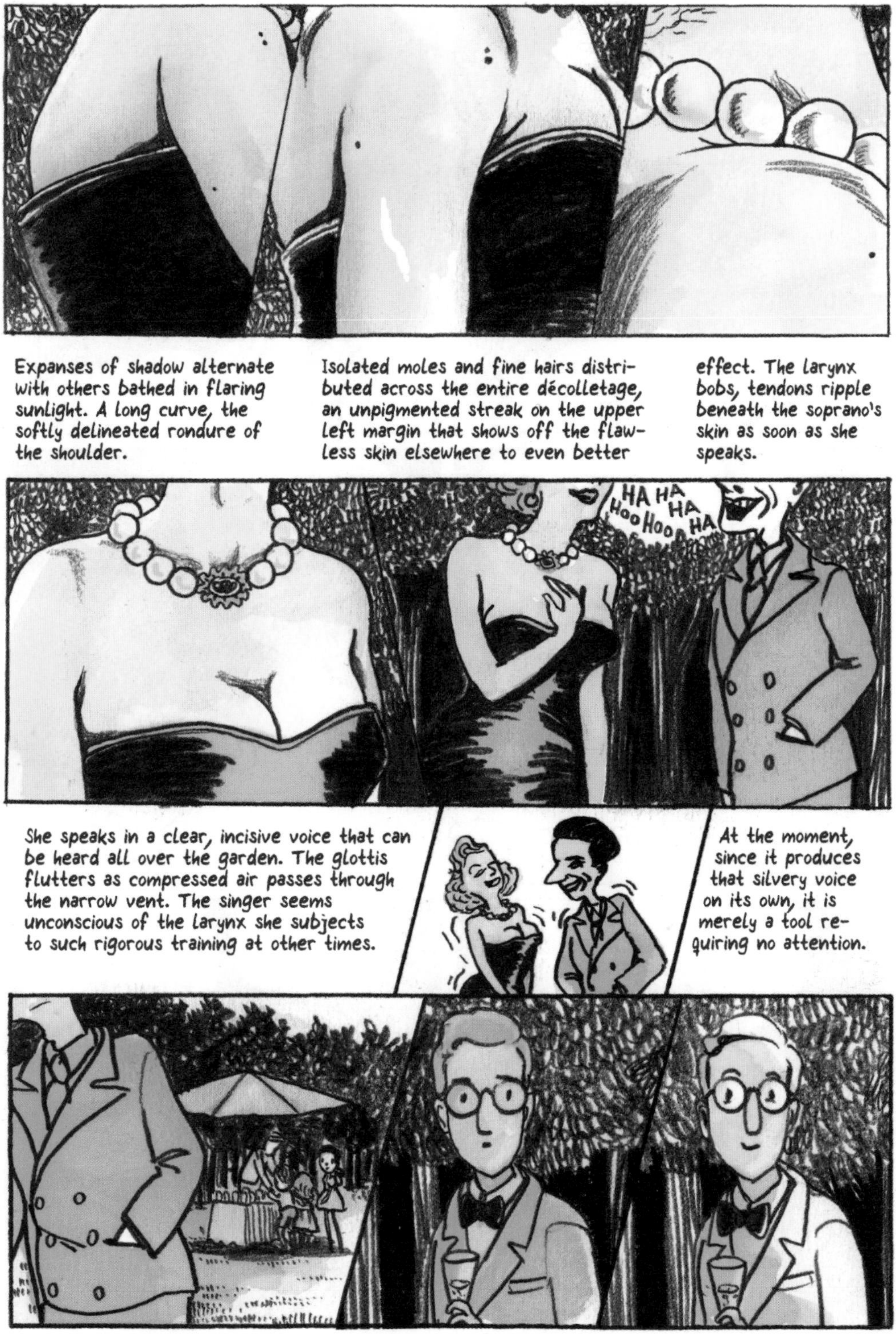
Expanses of shadow alternate with others bathed in flaring sunlight. A long curve, the softly delineated rondure of the shoulder.
Isolated moles and fine hairs distributed across the entire décolletage, an unpigmented streak on the upper left margin that shows off the flawless skin elsewhere to even better
effect. The larynx bobs, tendons ripple beneath the soprano's skin as soon as she speaks.
HA HA HA HA
HOO HOO
HA
She speaks in a clear, incisive voice that can be heard all over the garden. The glottis flutters as compressed air passes through the narrow vent. The singer seems unconscious of the larynx she subjects to such rigorous training at other times.
At the moment, since it produces that silvery voice on its own, it is merely a tool requiring no attention.

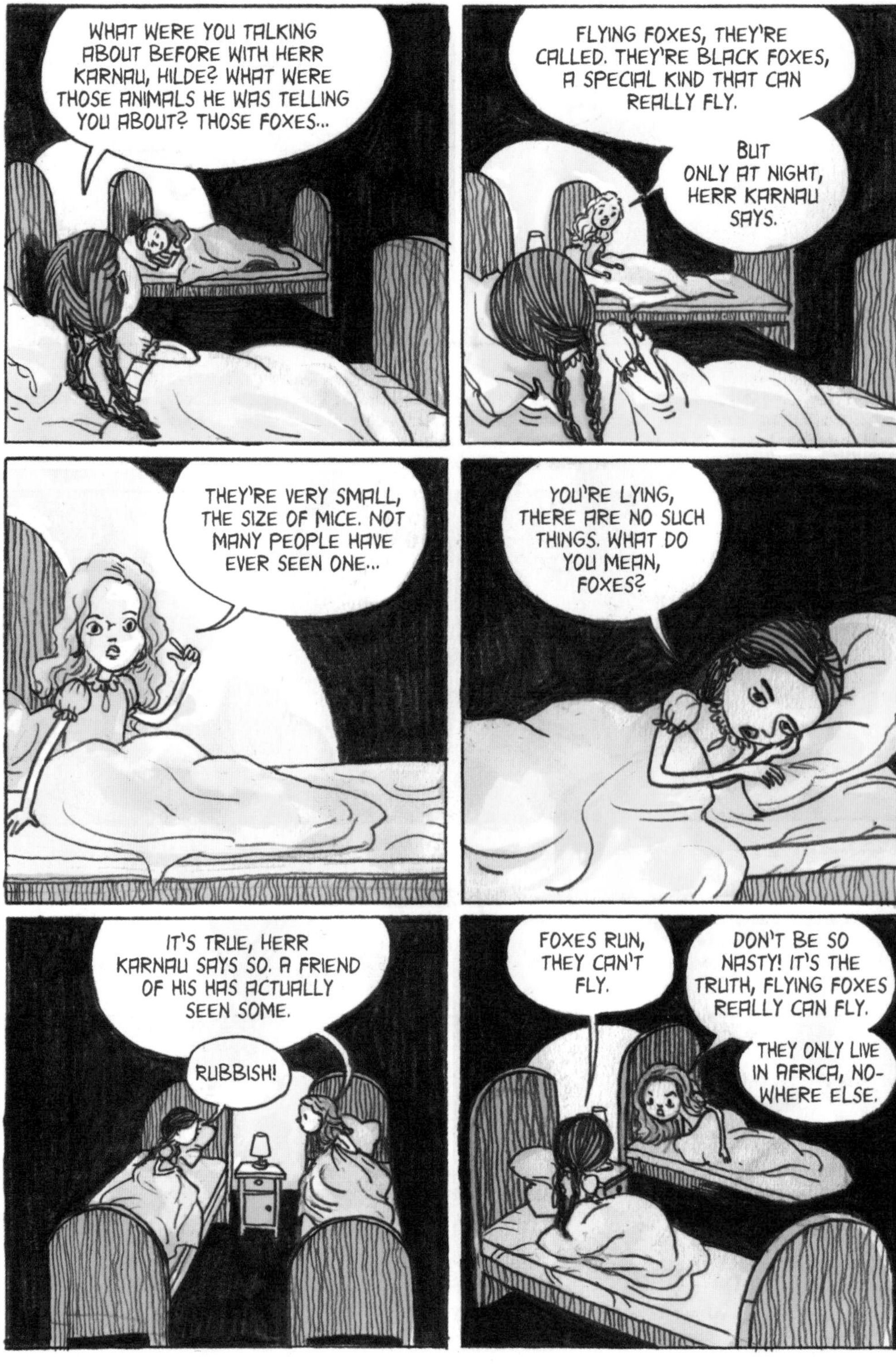
WHAT WERE YOU TALKING ABOUT BEFORE WITH HERR KARNAU, HILDE? WHAT WERE THOSE ANIMALS HE WAS TELLING YOU ABOUT? THOSE FOXES...
FLYING FOXES, THEY'RE CALLED. THEY'RE BLACK FOXES, A SPECIAL KIND THAT CAN REALLY FLY.
BUT ONLY AT NIGHT, HERR KARNAU SAYS.
THEY'RE VERY SMALL, THE SIZE OF MICE. NOT MANY PEOPLE HAVE EVER SEEN ONE...
YOU'RE LYING, THERE ARE NO SUCH THINGS. WHAT DO YOU MEAN, FOXES?
IT'S TRUE, HERR KARNAU SAYS SO. A FRIEND OF HIS HAS ACTUALLY SEEN SOME.
RUBBISH!
FOXES RUN, THEY CAN'T FLY.
DON'T BE SO NASTY! IT'S THE TRUTH, FLYING FOXES REALLY CAN FLY.
THEY ONLY LIVE IN AFRICA, NO-WHERE ELSE.

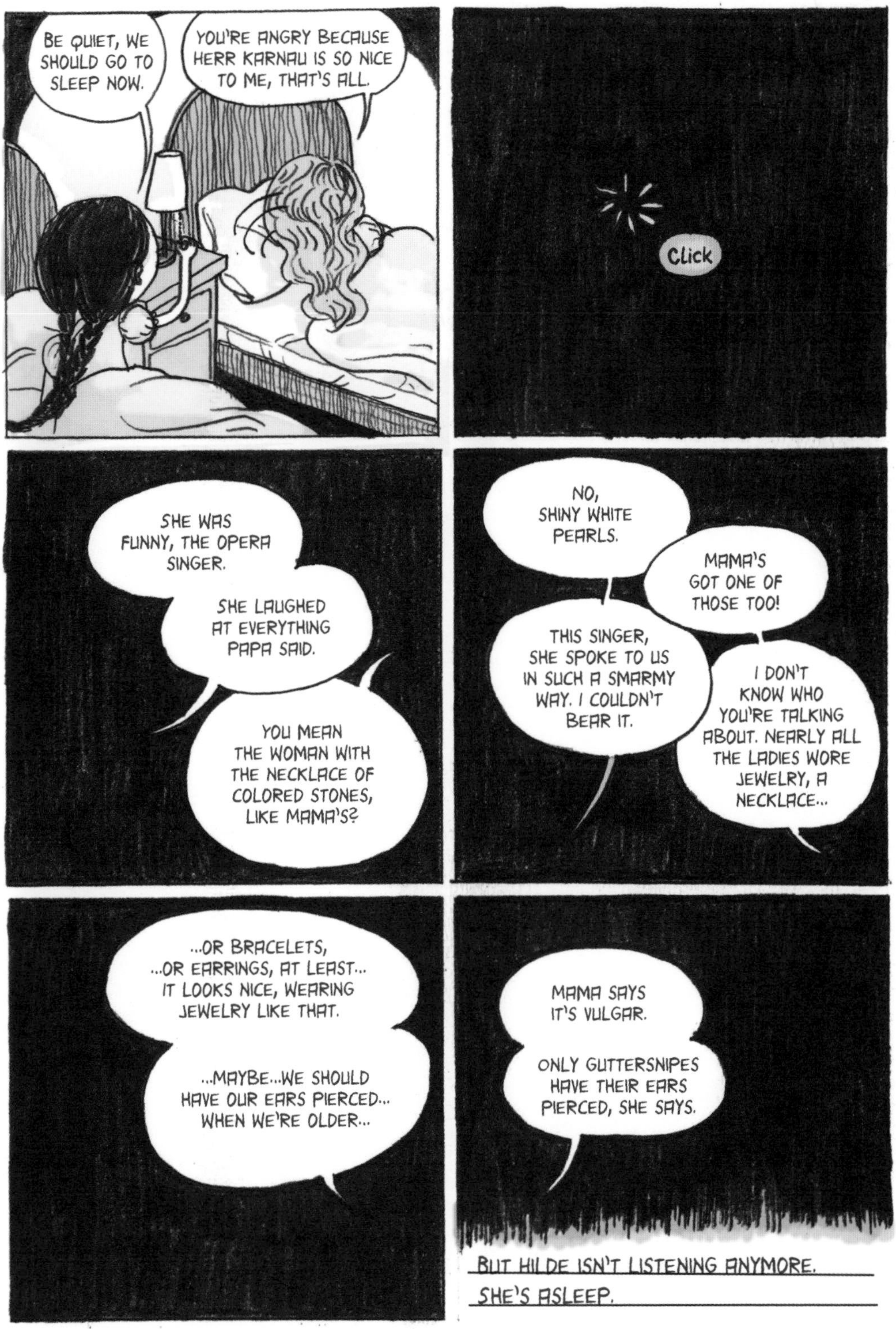
BE QUIET, WE SHOULD GO TO SLEEP NOW.
YOU'RE ANGRY BECAUSE HERR KARNAU IS SO NICE TO ME, THAT'S ALL.
Click
SHE WAS FUNNY, THE OPERA SINGER.
SHE LAUGHED AT EVERYTHING PAPA SAID.
YOU MEAN THE WOMAN WITH THE NECKLACE OF COLORED STONES, LIKE MAMA'S?
NO, SHINY WHITE PEARLS.
MAMA'S GOT ONE OF THOSE TOO!
THIS SINGER, SHE SPOKE TO US IN SUCH A SMARMY WAY. I COULDN'T BEAR IT.
I DON'T KNOW WHO YOU'RE TALKING ABOUT. NEARLY ALL THE LADIES WORE JEWELRY, A NECKLACE...
...OR BRACELETS, ...OR EARRINGS, AT LEAST... IT LOOKS NICE, WEARING JEWELRY LIKE THAT.
...MAYBE...WE SHOULD HAVE OUR EARS PIERCED... WHEN WE'RE OLDER...
MAMA SAYS IT'S VULGAR.
ONLY GUTTERSNIPES HAVE THEIR EARS PIERCED, SHE SAYS.
BUT HILDE ISN'T LISTENING ANYMORE.
SHE'S ASLEEP.

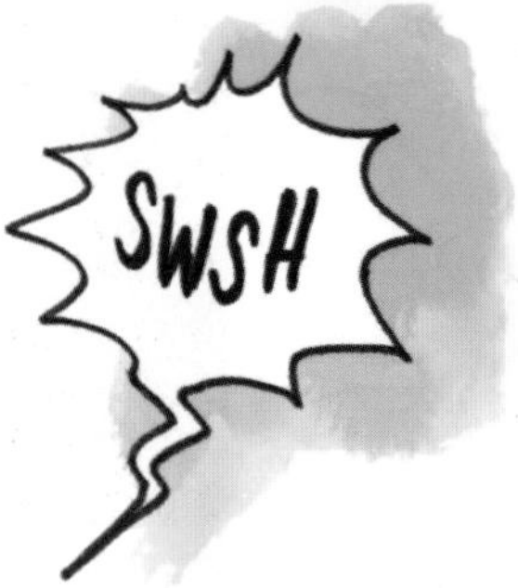
SWSH

III.

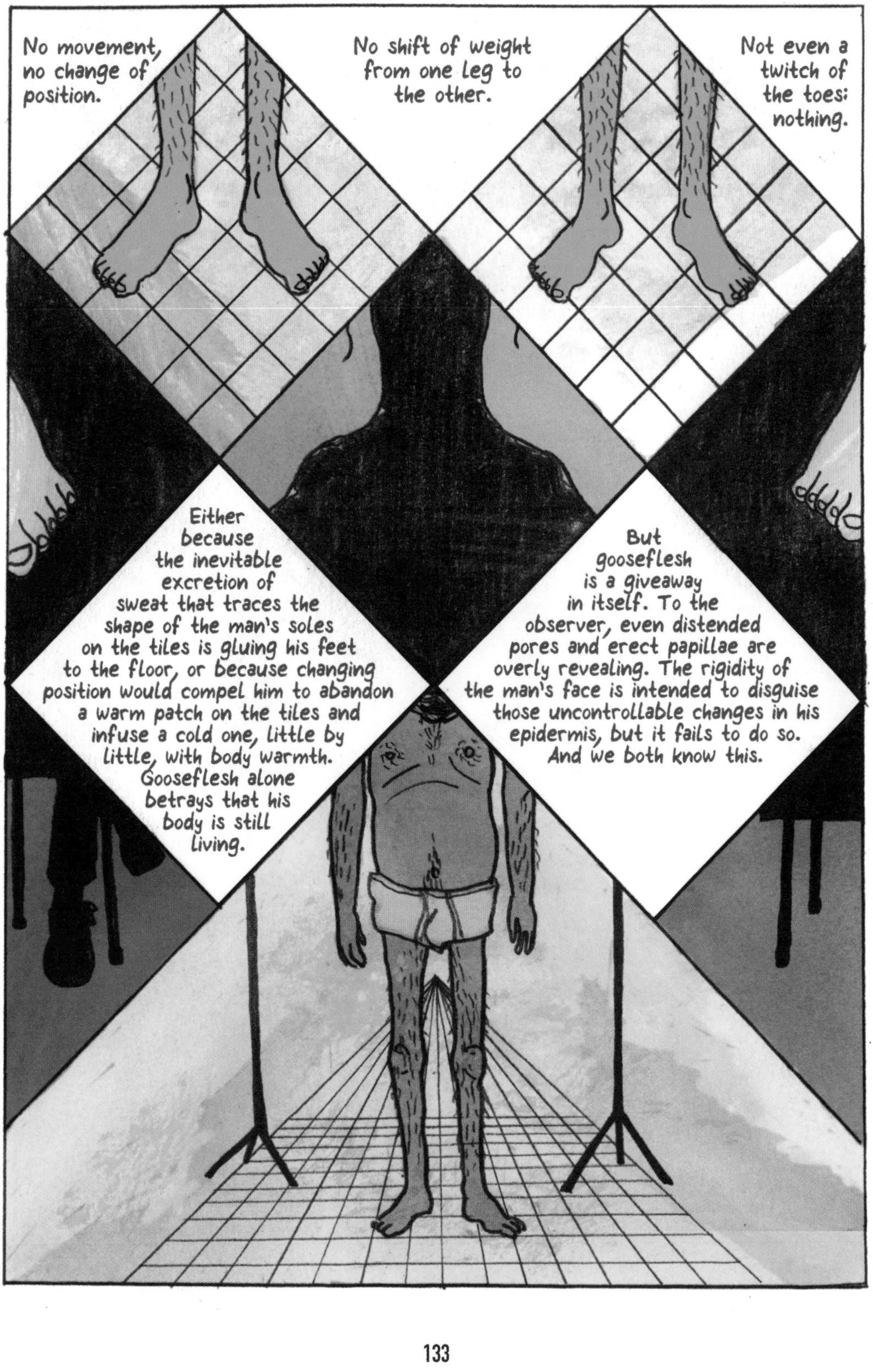

No movement, no change of position.
No shift of weight from one leg to the other.
Not even a twitch of the toes: nothing.
Either because the inevitable excretion of sweat that traces the shape of the man's soles on the tiles is gluing his feet to the floor, or because changing position would compel him to abandon a warm patch on the tiles and infuse a cold one, little by little, with body warmth. Gooseflesh alone betrays that his body is still living.
But gooseflesh is a giveaway in itself. To the observer, even distended pores and erect papillae are overly revealing. The rigidity of the man's face is intended to disguise those uncontrollable changes in his epidermis, but it fails to do so. And we both know this.

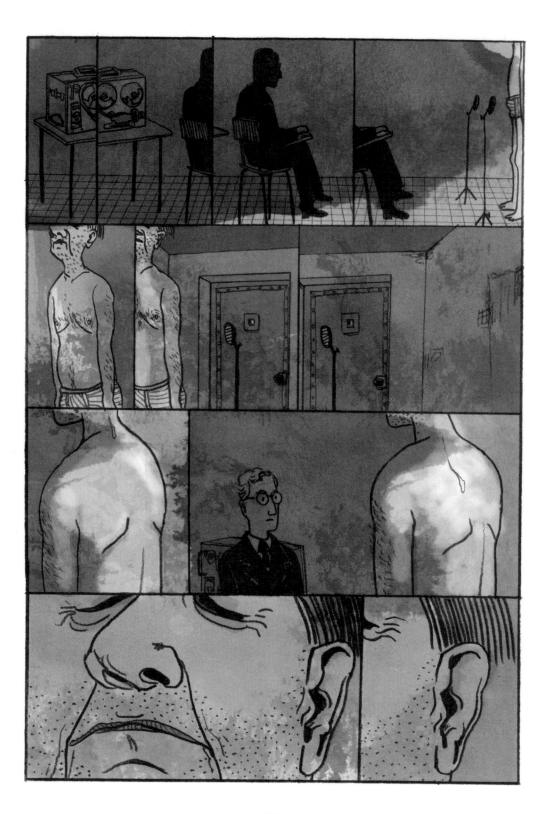

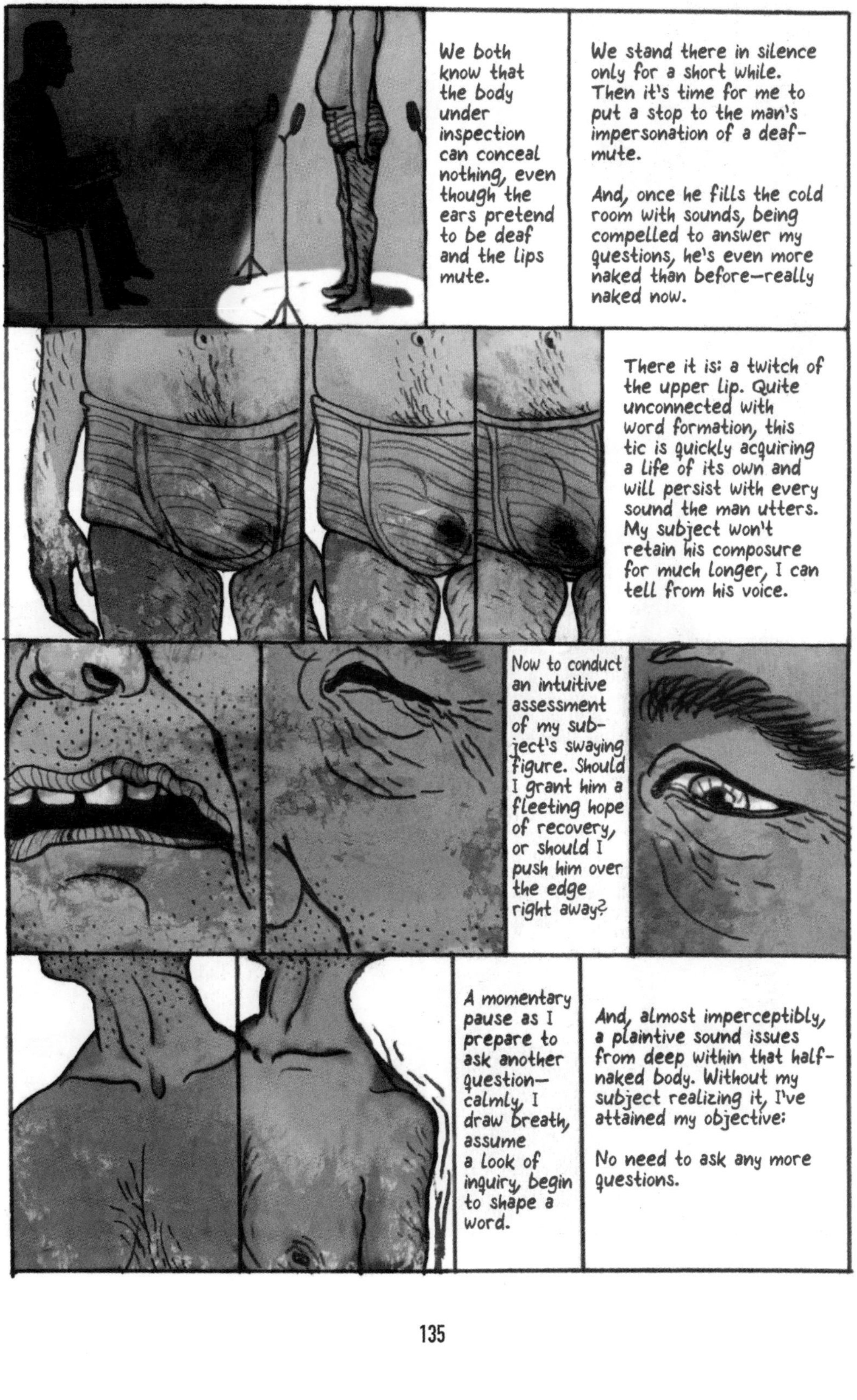

We both know that the body under inspection can conceal nothing, even though the ears pretend to be deaf and the lips mute.

We stand there in silence only for a short while. Then it's time for me to put a stop to the man's impersonation of a deaf-mute.

And, once he fills the cold room with sounds, being compelled to answer my questions, he's even more naked than before—really naked now.

There it is: a twitch of the upper lip. Quite unconnected with word formation, this tic is quickly acquiring a life of its own and will persist with every sound the man utters. My subject won't retain his composure for much longer, I can tell from his voice.

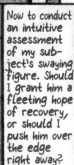

Now to conduct an intuitive assessment of my subject's swaying figure. Should I grant him a fleeting hope of recovery, or should I push him over the edge right away?

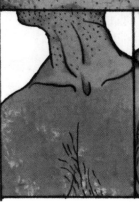

A momentary pause as I prepare to ask another question—calmly, I draw breath, assume a look of inquiry, begin to shape a word.

And, almost imperceptibly, a plaintive sound issues from deep within that half-naked body. Without my subject realizing it, I've attained my objective:

No need to ask any more questions.

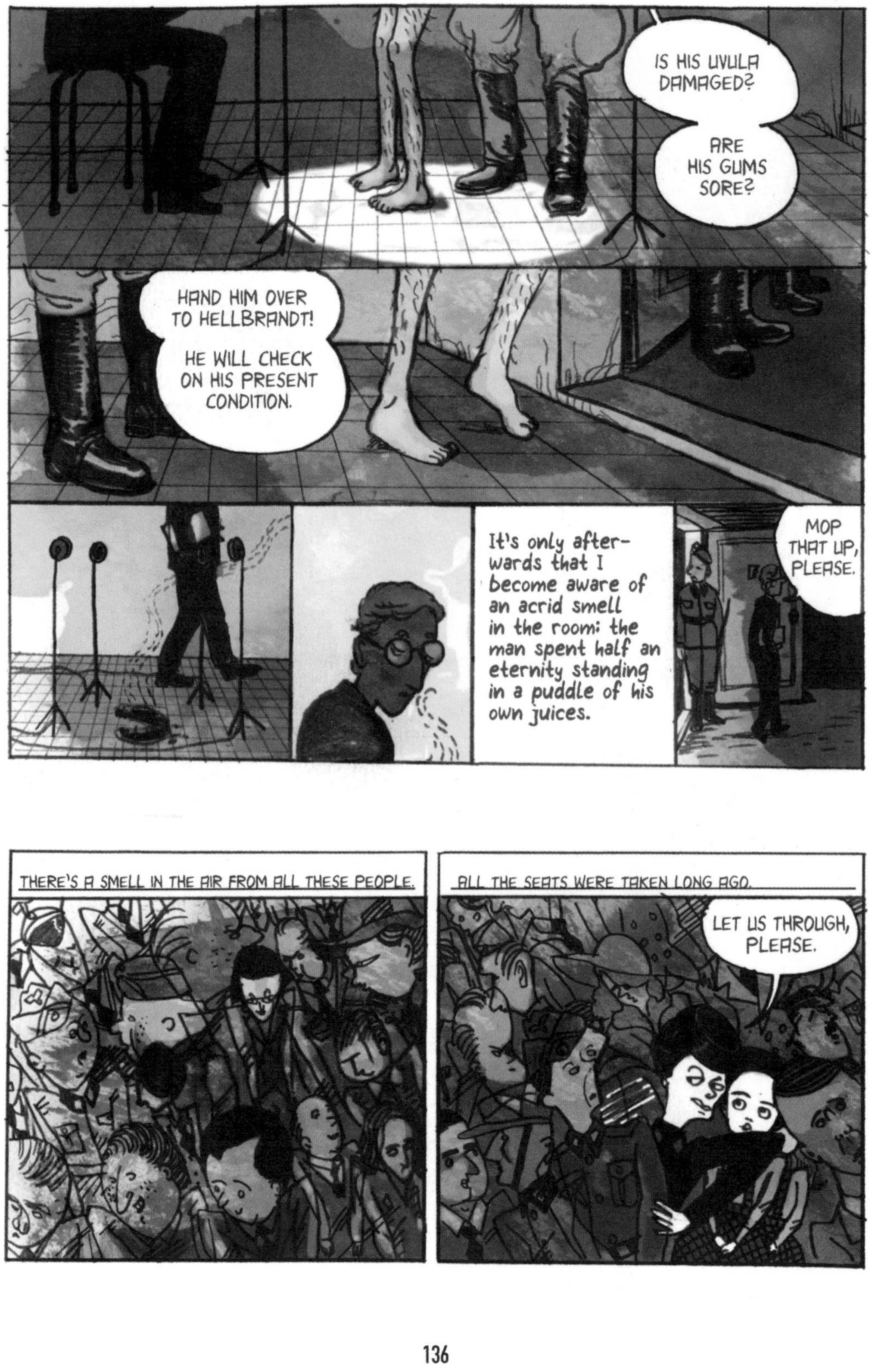
IS HIS UVULA DAMAGED?
ARE HIS GUMS SORE?
HAND HIM OVER TO HELLBRANDT!
HE WILL CHECK ON HIS PRESENT CONDITION.
It's only afterwards that I become aware of an acrid smell in the room: the man spent half an eternity standing in a puddle of his own juices.
MOP THAT UP, PLEASE.
THERE'S A SMELL IN THE AIR FROM ALL THESE PEOPLE.
ALL THE SEATS WERE TAKEN LONG AGO.
LET US THROUGH, PLEASE.

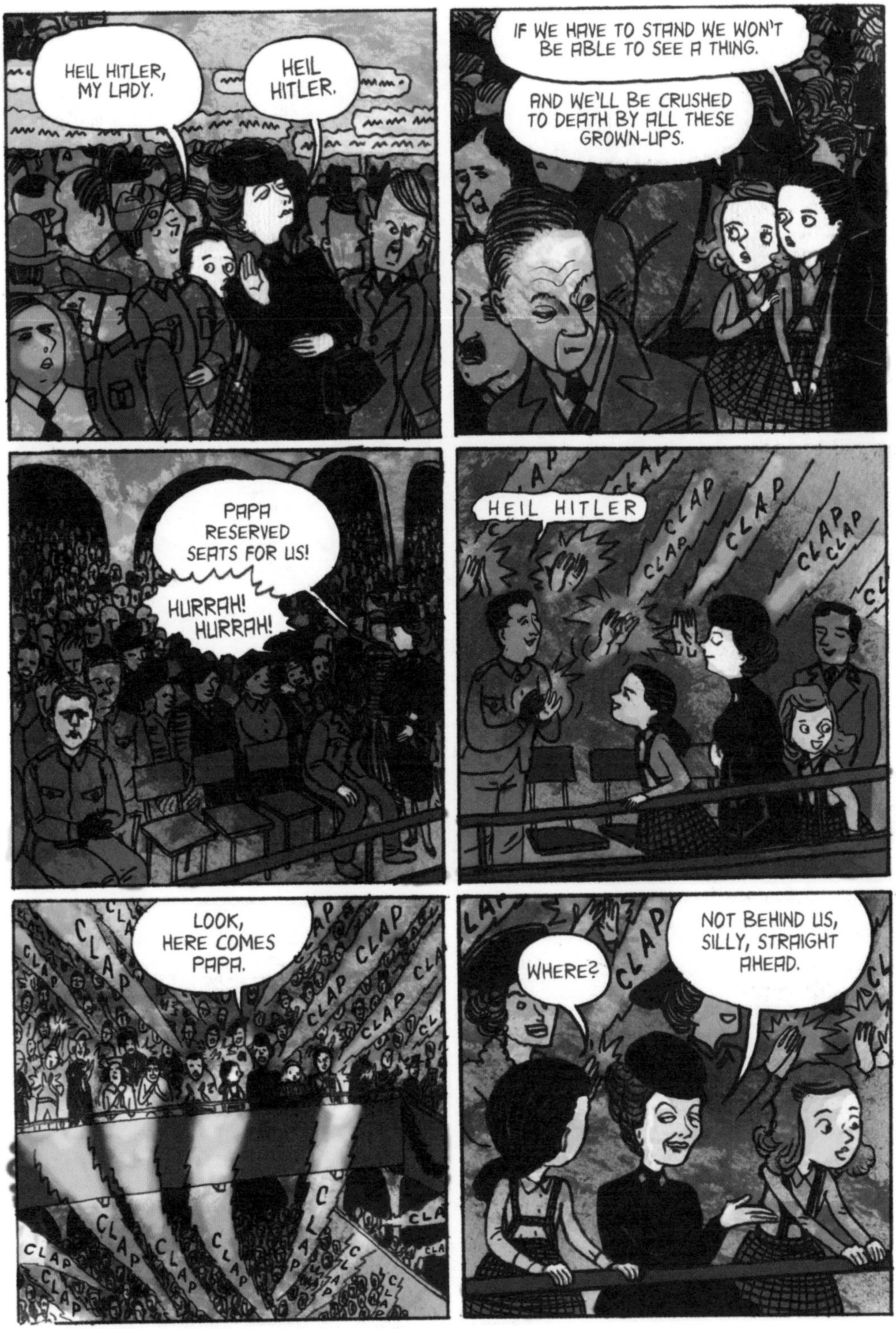
HEIL HITLER, MY LADY.
HEIL HITLER.
IF WE HAVE TO STAND WE WON'T BE ABLE TO SEE A THING.
AND WE'LL BE CRUSHED TO DEATH BY ALL THESE GROWN-UPS.
PAPA RESERVED SEATS FOR US!
HURRAH! HURRAH!
HEIL HITLER
CLAP CLAP CLAP CLAP CLAP
LOOK, HERE COMES PAPA.
CLAP CLAP CLAP CLAP
WHERE?
CLAP
NOT BEHIND US, SILLY, STRAIGHT AHEAD.

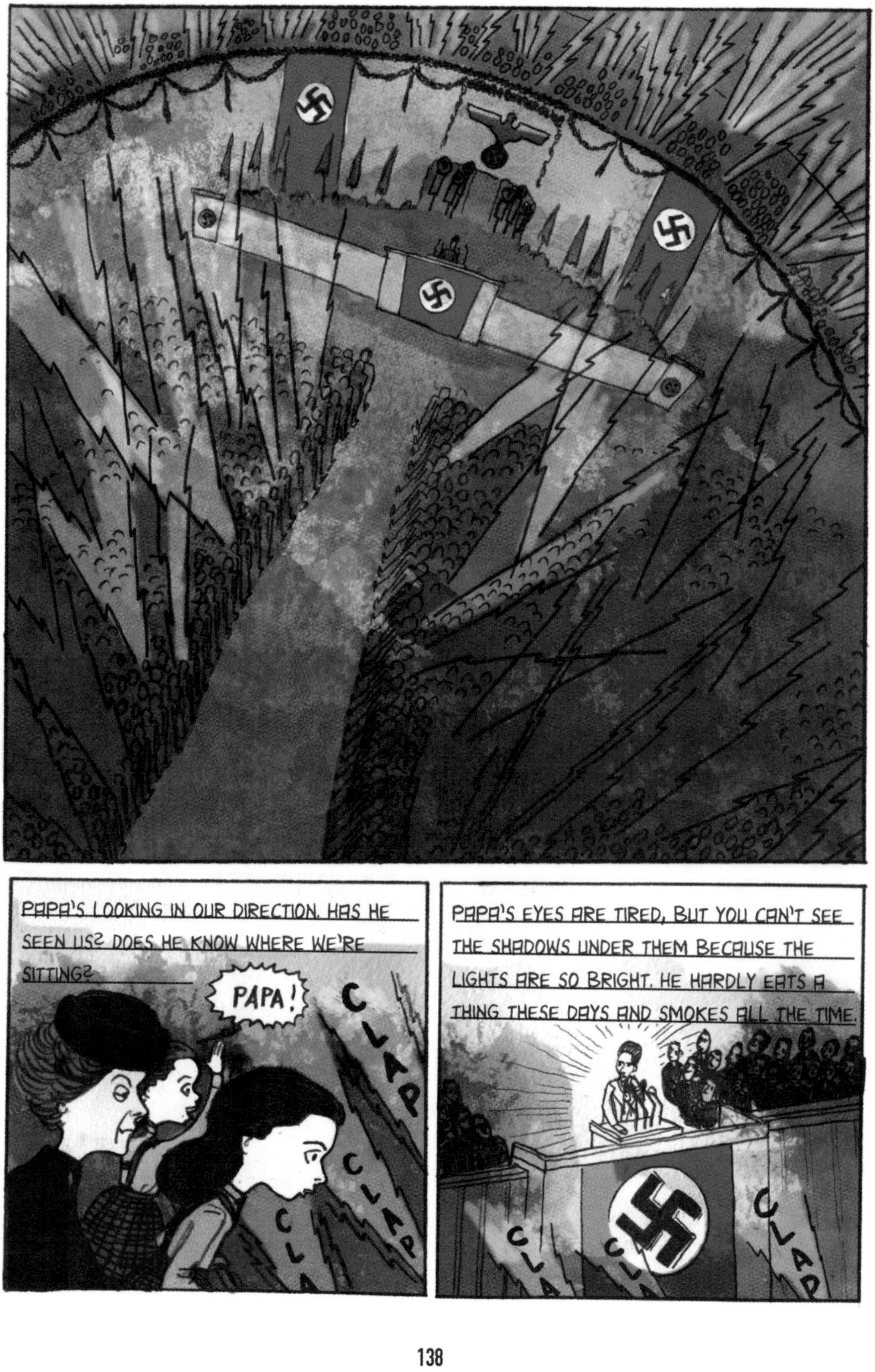
PAPA'S LOOKING IN OUR DIRECTION. HAS HE SEEN US? DOES HE KNOW WHERE WE'RE SITTING?
PAPA!
CLAP
CLAP
CLAP
PAPA'S EYES ARE TIRED, BUT YOU CAN'T SEE THE SHADOWS UNDER THEM BECAUSE THE LIGHTS ARE SO BRIGHT. HE HARDLY EATS A THING THESE DAYS AND SMOKES ALL THE TIME.
CLAP

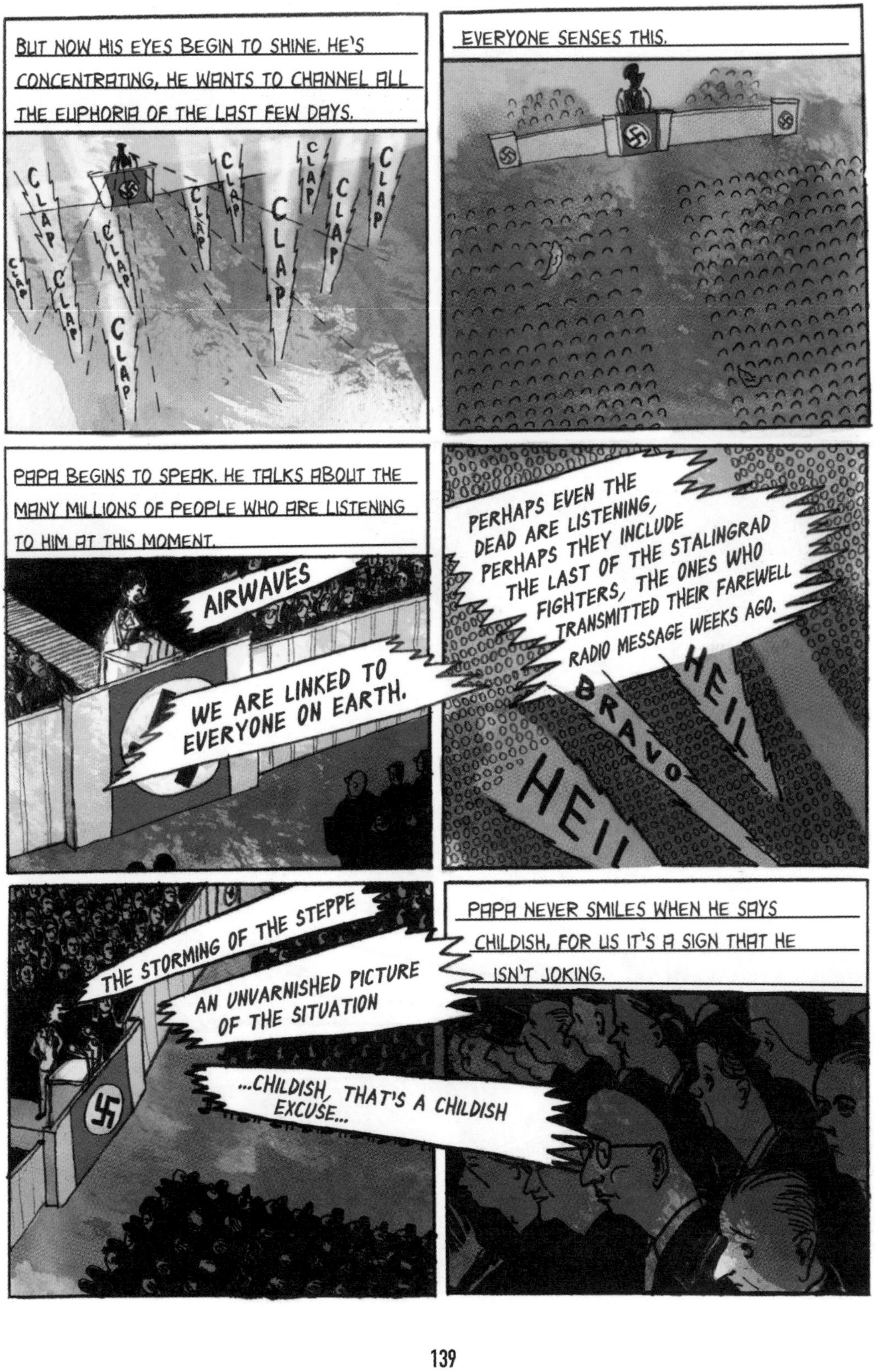
BUT NOW HIS EYES BEGIN TO SHINE. HE'S CONCENTRATING, HE WANTS TO CHANNEL ALL THE EUPHORIA OF THE LAST FEW DAYS.
CLAP CLAP CLAP CLAP CLAP CLAP CLAP CLAP CLAP CLAP CLAP CLAP
EVERYONE SENSES THIS.
PAPA BEGINS TO SPEAK. HE TALKS ABOUT THE MANY MILLIONS OF PEOPLE WHO ARE LISTENING TO HIM AT THIS MOMENT.
AIRWAVES
WE ARE LINKED TO EVERYONE ON EARTH.
PERHAPS EVEN THE DEAD ARE LISTENING, PERHAPS THEY INCLUDE THE LAST OF THE STALINGRAD FIGHTERS, THE ONES WHO TRANSMITTED THEIR FAREWELL RADIO MESSAGE WEEKS AGO.
HEIL
BRAVO
HEIL
THE STORMING OF THE STEPPE
AN UNVARNISHED PICTURE OF THE SITUATION
...CHILDISH, THAT'S A CHILDISH EXCUSE...
PAPA NEVER SMILES WHEN HE SAYS CHILDISH, FOR US IT'S A SIGN THAT HE ISN'T JOKING.

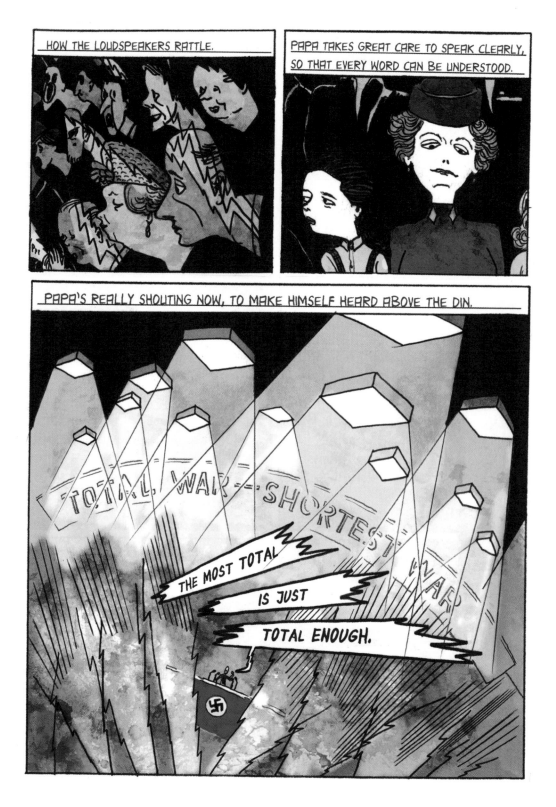

HOW THE LOUDSPEAKERS RATTLE.

PAPA TAKES GREAT CARE TO SPEAK CLEARLY, SO THAT EVERY WORD CAN BE UNDERSTOOD.

PAPA'S REALLY SHOUTING NOW, TO MAKE HIMSELF HEARD ABOVE THE DIN.

TOTAL WAR—SHORTEST WAR

THE MOST TOTAL IS JUST TOTAL ENOUGH.

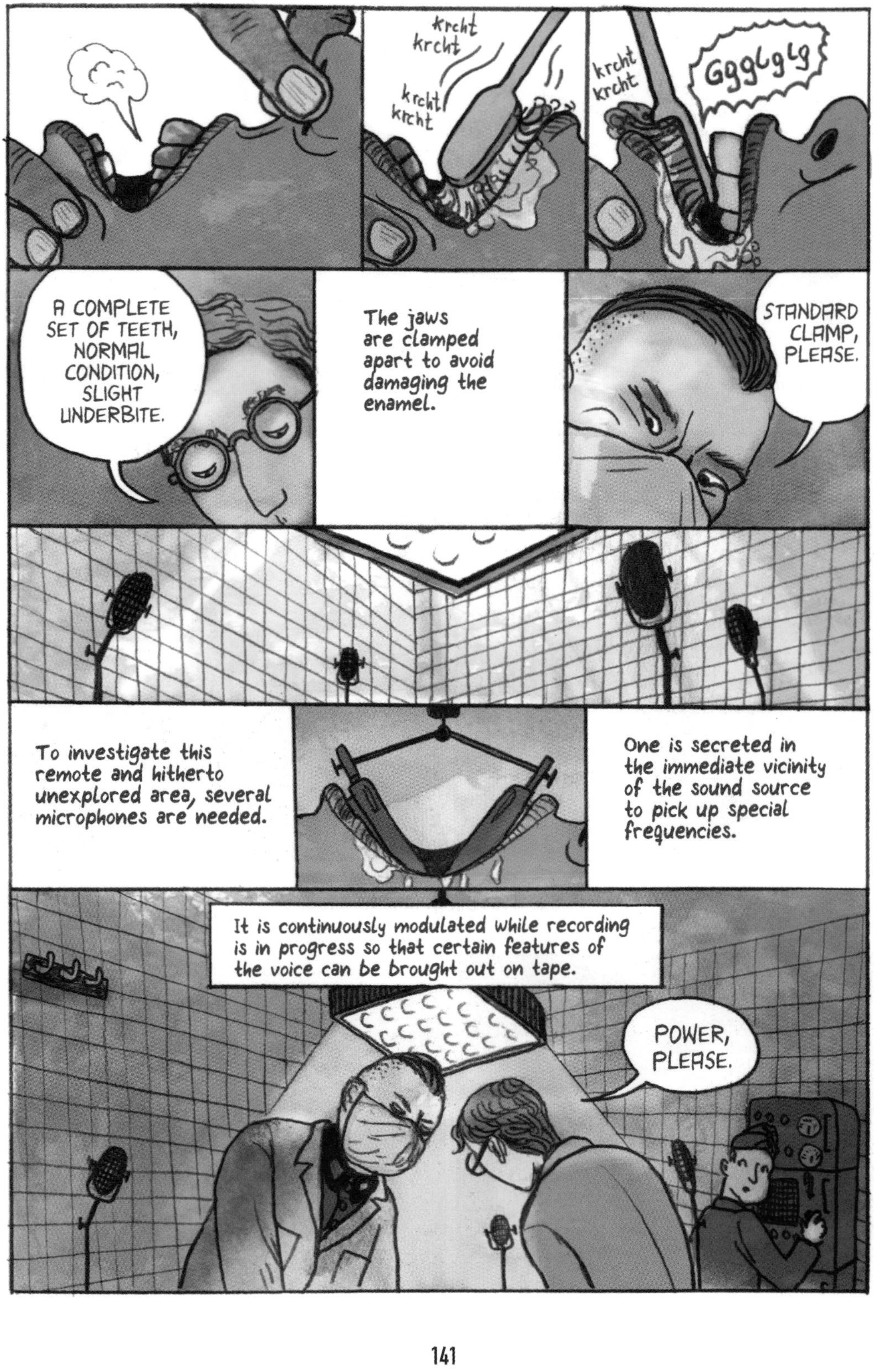
krcht
krcht
krcht
krcht
krcht
krcht
Gggᴸgᴸg
A COMPLETE SET OF TEETH, NORMAL CONDITION, SLIGHT UNDERBITE.
The jaws are clamped apart to avoid damaging the enamel.
STANDARD CLAMP, PLEASE.
To investigate this remote and hitherto unexplored area, several microphones are needed.
One is secreted in the immediate vicinity of the sound source to pick up special frequencies.
It is continuously modulated while recording is in progress so that certain features of the voice can be brought out on tape.
POWER, PLEASE.

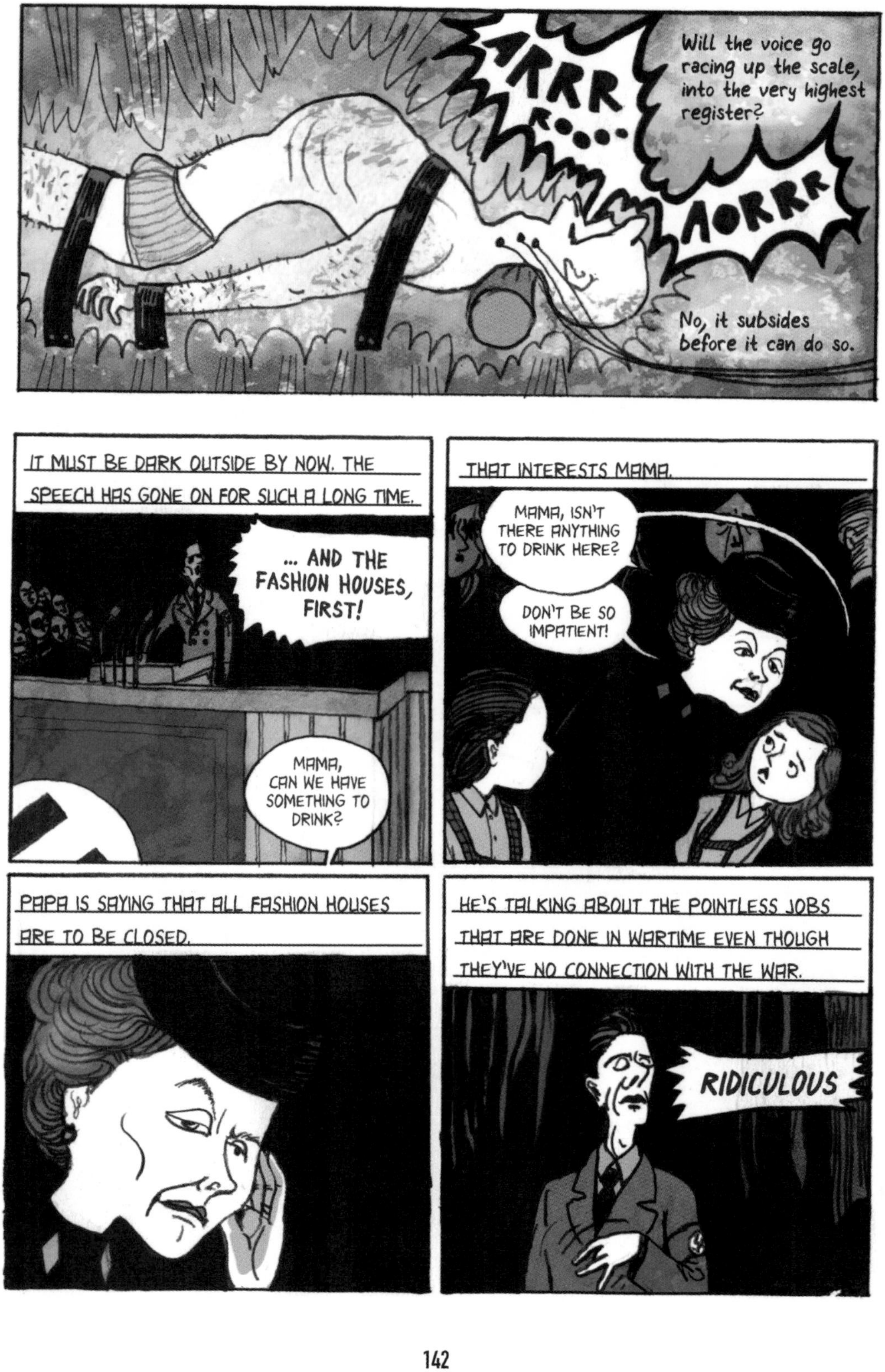
ARRR R....
Will the voice go racing up the scale, into the very highest register?
AORRR
No, it subsides before it can do so.
IT MUST BE DARK OUTSIDE BY NOW. THE SPEECH HAS GONE ON FOR SUCH A LONG TIME.
... AND THE FASHION HOUSES, FIRST!
MAMA, CAN WE HAVE SOMETHING TO DRINK?
THAT INTERESTS MAMA.
MAMA, ISN'T THERE ANYTHING TO DRINK HERE?
DON'T BE SO IMPATIENT!
PAPA IS SAYING THAT ALL FASHION HOUSES ARE TO BE CLOSED.
HE'S TALKING ABOUT THE POINTLESS JOBS THAT ARE DONE IN WARTIME EVEN THOUGH THEY'VE NO CONNECTION WITH THE WAR.
RIDICULOUS

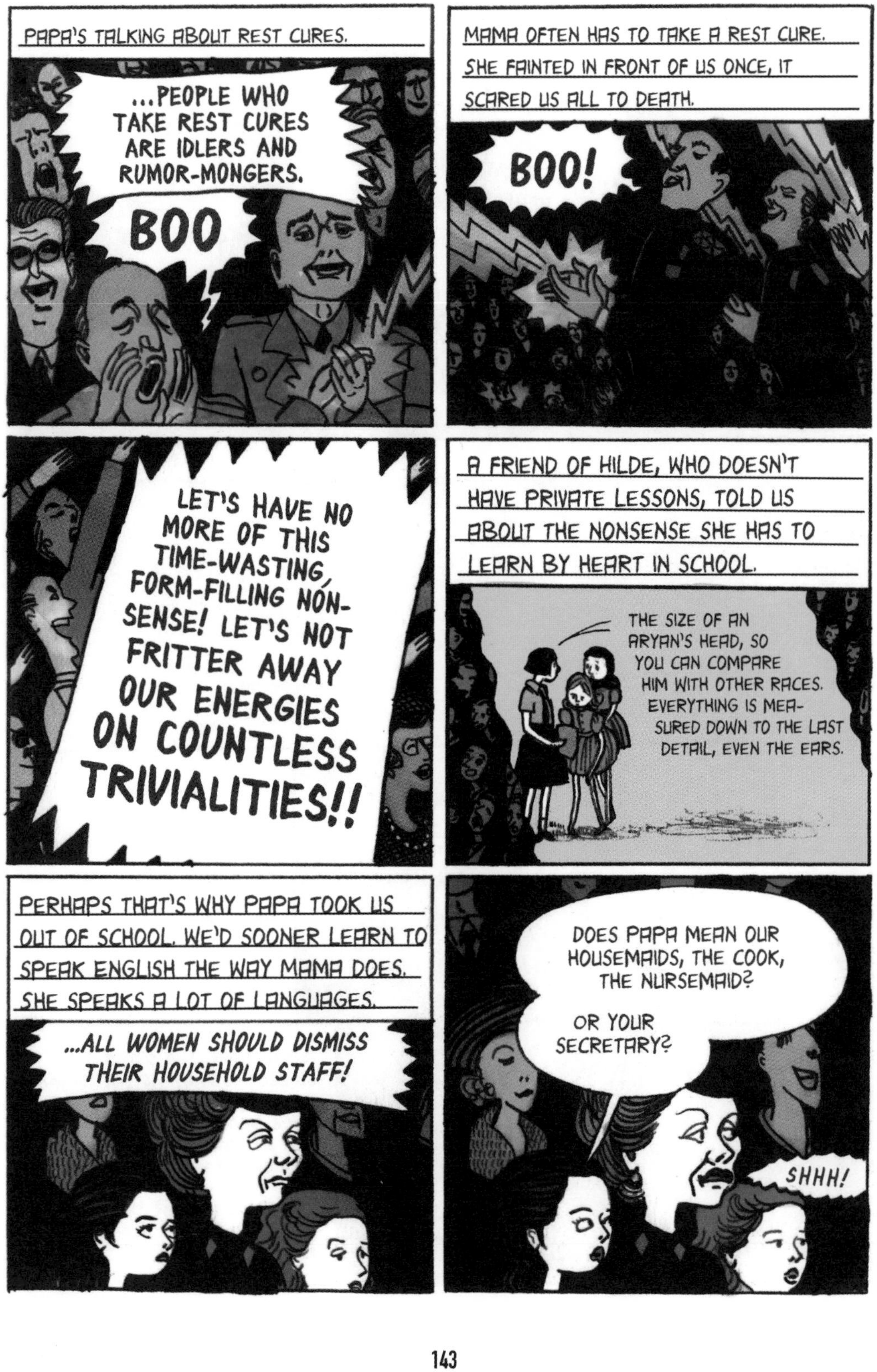
PAPA'S TALKING ABOUT REST CURES.
...PEOPLE WHO TAKE REST CURES ARE IDLERS AND RUMOR-MONGERS.
BOO
MAMA OFTEN HAS TO TAKE A REST CURE. SHE FAINTED IN FRONT OF US ONCE, IT SCARED US ALL TO DEATH.
BOO!
LET'S HAVE NO MORE OF THIS TIME-WASTING, FORM-FILLING NON-SENSE! LET'S NOT FRITTER AWAY OUR ENERGIES ON COUNTLESS TRIVIALITIES!!
A FRIEND OF HILDE, WHO DOESN'T HAVE PRIVATE LESSONS, TOLD US ABOUT THE NONSENSE SHE HAS TO LEARN BY HEART IN SCHOOL.
THE SIZE OF AN ARYAN'S HEAD, SO YOU CAN COMPARE HIM WITH OTHER RACES. EVERYTHING IS MEA-SURED DOWN TO THE LAST DETAIL, EVEN THE EARS.
PERHAPS THAT'S WHY PAPA TOOK US OUT OF SCHOOL. WE'D SOONER LEARN TO SPEAK ENGLISH THE WAY MAMA DOES. SHE SPEAKS A LOT OF LANGUAGES.
...ALL WOMEN SHOULD DISMISS THEIR HOUSEHOLD STAFF!
DOES PAPA MEAN OUR HOUSEMAIDS, THE COOK, THE NURSEMAID?
OR YOUR SECRETARY?
SHHH!

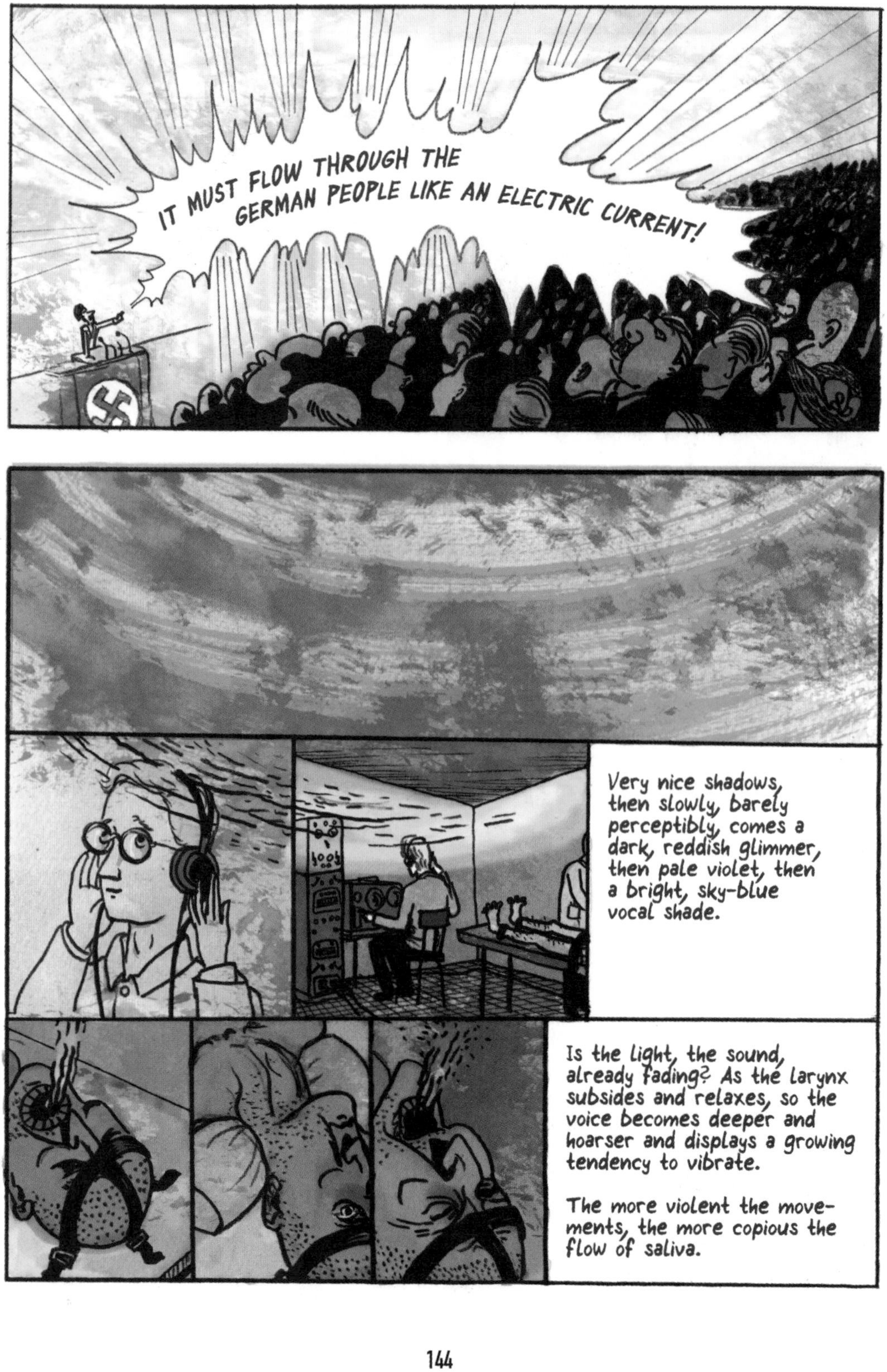
IT MUST FLOW THROUGH THE GERMAN PEOPLE LIKE AN ELECTRIC CURRENT!
Very nice shadows, then slowly, barely perceptibly, comes a dark, reddish glimmer, then pale violet, then a bright, sky-blue vocal shade.
Is the light, the sound, already fading? As the larynx subsides and relaxes, so the voice becomes deeper and hoarser and displays a growing tendency to vibrate.
The more violent the movements, the more copious the flow of saliva.

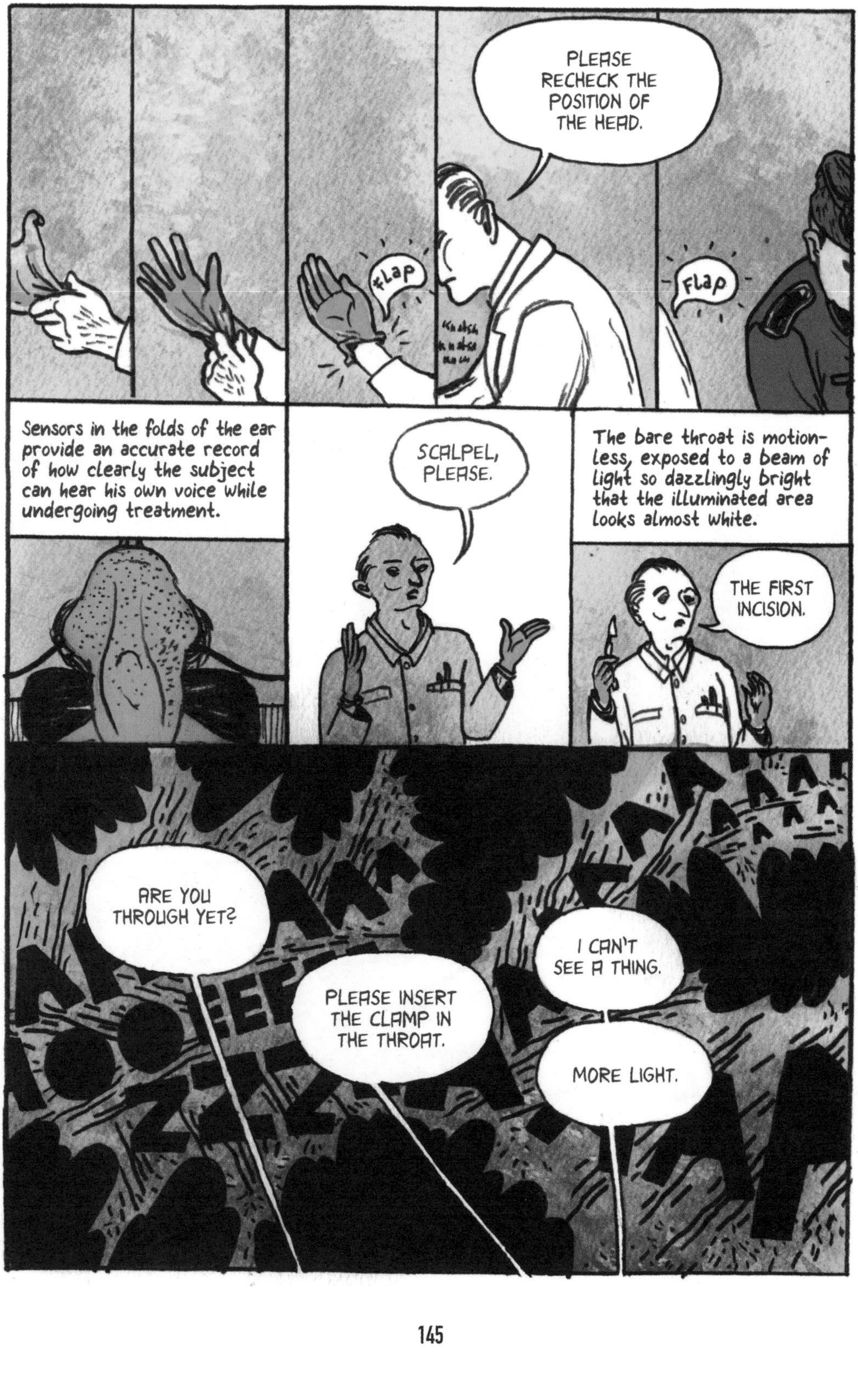
PLEASE RECHECK THE POSITION OF THE HEAD.
Flap
Flap
Sensors in the folds of the ear provide an accurate record of how clearly the subject can hear his own voice while undergoing treatment.
SCALPEL, PLEASE.
The bare throat is motionless, exposed to a beam of light so dazzlingly bright that the illuminated area looks almost white.
THE FIRST INCISION.
ARE YOU THROUGH YET?
PLEASE INSERT THE CLAMP IN THE THROAT.
I CAN'T SEE A THING.
MORE LIGHT.

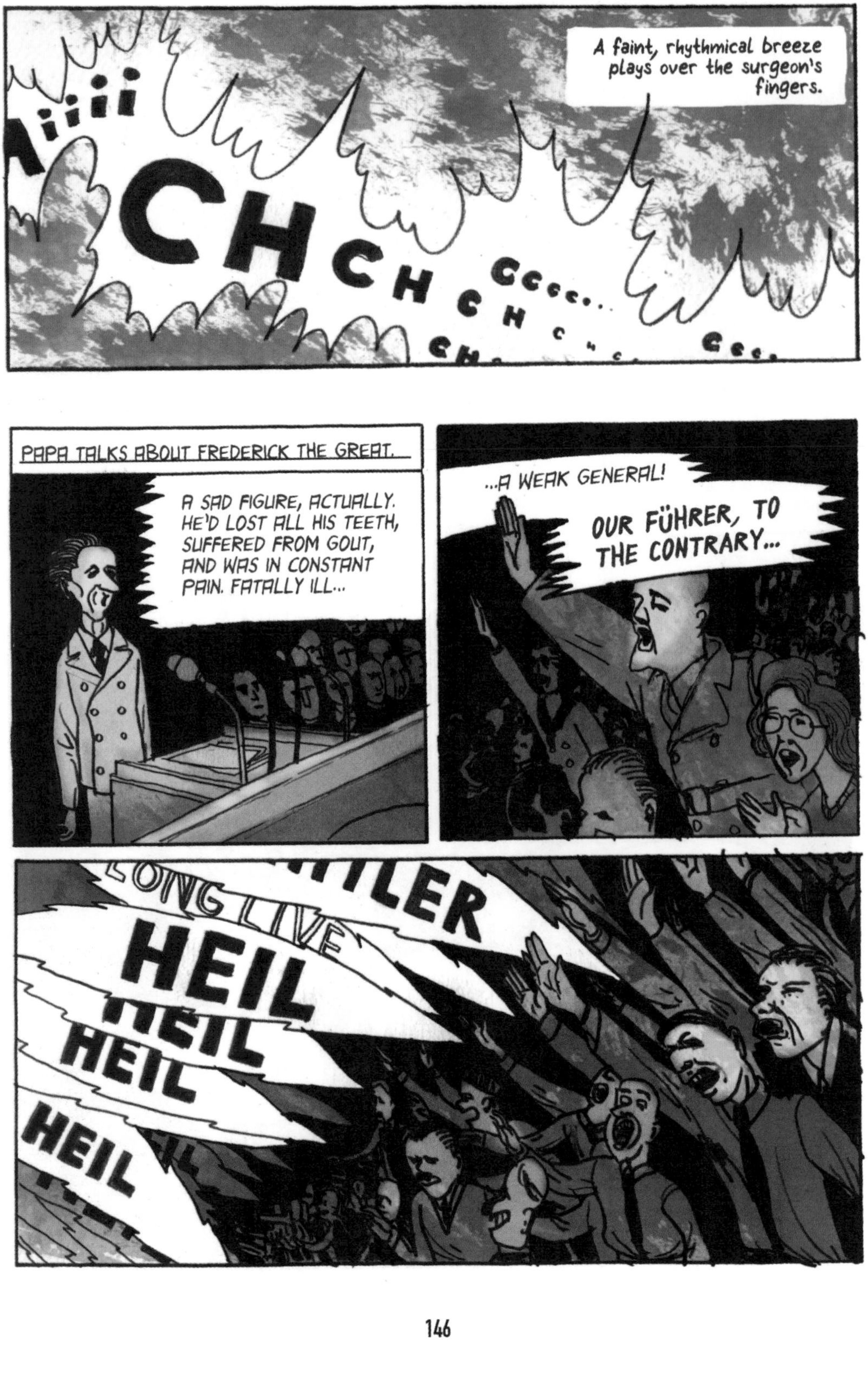
A faint, rhythmical breeze plays over the surgeon's fingers.
CH
PAPA TALKS ABOUT FREDERICK THE GREAT.
A SAD FIGURE, ACTUALLY. HE'D LOST ALL HIS TEETH, SUFFERED FROM GOUT, AND WAS IN CONSTANT PAIN. FATALLY ILL...
...A WEAK GENERAL!
OUR FÜHRER, TO THE CONTRARY...
LONG LIVE
HEIL
HEIL
HEIL
HEIL

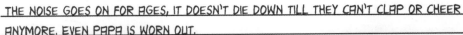
THE NOISE GOES ON FOR AGES, IT DOESN'T DIE DOWN TILL THEY CAN'T CLAP OR CHEER ANYMORE. EVEN PAPA IS WORN OUT.

SIEG HEIL

AND NOW TO MY FINAL POINT

IT'S TIME WE WENT HOME. THE LITTLE ONES WON'T BELIEVE US WHEN WE TELL THEM WHAT WE'VE SEEN AND HEARD HERE.

IT'S SO STUFFY IN HERE, WE COULD DO WITH SOME FRESH AIR. THERE AREN'T ANY WINDOWS, EITHER.

BUT PAPA DOESN'T STOP SPEAKING.

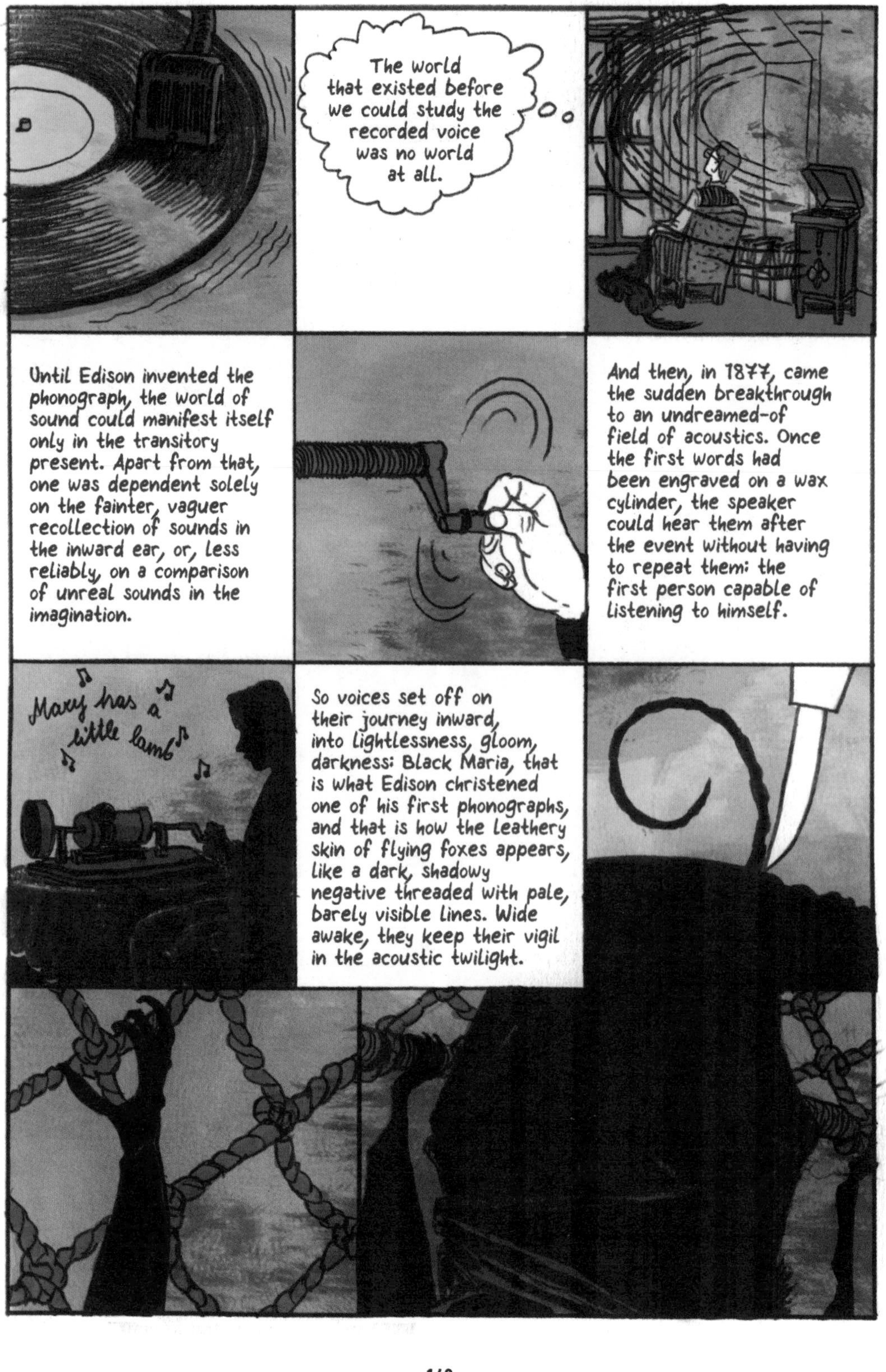
The world that existed before we could study the recorded voice was no world at all.
Until Edison invented the phonograph, the world of sound could manifest itself only in the transitory present. Apart from that, one was dependent solely on the fainter, vaguer recollection of sounds in the inward ear, or, less reliably, on a comparison of unreal sounds in the imagination.
And then, in 1877, came the sudden breakthrough to an undreamed-of field of acoustics. Once the first words had been engraved on a wax cylinder, the speaker could hear them after the event without having to repeat them: the first person capable of listening to himself.
Mary has a little lamb
So voices set off on their journey inward, into lightlessness, gloom, darkness: Black Maria, that is what Edison christened one of his first phonographs, and that is how the leathery skin of flying foxes appears, like a dark, shadowy negative threaded with pale, barely visible lines. Wide awake, they keep their vigil in the acoustic twilight.

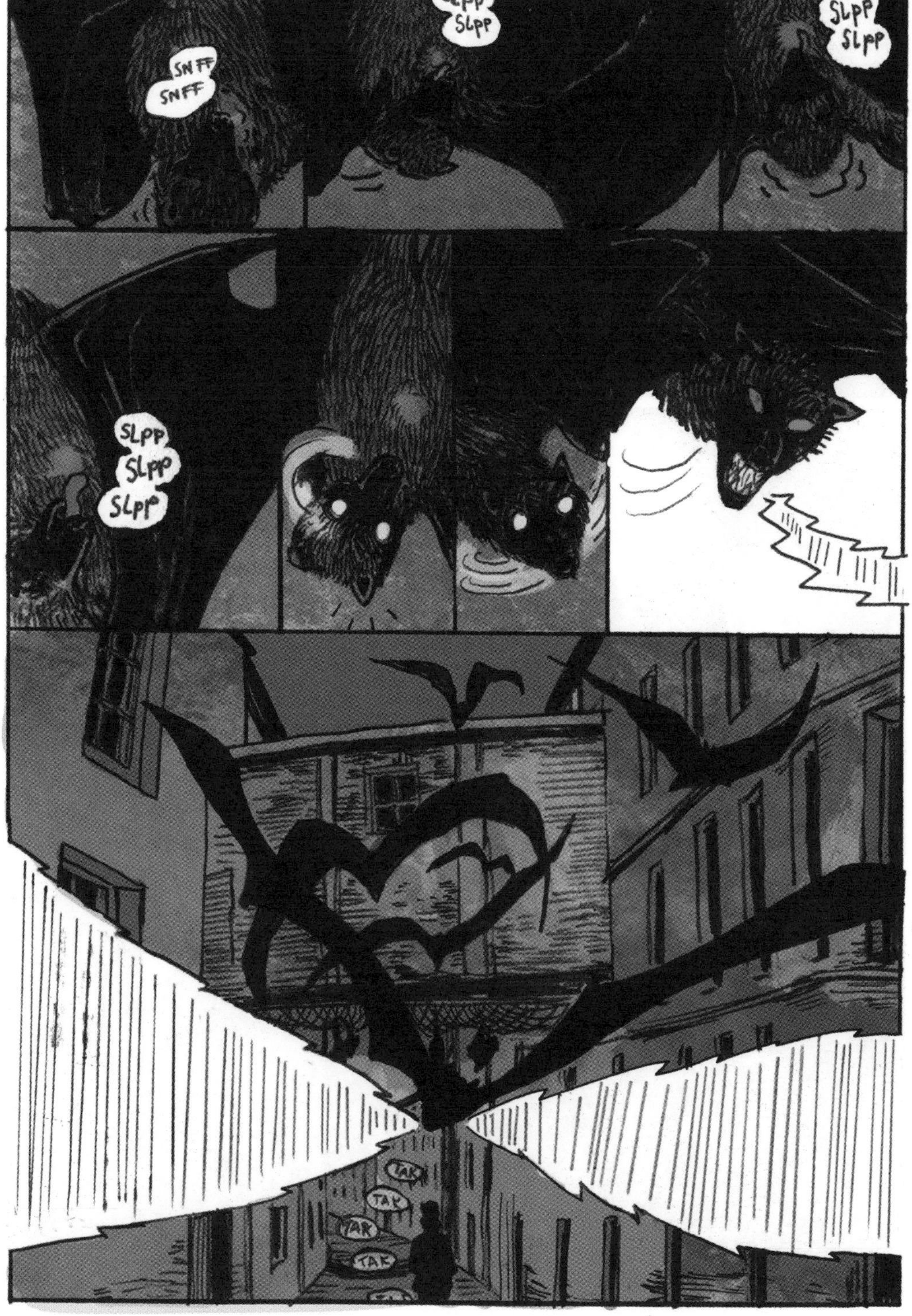

SNFF
SNFF
SLPP
SLPP
SLPP
SLPP
SLPP
SLPP
SLPP
TAK
TAK
TAK
TAK

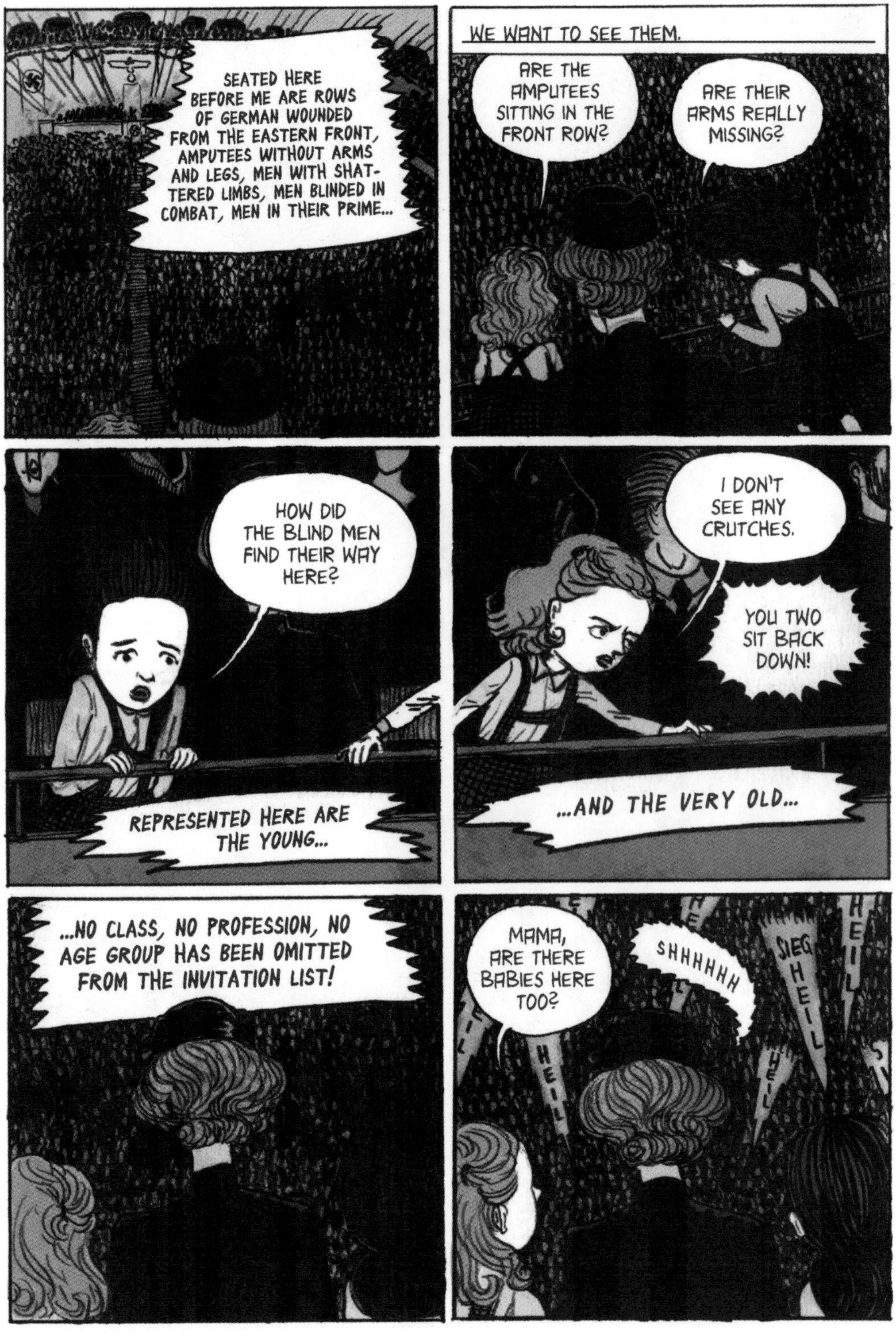
SEATED HERE BEFORE ME ARE ROWS OF GERMAN WOUNDED FROM THE EASTERN FRONT, AMPUTEES WITHOUT ARMS AND LEGS, MEN WITH SHATTERED LIMBS, MEN BLINDED IN COMBAT, MEN IN THEIR PRIME...
WE WANT TO SEE THEM.
ARE THE AMPUTEES SITTING IN THE FRONT ROW?
ARE THEIR ARMS REALLY MISSING?
HOW DID THE BLIND MEN FIND THEIR WAY HERE?
REPRESENTED HERE ARE THE YOUNG...
I DON'T SEE ANY CRUTCHES.
YOU TWO SIT BACK DOWN!
...AND THE VERY OLD...
...NO CLASS, NO PROFESSION, NO AGE GROUP HAS BEEN OMITTED FROM THE INVITATION LIST!
MAMA, ARE THERE BABIES HERE TOO?
SHHHHHH
SIEG HEIL
HEIL
HEIL
HEIL

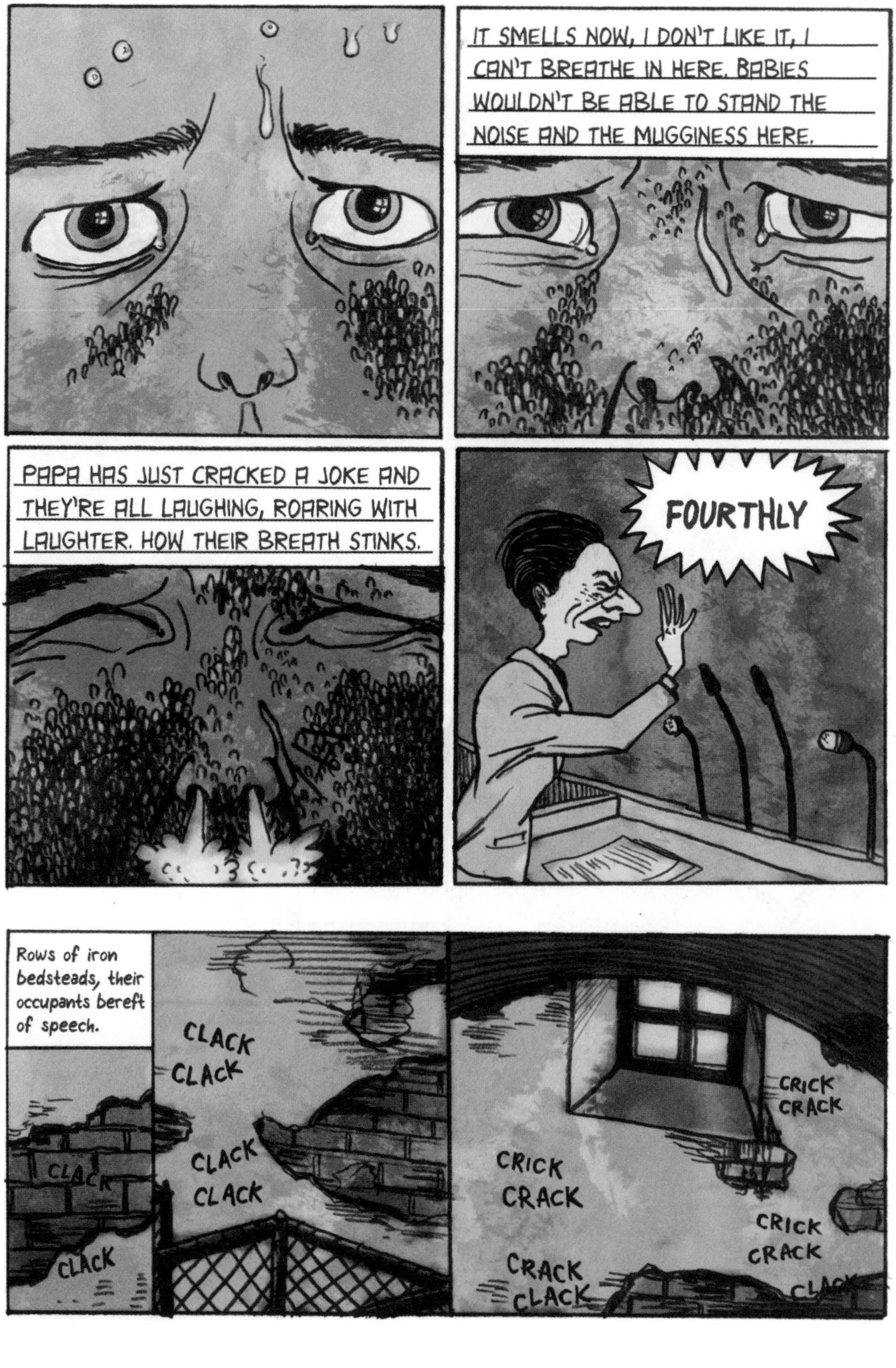
IT SMELLS NOW, I DON'T LIKE IT, I CAN'T BREATHE IN HERE. BABIES WOULDN'T BE ABLE TO STAND THE NOISE AND THE MUGGINESS HERE.
PAPA HAS JUST CRACKED A JOKE AND THEY'RE ALL LAUGHING, ROARING WITH LAUGHTER. HOW THEIR BREATH STINKS.
FOURTHLY
Rows of iron bedsteads, their occupants bereft of speech.
CLACK
CLACK
CLACK
CLACK
CLACK
CLACK
CLACK
CRICK CRACK
CRICK CRACK
CRICK CRACK
CRACK CLACK

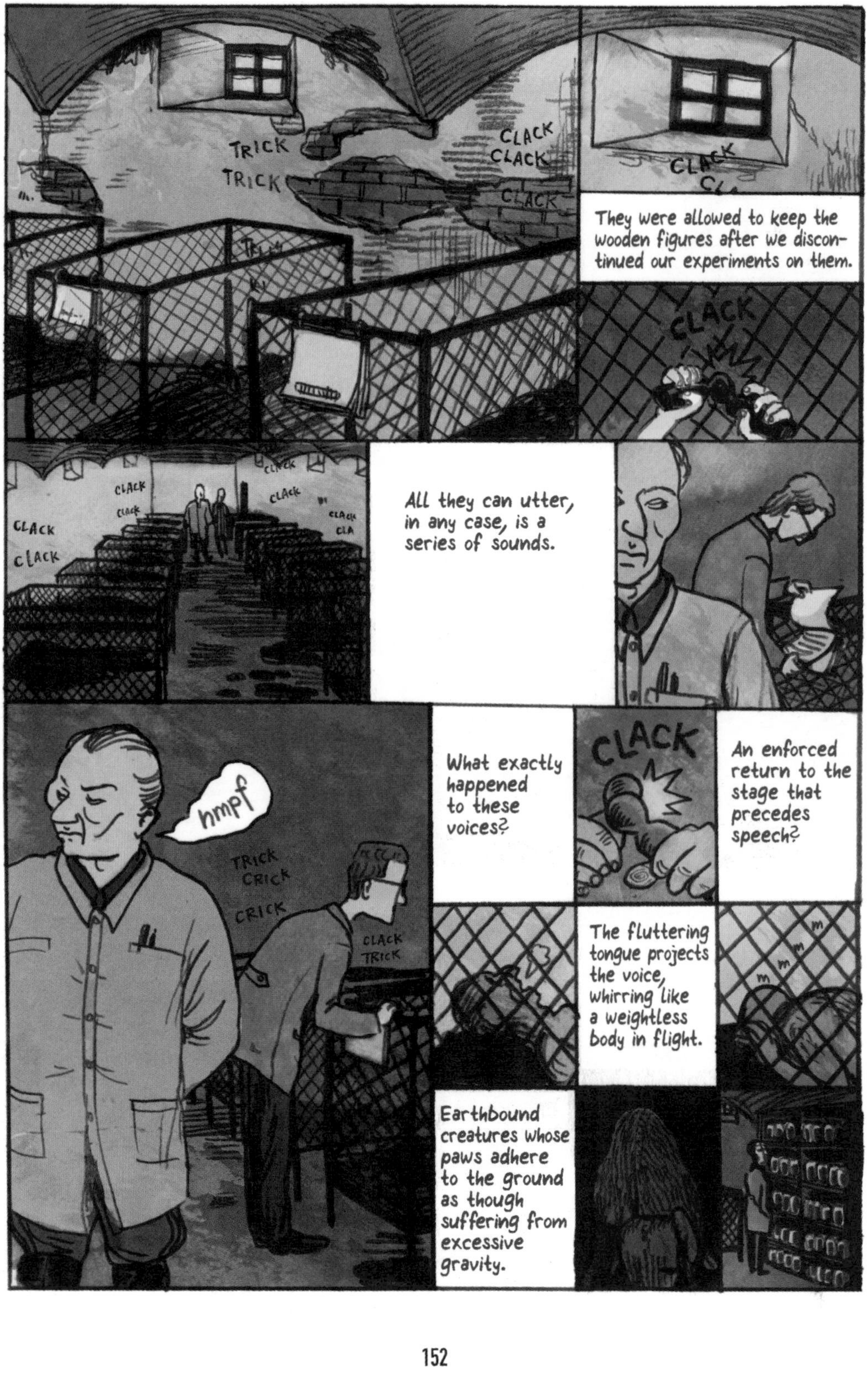
TRICK
TRICK
CLACK
CLACK
CLACK
They were allowed to keep the wooden figures after we discontinued our experiments on them.
CLACK
CLACK
CLACK
All they can utter, in any case, is a series of sounds.
hmpf
TRICK
CRICK
CRICK
CLACK
TRICK
What exactly happened to these voices?
CLACK
An enforced return to the stage that precedes speech?
The fluttering tongue projects the voice, whirring like a weightless body in flight.
Earthbound creatures whose paws adhere to the ground as though suffering from excessive gravity.

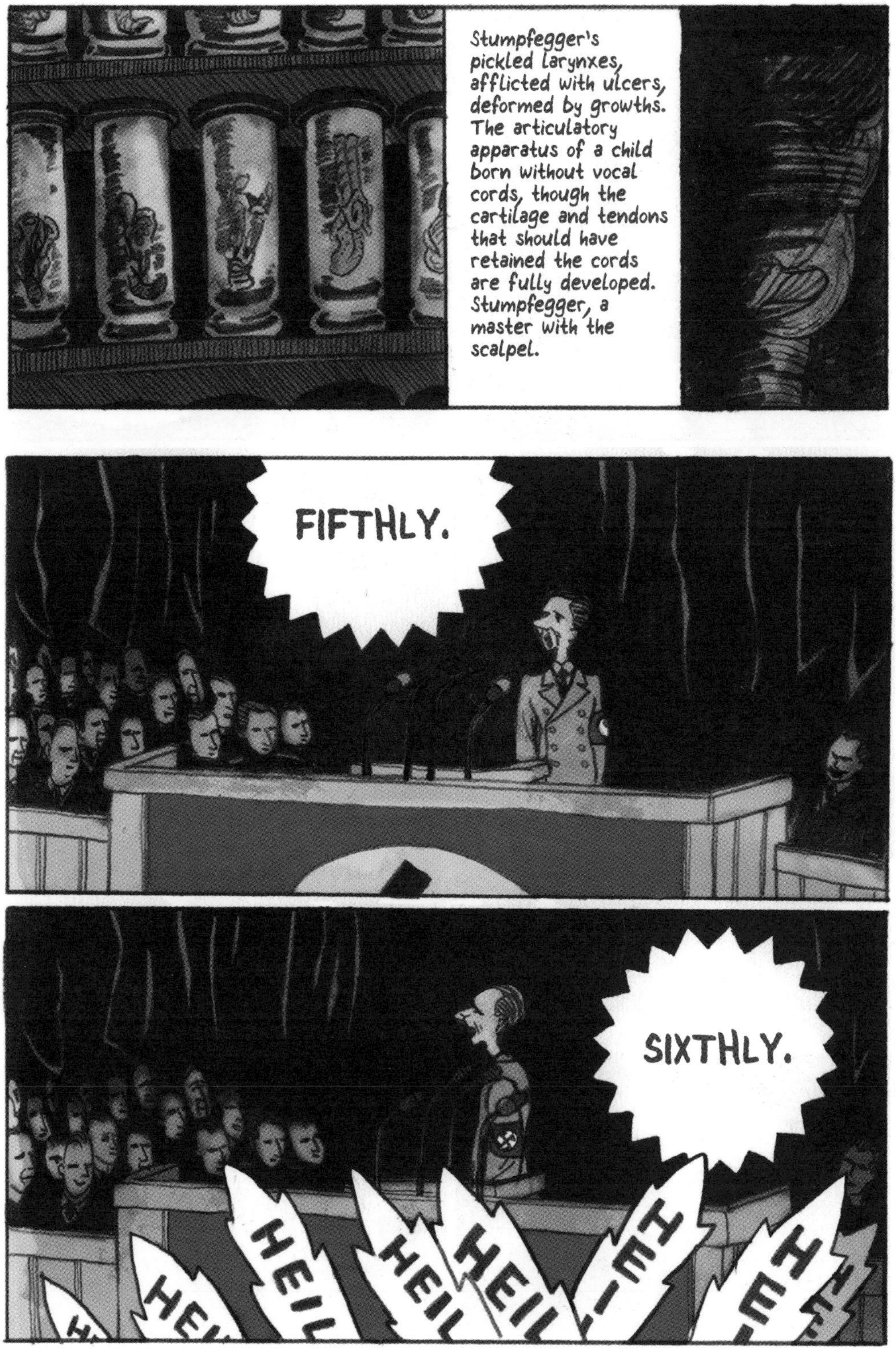
Stumpfegger's pickled larynxes, afflicted with ulcers, deformed by growths. The articulatory apparatus of a child born without vocal cords, though the cartilage and tendons that should have retained the cords are fully developed. Stumpfegger, a master with the scalpel.
FIFTHLY.
SIXTHLY.
HEIL
HEIL
HEIL

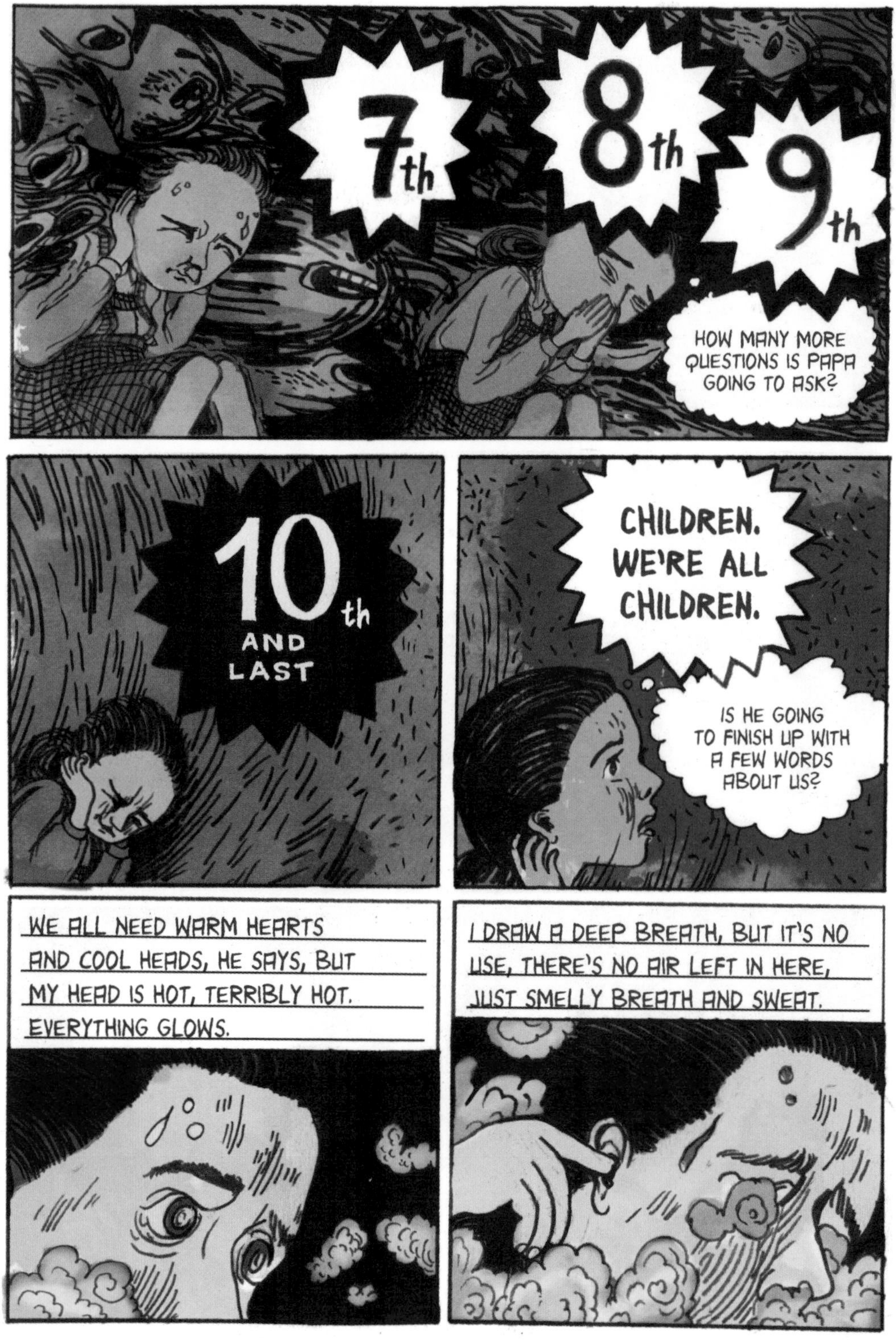
7th
8th
9th
HOW MANY MORE QUESTIONS IS PAPA GOING TO ASK?
10th AND LAST
CHILDREN. WE'RE ALL CHILDREN.
IS HE GOING TO FINISH UP WITH A FEW WORDS ABOUT US?
WE ALL NEED WARM HEARTS AND COOL HEADS, HE SAYS, BUT MY HEAD IS HOT, TERRIBLY HOT. EVERYTHING GLOWS.
I DRAW A DEEP BREATH, BUT IT'S NO USE, THERE'S NO AIR LEFT IN HERE, JUST SMELLY BREATH AND SWEAT.

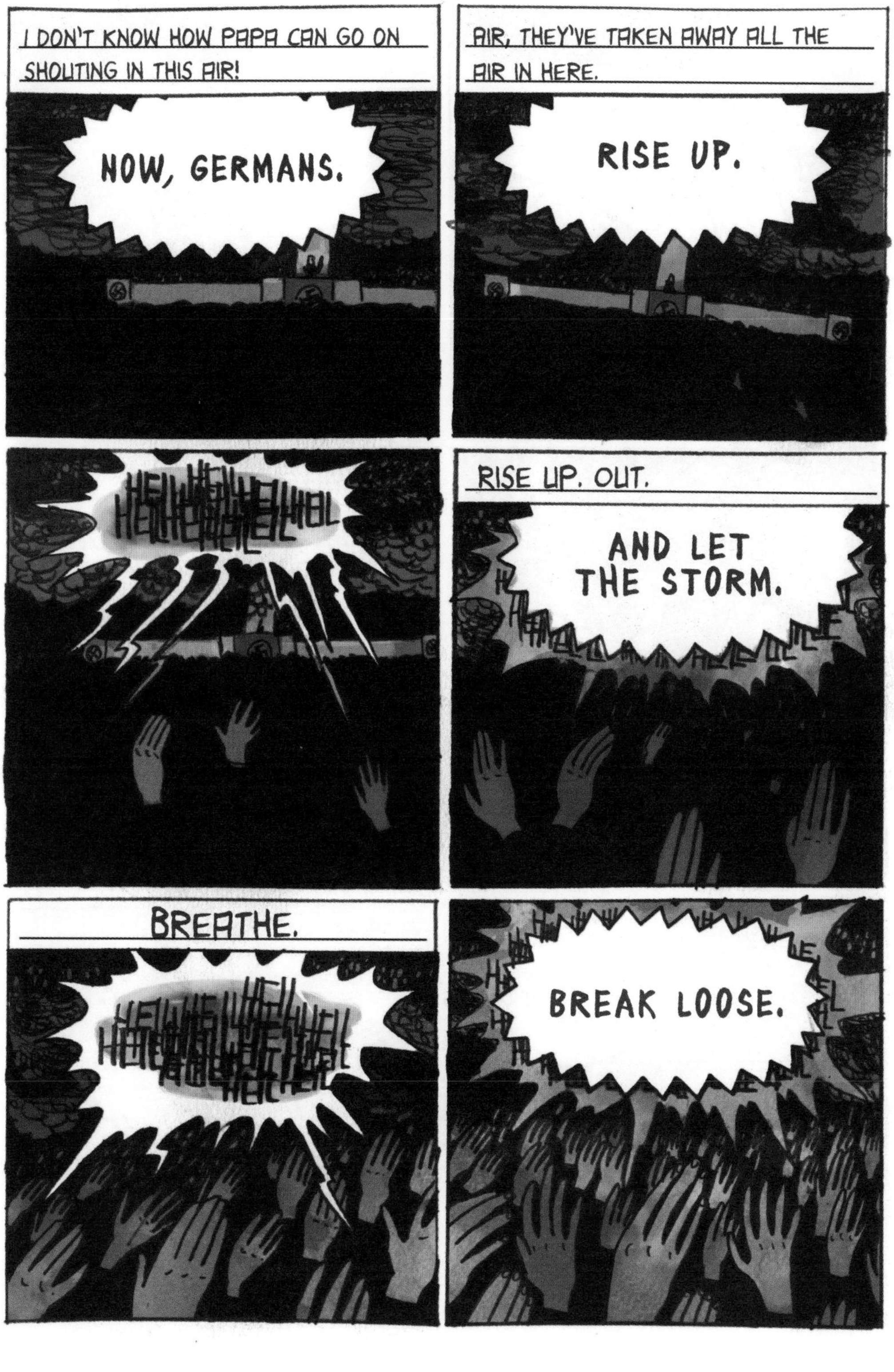
I DON'T KNOW HOW PAPA CAN GO ON SHOUTING IN THIS AIR!
NOW, GERMANS.
AIR, THEY'VE TAKEN AWAY ALL THE AIR IN HERE.
RISE UP.
RISE UP. OUT.
AND LET THE STORM.
BREATHE.
BREAK LOOSE.

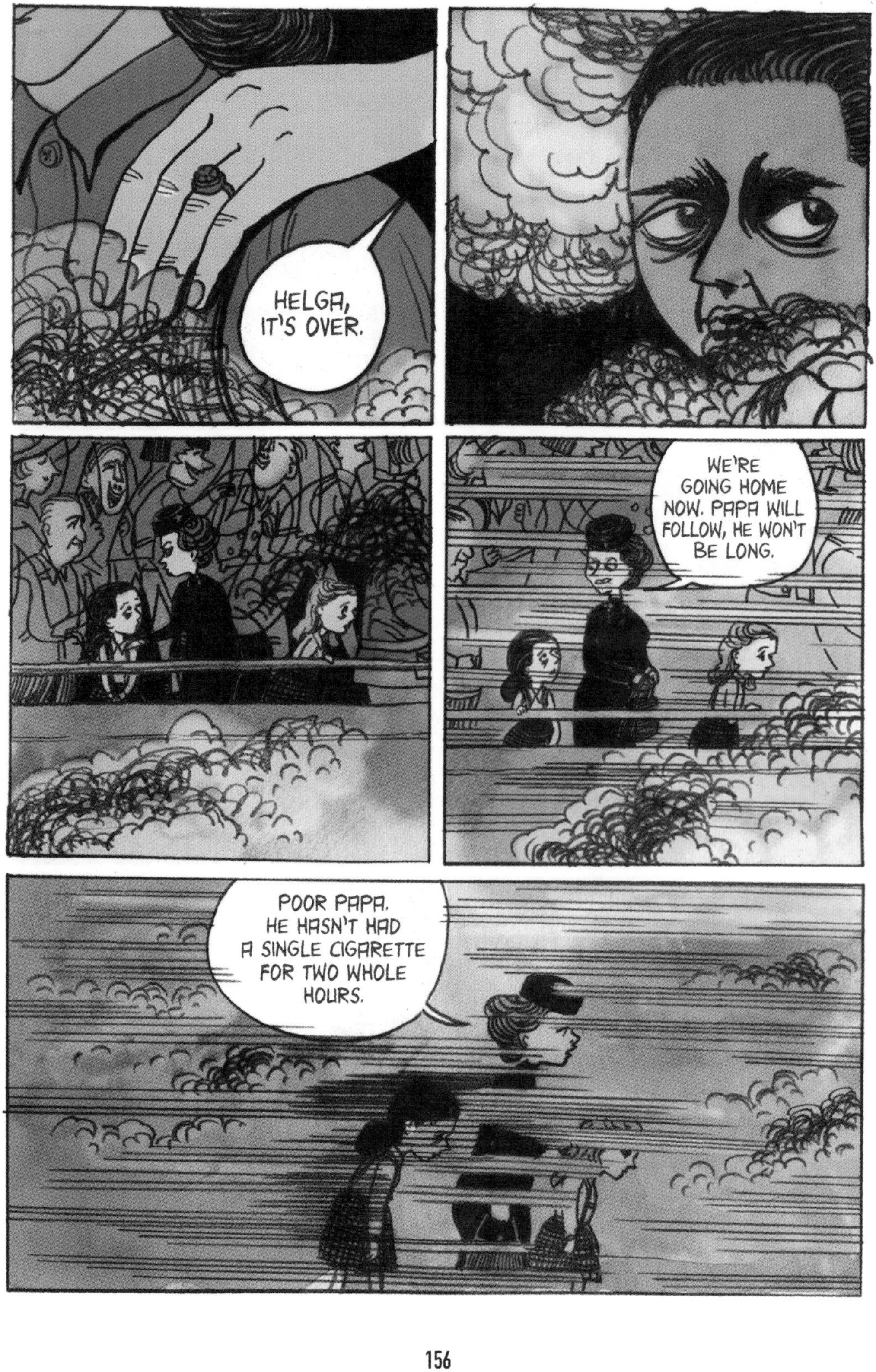
HELGA, IT'S OVER.
WE'RE GOING HOME NOW. PAPA WILL FOLLOW, HE WON'T BE LONG.
POOR PAPA. HE HASN'T HAD A SINGLE CIGARETTE FOR TWO WHOLE HOURS.

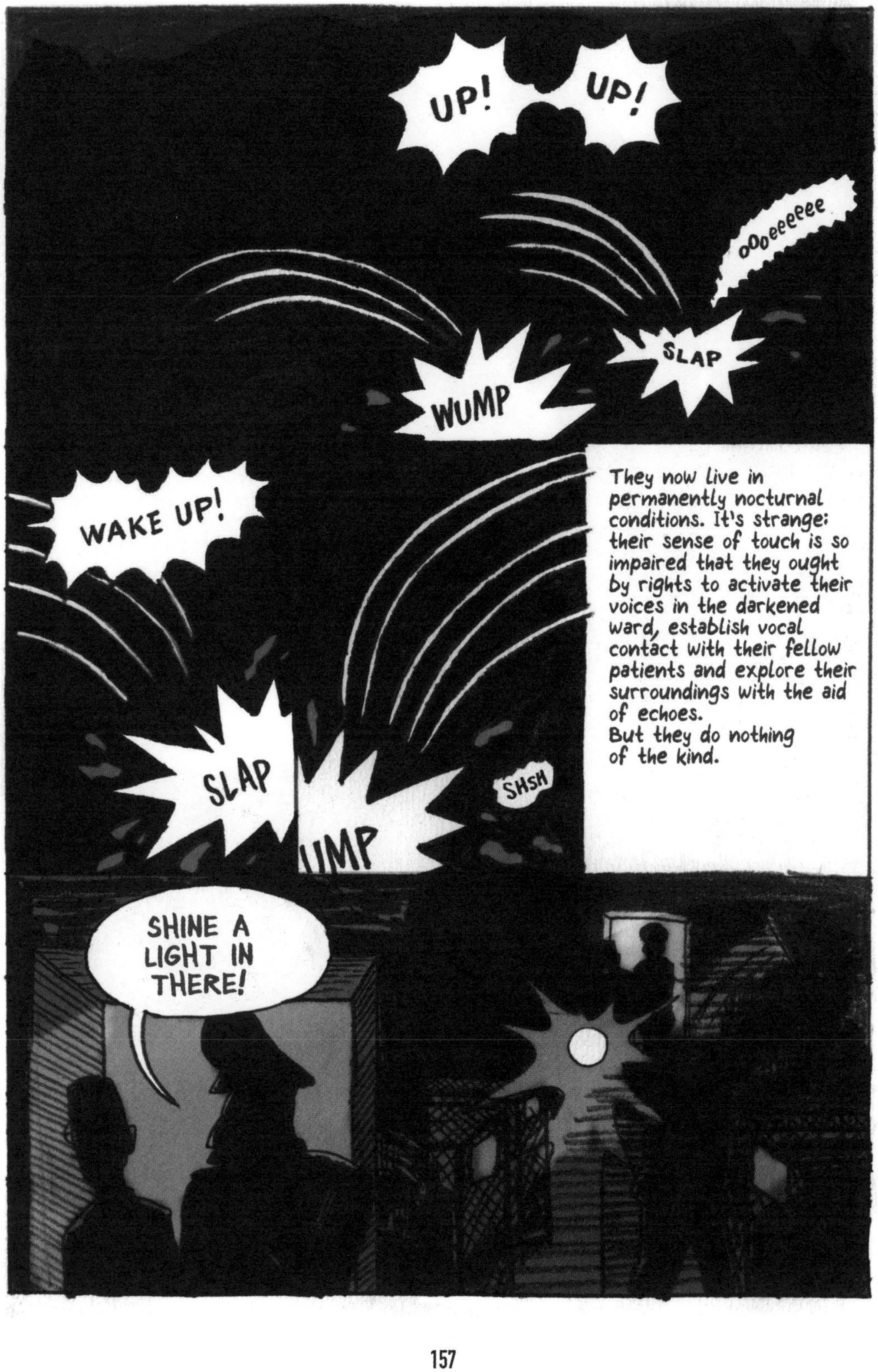
UP! UP!
oooeeeeee
WUMP
SLAP
WAKE UP!
They now live in permanently nocturnal conditions. It's strange: their sense of touch is so impaired that they ought by rights to activate their voices in the darkened ward, establish vocal contact with their fellow patients and explore their surroundings with the aid of echoes.
But they do nothing of the kind.
SLAP
UMP
SHSH
SHINE A LIGHT IN THERE!

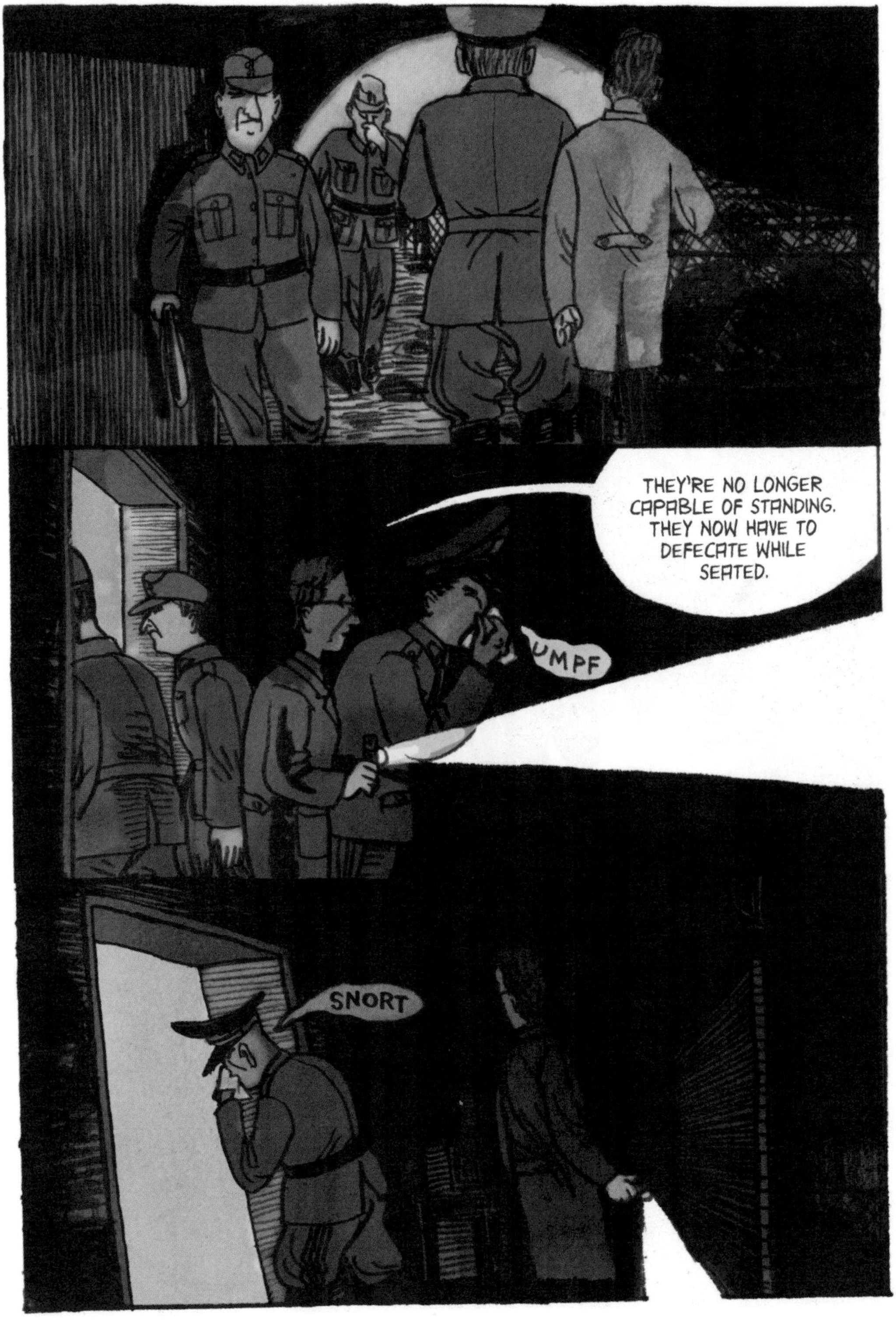
THEY'RE NO LONGER CAPABLE OF STANDING. THEY NOW HAVE TO DEFECATE WHILE SEATED.
UMPF
SNORT

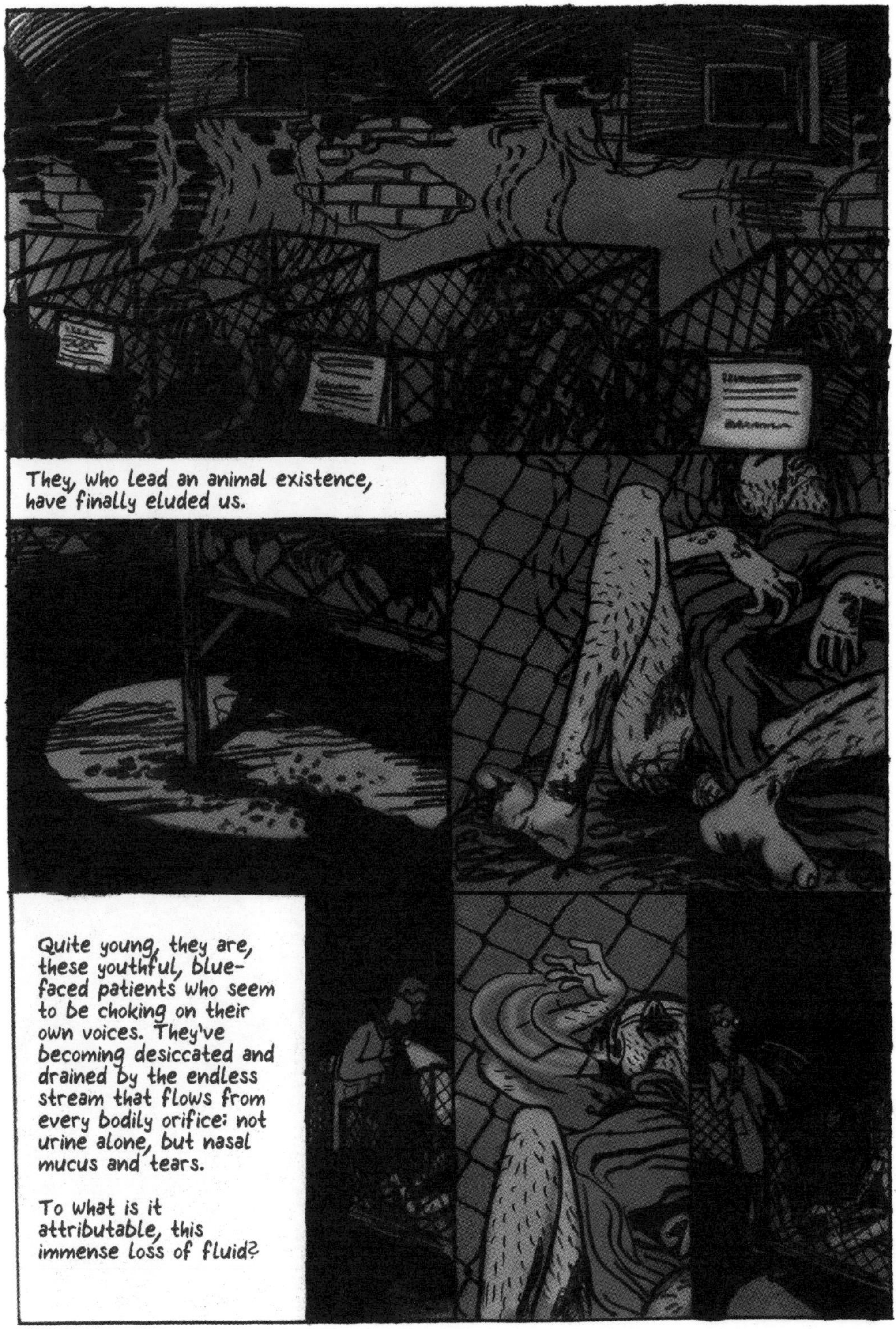
They, who lead an animal existence, have finally eluded us.
Quite young, they are, these youthful, blue-faced patients who seem to be choking on their own voices. They've becoming desiccated and drained by the endless stream that flows from every bodily orifice: not urine alone, but nasal mucus and tears.
To what is it attributable, this immense loss of fluid?

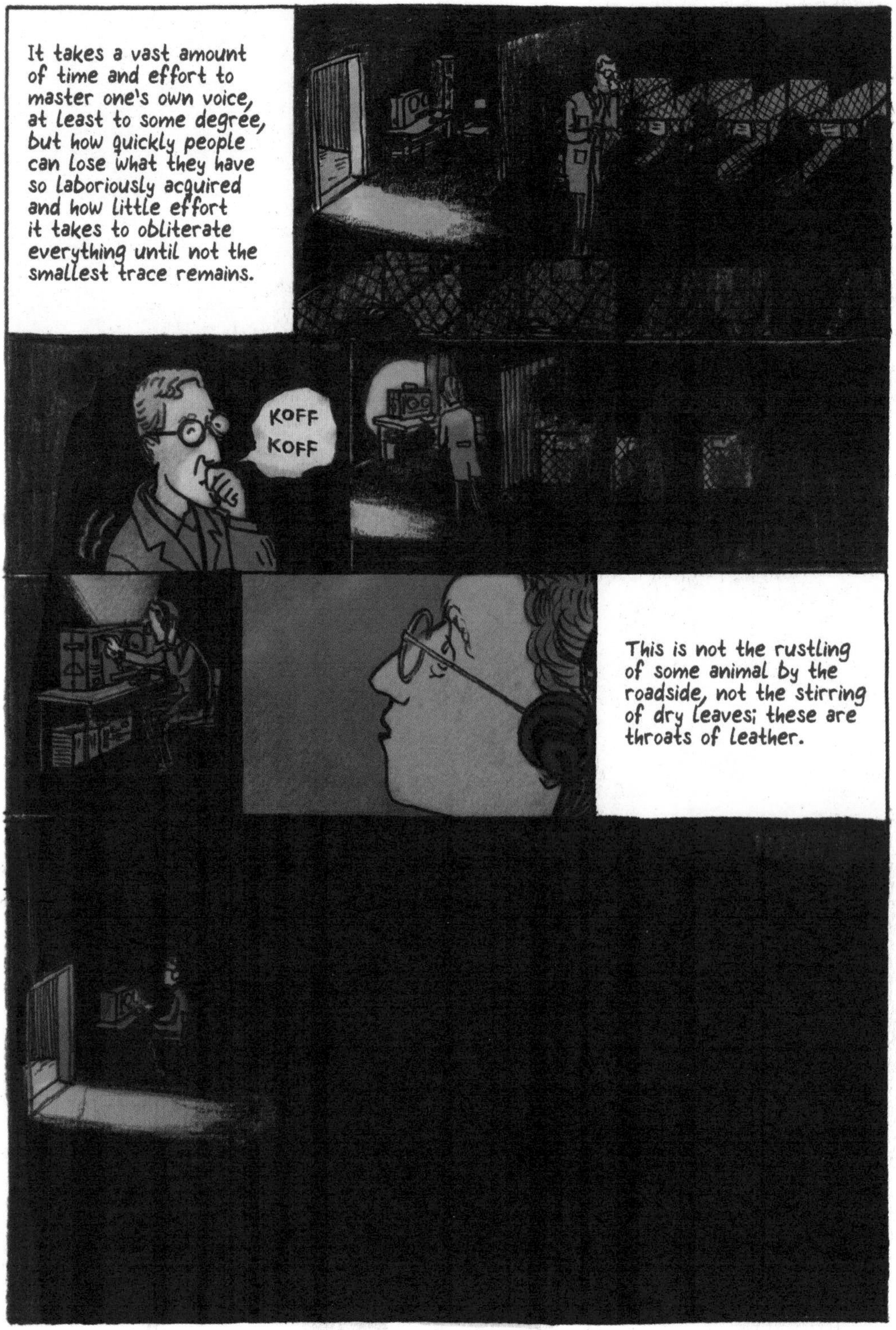

It takes a vast amount of time and effort to master one's own voice, at least to some degree, but how quickly people can lose what they have so laboriously acquired and how little effort it takes to obliterate everything until not the smallest trace remains.
KOFF KOFF
This is not the rustling of some animal by the roadside, not the stirring of dry leaves; these are throats of leather.

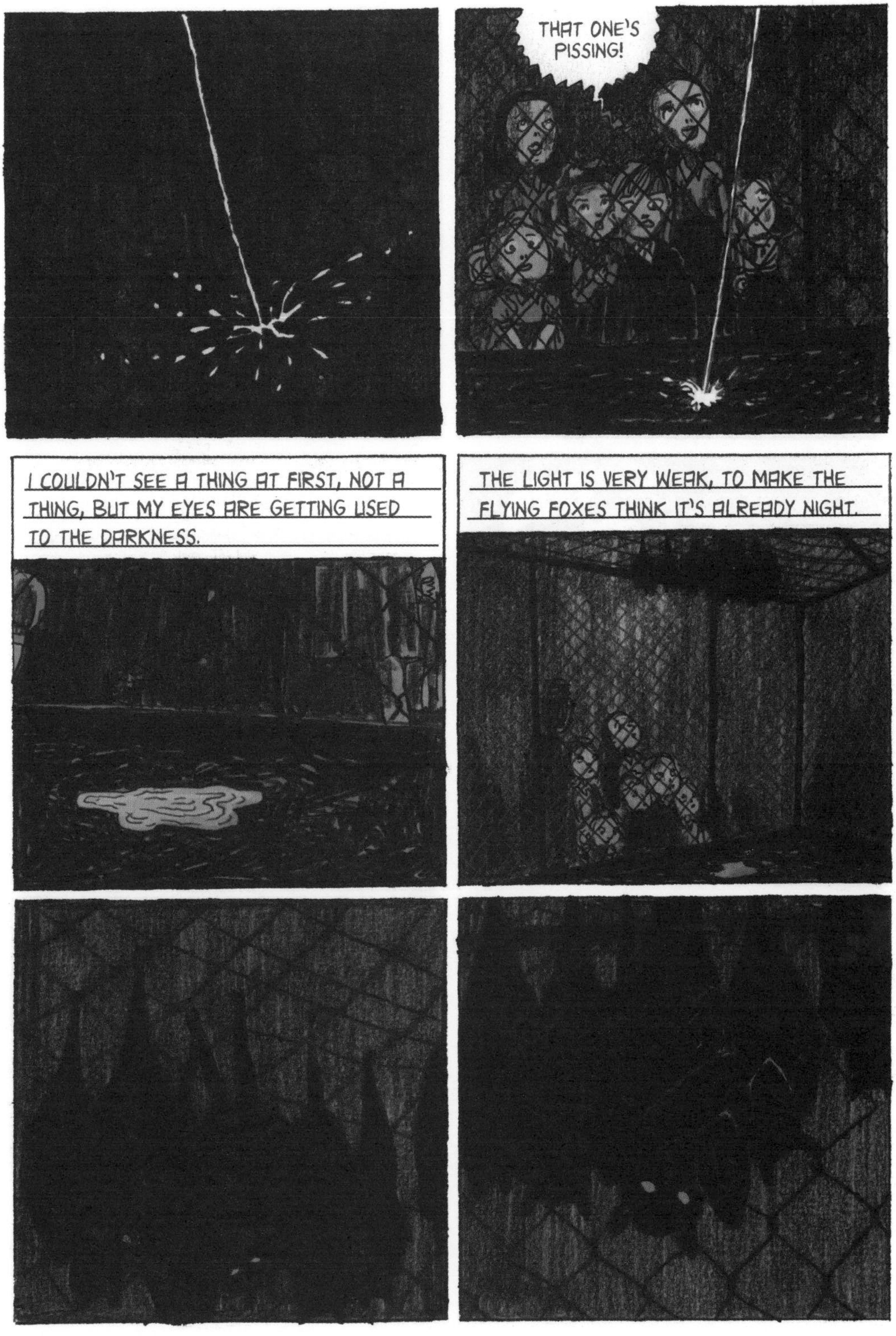
THAT ONE'S PISSING!
I COULDN'T SEE A THING AT FIRST, NOT A THING, BUT MY EYES ARE GETTING USED TO THE DARKNESS.
THE LIGHT IS VERY WEAK, TO MAKE THE FLYING FOXES THINK IT'S ALREADY NIGHT.

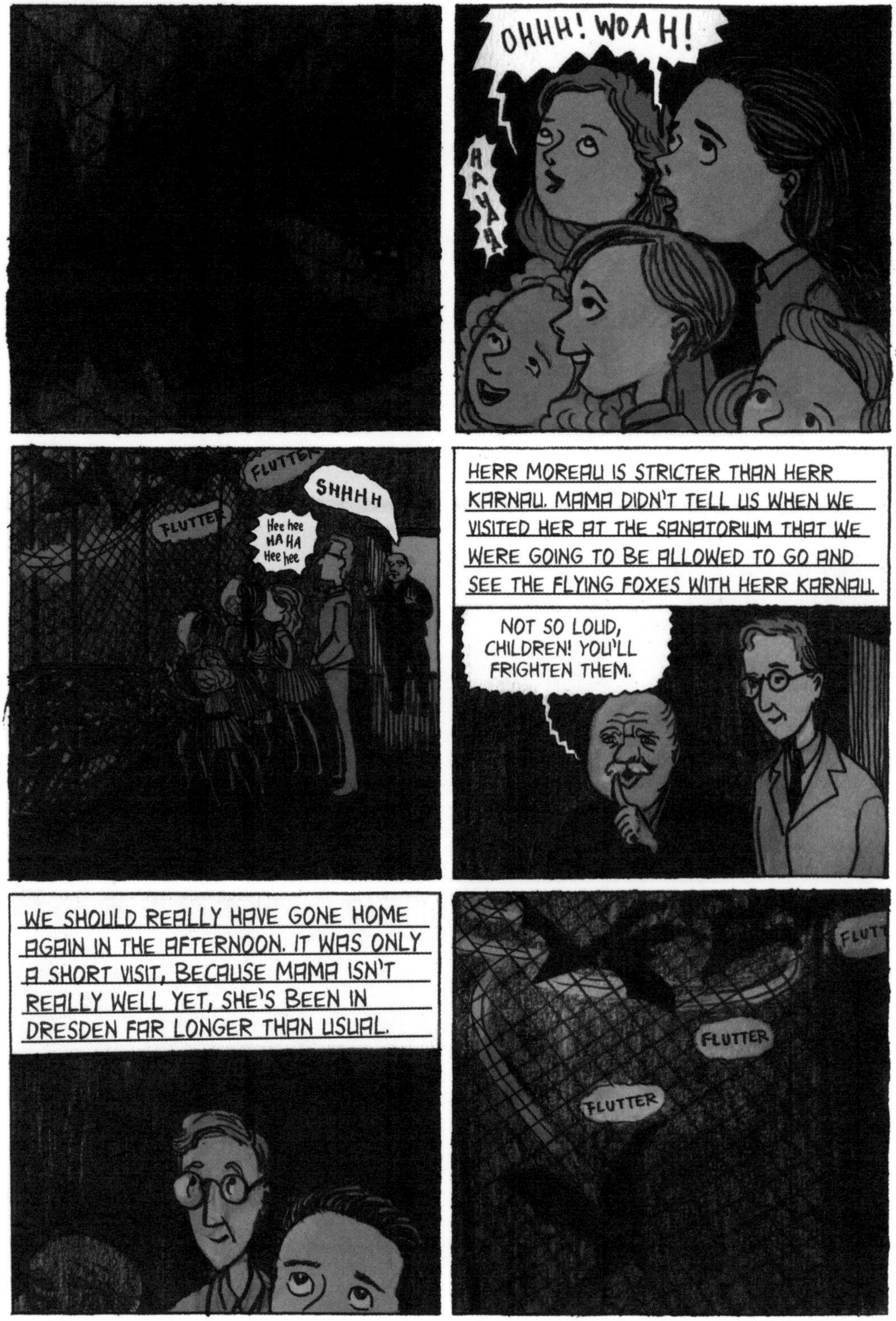
OHHH! WOAH!
HAHAHA
FLUTTER
FLUTTER
SHHHH
Hee hee
HA HA
Hee hee
HERR MOREAU IS STRICTER THAN HERR KARNAU. MAMA DIDN'T TELL US WHEN WE VISITED HER AT THE SANATORIUM THAT WE WERE GOING TO BE ALLOWED TO GO AND SEE THE FLYING FOXES WITH HERR KARNAU.
NOT SO LOUD, CHILDREN! YOU'LL FRIGHTEN THEM.
WE SHOULD REALLY HAVE GONE HOME AGAIN IN THE AFTERNOON. IT WAS ONLY A SHORT VISIT, BECAUSE MAMA ISN'T REALLY WELL YET, SHE'S BEEN IN DRESDEN FAR LONGER THAN USUAL.
FLUTTER
FLUTTER

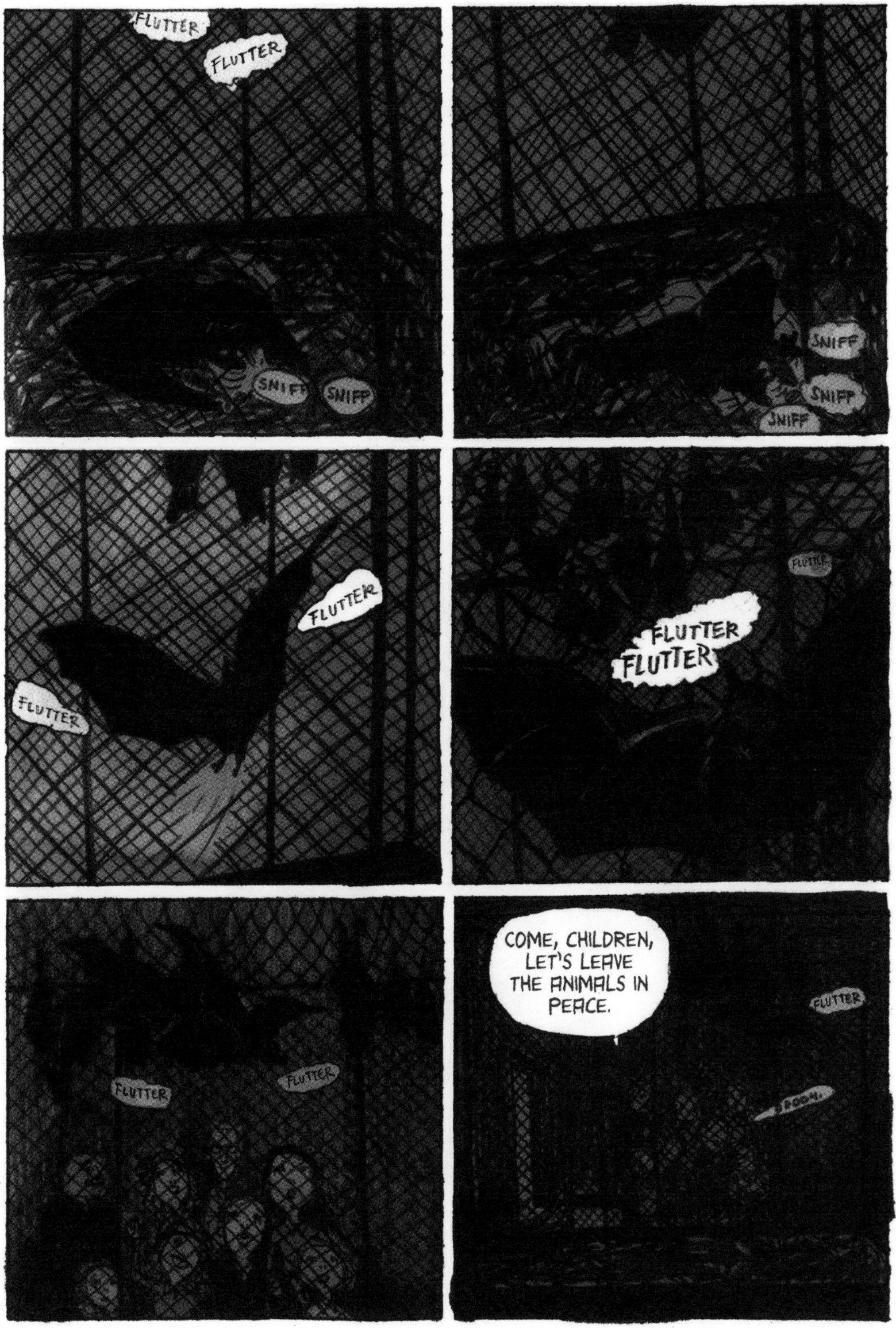
FLUTTER
FLUTTER
SNIFF
SNIFF
SNIFF
SNIFF
SNIFF
FLUTTER
FLUTTER
FLUTTER
FLUTTER
FLUTTER
FLUTTER
FLUTTER
COME, CHILDREN, LET'S LEAVE THE ANIMALS IN PEACE.
FLUTTER

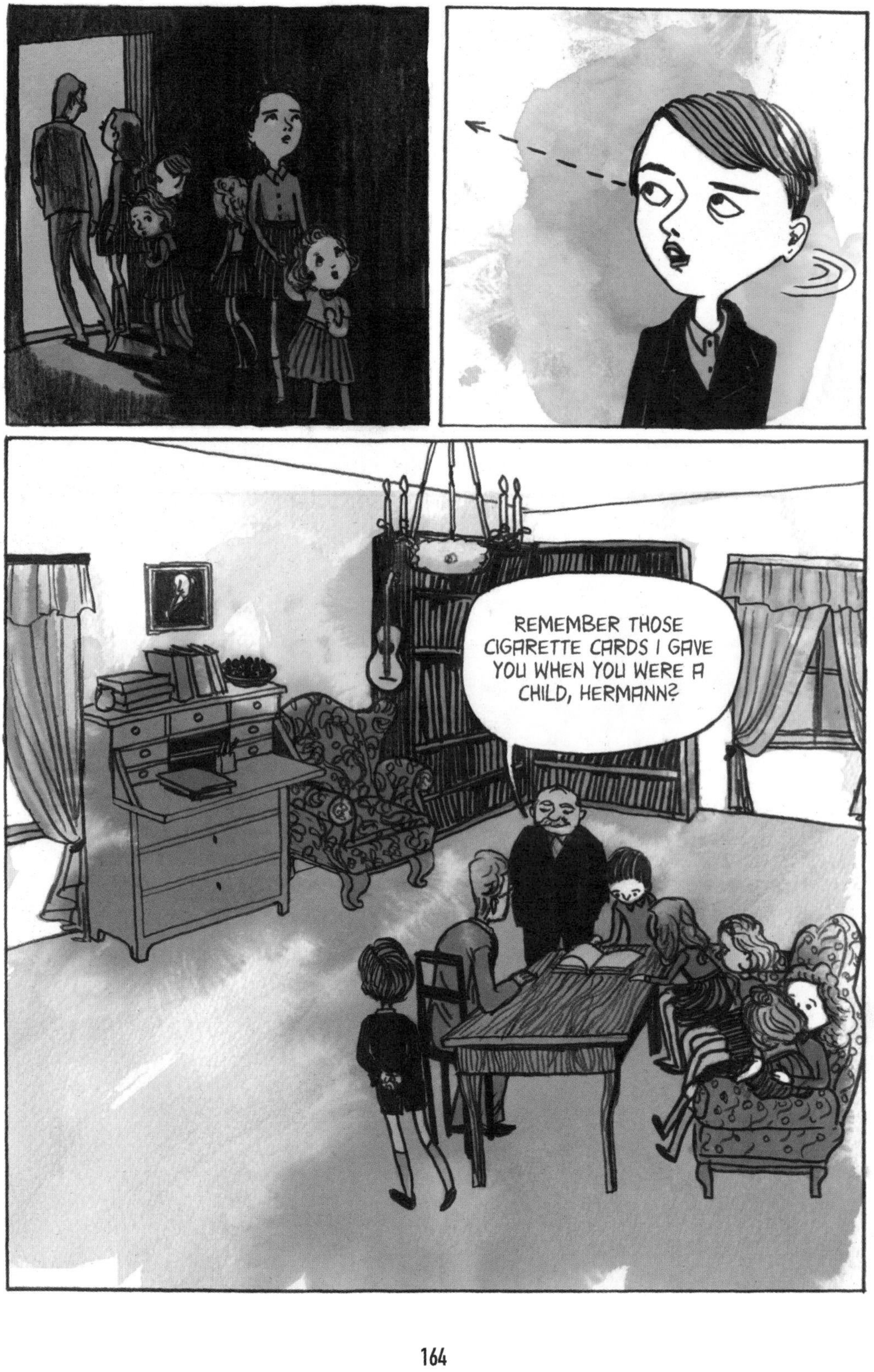
REMEMBER THOSE CIGARETTE CARDS I GAVE YOU WHEN YOU WERE A CHILD, HERMANN?

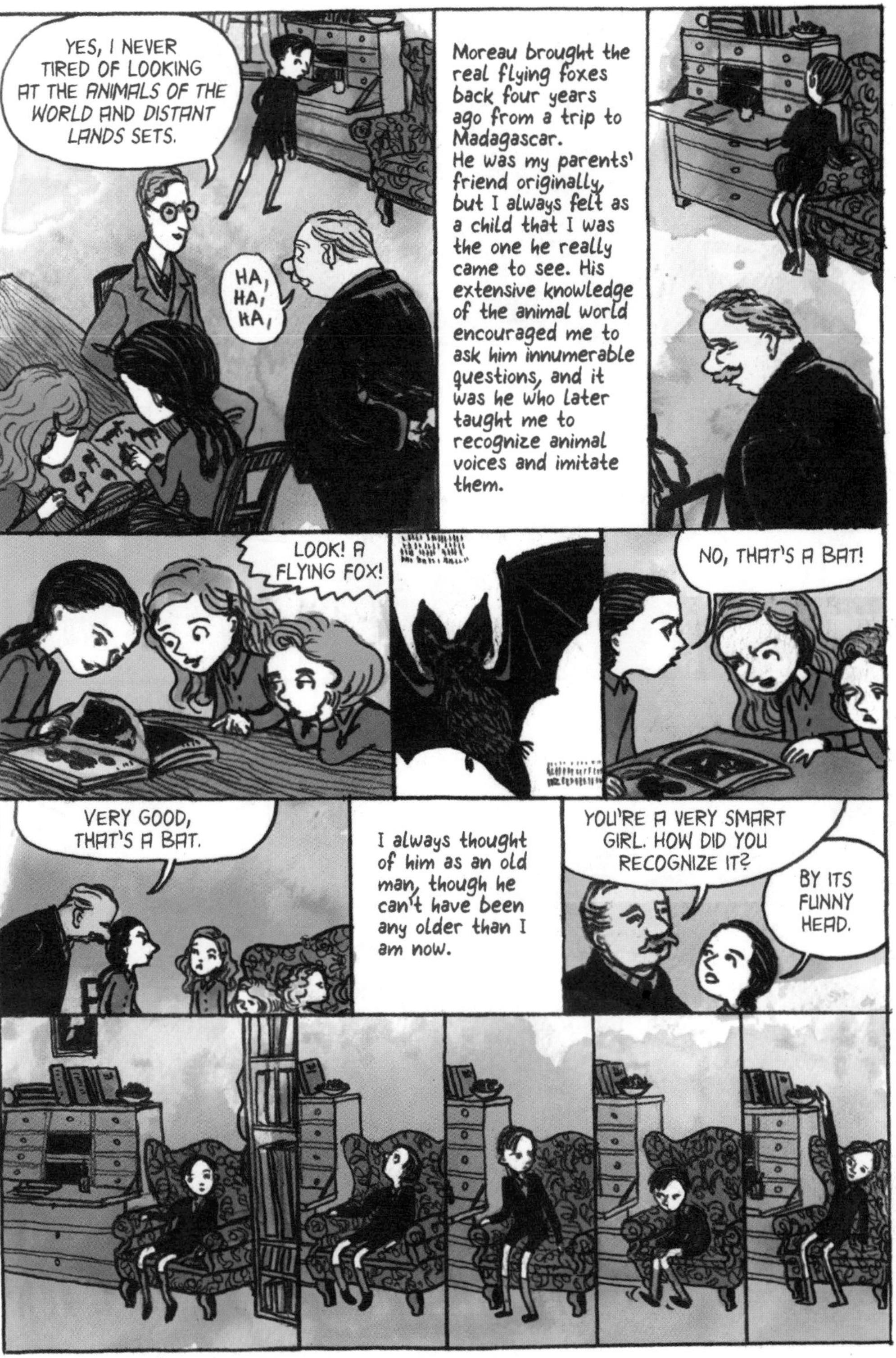
YES, I NEVER TIRED OF LOOKING AT THE ANIMALS OF THE WORLD AND DISTANT LANDS SETS.
HA, HA, HA,
Moreau brought the real flying foxes back four years ago from a trip to Madagascar.
He was my parents' friend originally, but I always felt as a child that I was the one he really came to see. His extensive knowledge of the animal world encouraged me to ask him innumerable questions, and it was he who later taught me to recognize animal voices and imitate them.
LOOK! A FLYING FOX!
NO, THAT'S A BAT!
VERY GOOD, THAT'S A BAT.
I always thought of him as an old man, though he can't have been any older than I am now.
YOU'RE A VERY SMART GIRL. HOW DID YOU RECOGNIZE IT?
BY ITS FUNNY HEAD.

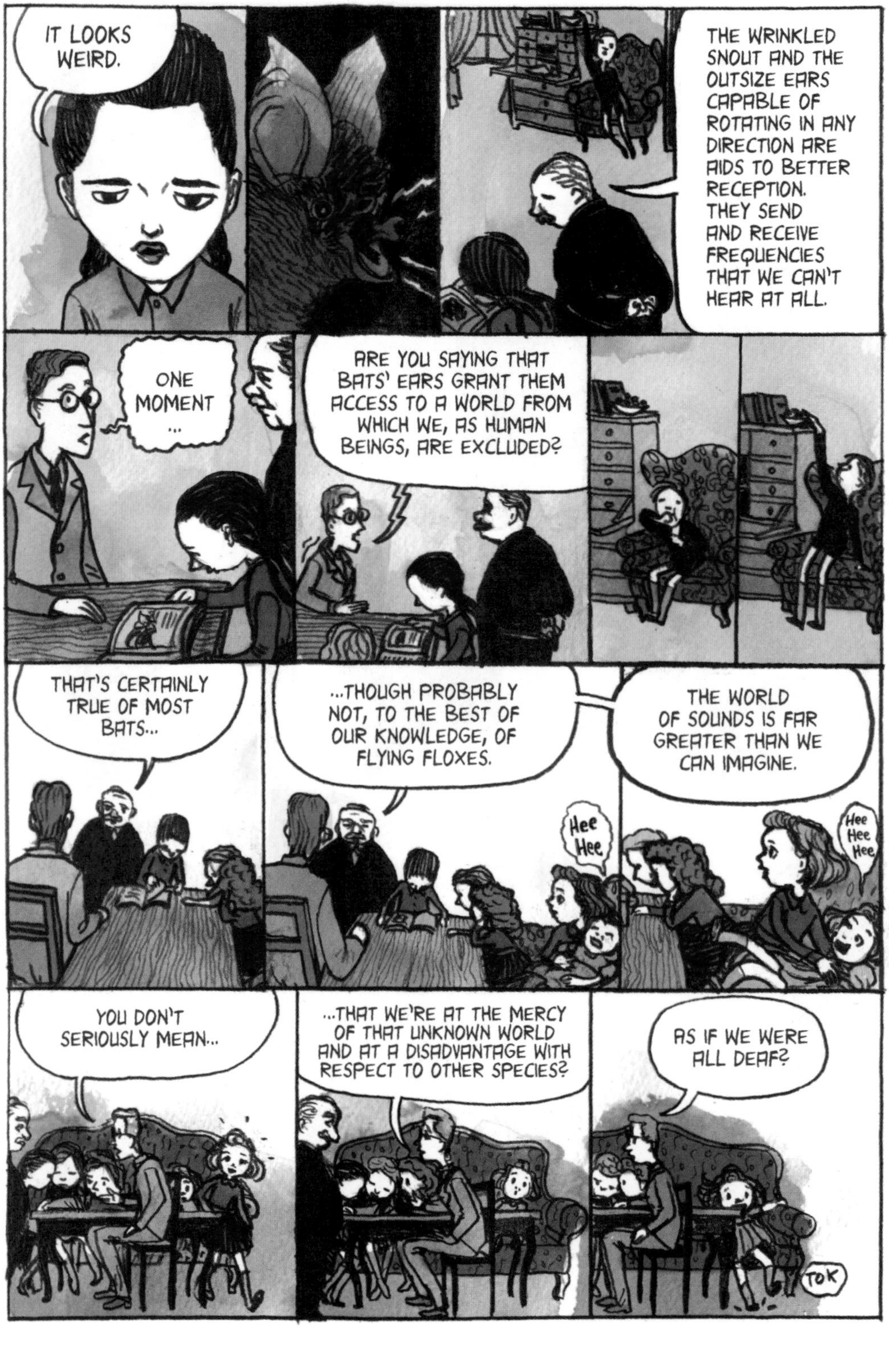
IT LOOKS WEIRD.
THE WRINKLED SNOUT AND THE OUTSIZE EARS CAPABLE OF ROTATING IN ANY DIRECTION ARE AIDS TO BETTER RECEPTION. THEY SEND AND RECEIVE FREQUENCIES THAT WE CAN'T HEAR AT ALL.
ONE MOMENT ...
ARE YOU SAYING THAT BATS' EARS GRANT THEM ACCESS TO A WORLD FROM WHICH WE, AS HUMAN BEINGS, ARE EXCLUDED?
THAT'S CERTAINLY TRUE OF MOST BATS...
...THOUGH PROBABLY NOT, TO THE BEST OF OUR KNOWLEDGE, OF FLYING FLOXES.
Hee Hee
THE WORLD OF SOUNDS IS FAR GREATER THAN WE CAN IMAGINE.
Hee Hee Hee
YOU DON'T SERIOUSLY MEAN...
...THAT WE'RE AT THE MERCY OF THAT UNKNOWN WORLD AND AT A DISADVANTAGE WITH RESPECT TO OTHER SPECIES?
AS IF WE WERE ALL DEAF?
TOK

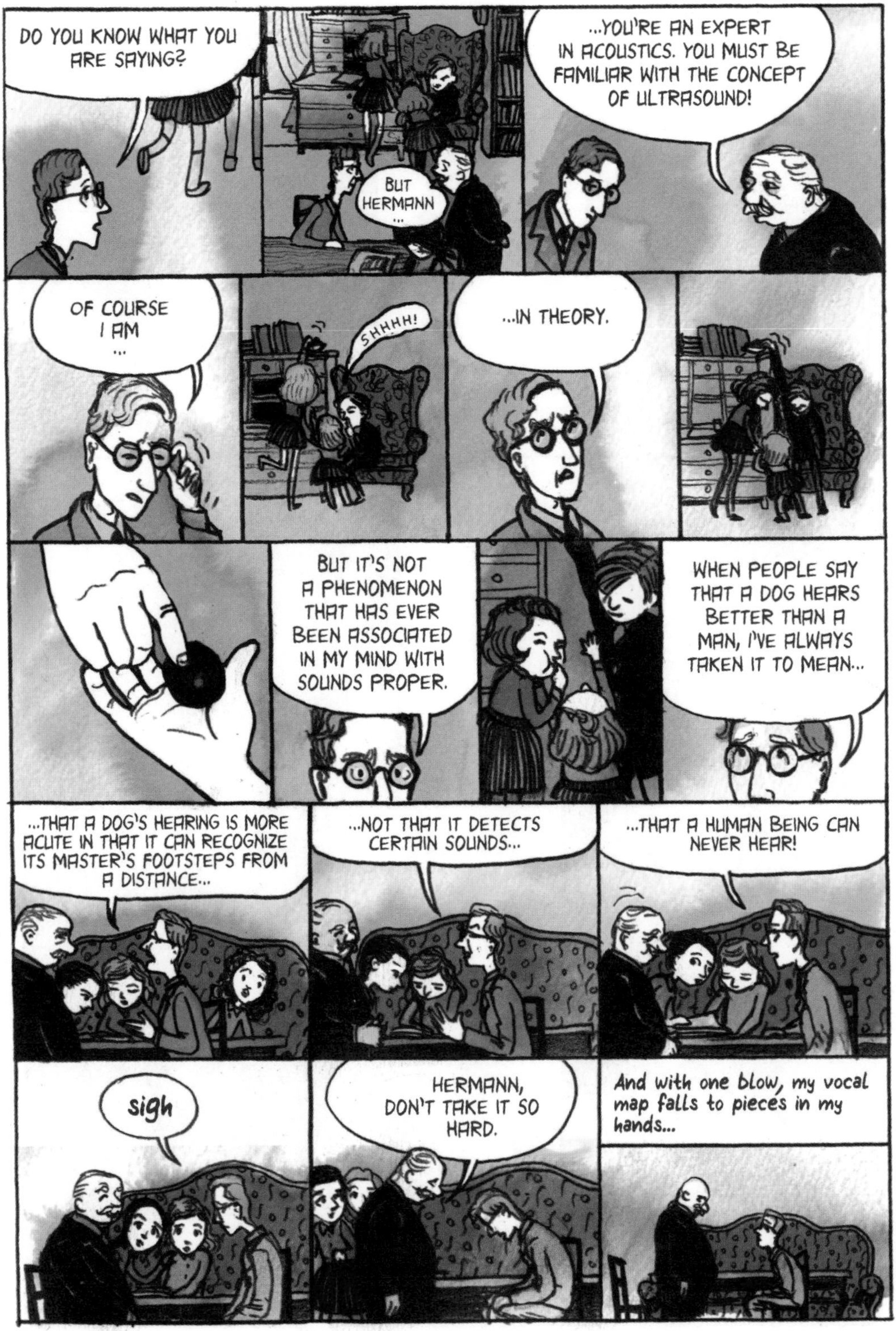
DO YOU KNOW WHAT YOU ARE SAYING?
BUT HERMANN ...
...YOU'RE AN EXPERT IN ACOUSTICS. YOU MUST BE FAMILIAR WITH THE CONCEPT OF ULTRASOUND!
OF COURSE I AM ...
SHHHH!
...IN THEORY.
BUT IT'S NOT A PHENOMENON THAT HAS EVER BEEN ASSOCIATED IN MY MIND WITH SOUNDS PROPER.
WHEN PEOPLE SAY THAT A DOG HEARS BETTER THAN A MAN, I'VE ALWAYS TAKEN IT TO MEAN...
...THAT A DOG'S HEARING IS MORE ACUTE IN THAT IT CAN RECOGNIZE ITS MASTER'S FOOTSTEPS FROM A DISTANCE...
...NOT THAT IT DETECTS CERTAIN SOUNDS...
...THAT A HUMAN BEING CAN NEVER HEAR!
sigh
HERMANN, DON'T TAKE IT SO HARD.
And with one blow, my vocal map falls to pieces in my hands...

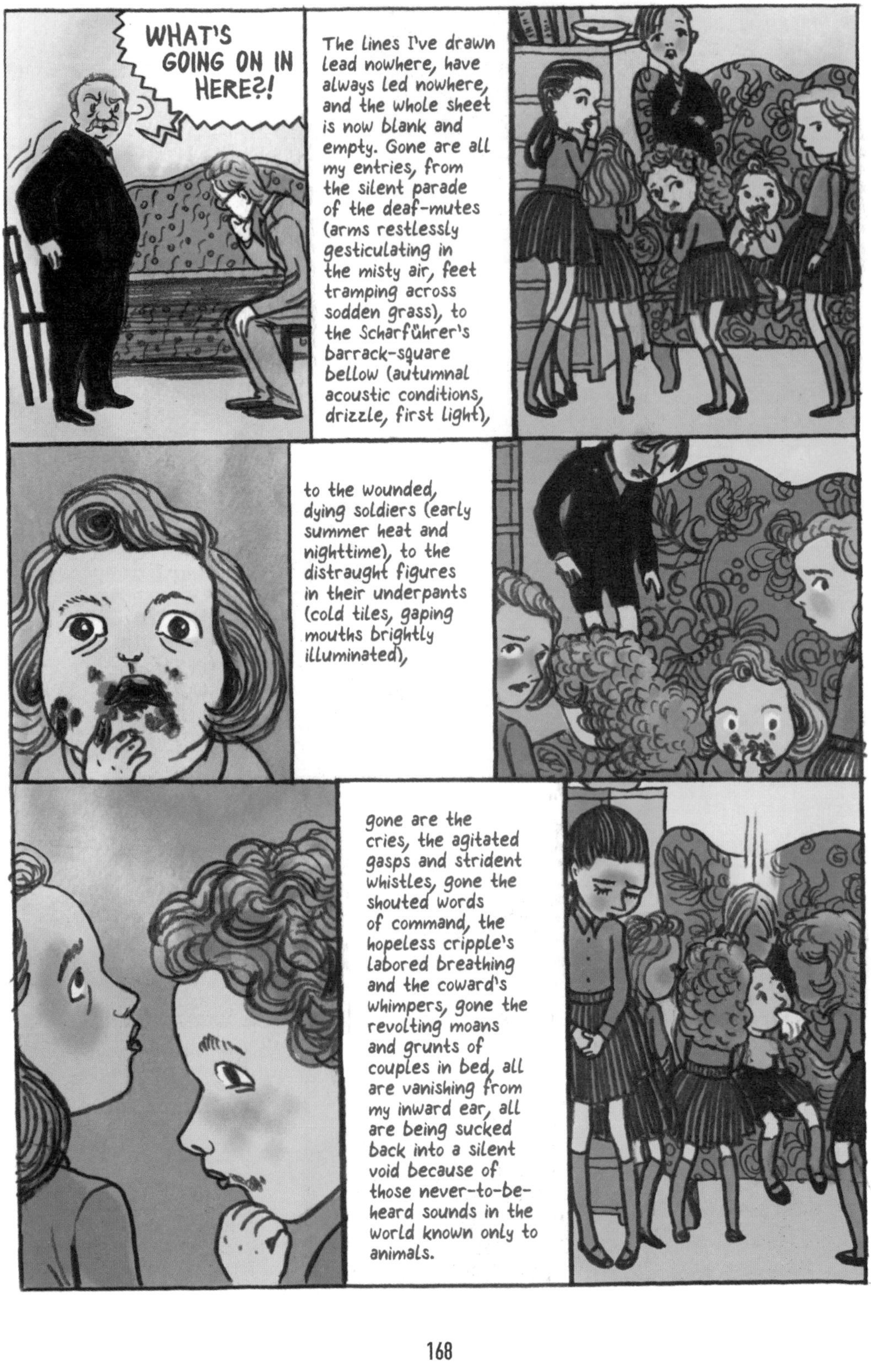
WHAT'S GOING ON IN HERE?!
The lines I've drawn lead nowhere, have always led nowhere, and the whole sheet is now blank and empty. Gone are all my entries, from the silent parade of the deaf-mutes (arms restlessly gesticulating in the misty air, feet tramping across sodden grass), to the Scharführer's barrack-square bellow (autumnal acoustic conditions, drizzle, first light),
to the wounded, dying soldiers (early summer heat and nighttime), to the distraught figures in their underpants (cold tiles, gaping mouths brightly illuminated),
gone are the cries, the agitated gasps and strident whistles, gone the shouted words of command, the hopeless cripple's labored breathing and the coward's whimpers, gone the revolting moans and grunts of couples in bed, all are vanishing from my inward ear, all are being sucked back into a silent void because of those never-to-be-heard sounds in the world known only to animals.

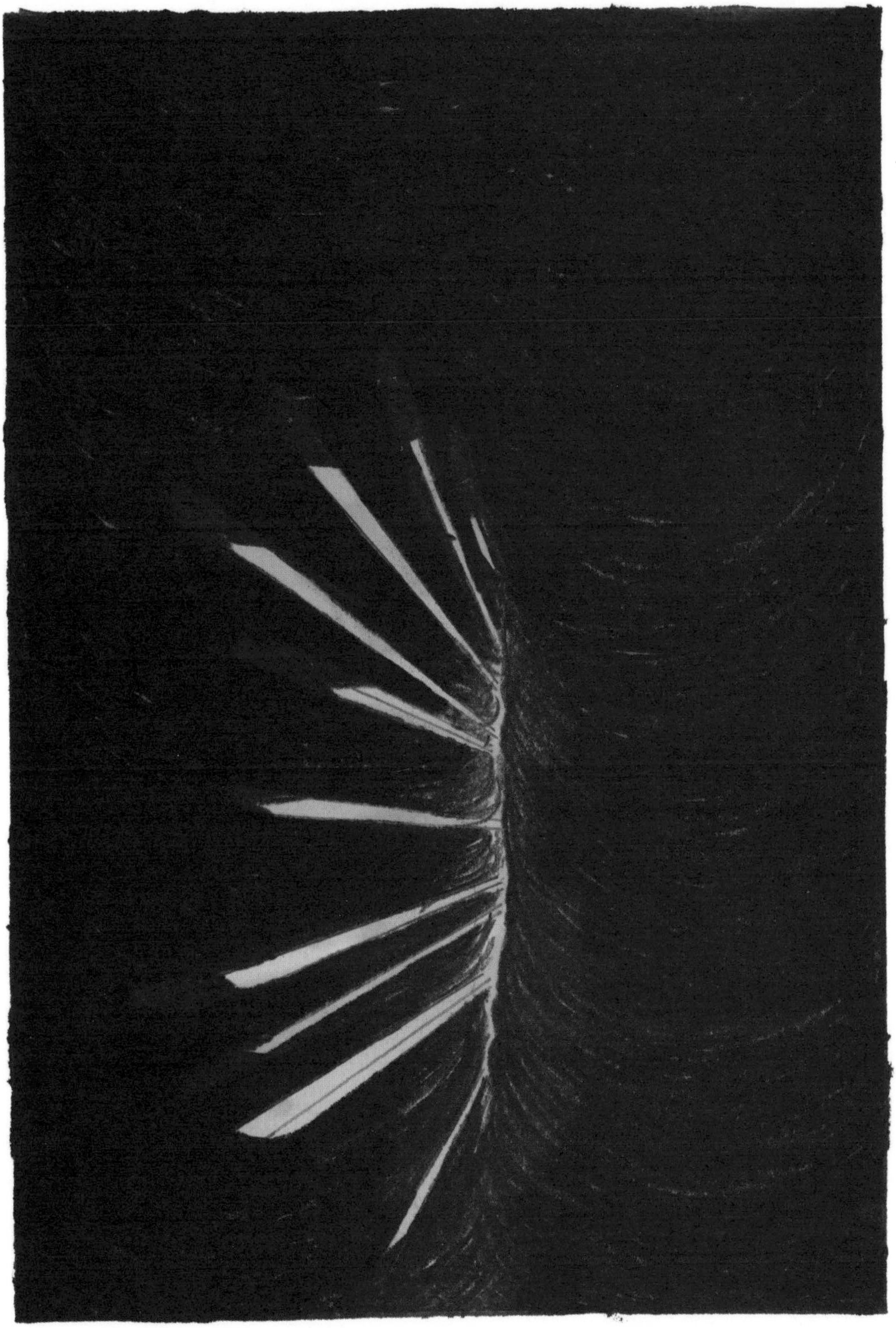

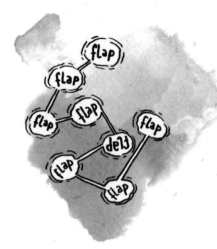

IV.

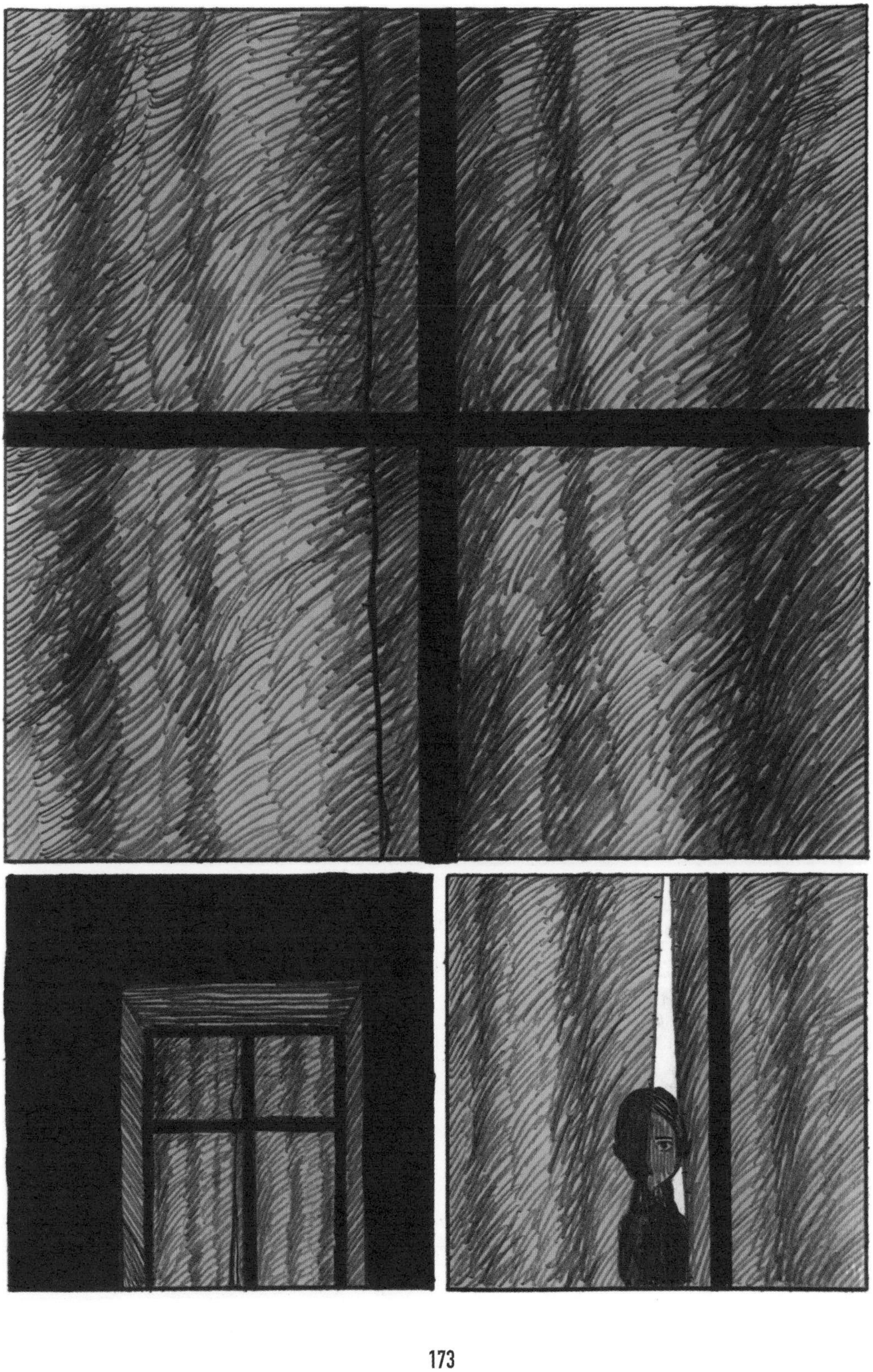

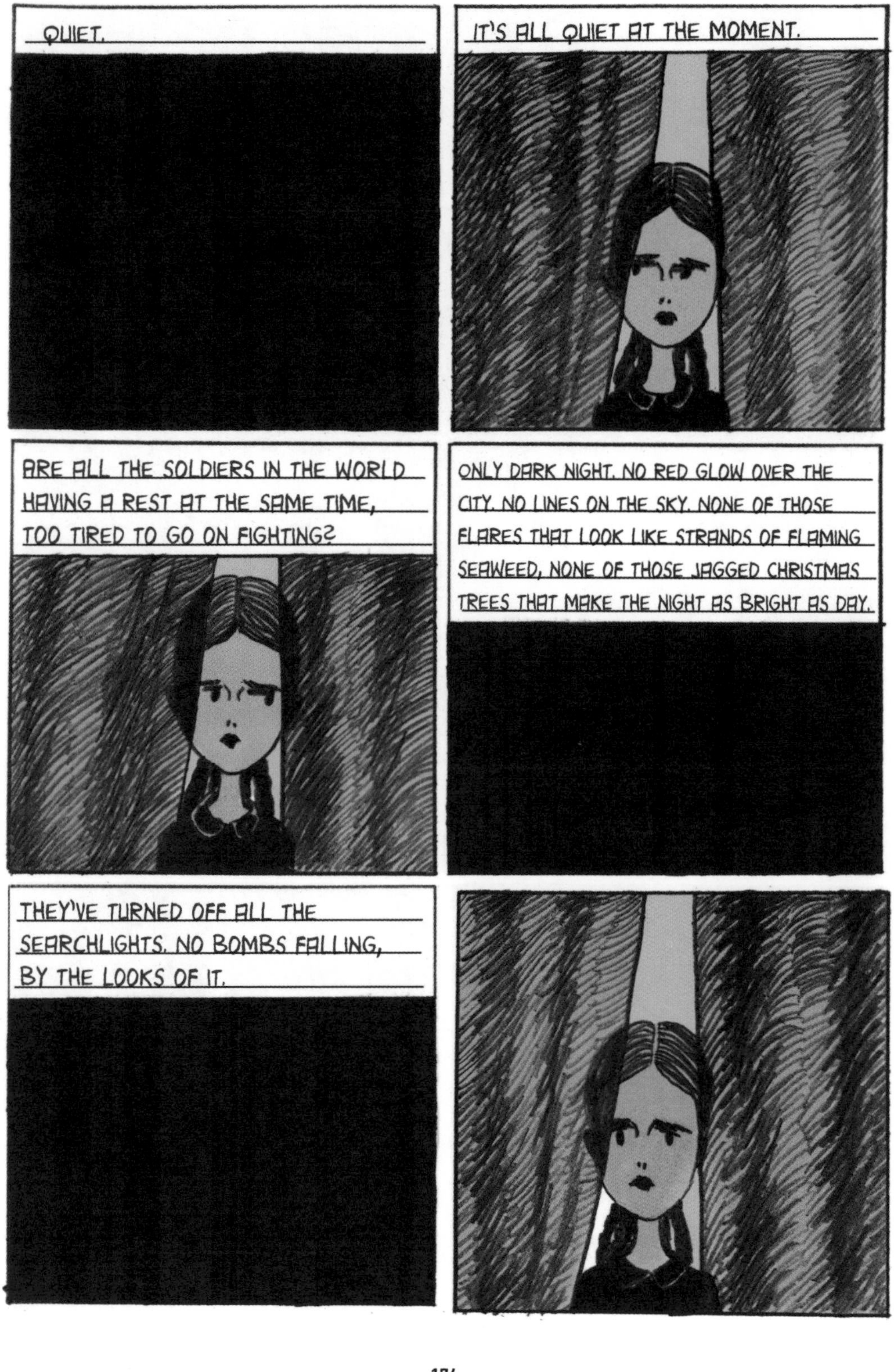
QUIET.
IT'S ALL QUIET AT THE MOMENT.
ARE ALL THE SOLDIERS IN THE WORLD HAVING A REST AT THE SAME TIME, TOO TIRED TO GO ON FIGHTING?
ONLY DARK NIGHT. NO RED GLOW OVER THE CITY. NO LINES ON THE SKY. NONE OF THOSE FLARES THAT LOOK LIKE STRANDS OF FLAMING SEAWEED, NONE OF THOSE JAGGED CHRISTMAS TREES THAT MAKE THE NIGHT AS BRIGHT AS DAY.
THEY'VE TURNED OFF ALL THE SEARCHLIGHTS. NO BOMBS FALLING, BY THE LOOKS OF IT.

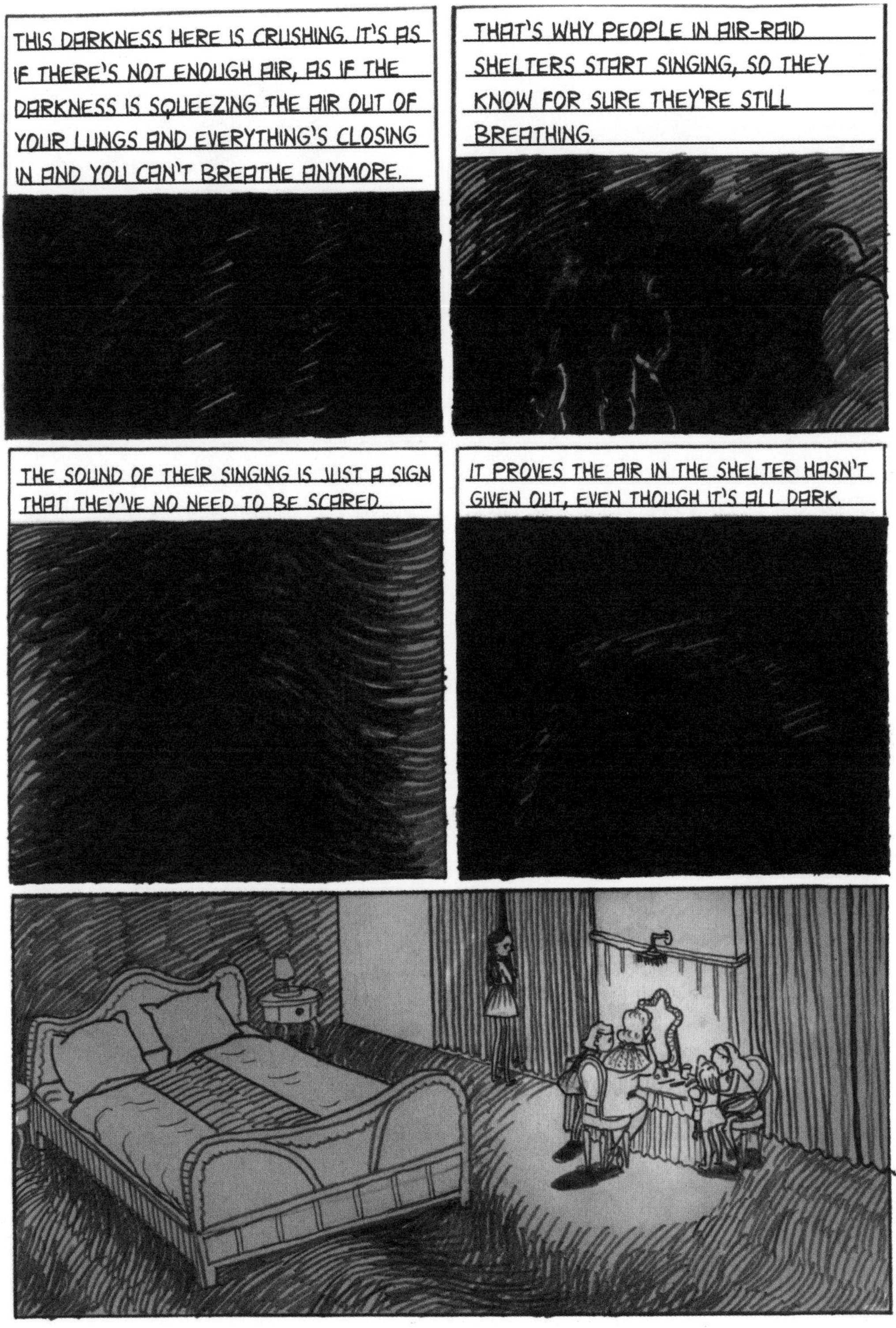

THIS DARKNESS HERE IS CRUSHING. IT'S AS IF THERE'S NOT ENOUGH AIR, AS IF THE DARKNESS IS SQUEEZING THE AIR OUT OF YOUR LUNGS AND EVERYTHING'S CLOSING IN AND YOU CAN'T BREATHE ANYMORE.
THAT'S WHY PEOPLE IN AIR-RAID SHELTERS START SINGING, SO THEY KNOW FOR SURE THEY'RE STILL BREATHING.
THE SOUND OF THEIR SINGING IS JUST A SIGN THAT THEY'VE NO NEED TO BE SCARED.
IT PROVES THE AIR IN THE SHELTER HASN'T GIVEN OUT, EVEN THOUGH IT'S ALL DARK.

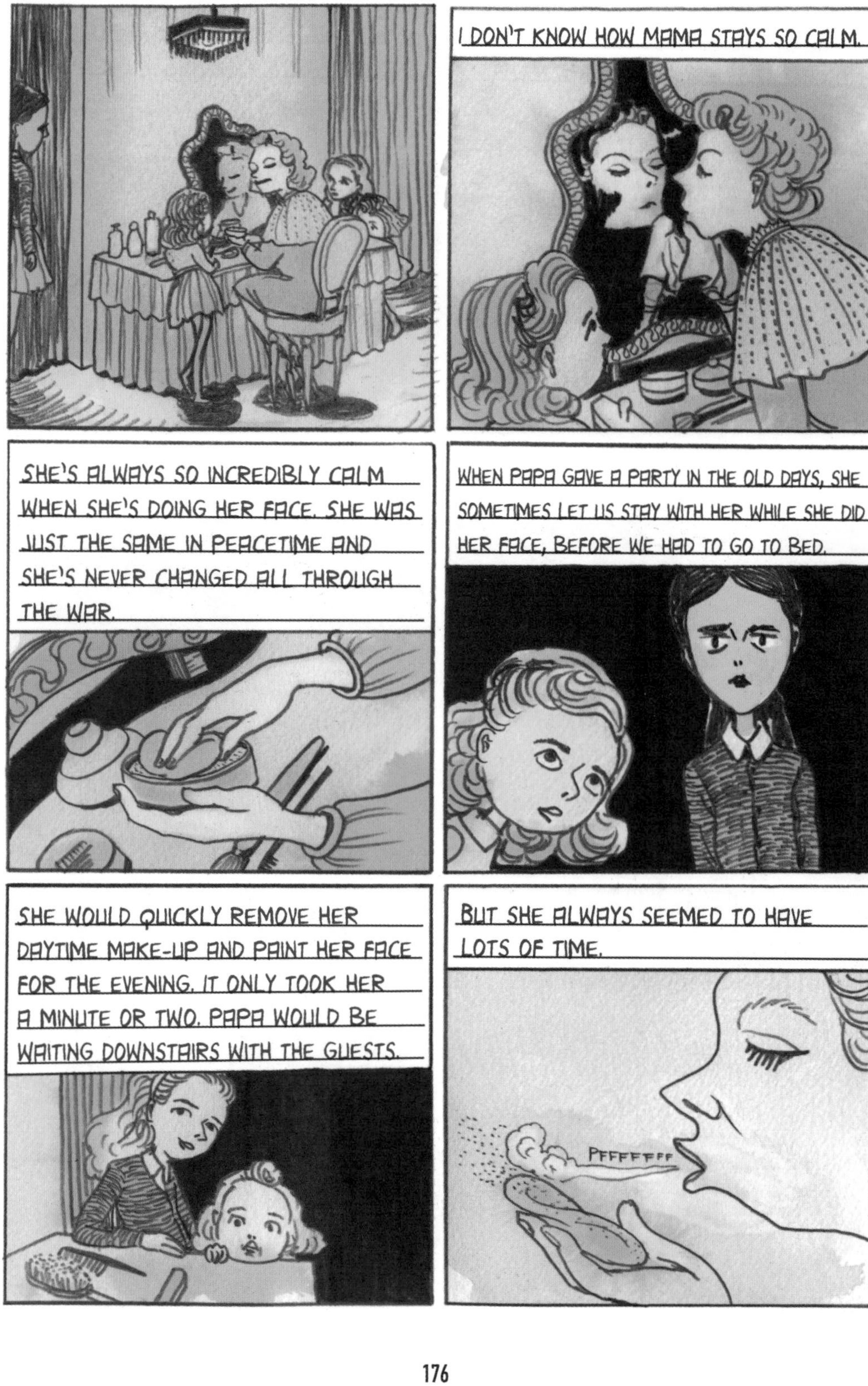
I DON'T KNOW HOW MAMA STAYS SO CALM.
SHE'S ALWAYS SO INCREDIBLY CALM WHEN SHE'S DOING HER FACE. SHE WAS JUST THE SAME IN PEACETIME AND SHE'S NEVER CHANGED ALL THROUGH THE WAR.
WHEN PAPA GAVE A PARTY IN THE OLD DAYS, SHE SOMETIMES LET US STAY WITH HER WHILE SHE DID HER FACE, BEFORE WE HAD TO GO TO BED.
SHE WOULD QUICKLY REMOVE HER DAYTIME MAKE-UP AND PAINT HER FACE FOR THE EVENING. IT ONLY TOOK HER A MINUTE OR TWO. PAPA WOULD BE WAITING DOWNSTAIRS WITH THE GUESTS.
BUT SHE ALWAYS SEEMED TO HAVE LOTS OF TIME.
PFFFFFFF

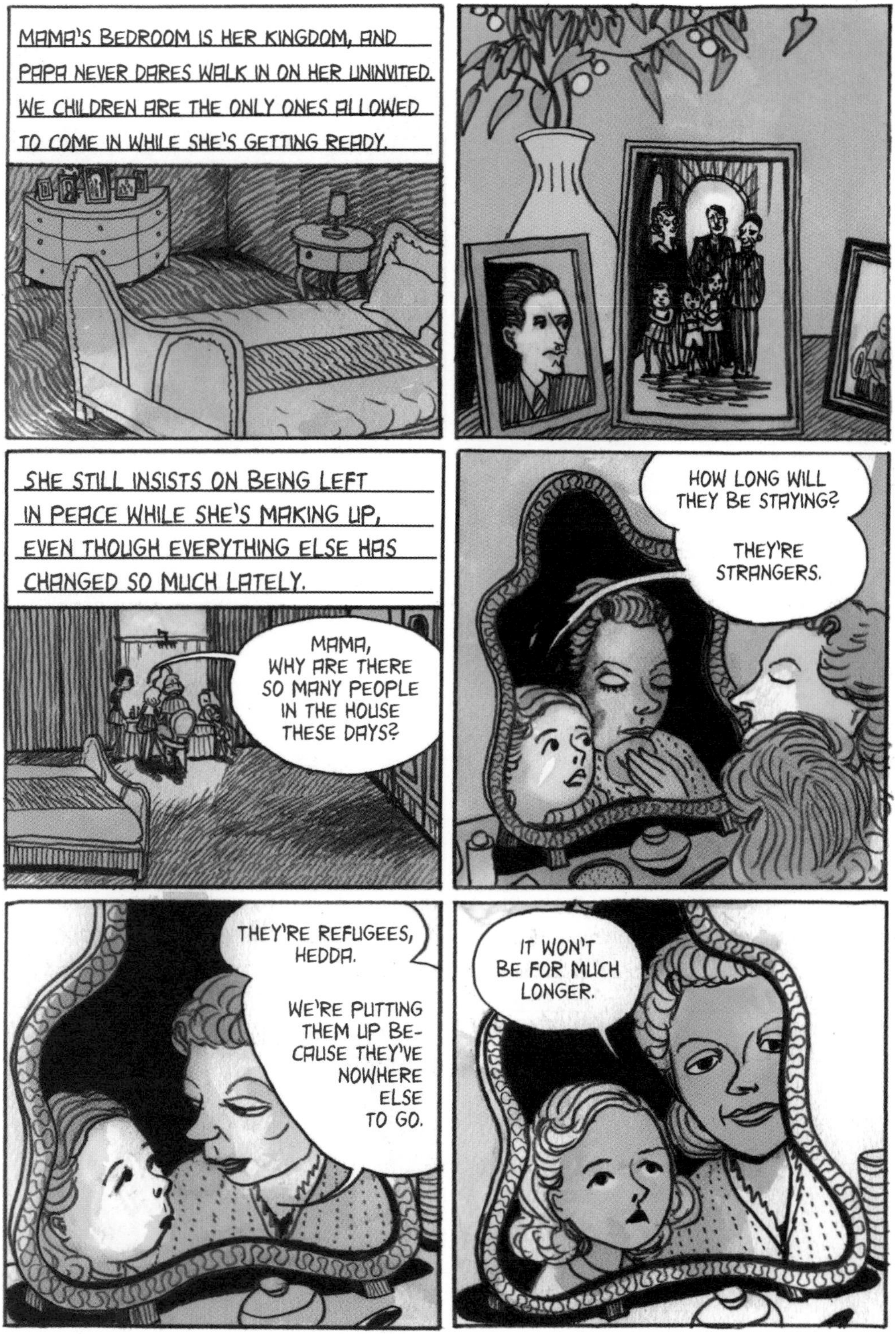
MAMA'S BEDROOM IS HER KINGDOM, AND PAPA NEVER DARES WALK IN ON HER UNINVITED. WE CHILDREN ARE THE ONLY ONES ALLOWED TO COME IN WHILE SHE'S GETTING READY.
SHE STILL INSISTS ON BEING LEFT IN PEACE WHILE SHE'S MAKING UP, EVEN THOUGH EVERYTHING ELSE HAS CHANGED SO MUCH LATELY.
MAMA, WHY ARE THERE SO MANY PEOPLE IN THE HOUSE THESE DAYS?
HOW LONG WILL THEY BE STAYING?
THEY'RE STRANGERS.
THEY'RE REFUGEES, HEDDA.
WE'RE PUTTING THEM UP BE-CAUSE THEY'VE NOWHERE ELSE TO GO.
IT WON'T BE FOR MUCH LONGER.

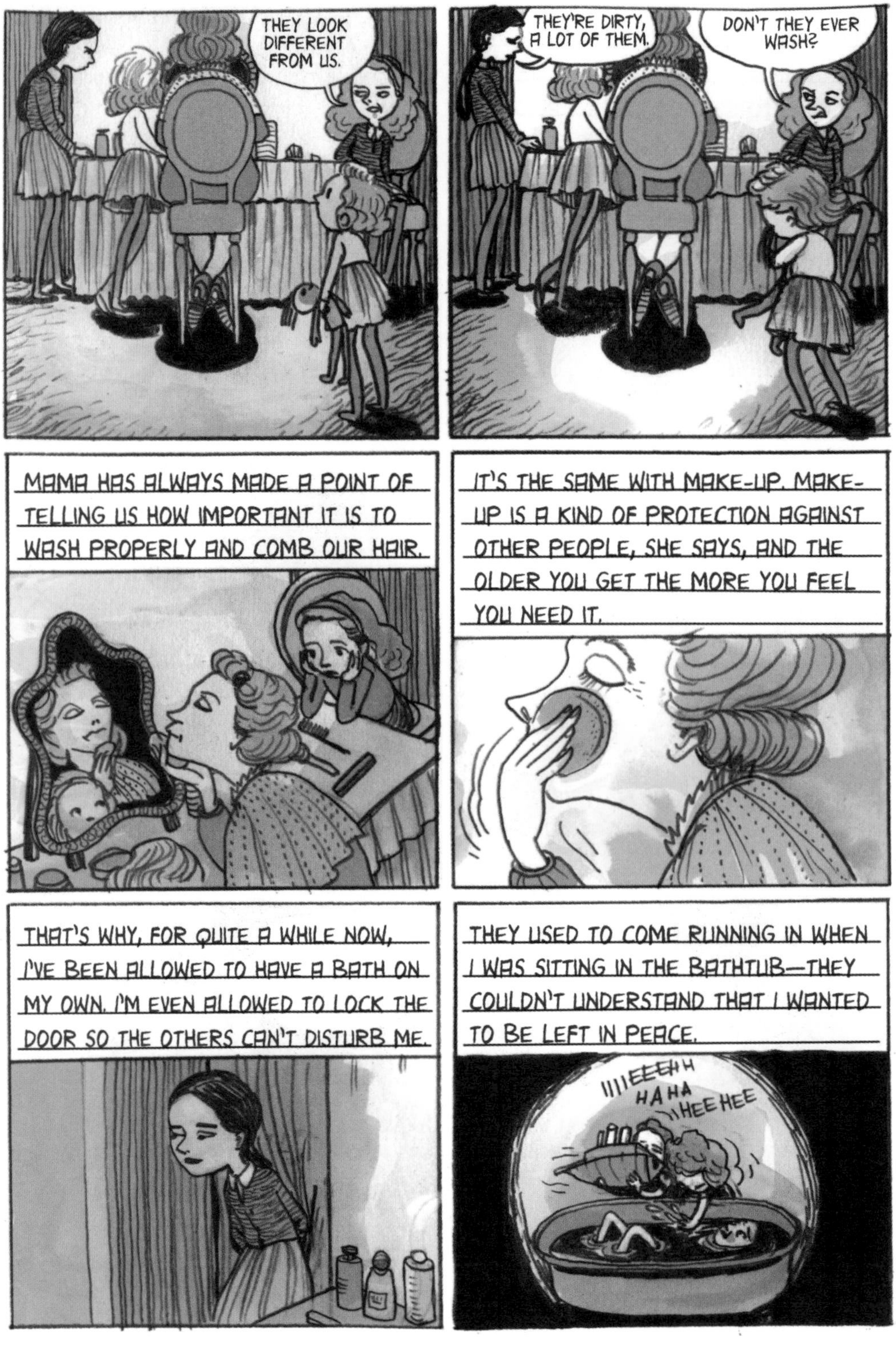
THEY LOOK DIFFERENT FROM US.
THEY'RE DIRTY, A LOT OF THEM.
DON'T THEY EVER WASH?
MAMA HAS ALWAYS MADE A POINT OF TELLING US HOW IMPORTANT IT IS TO WASH PROPERLY AND COMB OUR HAIR.
IT'S THE SAME WITH MAKE-UP. MAKE-UP IS A KIND OF PROTECTION AGAINST OTHER PEOPLE, SHE SAYS, AND THE OLDER YOU GET THE MORE YOU FEEL YOU NEED IT.
THAT'S WHY, FOR QUITE A WHILE NOW, I'VE BEEN ALLOWED TO HAVE A BATH ON MY OWN. I'M EVEN ALLOWED TO LOCK THE DOOR SO THE OTHERS CAN'T DISTURB ME.
THEY USED TO COME RUNNING IN WHEN I WAS SITTING IN THE BATHTUB—THEY COULDN'T UNDERSTAND THAT I WANTED TO BE LEFT IN PEACE.
HAHA
HEE HEE

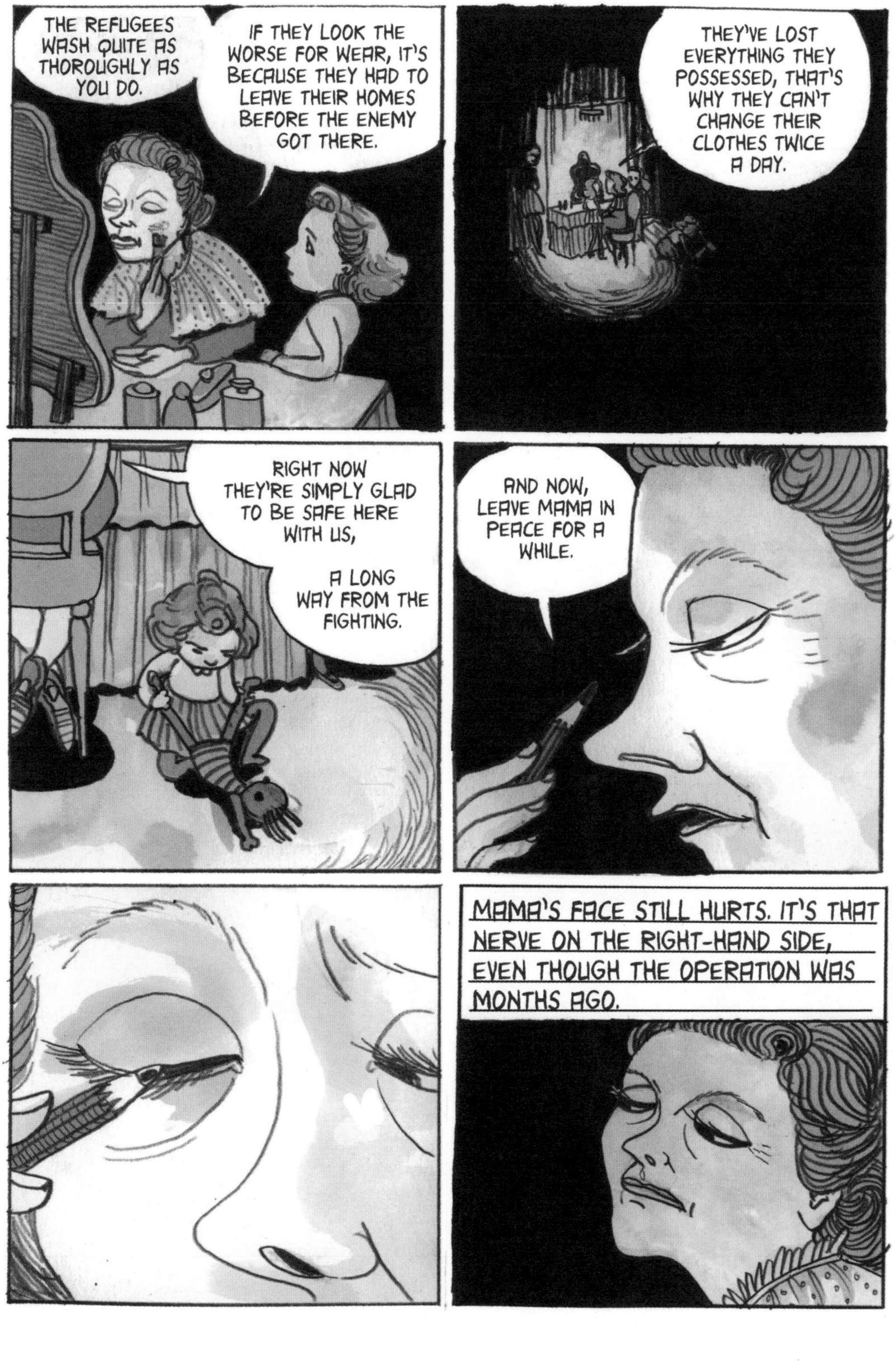
THE REFUGEES WASH QUITE AS THOROUGHLY AS YOU DO.
IF THEY LOOK THE WORSE FOR WEAR, IT'S BECAUSE THEY HAD TO LEAVE THEIR HOMES BEFORE THE ENEMY GOT THERE.
THEY'VE LOST EVERYTHING THEY POSSESSED, THAT'S WHY THEY CAN'T CHANGE THEIR CLOTHES TWICE A DAY.
RIGHT NOW THEY'RE SIMPLY GLAD TO BE SAFE HERE WITH US,
A LONG WAY FROM THE FIGHTING.
AND NOW, LEAVE MAMA IN PEACE FOR A WHILE.
MAMA'S FACE STILL HURTS. IT'S THAT NERVE ON THE RIGHT-HAND SIDE, EVEN THOUGH THE OPERATION WAS MONTHS AGO.

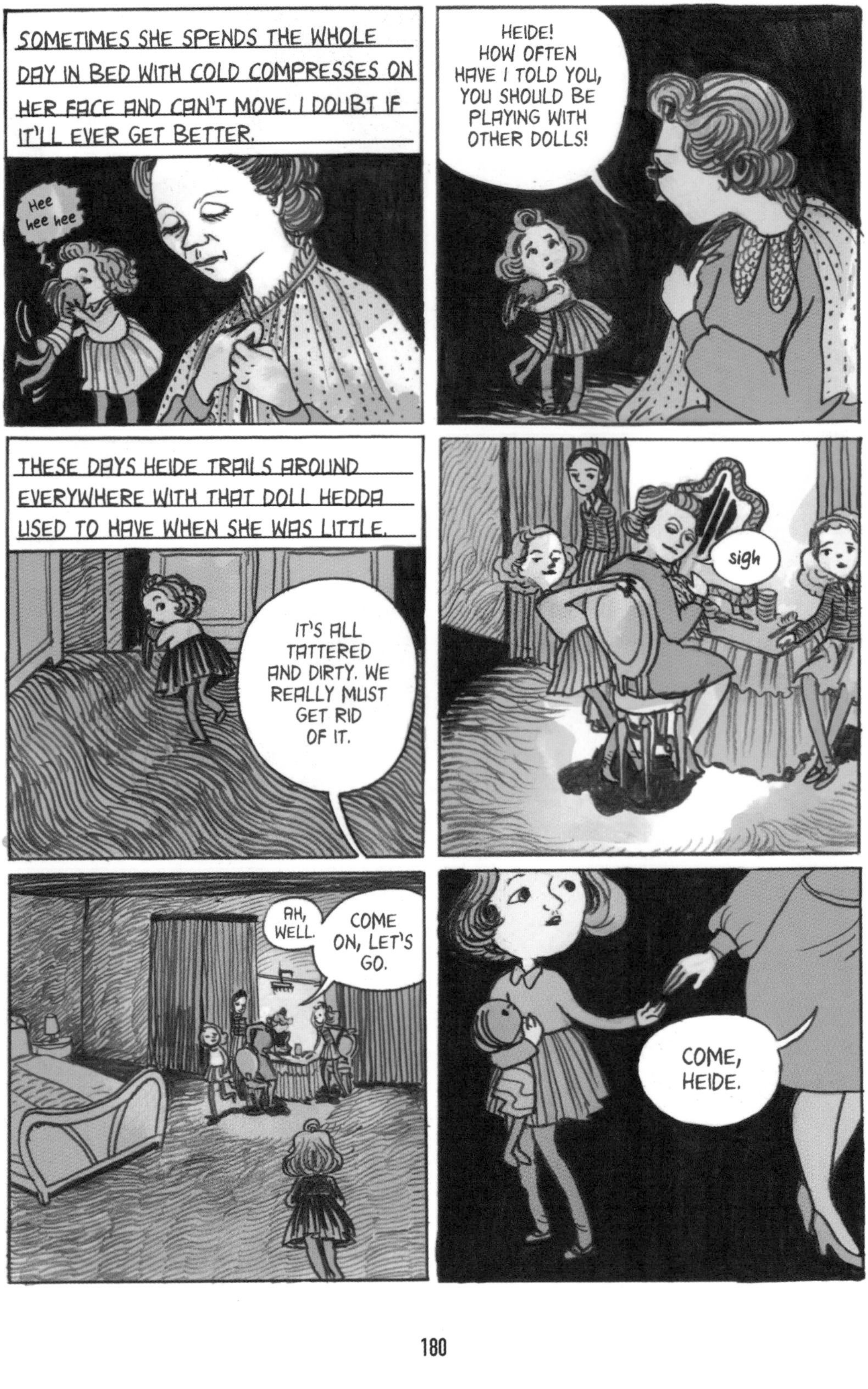
SOMETIMES SHE SPENDS THE WHOLE DAY IN BED WITH COLD COMPRESSES ON HER FACE AND CAN'T MOVE. I DOUBT IF IT'LL EVER GET BETTER.
Hee hee hee
HEIDE! HOW OFTEN HAVE I TOLD YOU, YOU SHOULD BE PLAYING WITH OTHER DOLLS!
THESE DAYS HEIDE TRAILS AROUND EVERYWHERE WITH THAT DOLL HEDDA USED TO HAVE WHEN SHE WAS LITTLE.
IT'S ALL TATTERED AND DIRTY. WE REALLY MUST GET RID OF IT.
sigh
AH, WELL.
COME ON, LET'S GO.
COME, HEIDE.

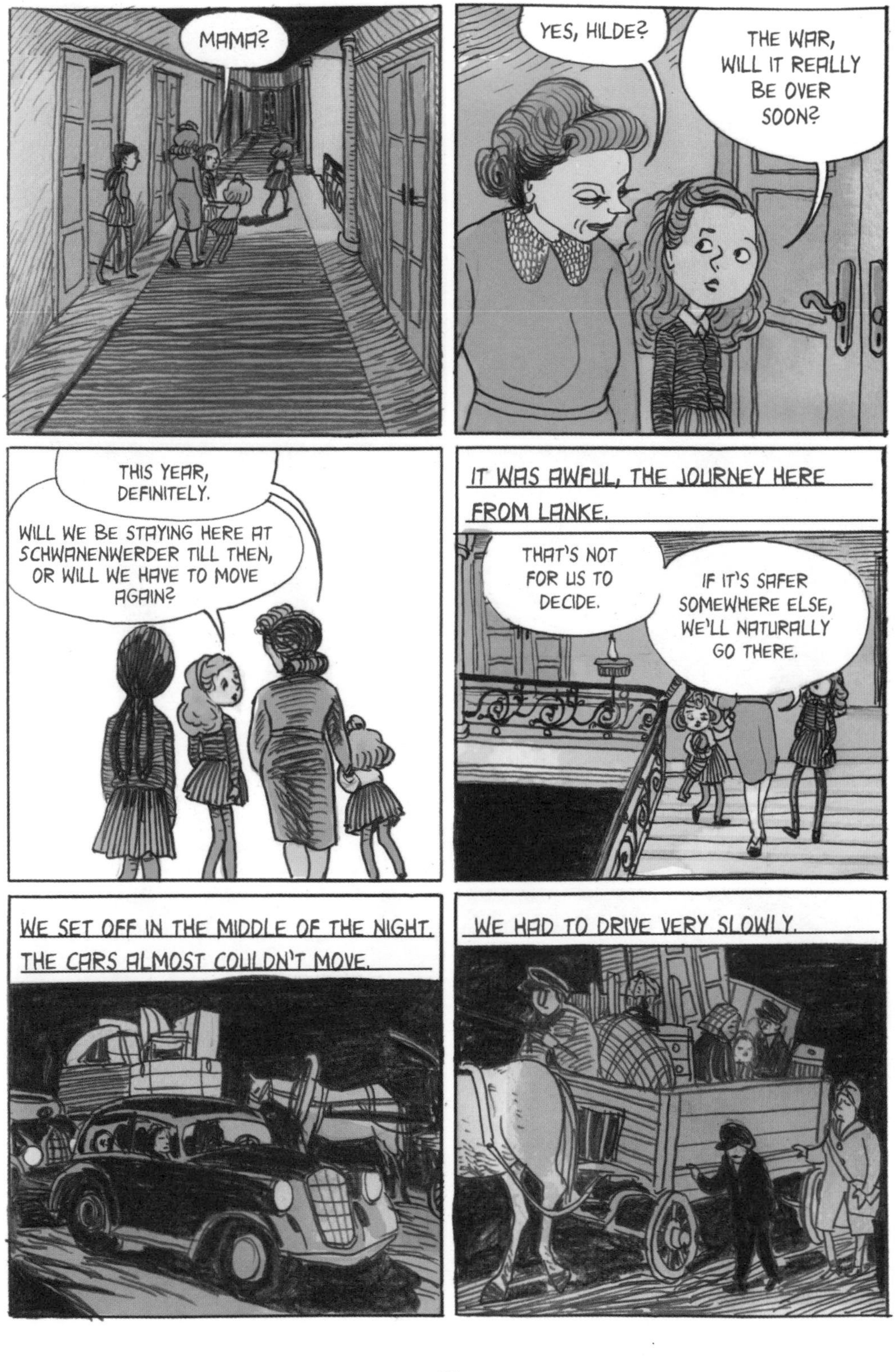
MAMA?
YES, HILDE?
THE WAR, WILL IT REALLY BE OVER SOON?
THIS YEAR, DEFINITELY.
WILL WE BE STAYING HERE AT SCHWANENWERDER TILL THEN, OR WILL WE HAVE TO MOVE AGAIN?
IT WAS AWFUL, THE JOURNEY HERE FROM LANKE.
THAT'S NOT FOR US TO DECIDE.
IF IT'S SAFER SOMEWHERE ELSE, WE'LL NATURALLY GO THERE.
WE SET OFF IN THE MIDDLE OF THE NIGHT. THE CARS ALMOST COULDN'T MOVE.
WE HAD TO DRIVE VERY SLOWLY.

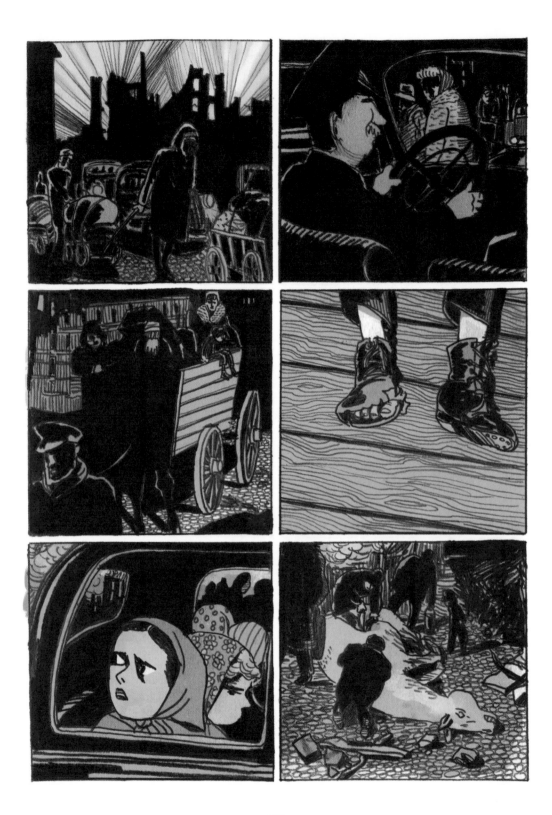

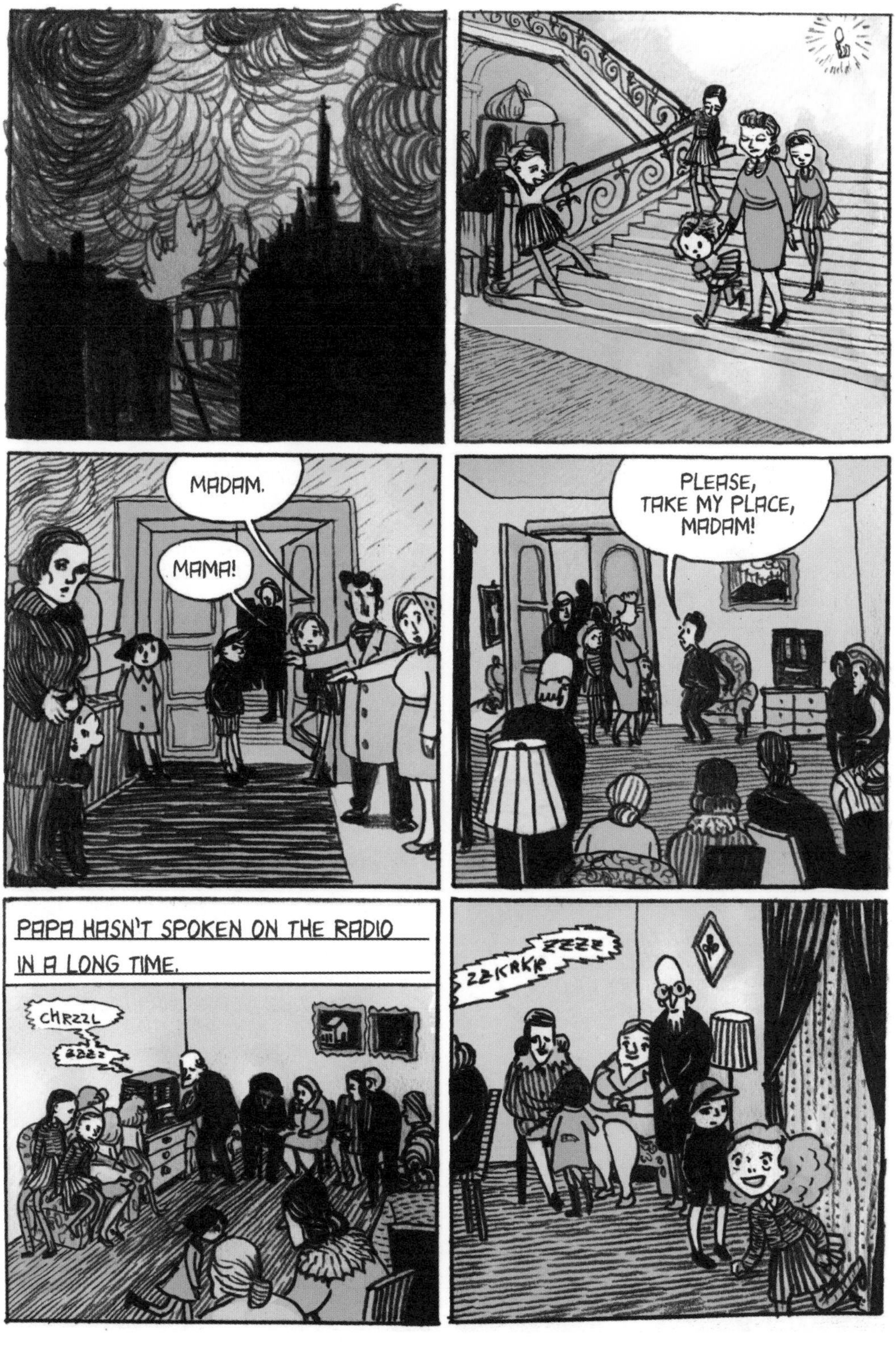
MADAM.
MAMA!
PLEASE, TAKE MY PLACE, MADAM!
PAPA HASN'T SPOKEN ON THE RADIO IN A LONG TIME.
CHRZZL
ZZZZ
ZZKRKR
ZZZZ

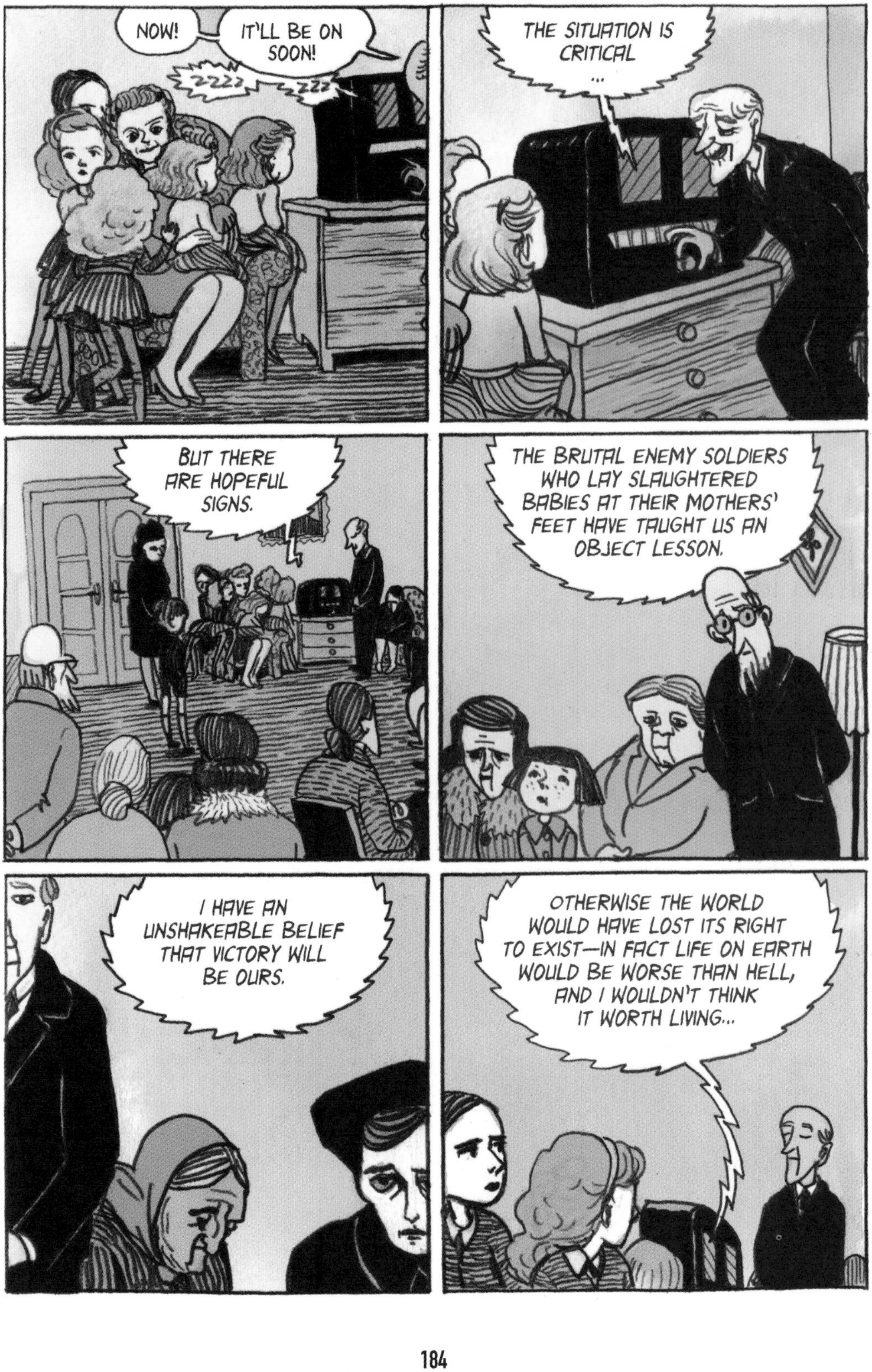
NOW!
IT'LL BE ON SOON!
ZZZZ
ZZZ
THE SITUATION IS CRITICAL ...
BUT THERE ARE HOPEFUL SIGNS.
THE BRUTAL ENEMY SOLDIERS WHO LAY SLAUGHTERED BABIES AT THEIR MOTHERS' FEET HAVE TAUGHT US AN OBJECT LESSON.
I HAVE AN UNSHAKEABLE BELIEF THAT VICTORY WILL BE OURS.
OTHERWISE THE WORLD WOULD HAVE LOST ITS RIGHT TO EXIST—IN FACT LIFE ON EARTH WOULD BE WORSE THAN HELL, AND I WOULDN'T THINK IT WORTH LIVING...

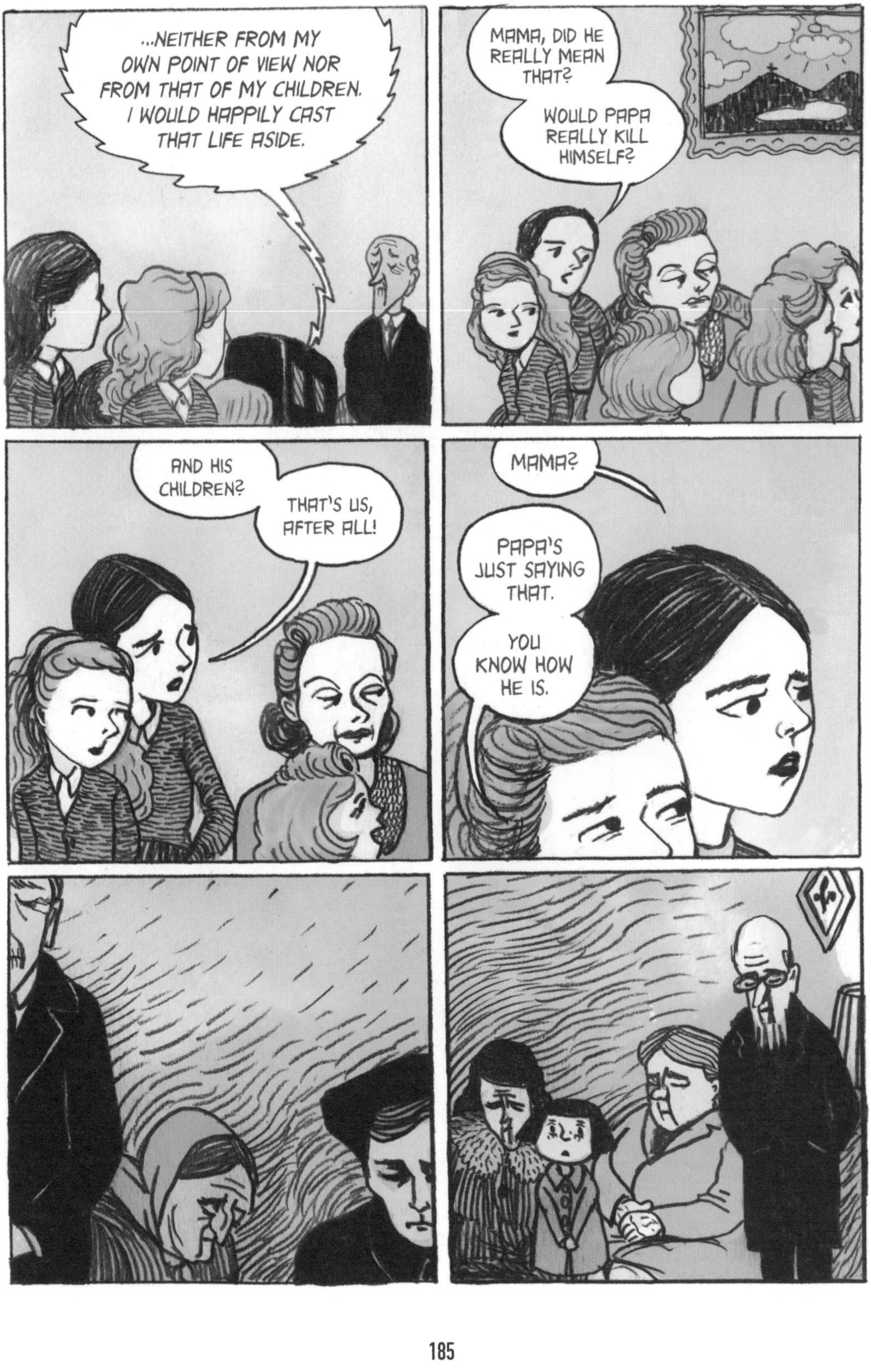
...NEITHER FROM MY OWN POINT OF VIEW NOR FROM THAT OF MY CHILDREN. I WOULD HAPPILY CAST THAT LIFE ASIDE.
MAMA, DID HE REALLY MEAN THAT?
WOULD PAPA REALLY KILL HIMSELF?
AND HIS CHILDREN?
THAT'S US, AFTER ALL!
MAMA?
PAPA'S JUST SAYING THAT.
YOU KNOW HOW HE IS.

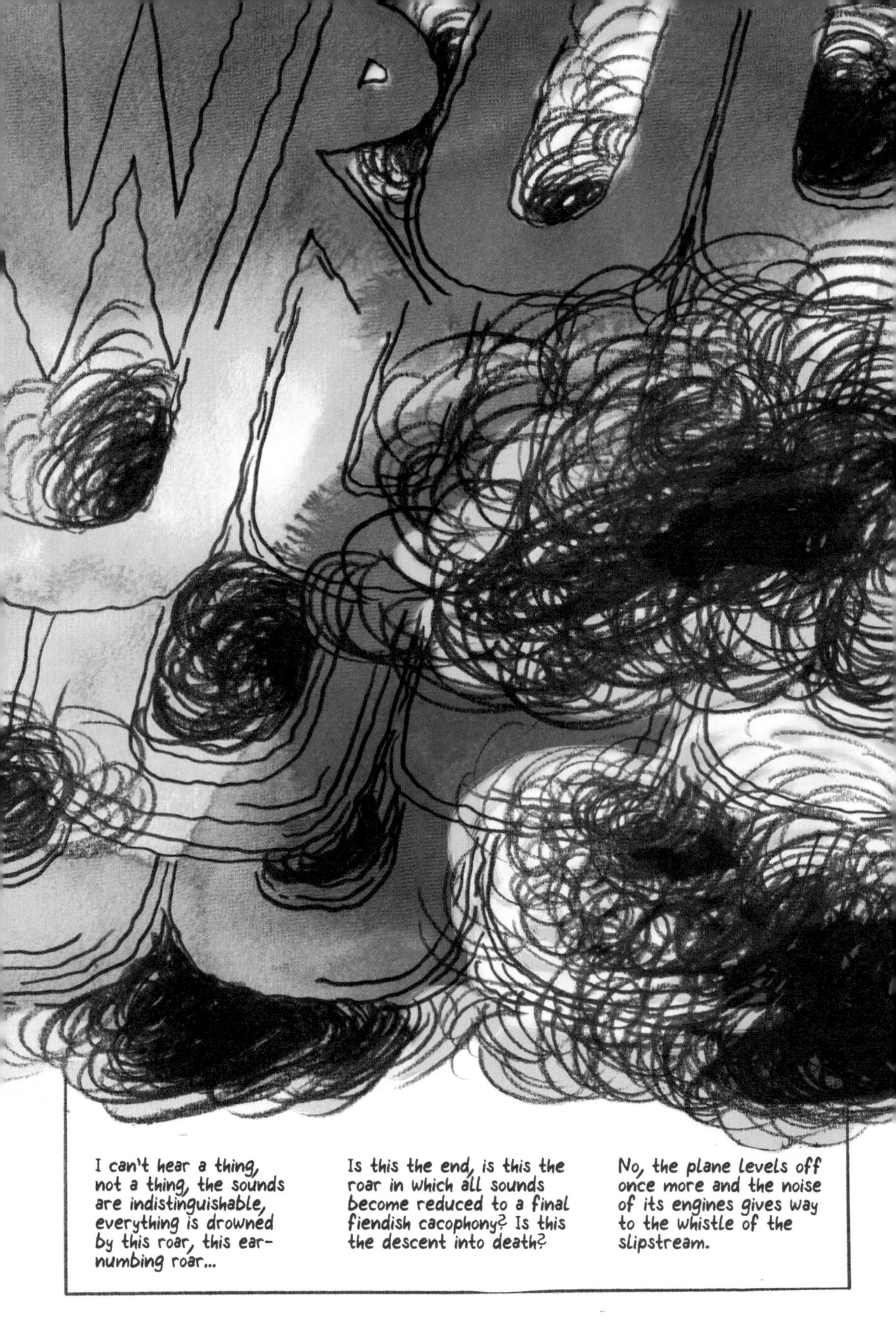
I can't hear a thing, not a thing, the sounds are indistinguishable, everything is drowned by this roar, this ear-numbing roar...
Is this the end, is this the roar in which all sounds become reduced to a final fiendish cacophony? Is this the descent into death?
No, the plane levels off once more and the noise of its engines gives way to the whistle of the slipstream.

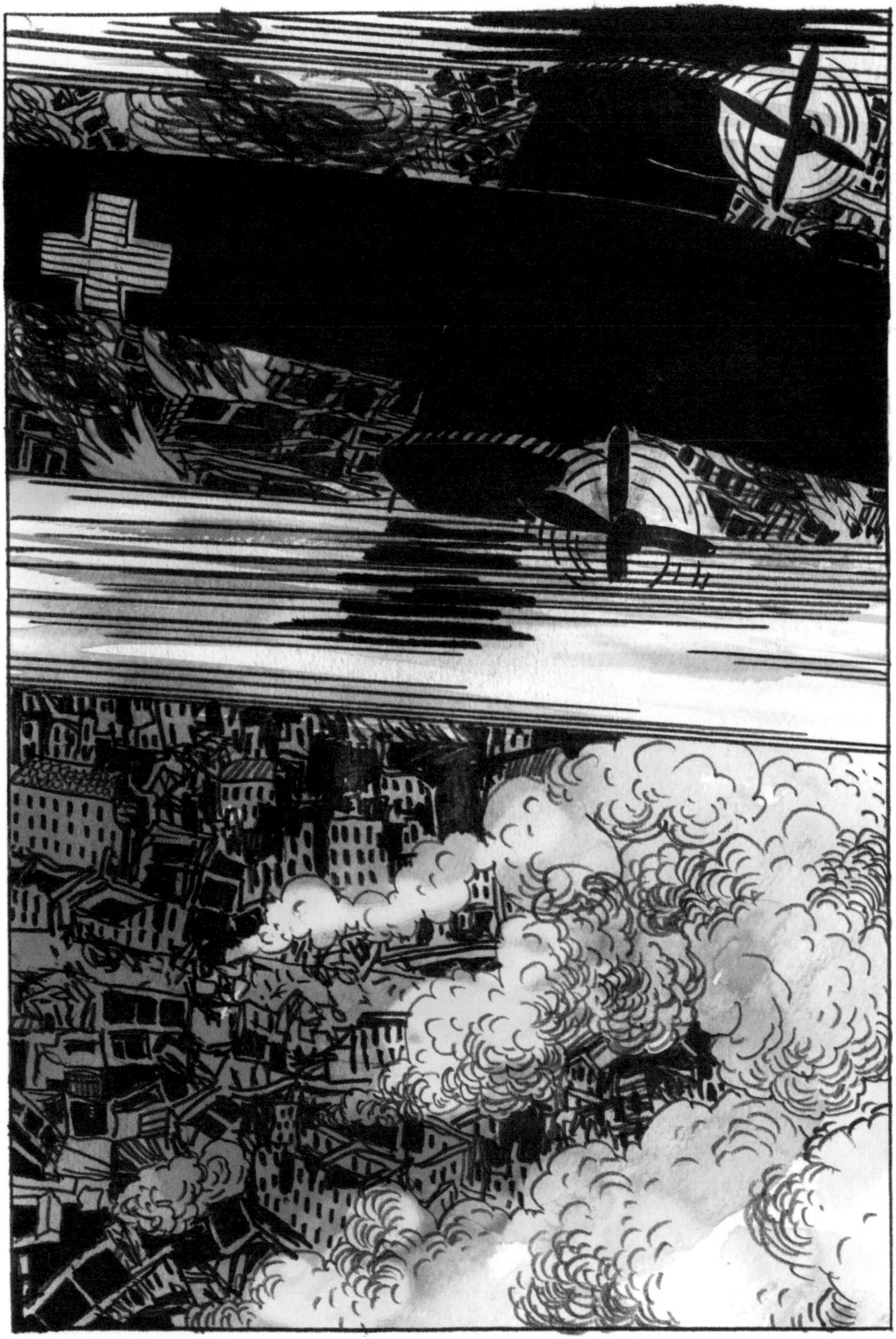

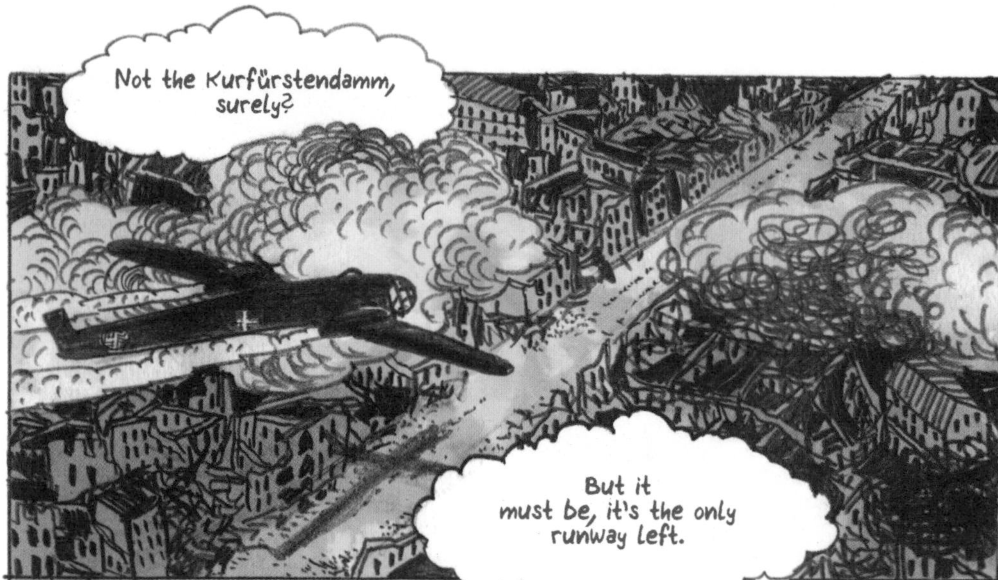
Not the Kurfürstendamm, surely?
But it must be, it's the only runway left.

Every tree in the avenue has been felled and the tramlines are obscured by a layer of bulldozed, steamrollered rubble. One detail after another flashes past at lightning speed.

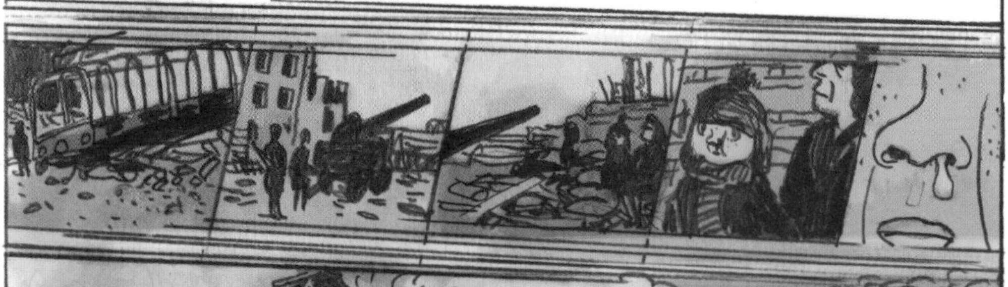

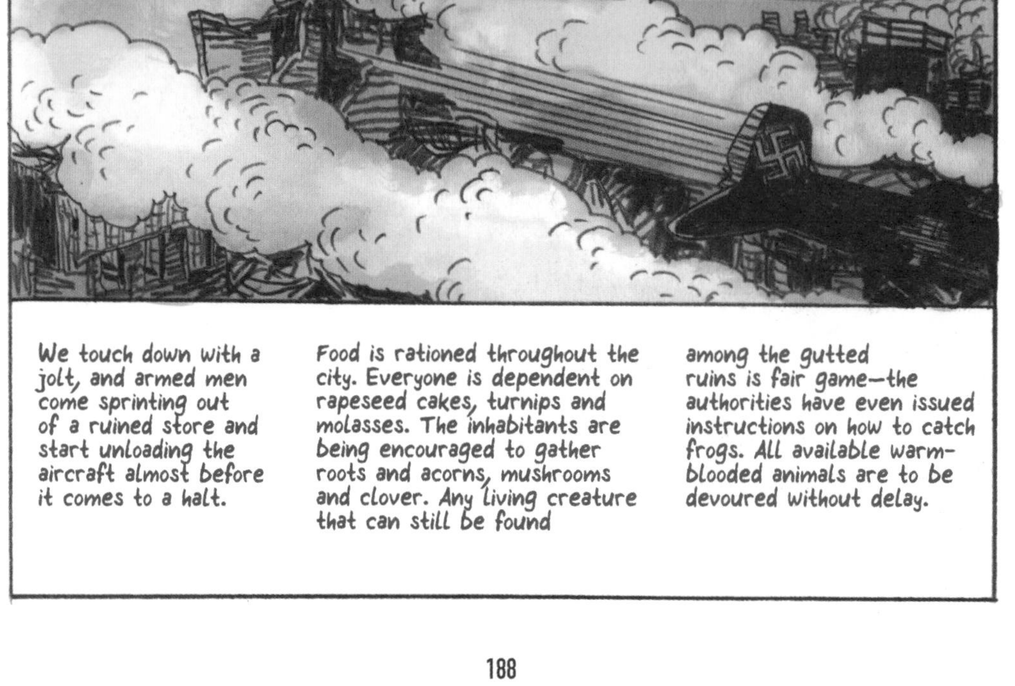

We touch down with a jolt, and armed men come sprinting out of a ruined store and start unloading the aircraft almost before it comes to a halt.

Food is rationed throughout the city. Everyone is dependent on rapeseed cakes, turnips and molasses. The inhabitants are being encouraged to gather roots and acorns, mushrooms and clover. Any living creature that can still be found among the gutted ruins is fair game—the authorities have even issued instructions on how to catch frogs. All available warm-blooded animals are to be devoured without delay.

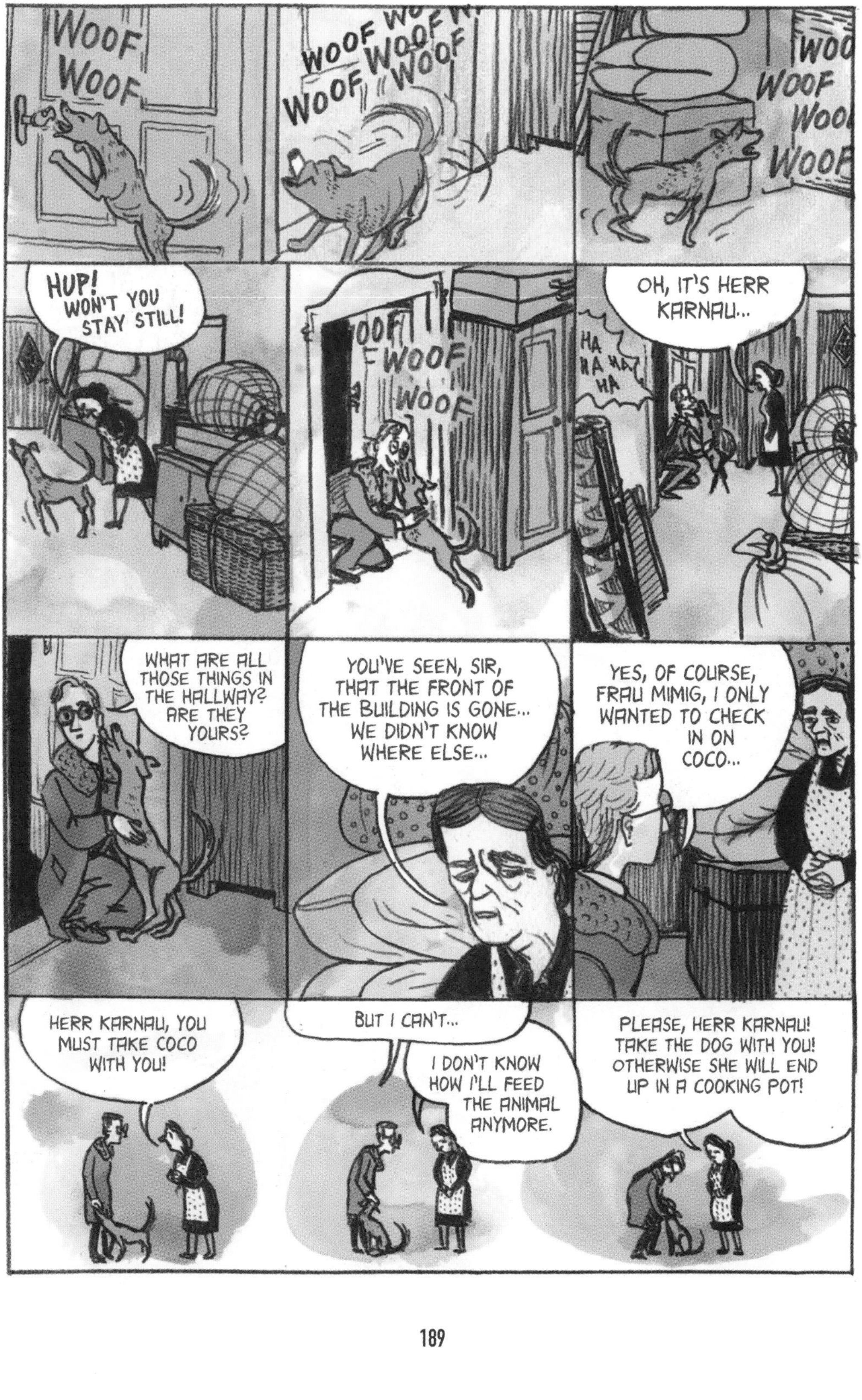
WOOF
WOOF
WOOF WOOF WOOF
WOOF WOOF
WOO
WOOF
WOO
WOOF
HUP! WON'T YOU STAY STILL!
OOF WOOF WOOF
HA HA HA HA
OH, IT'S HERR KARNAU...
WHAT ARE ALL THOSE THINGS IN THE HALLWAY? ARE THEY YOURS?
YOU'VE SEEN, SIR, THAT THE FRONT OF THE BUILDING IS GONE... WE DIDN'T KNOW WHERE ELSE...
YES, OF COURSE, FRAU MIMIG, I ONLY WANTED TO CHECK IN ON COCO...
HERR KARNAU, YOU MUST TAKE COCO WITH YOU!
BUT I CAN'T...
I DON'T KNOW HOW I'LL FEED THE ANIMAL ANYMORE.
PLEASE, HERR KARNAU! TAKE THE DOG WITH YOU! OTHERWISE SHE WILL END UP IN A COOKING POT!

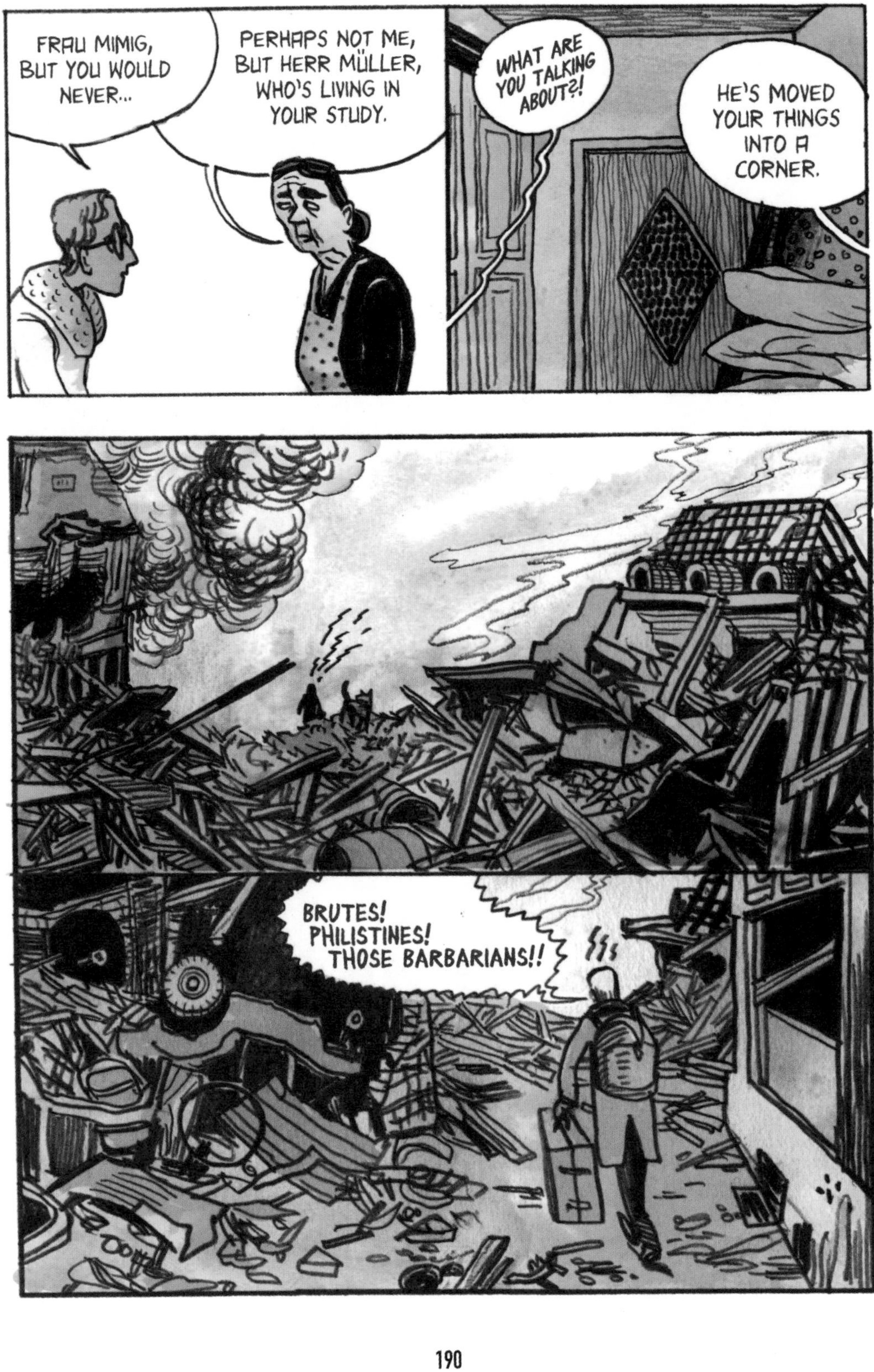
FRAU MIMIG, BUT YOU WOULD NEVER...
PERHAPS NOT ME, BUT HERR MÜLLER, WHO'S LIVING IN YOUR STUDY.
WHAT ARE YOU TALKING ABOUT?!
HE'S MOVED YOUR THINGS INTO A CORNER.
BRUTES! PHILISTINES! THOSE BARBARIANS!!

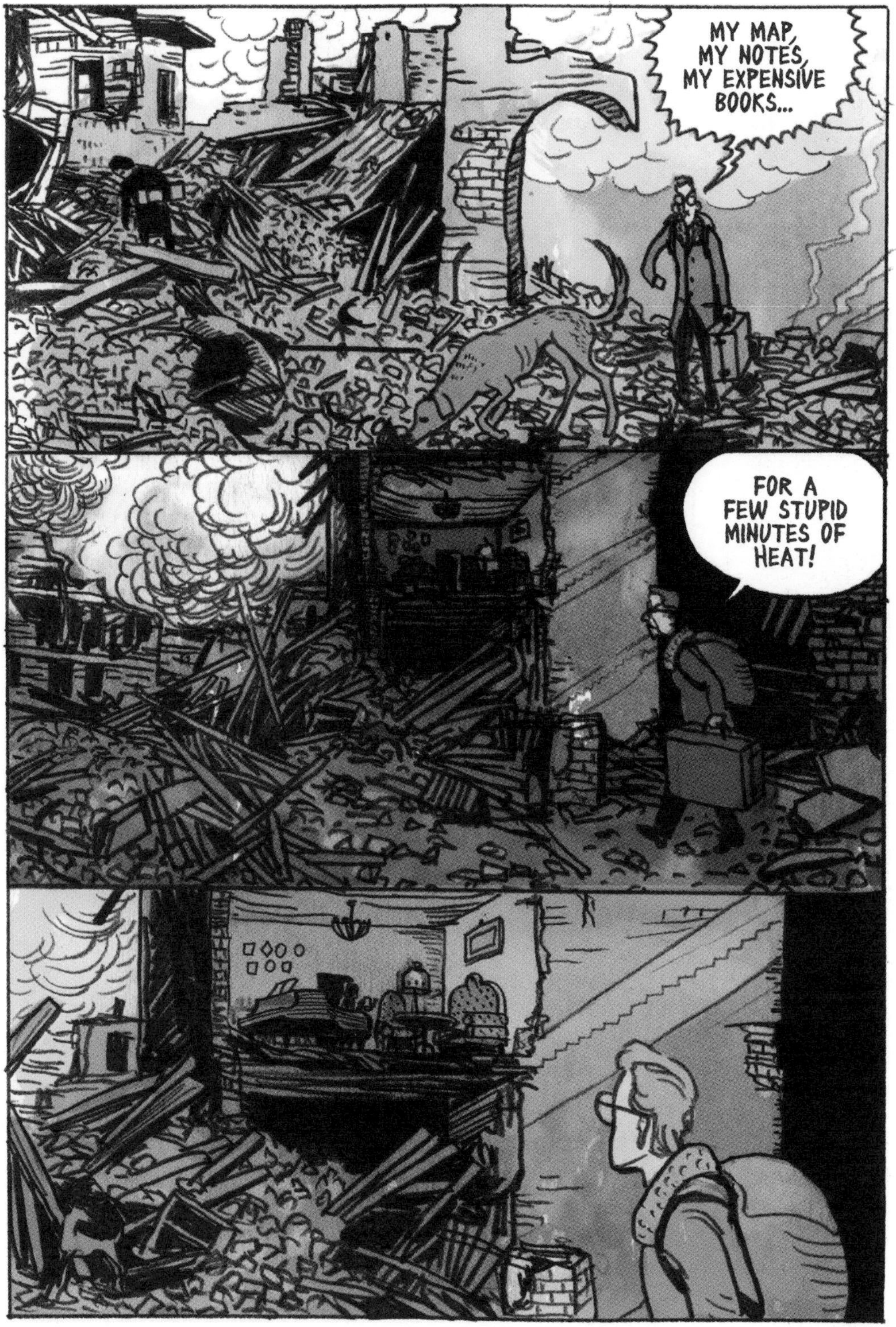
MY MAP, MY NOTES, MY EXPENSIVE BOOKS...
FOR A FEW STUPID MINUTES OF HEAT!

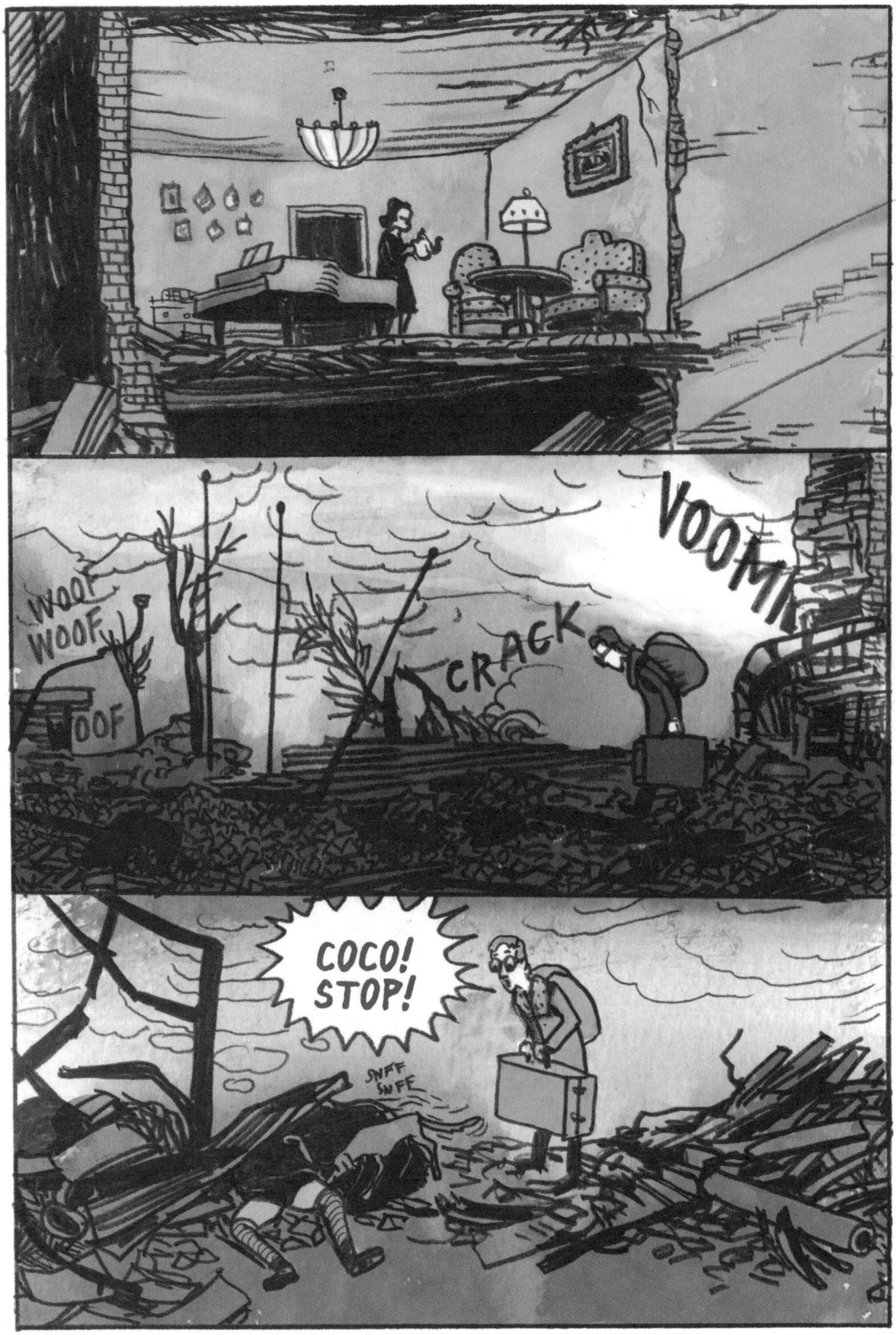
WOOF
WOOF
WOOF
CRACK
VOOM
COCO! STOP!
SNFF SNFF

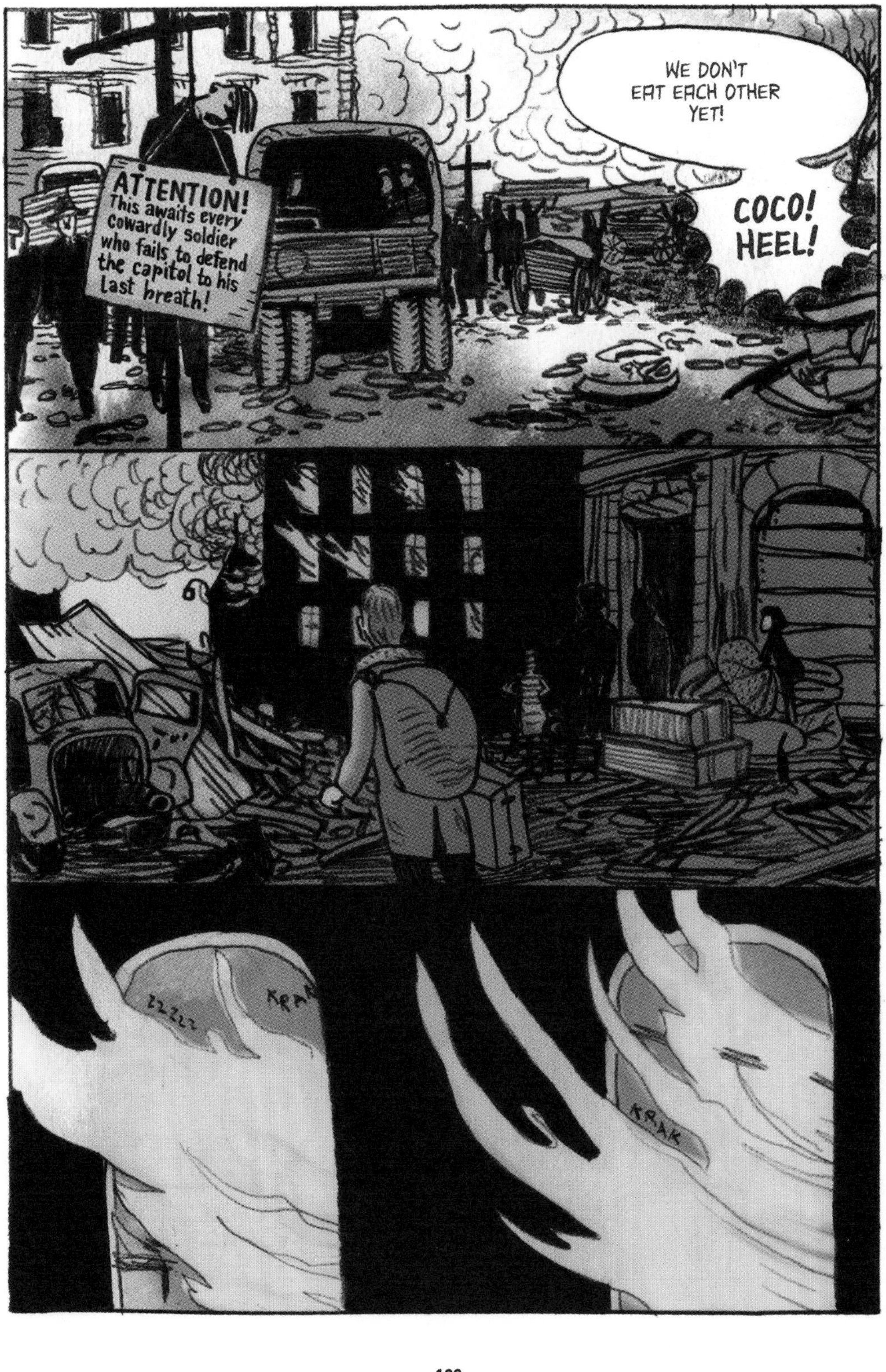
ATTENTION! This awaits every cowardly soldier who fails to defend the capitol to his last breath!
WE DON'T EAT EACH OTHER YET!
COCO! HEEL!
KRAK
KRAK

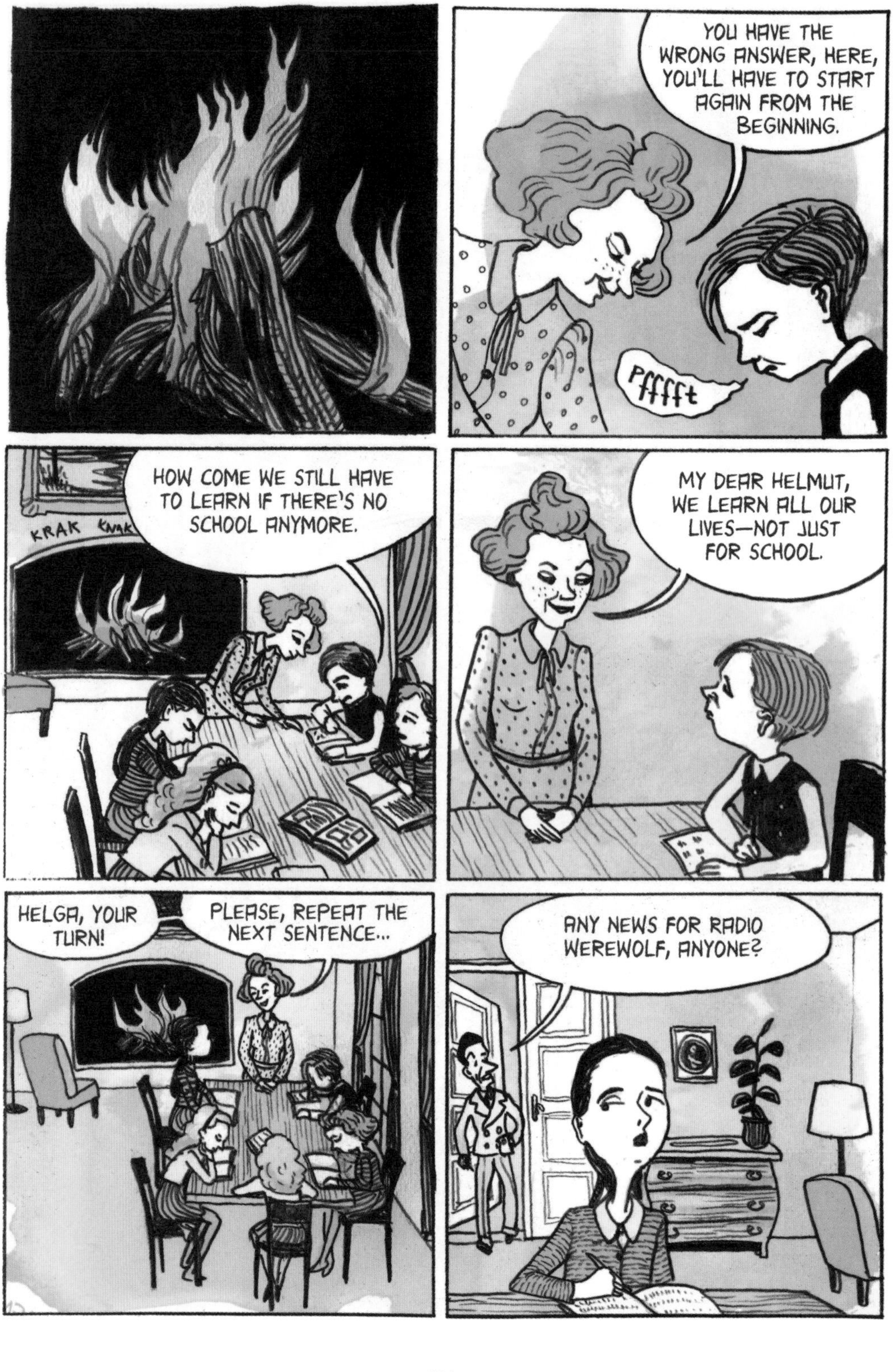
YOU HAVE THE WRONG ANSWER, HERE, YOU'LL HAVE TO START AGAIN FROM THE BEGINNING.
Pfffft
HOW COME WE STILL HAVE TO LEARN IF THERE'S NO SCHOOL ANYMORE.
KRAK KNAK
MY DEAR HELMUT, WE LEARN ALL OUR LIVES—NOT JUST FOR SCHOOL.
HELGA, YOUR TURN!
PLEASE, REPEAT THE NEXT SENTENCE...
ANY NEWS FOR RADIO WEREWOLF, ANYONE?

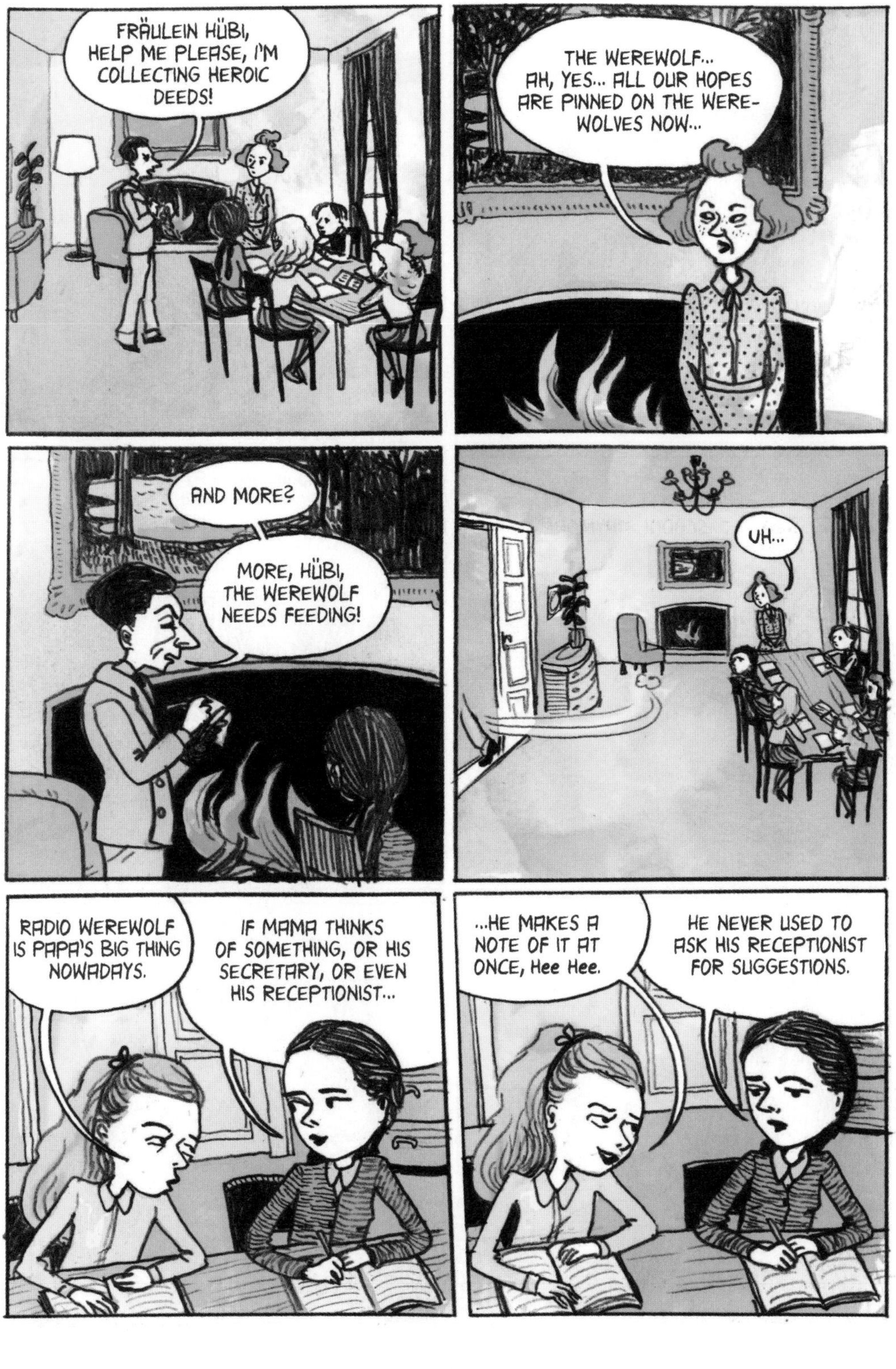
FRÄULEIN HÜBI, HELP ME PLEASE, I'M COLLECTING HEROIC DEEDS!
THE WEREWOLF... AH, YES... ALL OUR HOPES ARE PINNED ON THE WERE-WOLVES NOW...
AND MORE?
MORE, HÜBI, THE WEREWOLF NEEDS FEEDING!
UH...
RADIO WEREWOLF IS PAPA'S BIG THING NOWADAYS.
IF MAMA THINKS OF SOMETHING, OR HIS SECRETARY, OR EVEN HIS RECEPTIONIST...
...HE MAKES A NOTE OF IT AT ONCE, Hee Hee.
HE NEVER USED TO ASK HIS RECEPTIONIST FOR SUGGESTIONS.

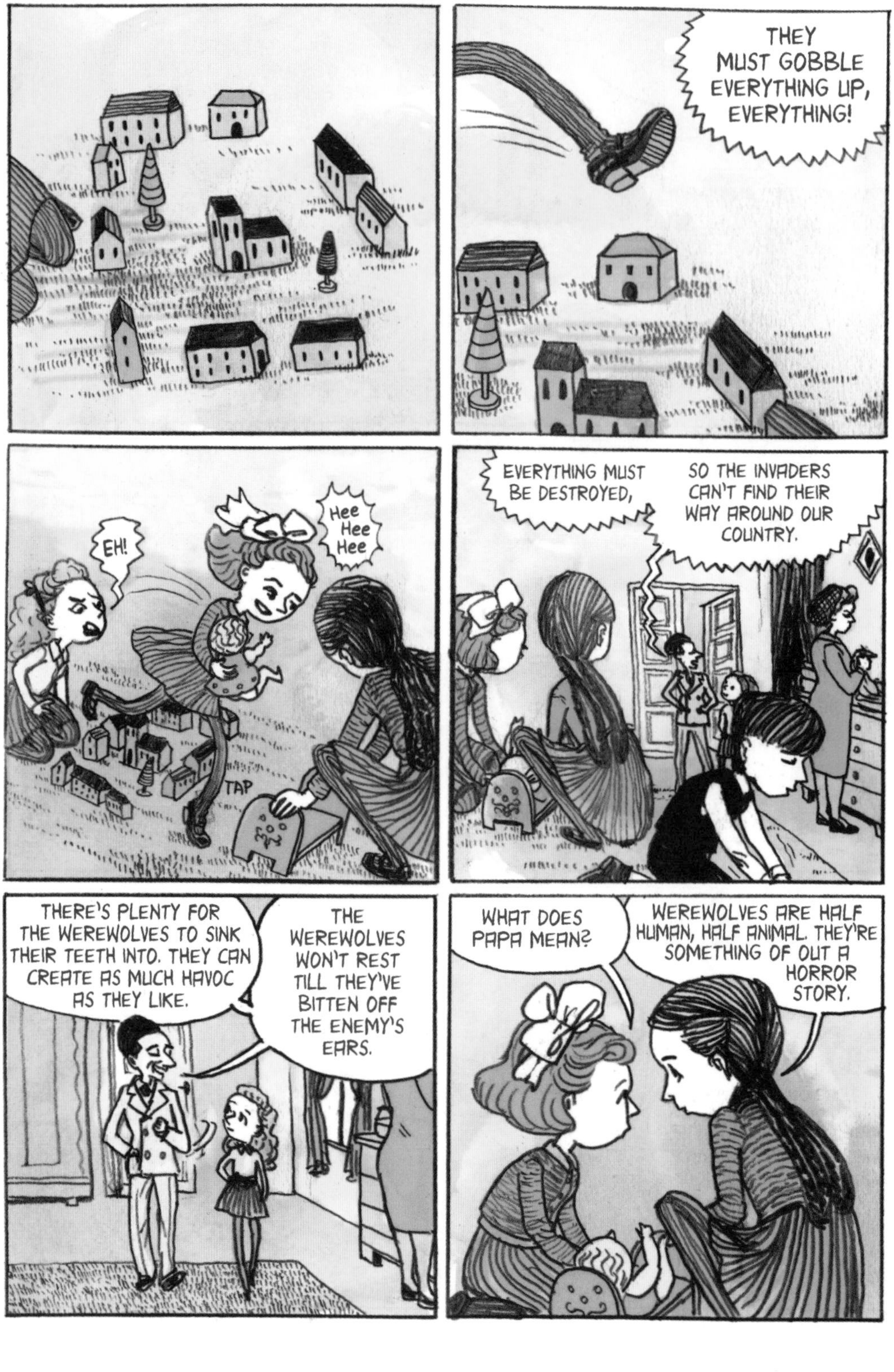
THEY MUST GOBBLE EVERYTHING UP, EVERYTHING!
EH!
Hee Hee Hee
TAP
EVERYTHING MUST BE DESTROYED,
SO THE INVADERS CAN'T FIND THEIR WAY AROUND OUR COUNTRY.
THERE'S PLENTY FOR THE WEREWOLVES TO SINK THEIR TEETH INTO. THEY CAN CREATE AS MUCH HAVOC AS THEY LIKE.
THE WEREWOLVES WON'T REST TILL THEY'VE BITTEN OFF THE ENEMY'S EARS.
WHAT DOES PAPA MEAN?
WEREWOLVES ARE HALF HUMAN, HALF ANIMAL. THEY'RE SOMETHING OF OUT A HORROR STORY.

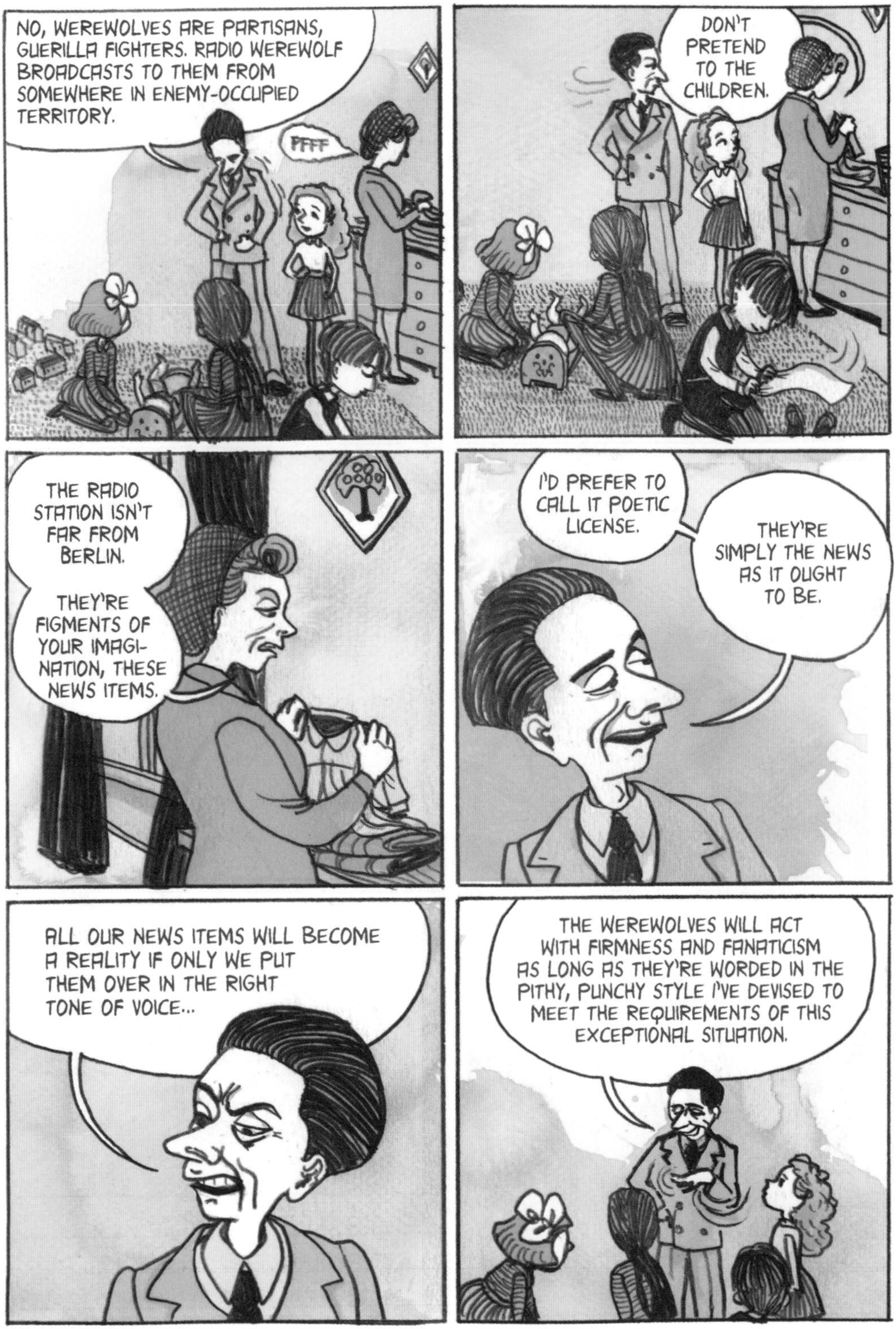

NO, WEREWOLVES ARE PARTISANS, GUERILLA FIGHTERS. RADIO WEREWOLF BROADCASTS TO THEM FROM SOMEWHERE IN ENEMY-OCCUPIED TERRITORY.
PFFF
DON'T PRETEND TO THE CHILDREN.
THE RADIO STATION ISN'T FAR FROM BERLIN.
THEY'RE FIGMENTS OF YOUR IMAGI-NATION, THESE NEWS ITEMS.
I'D PREFER TO CALL IT POETIC LICENSE.
THEY'RE SIMPLY THE NEWS AS IT OUGHT TO BE.
ALL OUR NEWS ITEMS WILL BECOME A REALITY IF ONLY WE PUT THEM OVER IN THE RIGHT TONE OF VOICE...
THE WEREWOLVES WILL ACT WITH FIRMNESS AND FANATICISM AS LONG AS THEY'RE WORDED IN THE PITHY, PUNCHY STYLE I'VE DEVISED TO MEET THE REQUIREMENTS OF THIS EXCEPTIONAL SITUATION.

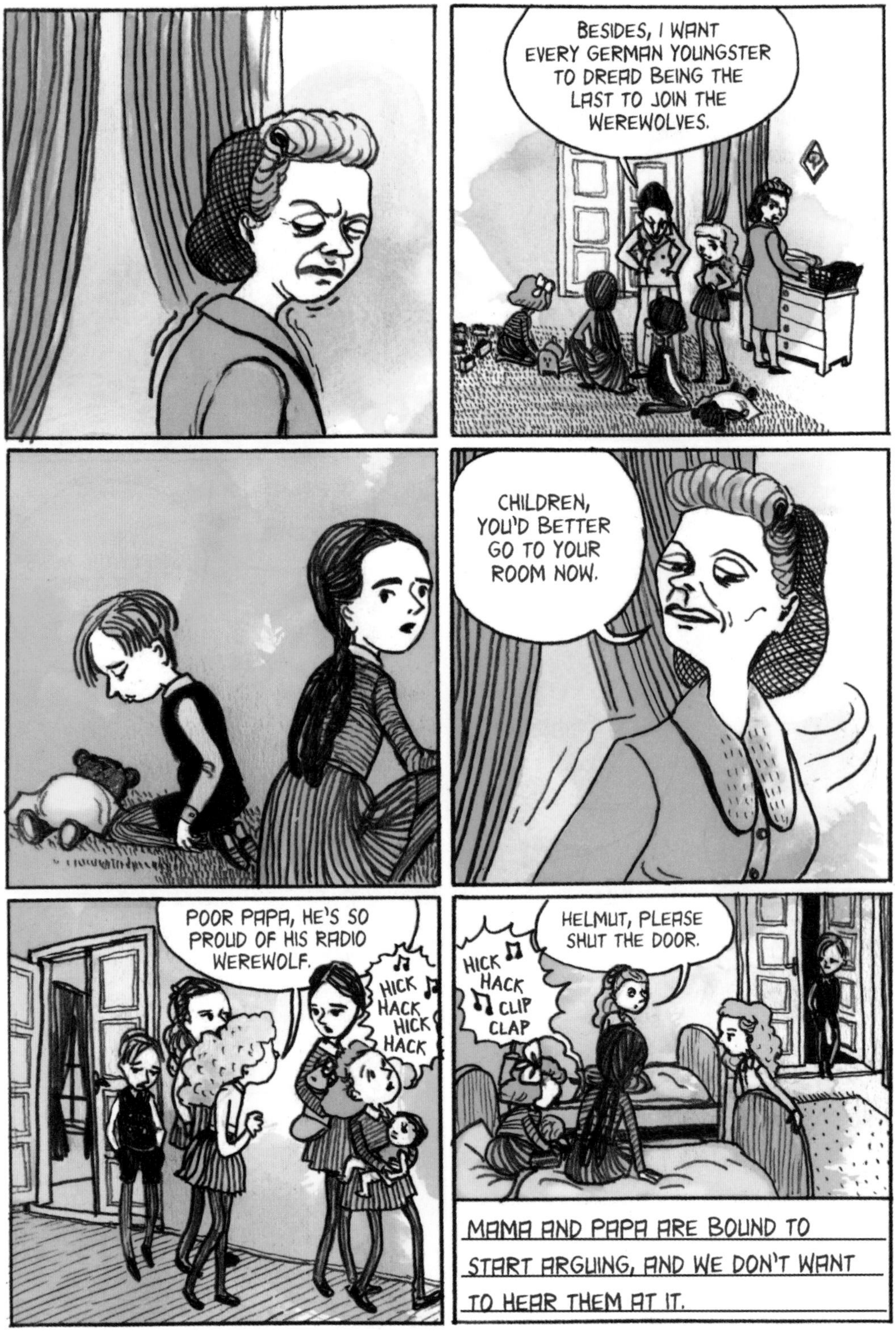
BESIDES, I WANT EVERY GERMAN YOUNGSTER TO DREAD BEING THE LAST TO JOIN THE WEREWOLVES.
CHILDREN, YOU'D BETTER GO TO YOUR ROOM NOW.
POOR PAPA, HE'S SO PROUD OF HIS RADIO WEREWOLF.
HICK HACK HICK HACK
HELMUT, PLEASE SHUT THE DOOR.
HICK HACK CLIP CLAP
MAMA AND PAPA ARE BOUND TO START ARGUING, AND WE DON'T WANT TO HEAR THEM AT IT.

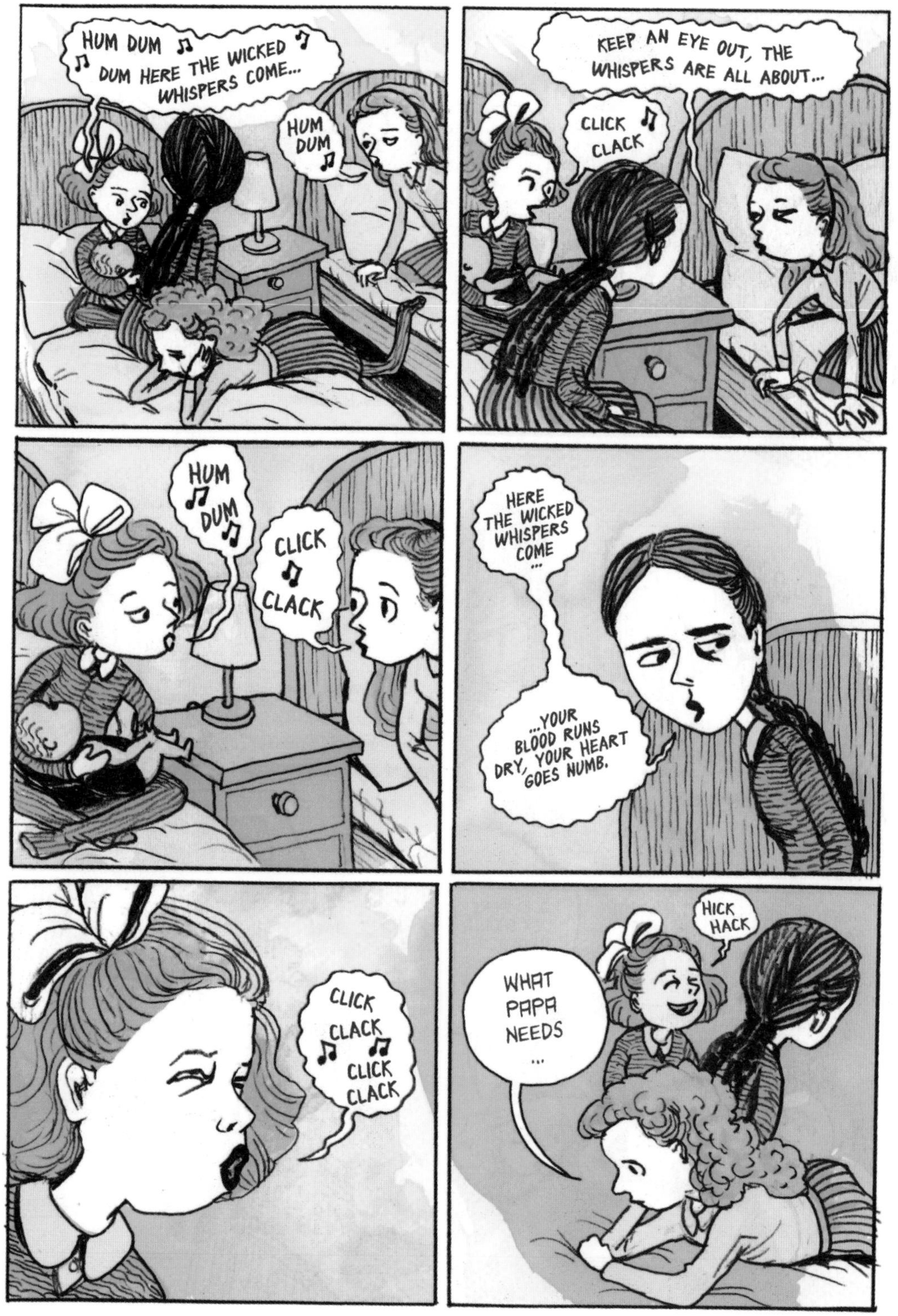
HUM DUM ♫ ♫ DUM HERE THE WICKED ♫ WHISPERS COME...
HUM DUM ♫
KEEP AN EYE OUT, THE WHISPERS ARE ALL ABOUT...
CLICK ♫ CLACK
HUM ♫ DUM ♫
CLICK ♫ CLACK
HERE THE WICKED WHISPERS COME ...
...YOUR BLOOD RUNS DRY, YOUR HEART GOES NUMB.
CLICK CLACK ♫ ♫ CLICK CLACK
HICK HACK
WHAT PAPA NEEDS ...

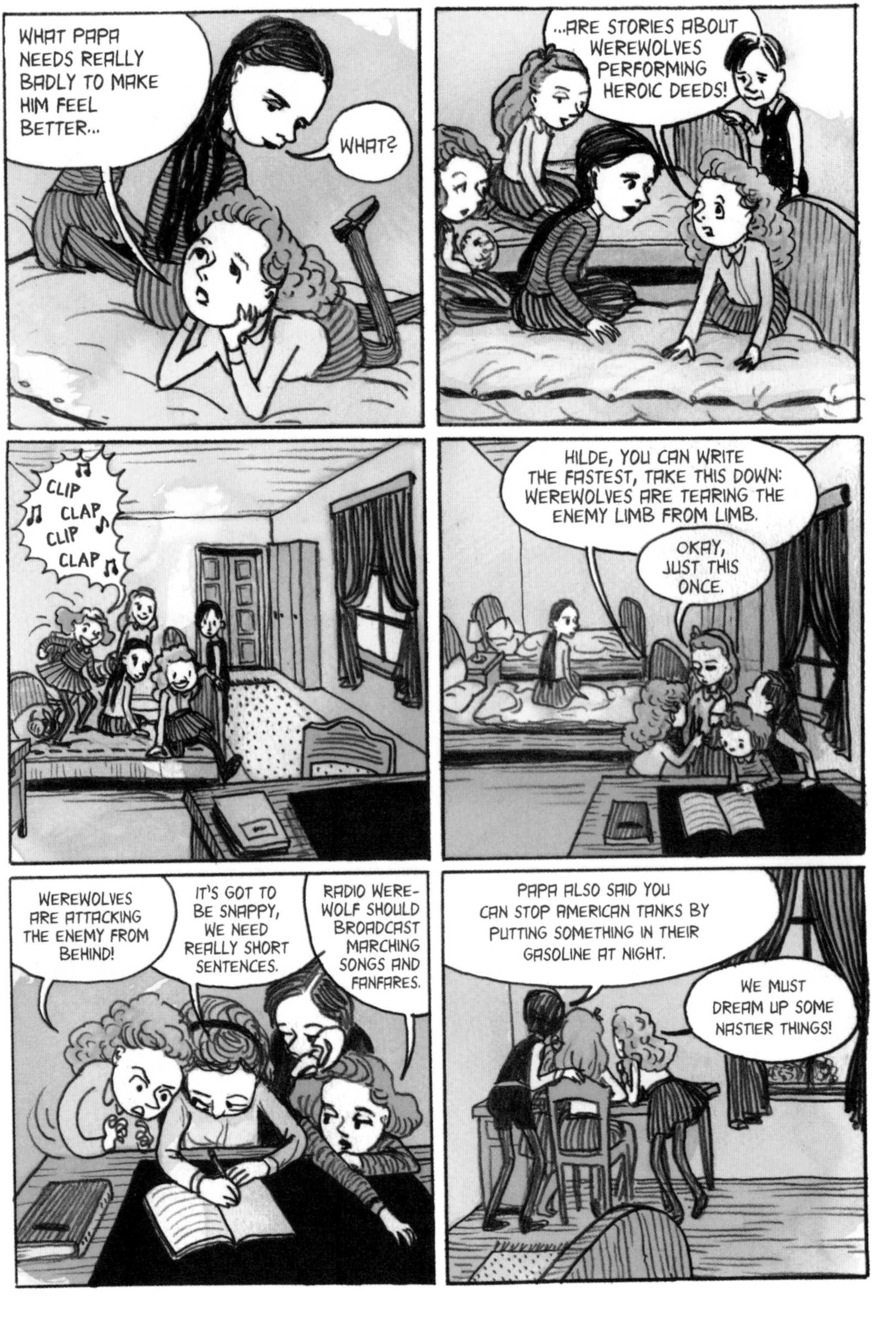
WHAT PAPA NEEDS REALLY BADLY TO MAKE HIM FEEL BETTER...
WHAT?
...ARE STORIES ABOUT WEREWOLVES PERFORMING HEROIC DEEDS!
CLIP CLAP CLIP CLAP
HILDE, YOU CAN WRITE THE FASTEST, TAKE THIS DOWN: WEREWOLVES ARE TEARING THE ENEMY LIMB FROM LIMB.
OKAY, JUST THIS ONCE.
WEREWOLVES ARE ATTACKING THE ENEMY FROM BEHIND!
IT'S GOT TO BE SNAPPY, WE NEED REALLY SHORT SENTENCES.
RADIO WERE-WOLF SHOULD BROADCAST MARCHING SONGS AND FANFARES.
PAPA ALSO SAID YOU CAN STOP AMERICAN TANKS BY PUTTING SOMETHING IN THEIR GASOLINE AT NIGHT.
WE MUST DREAM UP SOME NASTIER THINGS!

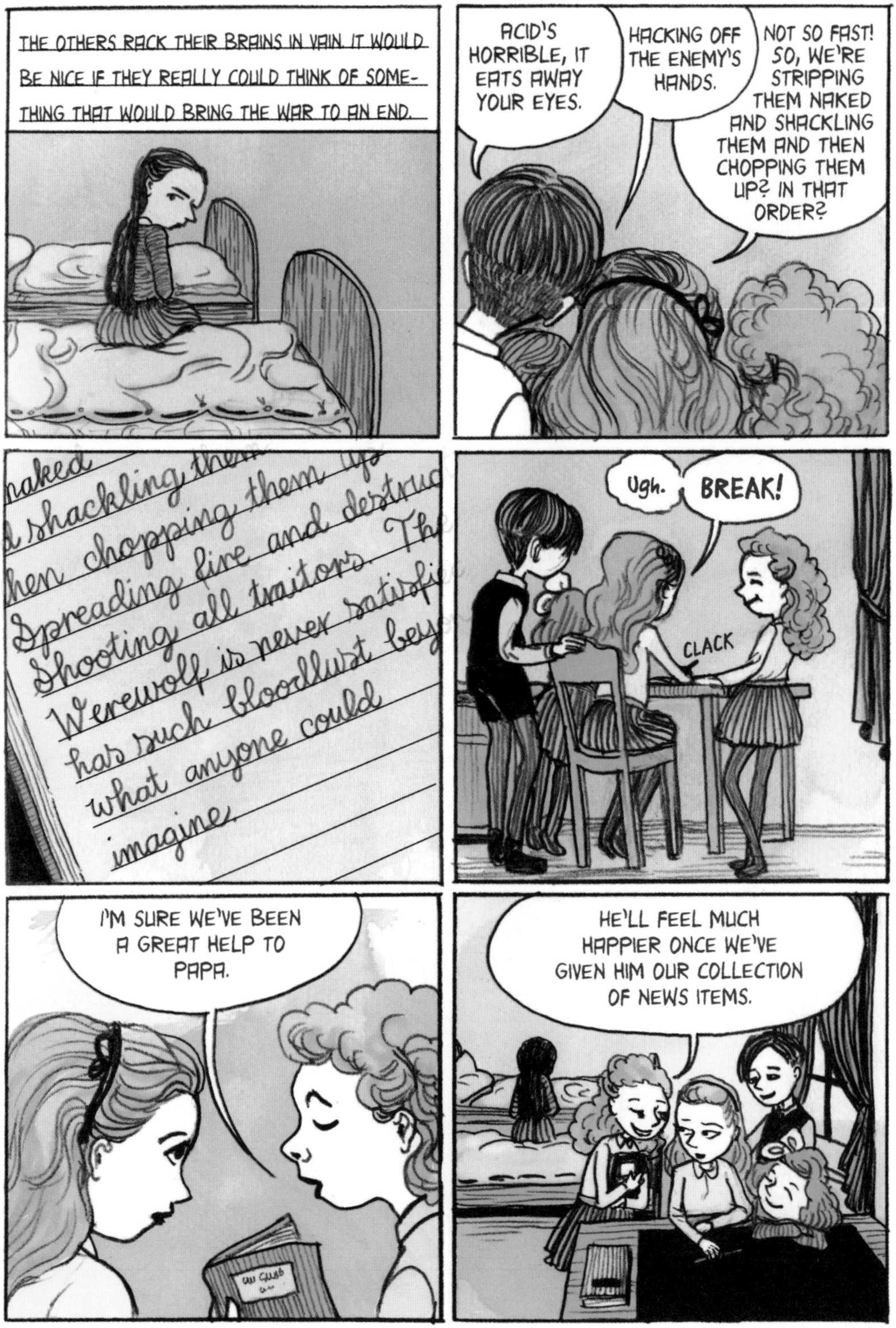
THE OTHERS RACK THEIR BRAINS IN VAIN. IT WOULD BE NICE IF THEY REALLY COULD THINK OF SOMETHING THAT WOULD BRING THE WAR TO AN END.
ACID'S HORRIBLE, IT EATS AWAY YOUR EYES.
HACKING OFF THE ENEMY'S HANDS.
NOT SO FAST! SO, WE'RE STRIPPING THEM NAKED AND SHACKLING THEM AND THEN CHOPPING THEM UP? IN THAT ORDER?
naked
shackling them
then chopping them up
Spreading fire and destruc
Shooting all traitors. The
Werewolf is never satisfie
has such bloodlust beyo
what anyone could
imagine.
Ugh.
BREAK!
CLACK
I'M SURE WE'VE BEEN A GREAT HELP TO PAPA.
HE'LL FEEL MUCH HAPPIER ONCE WE'VE GIVEN HIM OUR COLLECTION OF NEWS ITEMS.

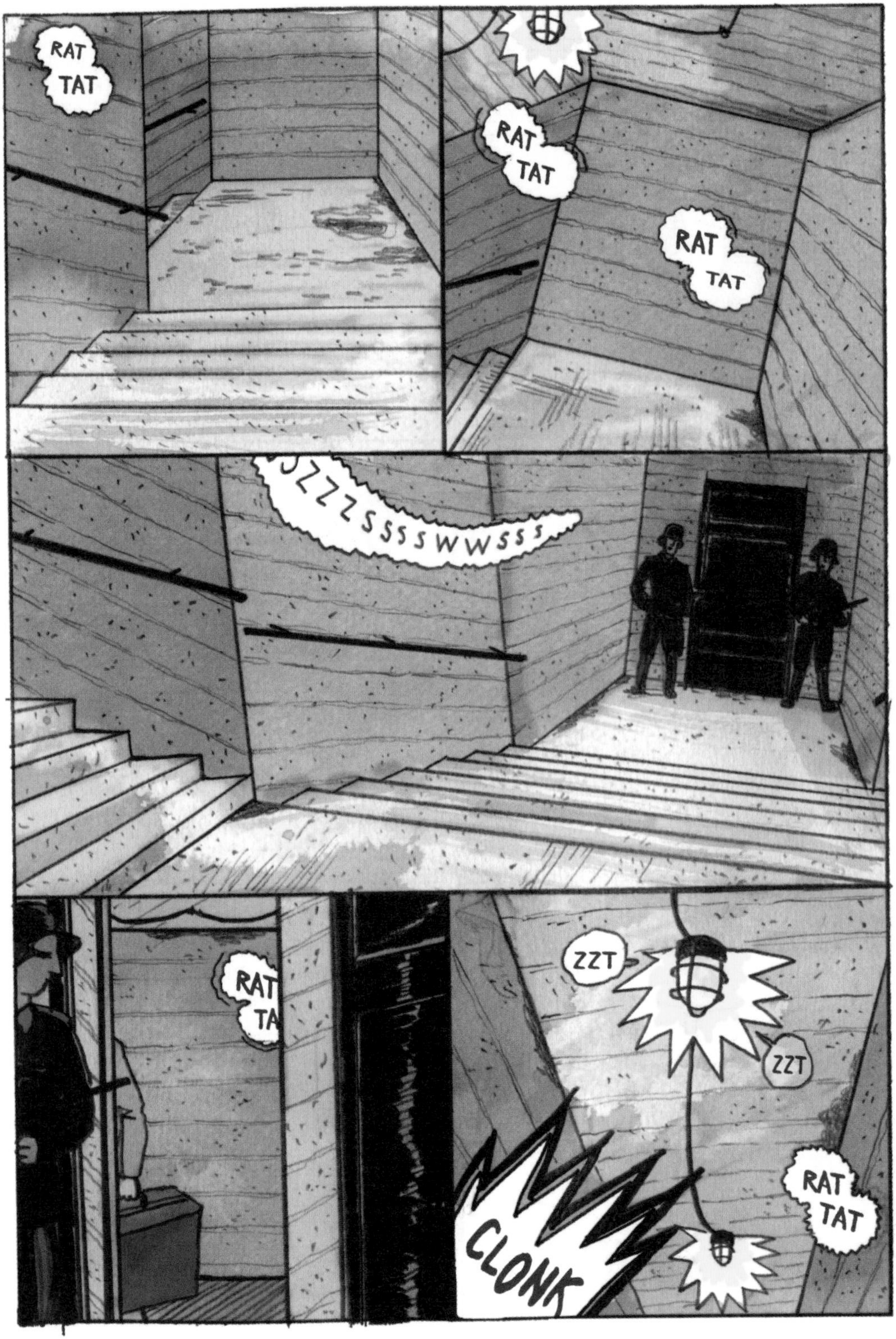
RAT TAT
RAT TAT
RAT TAT
ZZZSSSSWWSSS
RAT
ZZT
ZZT
CLONK
RAT TAT

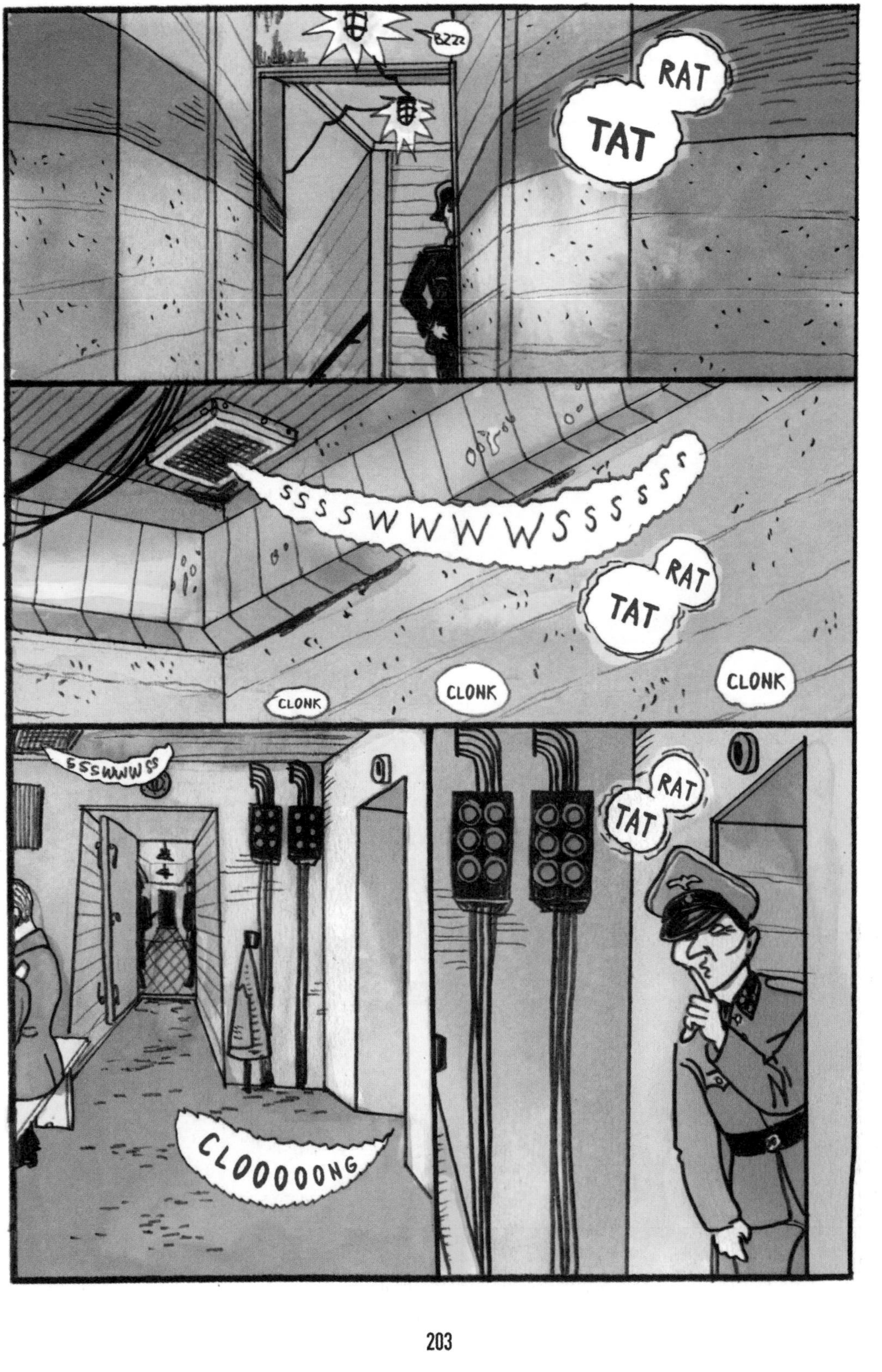
BZZZ
RAT
TAT
SSSSWWWWWSSSSSSS
RAT
TAT
CLONK
CLONK
CLONK
SSSWWWSS
CLOOOOOONG
RAT
TAT

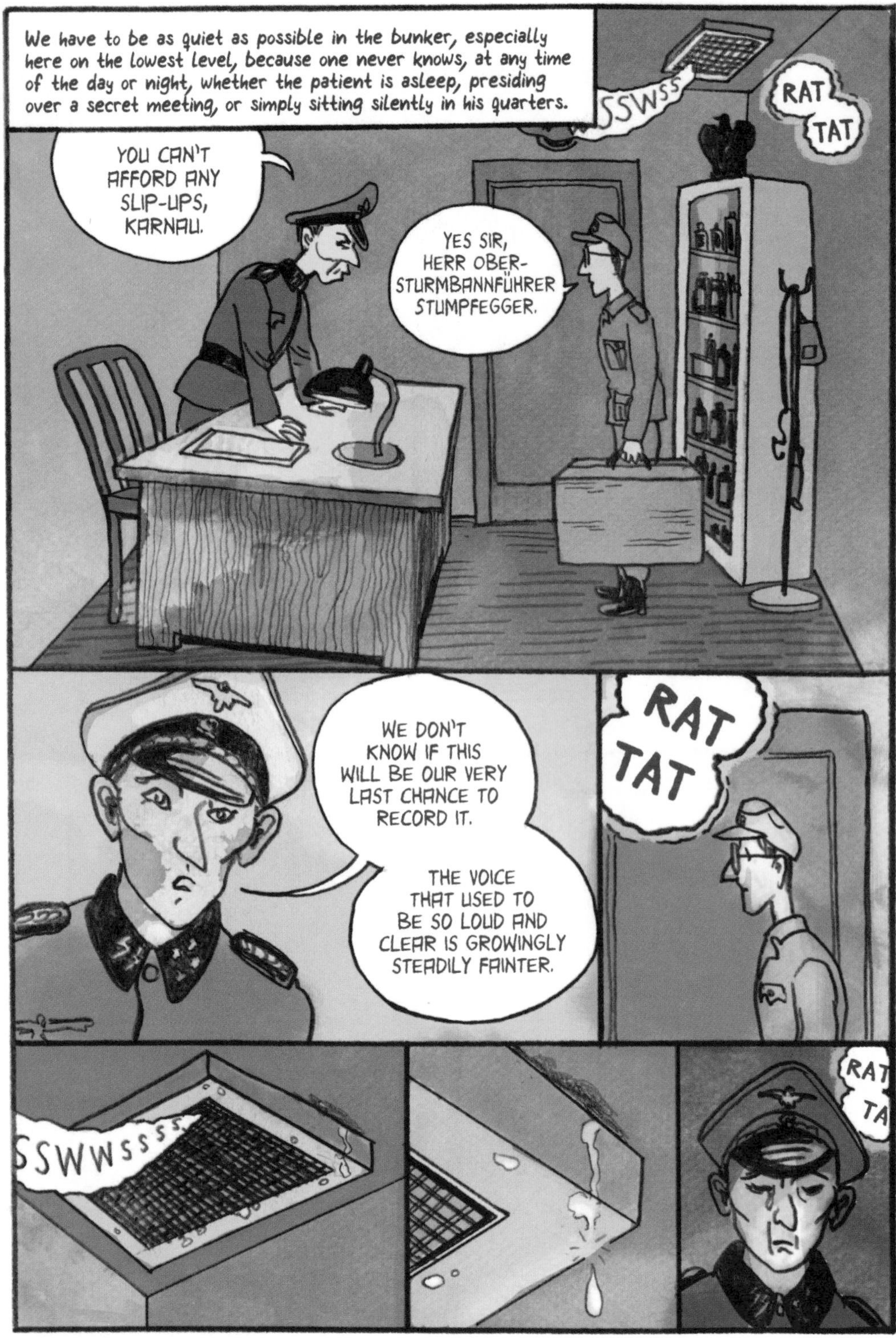
We have to be as quiet as possible in the bunker, especially here on the lowest level, because one never knows, at any time of the day or night, whether the patient is asleep, presiding over a secret meeting, or simply sitting silently in his quarters.
SSWSS
RAT TAT
YOU CAN'T AFFORD ANY SLIP-UPS, KARNAU.
YES SIR, HERR OBER-STURMBANNFÜHRER STUMPFEGGER.
WE DON'T KNOW IF THIS WILL BE OUR VERY LAST CHANCE TO RECORD IT.
THE VOICE THAT USED TO BE SO LOUD AND CLEAR IS GROWINGLY STEADILY FAINTER.
RAT TAT
SSWWSSSS
RAT
TA

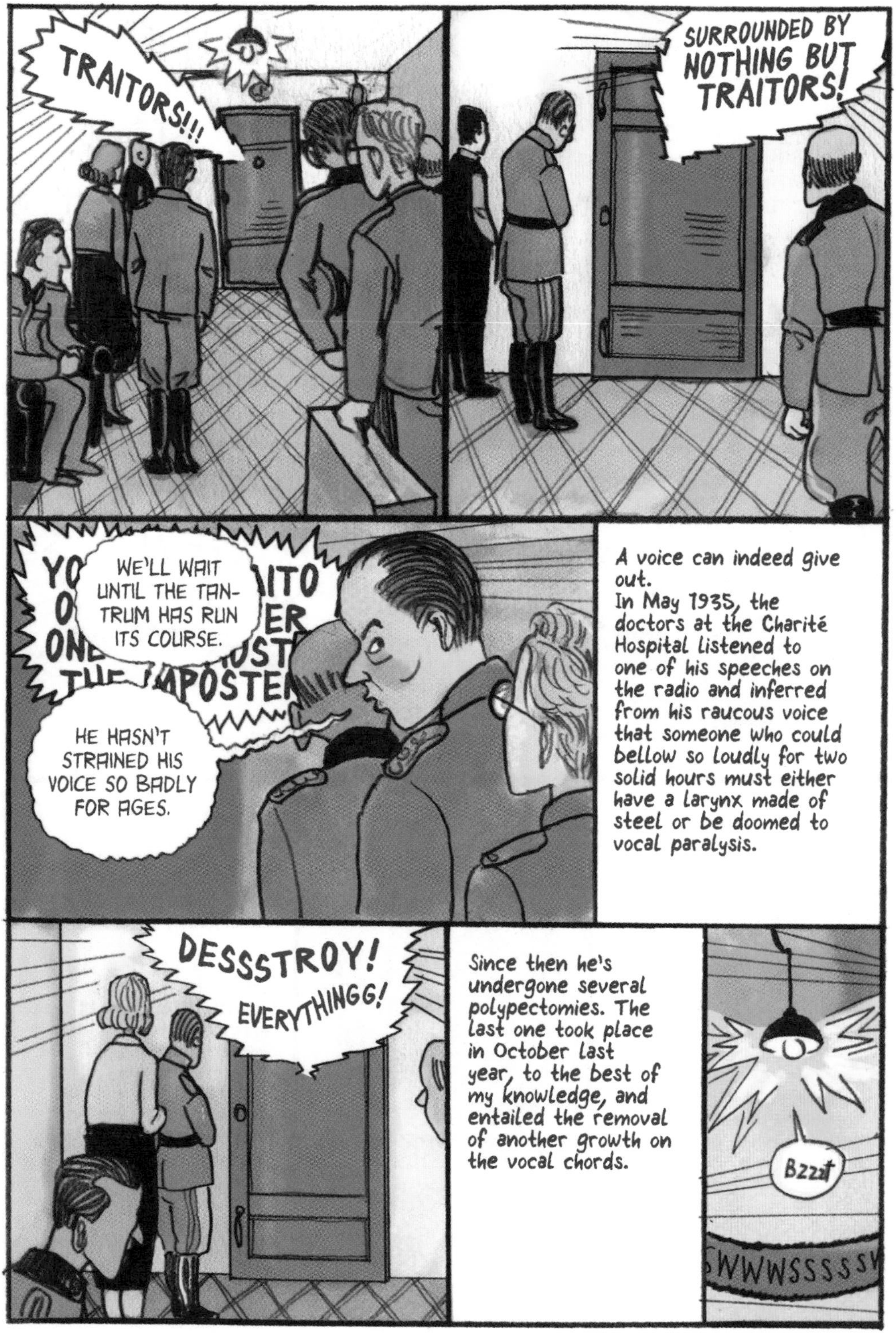
TRAITORS!!!
SURROUNDED BY NOTHING BUT TRAITORS!
WE'LL WAIT UNTIL THE TANTRUM HAS RUN ITS COURSE.
HE HASN'T STRAINED HIS VOICE SO BADLY FOR AGES.
A voice can indeed give out.
In May 1935, the doctors at the Charité Hospital listened to one of his speeches on the radio and inferred from his raucous voice that someone who could bellow so loudly for two solid hours must either have a larynx made of steel or be doomed to vocal paralysis.
DESSSTROY!
EVERYTHINGG!
Since then he's undergone several polypectomies. The last one took place in October last year, to the best of my knowledge, and entailed the removal of another growth on the vocal chords.
Bzzzt
SWWWSSSSSSV

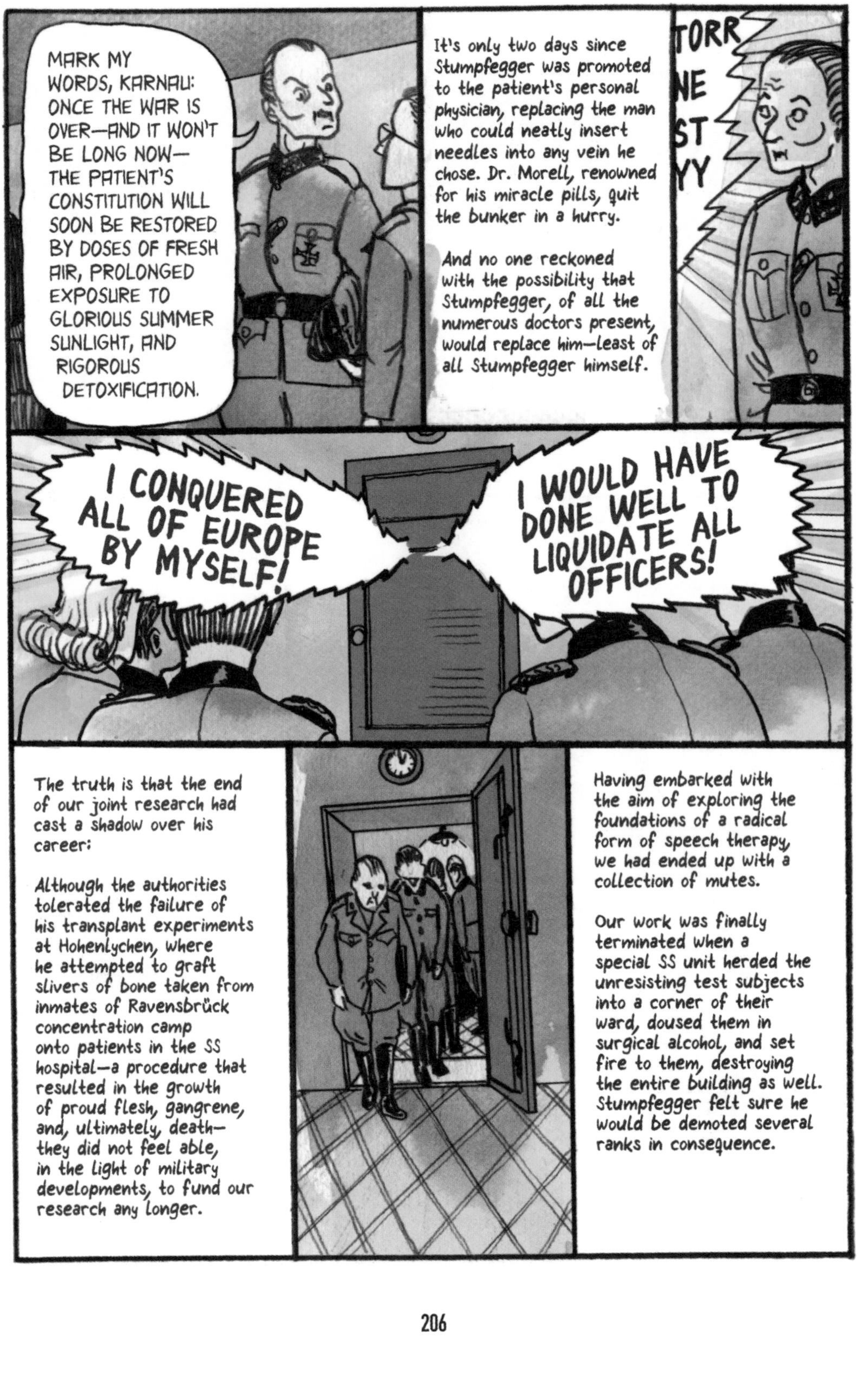
MARK MY WORDS, KARNAU: ONCE THE WAR IS OVER—AND IT WON'T BE LONG NOW—THE PATIENT'S CONSTITUTION WILL SOON BE RESTORED BY DOSES OF FRESH AIR, PROLONGED EXPOSURE TO GLORIOUS SUMMER SUNLIGHT, AND RIGOROUS DETOXIFICATION.
It's only two days since Stumpfegger was promoted to the patient's personal physician, replacing the man who could neatly insert needles into any vein he chose. Dr. Morell, renowned for his miracle pills, quit the bunker in a hurry.
And no one reckoned with the possibility that Stumpfegger, of all the numerous doctors present, would replace him—least of all Stumpfegger himself.
TORR
NE
ST
YY
I CONQUERED ALL OF EUROPE BY MYSELF!
I WOULD HAVE DONE WELL TO LIQUIDATE ALL OFFICERS!
The truth is that the end of our joint research had cast a shadow over his career:
Although the authorities tolerated the failure of his transplant experiments at Hohenlychen, where he attempted to graft slivers of bone taken from inmates of Ravensbrück concentration camp onto patients in the SS hospital—a procedure that resulted in the growth of proud flesh, gangrene, and, ultimately, death—they did not feel able, in the light of military developments, to fund our research any longer.
Having embarked with the aim of exploring the foundations of a radical form of speech therapy, we had ended up with a collection of mutes.
Our work was finally terminated when a special SS unit herded the unresisting test subjects into a corner of their ward, doused them in surgical alcohol, and set fire to them, destroying the entire building as well. Stumpfegger felt sure he would be demoted several ranks in consequence.

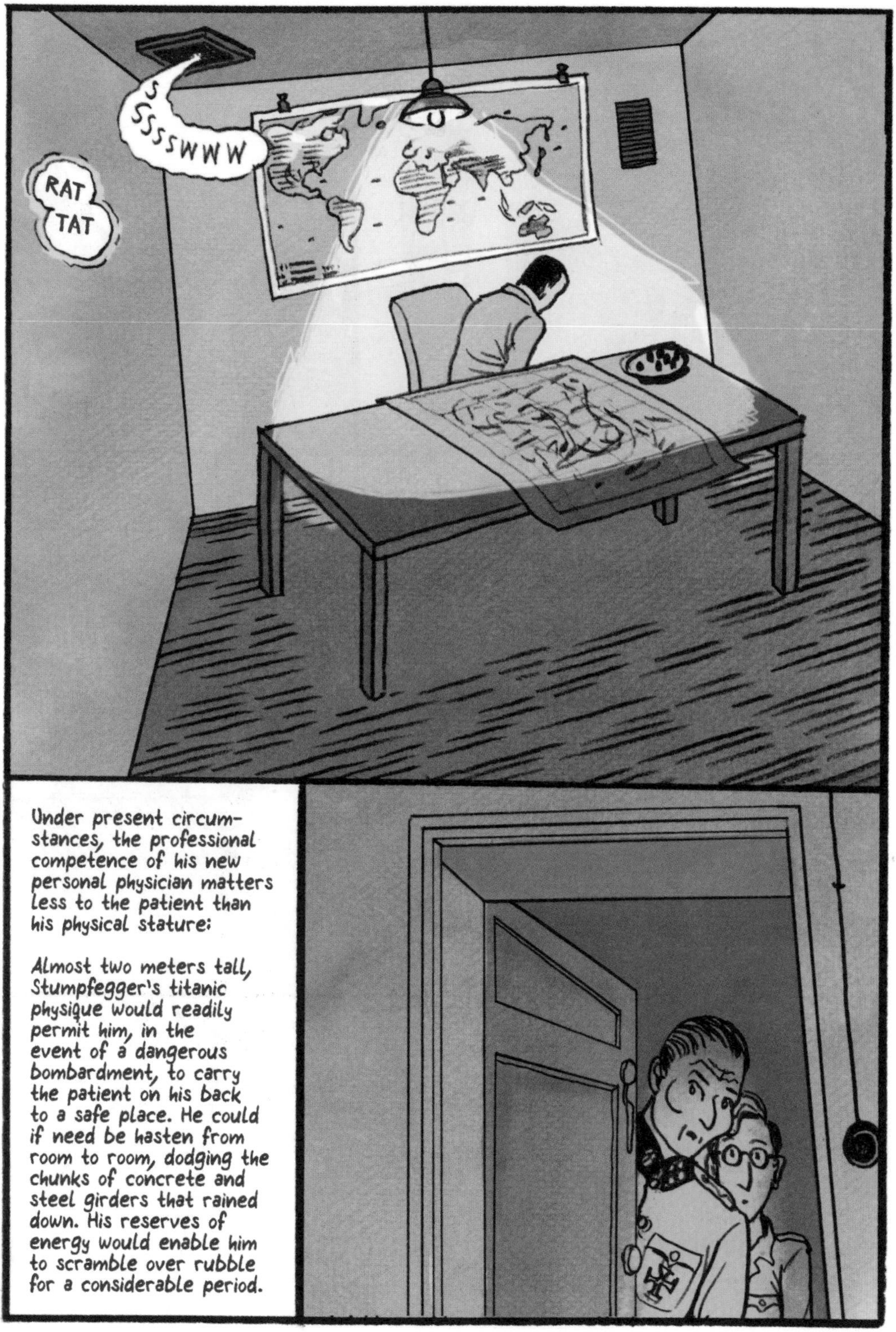
SSSSSWWW
RAT TAT
Under present circumstances, the professional competence of his new personal physician matters less to the patient than his physical stature:
Almost two meters tall, Stumpfegger's titanic physique would readily permit him, in the event of a dangerous bombardment, to carry the patient on his back to a safe place. He could if need be hasten from room to room, dodging the chunks of concrete and steel girders that rained down. His reserves of energy would enable him to scramble over rubble for a considerable period.

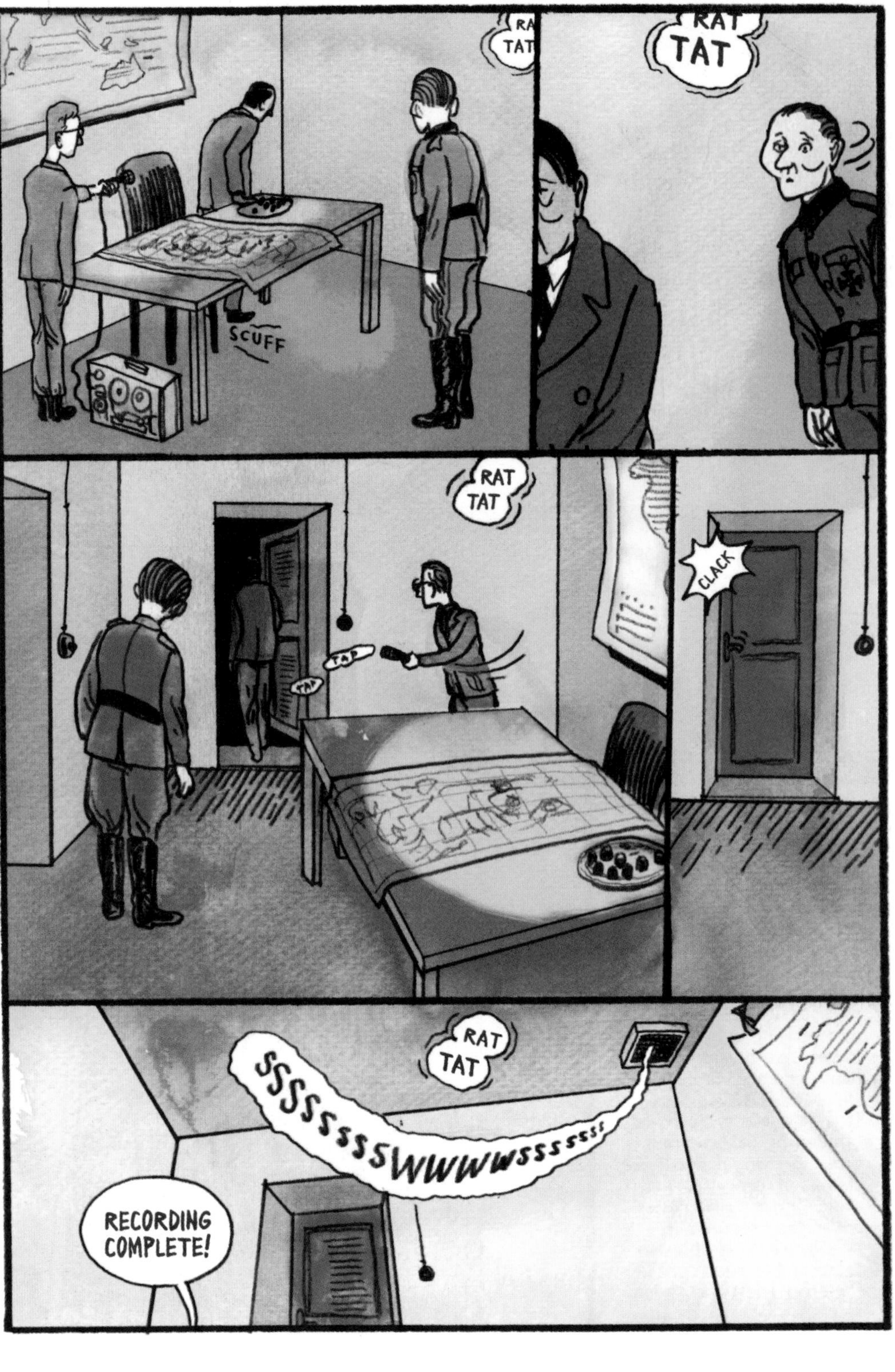

RAT TAT
SCUFF
RAT TAT
RAT TAT
TAP
TAP
CLACK
RAT TAT
SSSSSSSSSWWWWSSSSSSSS
RECORDING COMPLETE!

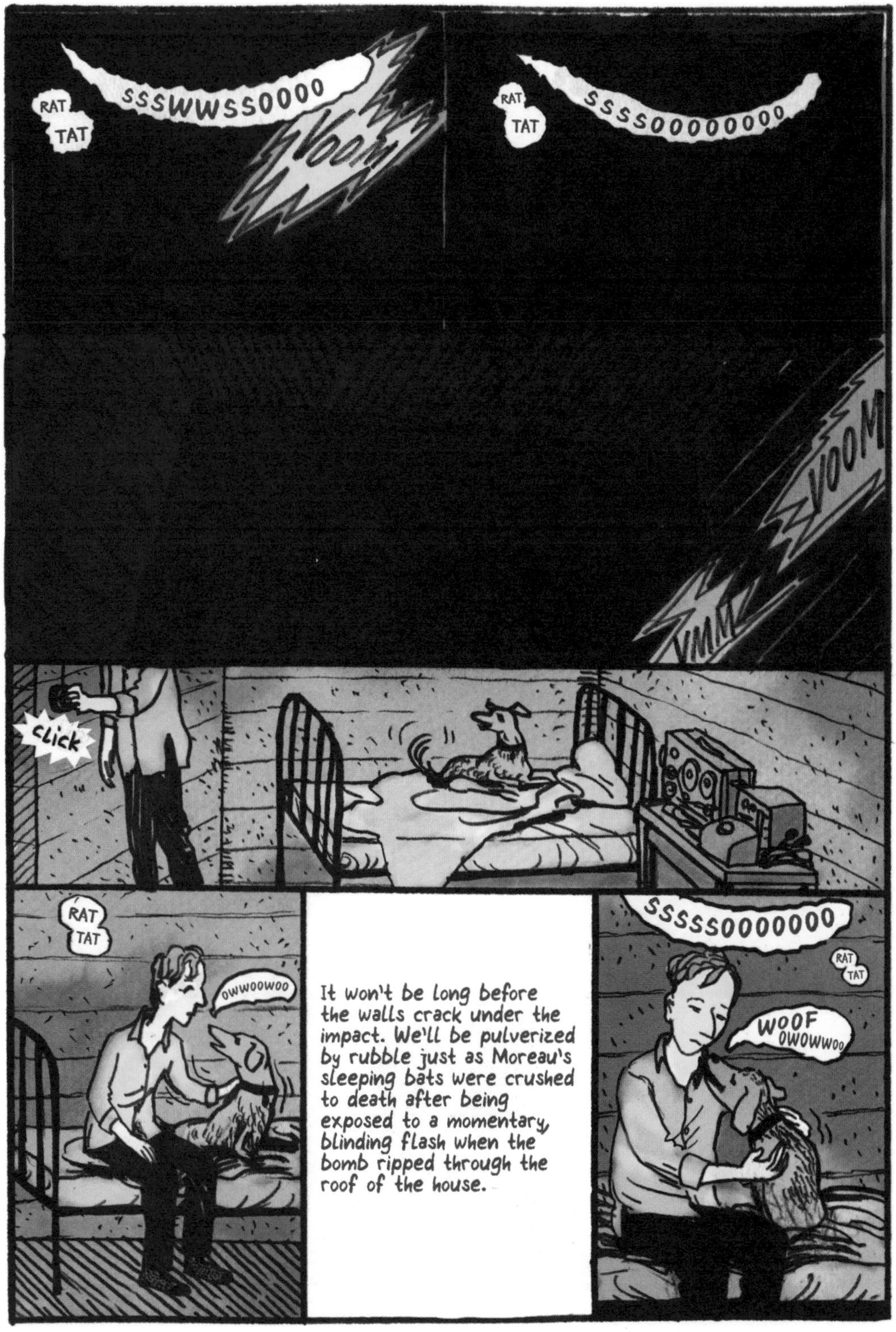
RAT
TAT
SSSWWSSOOOO
VOOM
RAT
TAT
SSSSOOOOOOOOO
VOOM
VMM
CLICK
RAT
TAT
OWWOOWOO
It won't be long before the walls crack under the impact. We'll be pulverized by rubble just as Moreau's sleeping bats were crushed to death after being exposed to a momentary, blinding flash when the bomb ripped through the roof of the house.
SSSSSOOOOOOOO
RAT
TAT
WOOF
OWOWWOO

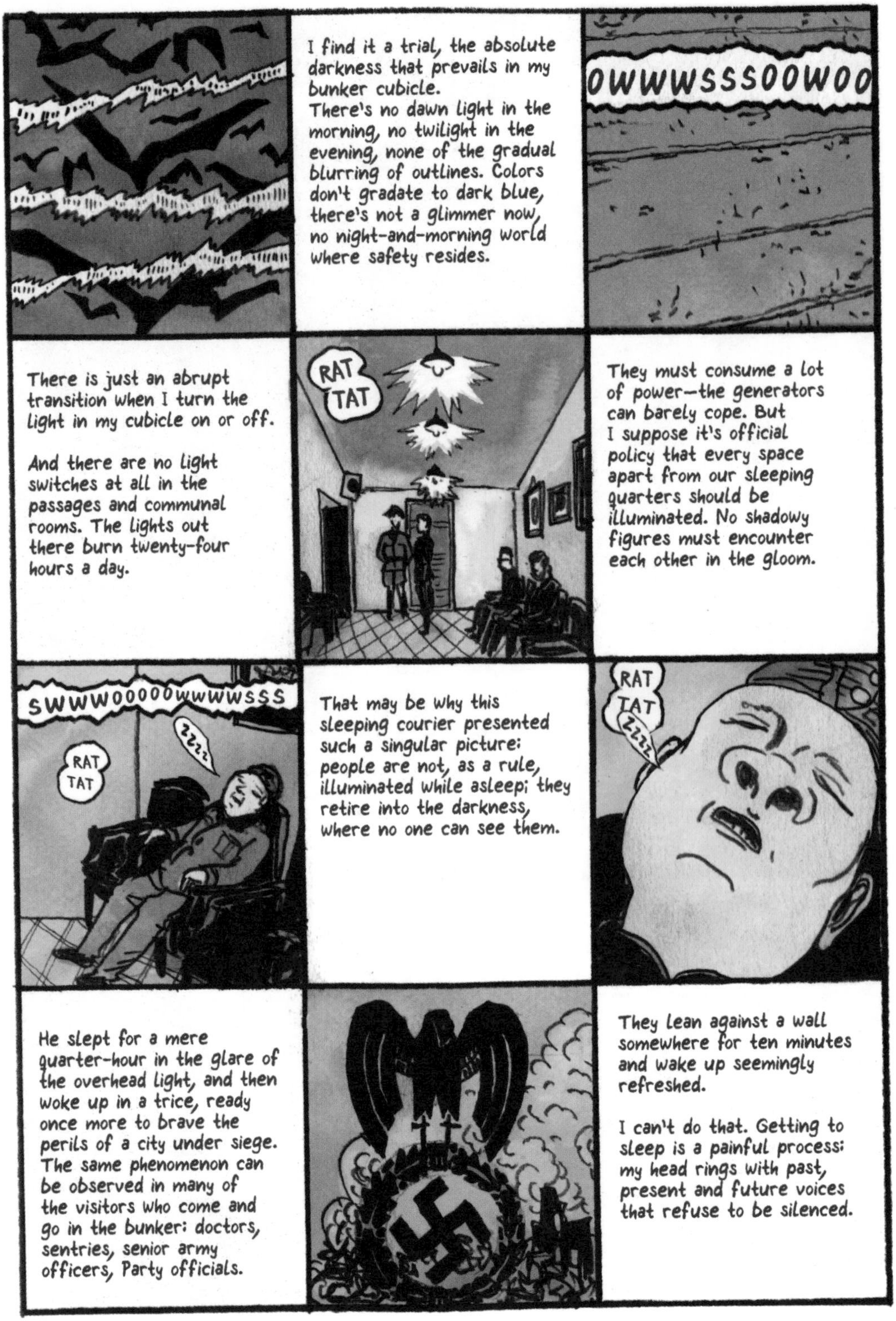
I find it a trial, the absolute darkness that prevails in my bunker cubicle.
There's no dawn light in the morning, no twilight in the evening, none of the gradual blurring of outlines. Colors don't gradate to dark blue, there's not a glimmer now, no night-and-morning world where safety resides.
OWWWSSSOOWOO
There is just an abrupt transition when I turn the light in my cubicle on or off.
And there are no light switches at all in the passages and communal rooms. The lights out there burn twenty-four hours a day.
RAT TAT
They must consume a lot of power—the generators can barely cope. But I suppose it's official policy that every space apart from our sleeping quarters should be illuminated. No shadowy figures must encounter each other in the gloom.
SWWWOOOOOWWWWSSS
RAT TAT
Zzzz
That may be why this sleeping courier presented such a singular picture: people are not, as a rule, illuminated while asleep; they retire into the darkness, where no one can see them.
RAT TAT
Zzzz
He slept for a mere quarter-hour in the glare of the overhead light, and then woke up in a trice, ready once more to brave the perils of a city under siege. The same phenomenon can be observed in many of the visitors who come and go in the bunker: doctors, sentries, senior army officers, Party officials.
They lean against a wall somewhere for ten minutes and wake up seemingly refreshed.
I can't do that. Getting to sleep is a painful process: my head rings with past, present and future voices that refuse to be silenced.

SSSWWWWWSSSS

RAT
TAT

The artificial light in which we have now been living for so many days even affects the acoustics:

All voices sound a full tone lower, all noises muffled and indistinct.

RAT
TAT

SSSSSWWWWWSSSSSWWW

We no longer venture to cite the time of day or night with any certainty. When someone visits from the outside world, he's promptly surrounded.

ARE THE NIGHTS GETTING MILDER?

DOES IT EVEN GET A BIT HOT, NOW, OUT IN THE SUN?

WHAT ABOUT THE REDDISH GLOW THE EVENING SKY TAKES ON IN SPRINGTIME? CAN YOU TELL IT FROM THE REFLECTION OF THE FIRES IN THE SUBURBS?

WHENEVER THE SMOKE CLEARS, SURE, NO PROBLEM.

Then everyone sinks back into the artificial light.

RAT
TAT

SSSSWWW

The bunker's entire ventilation system is on the verge of collapse. The stale air is no longer being fully extracted, so we filter the remaining oxygen from it by breathing faster than normal. Fainting fits are becoming more frequent. The ventilators themselves may be clogged with swarms of fruit flies sucked in from the kitchen.

RAT
TA
SSS SSSWWW

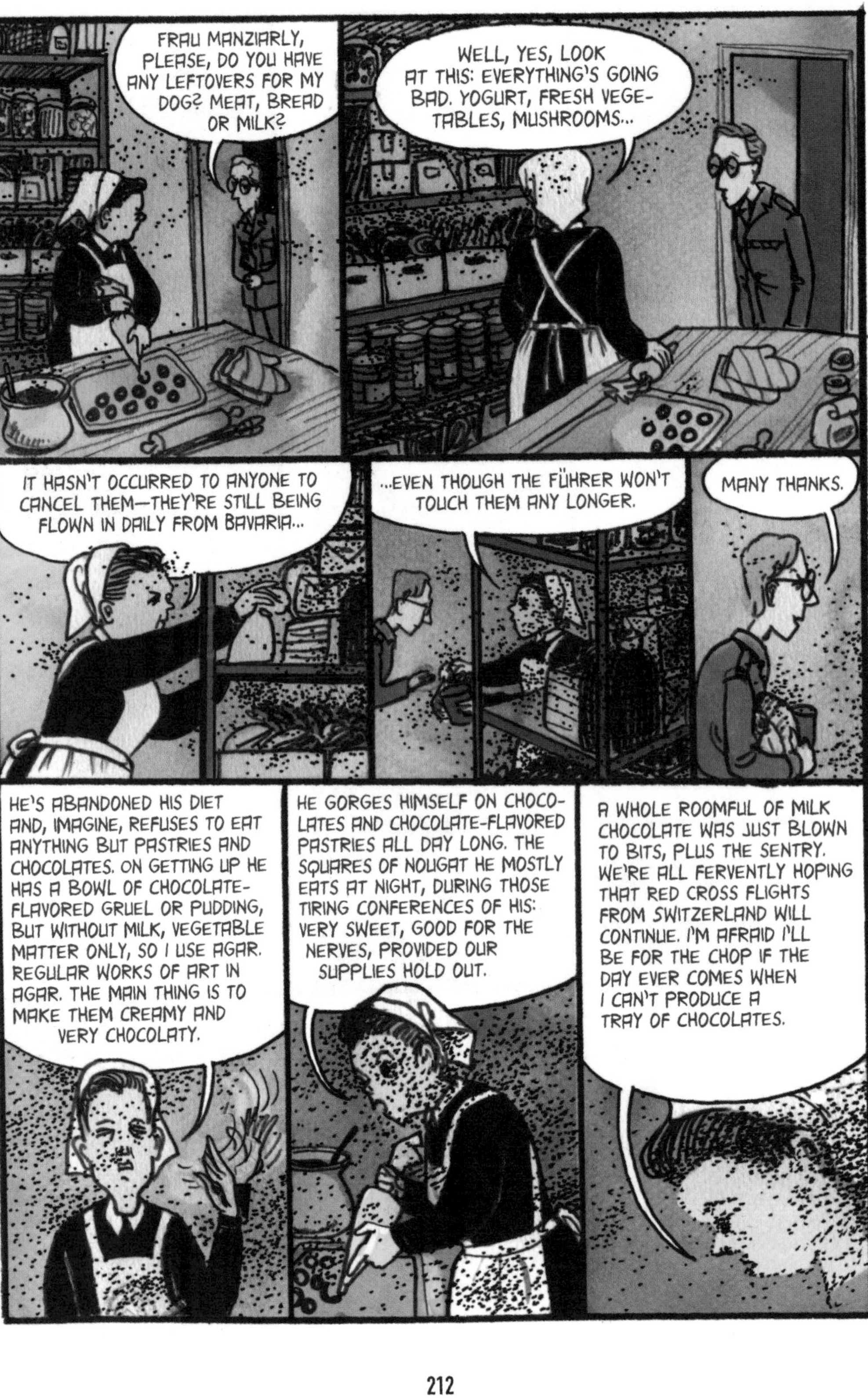
FRAU MANZIARLY, PLEASE, DO YOU HAVE ANY LEFTOVERS FOR MY DOG? MEAT, BREAD OR MILK?
WELL, YES, LOOK AT THIS: EVERYTHING'S GOING BAD. YOGURT, FRESH VEGETABLES, MUSHROOMS...
IT HASN'T OCCURRED TO ANYONE TO CANCEL THEM—THEY'RE STILL BEING FLOWN IN DAILY FROM BAVARIA...
...EVEN THOUGH THE FÜHRER WON'T TOUCH THEM ANY LONGER.
MANY THANKS.
HE'S ABANDONED HIS DIET AND, IMAGINE, REFUSES TO EAT ANYTHING BUT PASTRIES AND CHOCOLATES. ON GETTING UP HE HAS A BOWL OF CHOCOLATE-FLAVORED GRUEL OR PUDDING, BUT WITHOUT MILK, VEGETABLE MATTER ONLY, SO I USE AGAR. REGULAR WORKS OF ART IN AGAR. THE MAIN THING IS TO MAKE THEM CREAMY AND VERY CHOCOLATY.
HE GORGES HIMSELF ON CHOCOLATES AND CHOCOLATE-FLAVORED PASTRIES ALL DAY LONG. THE SQUARES OF NOUGAT HE MOSTLY EATS AT NIGHT, DURING THOSE TIRING CONFERENCES OF HIS: VERY SWEET, GOOD FOR THE NERVES, PROVIDED OUR SUPPLIES HOLD OUT.
A WHOLE ROOMFUL OF MILK CHOCOLATE WAS JUST BLOWN TO BITS, PLUS THE SENTRY. WE'RE ALL FERVENTLY HOPING THAT RED CROSS FLIGHTS FROM SWITZERLAND WILL CONTINUE. I'M AFRAID I'LL BE FOR THE CHOP IF THE DAY EVER COMES WHEN I CAN'T PRODUCE A TRAY OF CHOCOLATES.

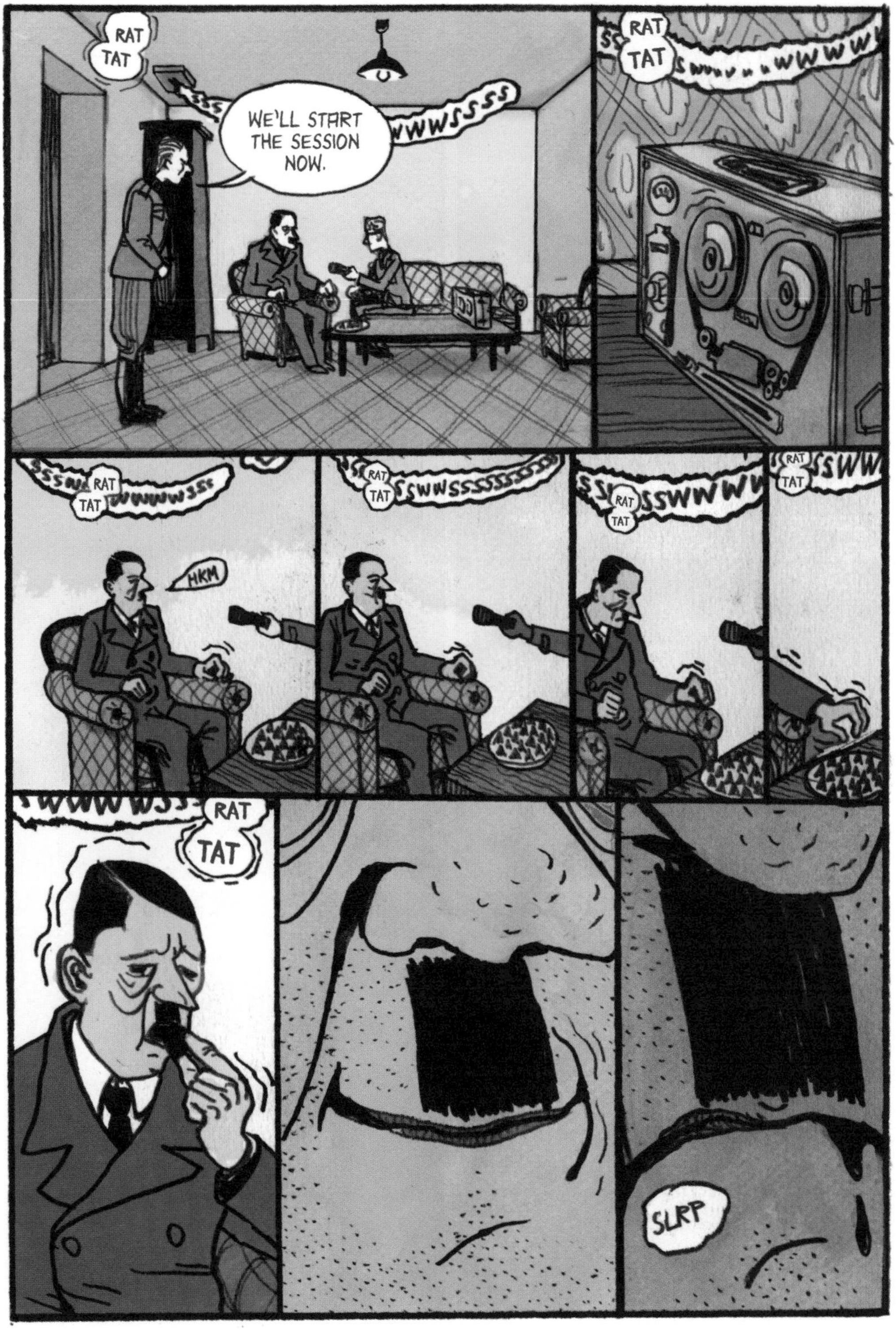
RAT
TAT
WE'LL START THE SESSION NOW.
RAT
TAT
RAT
TAT
HKM
RAT
TAT
RAT
TAT
RAT
TAT
RAT
TAT
SLRP

PANT

PANT

PANT PANT

PANT

PANT
PANT

THEY KNOW THEIR VICTIMS ARE DEFENSE-
LESS BECAUSE THEY CAN HEAR THEIR QUIET
BREATHING FROM A LONG WAY OFF.

ZZZZ ZZ
ZZ ZZZ ZZZZ

ZZZZ ZZZZ

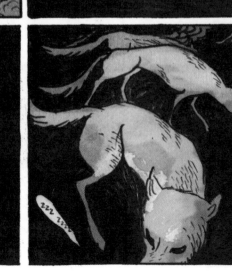

PAPA, PAPA,
LOOK, WE'VE WRITTEN
SO MANY WEREWOLF
STORIES FOR YOU!

THAT'S SO NICE, THANK
YOU, HOLDE.

I WROTE THEM,
ACTUALLY, THE OTHERS
JUST DICTATED THEM.

ZZZ ZZZZ

214

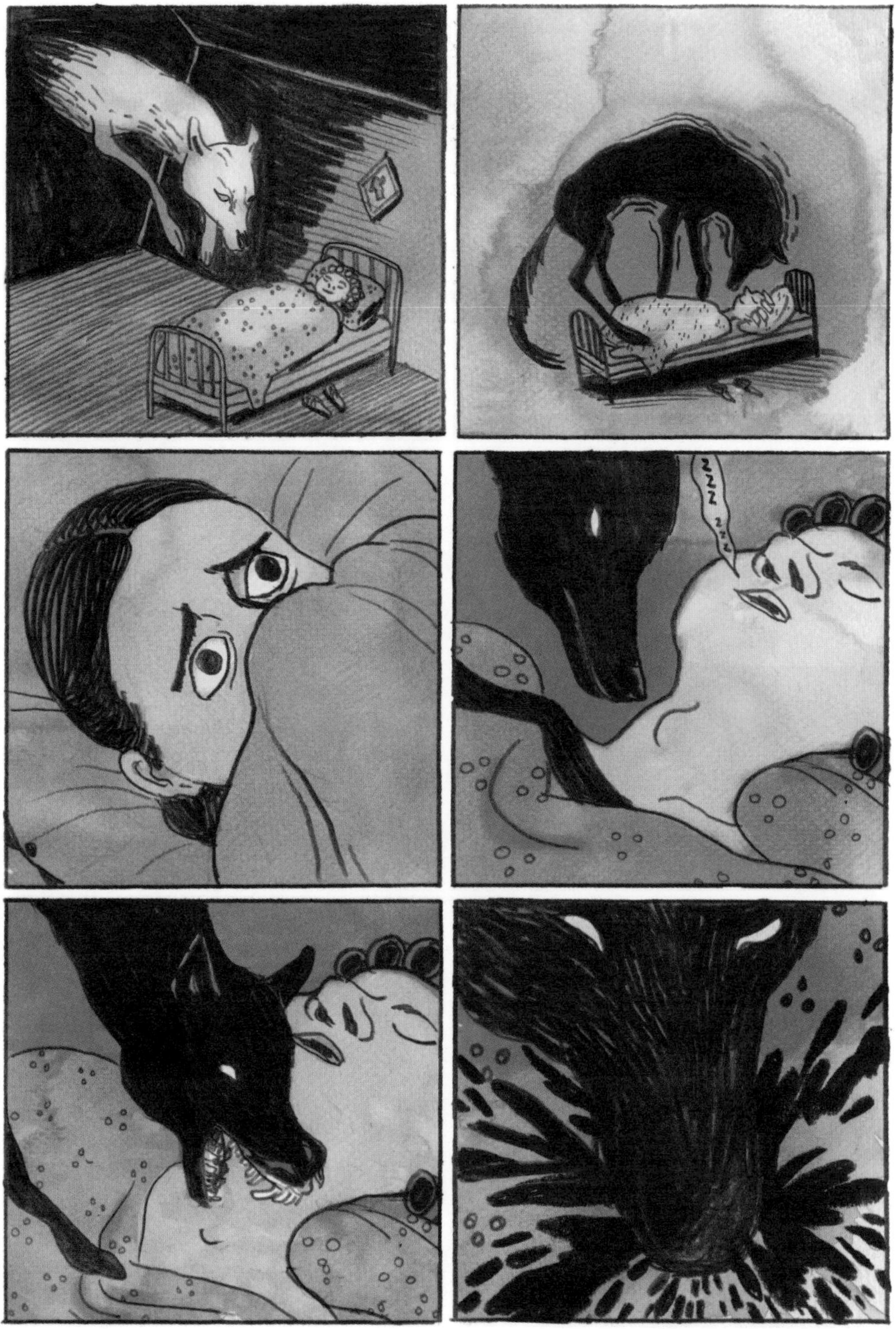
ZZZzzz

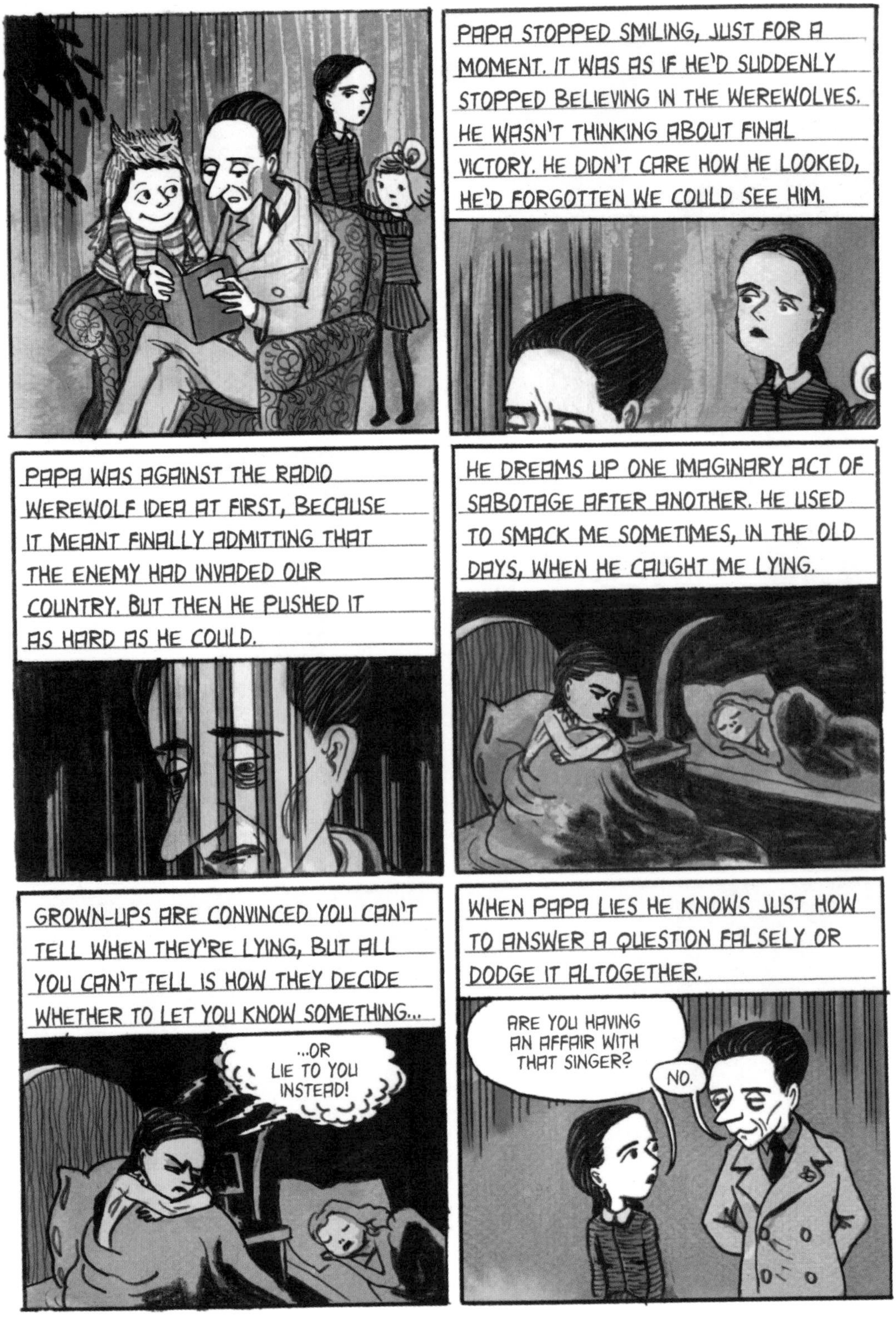
PAPA STOPPED SMILING, JUST FOR A MOMENT. IT WAS AS IF HE'D SUDDENLY STOPPED BELIEVING IN THE WEREWOLVES. HE WASN'T THINKING ABOUT FINAL VICTORY. HE DIDN'T CARE HOW HE LOOKED, HE'D FORGOTTEN WE COULD SEE HIM.
PAPA WAS AGAINST THE RADIO WEREWOLF IDEA AT FIRST, BECAUSE IT MEANT FINALLY ADMITTING THAT THE ENEMY HAD INVADED OUR COUNTRY. BUT THEN HE PUSHED IT AS HARD AS HE COULD.
HE DREAMS UP ONE IMAGINARY ACT OF SABOTAGE AFTER ANOTHER. HE USED TO SMACK ME SOMETIMES, IN THE OLD DAYS, WHEN HE CAUGHT ME LYING.
GROWN-UPS ARE CONVINCED YOU CAN'T TELL WHEN THEY'RE LYING, BUT ALL YOU CAN'T TELL IS HOW THEY DECIDE WHETHER TO LET YOU KNOW SOMETHING...
...OR LIE TO YOU INSTEAD!
WHEN PAPA LIES HE KNOWS JUST HOW TO ANSWER A QUESTION FALSELY OR DODGE IT ALTOGETHER.
ARE YOU HAVING AN AFFAIR WITH THAT SINGER?
NO.

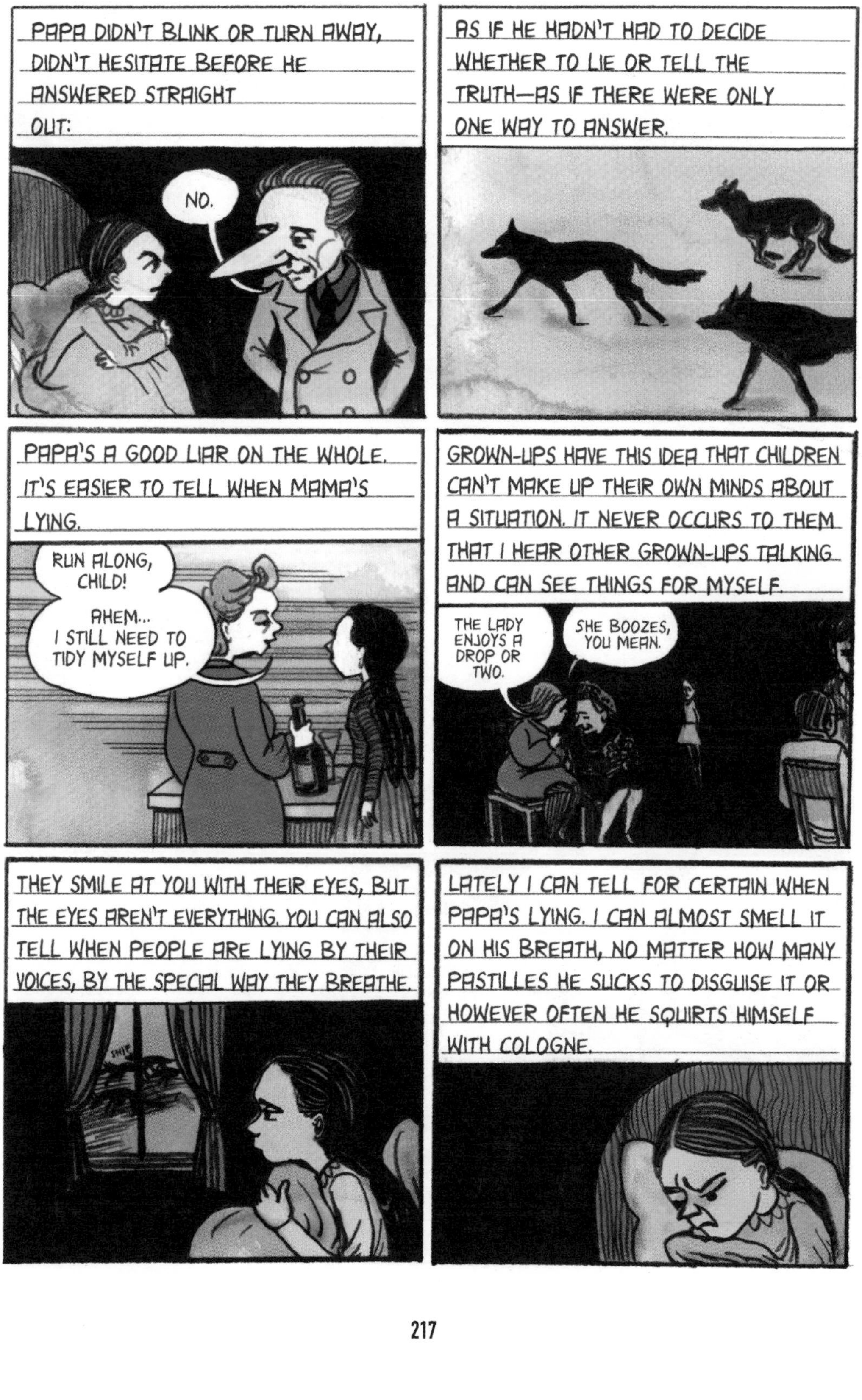
PAPA DIDN'T BLINK OR TURN AWAY, DIDN'T HESITATE BEFORE HE ANSWERED STRAIGHT OUT:
NO.
AS IF HE HADN'T HAD TO DECIDE WHETHER TO LIE OR TELL THE TRUTH—AS IF THERE WERE ONLY ONE WAY TO ANSWER.
PAPA'S A GOOD LIAR ON THE WHOLE. IT'S EASIER TO TELL WHEN MAMA'S LYING.
RUN ALONG, CHILD!
AHEM... I STILL NEED TO TIDY MYSELF UP.
GROWN-UPS HAVE THIS IDEA THAT CHILDREN CAN'T MAKE UP THEIR OWN MINDS ABOUT A SITUATION. IT NEVER OCCURS TO THEM THAT I HEAR OTHER GROWN-UPS TALKING AND CAN SEE THINGS FOR MYSELF.
THE LADY ENJOYS A DROP OR TWO.
SHE BOOZES, YOU MEAN.
THEY SMILE AT YOU WITH THEIR EYES, BUT THE EYES AREN'T EVERYTHING. YOU CAN ALSO TELL WHEN PEOPLE ARE LYING BY THEIR VOICES, BY THE SPECIAL WAY THEY BREATHE.
LATELY I CAN TELL FOR CERTAIN WHEN PAPA'S LYING. I CAN ALMOST SMELL IT ON HIS BREATH, NO MATTER HOW MANY PASTILLES HE SUCKS TO DISGUISE IT OR HOWEVER OFTEN HE SQUIRTS HIMSELF WITH COLOGNE.

April 24.
An absolute disaster:
RAT
TAT
The patient is refusing chocolate-flavored dishes of any kind, even pastries. He now insists on straight chocolate, the kind that melts in your mouth without having to be chewed or sucked. It dissolves of its own accord, diffuses itself through the oral cavity, and coats the teeth and gums with a thin film of creamy cocoa.
Bzzz
RAT
TAT
Bzzz
RAT
TAT
THERE'S NO HOPE NOW.
THIS IS THE BEGINNING OF THE END.
RAT
TAT

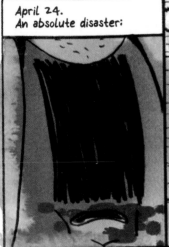

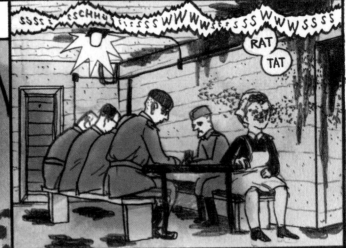

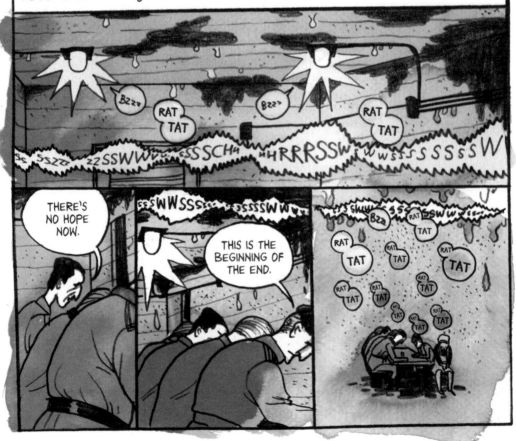

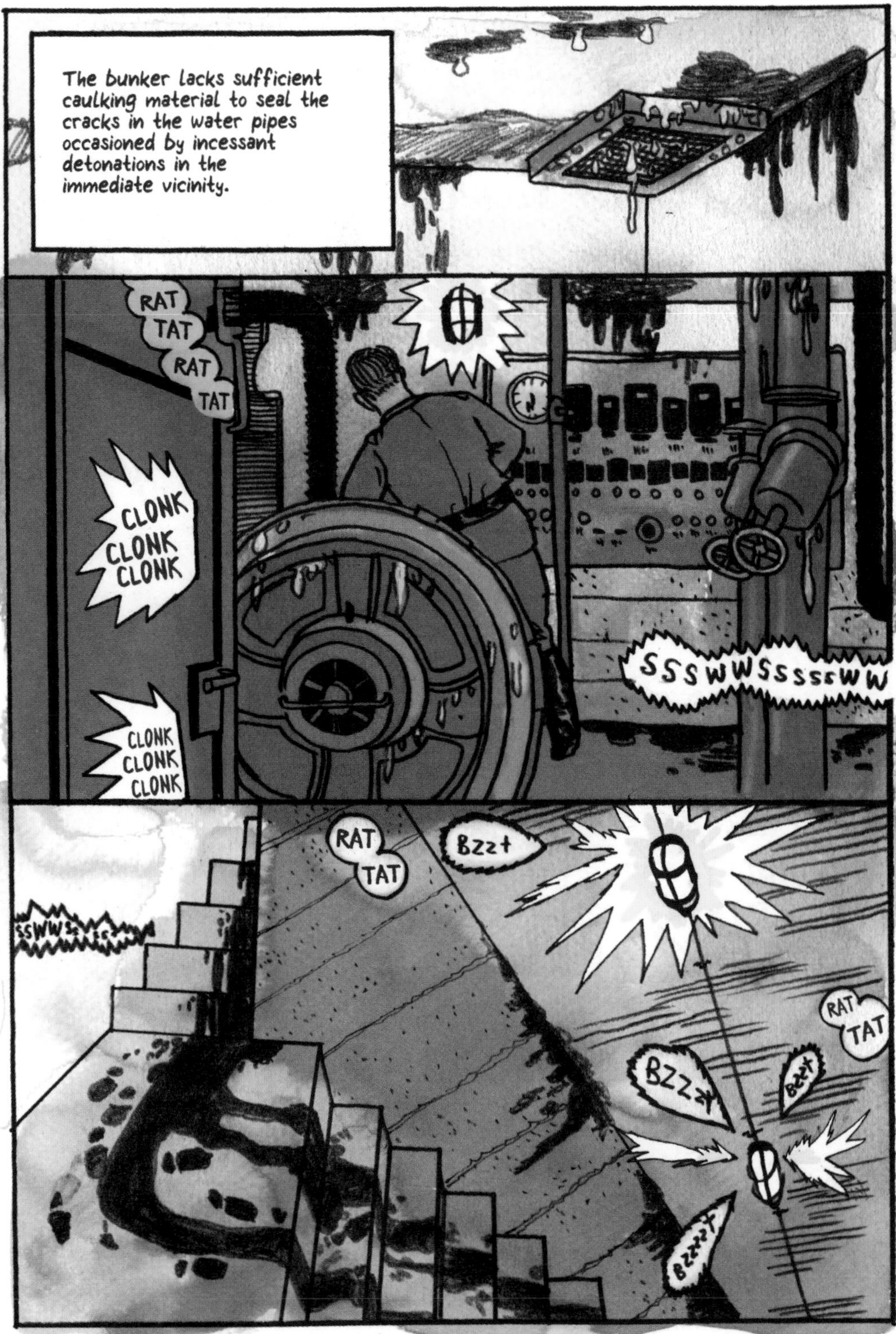

The bunker lacks sufficient caulking material to seal the cracks in the water pipes occasioned by incessant detonations in the immediate vicinity.
RAT TAT RAT TAT
CLONK CLONK CLONK
CLONK CLONK CLONK
SSSWWSSSSSWW
RAT TAT
Bzzt
RAT TAT
BZZZT
Bzzt

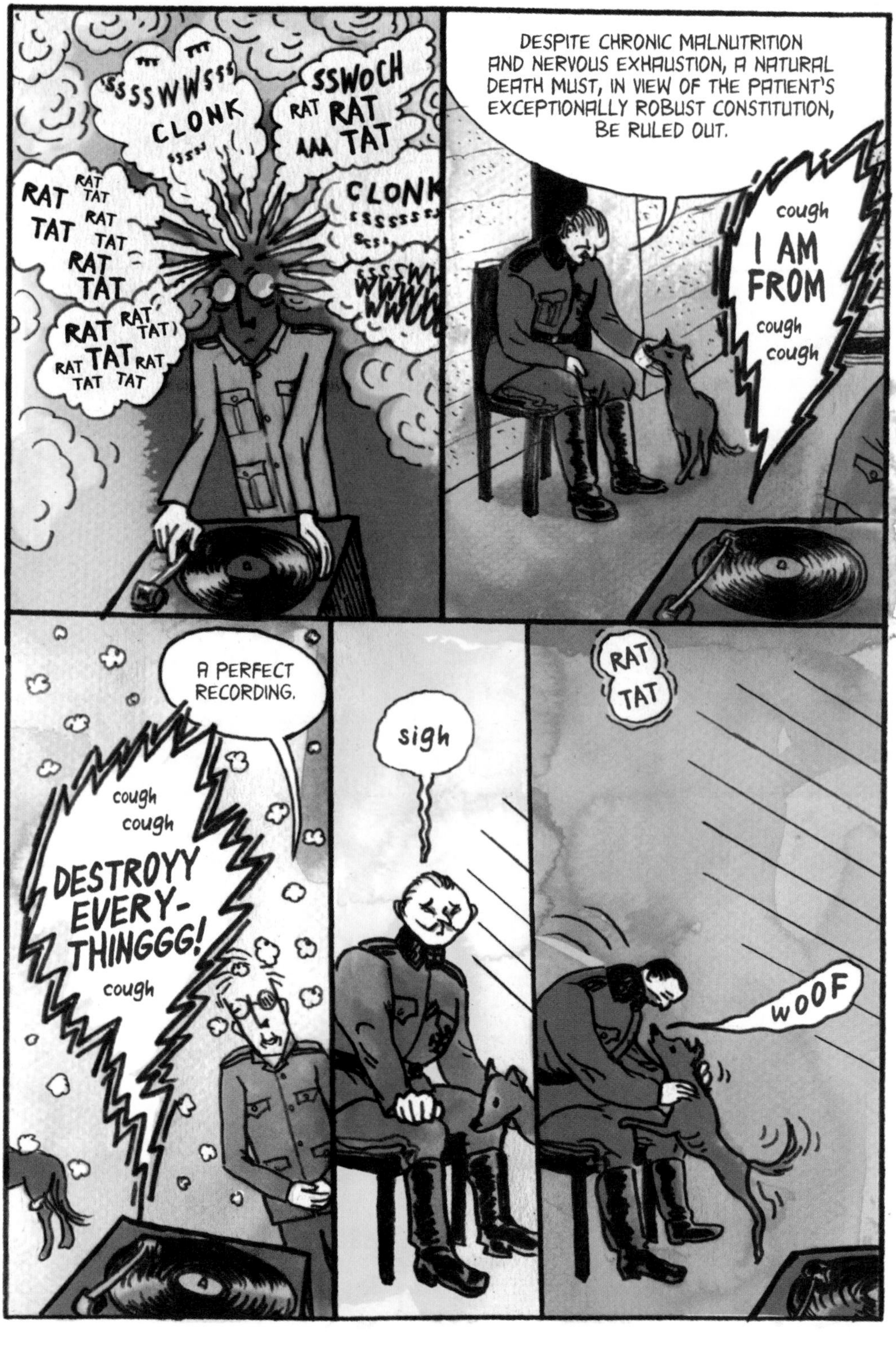
SSSSWWSSS
CLONK
SSSSS
SSWOCH
RAT RAT
AAA TAT
RAT
RAT TAT
TAT RAT
TAT
RAT
TAT
RAT RAT TAT
RAT TAT RAT
TAT TAT
CLONK
SSSSSSSS
SSSS
DESPITE CHRONIC MALNUTRITION AND NERVOUS EXHAUSTION, A NATURAL DEATH MUST, IN VIEW OF THE PATIENT'S EXCEPTIONALLY ROBUST CONSTITUTION, BE RULED OUT.
cough
I AM FROM
cough
cough
A PERFECT RECORDING.
cough
cough
DESTROYY EVERY-THINGGG!
cough
sigh
RAT
TAT
WOOF

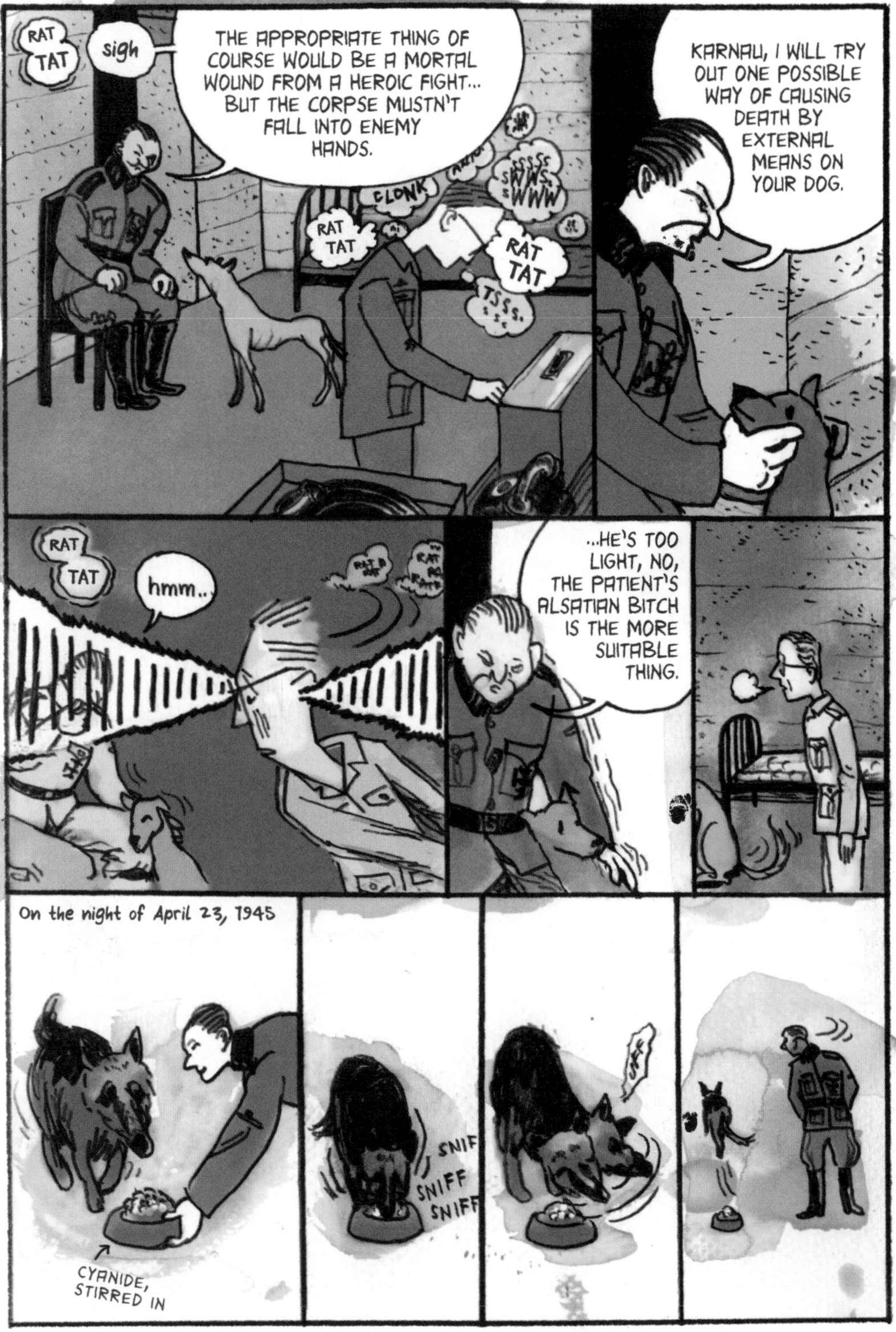
RAT TAT
sigh
THE APPROPRIATE THING OF COURSE WOULD BE A MORTAL WOUND FROM A HEROIC FIGHT... BUT THE CORPSE MUSTN'T FALL INTO ENEMY HANDS.
CLONK
RAT TAT
RAT TAT
TSSSS
KARNAU, I WILL TRY OUT ONE POSSIBLE WAY OF CAUSING DEATH BY EXTERNAL MEANS ON YOUR DOG.
RAT TAT
hmm...
...HE'S TOO LIGHT, NO, THE PATIENT'S ALSATIAN BITCH IS THE MORE SUITABLE THING.
On the night of April 23, 1945
CYANIDE, STIRRED IN
SNIF
SNIFF
SNIFF

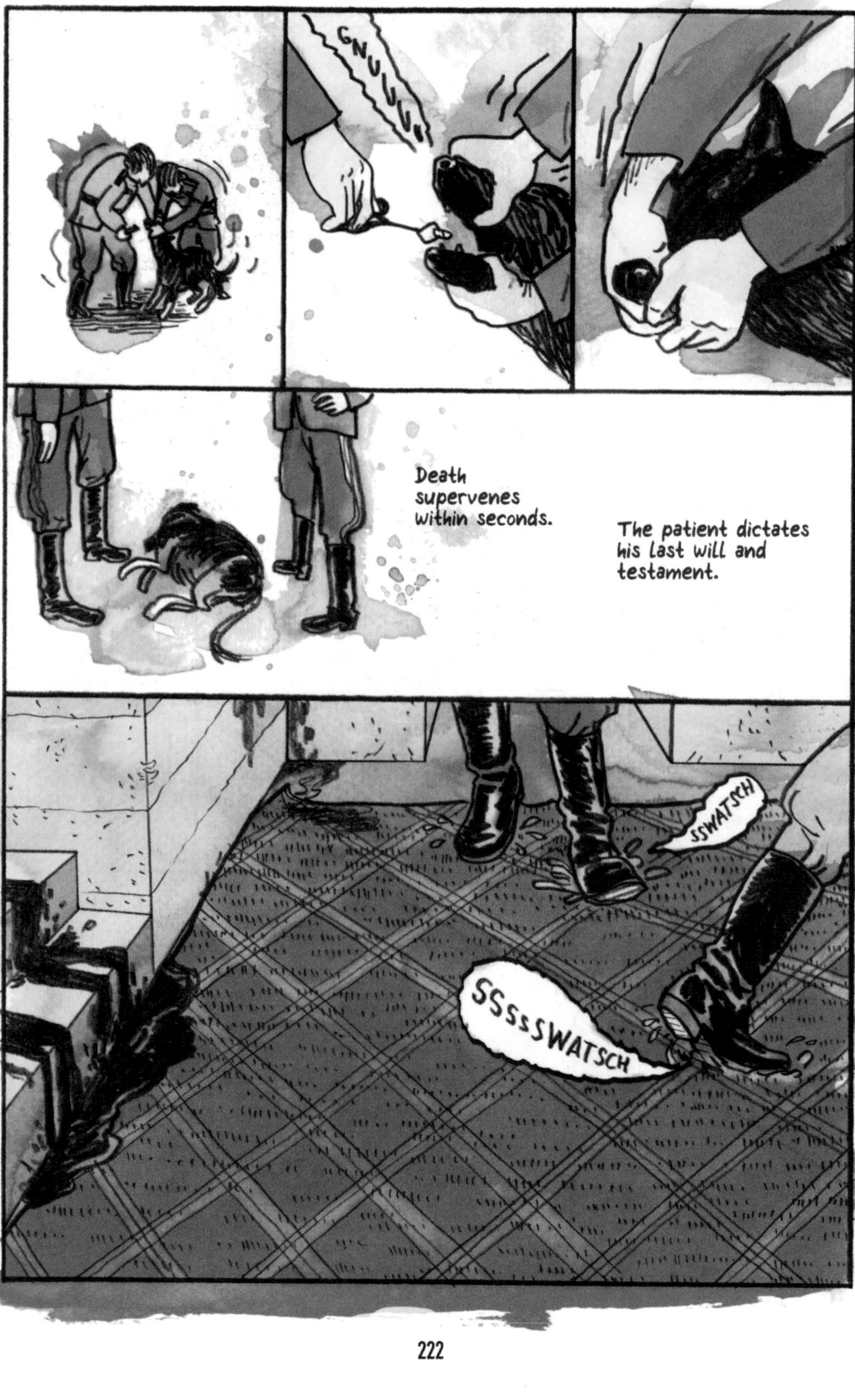
GNUUUU
Death supervenes within seconds.
The patient dictates his last will and testament.
SSWATSCH
SSsssWATSCH

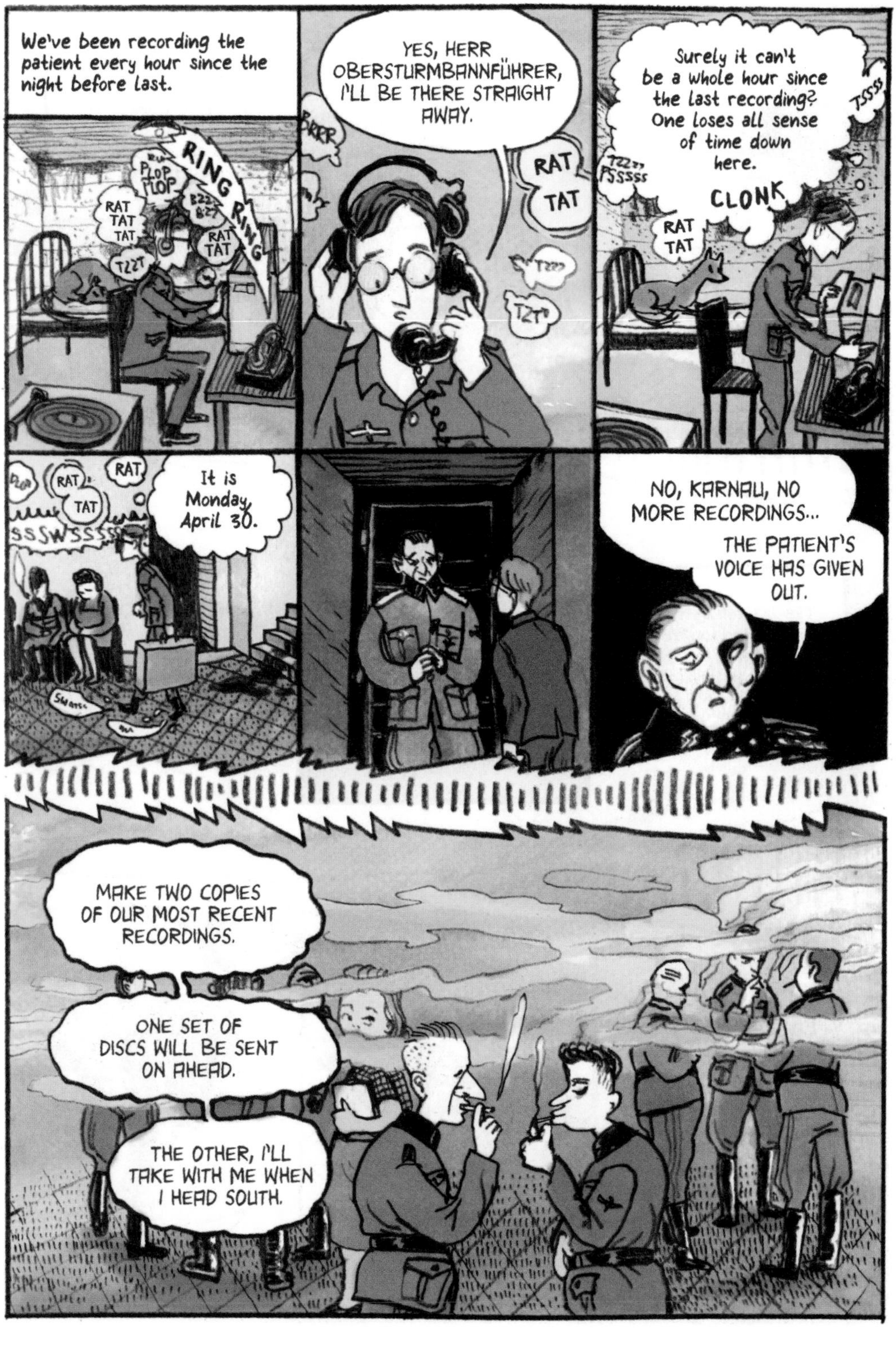
We've been recording the patient every hour since the night before last.
RING RING
PLOP PLOP
RAT TAT TAT
RAT TAT
TZZT
YES, HERR OBERSTURMBANNFÜHRER, I'LL BE THERE STRAIGHT AWAY.
BRRR
RAT TAT
Surely it can't be a whole hour since the last recording? One loses all sense of time down here.
TSSSS
CLONK
RAT TAT
RAT TAT
It is Monday, April 30.
SSSWSSSS
NO, KARNAU, NO MORE RECORDINGS...
THE PATIENT'S VOICE HAS GIVEN OUT.
MAKE TWO COPIES OF OUR MOST RECENT RECORDINGS.
ONE SET OF DISCS WILL BE SENT ON AHEAD.
THE OTHER, I'LL TAKE WITH ME WHEN I HEAD SOUTH.

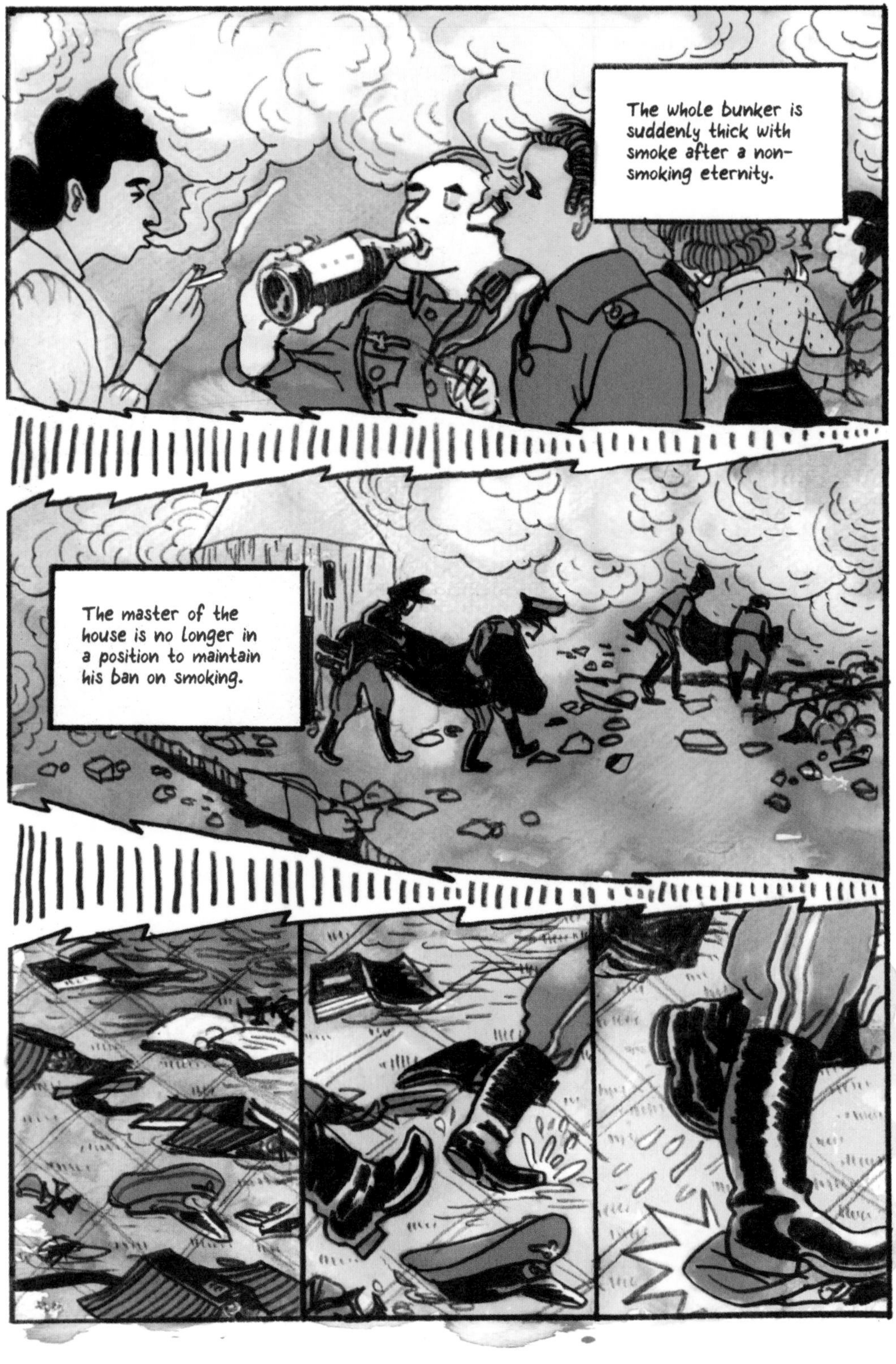
The whole bunker is suddenly thick with smoke after a non-smoking eternity.
The master of the house is no longer in a position to maintain his ban on smoking.

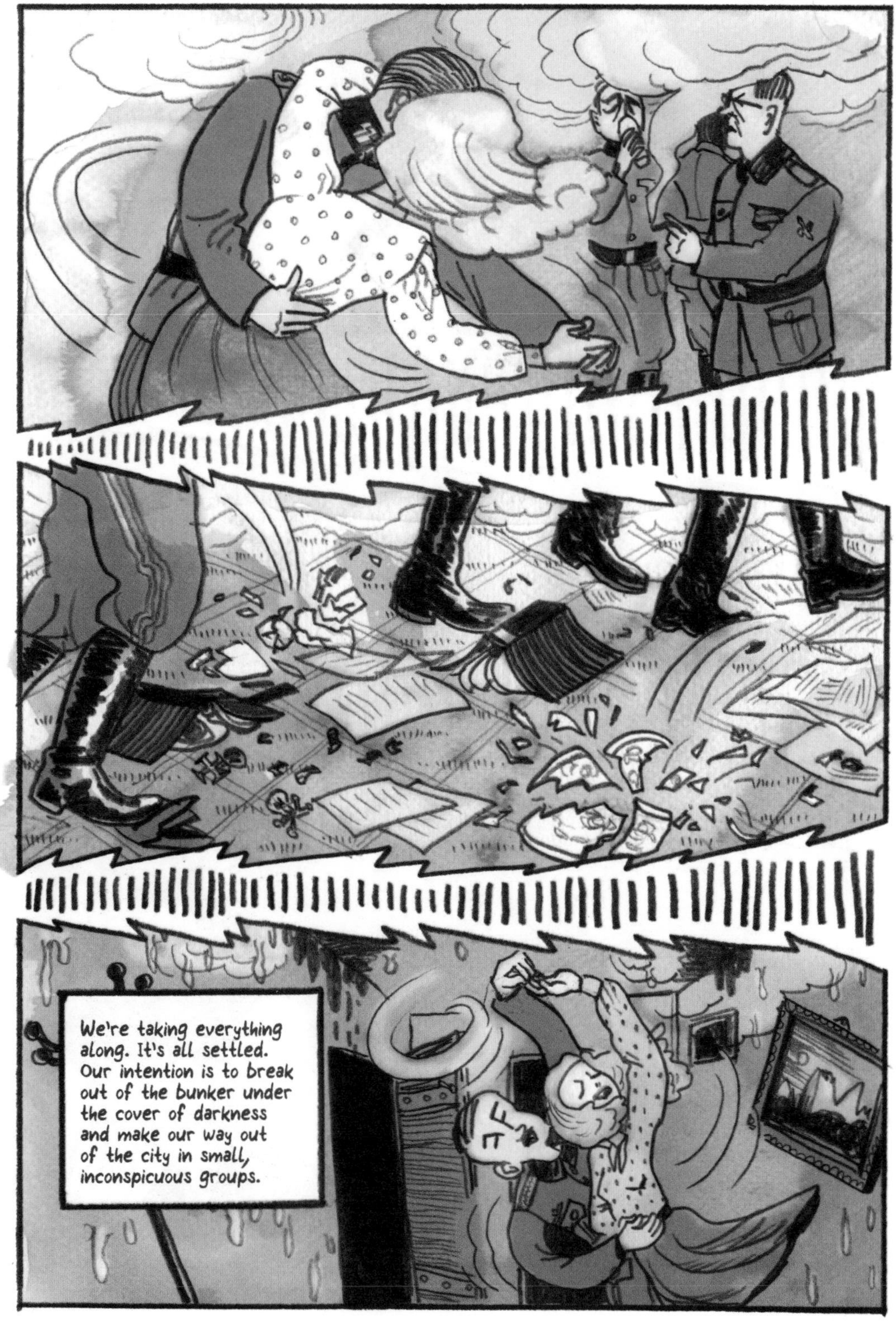
We're taking everything along. It's all settled. Our intention is to break out of the bunker under the cover of darkness and make our way out of the city in small, inconspicuous groups.

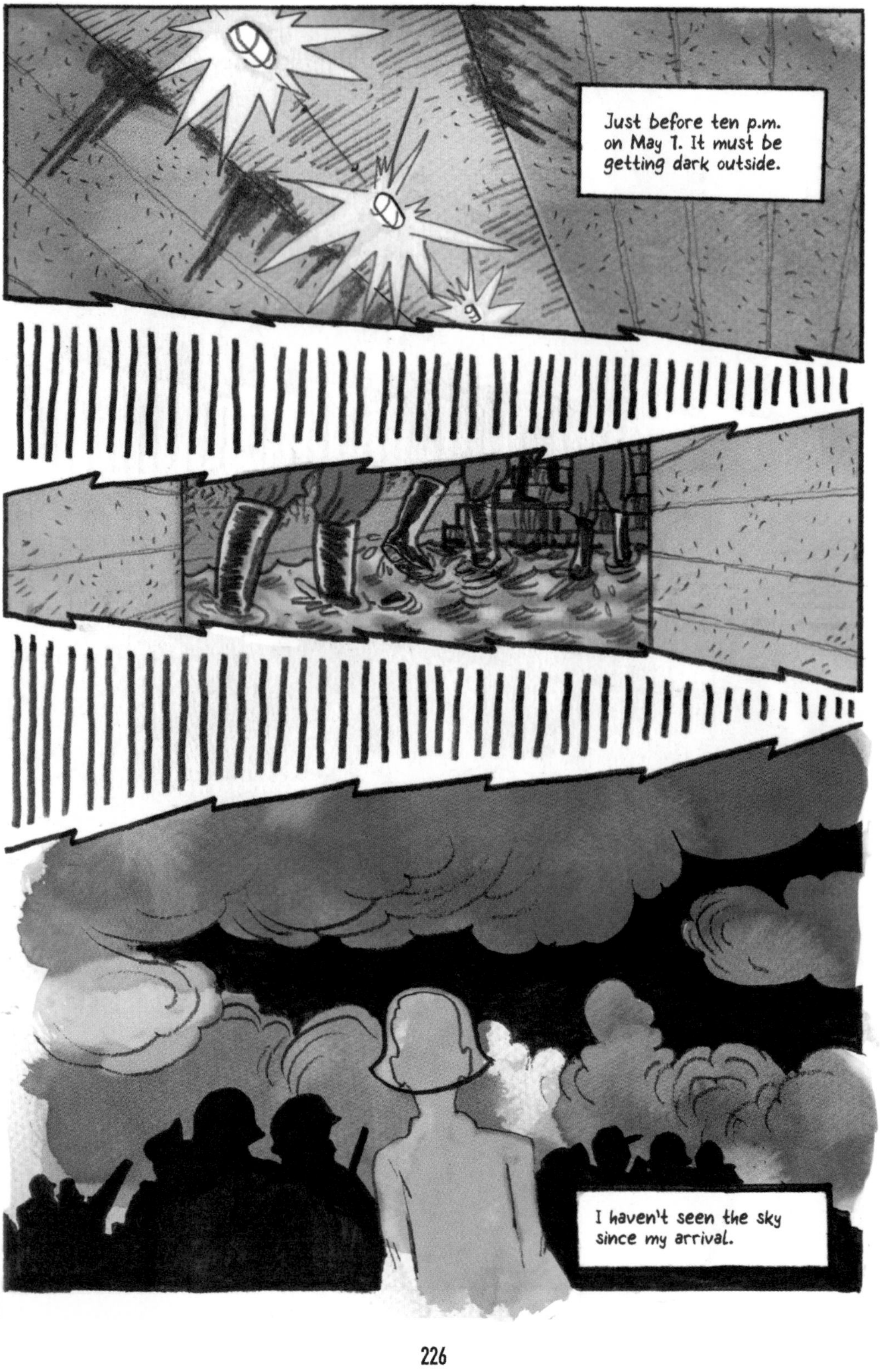
Just before ten p.m. on May 7. It must be getting dark outside.
I haven't seen the sky since my arrival.

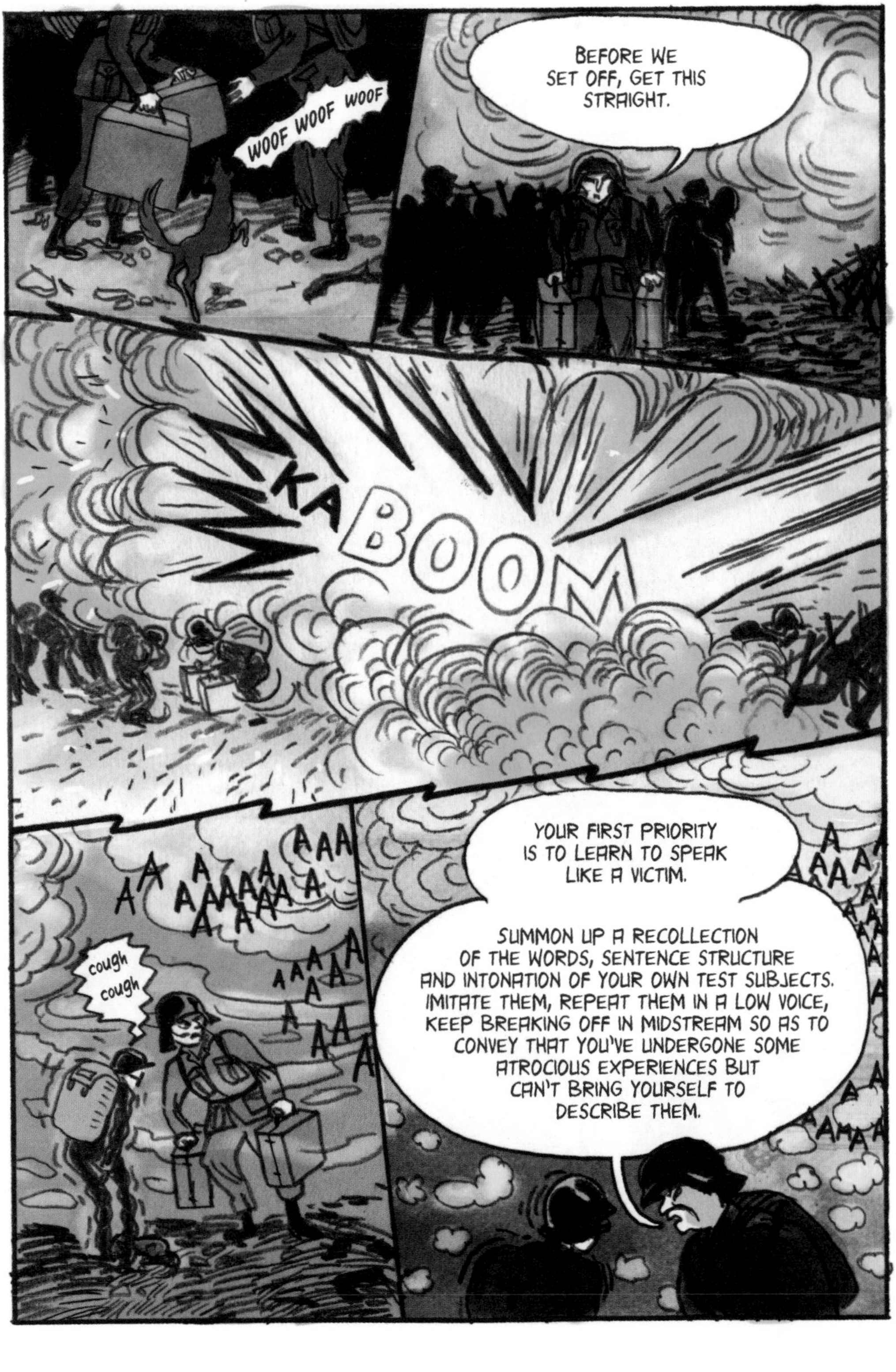
WOOF WOOF WOOF
BEFORE WE SET OFF, GET THIS STRAIGHT.
KABOOM
YOUR FIRST PRIORITY IS TO LEARN TO SPEAK LIKE A VICTIM.
SUMMON UP A RECOLLECTION OF THE WORDS, SENTENCE STRUCTURE AND INTONATION OF YOUR OWN TEST SUBJECTS. IMITATE THEM, REPEAT THEM IN A LOW VOICE, KEEP BREAKING OFF IN MIDSTREAM SO AS TO CONVEY THAT YOU'VE UNDERGONE SOME ATROCIOUS EXPERIENCES BUT CAN'T BRING YOURSELF TO DESCRIBE THEM.
cough cough

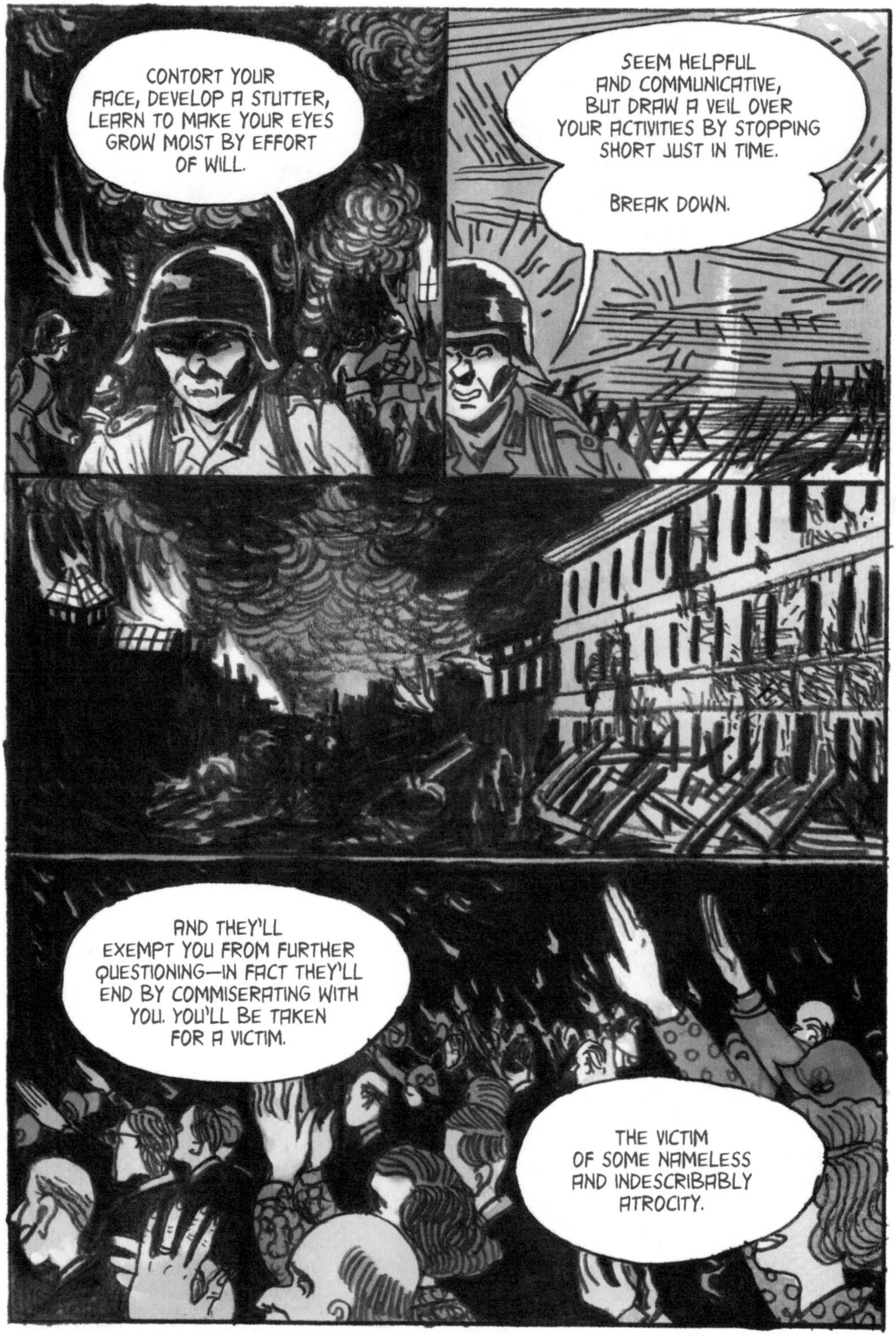
CONTORT YOUR FACE, DEVELOP A STUTTER, LEARN TO MAKE YOUR EYES GROW MOIST BY EFFORT OF WILL.
SEEM HELPFUL AND COMMUNICATIVE, BUT DRAW A VEIL OVER YOUR ACTIVITIES BY STOPPING SHORT JUST IN TIME.
BREAK DOWN.
AND THEY'LL EXEMPT YOU FROM FURTHER QUESTIONING—IN FACT THEY'LL END BY COMMISERATING WITH YOU. YOU'LL BE TAKEN FOR A VICTIM.
THE VICTIM OF SOME NAMELESS AND INDESCRIBABLY ATROCITY.

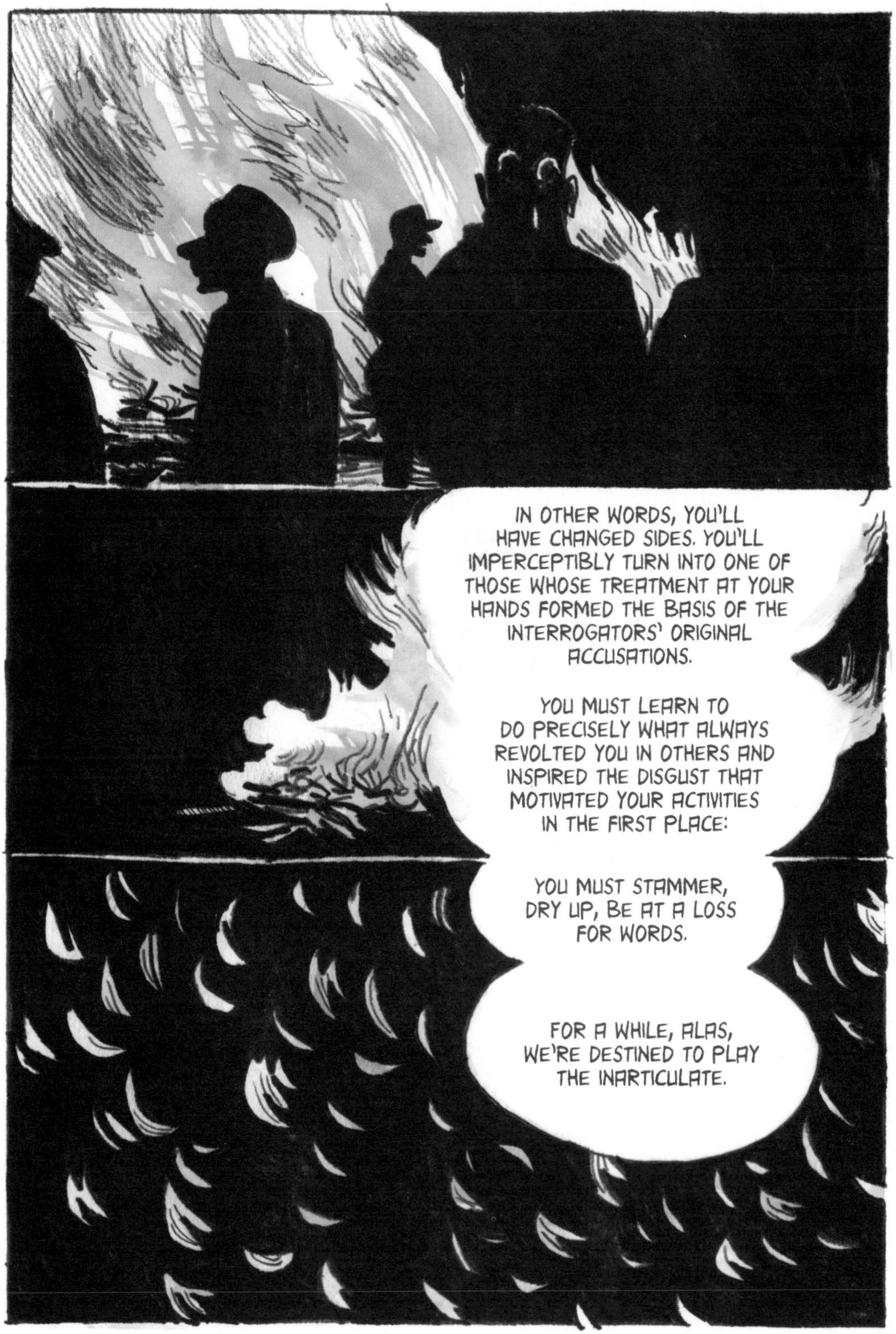
IN OTHER WORDS, YOU'LL HAVE CHANGED SIDES. YOU'LL IMPERCEPTIBLY TURN INTO ONE OF THOSE WHOSE TREATMENT AT YOUR HANDS FORMED THE BASIS OF THE INTERROGATORS' ORIGINAL ACCUSATIONS.
YOU MUST LEARN TO DO PRECISELY WHAT ALWAYS REVOLTED YOU IN OTHERS AND INSPIRED THE DISGUST THAT MOTIVATED YOUR ACTIVITIES IN THE FIRST PLACE:
YOU MUST STAMMER, DRY UP, BE AT A LOSS FOR WORDS.
FOR A WHILE, ALAS, WE'RE DESTINED TO PLAY THE INARTICULATE.

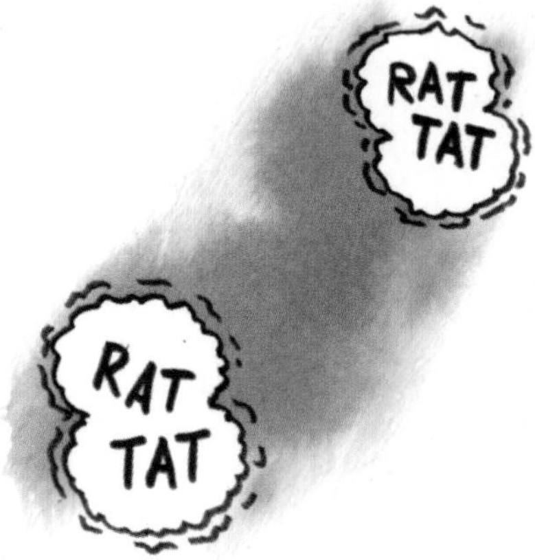
RAT TAT
RAT TAT

V.

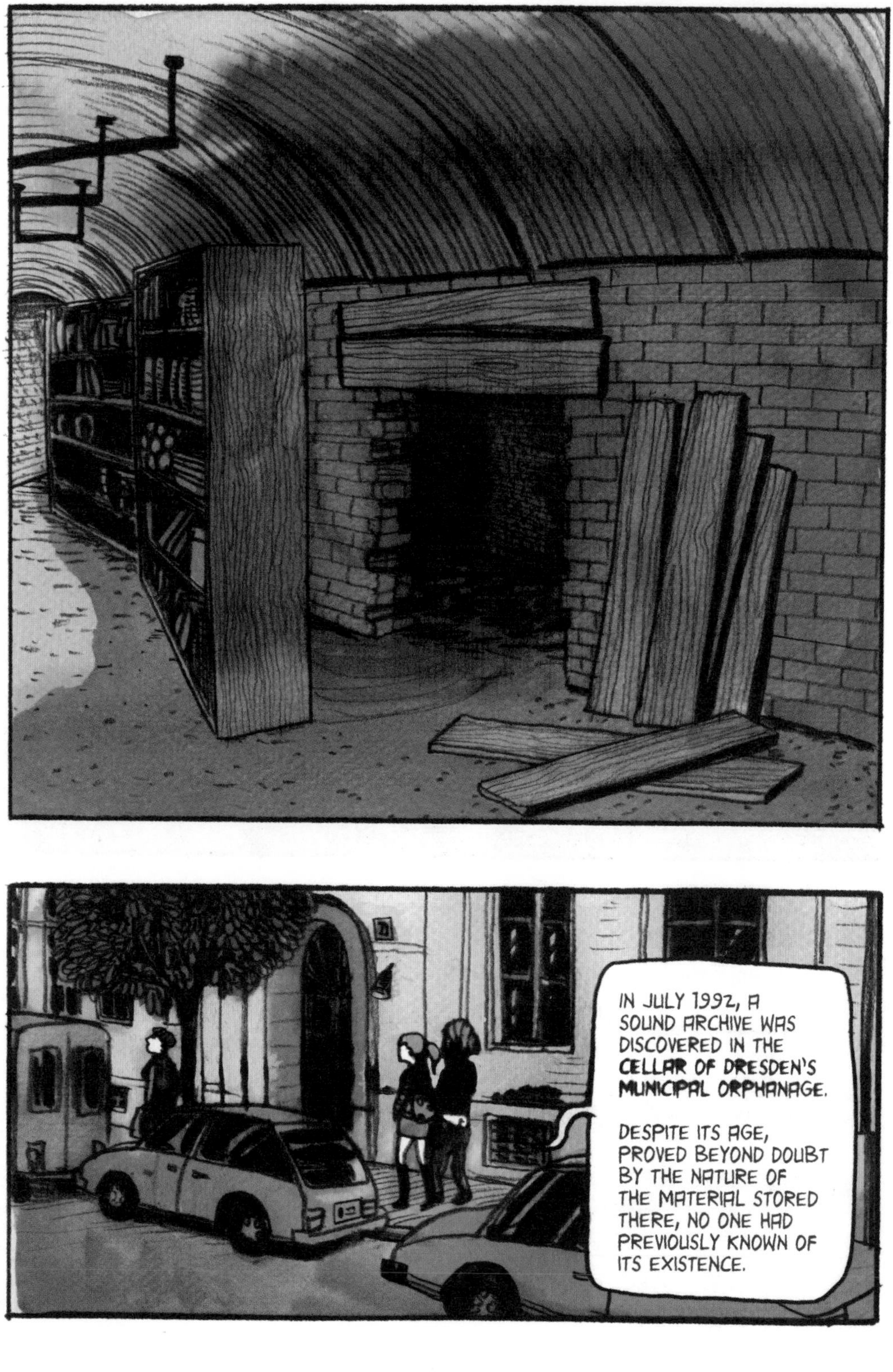
IN JULY 1992, A SOUND ARCHIVE WAS DISCOVERED IN THE **CELLAR OF DRESDEN'S MUNICIPAL ORPHANAGE.**
DESPITE ITS AGE, PROVED BEYOND DOUBT BY THE NATURE OF THE MATERIAL STORED THERE, NO ONE HAD PREVIOUSLY KNOWN OF ITS EXISTENCE.

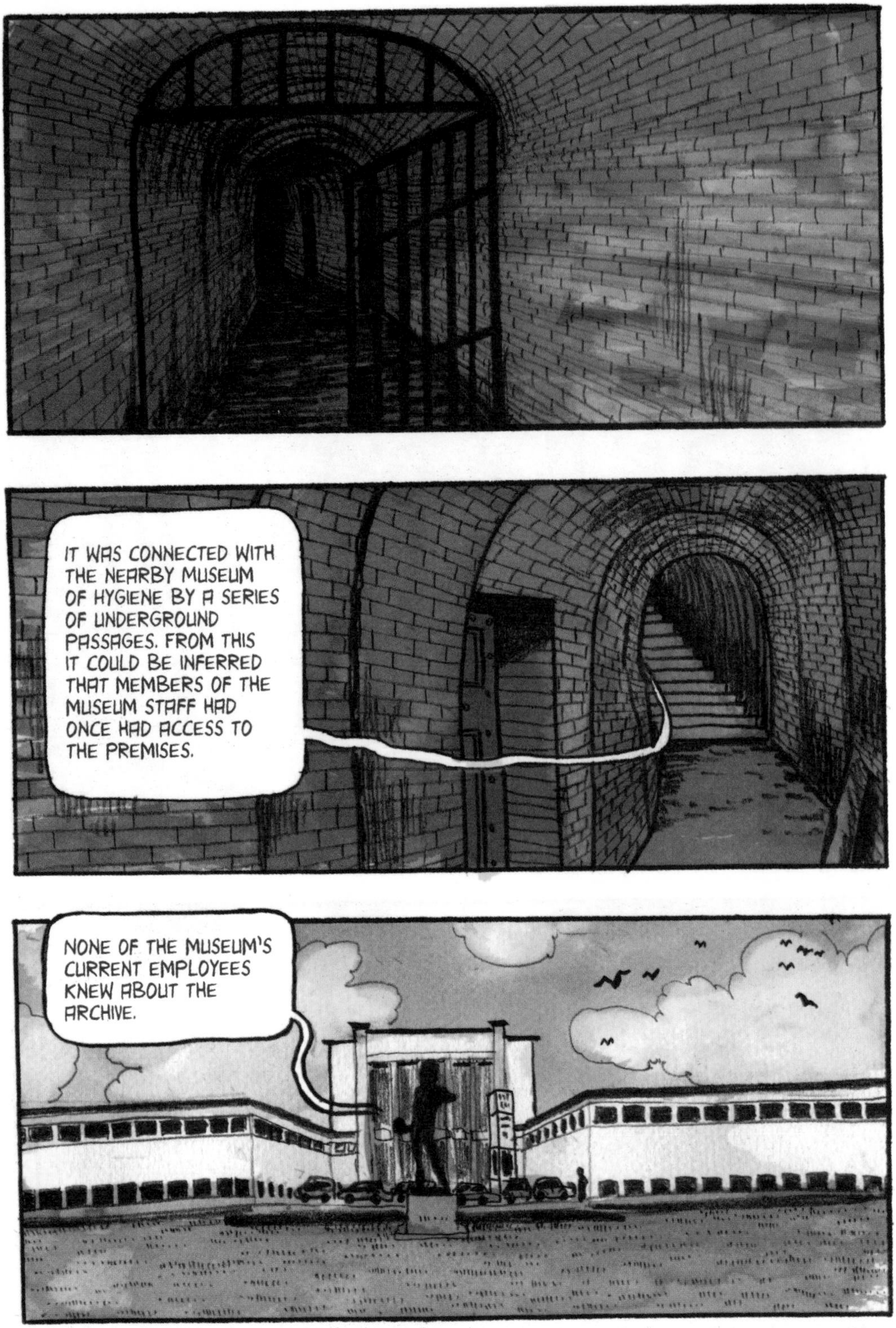
IT WAS CONNECTED WITH THE NEARBY MUSEUM OF HYGIENE BY A SERIES OF UNDERGROUND PASSAGES. FROM THIS IT COULD BE INFERRED THAT MEMBERS OF THE MUSEUM STAFF HAD ONCE HAD ACCESS TO THE PREMISES.
NONE OF THE MUSEUM'S CURRENT EMPLOYEES KNEW ABOUT THE ARCHIVE.

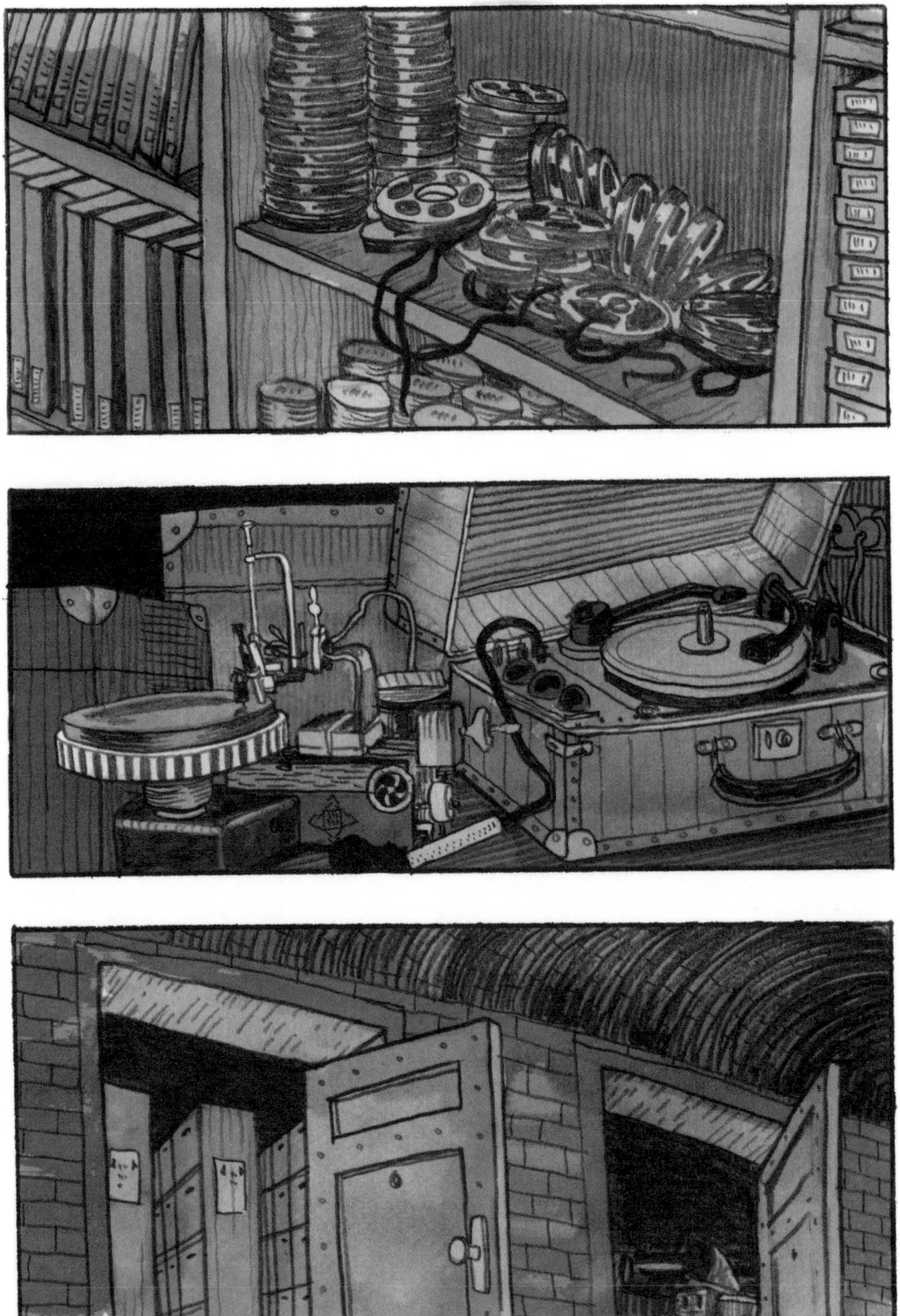

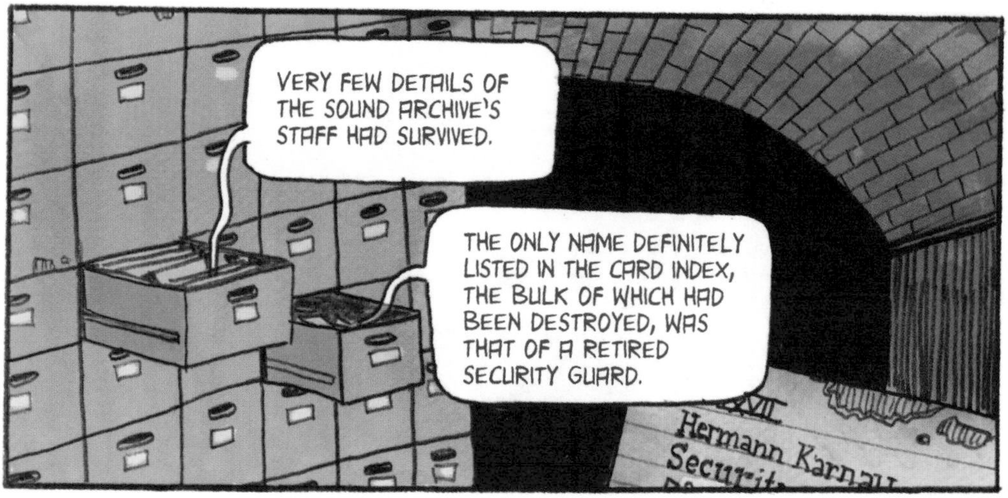
VERY FEW DETAILS OF THE SOUND ARCHIVE'S STAFF HAD SURVIVED.
THE ONLY NAME DEFINITELY LISTED IN THE CARD INDEX, THE BULK OF WHICH HAD BEEN DESTROYED, WAS THAT OF A RETIRED SECURITY GUARD.
Hermann Karnau

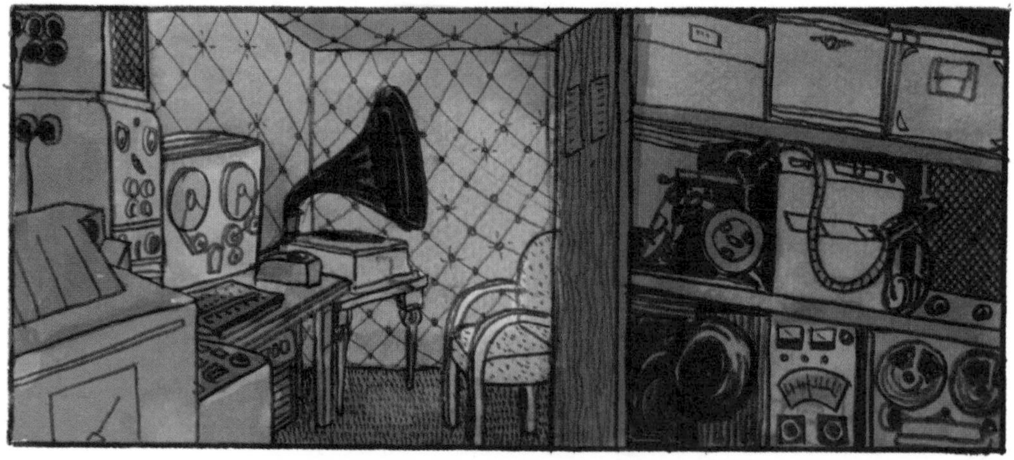

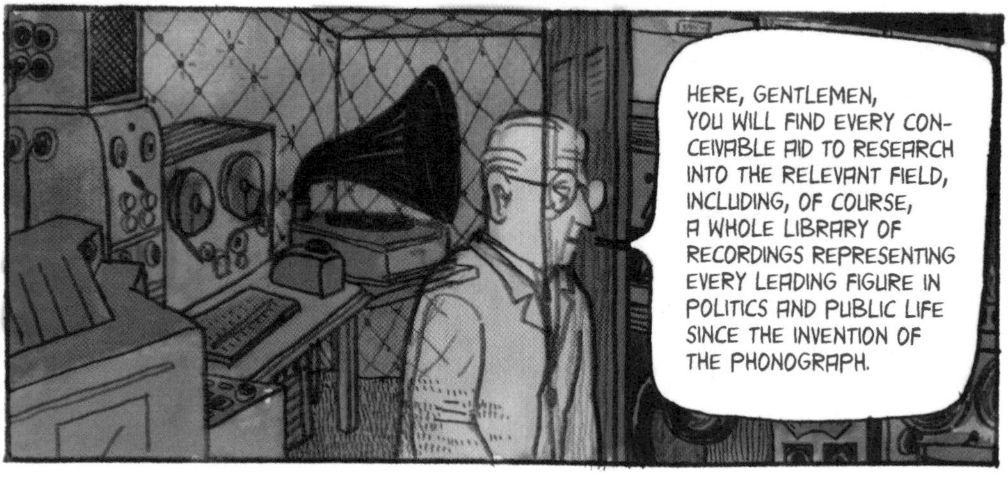
HERE, GENTLEMEN, YOU WILL FIND EVERY CONCEIVABLE AID TO RESEARCH INTO THE RELEVANT FIELD, INCLUDING, OF COURSE, A WHOLE LIBRARY OF RECORDINGS REPRESENTING EVERY LEADING FIGURE IN POLITICS AND PUBLIC LIFE SINCE THE INVENTION OF THE PHONOGRAPH.

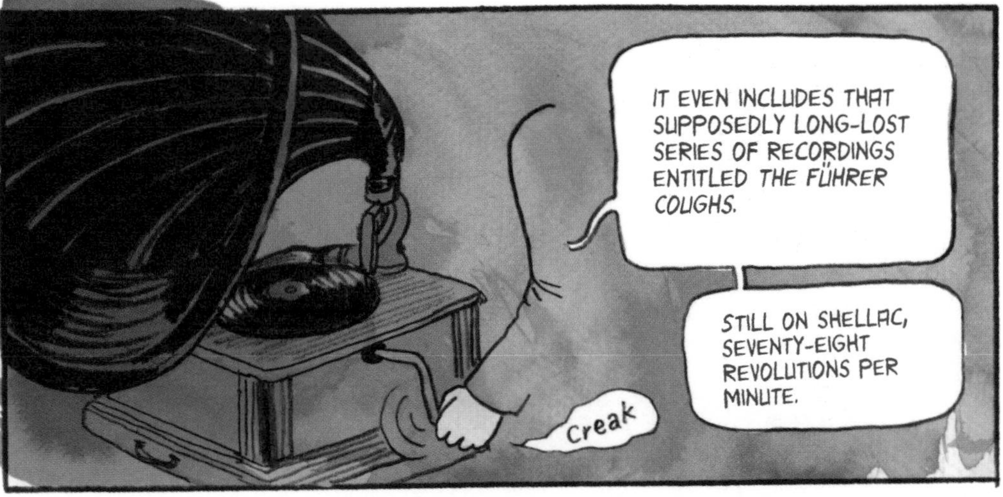
IT EVEN INCLUDES THAT SUPPOSEDLY LONG-LOST SERIES OF RECORDINGS ENTITLED *THE FÜHRER COUGHS*.
STILL ON SHELLAC, SEVENTY-EIGHT REVOLUTIONS PER MINUTE.
creak

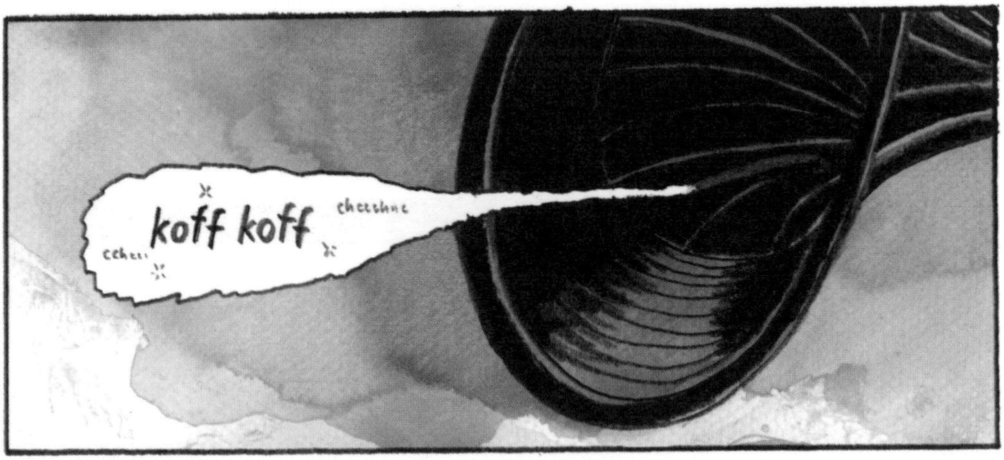
koff koff

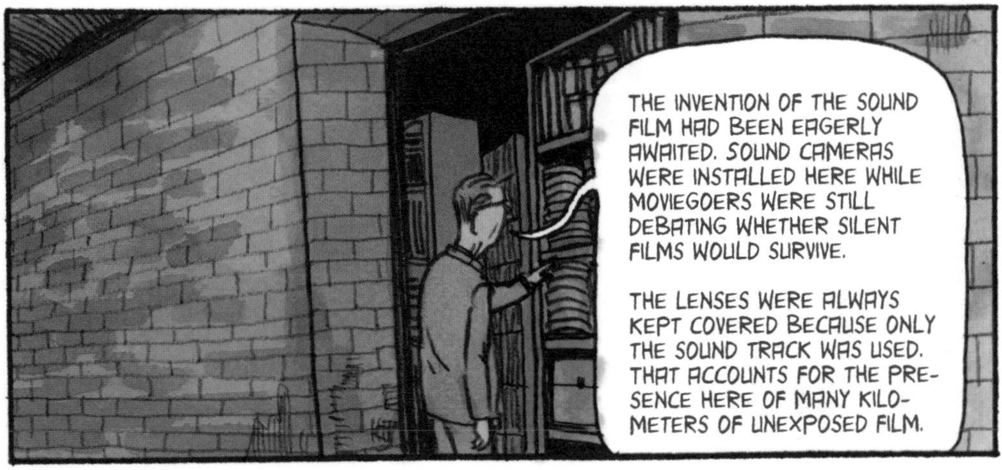
THE INVENTION OF THE SOUND FILM HAD BEEN EAGERLY AWAITED. SOUND CAMERAS WERE INSTALLED HERE WHILE MOVIEGOERS WERE STILL DEBATING WHETHER SILENT FILMS WOULD SURVIVE.
THE LENSES WERE ALWAYS KEPT COVERED BECAUSE ONLY THE SOUND TRACK WAS USED. THAT ACCOUNTS FOR THE PRESENCE HERE OF MANY KILOMETERS OF UNEXPOSED FILM.

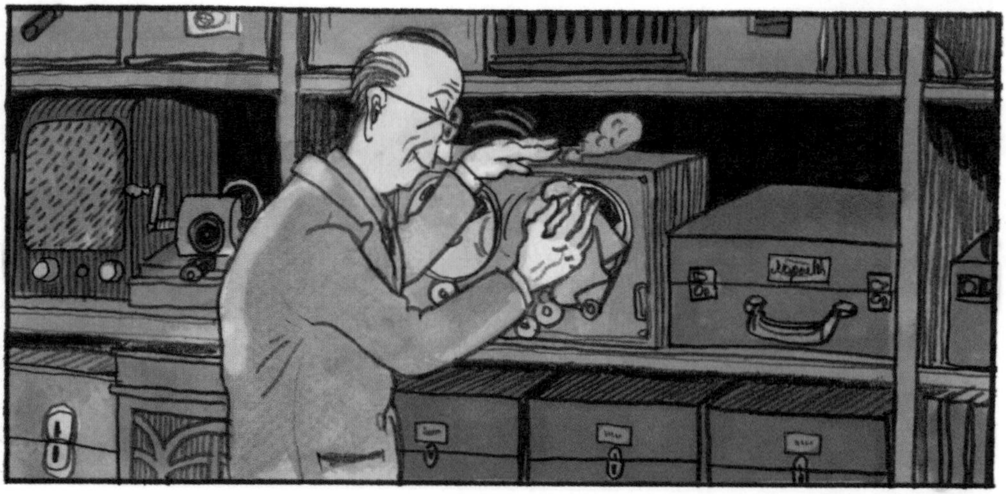

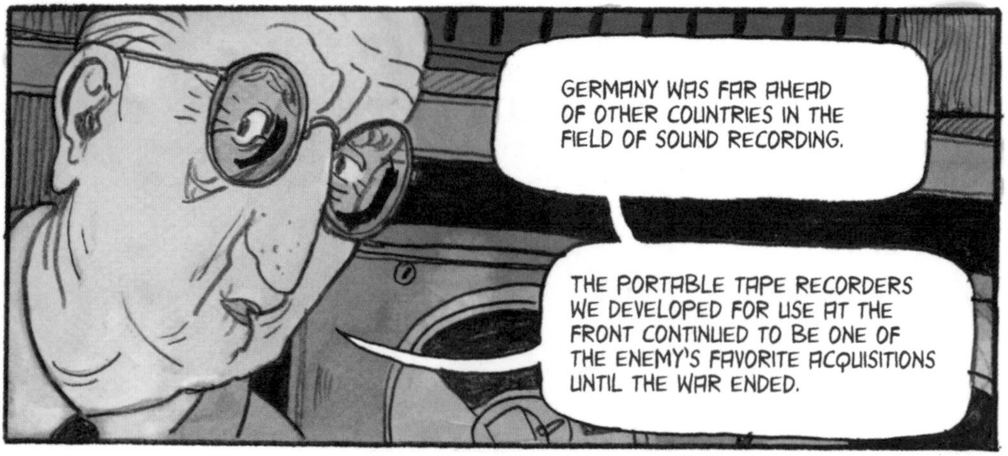
GERMANY WAS FAR AHEAD OF OTHER COUNTRIES IN THE FIELD OF SOUND RECORDING.
THE PORTABLE TAPE RECORDERS WE DEVELOPED FOR USE AT THE FRONT CONTINUED TO BE ONE OF THE ENEMY'S FAVORITE ACQUISITIONS UNTIL THE WAR ENDED.

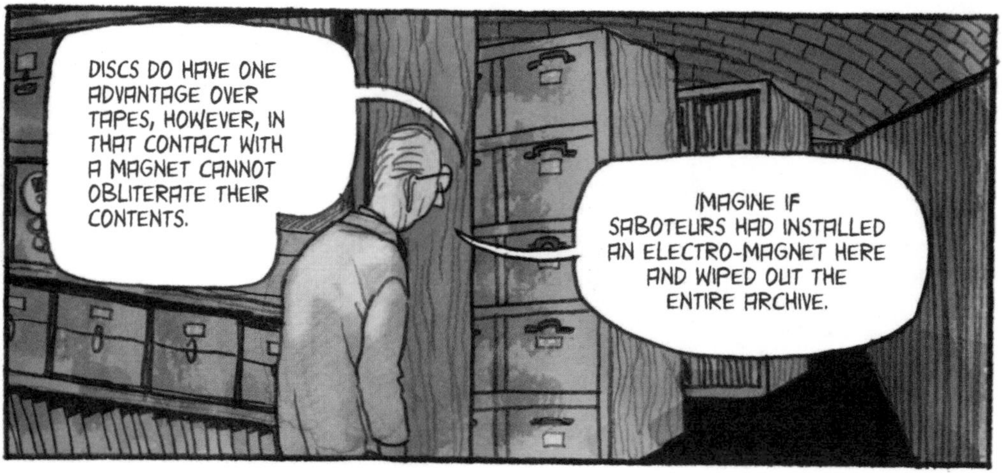
DISCS DO HAVE ONE ADVANTAGE OVER TAPES, HOWEVER, IN THAT CONTACT WITH A MAGNET CANNOT OBLITERATE THEIR CONTENTS.
IMAGINE IF SABOTEURS HAD INSTALLED AN ELECTRO-MAGNET HERE AND WIPED OUT THE ENTIRE ARCHIVE.

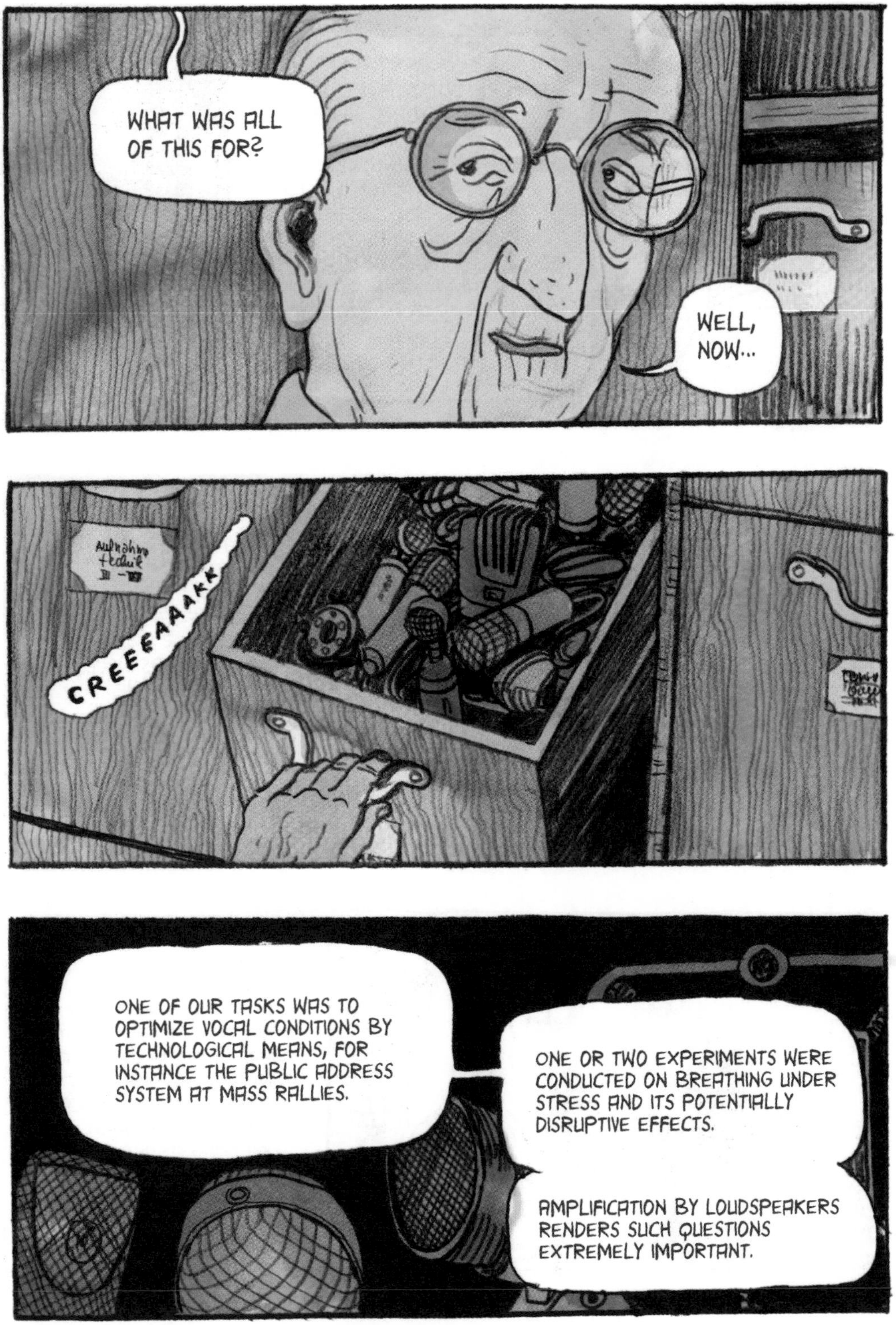
WHAT WAS ALL OF THIS FOR?
WELL, NOW...
CREEEAAAKK
ONE OF OUR TASKS WAS TO OPTIMIZE VOCAL CONDITIONS BY TECHNOLOGICAL MEANS, FOR INSTANCE THE PUBLIC ADDRESS SYSTEM AT MASS RALLIES.
ONE OR TWO EXPERIMENTS WERE CONDUCTED ON BREATHING UNDER STRESS AND ITS POTENTIALLY DISRUPTIVE EFFECTS.
AMPLIFICATION BY LOUDSPEAKERS RENDERS SUCH QUESTIONS EXTREMELY IMPORTANT.

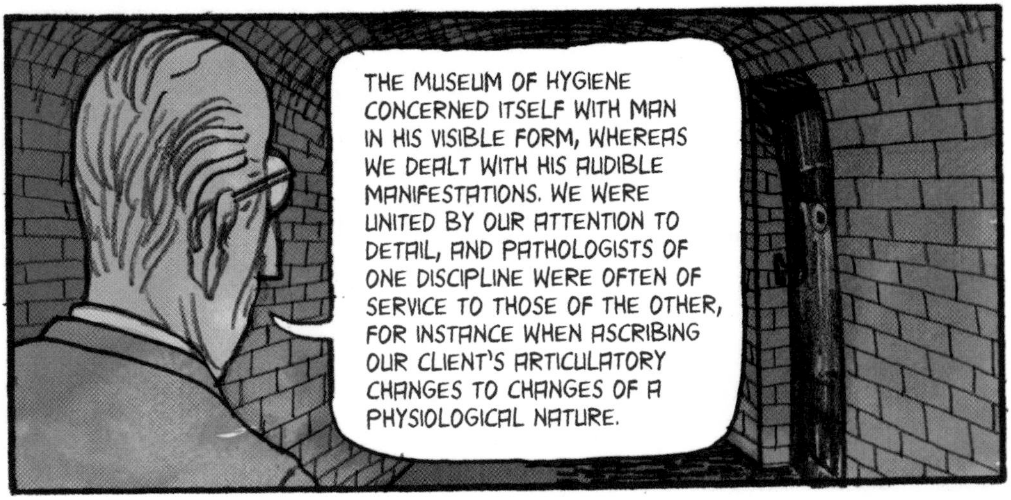
THE MUSEUM OF HYGIENE CONCERNED ITSELF WITH MAN IN HIS VISIBLE FORM, WHEREAS WE DEALT WITH HIS AUDIBLE MANIFESTATIONS. WE WERE UNITED BY OUR ATTENTION TO DETAIL, AND PATHOLOGISTS OF ONE DISCIPLINE WERE OFTEN OF SERVICE TO THOSE OF THE OTHER, FOR INSTANCE WHEN ASCRIBING OUR CLIENT'S ARTICULATORY CHANGES TO CHANGES OF A PHYSIOLOGICAL NATURE.

KARNAU PROVED TO BE EXTREMELY TALKATIVE; MORE THAN THAT, HE POSSESSED A KNOWLEDGE OF TECHNICAL MATTERS THAT WAS WHOLLY AT ODDS WITH HIS STATUS AS A SECURITY GUARD. HE SOMETIMES STRAYED INTO REMINISCENCES.

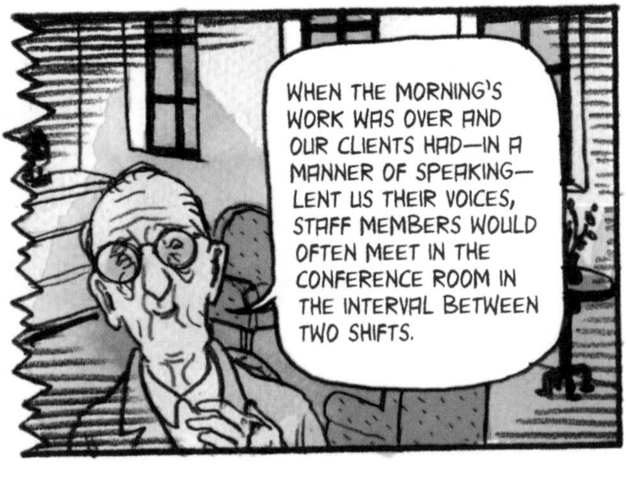
WHEN THE MORNING'S WORK WAS OVER AND OUR CLIENTS HAD—IN A MANNER OF SPEAKING—LENT US THEIR VOICES, STAFF MEMBERS WOULD OFTEN MEET IN THE CONFERENCE ROOM IN THE INTERVAL BETWEEN TWO SHIFTS.

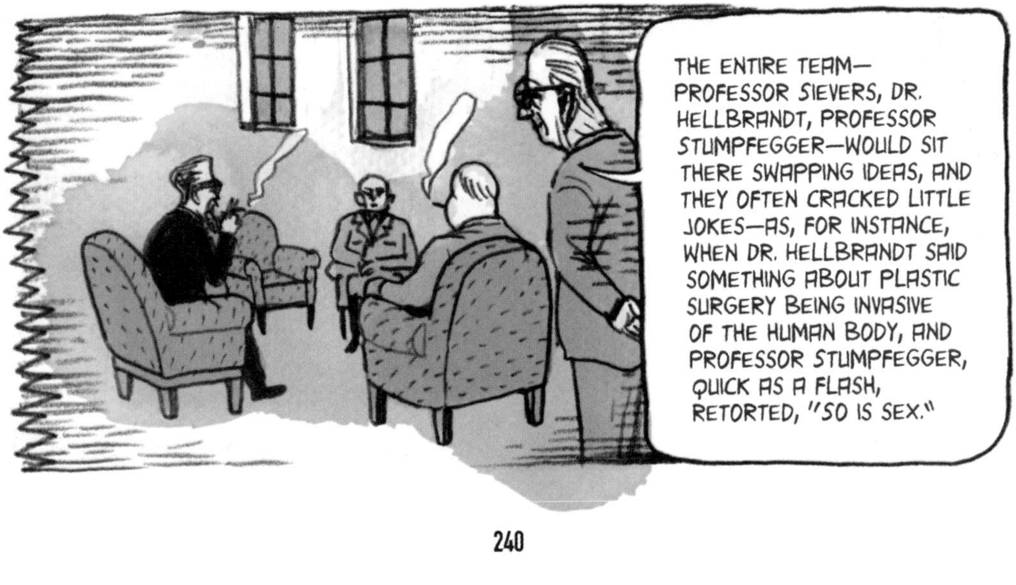
THE ENTIRE TEAM—PROFESSOR SIEVERS, DR. HELLBRANDT, PROFESSOR STUMPFEGGER—WOULD SIT THERE SWAPPING IDEAS, AND THEY OFTEN CRACKED LITTLE JOKES—AS, FOR INSTANCE, WHEN DR. HELLBRANDT SAID SOMETHING ABOUT PLASTIC SURGERY BEING INVASIVE OF THE HUMAN BODY, AND PROFESSOR STUMPFEGGER, QUICK AS A FLASH, RETORTED, "SO IS SEX."

KARNAU'S DETAILED KNOWLEDGE AROUSED A SUSPICION THAT HE HAD NOT MERELY BEEN IN CHARGE OF SECURITY, AS HE STEADFASTLY MAINTAINED, BUT MUST HAVE HELD A FAR MORE RESPONSIBLE POSITION.

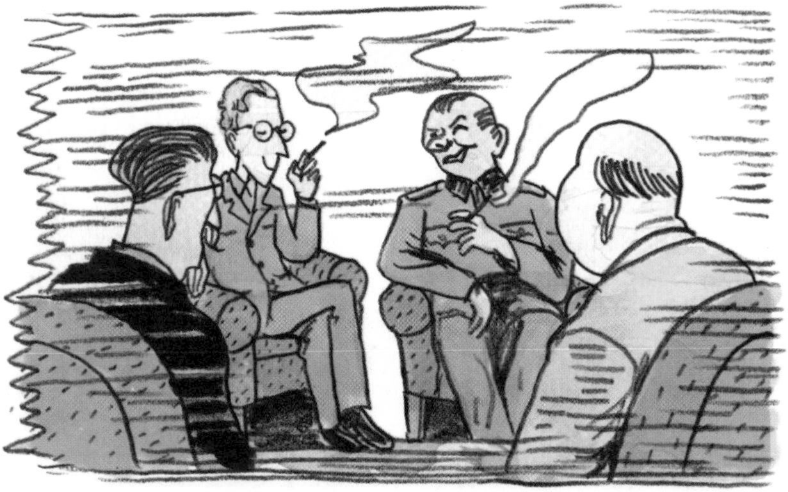

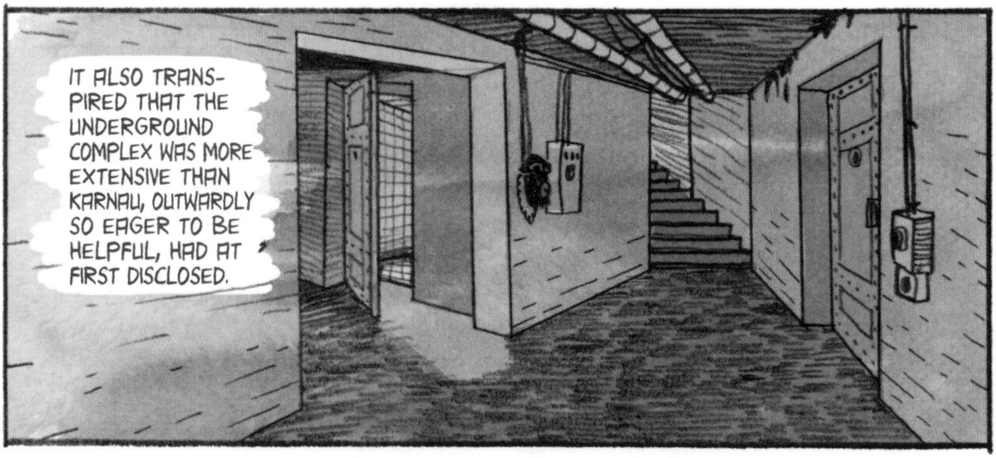
IT ALSO TRANSPIRED THAT THE UNDERGROUND COMPLEX WAS MORE EXTENSIVE THAN KARNAU, OUTWARDLY SO EAGER TO BE HELPFUL, HAD AT FIRST DISCLOSED.

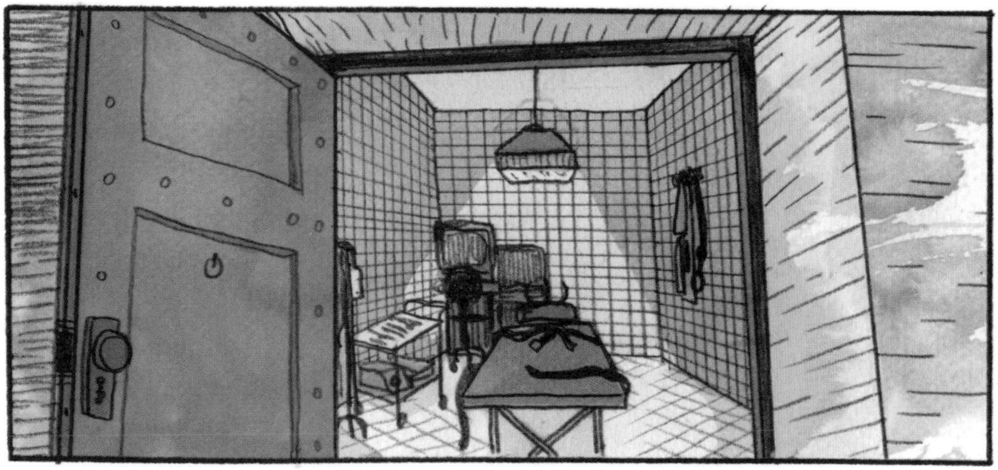

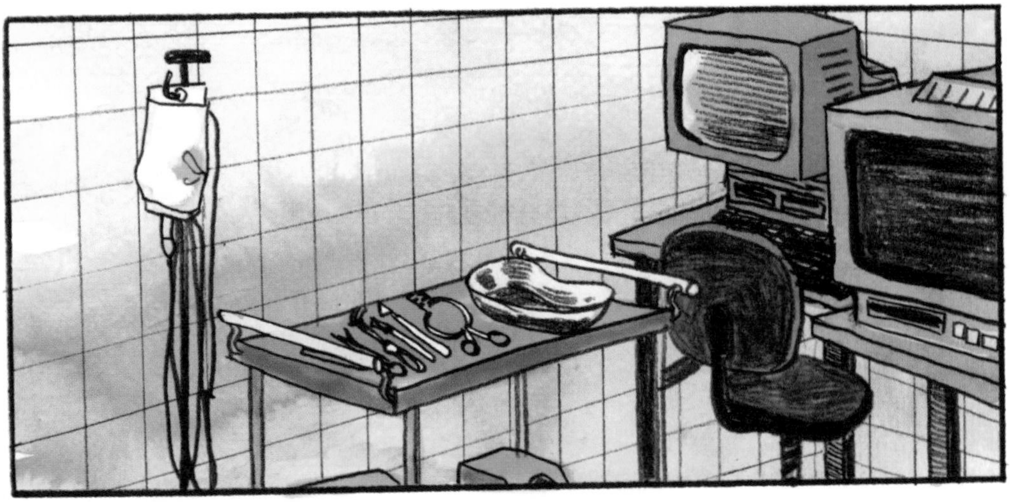

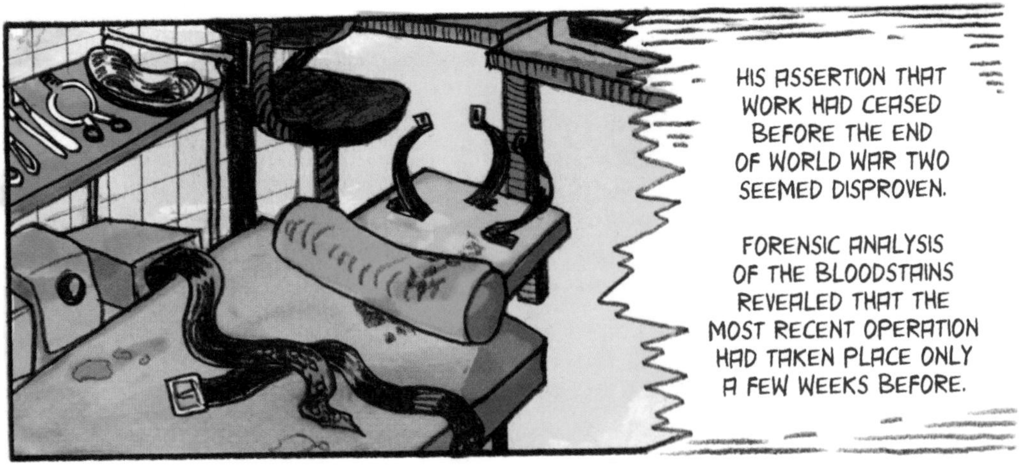
HIS ASSERTION THAT WORK HAD CEASED BEFORE THE END OF WORLD WAR TWO SEEMED DISPROVEN.
FORENSIC ANALYSIS OF THE BLOODSTAINS REVEALED THAT THE MOST RECENT OPERATION HAD TAKEN PLACE ONLY A FEW WEEKS BEFORE.

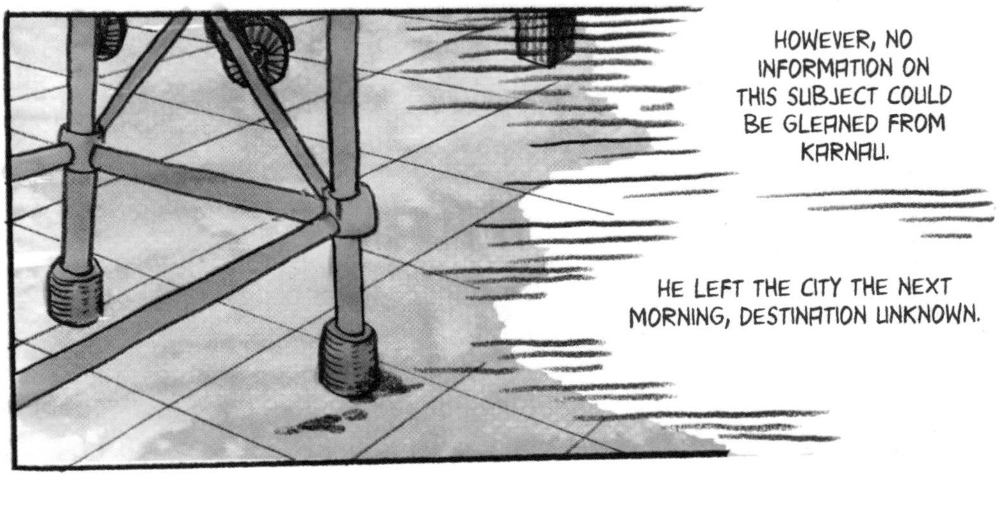
HOWEVER, NO INFORMATION ON THIS SUBJECT COULD BE GLEANED FROM KARNAU.
HE LEFT THE CITY THE NEXT MORNING, DESTINATION UNKNOWN.

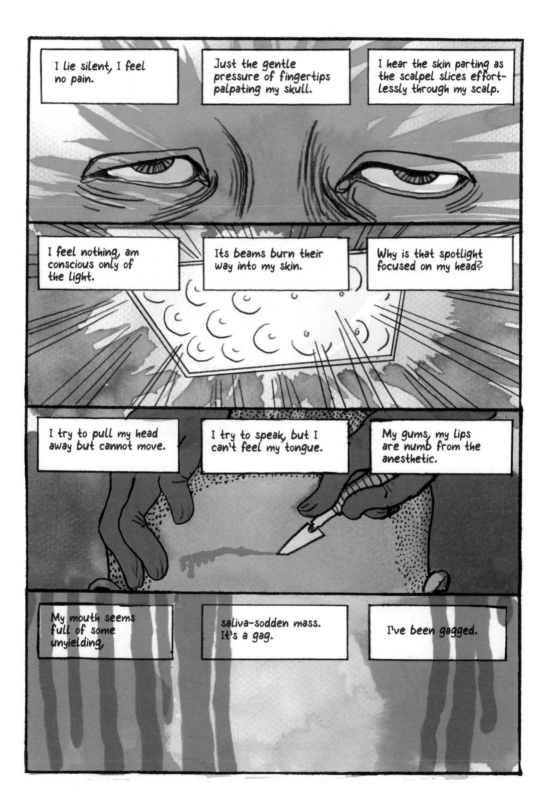

I *lie* silent, I feel no pain.

Just the gentle pressure of fingertips palpating my skull.

I hear the skin parting as the scalpel slices effort- lessly through my scalp.

I *feel* nothing, am conscious only of the light.

Its beams burn their way into my skin.

Why is that spotlight focused on my head?

I try to pull my head away but cannot move.

I try to speak, but I can't feel my tongue.

My gums, my lips are numb from the anesthetic.

My mouth seems full of some unyielding,

saliva-sodden mass. It's a gag.

I've been *gagged.*

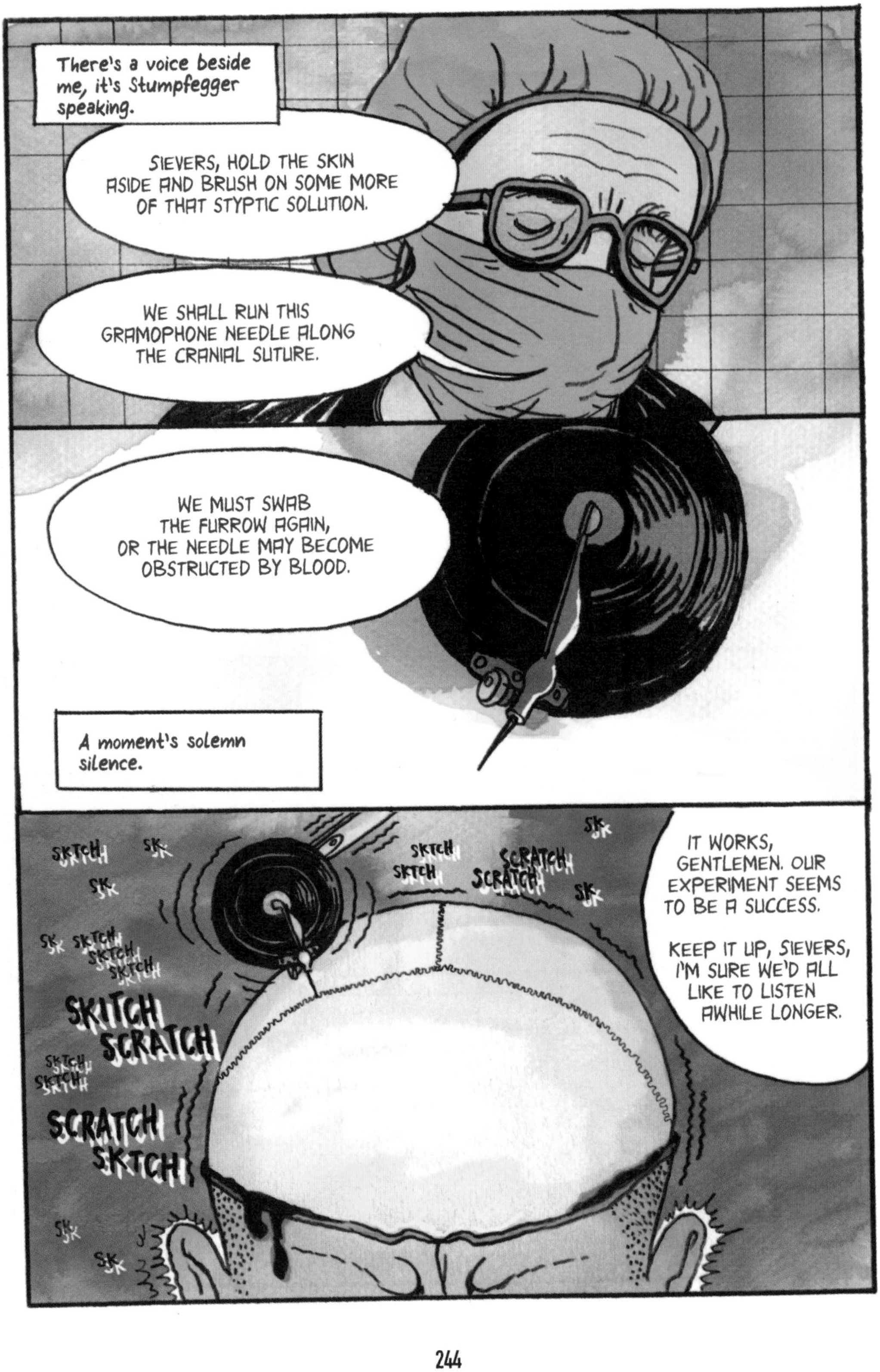
There's a voice beside me, it's Stumpfegger speaking.
SIEVERS, HOLD THE SKIN ASIDE AND BRUSH ON SOME MORE OF THAT STYPTIC SOLUTION.
WE SHALL RUN THIS GRAMOPHONE NEEDLE ALONG THE CRANIAL SUTURE.
WE MUST SWAB THE FURROW AGAIN, OR THE NEEDLE MAY BECOME OBSTRUCTED BY BLOOD.
A moment's solemn silence.
SKTCH SK SK SKTCH SKTCH SCRATCH SCRATCH SK SK
SK SKTCH SKTCH SKTCH
SKITCH SCRATCH
SKTCH SKTCH
SCRATCH SKTCH
SK SK
IT WORKS, GENTLEMEN. OUR EXPERIMENT SEEMS TO BE A SUCCESS.
KEEP IT UP, SIEVERS, I'M SURE WE'D ALL LIKE TO LISTEN AWHILE LONGER.

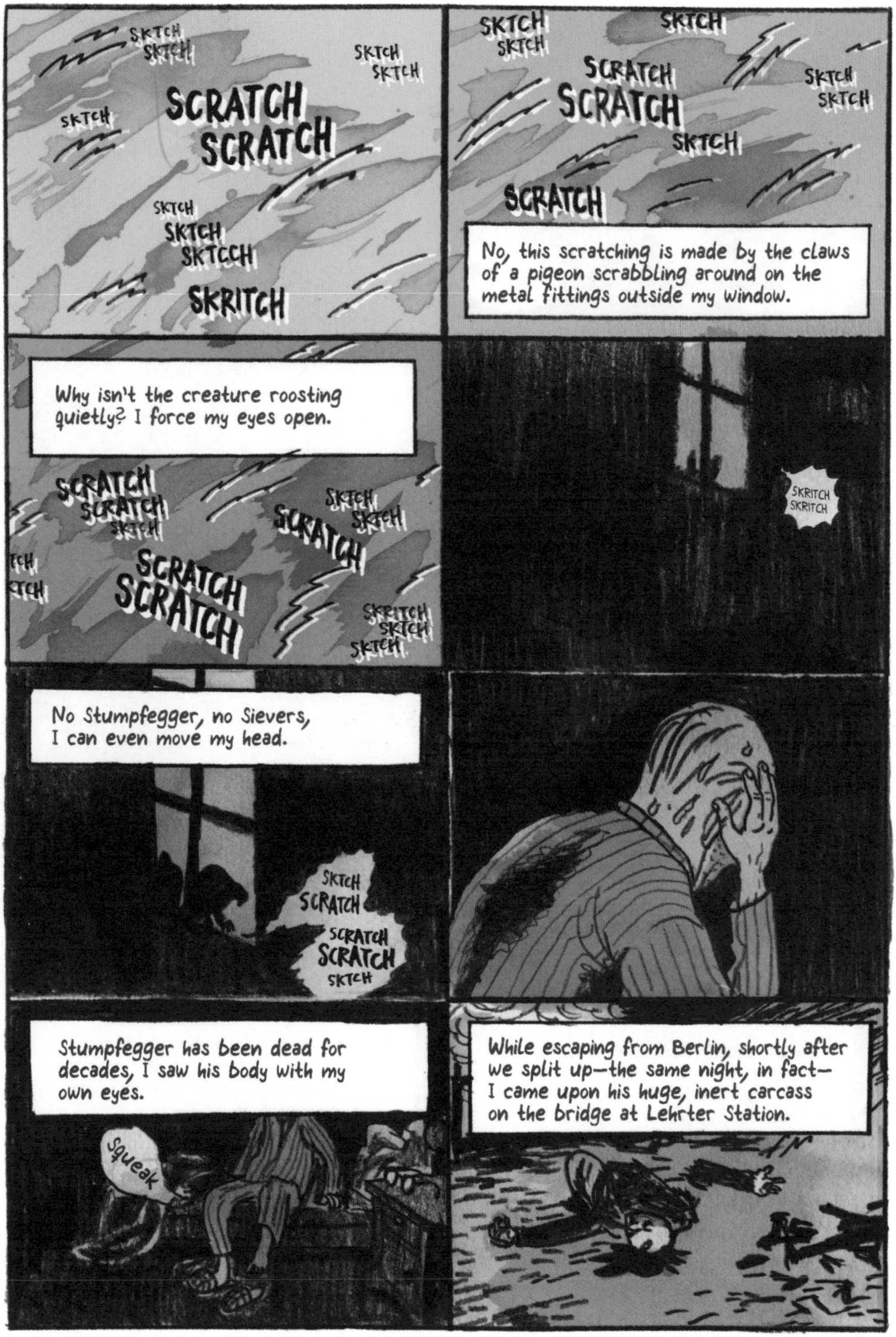
SKTCH
SKTCH
SKTCH
SKTCH
SCRATCH
SCRATCH
SKTCH
SKTCH
SKTCH
SKTCCH
SKRITCH
SKTCH
SKTCH
SKTCH
SCRATCH
SCRATCH
SKTCH
SKTCH
SKTCH
SCRATCH
No, this scratching is made by the claws of a pigeon scrabbling around on the metal fittings outside my window.
Why isn't the creature roosting quietly? I force my eyes open.
SCRATCH
SCRATCH
SKTCH
SKTCH
SKTCH
SCRATCH
SCRATCH
SCRATCH
SKRITCH
SKTCH
SKTCH
SKRITCH
SKRITCH
No Stumpfegger, no Sievers, I can even move my head.
SKTCH
SCRATCH
SCRATCH
SCRATCH
SKTCH
Stumpfegger has been dead for decades, I saw his body with my own eyes.
Squeak
While escaping from Berlin, shortly after we split up—the same night, in fact—I came upon his huge, inert carcass on the bridge at Lehrter Station.

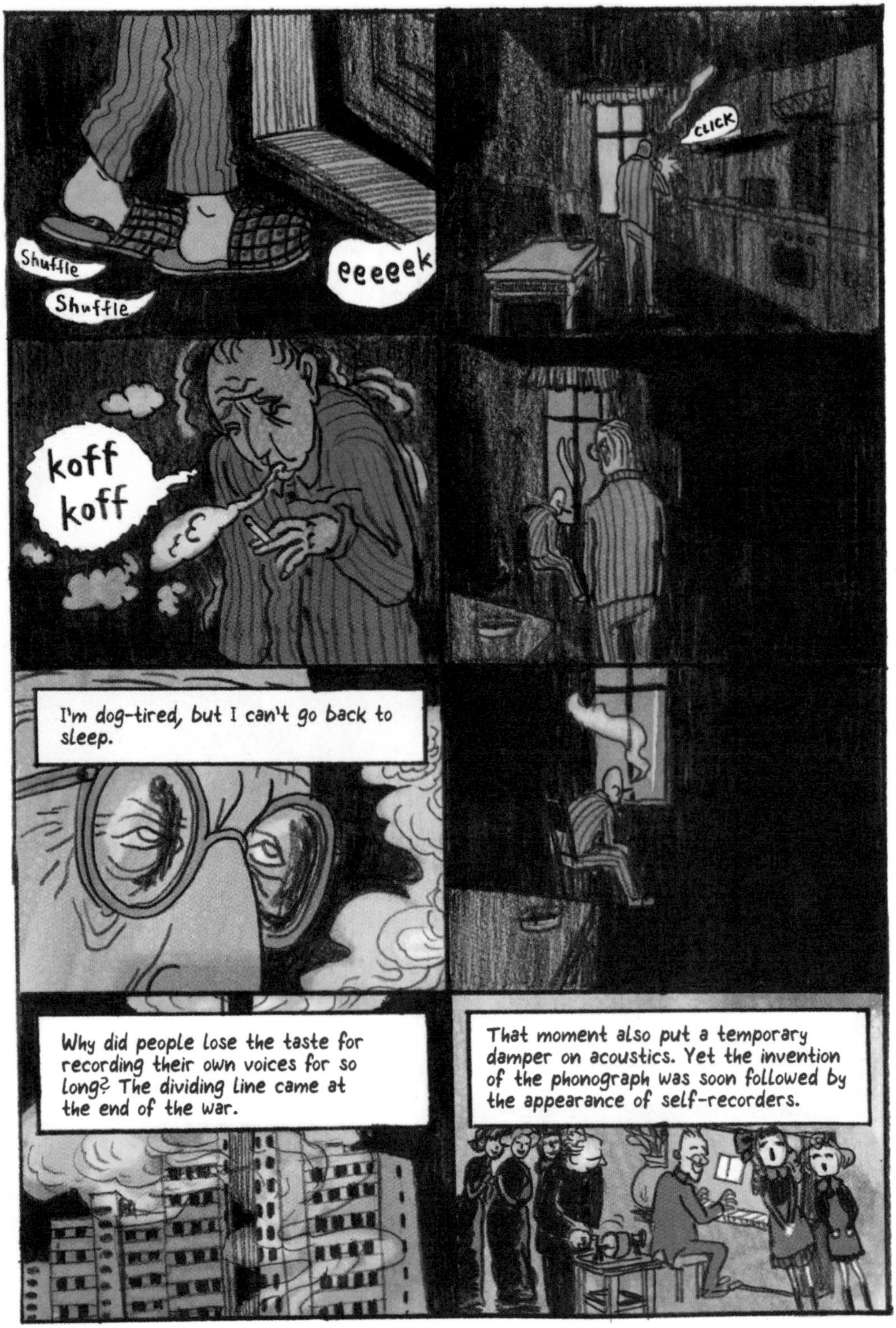

Shuffle
Shuffle
eeeeek
CLICK
koff
koff
I'm dog-tired, but I can't go back to sleep.
Why did people lose the taste for recording their own voices for so long? The dividing line came at the end of the war.
That moment also put a temporary damper on acoustics. Yet the invention of the phonograph was soon followed by the appearance of self-recorders.

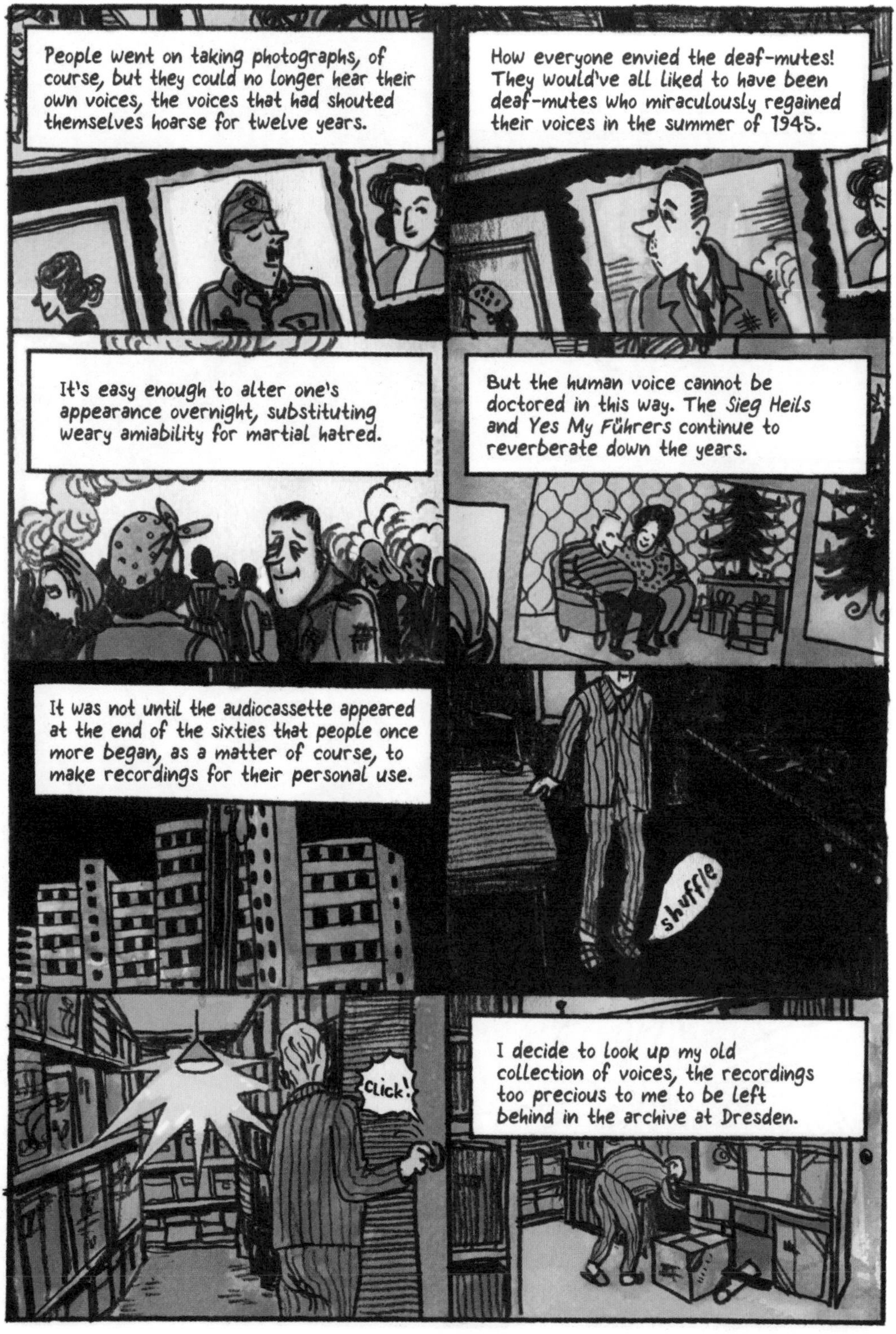

People went on taking photographs, of course, but they could no longer hear their own voices, the voices that had shouted themselves hoarse for twelve years.
How everyone envied the deaf-mutes! They would've all liked to have been deaf-mutes who miraculously regained their voices in the summer of 1945.
It's easy enough to alter one's appearance overnight, substituting weary amiability for martial hatred.
But the human voice cannot be doctored in this way. The *Sieg Heils* and *Yes My Führers* continue to reverberate down the years.
It was not until the audiocassette appeared at the end of the sixties that people once more began, as a matter of course, to make recordings for their personal use.
shuffle
CLICK!
I decide to look up my old collection of voices, the recordings too precious to me to be left behind in the archive at Dresden.

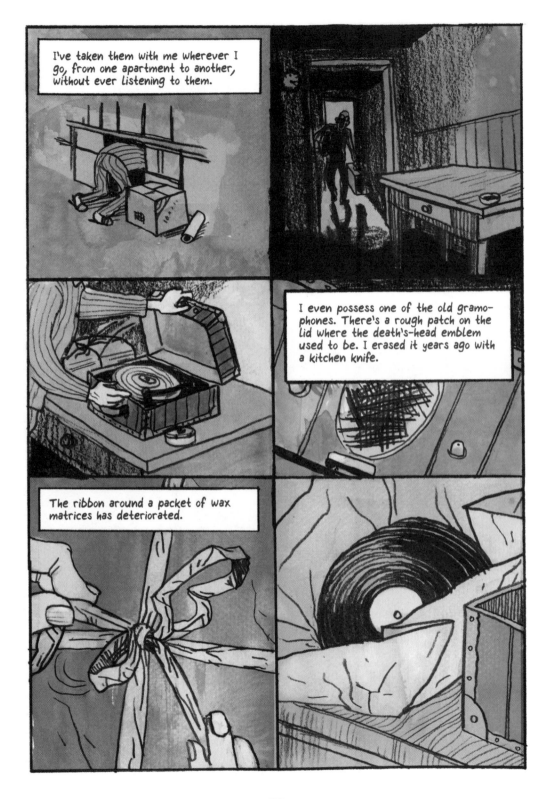

I've taken them with me wherever I go, from one apartment to another, without ever listening to them.

I even possess one of the old gramophones. There's a rough patch on the lid where the death's-head emblem used to be. I erased it years ago with a kitchen knife.

The ribbon around a packet of wax matrices has deteriorated.

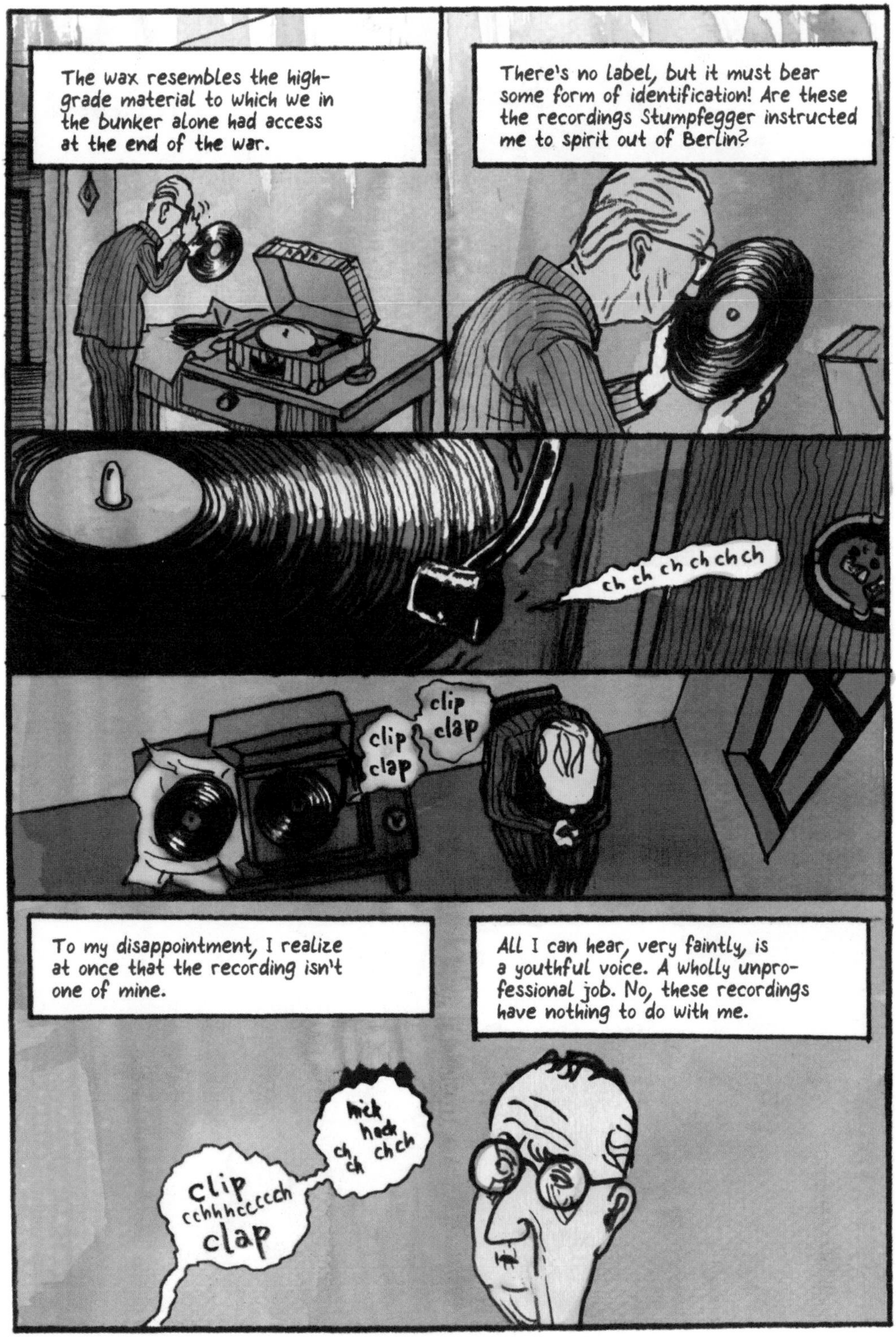
The wax resembles the high-grade material to which we in the bunker alone had access at the end of the war.
There's no label, but it must bear some form of identification! Are these the recordings Stumpfegger instructed me to spirit out of Berlin?
ch ch ch ch ch ch ch
clip clap
clip clap
To my disappointment, I realize at once that the recording isn't one of mine.
All I can hear, very faintly, is a youthful voice. A wholly unprofessional job. No, these recordings have nothing to do with me.
clip cchhhcccccch clap
hick hack ch ch chch

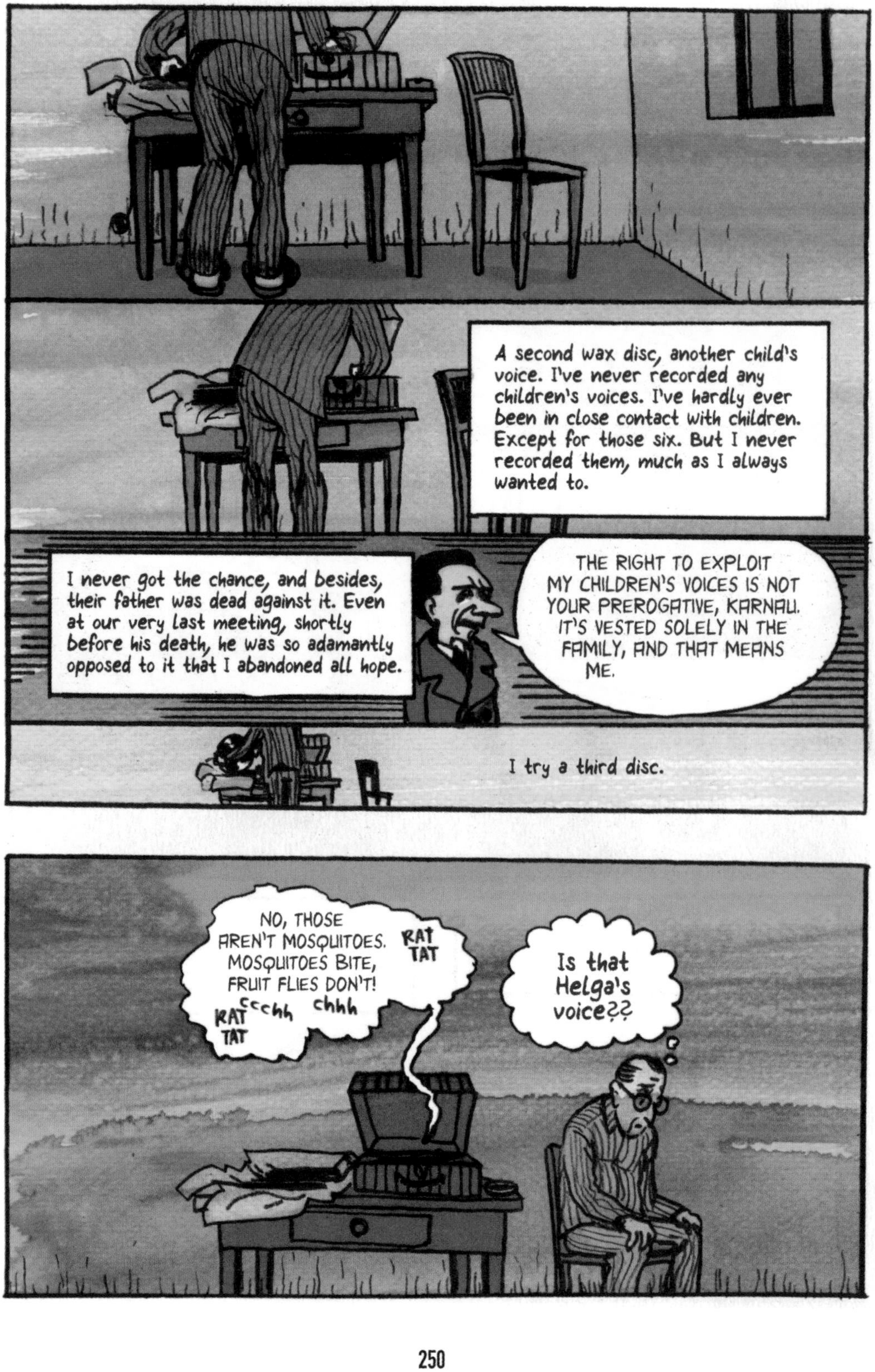
A second wax disc, another child's voice. I've never recorded any children's voices. I've hardly ever been in close contact with children. Except for those six. But I never recorded them, much as I always wanted to.
I never got the chance, and besides, their father was dead against it. Even at our very last meeting, shortly before his death, he was so adamantly opposed to it that I abandoned all hope.
THE RIGHT TO EXPLOIT MY CHILDREN'S VOICES IS NOT YOUR PREROGATIVE, KARNAU. IT'S VESTED SOLELY IN THE FAMILY, AND THAT MEANS ME.
I try a third disc.
NO, THOSE AREN'T MOSQUITOES. MOSQUITOES BITE, FRUIT FLIES DON'T!
RAT TAT
ccchh chhh
RAT TAT
Is that Helga's voice??

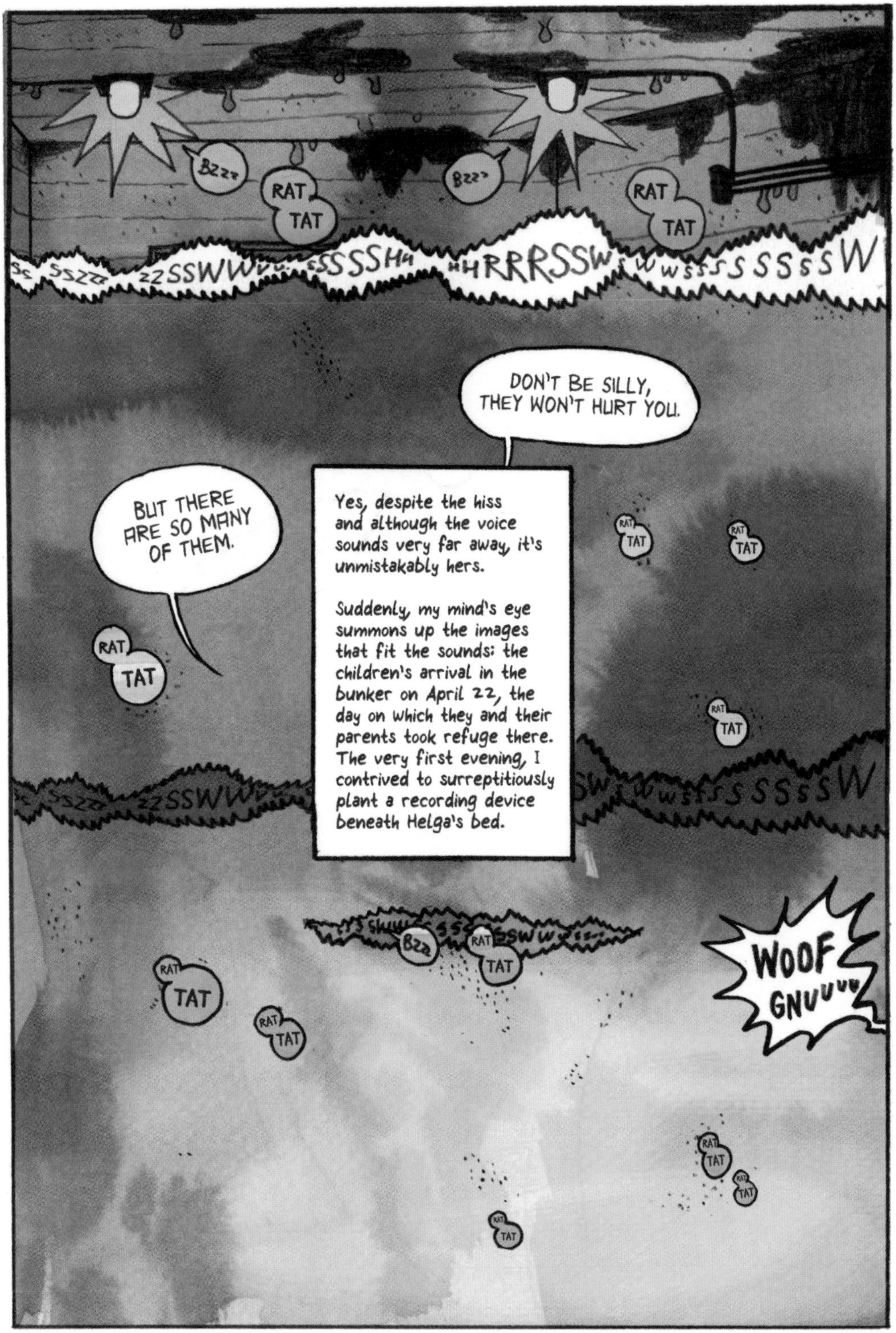

BZZZ
RAT TAT
BZZZ
RAT TAT
SSZZZ ZZSSWW SSSSH HRRRSSW WWSSSSSSSSW
DON'T BE SILLY, THEY WON'T HURT YOU.
BUT THERE ARE SO MANY OF THEM.
Yes, despite the hiss and although the voice sounds very far away, it's unmistakably hers.
Suddenly, my mind's eye summons up the images that fit the sounds: the children's arrival in the bunker on April 22, the day on which they and their parents took refuge there. The very first evening, I contrived to surreptitiously plant a recording device beneath Helga's bed.
RAT TAT
RAT TAT
RAT TAT
RAT TAT
WOOF GNUUUU
RAT TAT
RAT TAT
RAT TAT

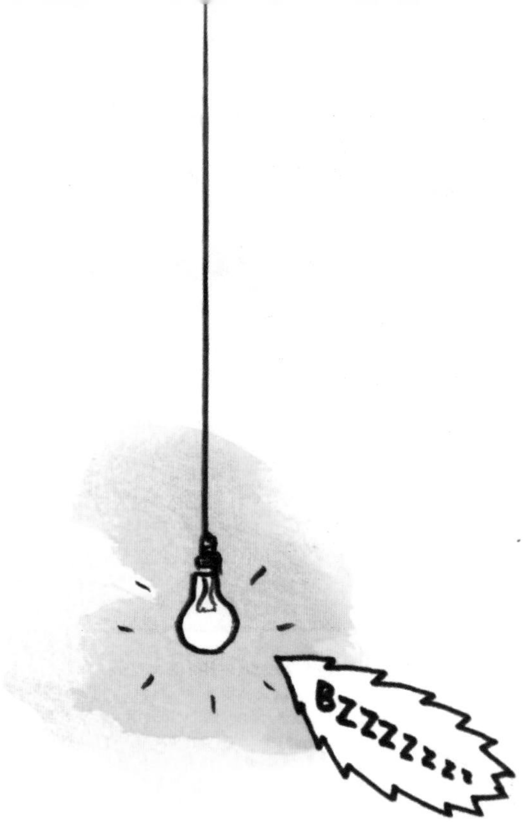
BZZZZZZZ

VI.

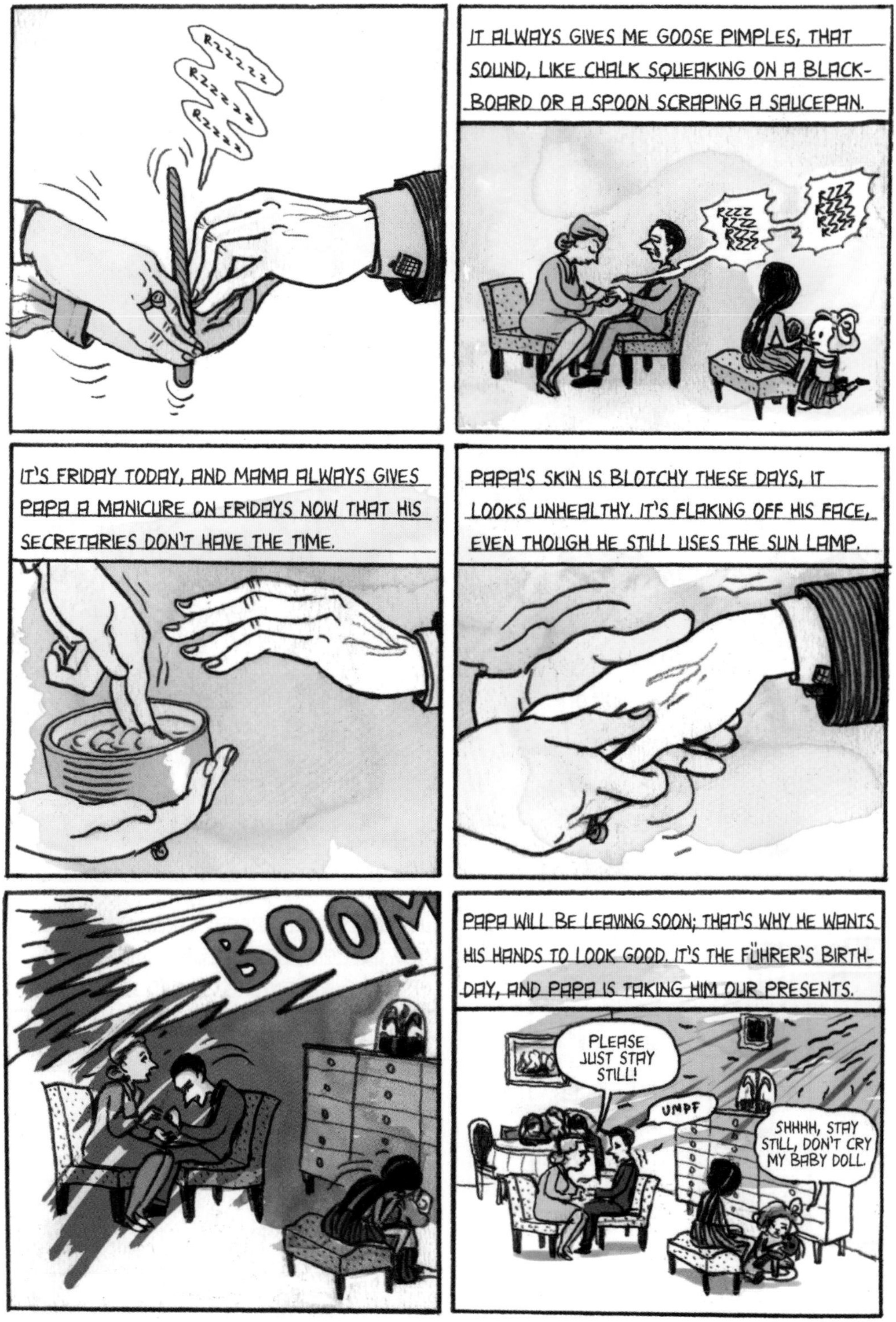
RZZZZZZ RZZZZZZ RZZZZZ
IT ALWAYS GIVES ME GOOSE PIMPLES, THAT SOUND, LIKE CHALK SQUEAKING ON A BLACK-BOARD OR A SPOON SCRAPING A SAUCEPAN.
RZZZ RZZZ RZZZ RZZZ
RZZZ RZZZ RZZZ RZZZ
IT'S FRIDAY TODAY, AND MAMA ALWAYS GIVES PAPA A MANICURE ON FRIDAYS NOW THAT HIS SECRETARIES DON'T HAVE THE TIME.
PAPA'S SKIN IS BLOTCHY THESE DAYS, IT LOOKS UNHEALTHY. IT'S FLAKING OFF HIS FACE, EVEN THOUGH HE STILL USES THE SUN LAMP.
BOOM
PAPA WILL BE LEAVING SOON; THAT'S WHY HE WANTS HIS HANDS TO LOOK GOOD. IT'S THE FÜHRER'S BIRTH-DAY, AND PAPA IS TAKING HIM OUR PRESENTS.
PLEASE JUST STAY STILL!
UMPF
SHHHH, STAY STILL, DON'T CRY MY BABY DOLL.

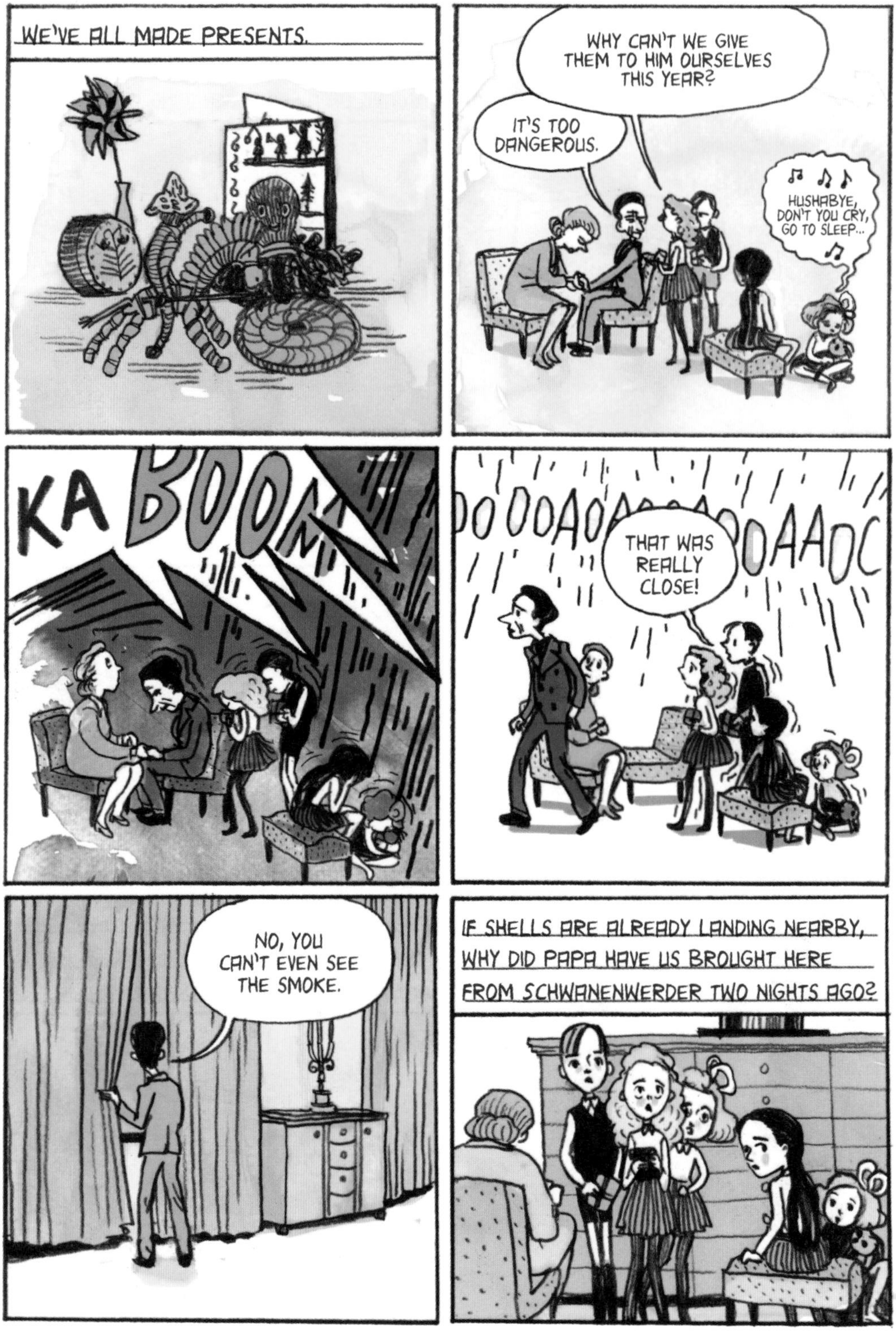
WE'VE ALL MADE PRESENTS.
WHY CAN'T WE GIVE THEM TO HIM OURSELVES THIS YEAR?
IT'S TOO DANGEROUS.
HUSHABYE, DON'T YOU CRY, GO TO SLEEP...
KA BOOM
OOOAOAAOOOAAADO
THAT WAS REALLY CLOSE!
NO, YOU CAN'T EVEN SEE THE SMOKE.
IF SHELLS ARE ALREADY LANDING NEARBY, WHY DID PAPA HAVE US BROUGHT HERE FROM SCHWANENWERDER TWO NIGHTS AGO?

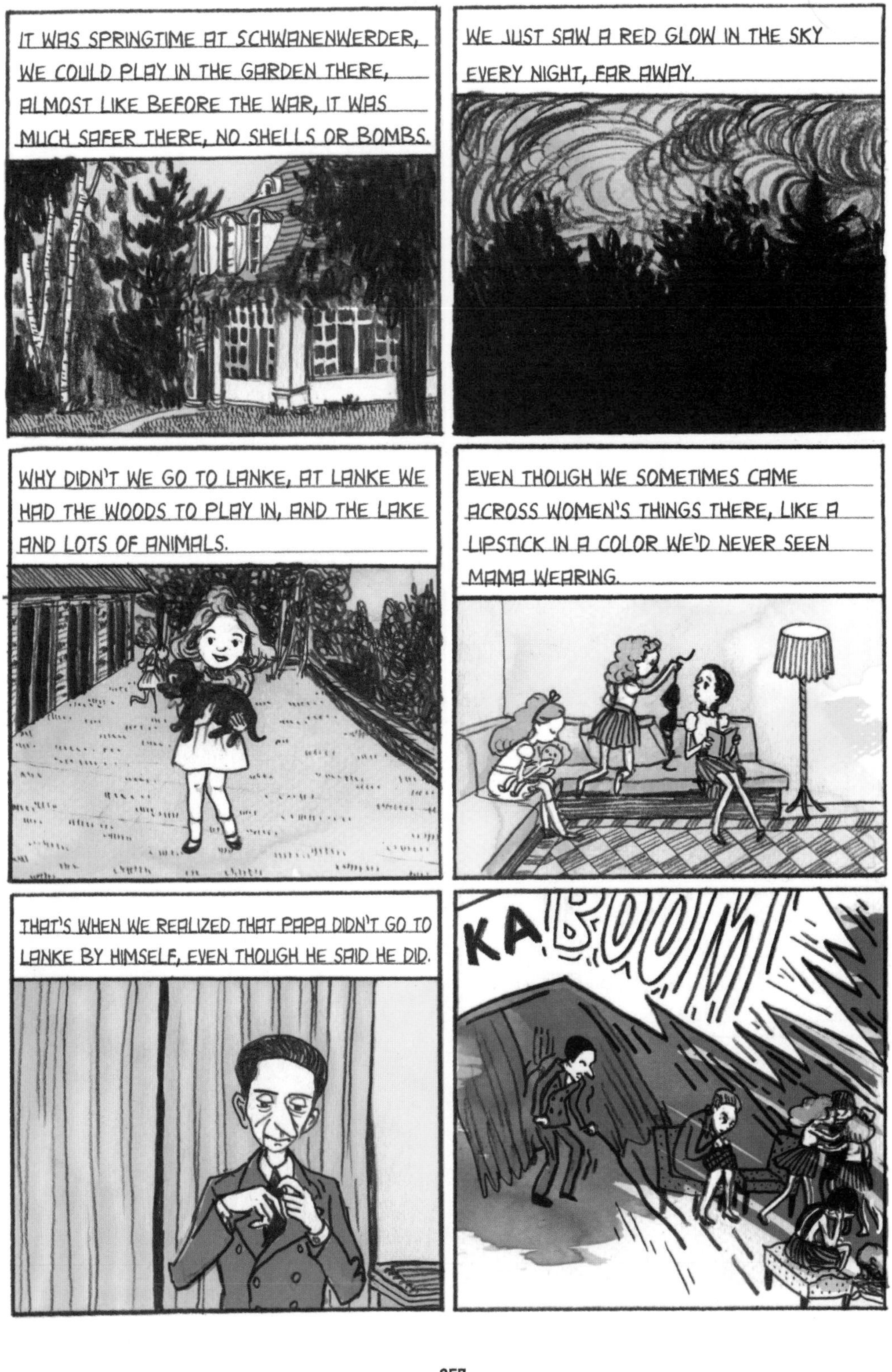
IT WAS SPRINGTIME AT SCHWANENWERDER, WE COULD PLAY IN THE GARDEN THERE, ALMOST LIKE BEFORE THE WAR, IT WAS MUCH SAFER THERE, NO SHELLS OR BOMBS.
WE JUST SAW A RED GLOW IN THE SKY EVERY NIGHT, FAR AWAY.
WHY DIDN'T WE GO TO LANKE, AT LANKE WE HAD THE WOODS TO PLAY IN, AND THE LAKE AND LOTS OF ANIMALS.
EVEN THOUGH WE SOMETIMES CAME ACROSS WOMEN'S THINGS THERE, LIKE A LIPSTICK IN A COLOR WE'D NEVER SEEN MAMA WEARING.
THAT'S WHEN WE REALIZED THAT PAPA DIDN'T GO TO LANKE BY HIMSELF, EVEN THOUGH HE SAID HE DID.
KABOOM!

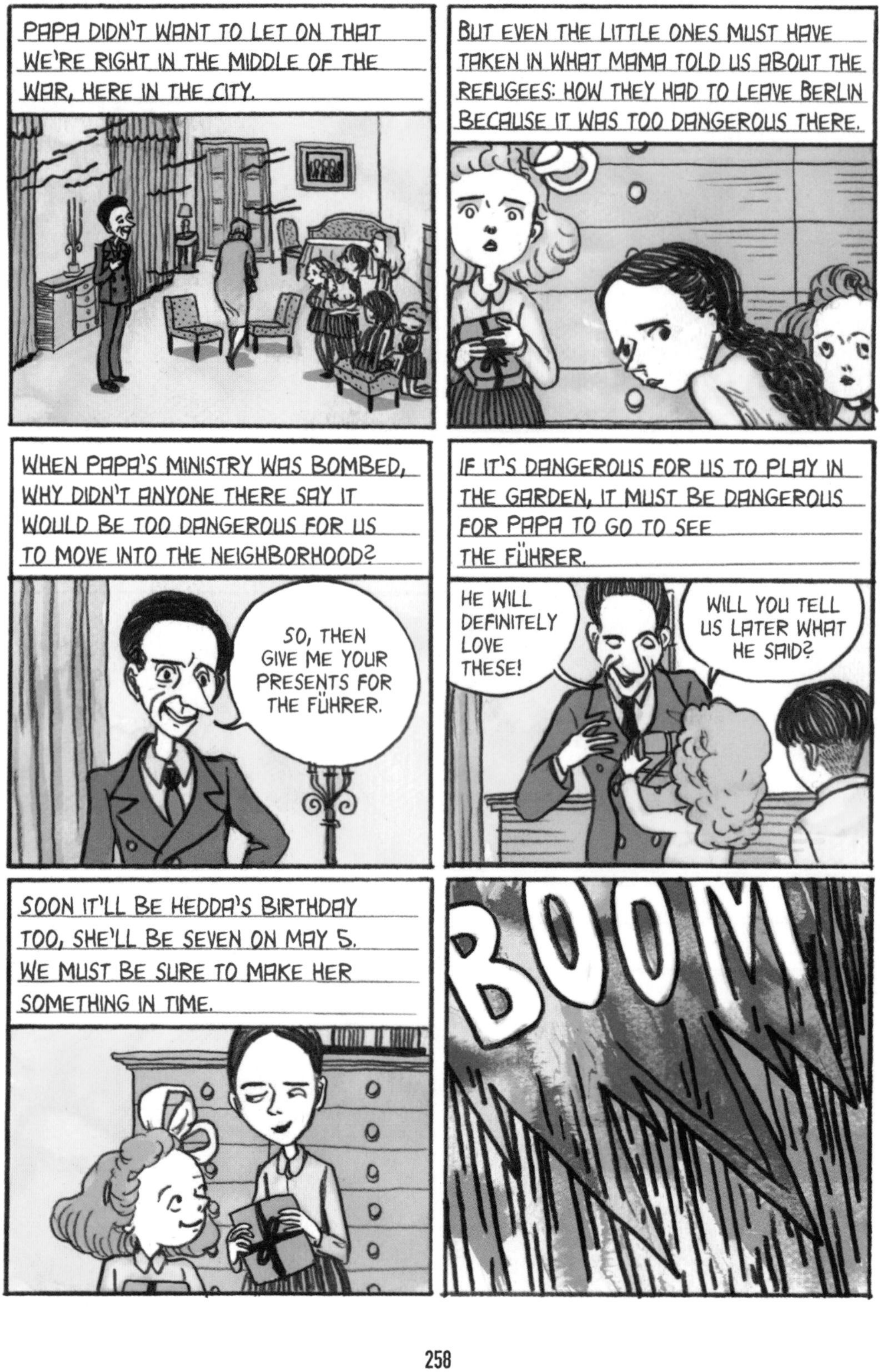
PAPA DIDN'T WANT TO LET ON THAT WE'RE RIGHT IN THE MIDDLE OF THE WAR, HERE IN THE CITY.
BUT EVEN THE LITTLE ONES MUST HAVE TAKEN IN WHAT MAMA TOLD US ABOUT THE REFUGEES: HOW THEY HAD TO LEAVE BERLIN BECAUSE IT WAS TOO DANGEROUS THERE.
WHEN PAPA'S MINISTRY WAS BOMBED, WHY DIDN'T ANYONE THERE SAY IT WOULD BE TOO DANGEROUS FOR US TO MOVE INTO THE NEIGHBORHOOD?
SO, THEN GIVE ME YOUR PRESENTS FOR THE FÜHRER.
IF IT'S DANGEROUS FOR US TO PLAY IN THE GARDEN, IT MUST BE DANGEROUS FOR PAPA TO GO TO SEE THE FÜHRER.
HE WILL DEFINITELY LOVE THESE!
WILL YOU TELL US LATER WHAT HE SAID?
SOON IT'LL BE HEDDA'S BIRTHDAY TOO, SHE'LL BE SEVEN ON MAY 5. WE MUST BE SURE TO MAKE HER SOMETHING IN TIME.
BOOM

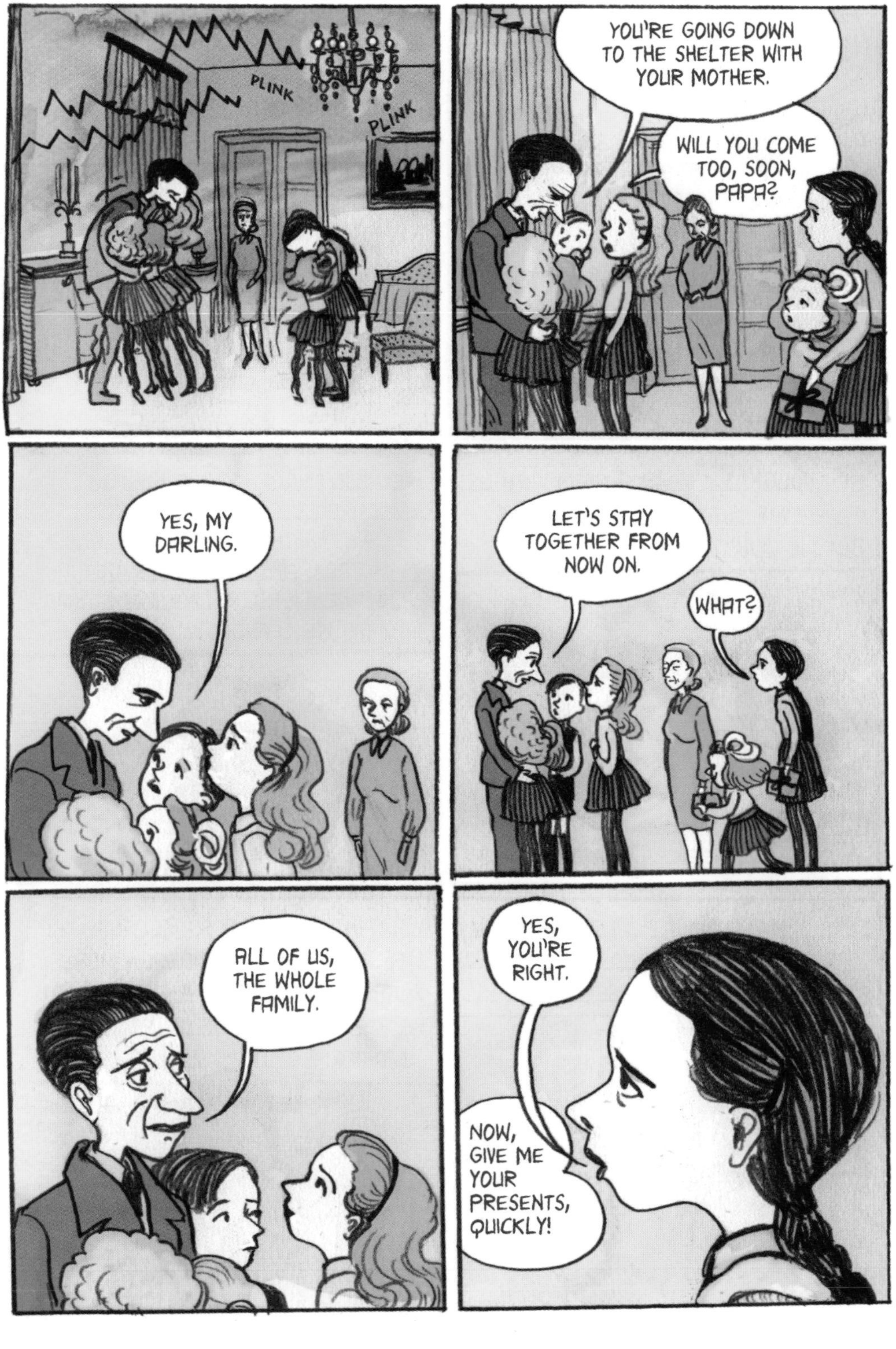
PLINK
PLINK
YOU'RE GOING DOWN TO THE SHELTER WITH YOUR MOTHER.
WILL YOU COME TOO, SOON, PAPA?
YES, MY DARLING.
LET'S STAY TOGETHER FROM NOW ON.
WHAT?
ALL OF US, THE WHOLE FAMILY.
YES, YOU'RE RIGHT.
NOW, GIVE ME YOUR PRESENTS, QUICKLY!

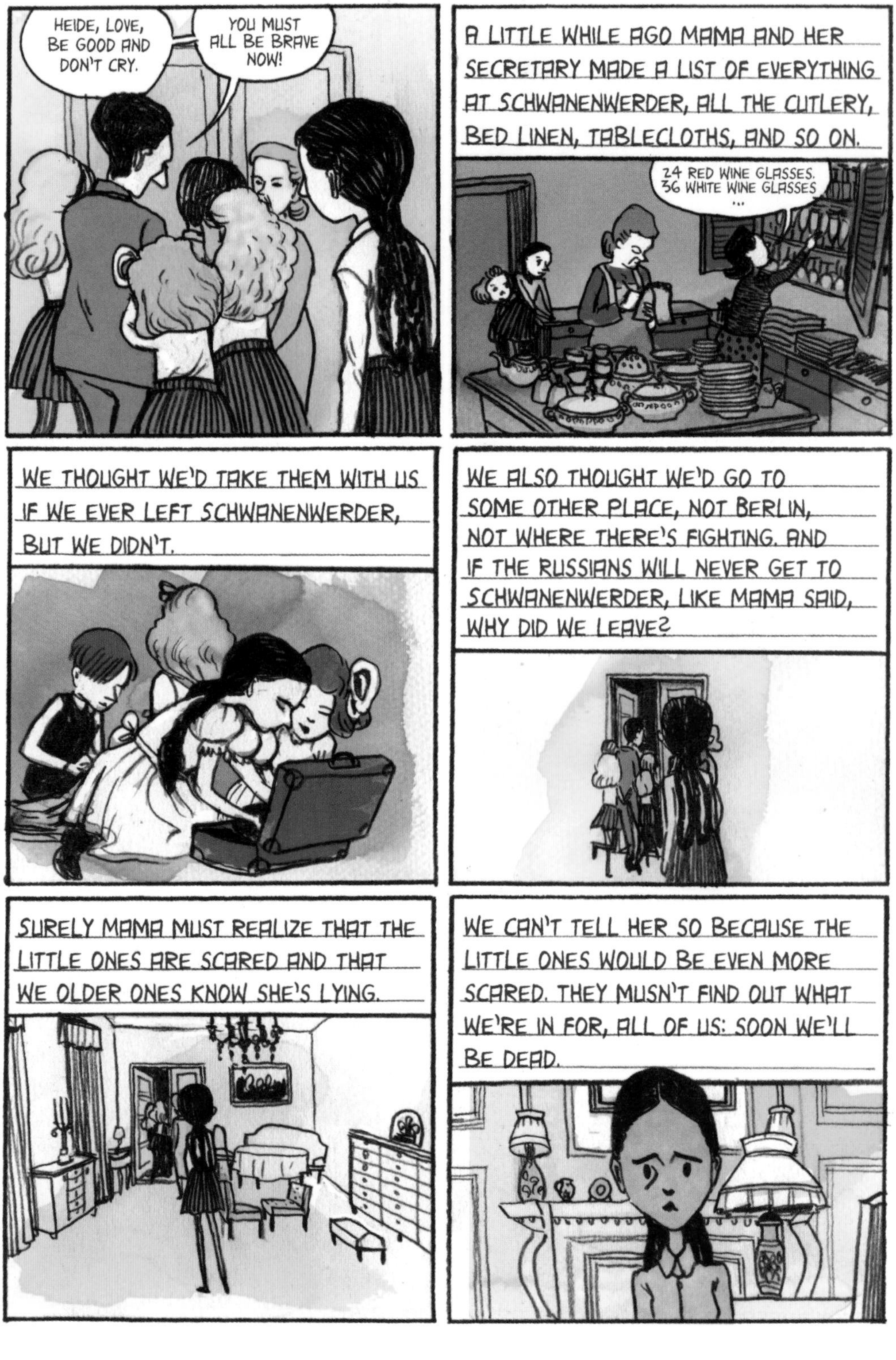
HEIDE, LOVE, BE GOOD AND DON'T CRY.
YOU MUST ALL BE BRAVE NOW!
A LITTLE WHILE AGO MAMA AND HER SECRETARY MADE A LIST OF EVERYTHING AT SCHWANENWERDER, ALL THE CUTLERY, BED LINEN, TABLECLOTHS, AND SO ON.
24 RED WINE GLASSES. 36 WHITE WINE GLASSES ...
WE THOUGHT WE'D TAKE THEM WITH US IF WE EVER LEFT SCHWANENWERDER, BUT WE DIDN'T.
WE ALSO THOUGHT WE'D GO TO SOME OTHER PLACE, NOT BERLIN, NOT WHERE THERE'S FIGHTING. AND IF THE RUSSIANS WILL NEVER GET TO SCHWANENWERDER, LIKE MAMA SAID, WHY DID WE LEAVE?
SURELY MAMA MUST REALIZE THAT THE LITTLE ONES ARE SCARED AND THAT WE OLDER ONES KNOW SHE'S LYING.
WE CAN'T TELL HER SO BECAUSE THE LITTLE ONES WOULD BE EVEN MORE SCARED. THEY MUSN'T FIND OUT WHAT WE'RE IN FOR, ALL OF US: SOON WE'LL BE DEAD.

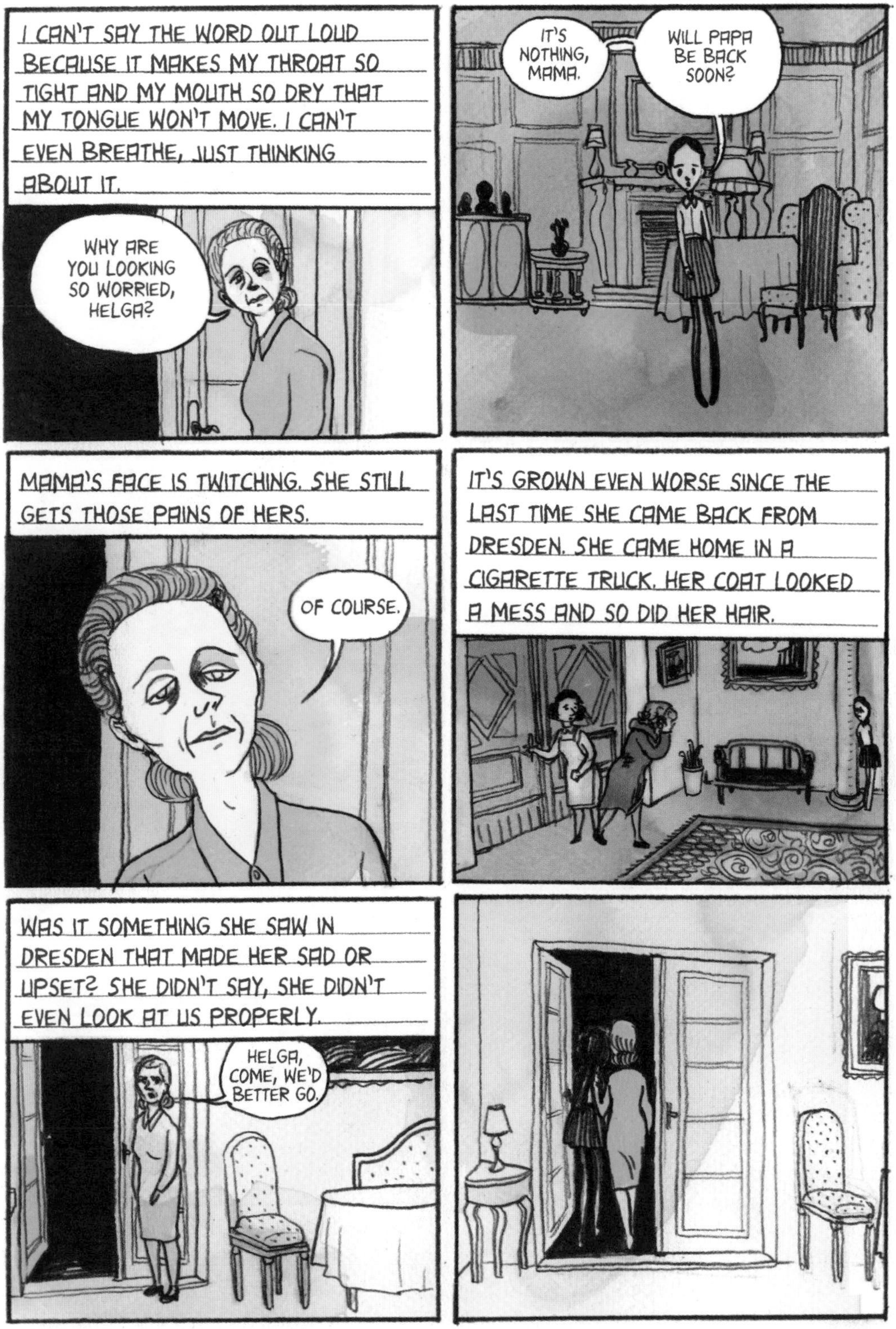
I CAN'T SAY THE WORD OUT LOUD BECAUSE IT MAKES MY THROAT SO TIGHT AND MY MOUTH SO DRY THAT MY TONGUE WON'T MOVE. I CAN'T EVEN BREATHE, JUST THINKING ABOUT IT.
WHY ARE YOU LOOKING SO WORRIED, HELGA?
IT'S NOTHING, MAMA.
WILL PAPA BE BACK SOON?
MAMA'S FACE IS TWITCHING. SHE STILL GETS THOSE PAINS OF HERS.
OF COURSE.
IT'S GROWN EVEN WORSE SINCE THE LAST TIME SHE CAME BACK FROM DRESDEN. SHE CAME HOME IN A CIGARETTE TRUCK. HER COAT LOOKED A MESS AND SO DID HER HAIR.
WAS IT SOMETHING SHE SAW IN DRESDEN THAT MADE HER SAD OR UPSET? SHE DIDN'T SAY, SHE DIDN'T EVEN LOOK AT US PROPERLY.
HELGA, COME, WE'D BETTER GO.

NOBODY CLEANS THE PLACE ANYMORE.

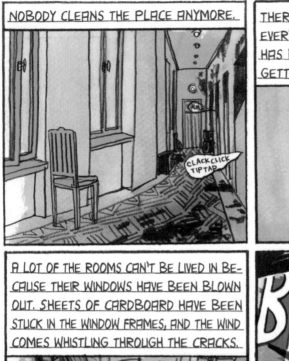

CLACK CLICK
TIPTAP

THERE ARE PEOPLE SITTING WORKING IN EVERY ROOM NOW THAT PAPA'S MINISTRY HAS BEEN DESTROYED. THE ROOMS ARE GETTING MORE AND MORE CROWDED.

CLICK
CLACK C

A LOT OF THE ROOMS CAN'T BE LIVED IN BE-CAUSE THEIR WINDOWS HAVE BEEN BLOWN OUT. SHEETS OF CARDBOARD HAVE BEEN STUCK IN THE WINDOW FRAMES, AND THE WIND COMES WHISTLING THROUGH THE CRACKS.

BOOM

HELGA, HAVE THEY HIT THE UPSTAIRS YET?

NO, HELMUT, EVERYTHING'S FINE.

WAAAAAHHHH

WE CHILDREN GO DOWN TO THE SHELTER, BUT THE OTHERS HAVE TO STAY UPSTAIRS AND KEEP WORKING.

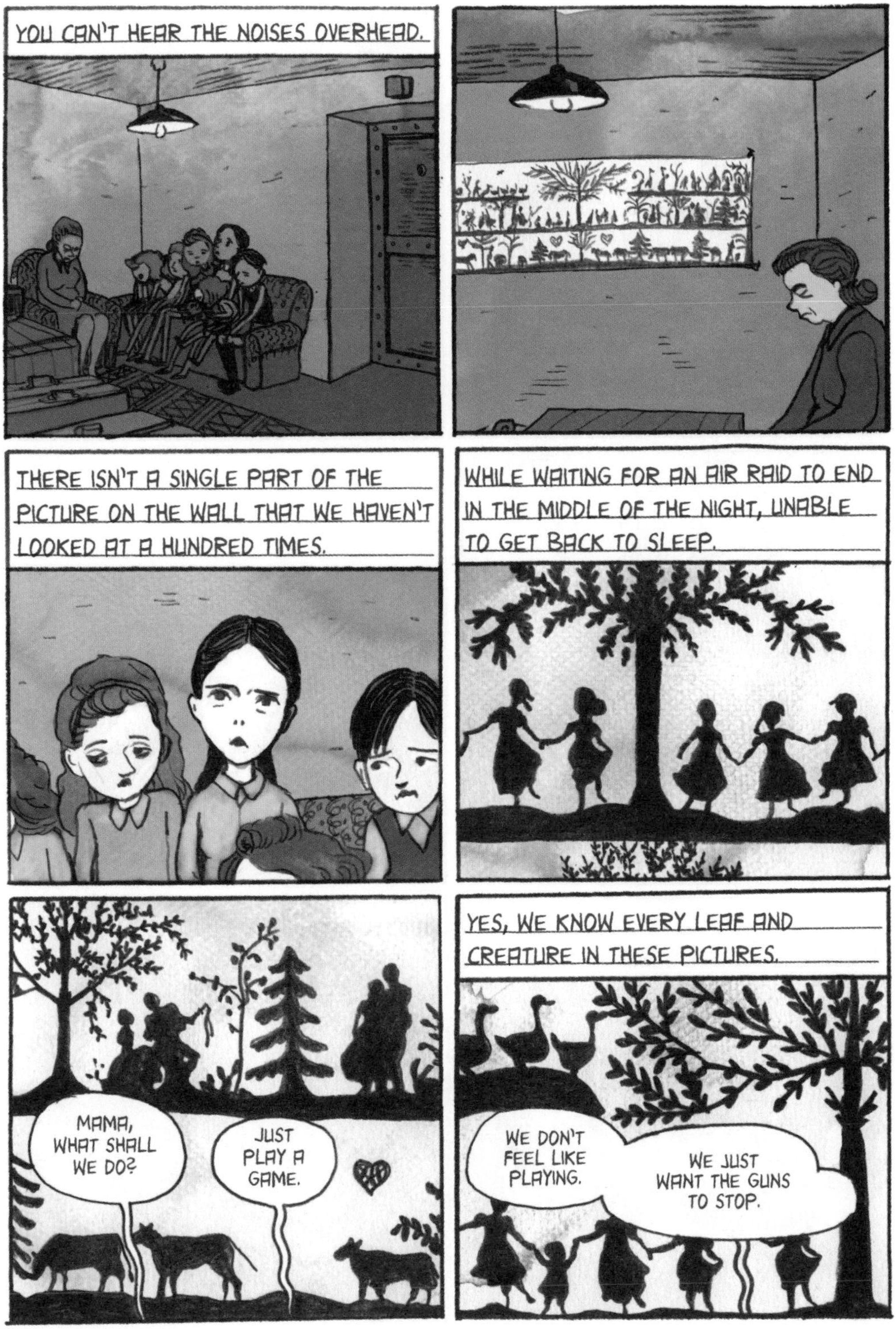

YOU CAN'T HEAR THE NOISES OVERHEAD.
THERE ISN'T A SINGLE PART OF THE PICTURE ON THE WALL THAT WE HAVEN'T LOOKED AT A HUNDRED TIMES.
WHILE WAITING FOR AN AIR RAID TO END IN THE MIDDLE OF THE NIGHT, UNABLE TO GET BACK TO SLEEP.
MAMA, WHAT SHALL WE DO?
JUST PLAY A GAME.
YES, WE KNOW EVERY LEAF AND CREATURE IN THESE PICTURES.
WE DON'T FEEL LIKE PLAYING.
WE JUST WANT THE GUNS TO STOP.

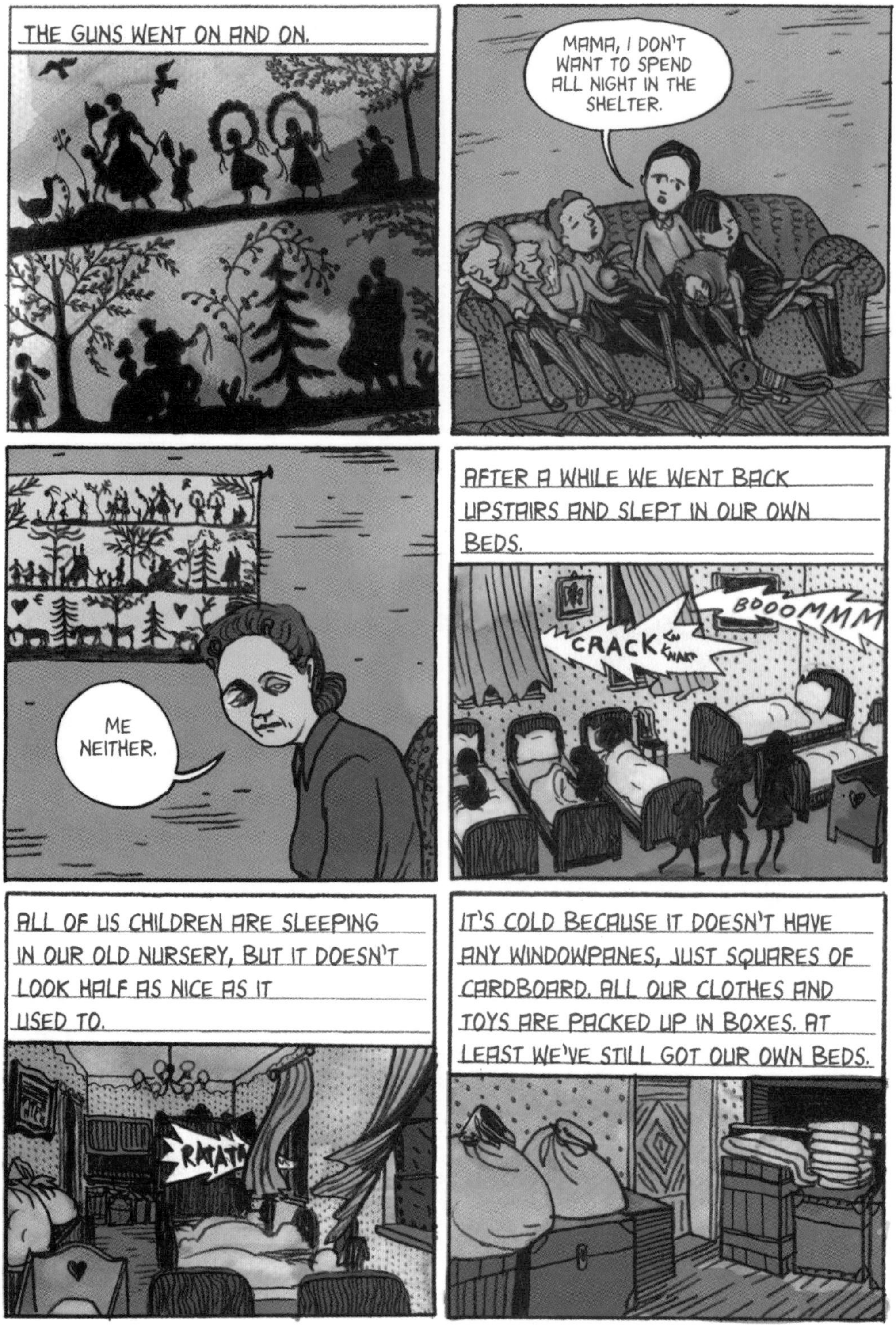
THE GUNS WENT ON AND ON.
MAMA, I DON'T WANT TO SPEND ALL NIGHT IN THE SHELTER.
ME NEITHER.
AFTER A WHILE WE WENT BACK UPSTAIRS AND SLEPT IN OUR OWN BEDS.
CRACK
BOOOMMM
ALL OF US CHILDREN ARE SLEEPING IN OUR OLD NURSERY, BUT IT DOESN'T LOOK HALF AS NICE AS IT USED TO.
IT'S COLD BECAUSE IT DOESN'T HAVE ANY WINDOWPANES, JUST SQUARES OF CARDBOARD. ALL OUR CLOTHES AND TOYS ARE PACKED UP IN BOXES. AT LEAST WE'VE STILL GOT OUR OWN BEDS.

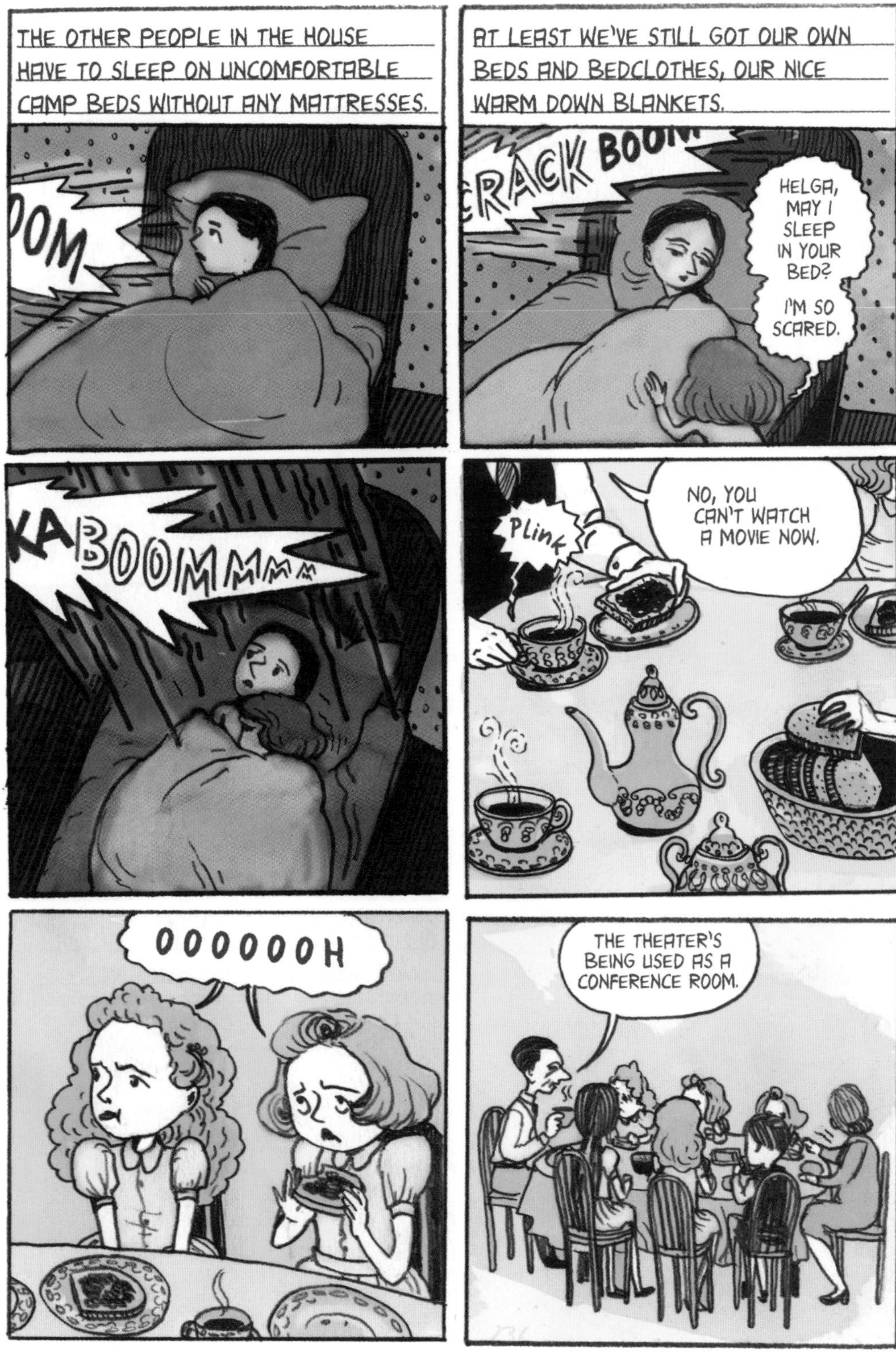
THE OTHER PEOPLE IN THE HOUSE HAVE TO SLEEP ON UNCOMFORTABLE CAMP BEDS WITHOUT ANY MATTRESSES.
AT LEAST WE'VE STILL GOT OUR OWN BEDS AND BEDCLOTHES, OUR NICE WARM DOWN BLANKETS.
OOM
CRACK BOOM
HELGA, MAY I SLEEP IN YOUR BED?
I'M SO SCARED.
KABOOMMMM
Plink
NO, YOU CAN'T WATCH A MOVIE NOW.
OOOOOOH
THE THEATER'S BEING USED AS A CONFERENCE ROOM.

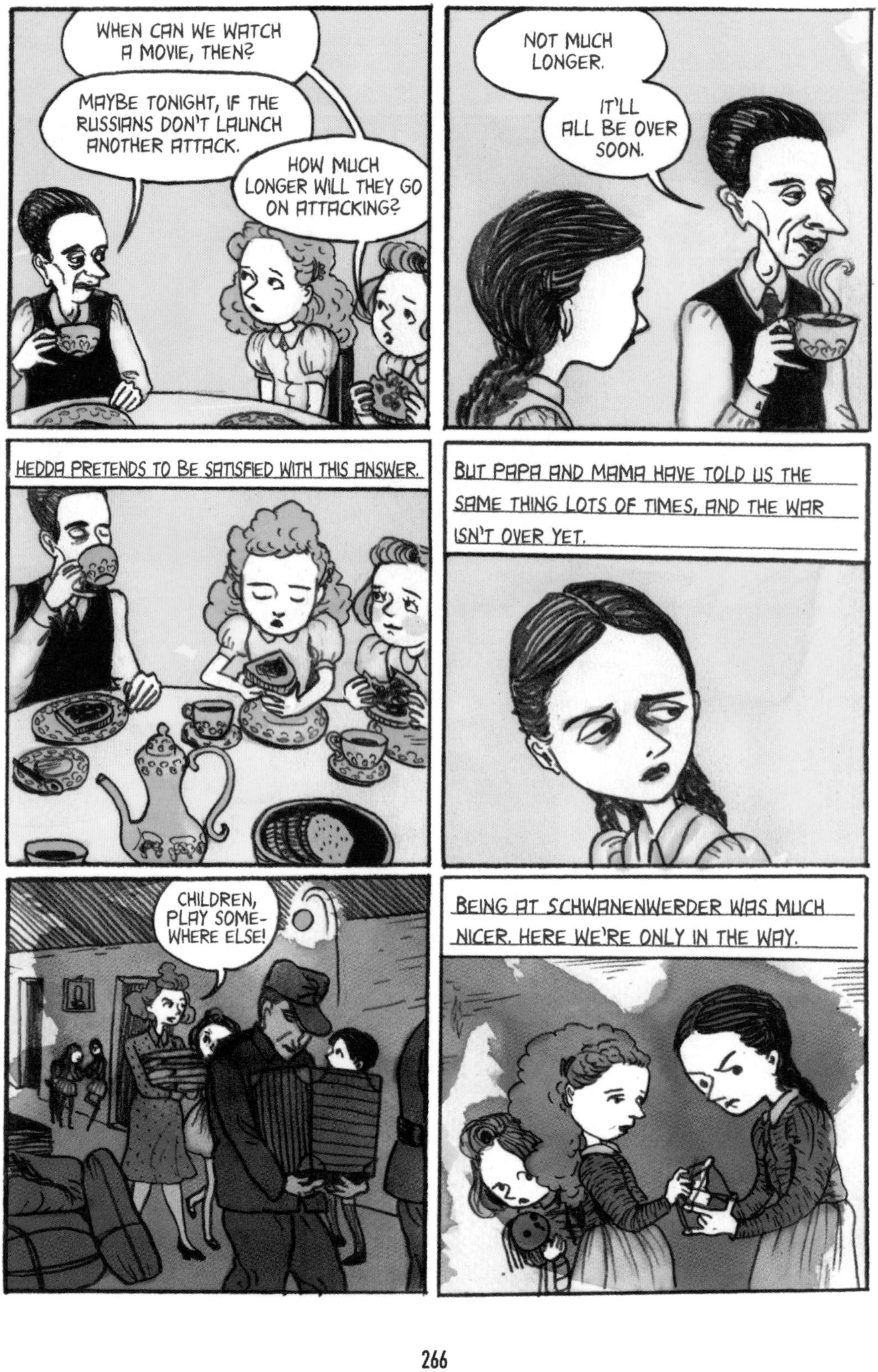
WHEN CAN WE WATCH A MOVIE, THEN?
MAYBE TONIGHT, IF THE RUSSIANS DON'T LAUNCH ANOTHER ATTACK.
HOW MUCH LONGER WILL THEY GO ON ATTACKING?
NOT MUCH LONGER.
IT'LL ALL BE OVER SOON.
HEDDA PRETENDS TO BE SATISFIED WITH THIS ANSWER.
BUT PAPA AND MAMA HAVE TOLD US THE SAME THING LOTS OF TIMES, AND THE WAR ISN'T OVER YET.
CHILDREN, PLAY SOME-WHERE ELSE!
BEING AT SCHWANENWERDER WAS MUCH NICER. HERE WE'RE ONLY IN THE WAY.

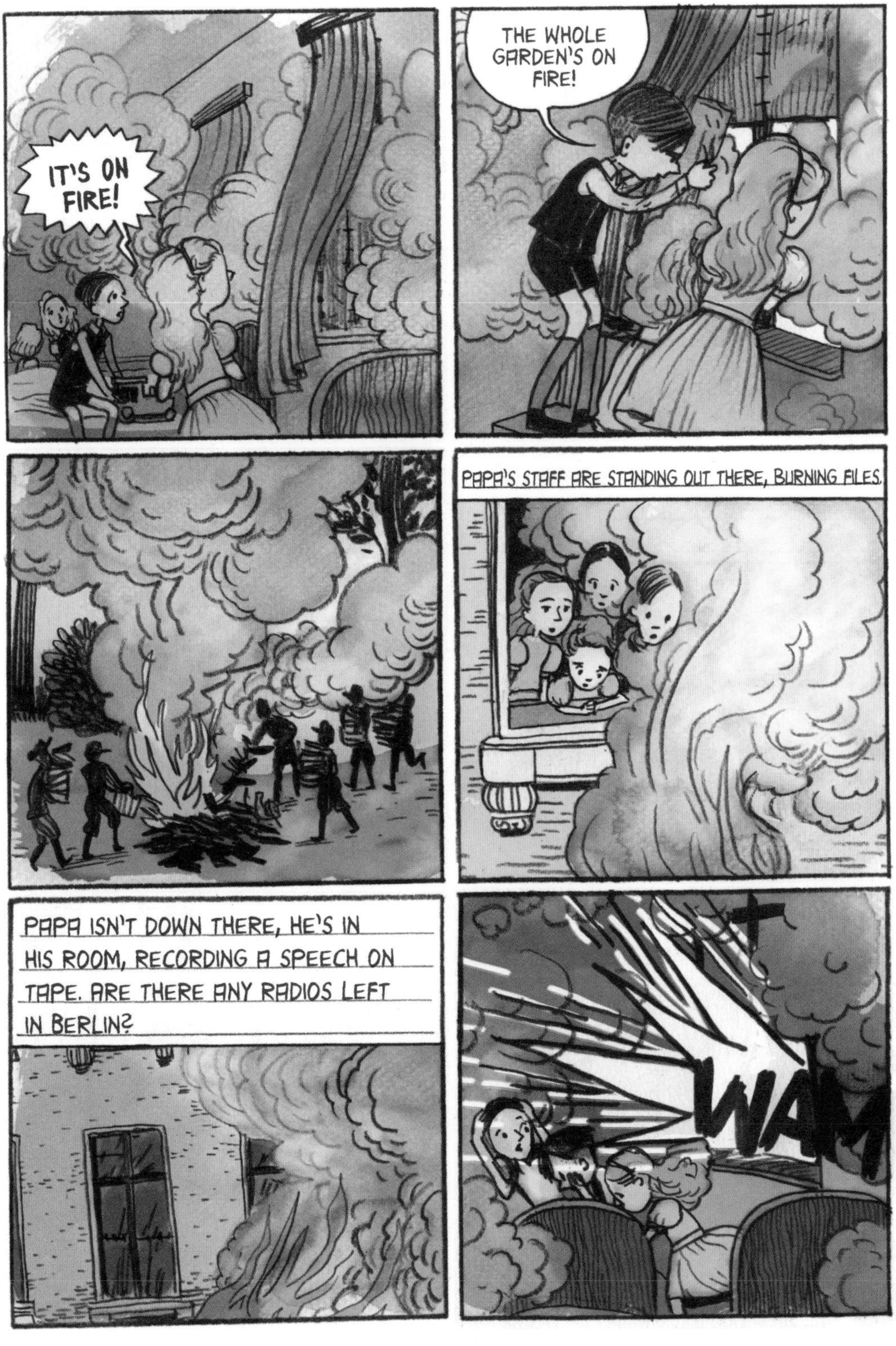
IT'S ON FIRE!
THE WHOLE GARDEN'S ON FIRE!
PAPA'S STAFF ARE STANDING OUT THERE, BURNING FILES.
PAPA ISN'T DOWN THERE, HE'S IN HIS ROOM, RECORDING A SPEECH ON TAPE. ARE THERE ANY RADIOS LEFT IN BERLIN?
WAM

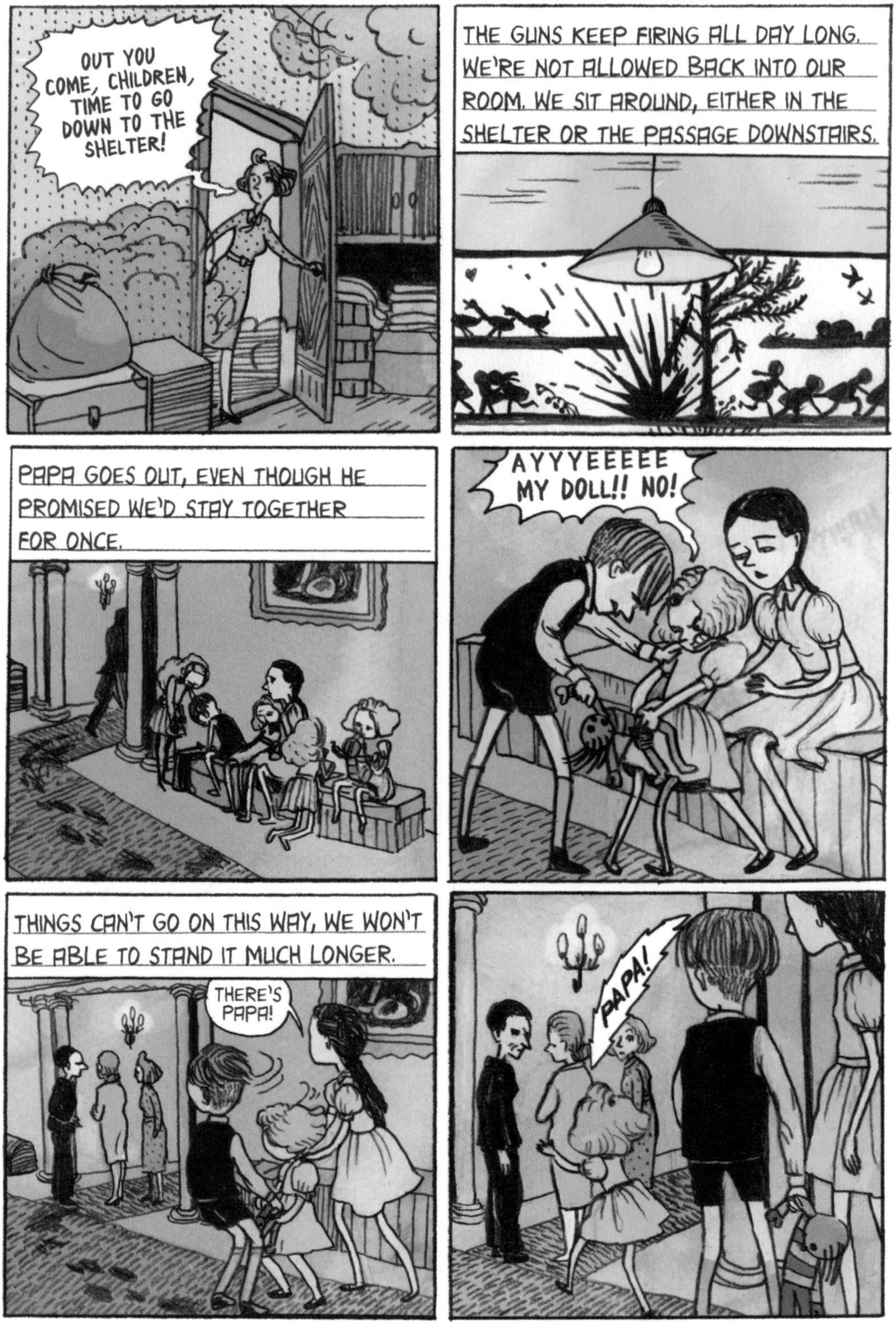
OUT YOU COME, CHILDREN, TIME TO GO DOWN TO THE SHELTER!
THE GUNS KEEP FIRING ALL DAY LONG. WE'RE NOT ALLOWED BACK INTO OUR ROOM. WE SIT AROUND, EITHER IN THE SHELTER OR THE PASSAGE DOWNSTAIRS.
PAPA GOES OUT, EVEN THOUGH HE PROMISED WE'D STAY TOGETHER FOR ONCE.
AYYYEEEEE MY DOLL!! NO!
THINGS CAN'T GO ON THIS WAY, WE WON'T BE ABLE TO STAND IT MUCH LONGER.
THERE'S PAPA!
PAPA!

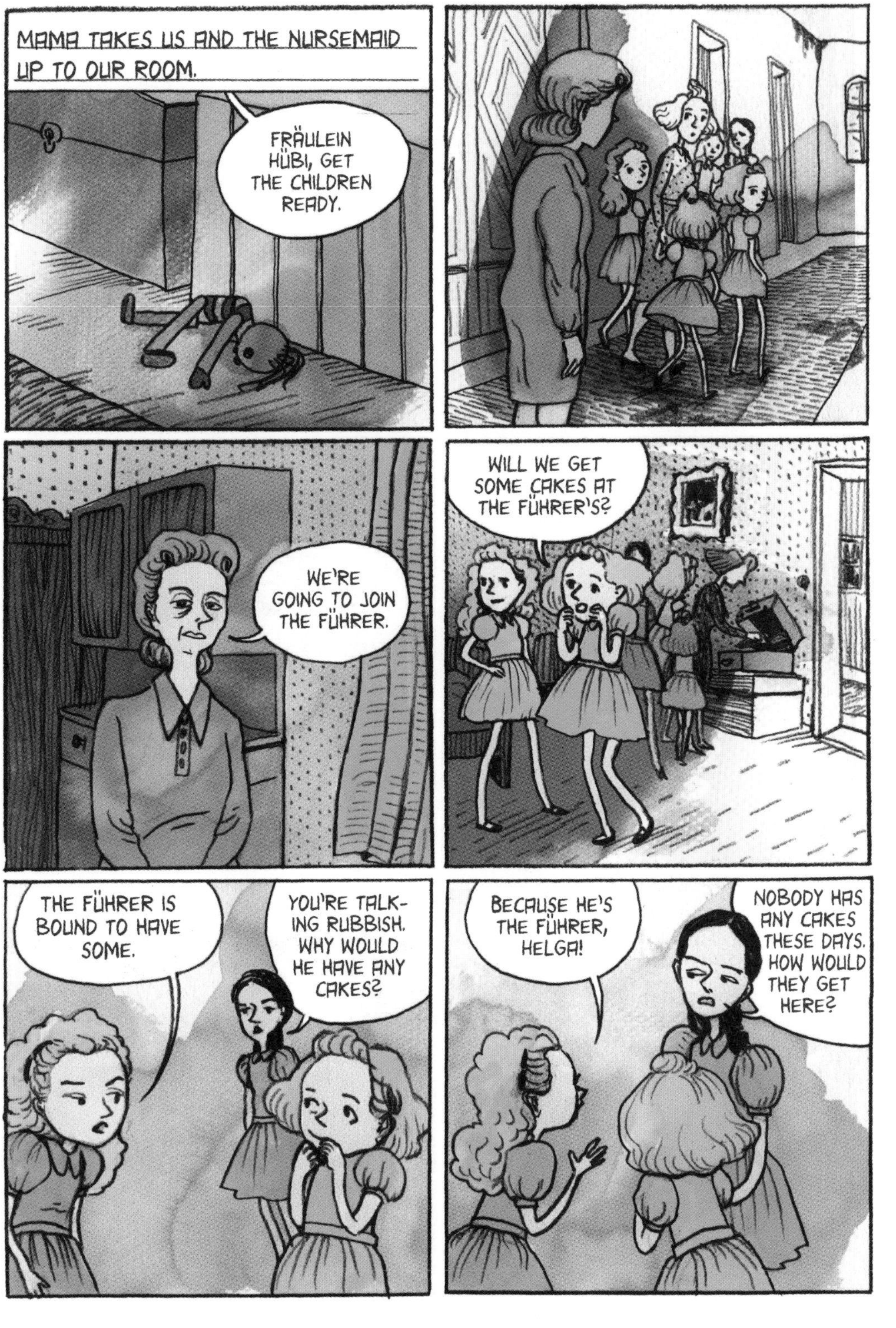
MAMA TAKES US AND THE NURSEMAID UP TO OUR ROOM.
FRÄULEIN HÜBI, GET THE CHILDREN READY.
WE'RE GOING TO JOIN THE FÜHRER.
WILL WE GET SOME CAKES AT THE FÜHRER'S?
THE FÜHRER IS BOUND TO HAVE SOME.
YOU'RE TALKING RUBBISH. WHY WOULD HE HAVE ANY CAKES?
BECAUSE HE'S THE FÜHRER, HELGA!
NOBODY HAS ANY CAKES THESE DAYS. HOW WOULD THEY GET HERE?

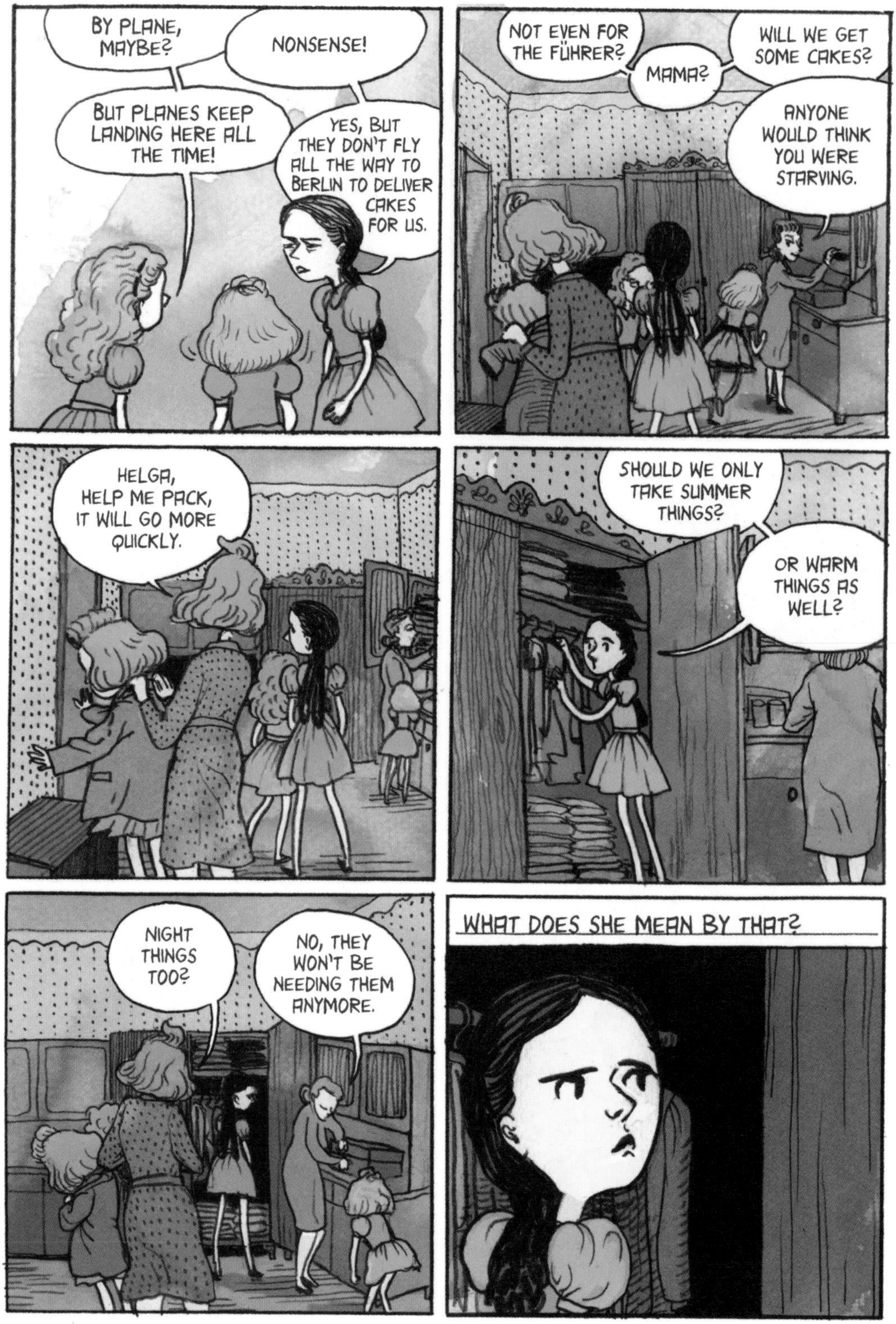
BY PLANE, MAYBE?
NONSENSE!
BUT PLANES KEEP LANDING HERE ALL THE TIME!
YES, BUT THEY DON'T FLY ALL THE WAY TO BERLIN TO DELIVER CAKES FOR US.
NOT EVEN FOR THE FÜHRER?
MAMA?
WILL WE GET SOME CAKES?
ANYONE WOULD THINK YOU WERE STARVING.
HELGA, HELP ME PACK, IT WILL GO MORE QUICKLY.
SHOULD WE ONLY TAKE SUMMER THINGS?
OR WARM THINGS AS WELL?
NIGHT THINGS TOO?
NO, THEY WON'T BE NEEDING THEM ANYMORE.
WHAT DOES SHE MEAN BY THAT?

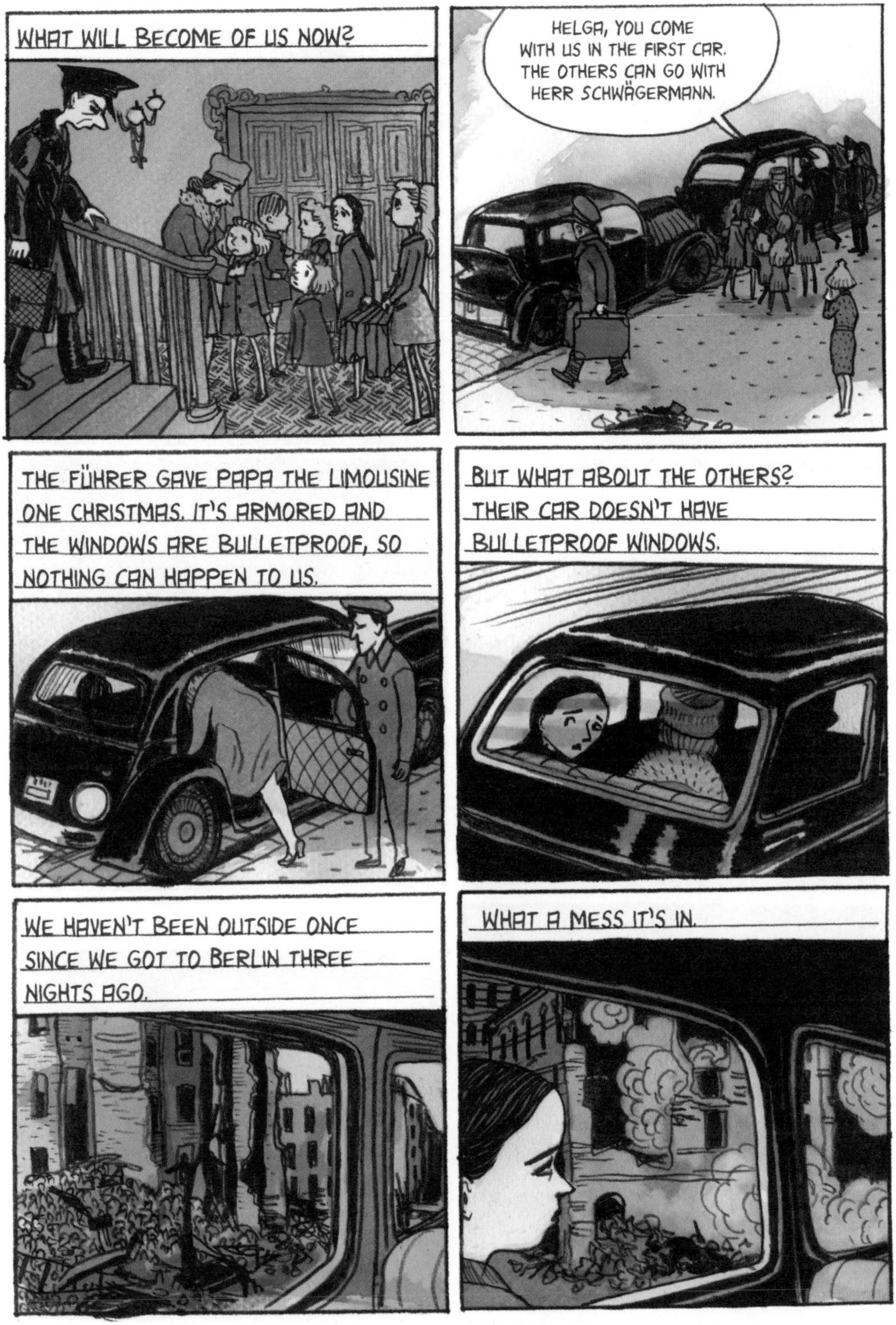
WHAT WILL BECOME OF US NOW?
HELGA, YOU COME WITH US IN THE FIRST CAR. THE OTHERS CAN GO WITH HERR SCHWÄGERMANN.
THE FÜHRER GAVE PAPA THE LIMOUSINE ONE CHRISTMAS. IT'S ARMORED AND THE WINDOWS ARE BULLETPROOF, SO NOTHING CAN HAPPEN TO US.
BUT WHAT ABOUT THE OTHERS? THEIR CAR DOESN'T HAVE BULLETPROOF WINDOWS.
WE HAVEN'T BEEN OUTSIDE ONCE SINCE WE GOT TO BERLIN THREE NIGHTS AGO.
WHAT A MESS IT'S IN.

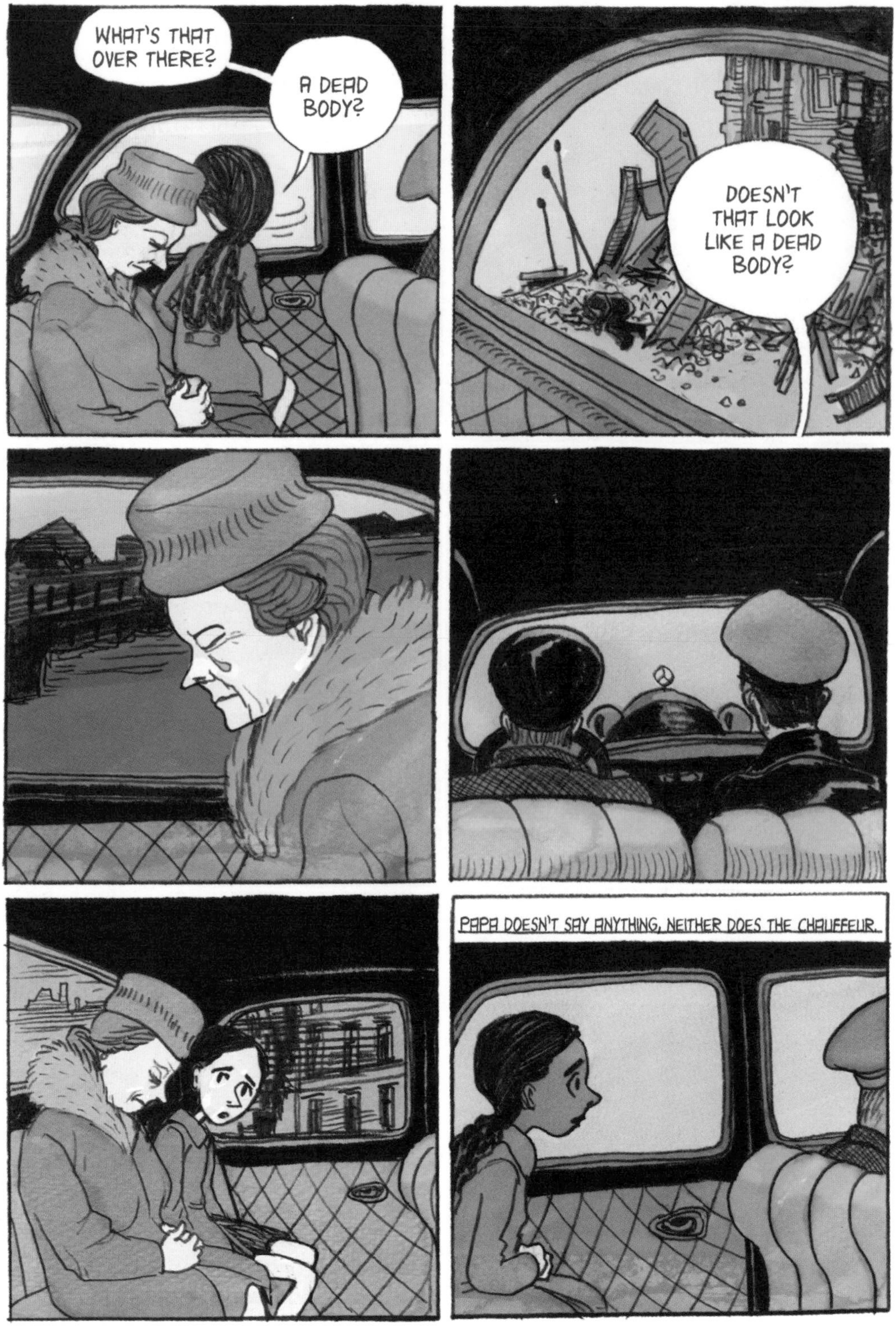
WHAT'S THAT OVER THERE?
A DEAD BODY?
DOESN'T THAT LOOK LIKE A DEAD BODY?
PAPA DOESN'T SAY ANYTHING, NEITHER DOES THE CHAUFFEUR.

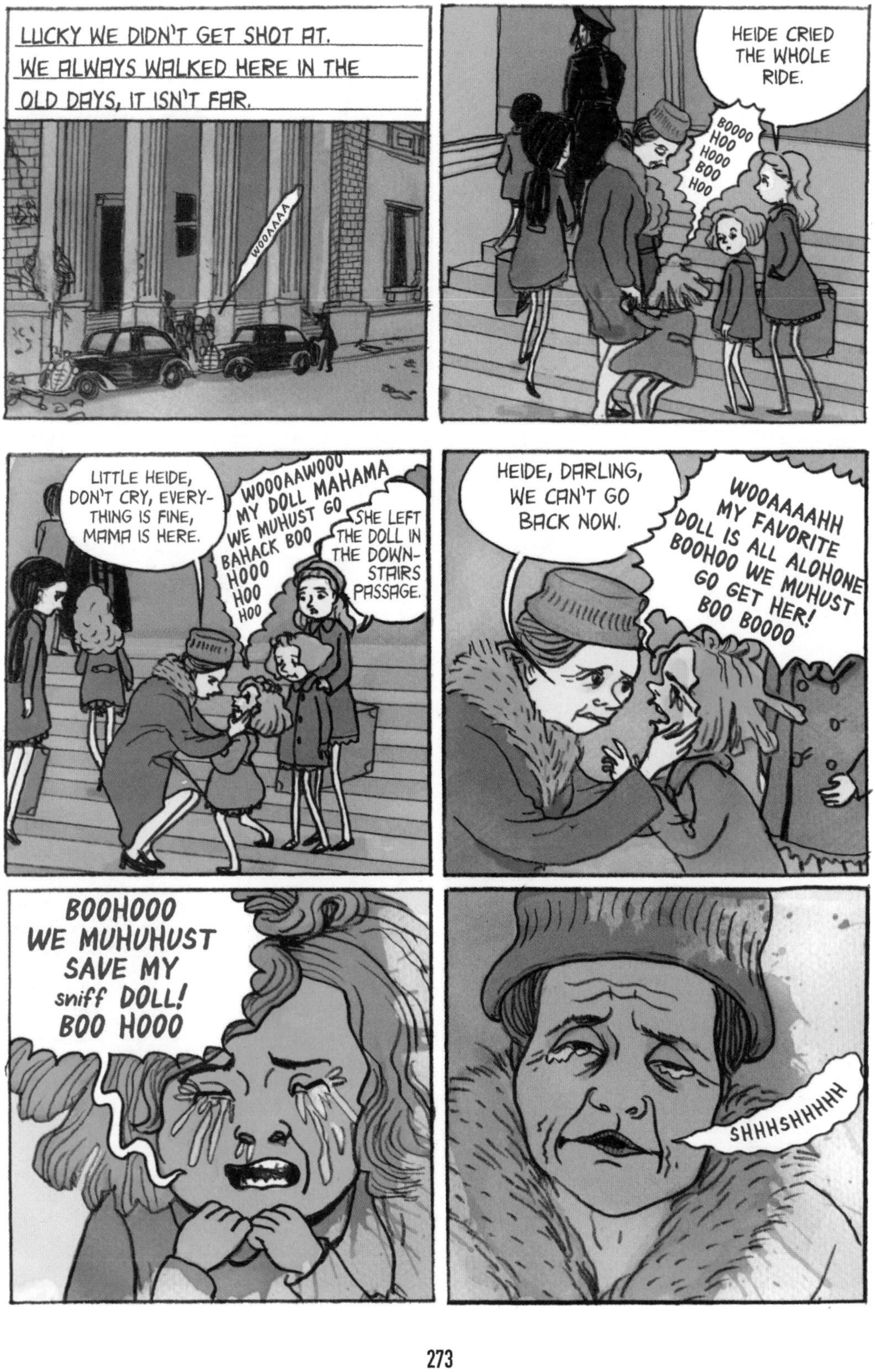

LUCKY WE DIDN'T GET SHOT AT.
WE ALWAYS WALKED HERE IN THE OLD DAYS, IT ISN'T FAR.
WOOAAAA
HEIDE CRIED THE WHOLE RIDE.
BOOOO HOO HOOO BOO HOO
LITTLE HEIDE, DON'T CRY, EVERY-THING IS FINE, MAMA IS HERE.
WOOOAAWOOO MY DOLL MAHAMA WE MUHUST GO BAHACK BOO HOOO HOO HOO
SHE LEFT THE DOLL IN THE DOWN-STAIRS PASSAGE.
HEIDE, DARLING, WE CAN'T GO BACK NOW.
WOOAAAAHH MY FAVORITE DOLL IS ALL ALOHONE BOOHOO WE MUHUST GO GET HER! BOO BOOOO
BOOHOOO WE MUHUHUST SAVE MY sniff DOLL! BOO HOOO
SHHHSHHHHH

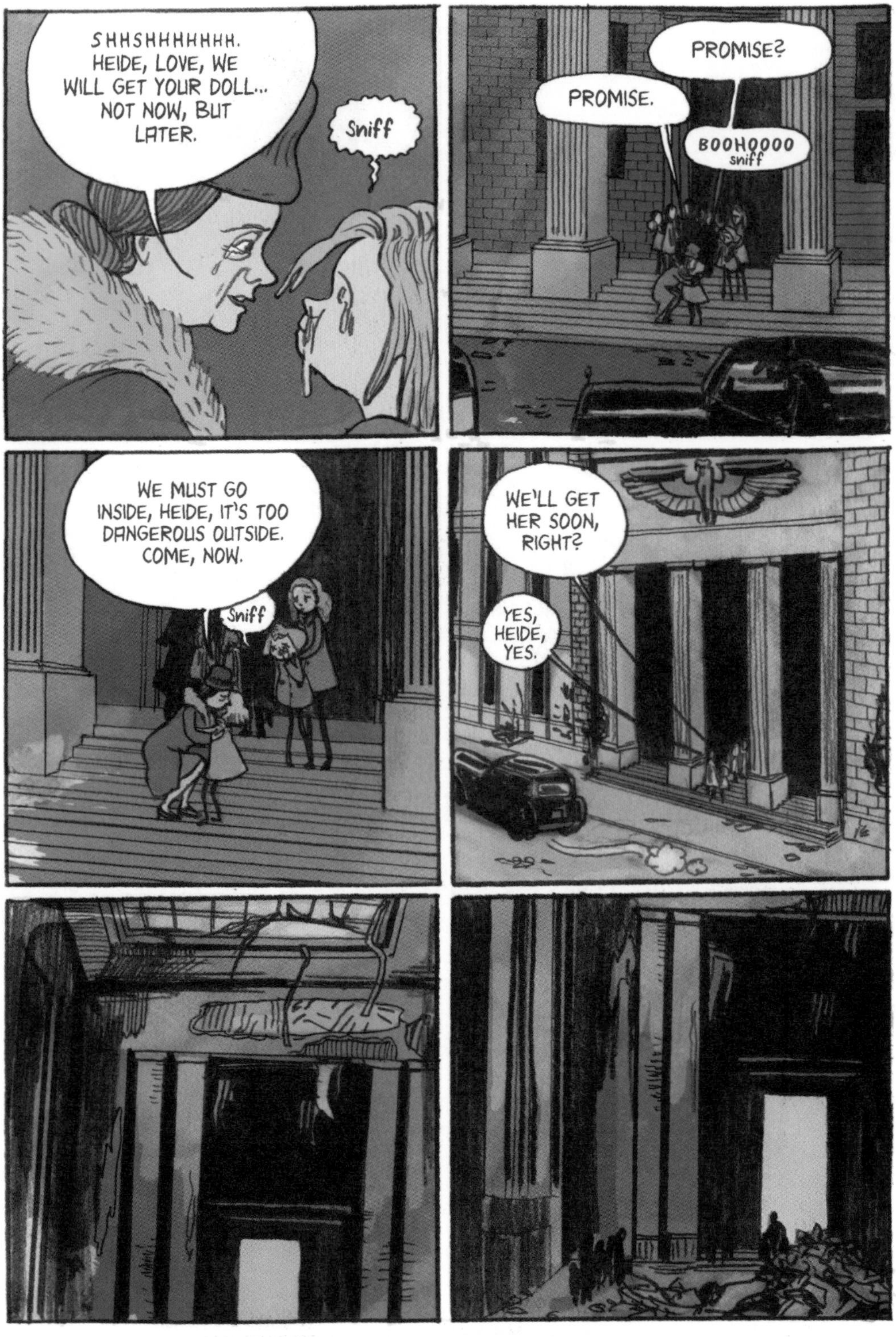
SHHSHHHHHHH.
HEIDE, LOVE, WE WILL GET YOUR DOLL... NOT NOW, BUT LATER.
Sniff
PROMISE?
PROMISE.
BOOHOOOO
sniff
WE MUST GO INSIDE, HEIDE, IT'S TOO DANGEROUS OUTSIDE. COME, NOW.
Sniff
WE'LL GET HER SOON, RIGHT?
YES, HEIDE, YES.

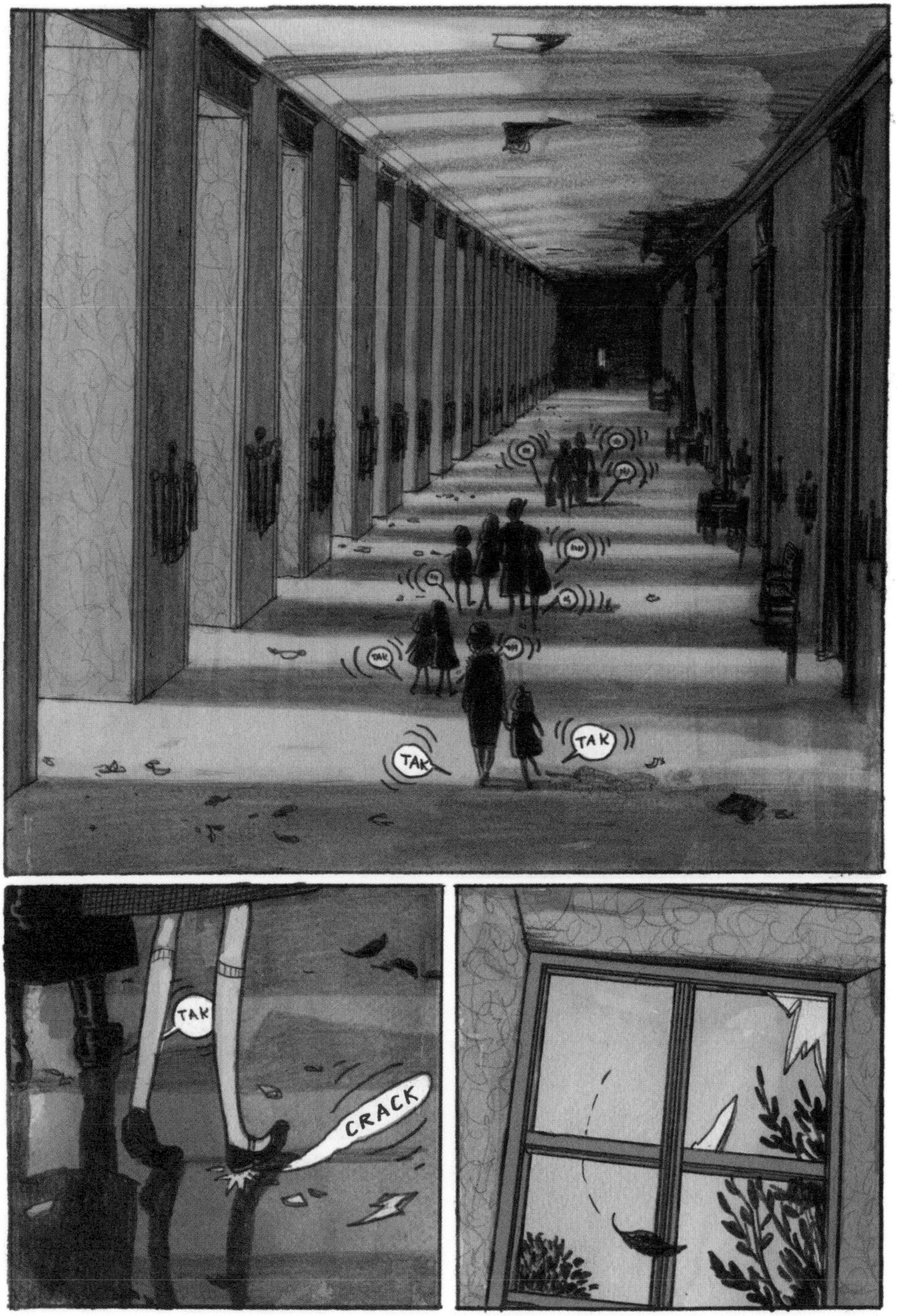
TAK
TAK
TAK
TAK
CRACK

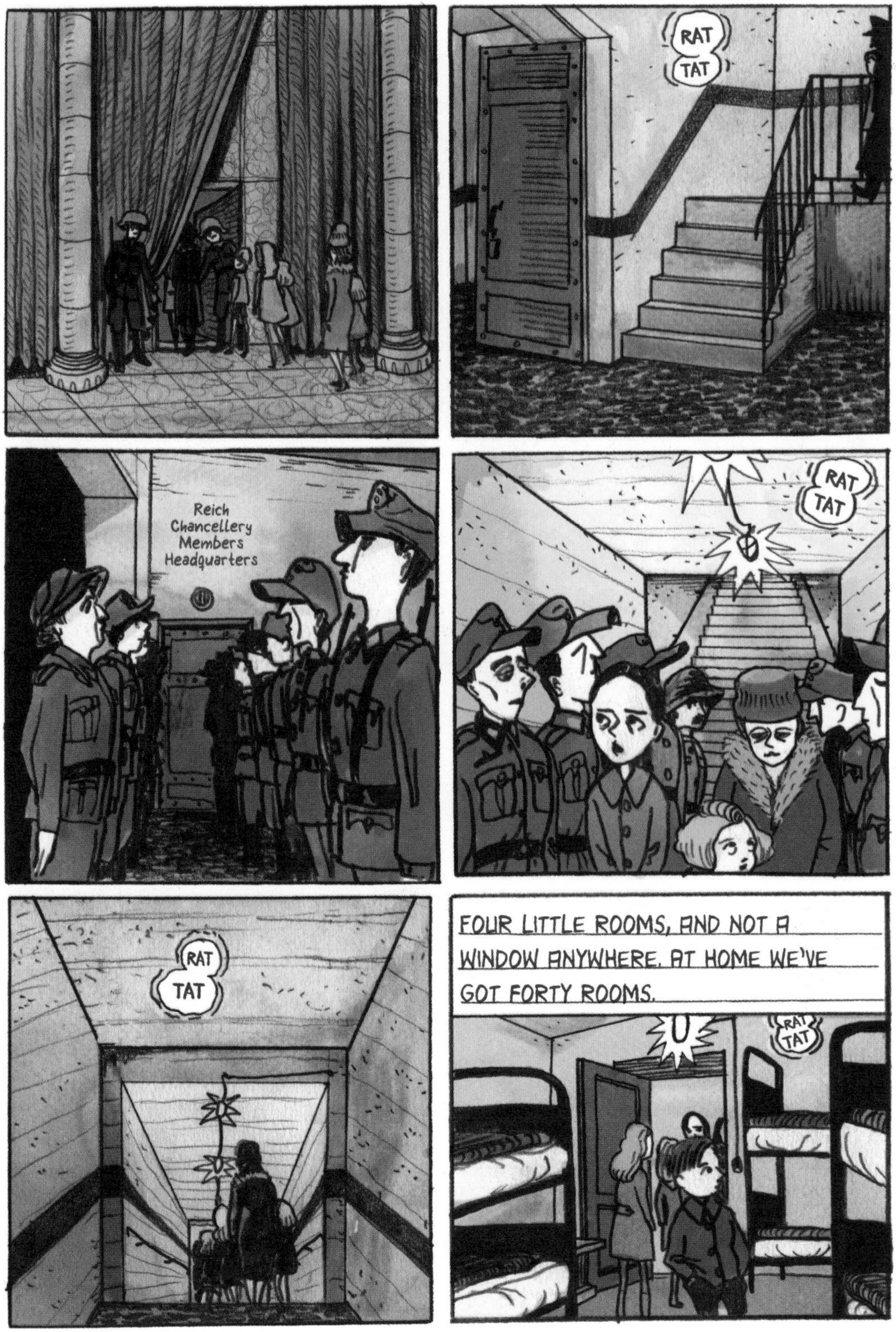
RAT
TAT
Reich Chancellery Members Headquarters
RAT
TAT
RAT
TAT
FOUR LITTLE ROOMS, AND NOT A WINDOW ANYWHERE. AT HOME WE'VE GOT FORTY ROOMS.
RAT
TAT

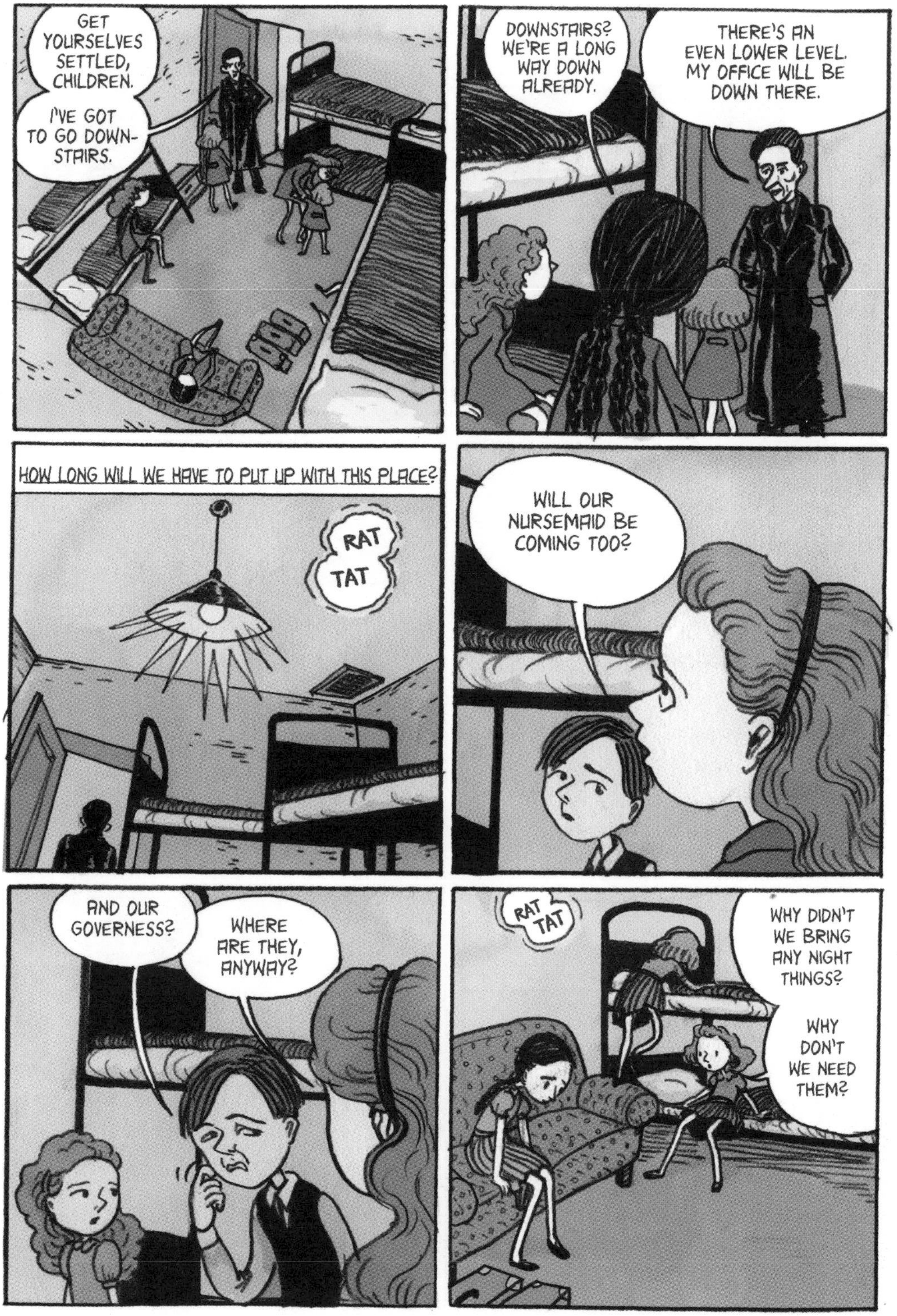
GET YOURSELVES SETTLED, CHILDREN.
I'VE GOT TO GO DOWN-STAIRS.
DOWNSTAIRS? WE'RE A LONG WAY DOWN ALREADY.
THERE'S AN EVEN LOWER LEVEL. MY OFFICE WILL BE DOWN THERE.
HOW LONG WILL WE HAVE TO PUT UP WITH THIS PLACE?
RAT TAT
WILL OUR NURSEMAID BE COMING TOO?
AND OUR GOVERNESS?
WHERE ARE THEY, ANYWAY?
RAT TAT
WHY DIDN'T WE BRING ANY NIGHT THINGS?
WHY DON'T WE NEED THEM?

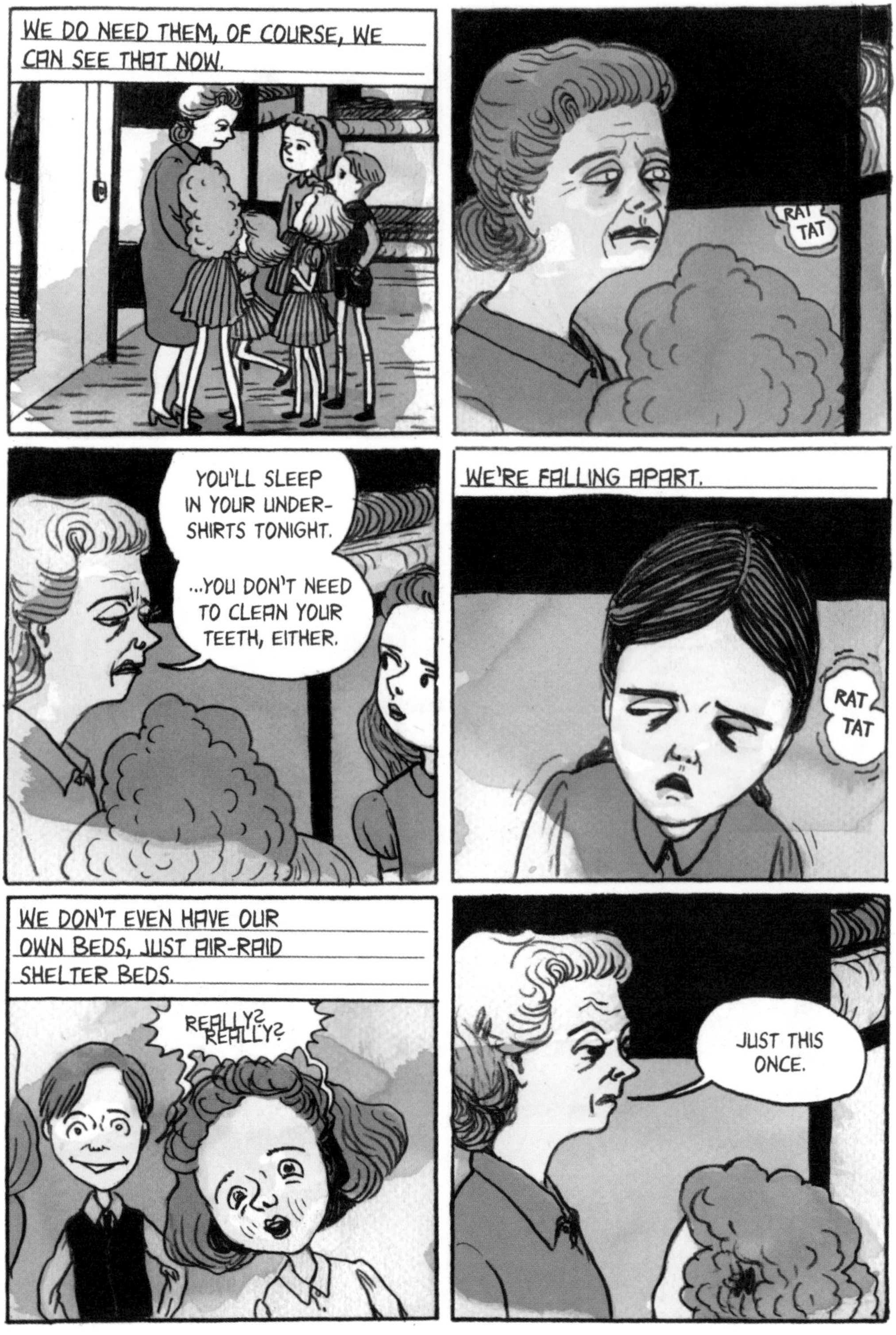
WE DO NEED THEM, OF COURSE, WE CAN SEE THAT NOW.
RAT TAT
YOU'LL SLEEP IN YOUR UNDER-SHIRTS TONIGHT.
...YOU DON'T NEED TO CLEAN YOUR TEETH, EITHER.
WE'RE FALLING APART.
RAT TAT
WE DON'T EVEN HAVE OUR OWN BEDS, JUST AIR-RAID SHELTER BEDS.
REALLY? REALLY?
JUST THIS ONCE.

AND YET WE HAVE THREE HOUSES! SCHWANENWERDER WAS THE NICEST, BECAUSE WE COULD INVITE FRIENDS HOME FROM SCHOOL.

WE WENT FOR BOAT RIDES THERE AND LEARNED TO SWIM.

OUR ROOMS AT THE TOWN HOUSE WERE LOVELY, AND WE OFTEN SAW PAPA DURING THE DAY WHEN WE WERE STAYING THERE. HE WOULD TAKE US OUT AND BUY US SOMETHING, EVERY TIME.

WE HAD SO MANY TOYS AT THE TOWN HOUSE, THEY WOULDN'T ALL FIT INTO THE NURSERY.

HERE WE'VE GOT NOTHING. THERE WEREN'T ANY CAKES AFTER ALL. IT'S BEEN ANOTHER MISERABLE DAY.

CLICK

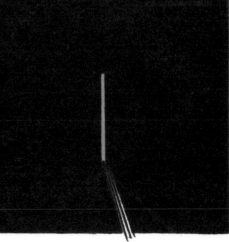

279

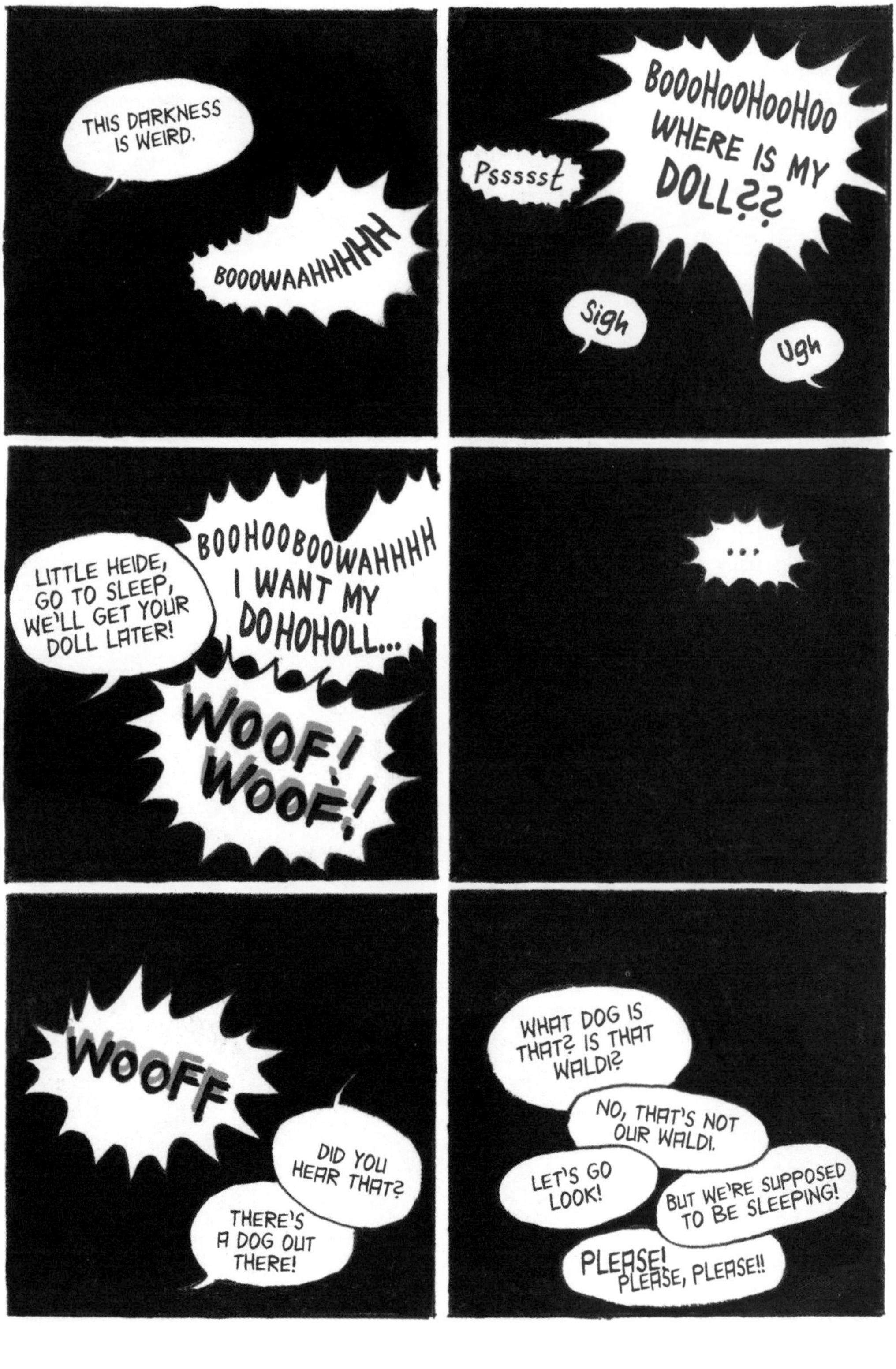

THIS DARKNESS IS WEIRD.
BOOOWAAHHHHH
Psssssst
BOOOHOOHOOHOO WHERE IS MY DOLL??
Sigh
Ugh
LITTLE HEIDE, GO TO SLEEP, WE'LL GET YOUR DOLL LATER!
BOOHOOBOOWAHHHH I WANT MY DOHOHOLL...
WOOF! WOOF!
...
WOOFF
DID YOU HEAR THAT?
THERE'S A DOG OUT THERE!
WHAT DOG IS THAT? IS THAT WALDI?
NO, THAT'S NOT OUR WALDI.
LET'S GO LOOK!
BUT WE'RE SUPPOSED TO BE SLEEPING!
PLEASE! PLEASE, PLEASE!!

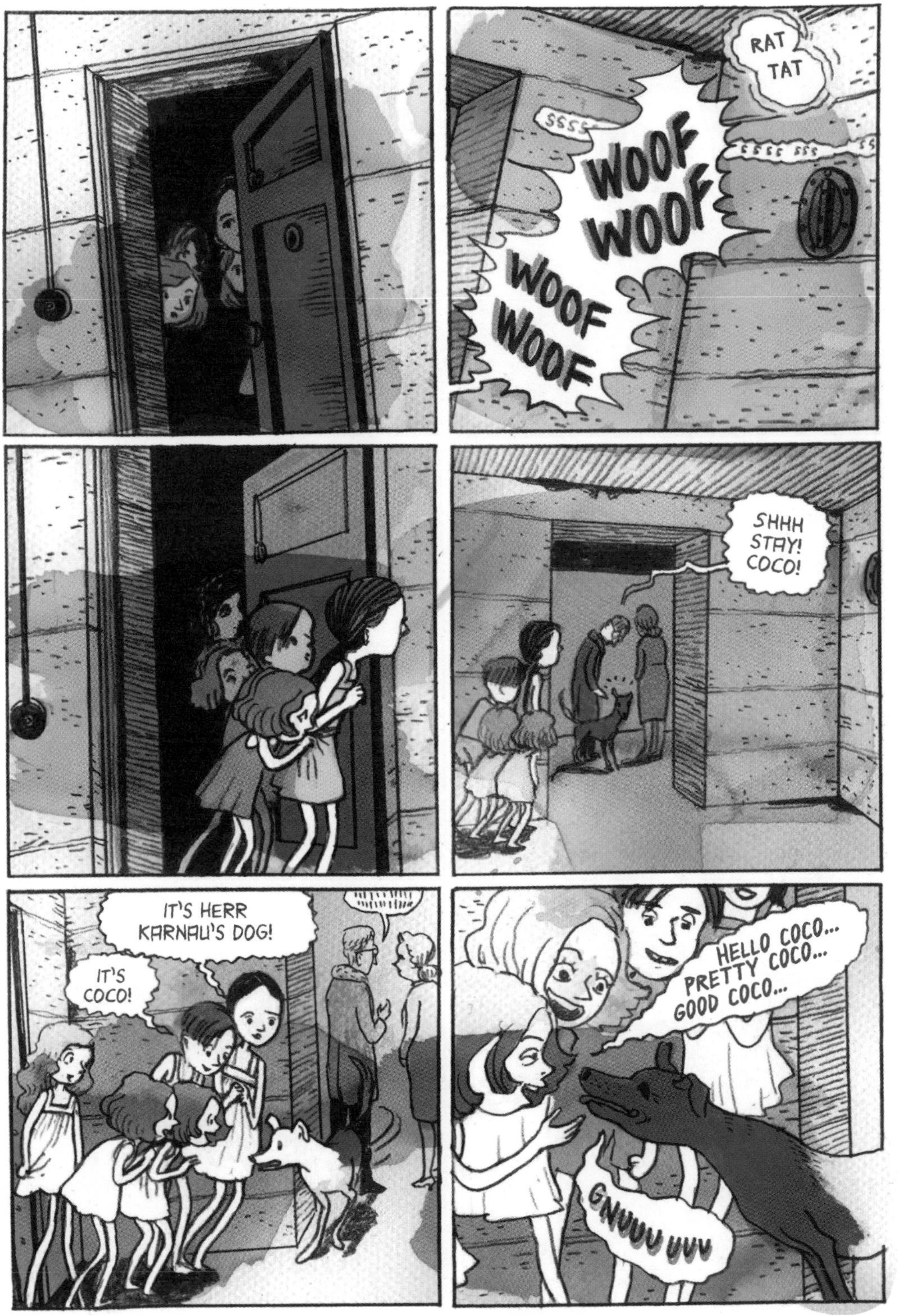
RAT
TAT
WOOF
WOOF
WOOF
WOOF
SHHH
STAY!
COCO!
IT'S HERR
KARNAU'S DOG!
IT'S
COCO!
HELLO COCO...
PRETTY COCO...
GOOD COCO...
GNUUU UUV

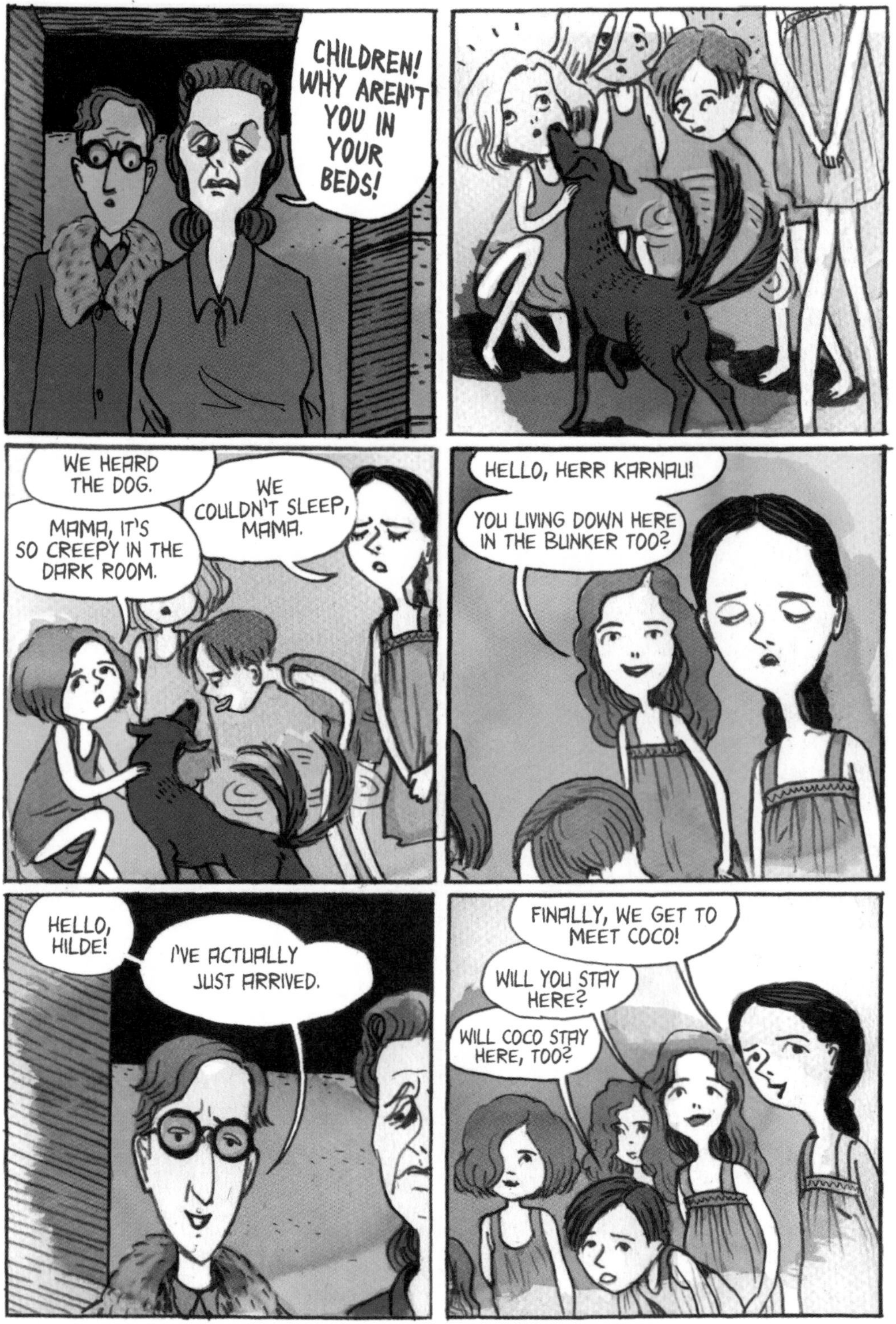
CHILDREN! WHY AREN'T YOU IN YOUR BEDS!
WE HEARD THE DOG.
MAMA, IT'S SO CREEPY IN THE DARK ROOM.
WE COULDN'T SLEEP, MAMA.
HELLO, HERR KARNAU!
YOU LIVING DOWN HERE IN THE BUNKER TOO?
HELLO, HILDE!
I'VE ACTUALLY JUST ARRIVED.
FINALLY, WE GET TO MEET COCO!
WILL YOU STAY HERE?
WILL COCO STAY HERE, TOO?

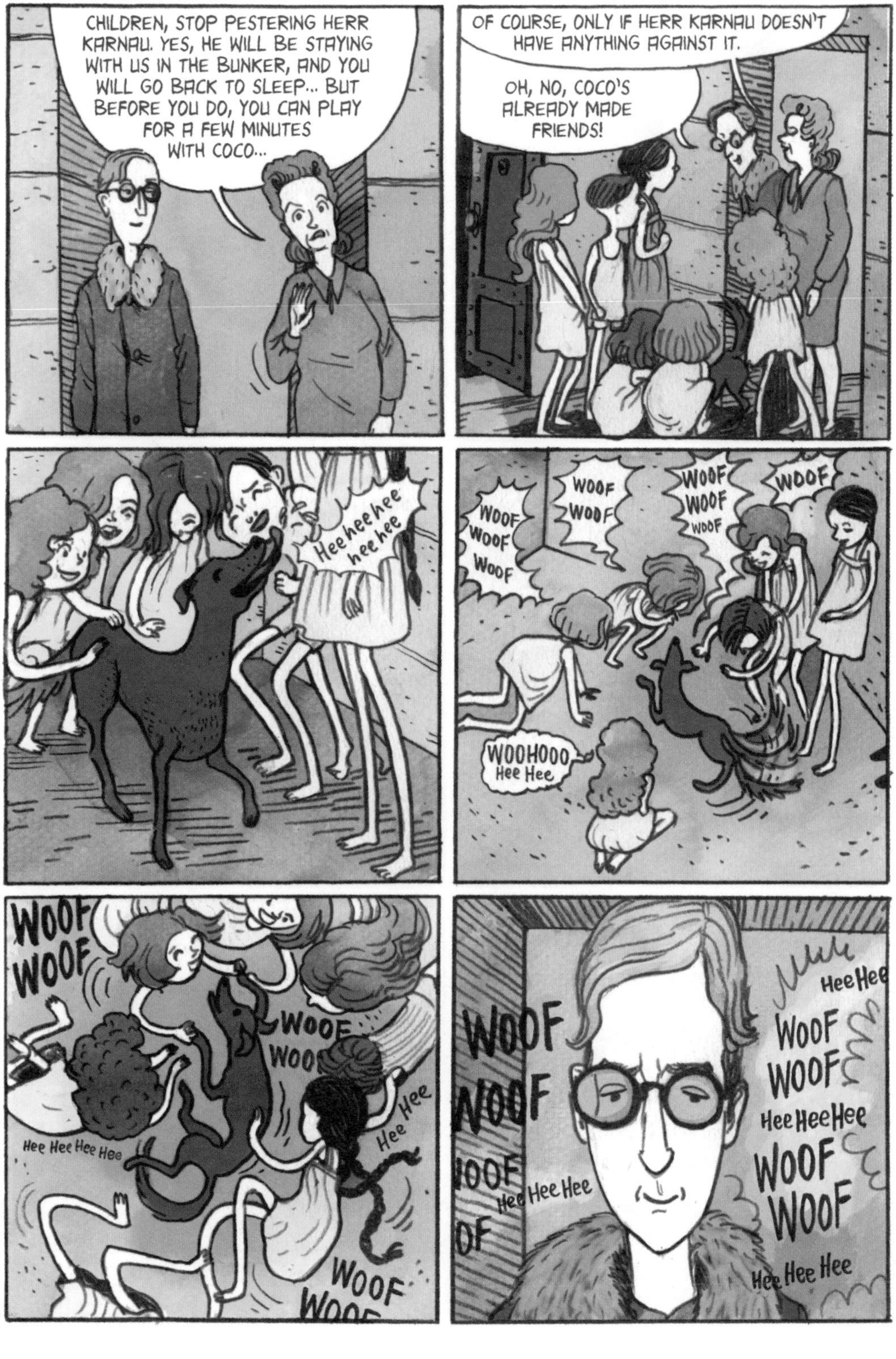
CHILDREN, STOP PESTERING HERR KARNAU. YES, HE WILL BE STAYING WITH US IN THE BUNKER, AND YOU WILL GO BACK TO SLEEP... BUT BEFORE YOU DO, YOU CAN PLAY FOR A FEW MINUTES WITH COCO...
OF COURSE, ONLY IF HERR KARNAU DOESN'T HAVE ANYTHING AGAINST IT.
OH, NO, COCO'S ALREADY MADE FRIENDS!
Hee hee hee hee hee
WOOF WOOF WOOF
WOOF WOOF
WOOF WOOF WOOF
WOOF
WOOHOOO Hee Hee
WOOF WOOF
WOOF WOOF
Hee Hee
Hee Hee Hee Hee
WOOF
Hee Hee
WOOF WOOF
WOOF WOOF
Hee Hee Hee
WOOF WOOF
Hee Hee Hee
Hee Hee Hee

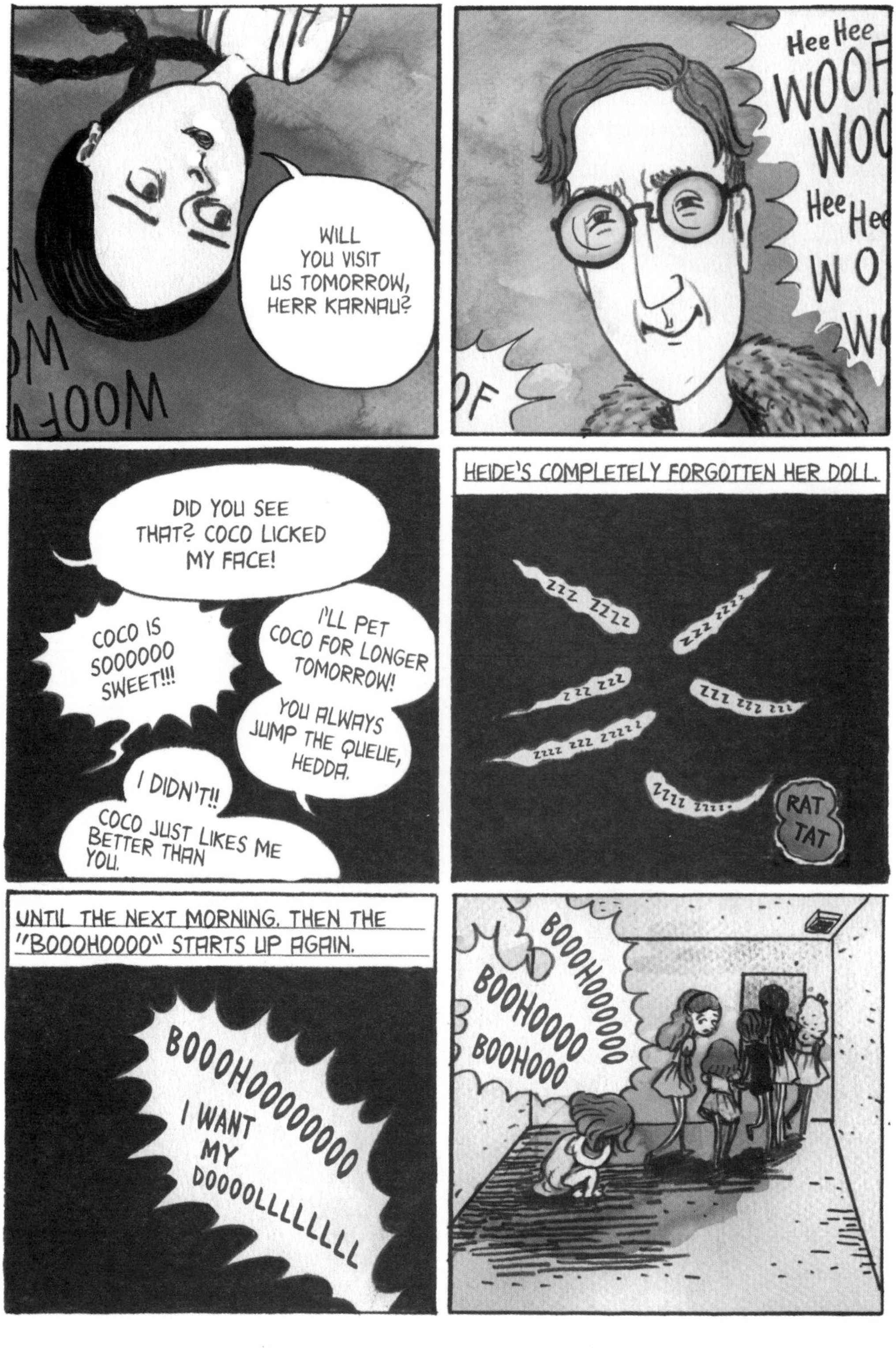
WOOF WO W
WILL YOU VISIT US TOMORROW, HERR KARNAU?
Hee Hee
WOOF
WOO
Hee Hee
W O
W
OF
DID YOU SEE THAT? COCO LICKED MY FACE!
COCO IS SOOOOOO SWEET!!!
I'LL PET COCO FOR LONGER TOMORROW!
YOU ALWAYS JUMP THE QUEUE, HEDDA.
I DIDN'T!!
COCO JUST LIKES ME BETTER THAN YOU.
HEIDE'S COMPLETELY FORGOTTEN HER DOLL.
RAT TAT
UNTIL THE NEXT MORNING. THEN THE "BOOOHOOOO" STARTS UP AGAIN.
BOOOHOOOOOOOO I WANT MY DOOOOLLLLLLLL
BOOOHOOOOOO
BOOHOOOO
BOOHOOO

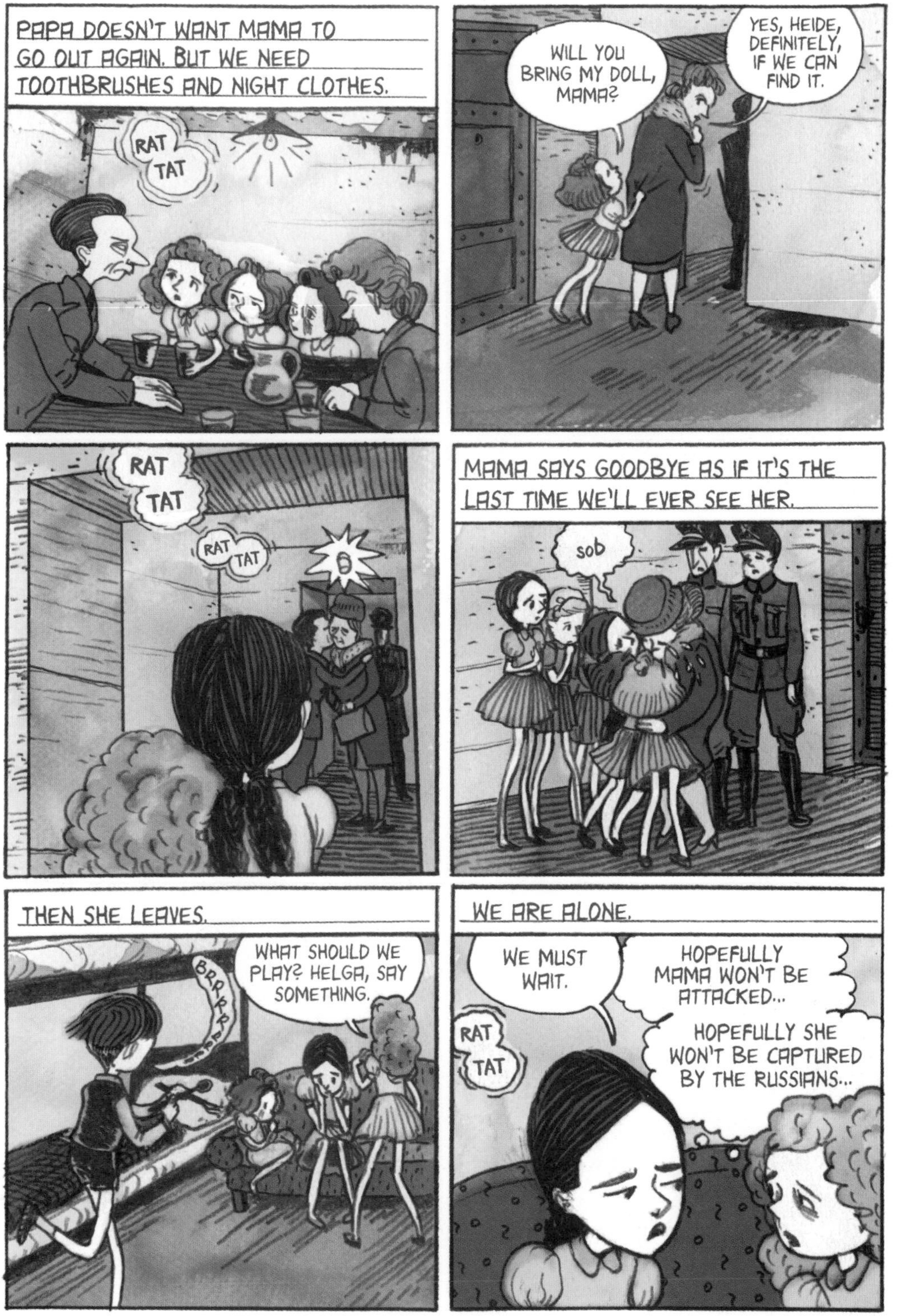
PAPA DOESN'T WANT MAMA TO GO OUT AGAIN. BUT WE NEED TOOTHBRUSHES AND NIGHT CLOTHES.
RAT TAT
WILL YOU BRING MY DOLL, MAMA?
YES, HEIDE, DEFINITELY, IF WE CAN FIND IT.
RAT TAT
RAT TAT
MAMA SAYS GOODBYE AS IF IT'S THE LAST TIME WE'LL EVER SEE HER.
sob
THEN SHE LEAVES.
BRRRRRR
WHAT SHOULD WE PLAY? HELGA, SAY SOMETHING.
WE ARE ALONE.
WE MUST WAIT.
HOPEFULLY MAMA WON'T BE ATTACKED...
HOPEFULLY SHE WON'T BE CAPTURED BY THE RUSSIANS...
RAT TAT

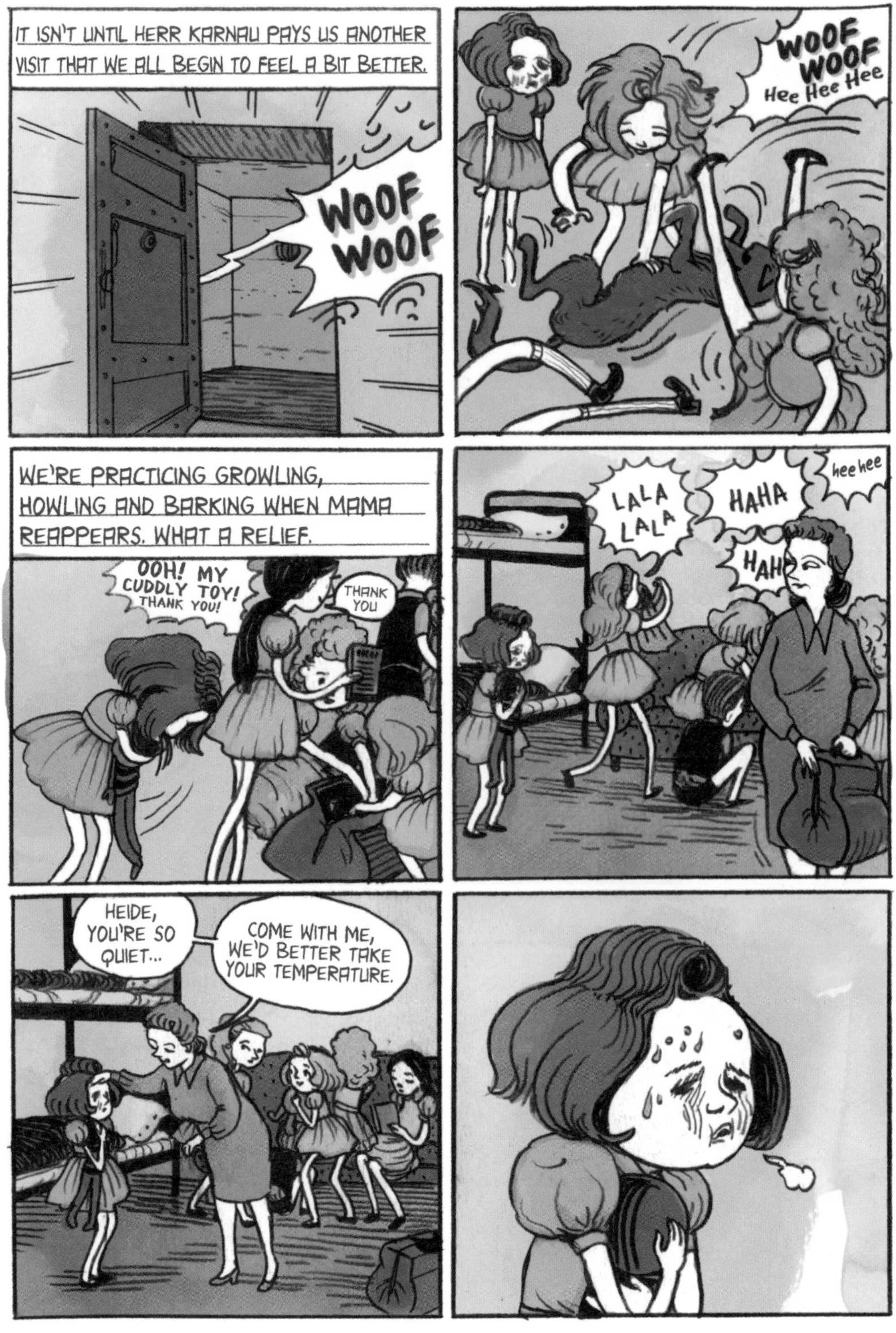
IT ISN'T UNTIL HERR KARNAU PAYS US ANOTHER VISIT THAT WE ALL BEGIN TO FEEL A BIT BETTER.
WOOF WOOF
WOOF WOOF
Hee Hee Hee
WE'RE PRACTICING GROWLING, HOWLING AND BARKING WHEN MAMA REAPPEARS. WHAT A RELIEF.
OOH! MY CUDDLY TOY! THANK YOU!
THANK YOU
LALA LALA
HAHA
hee hee
HAHA
HEIDE, YOU'RE SO QUIET...
COME WITH ME, WE'D BETTER TAKE YOUR TEMPERATURE.

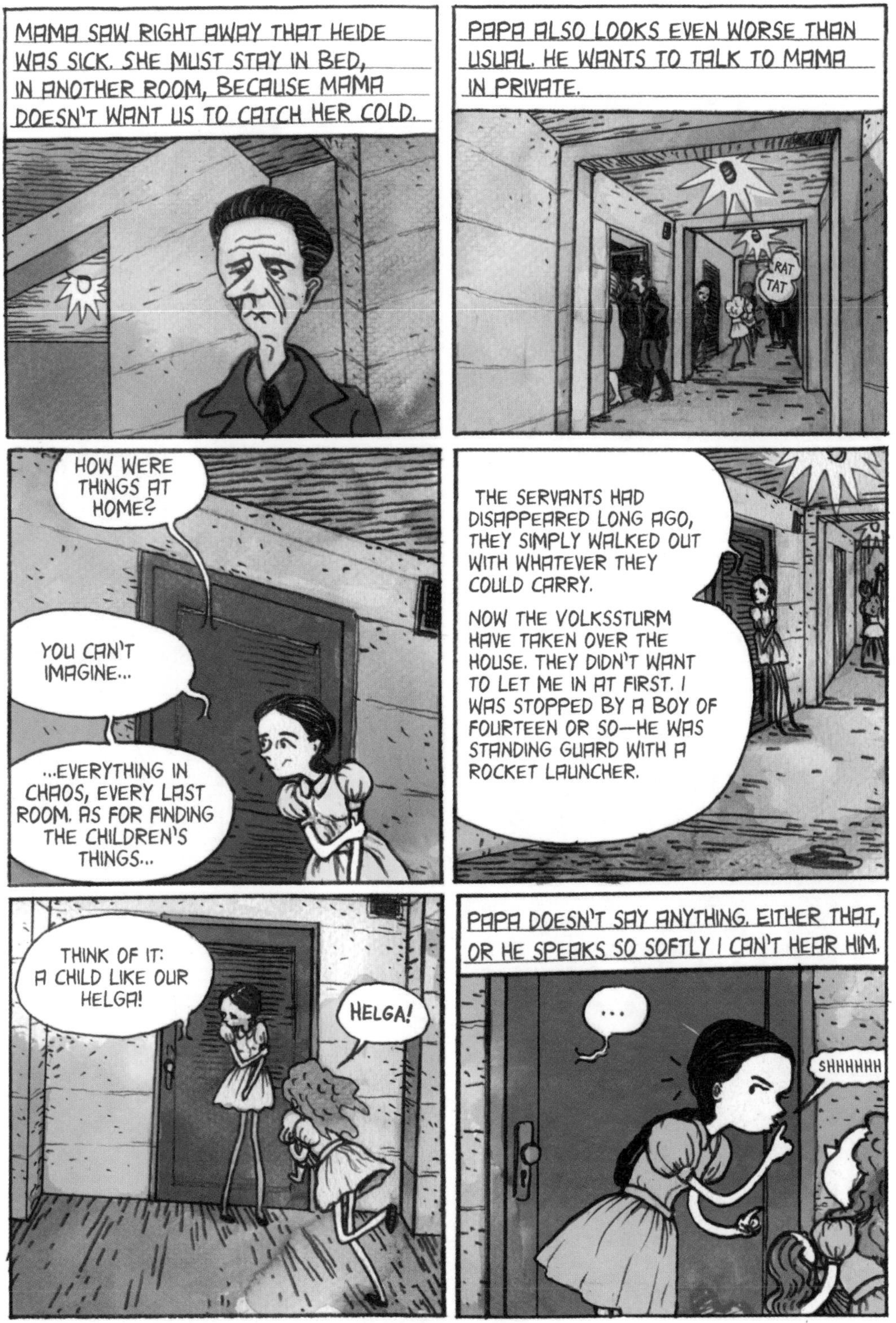
MAMA SAW RIGHT AWAY THAT HEIDE WAS SICK. SHE MUST STAY IN BED, IN ANOTHER ROOM, BECAUSE MAMA DOESN'T WANT US TO CATCH HER COLD.
PAPA ALSO LOOKS EVEN WORSE THAN USUAL. HE WANTS TO TALK TO MAMA IN PRIVATE.
RAT TAT
HOW WERE THINGS AT HOME?
YOU CAN'T IMAGINE...
...EVERYTHING IN CHAOS, EVERY LAST ROOM. AS FOR FINDING THE CHILDREN'S THINGS...
THE SERVANTS HAD DISAPPEARED LONG AGO, THEY SIMPLY WALKED OUT WITH WHATEVER THEY COULD CARRY.
NOW THE VOLKSSTURM HAVE TAKEN OVER THE HOUSE. THEY DIDN'T WANT TO LET ME IN AT FIRST. I WAS STOPPED BY A BOY OF FOURTEEN OR SO—HE WAS STANDING GUARD WITH A ROCKET LAUNCHER.
THINK OF IT: A CHILD LIKE OUR HELGA!
HELGA!
PAPA DOESN'T SAY ANYTHING. EITHER THAT, OR HE SPEAKS SO SOFTLY I CAN'T HEAR HIM.
...
SHHHHHH

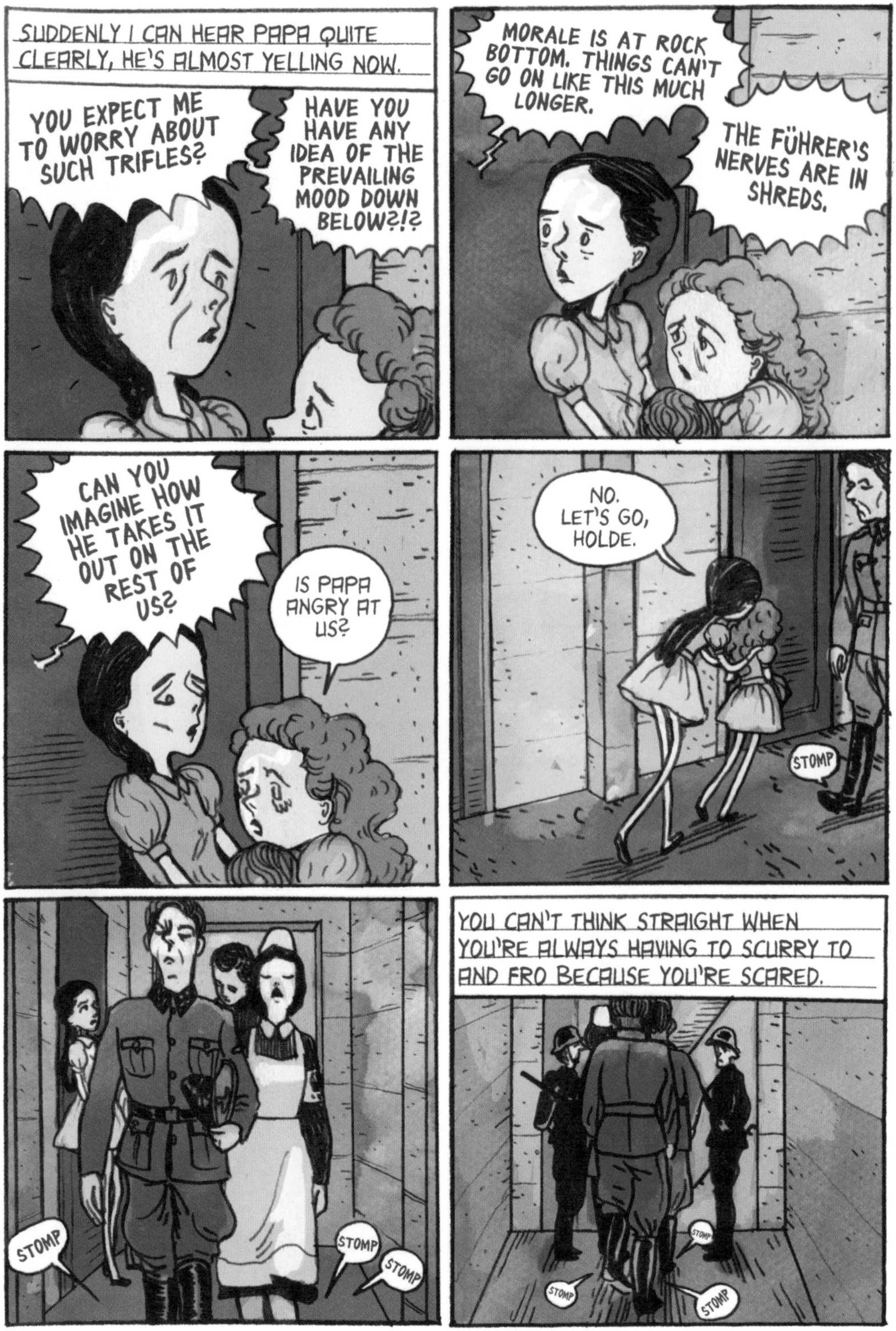
SUDDENLY I CAN HEAR PAPA QUITE CLEARLY, HE'S ALMOST YELLING NOW.
YOU EXPECT ME TO WORRY ABOUT SUCH TRIFLES?
HAVE YOU HAVE ANY IDEA OF THE PREVAILING MOOD DOWN BELOW?!?
MORALE IS AT ROCK BOTTOM. THINGS CAN'T GO ON LIKE THIS MUCH LONGER.
THE FÜHRER'S NERVES ARE IN SHREDS.
CAN YOU IMAGINE HOW HE TAKES IT OUT ON THE REST OF US?
IS PAPA ANGRY AT US?
NO. LET'S GO, HOLDE.
STOMP
STOMP
STOMP
STOMP
YOU CAN'T THINK STRAIGHT WHEN YOU'RE ALWAYS HAVING TO SCURRY TO AND FRO BECAUSE YOU'RE SCARED.
STOMP
STOMP
STOMP

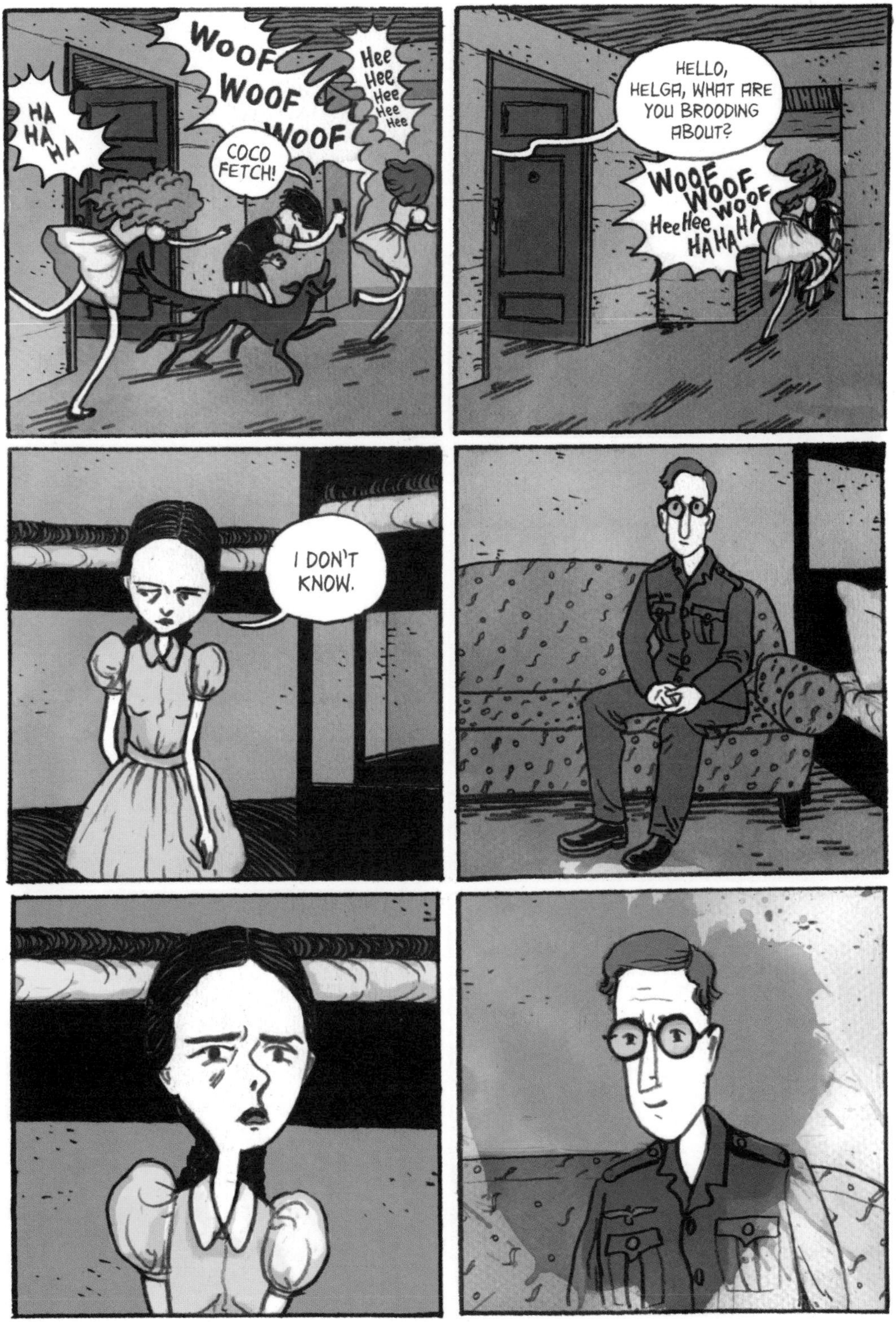
WOOF WOOF WOOF
HA HA HA
Hee Hee Hee Hee Hee
COCO FETCH!
HELLO, HELGA, WHAT ARE YOU BROODING ABOUT?
WOOF WOOF WOOF
Hee Hee HA HA HA
I DON'T KNOW.

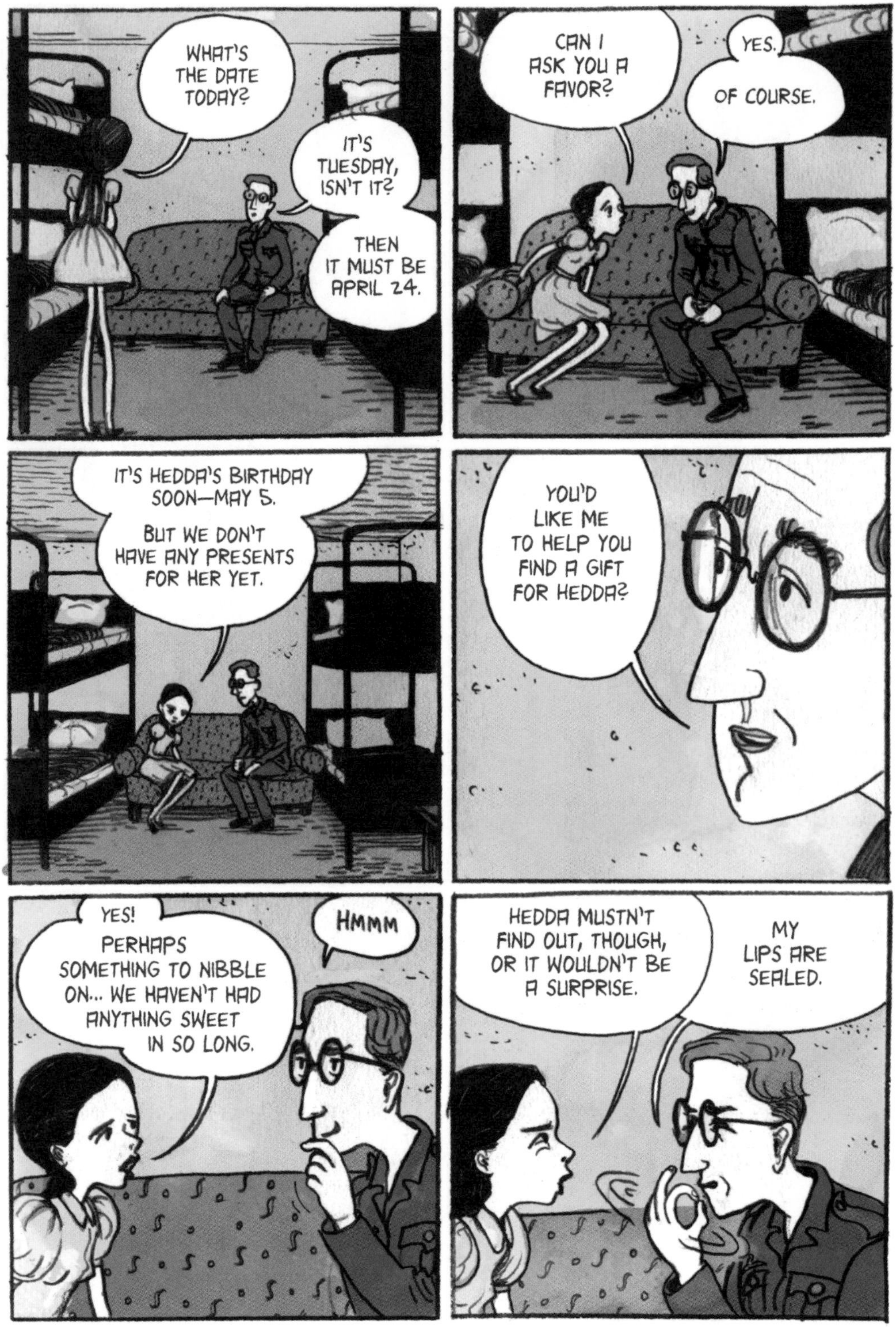
WHAT'S THE DATE TODAY?
IT'S TUESDAY, ISN'T IT?
THEN IT MUST BE APRIL 24.
CAN I ASK YOU A FAVOR?
YES.
OF COURSE.
IT'S HEDDA'S BIRTHDAY SOON—MAY 5.
BUT WE DON'T HAVE ANY PRESENTS FOR HER YET.
YOU'D LIKE ME TO HELP YOU FIND A GIFT FOR HEDDA?
YES!
PERHAPS SOMETHING TO NIBBLE ON... WE HAVEN'T HAD ANYTHING SWEET IN SO LONG.
HMMM
HEDDA MUSTN'T FIND OUT, THOUGH, OR IT WOULDN'T BE A SURPRISE.
MY LIPS ARE SEALED.

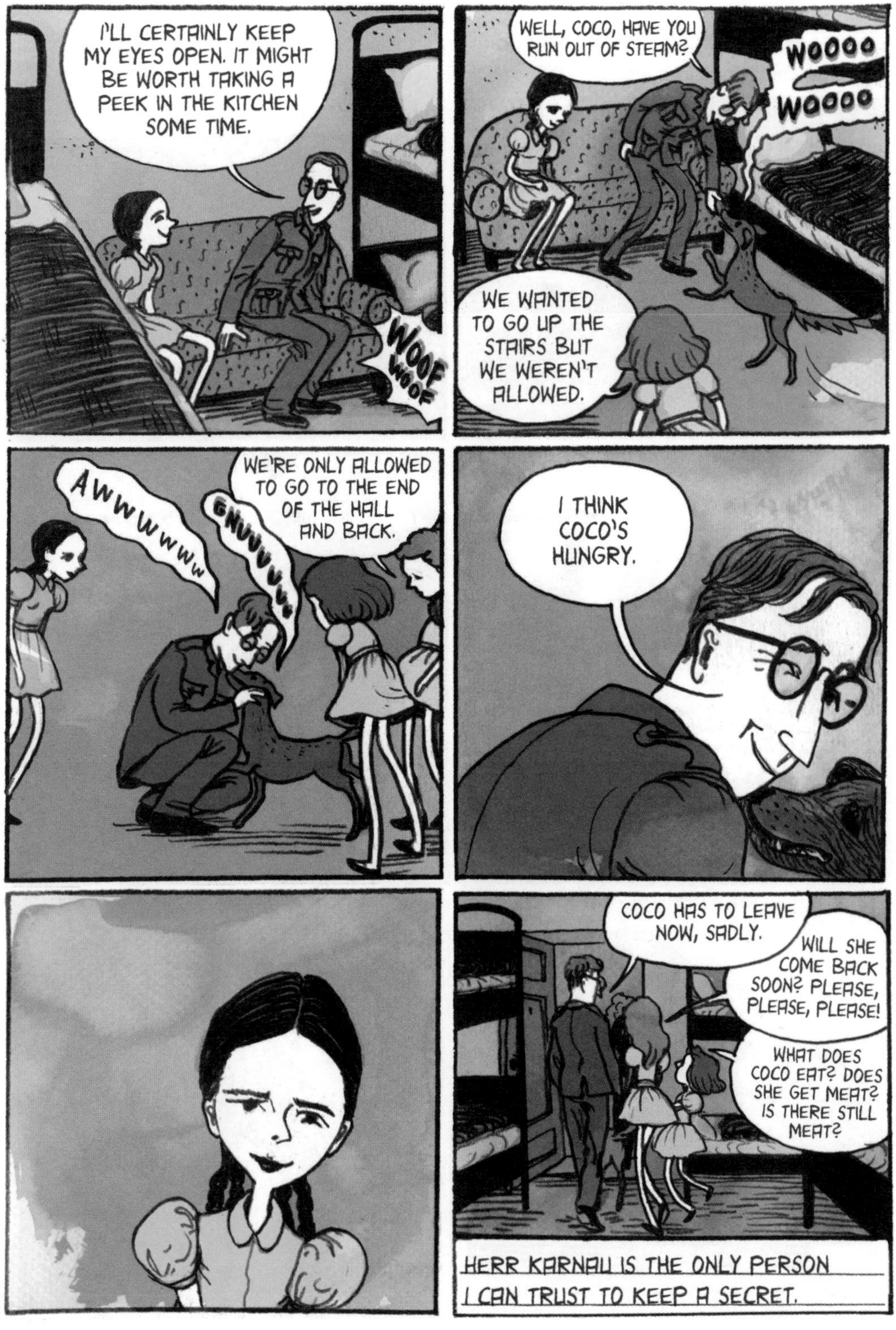
I'LL CERTAINLY KEEP MY EYES OPEN. IT MIGHT BE WORTH TAKING A PEEK IN THE KITCHEN SOME TIME.
WOOF WOOF
WELL, COCO, HAVE YOU RUN OUT OF STEAM?
WOOOO WOOOO
WE WANTED TO GO UP THE STAIRS BUT WE WEREN'T ALLOWED.
AWWWWWW
GNUUUUUU
WE'RE ONLY ALLOWED TO GO TO THE END OF THE HALL AND BACK.
I THINK COCO'S HUNGRY.
COCO HAS TO LEAVE NOW, SADLY.
WILL SHE COME BACK SOON? PLEASE, PLEASE, PLEASE!
WHAT DOES COCO EAT? DOES SHE GET MEAT? IS THERE STILL MEAT?
HERR KARNAU IS THE ONLY PERSON I CAN TRUST TO KEEP A SECRET.

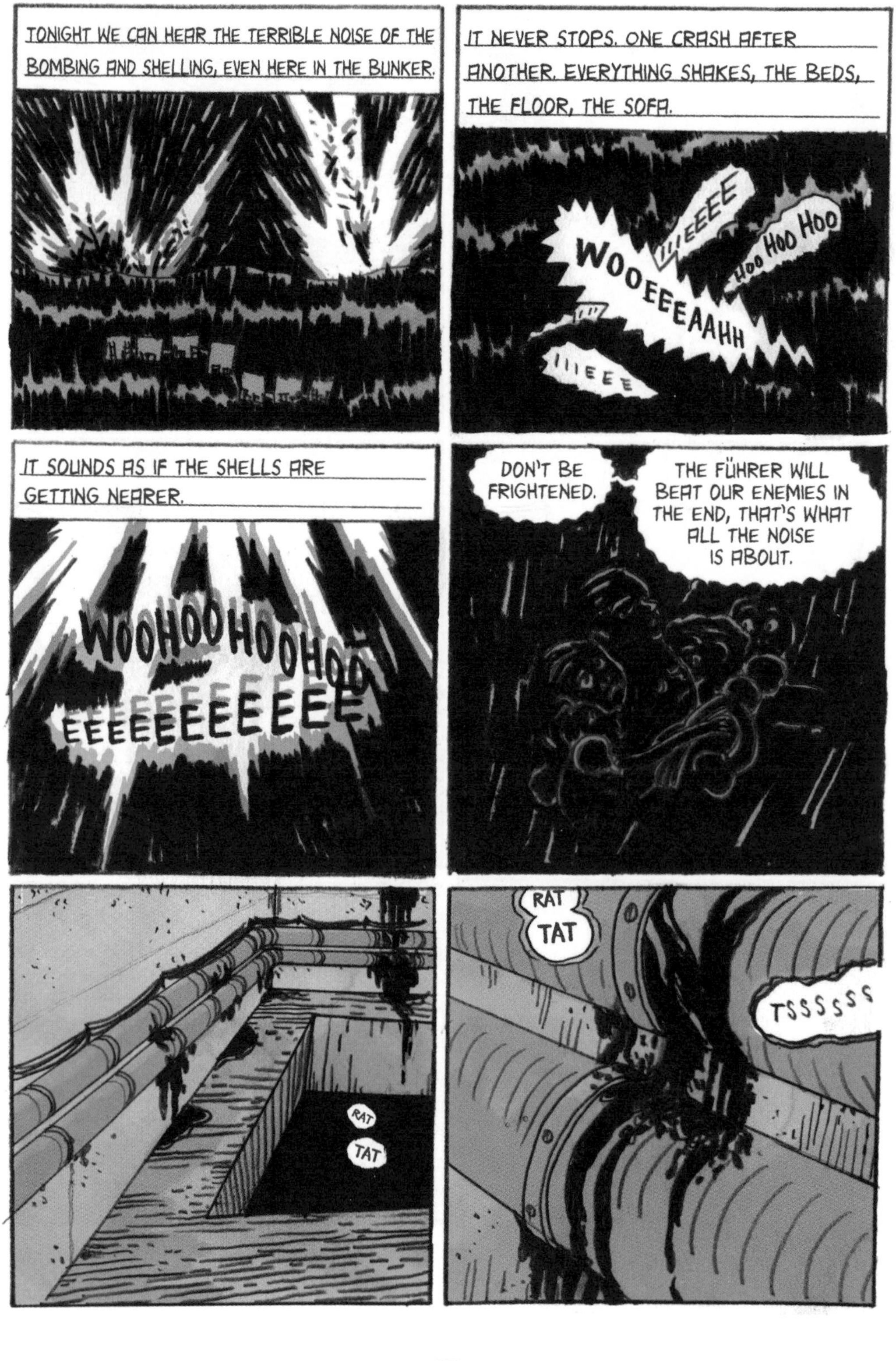
TONIGHT WE CAN HEAR THE TERRIBLE NOISE OF THE BOMBING AND SHELLING, EVEN HERE IN THE BUNKER.
IT NEVER STOPS. ONE CRASH AFTER ANOTHER. EVERYTHING SHAKES, THE BEDS, THE FLOOR, THE SOFA.
IIIEEEE
HOO HOO HOO
WOOEEEAAHH
IIIEEE
IT SOUNDS AS IF THE SHELLS ARE GETTING NEARER.
WOOHOOHOOHOO
EEEEEEEEEEE
DON'T BE FRIGHTENED.
THE FÜHRER WILL BEAT OUR ENEMIES IN THE END, THAT'S WHAT ALL THE NOISE IS ABOUT.
RAT
TAT
RAT
TAT
TSSSSSS

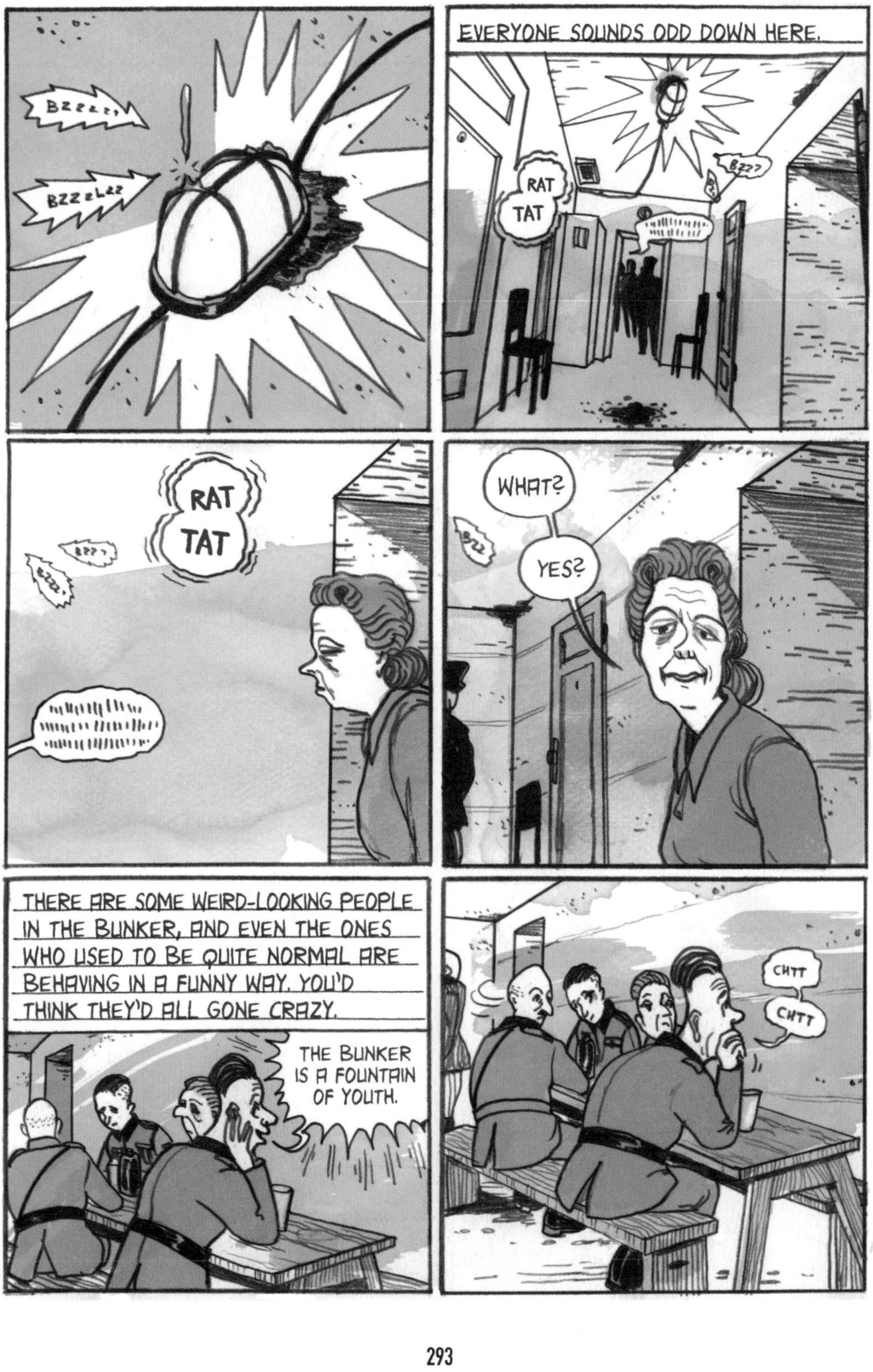

BZZZZ
BZZZLZZ
EVERYONE SOUNDS ODD DOWN HERE.
RAT TAT
BZZ?
RAT TAT
BZZ?
WHAT?
YES?
THERE ARE SOME WEIRD-LOOKING PEOPLE IN THE BUNKER, AND EVEN THE ONES WHO USED TO BE QUITE NORMAL ARE BEHAVING IN A FUNNY WAY. YOU'D THINK THEY'D ALL GONE CRAZY.
THE BUNKER IS A FOUNTAIN OF YOUTH.
CHTT
CHTT

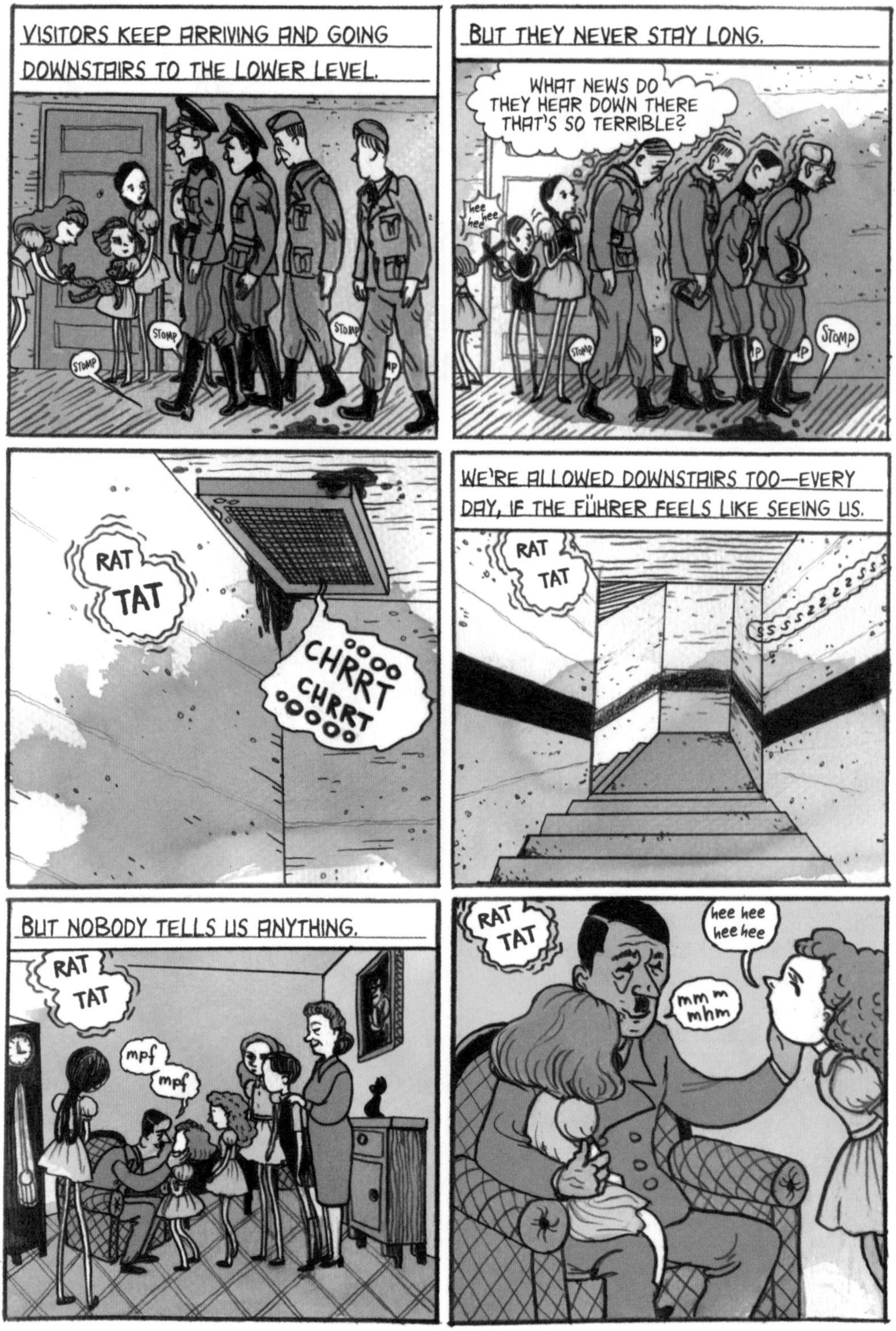
VISITORS KEEP ARRIVING AND GOING DOWNSTAIRS TO THE LOWER LEVEL.
STOMP
STOMP
STOMP
BUT THEY NEVER STAY LONG.
WHAT NEWS DO THEY HEAR DOWN THERE THAT'S SO TERRIBLE?
hee hee hee
STOMP
STOMP
RAT TAT
CHRRT CHRRT
WE'RE ALLOWED DOWNSTAIRS TOO—EVERY DAY, IF THE FÜHRER FEELS LIKE SEEING US.
RAT TAT
BUT NOBODY TELLS US ANYTHING.
RAT TAT
mpf mpf
RAT TAT
hee hee hee hee
mm m mhm

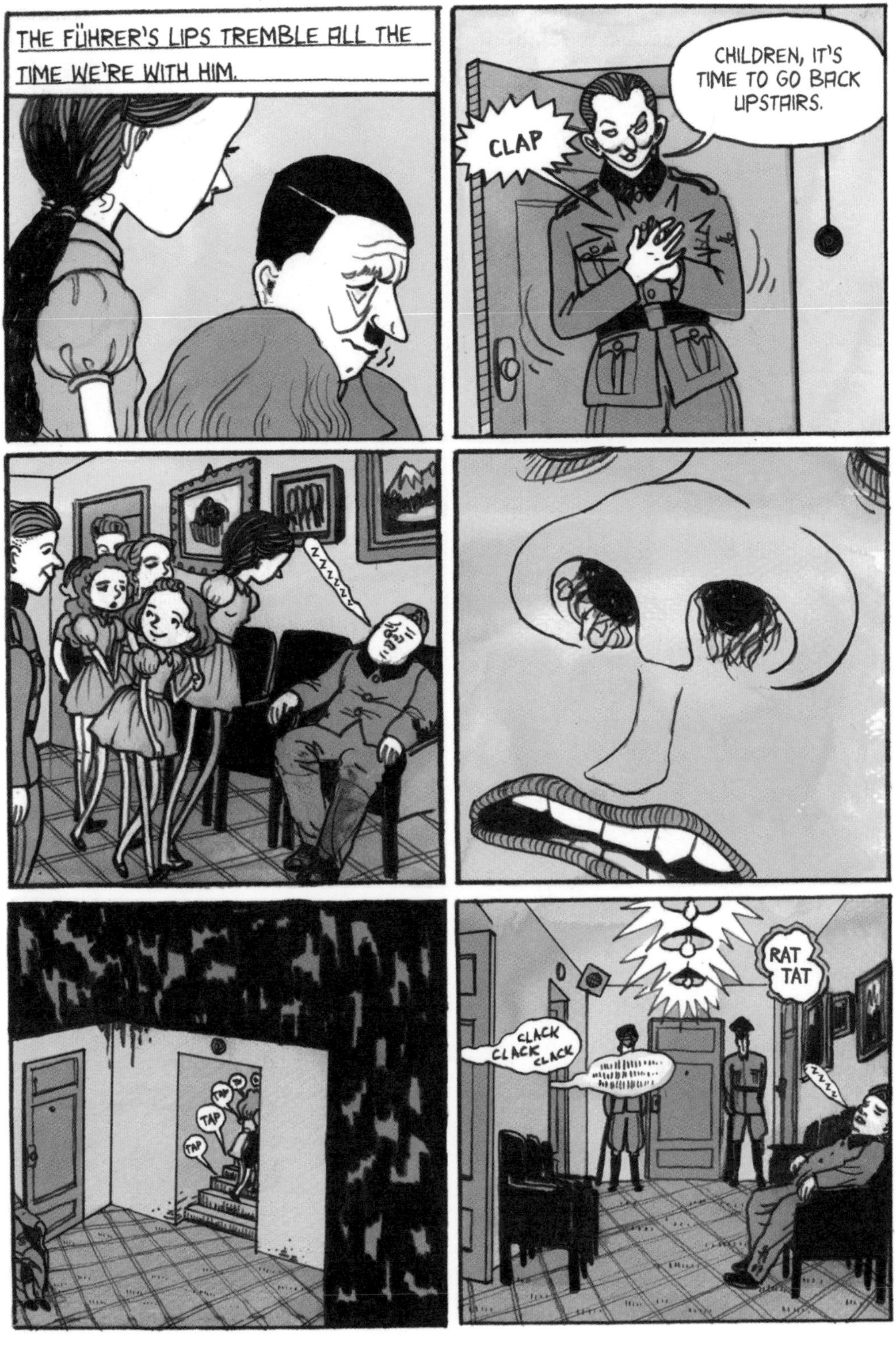
THE FÜHRER'S LIPS TREMBLE ALL THE TIME WE'RE WITH HIM.
CLAP
CHILDREN, IT'S TIME TO GO BACK UPSTAIRS.
ZZZZZZ
TAP
TAP
TAP
TAP
TAP
CLACK CLACK CLACK CLACK
RAT TAT
ZZZZZ

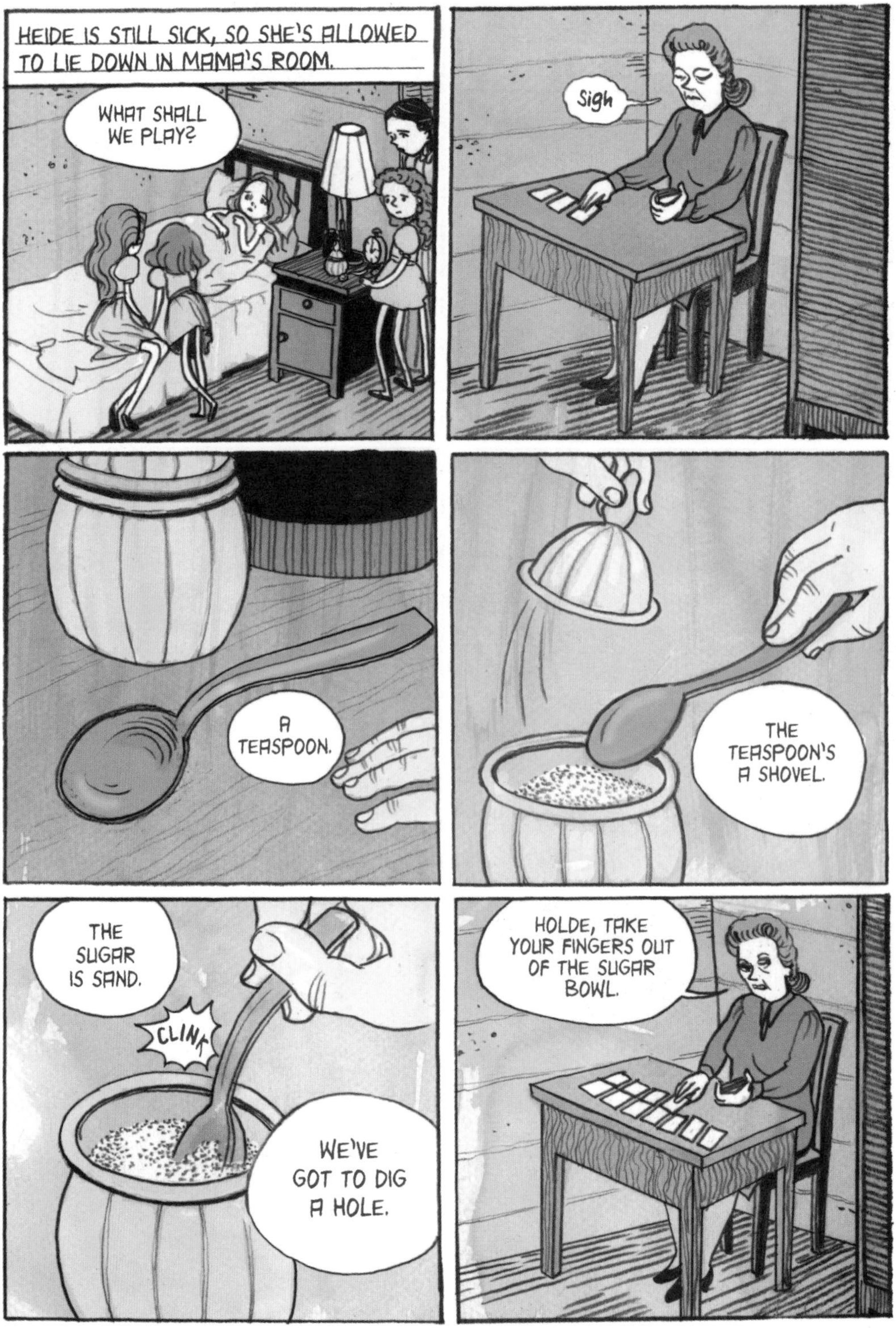
HEIDE IS STILL SICK, SO SHE'S ALLOWED TO LIE DOWN IN MAMA'S ROOM.
WHAT SHALL WE PLAY?
Sigh
A TEASPOON.
THE TEASPOON'S A SHOVEL.
THE SUGAR IS SAND.
CLINK
WE'VE GOT TO DIG A HOLE.
HOLDE, TAKE YOUR FINGERS OUT OF THE SUGAR BOWL.

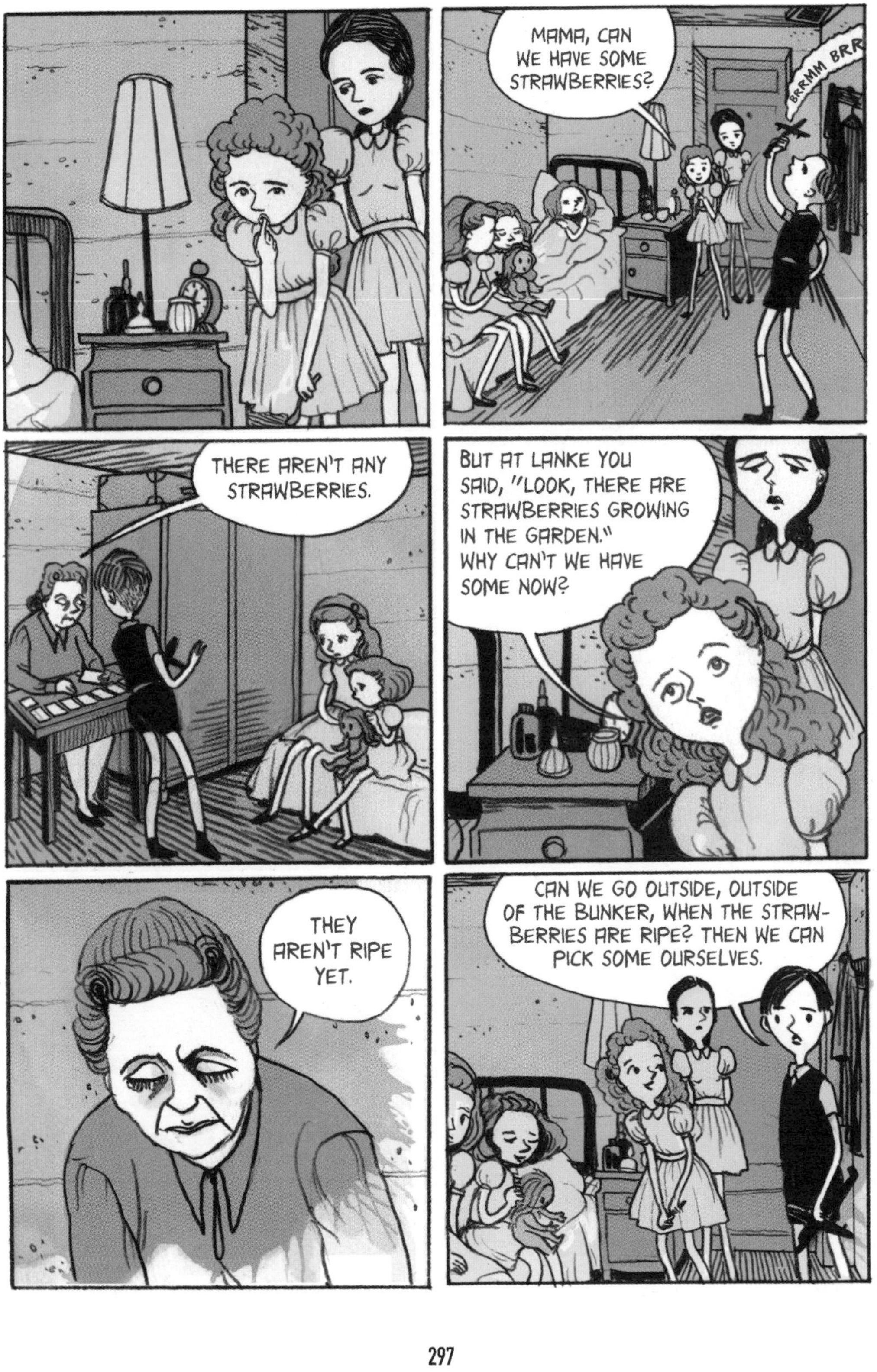
MAMA, CAN WE HAVE SOME STRAWBERRIES?
BRRMM BRR
THERE AREN'T ANY STRAWBERRIES.
BUT AT LANKE YOU SAID, "LOOK, THERE ARE STRAWBERRIES GROWING IN THE GARDEN." WHY CAN'T WE HAVE SOME NOW?
THEY AREN'T RIPE YET.
CAN WE GO OUTSIDE, OUTSIDE OF THE BUNKER, WHEN THE STRAW-BERRIES ARE RIPE? THEN WE CAN PICK SOME OURSELVES.

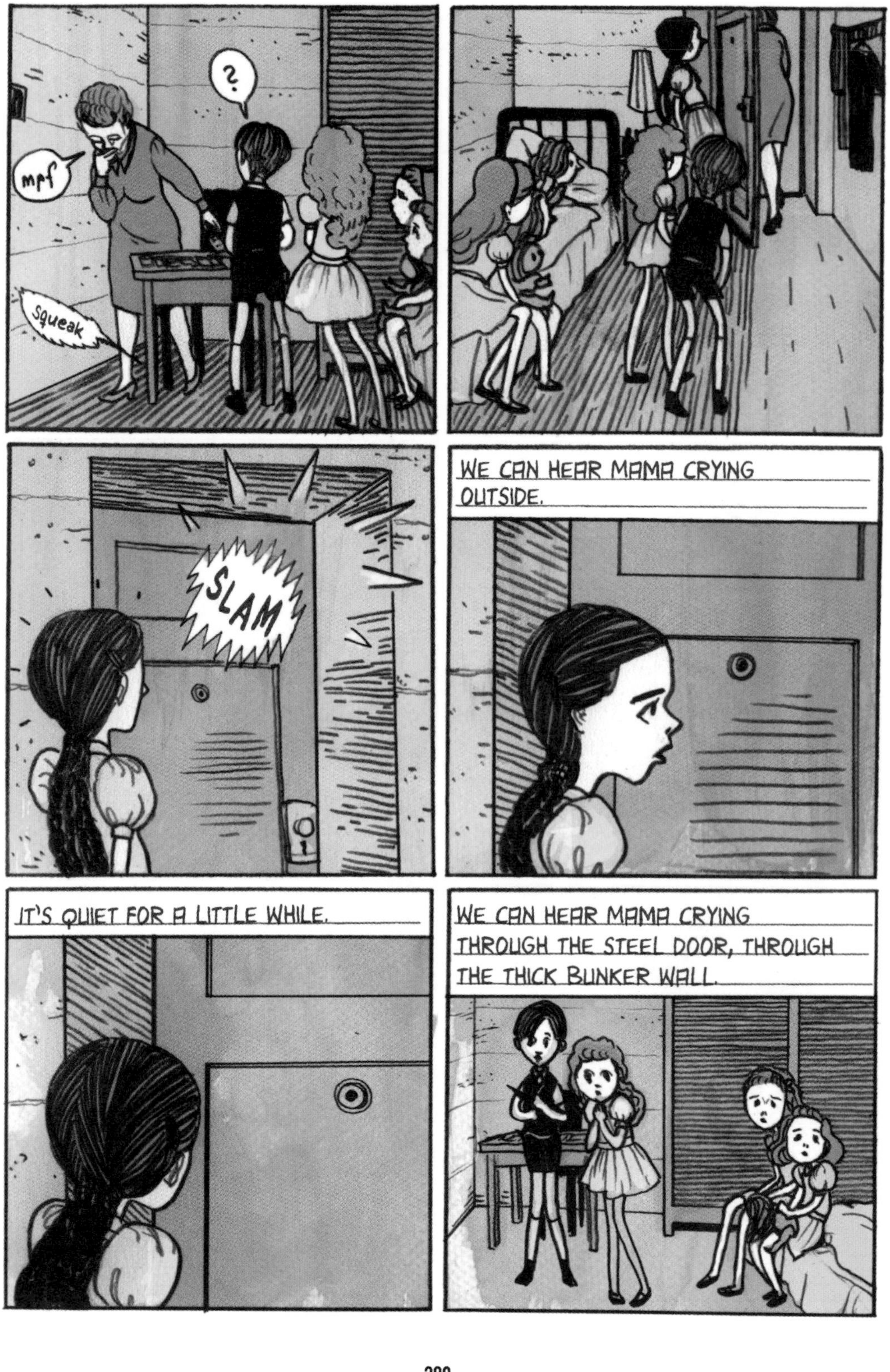
mpf
?
squeak
SLAM
WE CAN HEAR MAMA CRYING OUTSIDE.
IT'S QUIET FOR A LITTLE WHILE.
WE CAN HEAR MAMA CRYING THROUGH THE STEEL DOOR, THROUGH THE THICK BUNKER WALL.

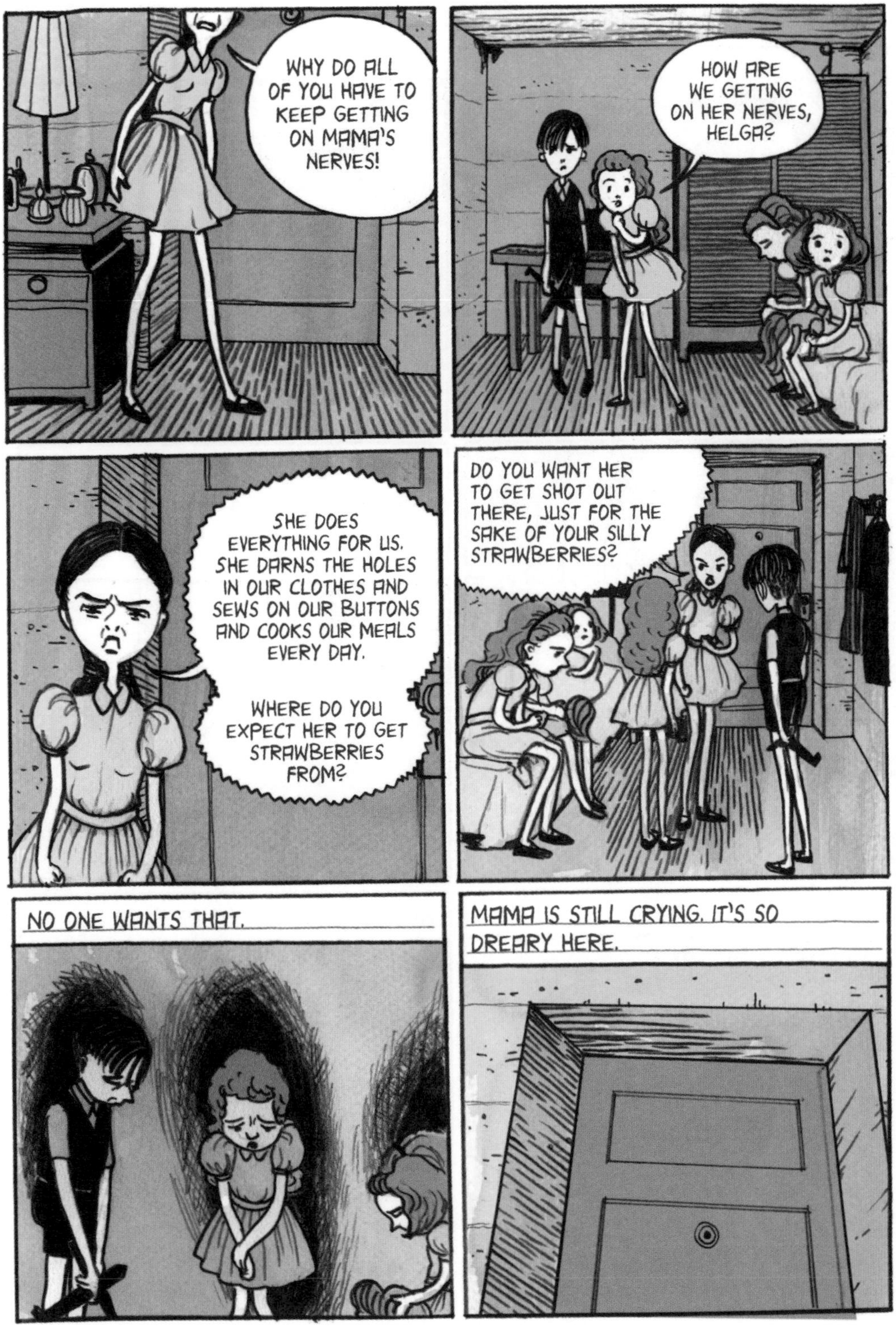
WHY DO ALL OF YOU HAVE TO KEEP GETTING ON MAMA'S NERVES!
HOW ARE WE GETTING ON HER NERVES, HELGA?
SHE DOES EVERYTHING FOR US. SHE DARNS THE HOLES IN OUR CLOTHES AND SEWS ON OUR BUTTONS AND COOKS OUR MEALS EVERY DAY.
WHERE DO YOU EXPECT HER TO GET STRAWBERRIES FROM?
DO YOU WANT HER TO GET SHOT OUT THERE, JUST FOR THE SAKE OF YOUR SILLY STRAWBERRIES?
NO ONE WANTS THAT.
MAMA IS STILL CRYING. IT'S SO DREARY HERE.

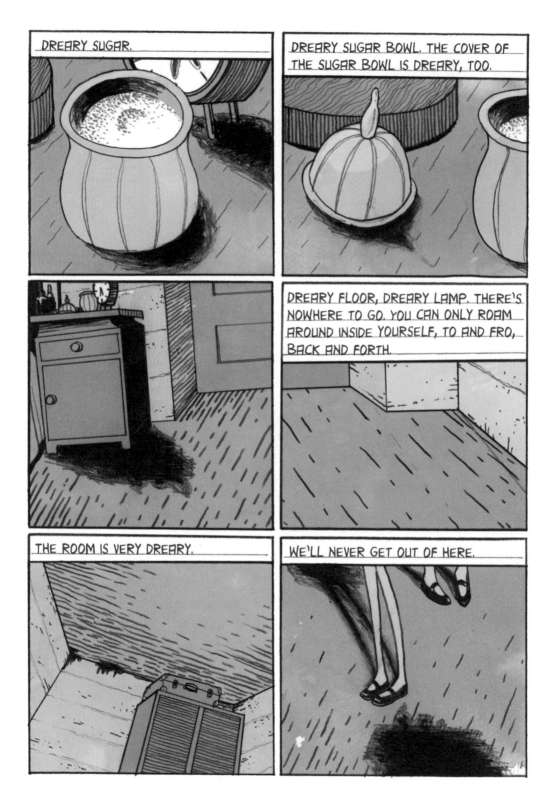

DREARY SUGAR.

DREARY SUGAR BOWL. THE COVER OF THE SUGAR BOWL IS DREARY, TOO.

DREARY FLOOR, DREARY LAMP. THERE'S NOWHERE TO GO. YOU CAN ONLY ROAM AROUND INSIDE YOURSELF, TO AND FRO, BACK AND FORTH.

THE ROOM IS VERY DREARY.

WE'LL NEVER GET OUT OF HERE.

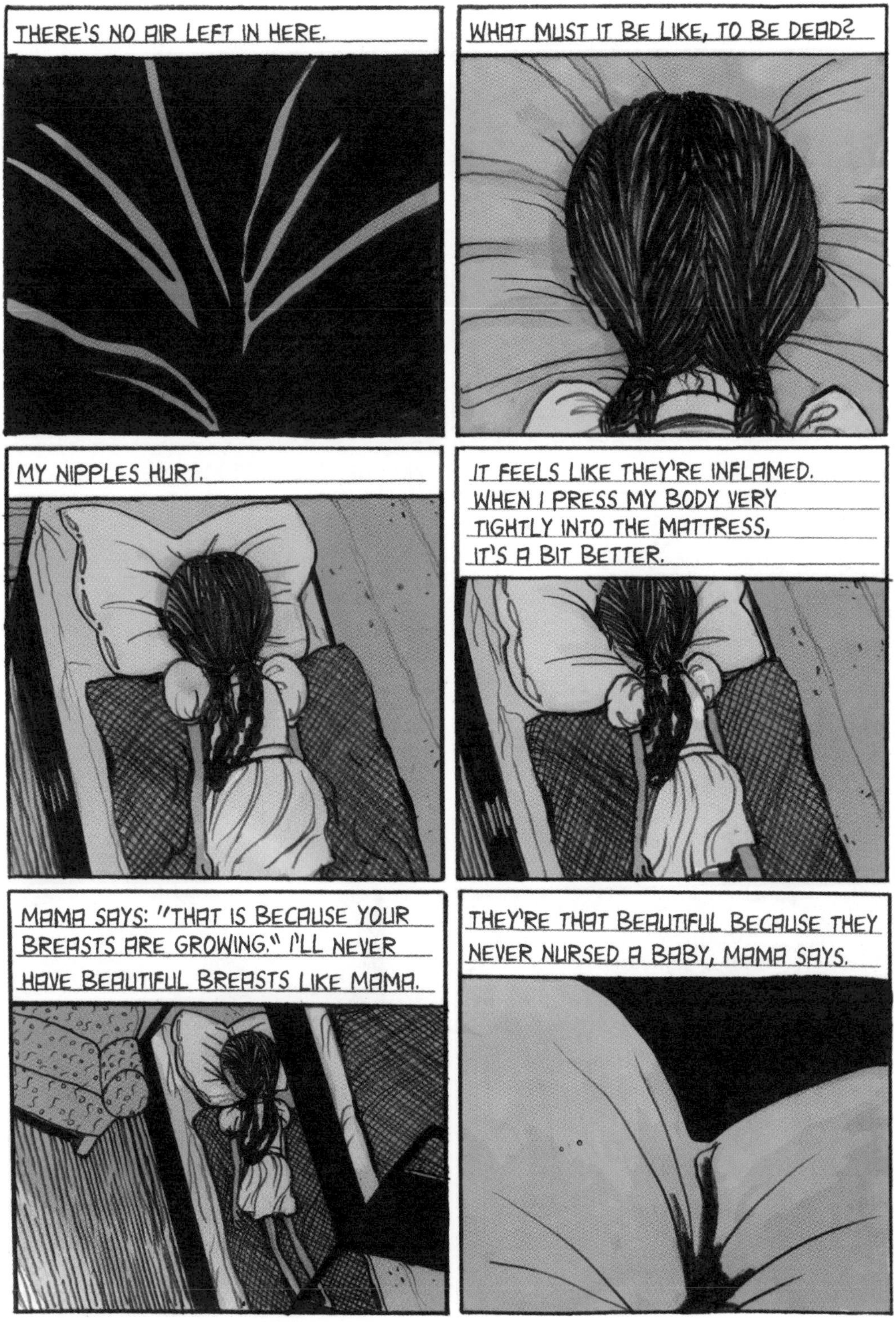
THERE'S NO AIR LEFT IN HERE.
WHAT MUST IT BE LIKE, TO BE DEAD?
MY NIPPLES HURT.
IT FEELS LIKE THEY'RE INFLAMED. WHEN I PRESS MY BODY VERY TIGHTLY INTO THE MATTRESS, IT'S A BIT BETTER.
MAMA SAYS: "THAT IS BECAUSE YOUR BREASTS ARE GROWING." I'LL NEVER HAVE BEAUTIFUL BREASTS LIKE MAMA.
THEY'RE THAT BEAUTIFUL BECAUSE THEY NEVER NURSED A BABY, MAMA SAYS.

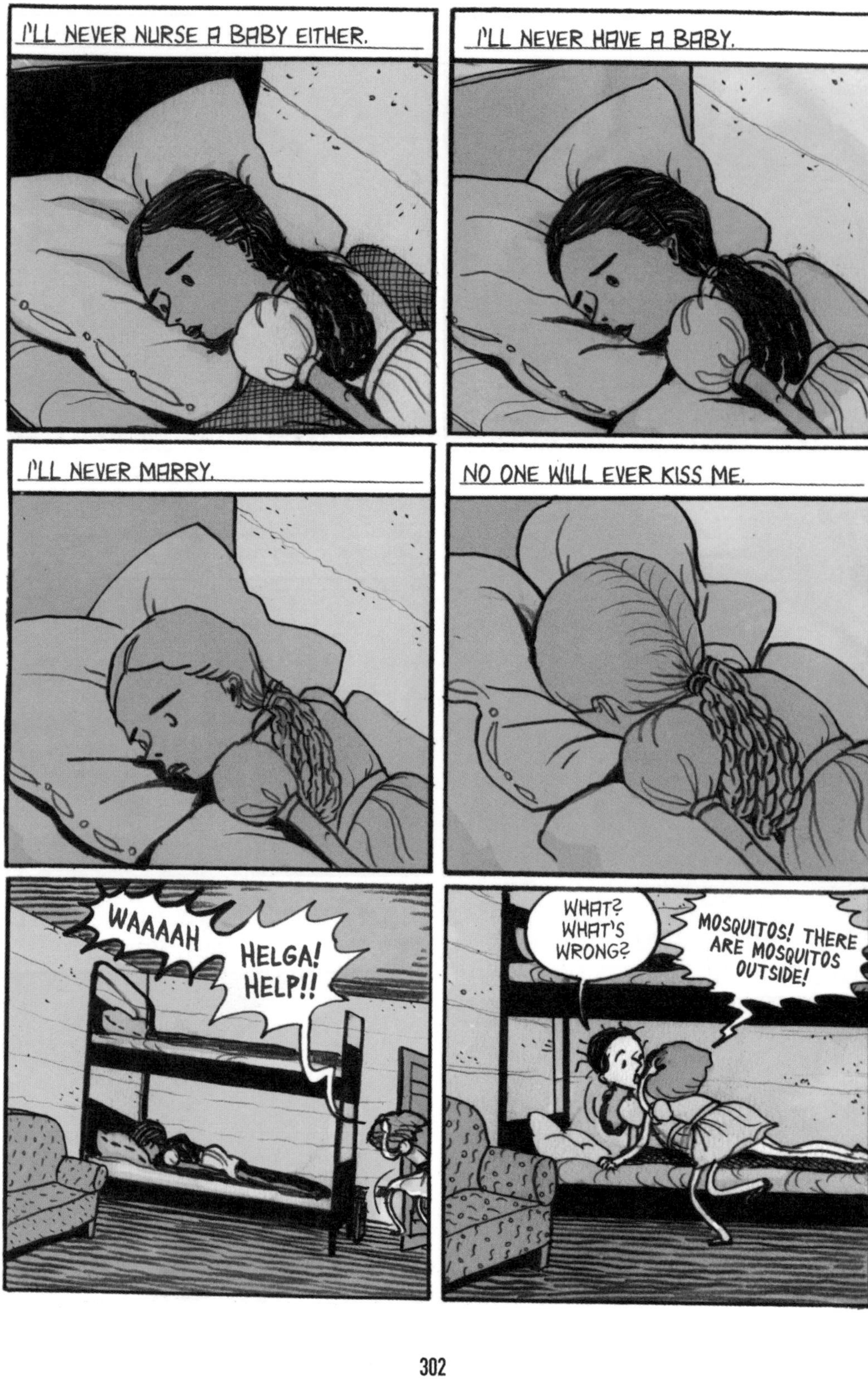
I'LL NEVER NURSE A BABY EITHER.
I'LL NEVER HAVE A BABY.
I'LL NEVER MARRY.
NO ONE WILL EVER KISS ME.
WAAAAH
HELGA! HELP!!
WHAT? WHAT'S WRONG?
MOSQUITOS! THERE ARE MOSQUITOS OUTSIDE!

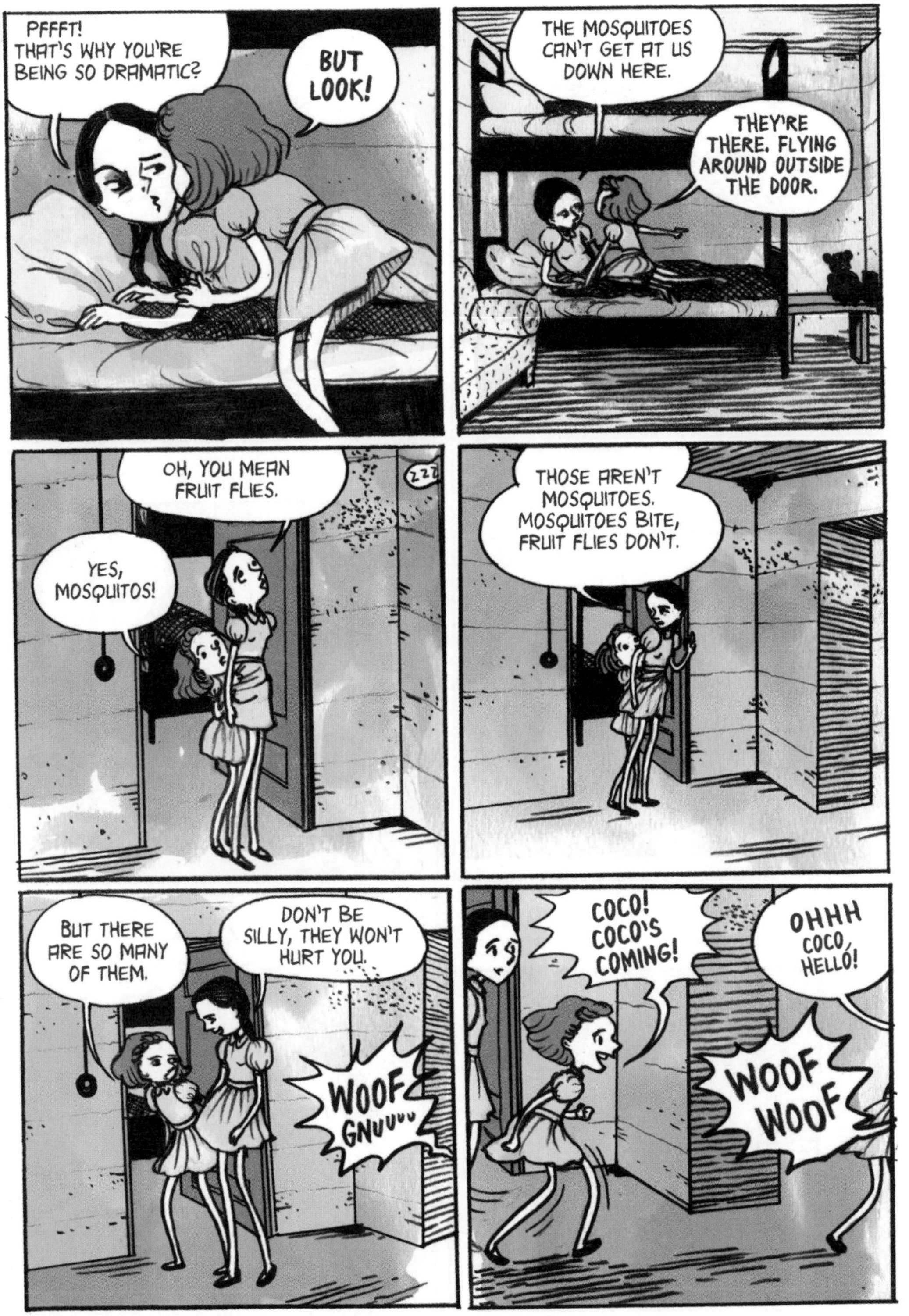
PFFFT! THAT'S WHY YOU'RE BEING SO DRAMATIC?
BUT LOOK!
THE MOSQUITOES CAN'T GET AT US DOWN HERE.
THEY'RE THERE. FLYING AROUND OUTSIDE THE DOOR.
OH, YOU MEAN FRUIT FLIES.
YES, MOSQUITOS!
THOSE AREN'T MOSQUITOES. MOSQUITOES BITE, FRUIT FLIES DON'T.
BUT THERE ARE SO MANY OF THEM.
DON'T BE SILLY, THEY WON'T HURT YOU.
WOOF GNUUUU
COCO! COCO'S COMING!
OHHH COCO, HELLÓ!
WOOF WOOF

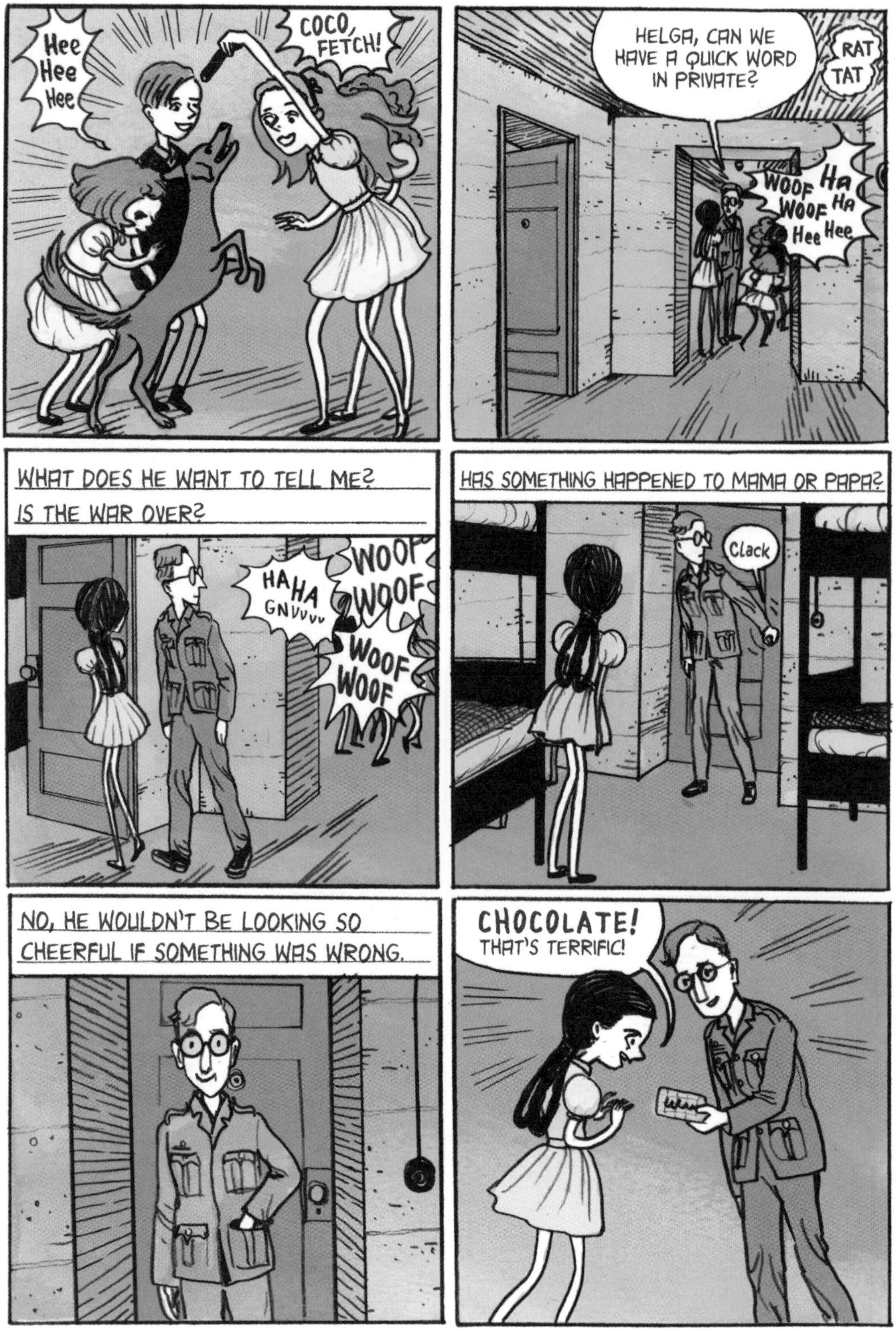
Hee Hee Hee
COCO, FETCH!
HELGA, CAN WE HAVE A QUICK WORD IN PRIVATE?
RAT TAT
WOOF WOOF
Ha Ha Hee Hee
WHAT DOES HE WANT TO TELL ME?
IS THE WAR OVER?
HA HA GNVVVV
WOOF WOOF
WOOF WOOF
HAS SOMETHING HAPPENED TO MAMA OR PAPA?
Clack
NO, HE WOULDN'T BE LOOKING SO CHEERFUL IF SOMETHING WAS WRONG.
CHOCOLATE! THAT'S TERRIFIC!

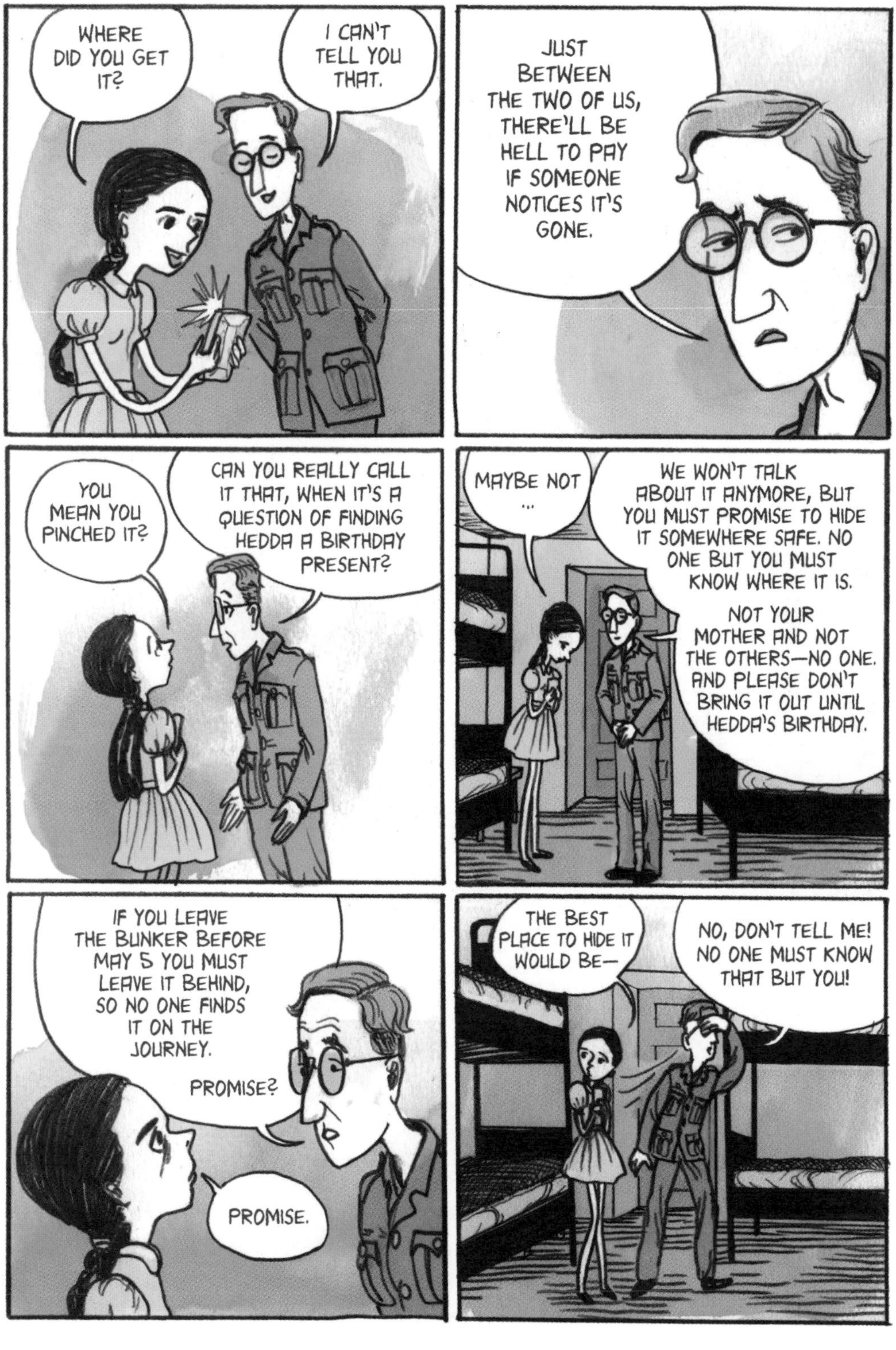
WHERE DID YOU GET IT?
I CAN'T TELL YOU THAT.
JUST BETWEEN THE TWO OF US, THERE'LL BE HELL TO PAY IF SOMEONE NOTICES IT'S GONE.
YOU MEAN YOU PINCHED IT?
CAN YOU REALLY CALL IT THAT, WHEN IT'S A QUESTION OF FINDING HEDDA A BIRTHDAY PRESENT?
MAYBE NOT ...
WE WON'T TALK ABOUT IT ANYMORE, BUT YOU MUST PROMISE TO HIDE IT SOMEWHERE SAFE. NO ONE BUT YOU MUST KNOW WHERE IT IS.
NOT YOUR MOTHER AND NOT THE OTHERS—NO ONE. AND PLEASE DON'T BRING IT OUT UNTIL HEDDA'S BIRTHDAY.
IF YOU LEAVE THE BUNKER BEFORE MAY 5 YOU MUST LEAVE IT BEHIND, SO NO ONE FINDS IT ON THE JOURNEY.
PROMISE?
PROMISE.
THE BEST PLACE TO HIDE IT WOULD BE—
NO, DON'T TELL ME! NO ONE MUST KNOW THAT BUT YOU!

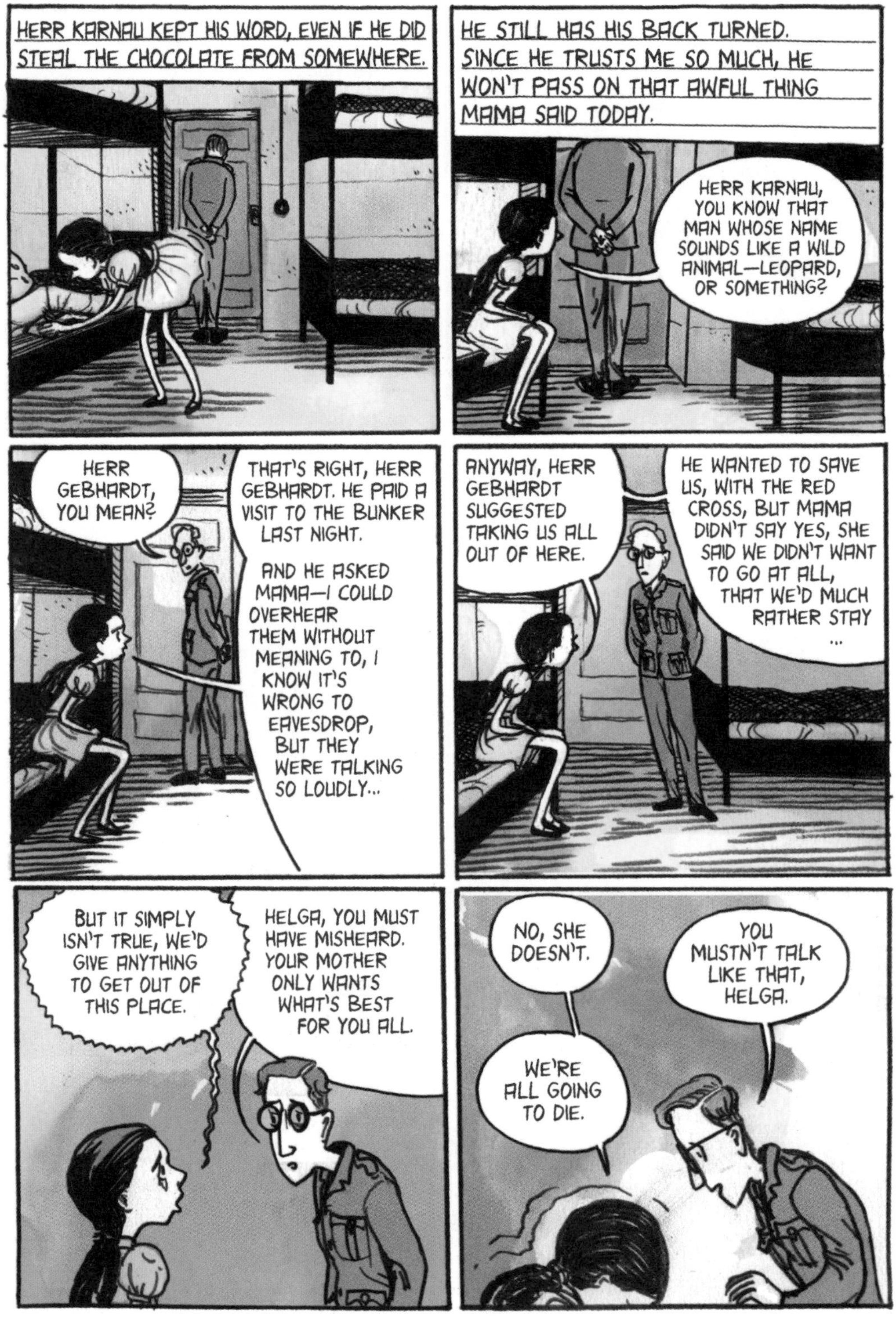

HERR KARNAU KEPT HIS WORD, EVEN IF HE DID STEAL THE CHOCOLATE FROM SOMEWHERE.
HE STILL HAS HIS BACK TURNED. SINCE HE TRUSTS ME SO MUCH, HE WON'T PASS ON THAT AWFUL THING MAMA SAID TODAY.
HERR KARNAU, YOU KNOW THAT MAN WHOSE NAME SOUNDS LIKE A WILD ANIMAL—LEOPARD, OR SOMETHING?
HERR GEBHARDT, YOU MEAN?
THAT'S RIGHT, HERR GEBHARDT. HE PAID A VISIT TO THE BUNKER LAST NIGHT.
AND HE ASKED MAMA—I COULD OVERHEAR THEM WITHOUT MEANING TO, I KNOW IT'S WRONG TO EAVESDROP, BUT THEY WERE TALKING SO LOUDLY...
ANYWAY, HERR GEBHARDT SUGGESTED TAKING US ALL OUT OF HERE.
HE WANTED TO SAVE US, WITH THE RED CROSS, BUT MAMA DIDN'T SAY YES, SHE SAID WE DIDN'T WANT TO GO AT ALL, THAT WE'D MUCH RATHER STAY ...
BUT IT SIMPLY ISN'T TRUE, WE'D GIVE ANYTHING TO GET OUT OF THIS PLACE.
HELGA, YOU MUST HAVE MISHEARD. YOUR MOTHER ONLY WANTS WHAT'S BEST FOR YOU ALL.
NO, SHE DOESN'T.
WE'RE ALL GOING TO DIE.
YOU MUSTN'T TALK LIKE THAT, HELGA.

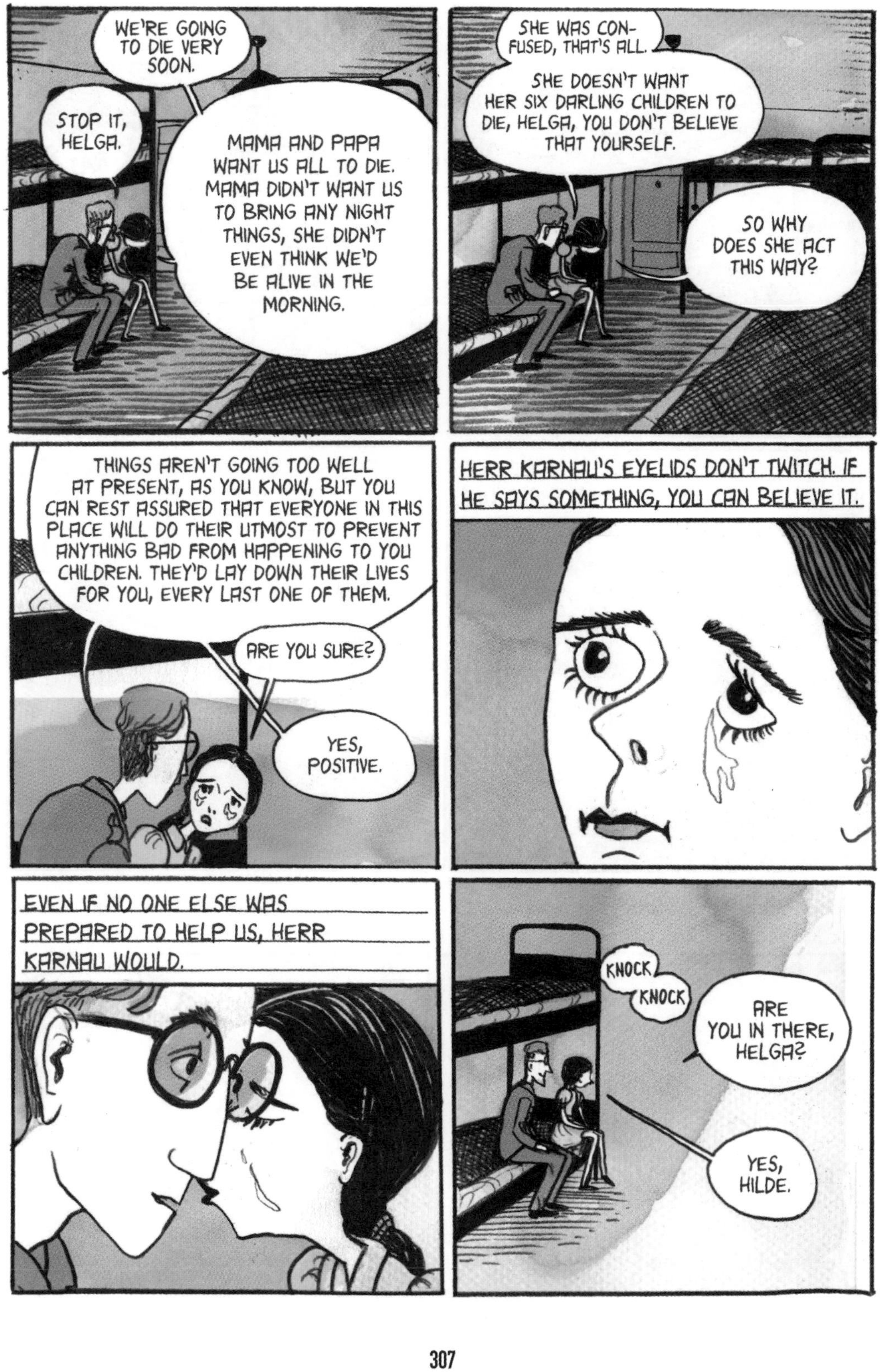
WE'RE GOING TO DIE VERY SOON.
STOP IT, HELGA.
MAMA AND PAPA WANT US ALL TO DIE. MAMA DIDN'T WANT US TO BRING ANY NIGHT THINGS, SHE DIDN'T EVEN THINK WE'D BE ALIVE IN THE MORNING.
SHE WAS CONFUSED, THAT'S ALL.
SHE DOESN'T WANT HER SIX DARLING CHILDREN TO DIE, HELGA, YOU DON'T BELIEVE THAT YOURSELF.
SO WHY DOES SHE ACT THIS WAY?
THINGS AREN'T GOING TOO WELL AT PRESENT, AS YOU KNOW, BUT YOU CAN REST ASSURED THAT EVERYONE IN THIS PLACE WILL DO THEIR UTMOST TO PREVENT ANYTHING BAD FROM HAPPENING TO YOU CHILDREN. THEY'D LAY DOWN THEIR LIVES FOR YOU, EVERY LAST ONE OF THEM.
ARE YOU SURE?
YES, POSITIVE.
HERR KARNAU'S EYELIDS DON'T TWITCH. IF HE SAYS SOMETHING, YOU CAN BELIEVE IT.
EVEN IF NO ONE ELSE WAS PREPARED TO HELP US, HERR KARNAU WOULD.
KNOCK
KNOCK
ARE YOU IN THERE, HELGA?
YES, HILDE.

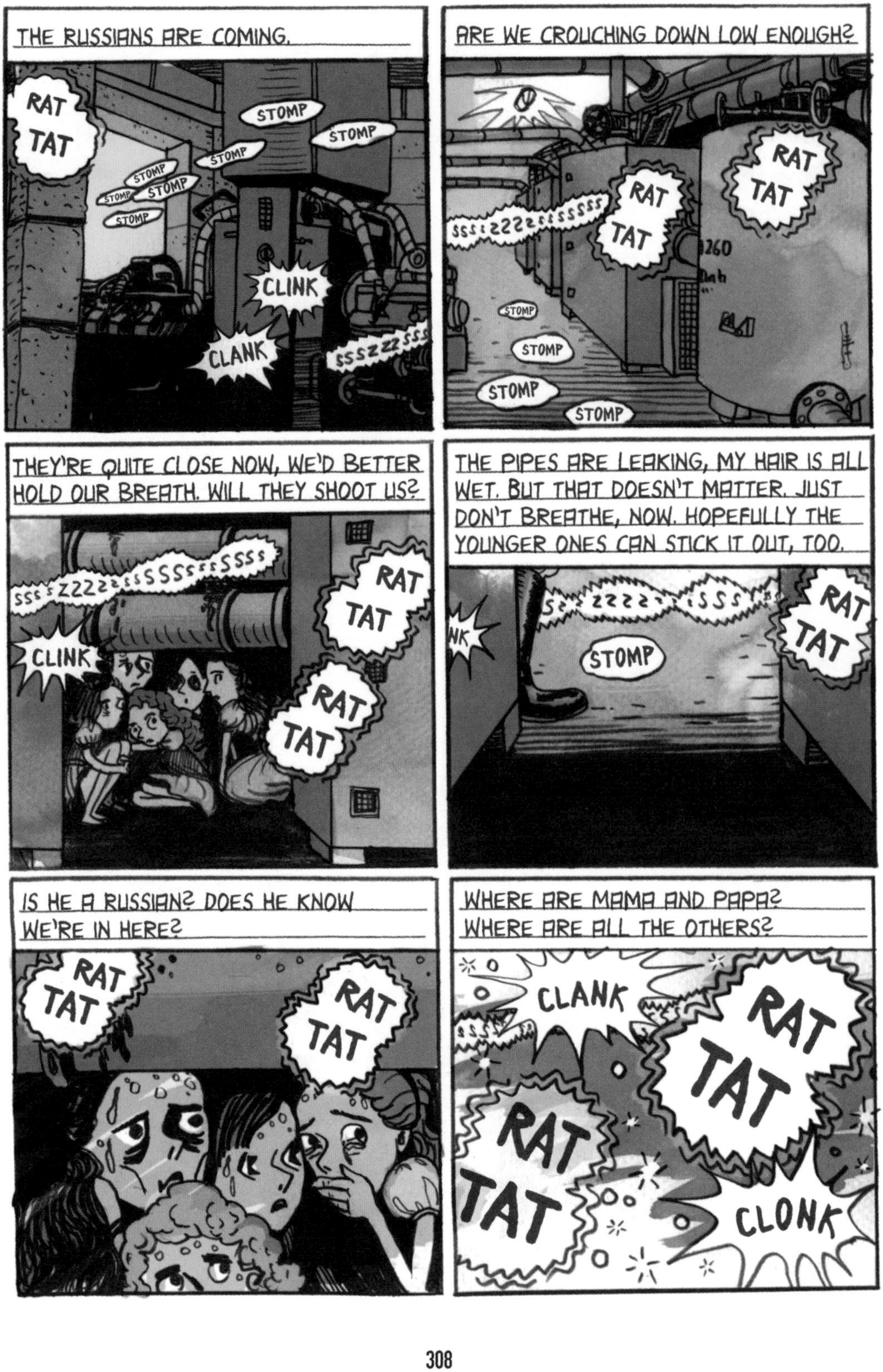
THE RUSSIANS ARE COMING.
RAT TAT
STOMP
STOMP
STOMP
STOMP
STOMP
STOMP
STOMP
CLINK
CLANK
SSSZZZSSS
ARE WE CROUCHING DOWN LOW ENOUGH?
RAT TAT
RAT TAT
SSSSZZZSSSSSSS
STOMP
STOMP
STOMP
STOMP
THEY'RE QUITE CLOSE NOW, WE'D BETTER HOLD OUR BREATH. WILL THEY SHOOT US?
SSSSZZZZSSSSSSSSSSS
RAT TAT
CLINK
RAT TAT
THE PIPES ARE LEAKING, MY HAIR IS ALL WET. BUT THAT DOESN'T MATTER. JUST DON'T BREATHE, NOW. HOPEFULLY THE YOUNGER ONES CAN STICK IT OUT, TOO.
ZZZZ
SSS
RAT TAT
STOMP
IS HE A RUSSIAN? DOES HE KNOW WE'RE IN HERE?
RAT TAT
RAT TAT
WHERE ARE MAMA AND PAPA? WHERE ARE ALL THE OTHERS?
CLANK
RAT TAT
RAT TAT
CLONK

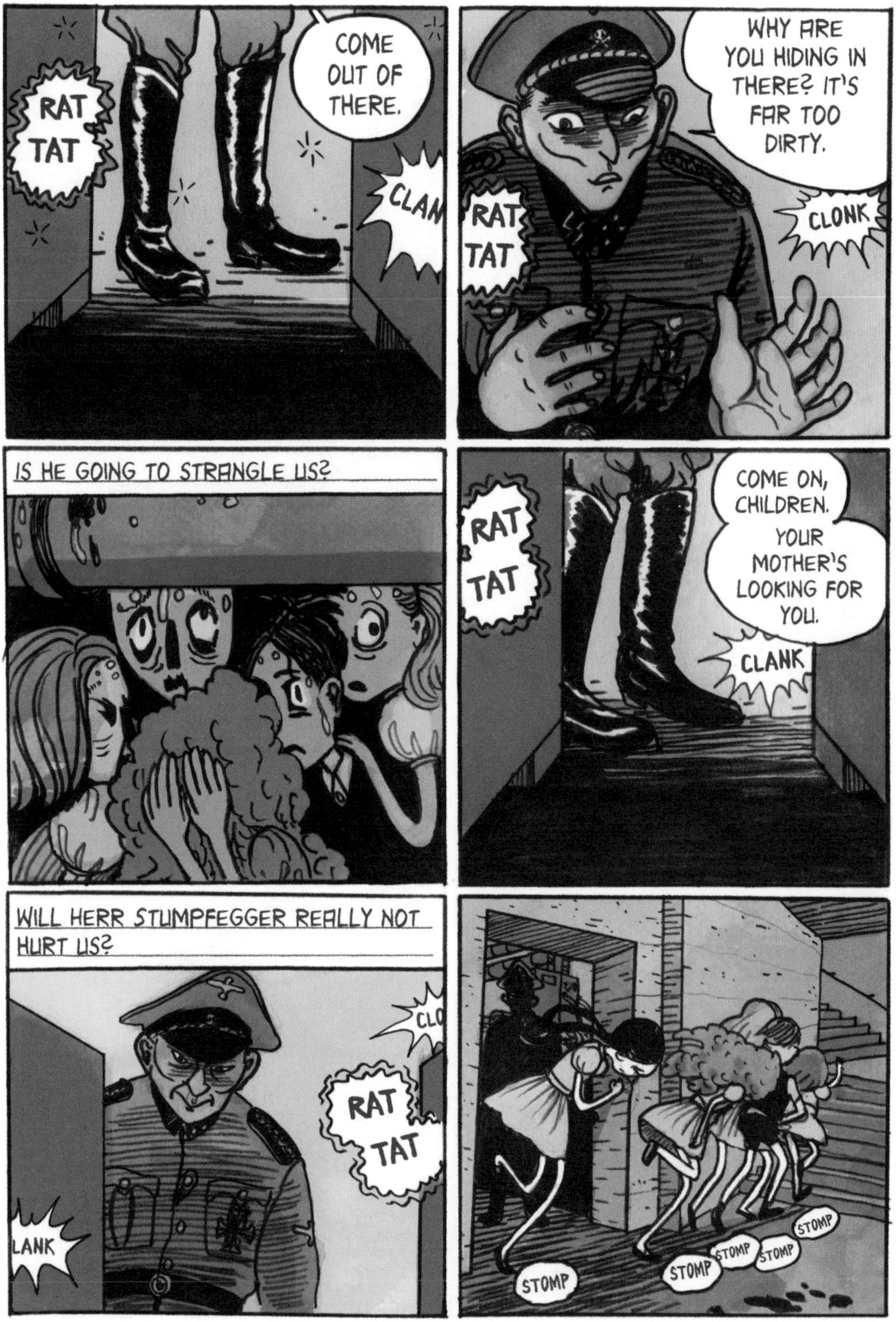
RAT TAT
COME OUT OF THERE.
CLAN
WHY ARE YOU HIDING IN THERE? IT'S FAR TOO DIRTY.
RAT TAT
CLONK
IS HE GOING TO STRANGLE US?
RAT TAT
COME ON, CHILDREN.
YOUR MOTHER'S LOOKING FOR YOU.
CLANK
WILL HERR STUMPFEGGER REALLY NOT HURT US?
CLO
RAT TAT
LANK
STOMP
STOMP
STOMP
STOMP
STOMP

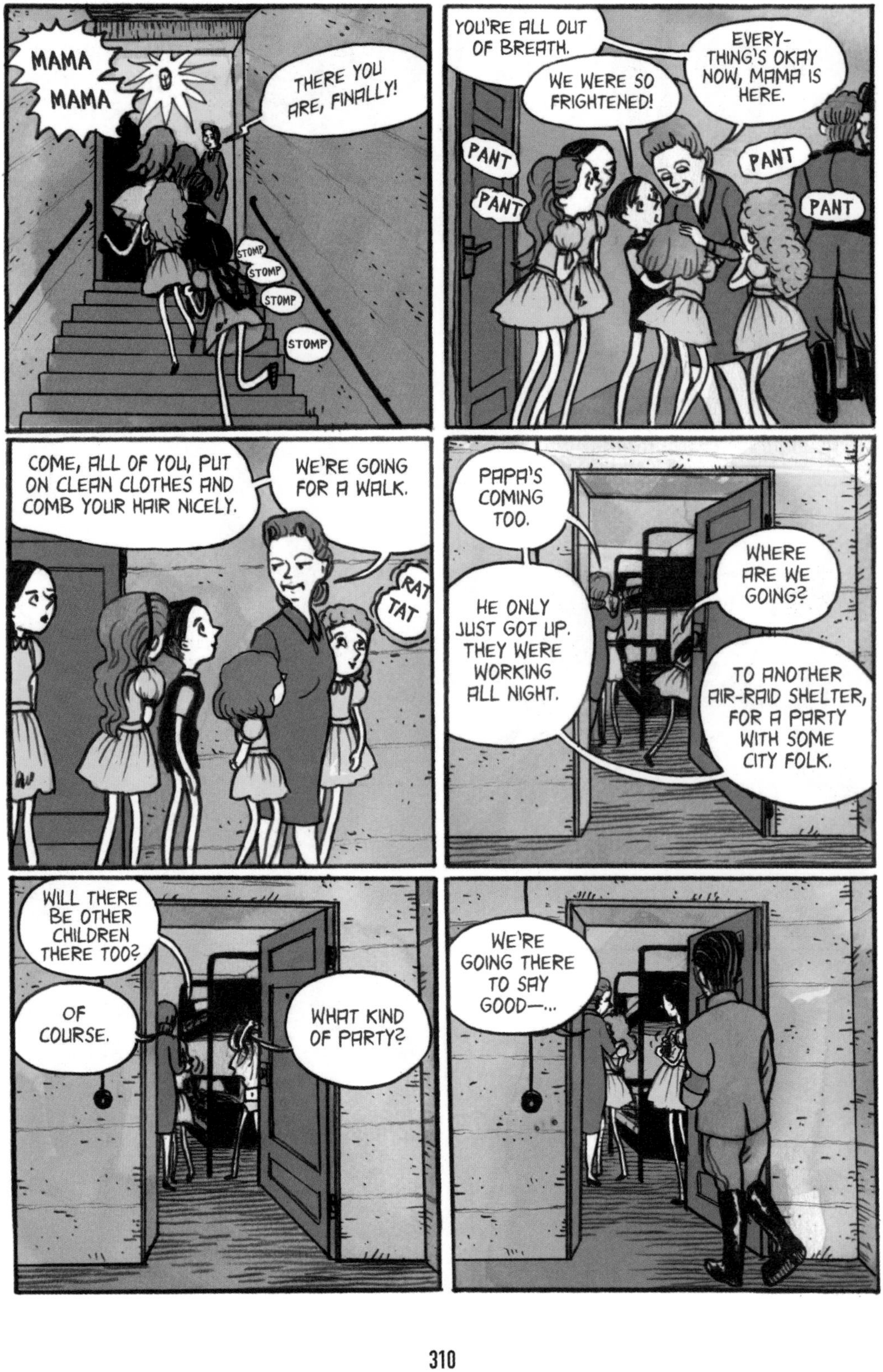
MAMA
MAMA
THERE YOU ARE, FINALLY!
STOMP
STOMP
STOMP
STOMP
YOU'RE ALL OUT OF BREATH.
WE WERE SO FRIGHTENED!
EVERY-THING'S OKAY NOW, MAMA IS HERE.
PANT
PANT
PANT
PANT
COME, ALL OF YOU, PUT ON CLEAN CLOTHES AND COMB YOUR HAIR NICELY.
WE'RE GOING FOR A WALK.
RAT TAT
PAPA'S COMING TOO.
HE ONLY JUST GOT UP. THEY WERE WORKING ALL NIGHT.
WHERE ARE WE GOING?
TO ANOTHER AIR-RAID SHELTER, FOR A PARTY WITH SOME CITY FOLK.
WILL THERE BE OTHER CHILDREN THERE TOO?
OF COURSE.
WHAT KIND OF PARTY?
WE'RE GOING THERE TO SAY GOOD—...

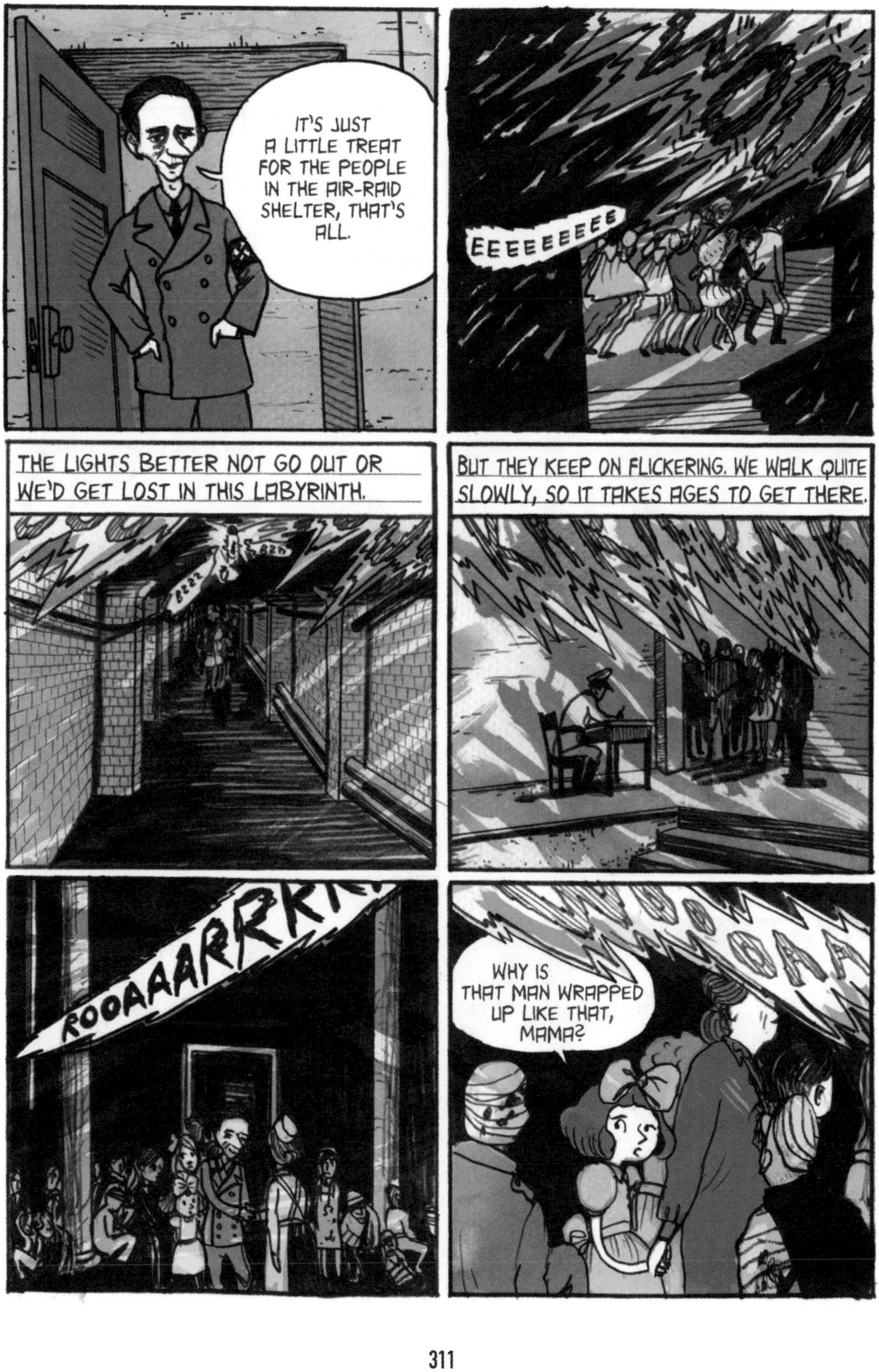
IT'S JUST A LITTLE TREAT FOR THE PEOPLE IN THE AIR-RAID SHELTER, THAT'S ALL.
EEEEEEEEE
THE LIGHTS BETTER NOT GO OUT OR WE'D GET LOST IN THIS LABYRINTH.
BZZZ
BUT THEY KEEP ON FLICKERING. WE WALK QUITE SLOWLY, SO IT TAKES AGES TO GET THERE.
ROOAAARRRR
WHY IS THAT MAN WRAPPED UP LIKE THAT, MAMA?

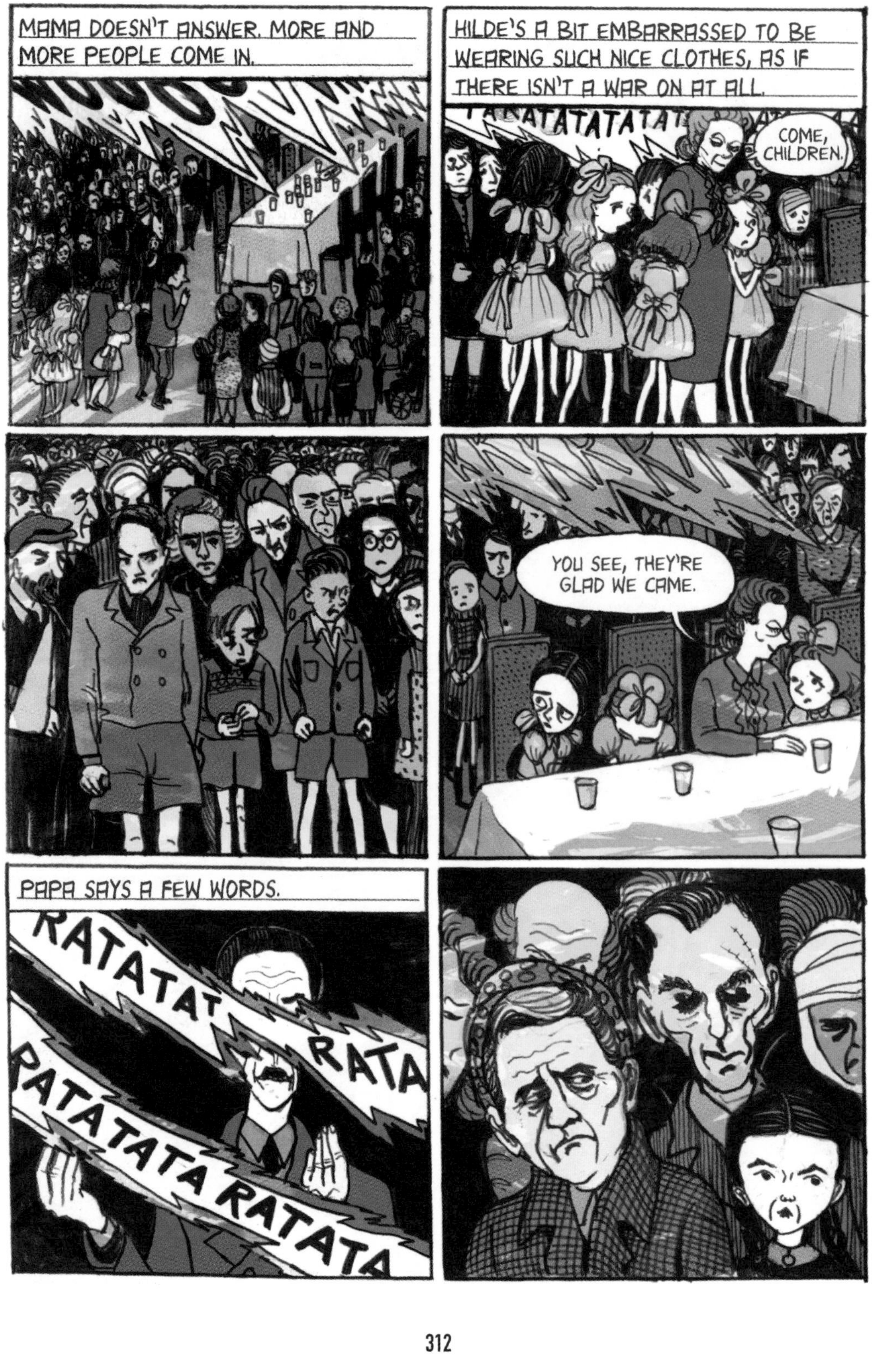
MAMA DOESN'T ANSWER. MORE AND MORE PEOPLE COME IN.
HILDE'S A BIT EMBARRASSED TO BE WEARING SUCH NICE CLOTHES, AS IF THERE ISN'T A WAR ON AT ALL.
RATATATATATAT
COME, CHILDREN.
YOU SEE, THEY'RE GLAD WE CAME.
PAPA SAYS A FEW WORDS.
RATATAT
RATA
RATATATA RATATATA

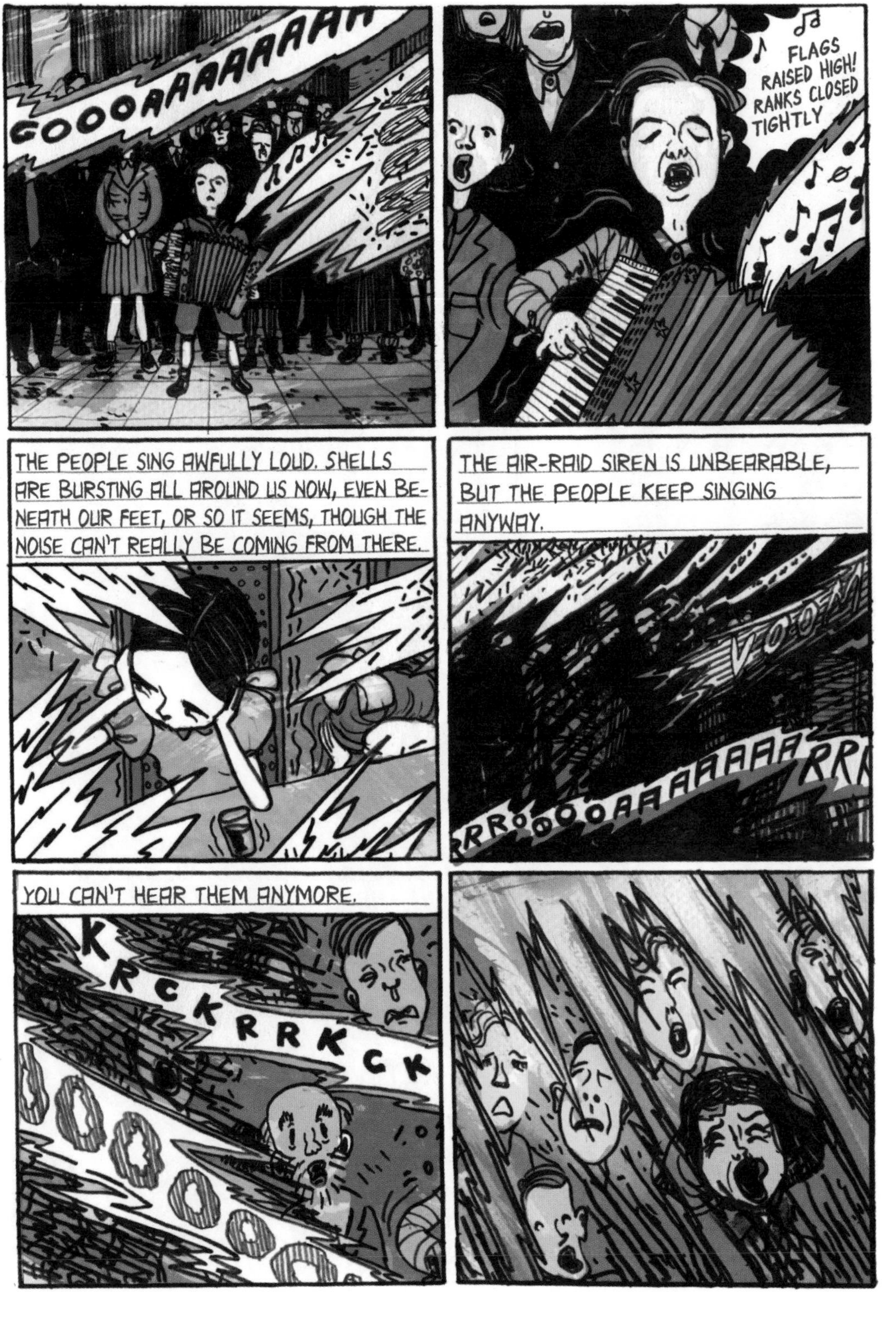
GOOOAAAAAAAAAH
FLAGS RAISED HIGH! RANKS CLOSED TIGHTLY
THE PEOPLE SING AWFULLY LOUD. SHELLS ARE BURSTING ALL AROUND US NOW, EVEN BENEATH OUR FEET, OR SO IT SEEMS, THOUGH THE NOISE CAN'T REALLY BE COMING FROM THERE.
THE AIR-RAID SIREN IS UNBEARABLE, BUT THE PEOPLE KEEP SINGING ANYWAY.
RRROOOOAAAAAAAAARRR
YOU CAN'T HEAR THEM ANYMORE.
KRCKRRRKCK

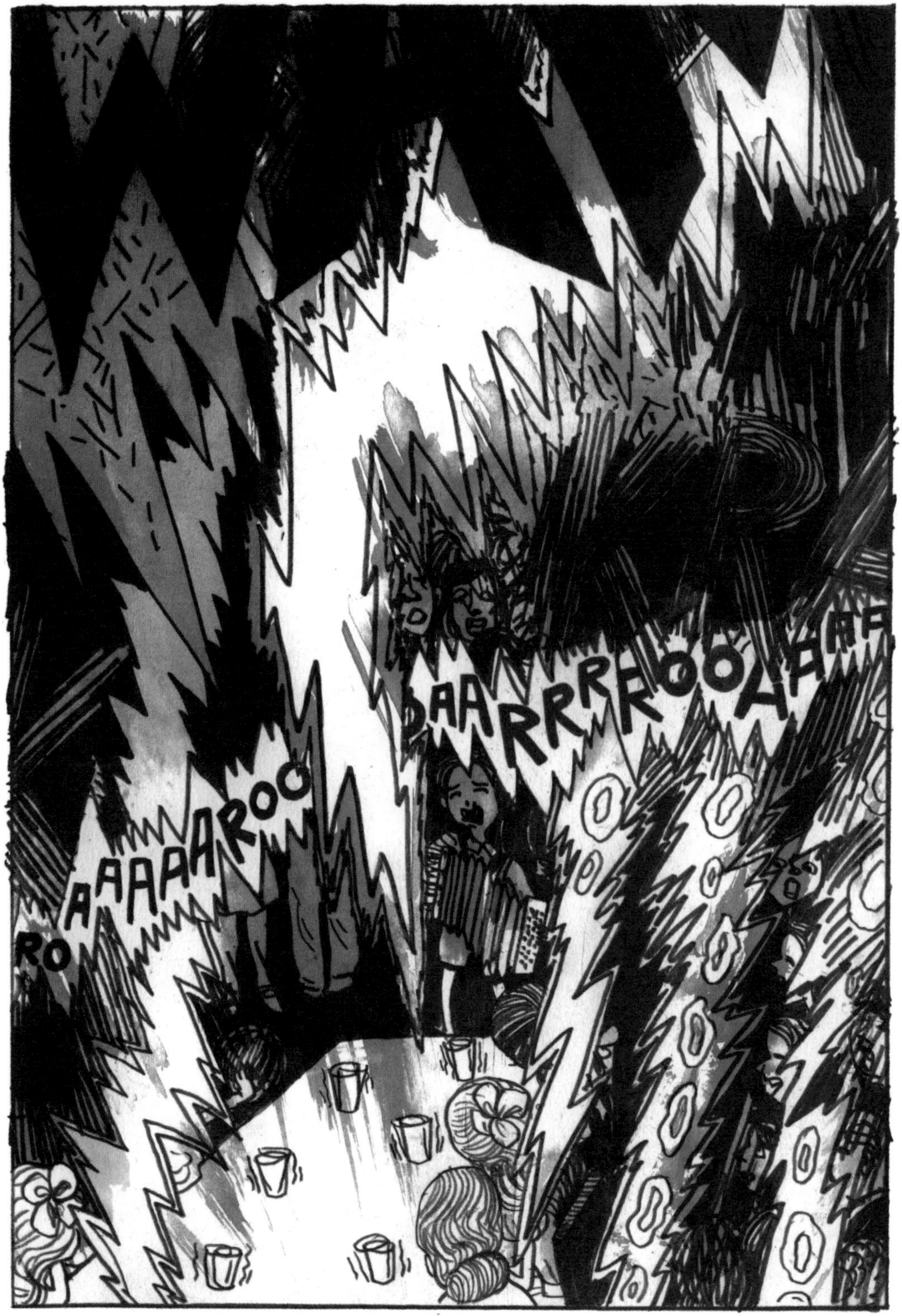
ROAAAAAROO
DAARRRRROOAAAA

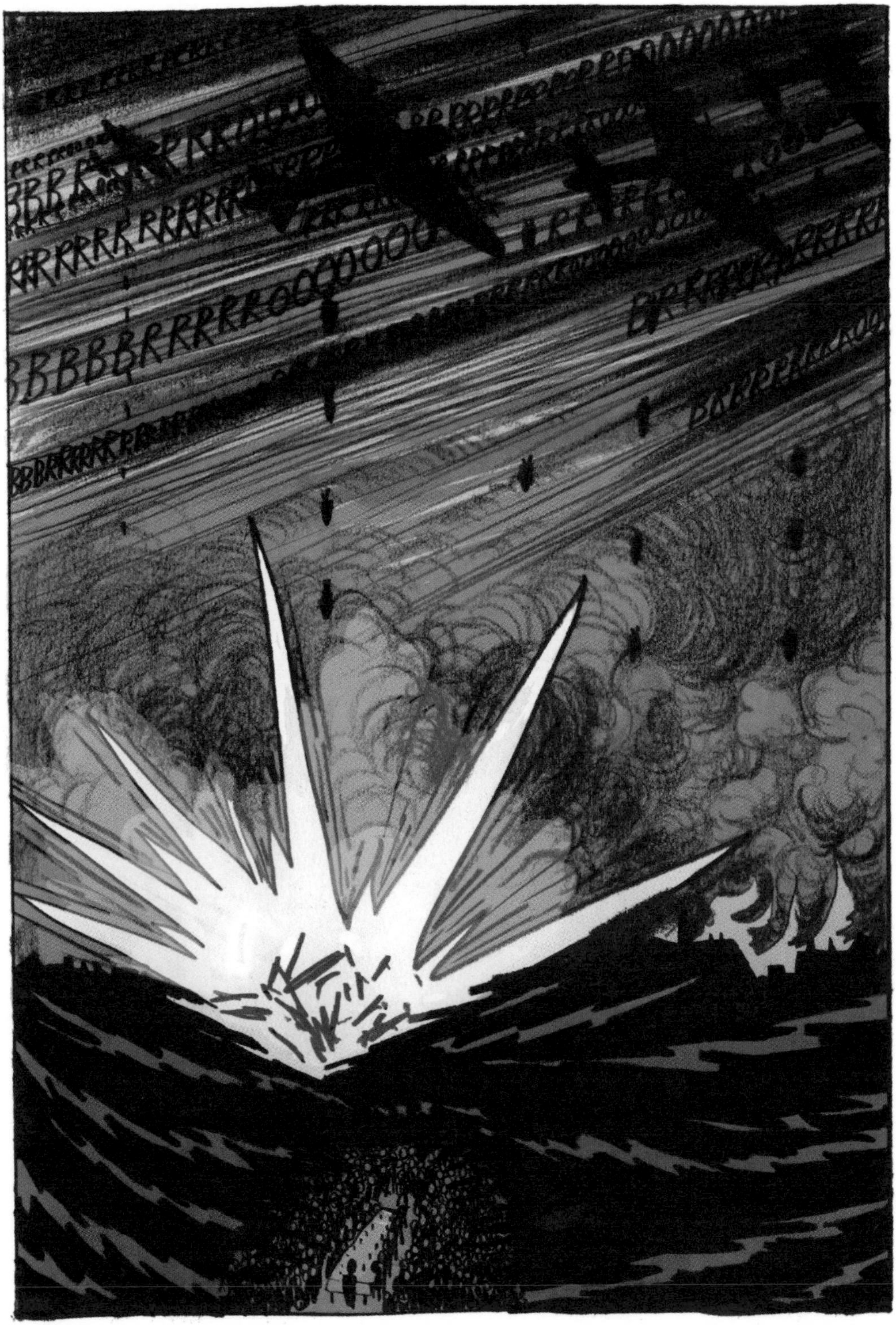

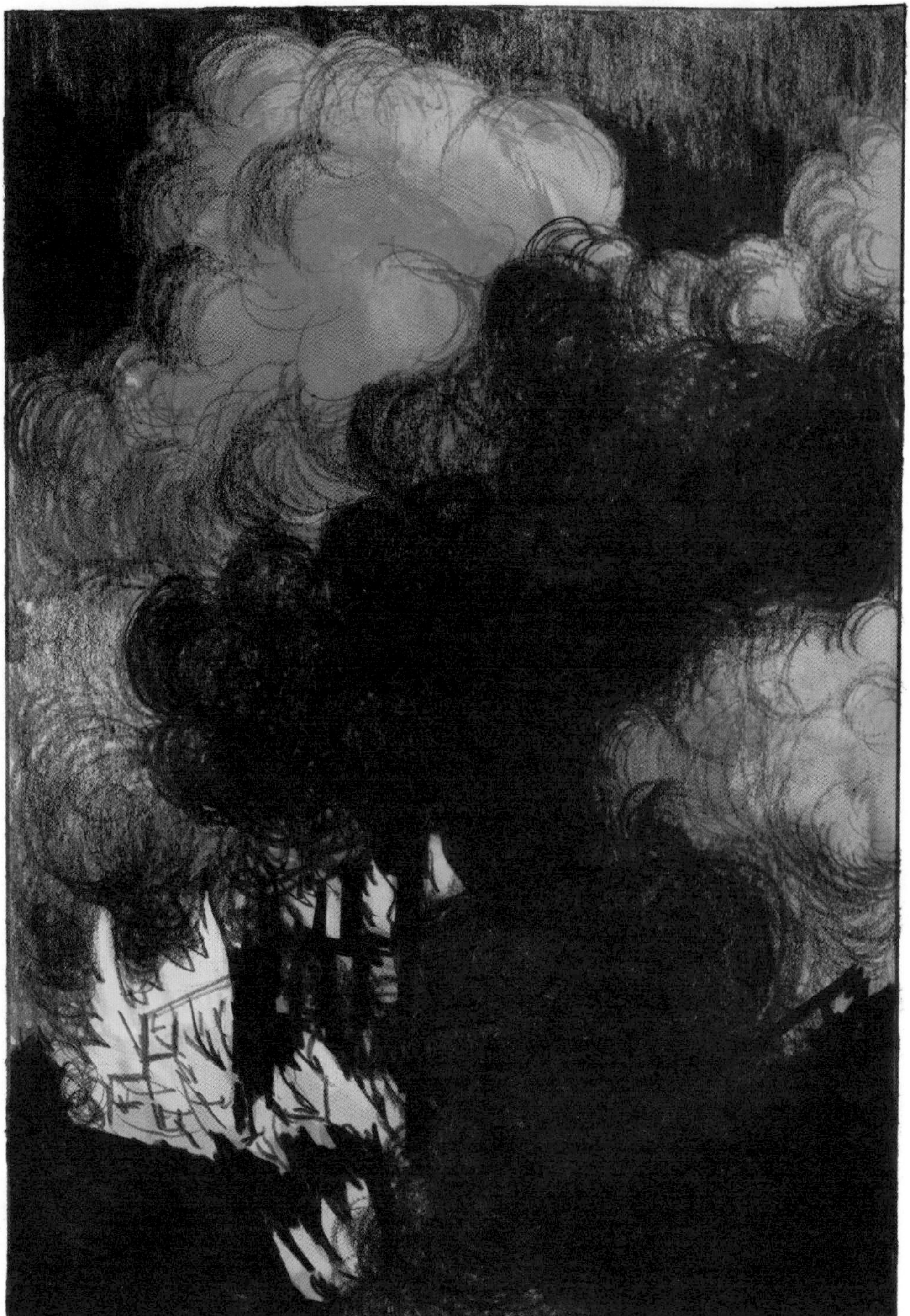

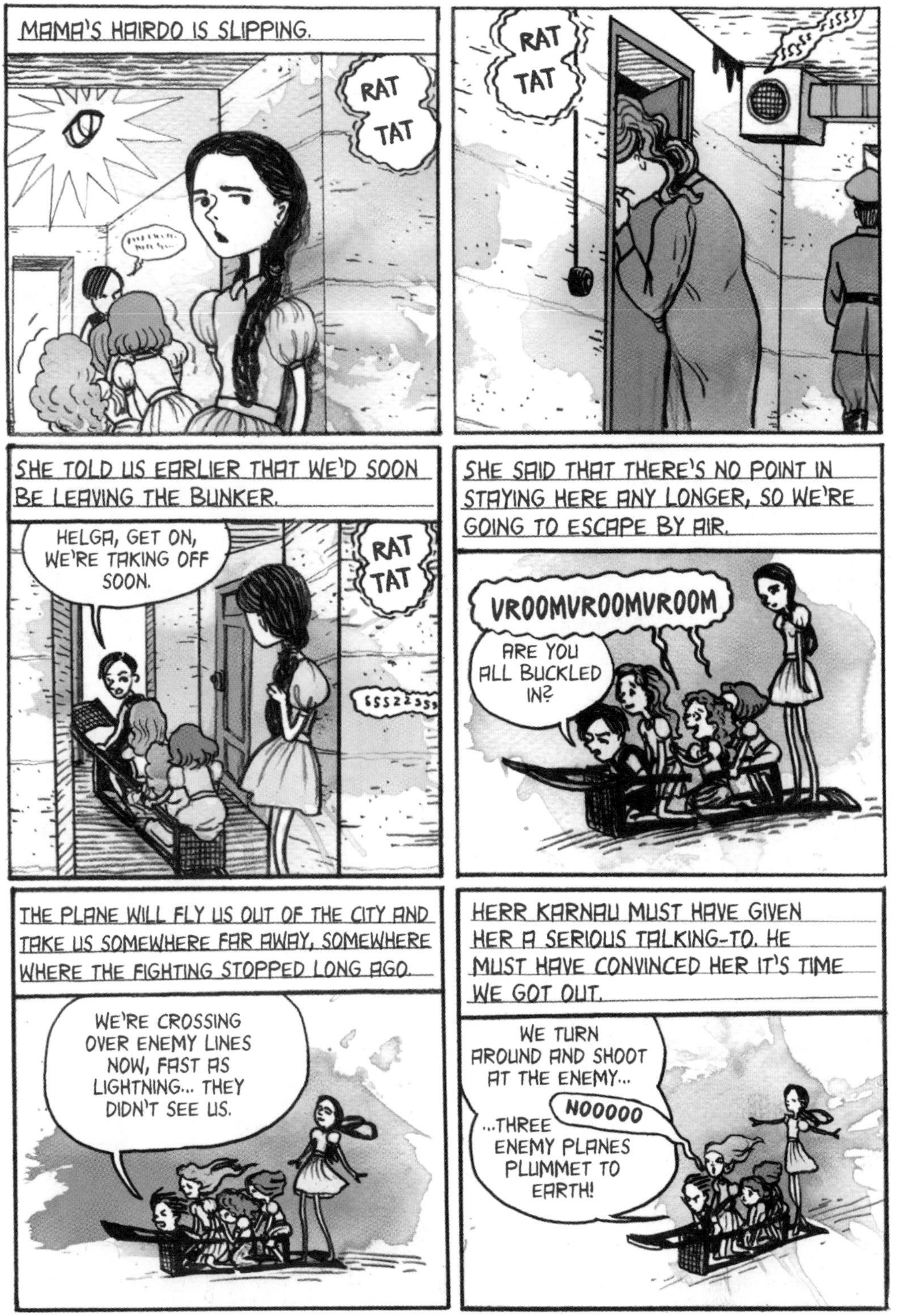
MAMA'S HAIRDO IS SLIPPING.
RAT TAT
RAT TAT
SHE TOLD US EARLIER THAT WE'D SOON BE LEAVING THE BUNKER.
HELGA, GET ON, WE'RE TAKING OFF SOON.
RAT TAT
SHE SAID THAT THERE'S NO POINT IN STAYING HERE ANY LONGER, SO WE'RE GOING TO ESCAPE BY AIR.
VROOMVROOMVROOM
ARE YOU ALL BUCKLED IN?
THE PLANE WILL FLY US OUT OF THE CITY AND TAKE US SOMEWHERE FAR AWAY, SOMEWHERE WHERE THE FIGHTING STOPPED LONG AGO.
WE'RE CROSSING OVER ENEMY LINES NOW, FAST AS LIGHTNING... THEY DIDN'T SEE US.
HERR KARNAU MUST HAVE GIVEN HER A SERIOUS TALKING-TO. HE MUST HAVE CONVINCED HER IT'S TIME WE GOT OUT.
WE TURN AROUND AND SHOOT AT THE ENEMY...
NOOOOO
...THREE ENEMY PLANES PLUMMET TO EARTH!

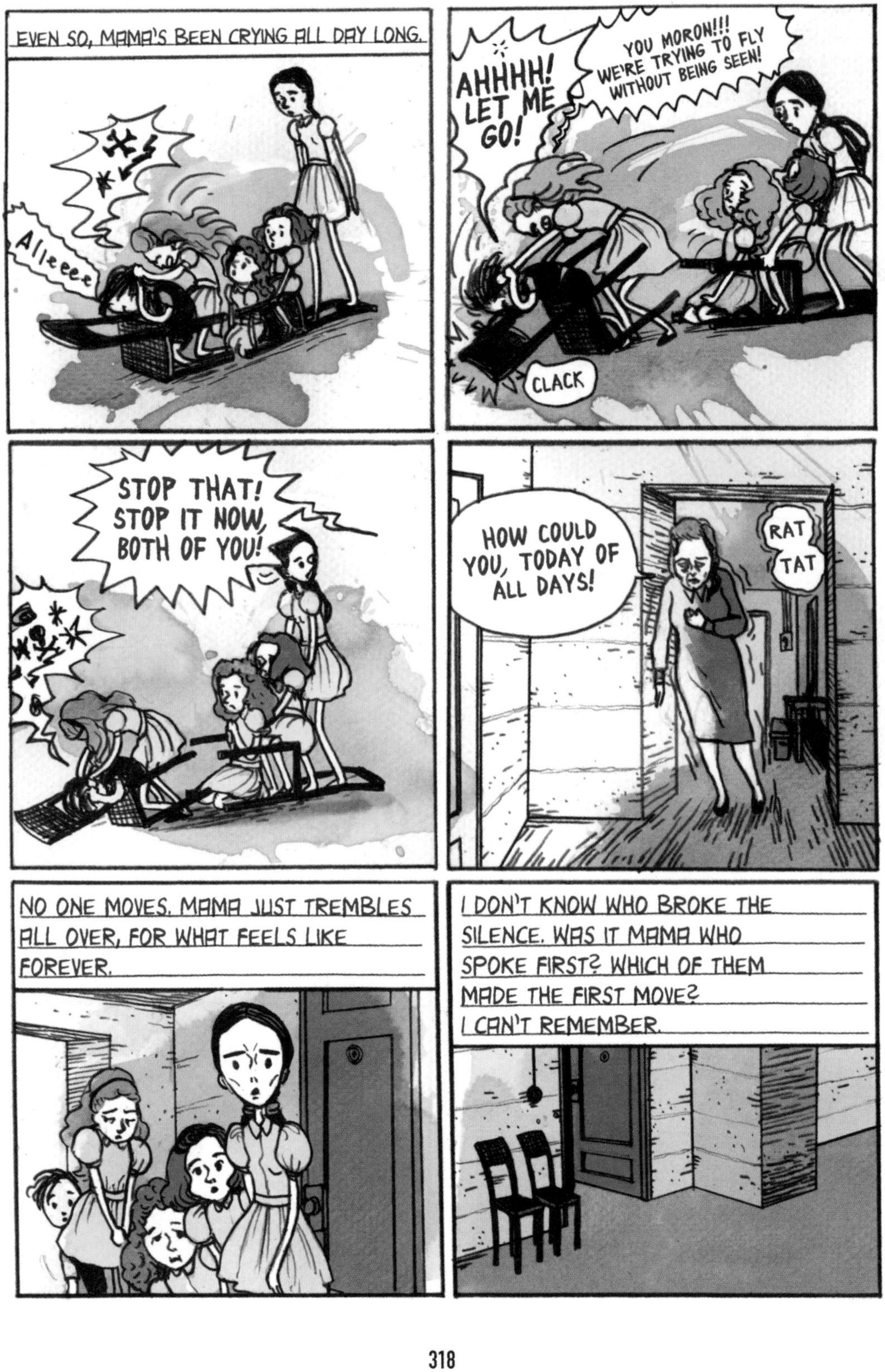
EVEN SO, MAMA'S BEEN CRYING ALL DAY LONG.
Alleeee
AHHHH! LET ME GO!
YOU MORON!!! WE'RE TRYING TO FLY WITHOUT BEING SEEN!
CLACK
STOP THAT! STOP IT NOW, BOTH OF YOU!
HOW COULD YOU, TODAY OF ALL DAYS!
RAT
TAT
NO ONE MOVES. MAMA JUST TREMBLES ALL OVER, FOR WHAT FEELS LIKE FOREVER.
I DON'T KNOW WHO BROKE THE SILENCE. WAS IT MAMA WHO SPOKE FIRST? WHICH OF THEM MADE THE FIRST MOVE? I CAN'T REMEMBER.

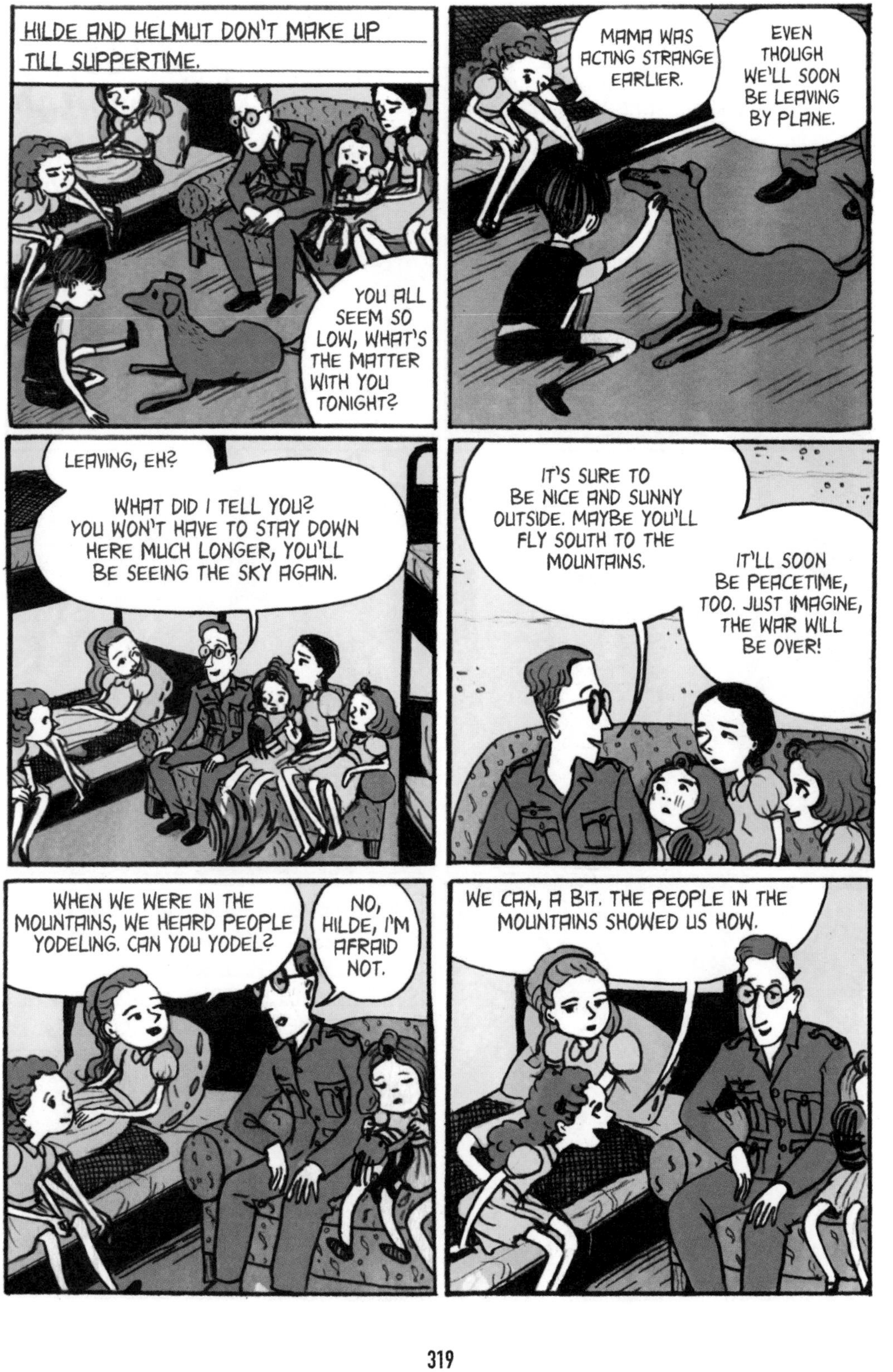
HILDE AND HELMUT DON'T MAKE UP TILL SUPPERTIME.
YOU ALL SEEM SO LOW, WHAT'S THE MATTER WITH YOU TONIGHT?
MAMA WAS ACTING STRANGE EARLIER.
EVEN THOUGH WE'LL SOON BE LEAVING BY PLANE.
LEAVING, EH?
WHAT DID I TELL YOU? YOU WON'T HAVE TO STAY DOWN HERE MUCH LONGER, YOU'LL BE SEEING THE SKY AGAIN.
IT'S SURE TO BE NICE AND SUNNY OUTSIDE. MAYBE YOU'LL FLY SOUTH TO THE MOUNTAINS.
IT'LL SOON BE PEACETIME, TOO. JUST IMAGINE, THE WAR WILL BE OVER!
WHEN WE WERE IN THE MOUNTAINS, WE HEARD PEOPLE YODELING. CAN YOU YODEL?
NO, HILDE, I'M AFRAID NOT.
WE CAN, A BIT. THE PEOPLE IN THE MOUNTAINS SHOWED US HOW.

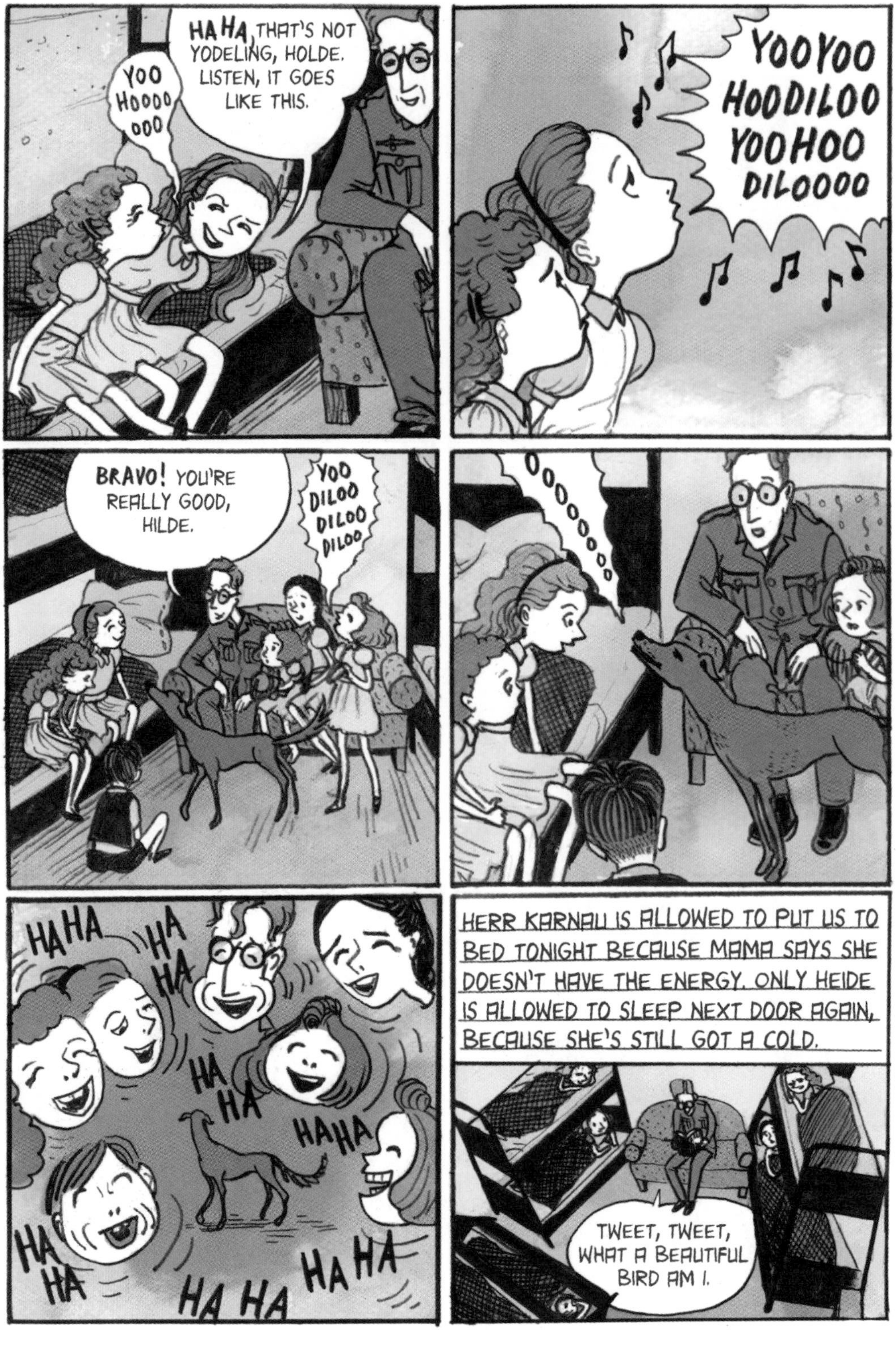
YOO HOOOO OOO
HAHA, THAT'S NOT YODELING, HOLDE. LISTEN, IT GOES LIKE THIS.
YOOYOO HOODILOO YOOHOO DILOOOO
BRAVO! YOU'RE REALLY GOOD, HILDE.
YOO DILOO DILOO DILOO
OOOOOOOOO
HAHA
HA HA HA
HA HA
HAHA
HA HA
HA HA
HAHA
HERR KARNAU IS ALLOWED TO PUT US TO BED TONIGHT BECAUSE MAMA SAYS SHE DOESN'T HAVE THE ENERGY. ONLY HEIDE IS ALLOWED TO SLEEP NEXT DOOR AGAIN, BECAUSE SHE'S STILL GOT A COLD.
TWEET, TWEET, WHAT A BEAUTIFUL BIRD AM I.

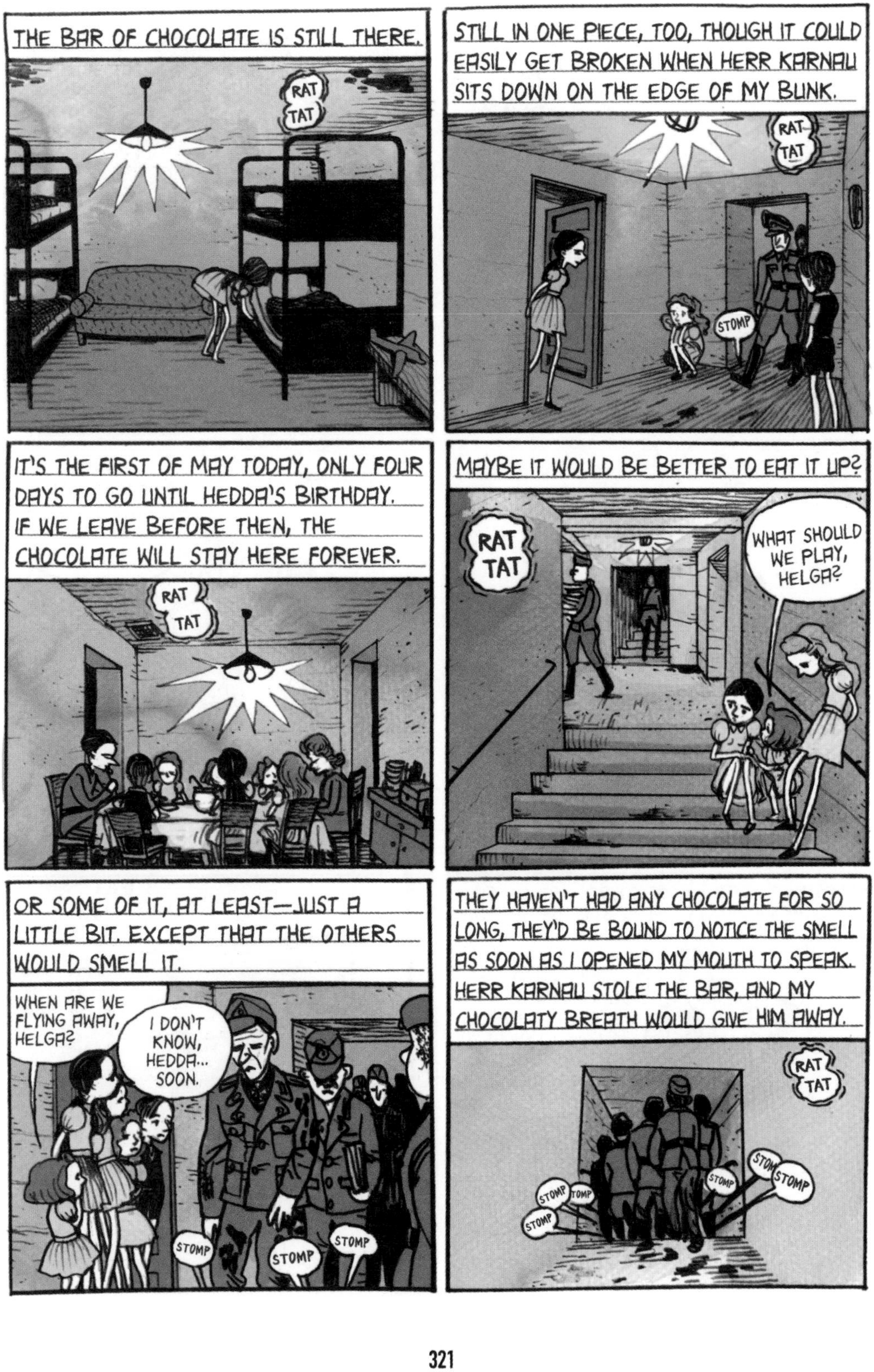
THE BAR OF CHOCOLATE IS STILL THERE.
RAT TAT
STILL IN ONE PIECE, TOO, THOUGH IT COULD EASILY GET BROKEN WHEN HERR KARNAU SITS DOWN ON THE EDGE OF MY BUNK.
RAT TAT
STOMP
IT'S THE FIRST OF MAY TODAY, ONLY FOUR DAYS TO GO UNTIL HEDDA'S BIRTHDAY. IF WE LEAVE BEFORE THEN, THE CHOCOLATE WILL STAY HERE FOREVER.
RAT TAT
MAYBE IT WOULD BE BETTER TO EAT IT UP?
RAT TAT
WHAT SHOULD WE PLAY, HELGA?
OR SOME OF IT, AT LEAST—JUST A LITTLE BIT. EXCEPT THAT THE OTHERS WOULD SMELL IT.
WHEN ARE WE FLYING AWAY, HELGA?
I DON'T KNOW, HEDDA... SOON.
STOMP
STOMP
STOMP
THEY HAVEN'T HAD ANY CHOCOLATE FOR SO LONG, THEY'D BE BOUND TO NOTICE THE SMELL AS SOON AS I OPENED MY MOUTH TO SPEAK. HERR KARNAU STOLE THE BAR, AND MY CHOCOLATY BREATH WOULD GIVE HIM AWAY.
RAT TAT
STOMP
STOMP
STOMP
STOMP
STOMP
STOMP

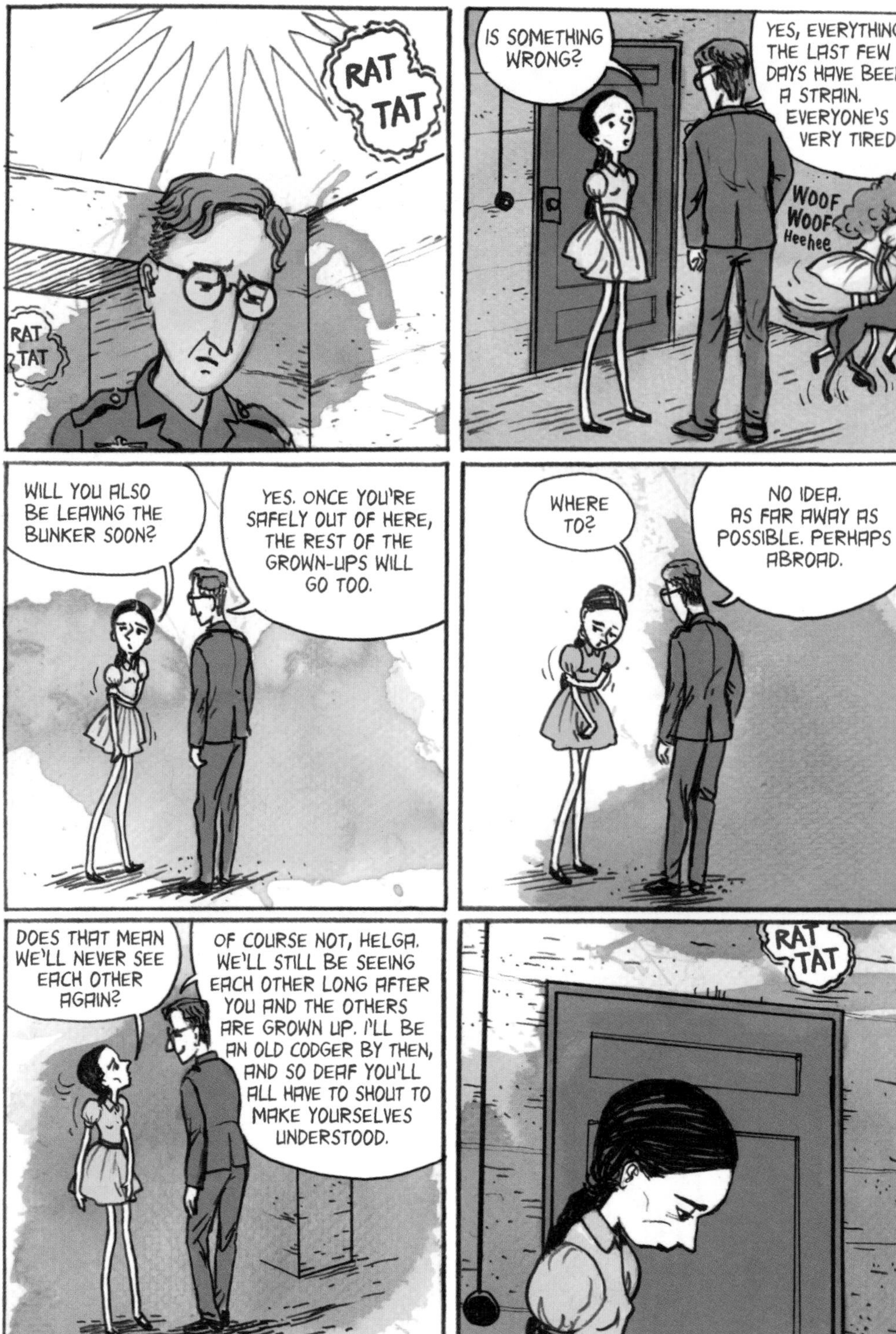
RAT TAT
RAT TAT
IS SOMETHING WRONG?
YES, EVERYTHING. THE LAST FEW DAYS HAVE BEEN A STRAIN. EVERYONE'S VERY TIRED.
WOOF WOOF
Heehee
WILL YOU ALSO BE LEAVING THE BUNKER SOON?
YES. ONCE YOU'RE SAFELY OUT OF HERE, THE REST OF THE GROWN-UPS WILL GO TOO.
WHERE TO?
NO IDEA. AS FAR AWAY AS POSSIBLE. PERHAPS ABROAD.
DOES THAT MEAN WE'LL NEVER SEE EACH OTHER AGAIN?
OF COURSE NOT, HELGA. WE'LL STILL BE SEEING EACH OTHER LONG AFTER YOU AND THE OTHERS ARE GROWN UP. I'LL BE AN OLD CODGER BY THEN, AND SO DEAF YOU'LL ALL HAVE TO SHOUT TO MAKE YOURSELVES UNDERSTOOD.
RAT TAT

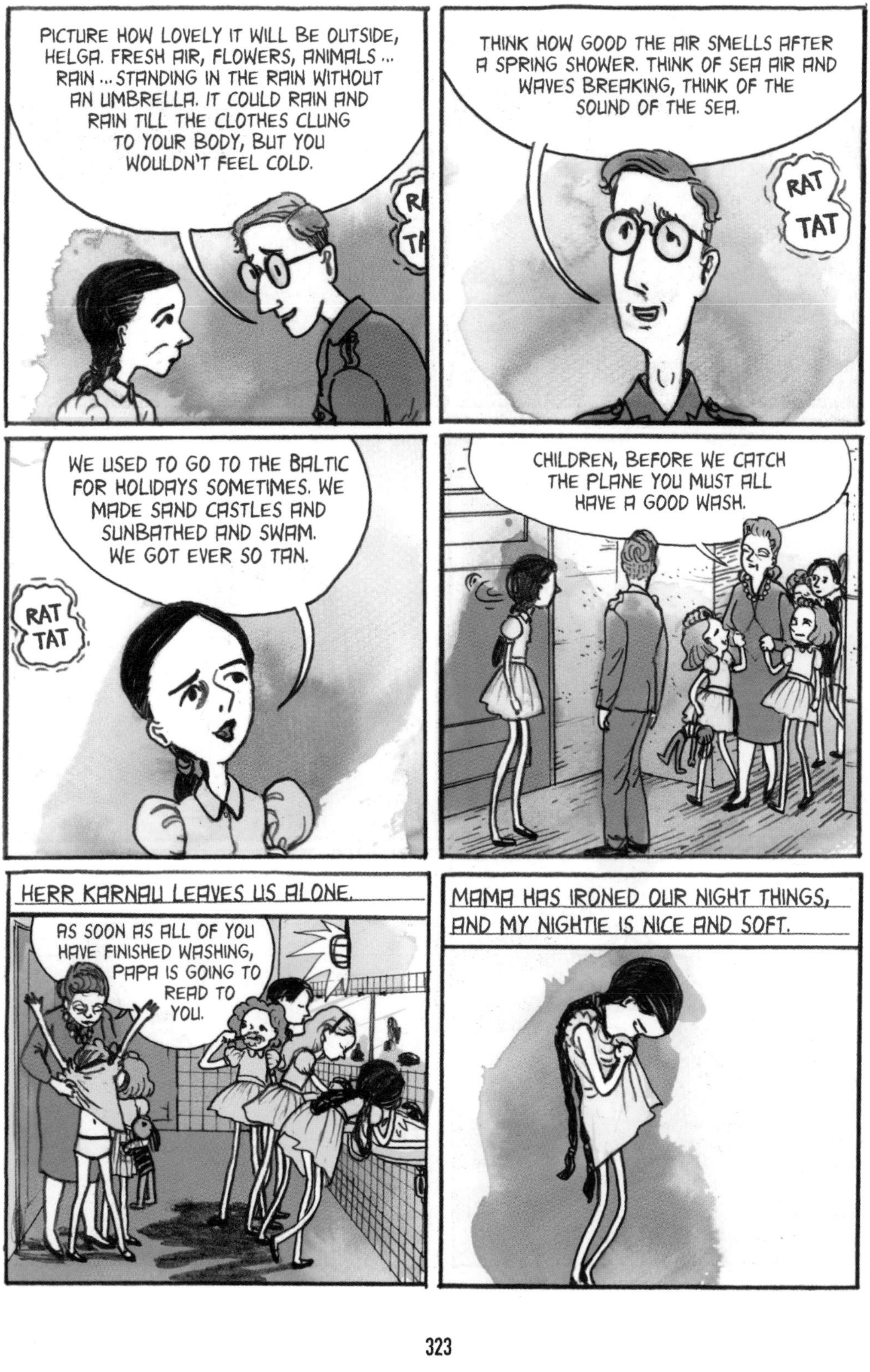
PICTURE HOW LOVELY IT WILL BE OUTSIDE, HELGA. FRESH AIR, FLOWERS, ANIMALS ... RAIN ... STANDING IN THE RAIN WITHOUT AN UMBRELLA. IT COULD RAIN AND RAIN TILL THE CLOTHES CLUNG TO YOUR BODY, BUT YOU WOULDN'T FEEL COLD.
THINK HOW GOOD THE AIR SMELLS AFTER A SPRING SHOWER. THINK OF SEA AIR AND WAVES BREAKING, THINK OF THE SOUND OF THE SEA.
RAT TAT
WE USED TO GO TO THE BALTIC FOR HOLIDAYS SOMETIMES. WE MADE SAND CASTLES AND SUNBATHED AND SWAM. WE GOT EVER SO TAN.
RAT TAT
CHILDREN, BEFORE WE CATCH THE PLANE YOU MUST ALL HAVE A GOOD WASH.
HERR KARNAU LEAVES US ALONE.
AS SOON AS ALL OF YOU HAVE FINISHED WASHING, PAPA IS GOING TO READ TO YOU.
MAMA HAS IRONED OUR NIGHT THINGS, AND MY NIGHTIE IS NICE AND SOFT.

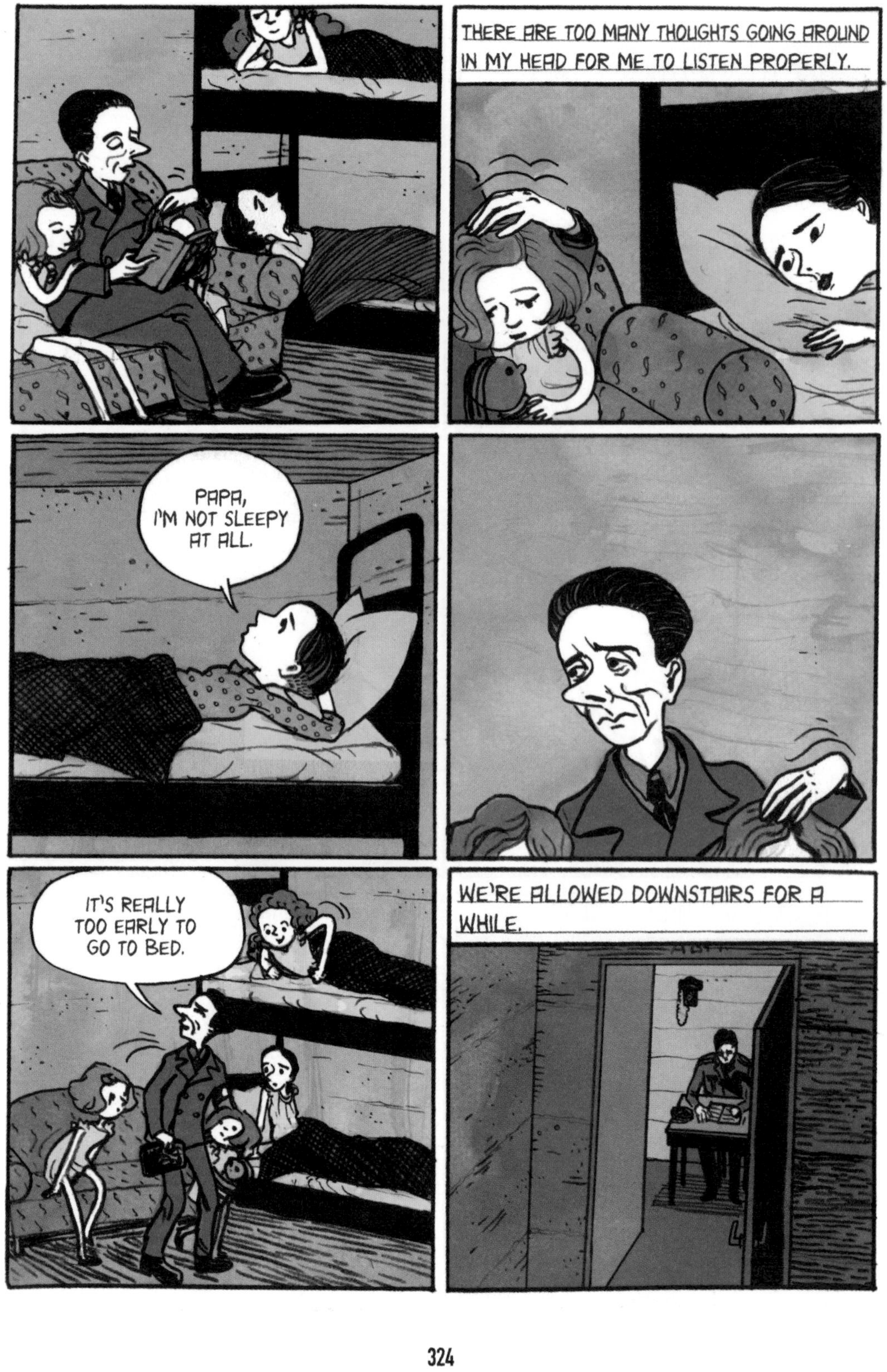
THERE ARE TOO MANY THOUGHTS GOING AROUND IN MY HEAD FOR ME TO LISTEN PROPERLY.
PAPA, I'M NOT SLEEPY AT ALL.
IT'S REALLY TOO EARLY TO GO TO BED.
WE'RE ALLOWED DOWNSTAIRS FOR A WHILE.

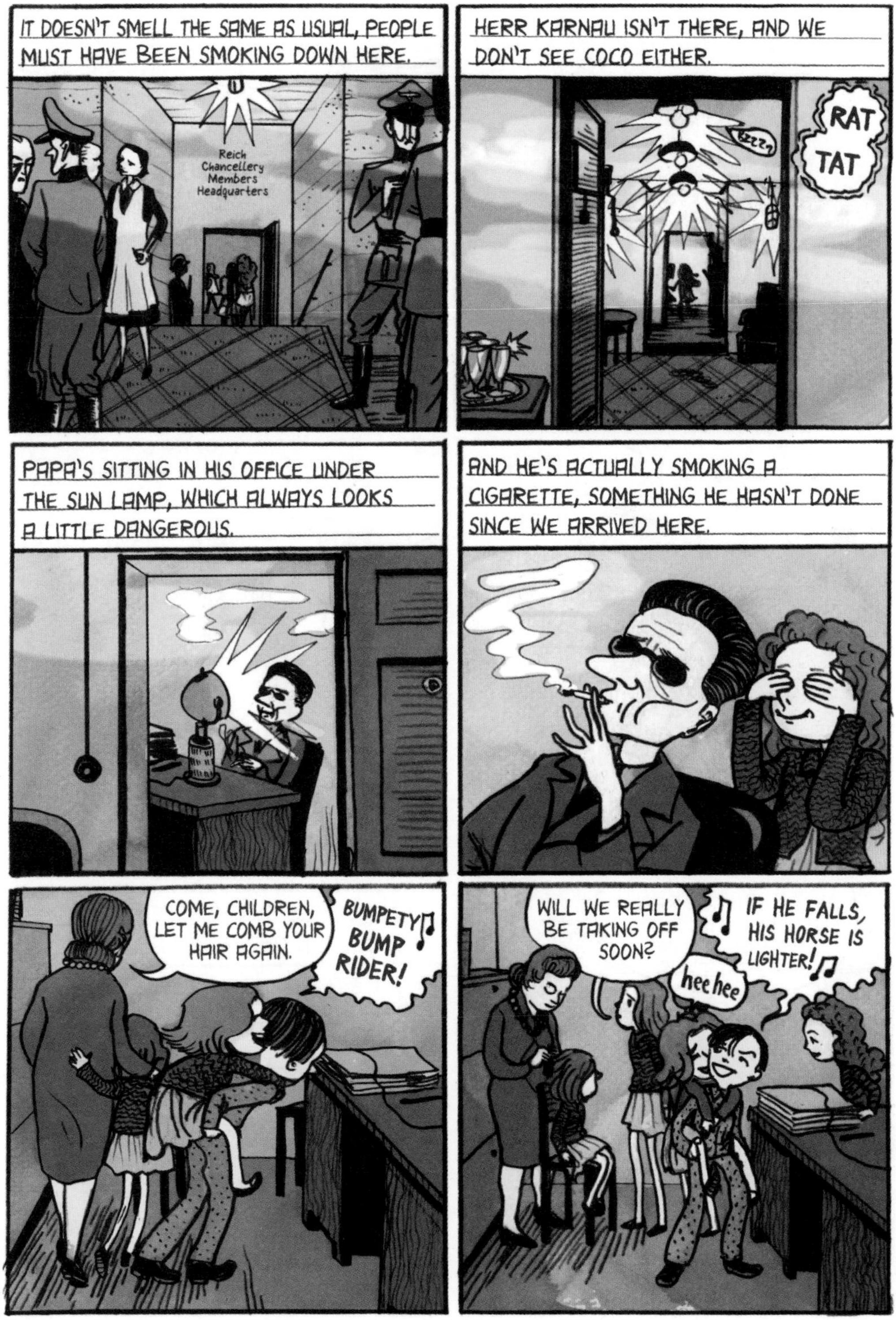
IT DOESN'T SMELL THE SAME AS USUAL, PEOPLE MUST HAVE BEEN SMOKING DOWN HERE.
Reich Chancellery Members Headquarters
HERR KARNAU ISN'T THERE, AND WE DON'T SEE COCO EITHER.
RAT TAT
PAPA'S SITTING IN HIS OFFICE UNDER THE SUN LAMP, WHICH ALWAYS LOOKS A LITTLE DANGEROUS.
AND HE'S ACTUALLY SMOKING A CIGARETTE, SOMETHING HE HASN'T DONE SINCE WE ARRIVED HERE.
COME, CHILDREN, LET ME COMB YOUR HAIR AGAIN.
BUMPETY BUMP RIDER!
WILL WE REALLY BE TAKING OFF SOON?
IF HE FALLS, HIS HORSE IS LIGHTER!
hee hee

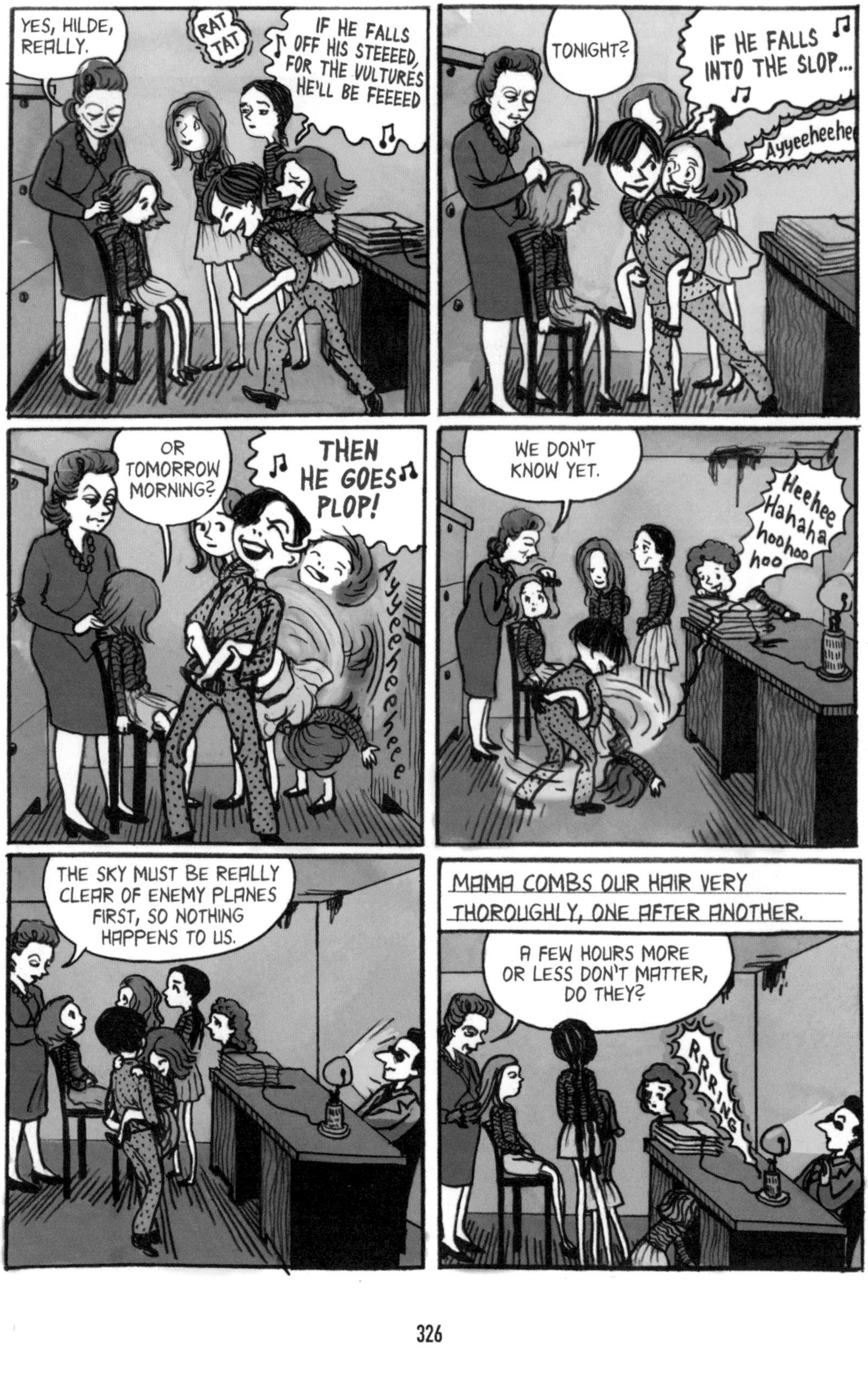
YES, HILDE, REALLY.
RAT TAT
IF HE FALLS OFF HIS STEEEED, FOR THE VULTURES HE'LL BE FEEEED
TONIGHT?
IF HE FALLS INTO THE SLOP...
Ayyeeheehe
OR TOMORROW MORNING?
THEN HE GOES PLOP!
Ayyeeheeheeheee
WE DON'T KNOW YET.
Heehee Hahaha hoohoo hoo
THE SKY MUST BE REALLY CLEAR OF ENEMY PLANES FIRST, SO NOTHING HAPPENS TO US.
MAMA COMBS OUR HAIR VERY THOROUGHLY, ONE AFTER ANOTHER.
A FEW HOURS MORE OR LESS DON'T MATTER, DO THEY?
RRRING

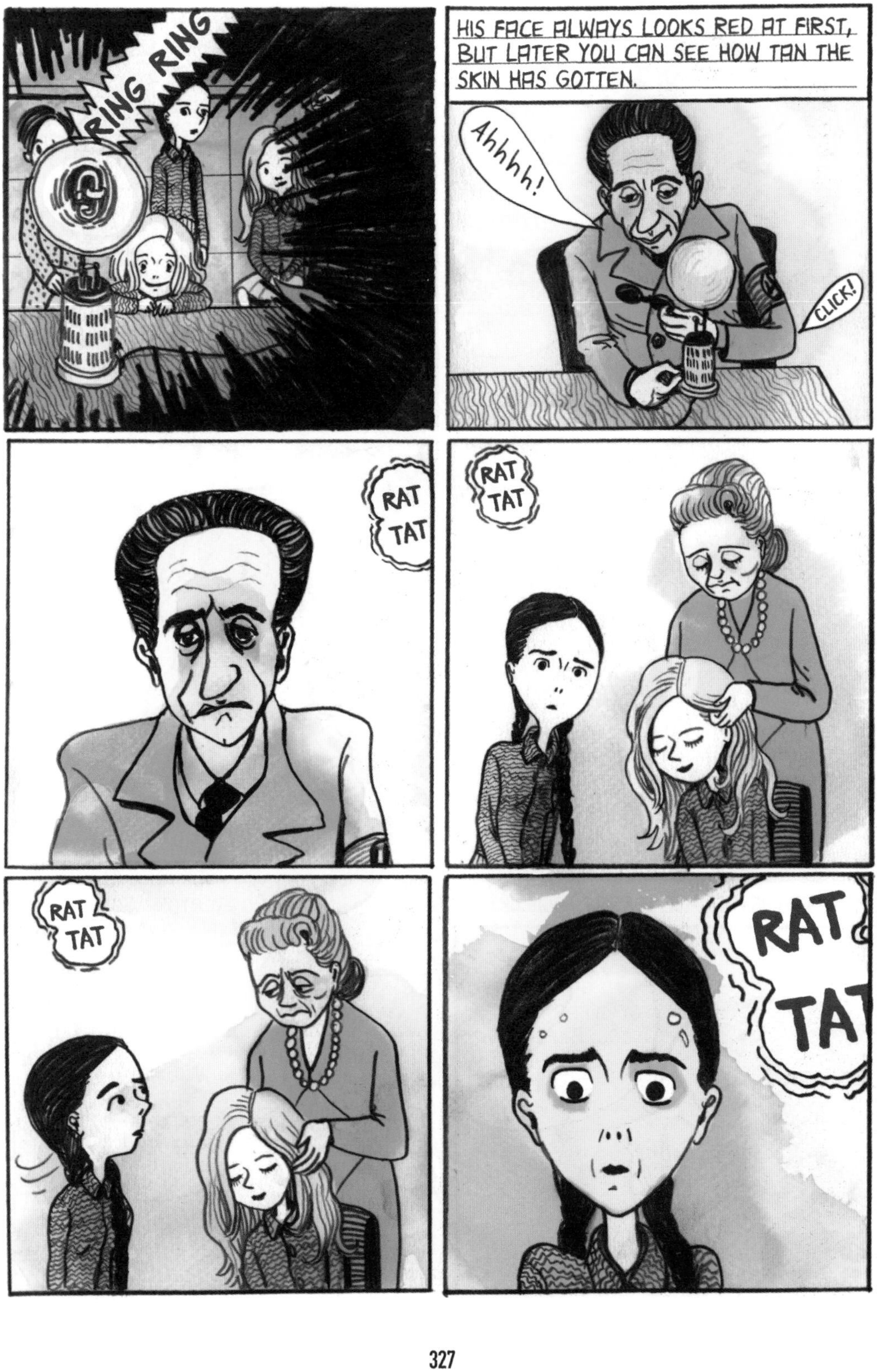
RING RING
HIS FACE ALWAYS LOOKS RED AT FIRST, BUT LATER YOU CAN SEE HOW TAN THE SKIN HAS GOTTEN.
Ahhhh!
CLICK!
RAT TAT
RAT TAT
RAT TAT
RAT TAT

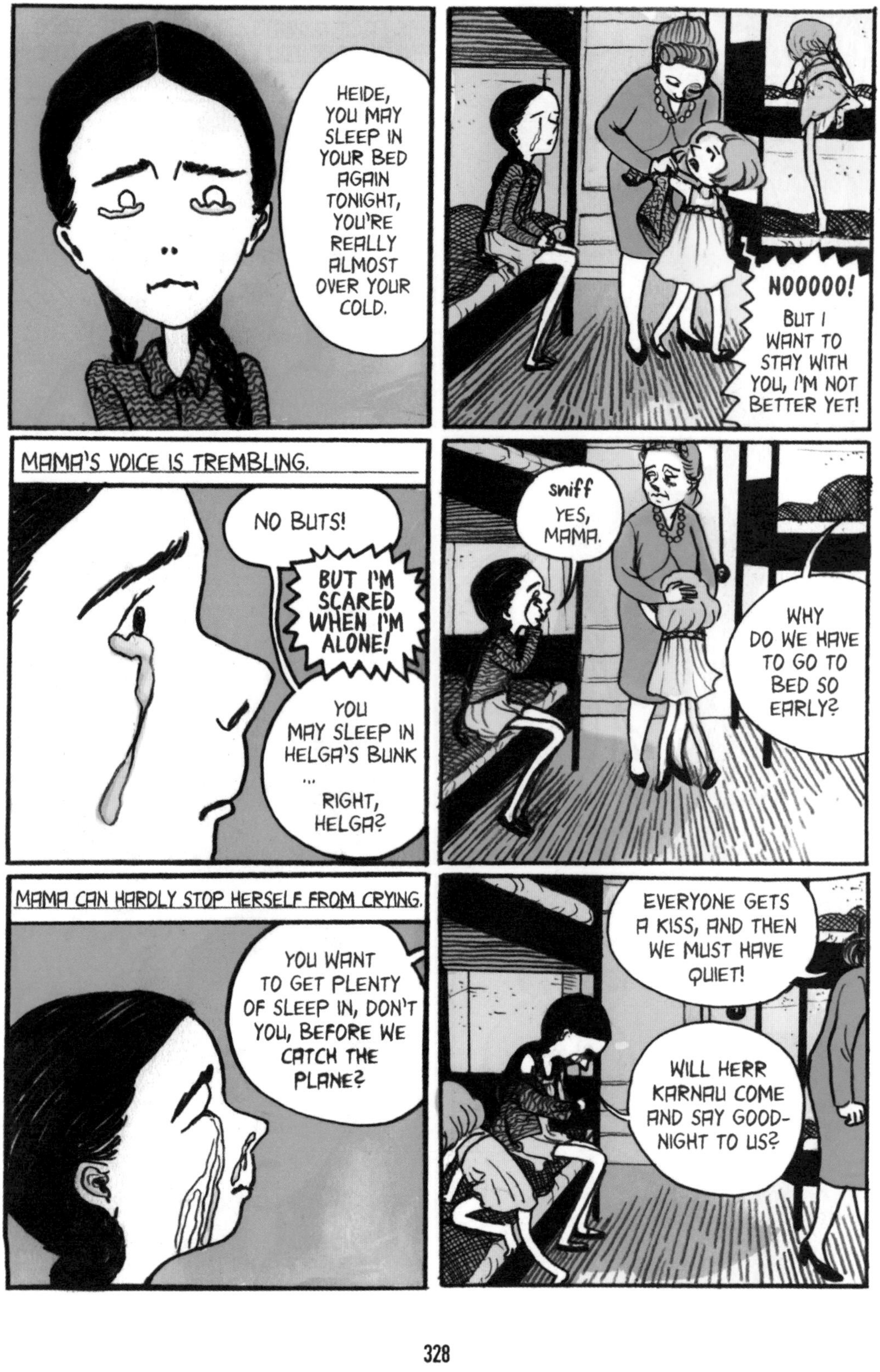
HEIDE, YOU MAY SLEEP IN YOUR BED AGAIN TONIGHT, YOU'RE REALLY ALMOST OVER YOUR COLD.
NOOOOO! BUT I WANT TO STAY WITH YOU, I'M NOT BETTER YET!
MAMA'S VOICE IS TREMBLING.
NO BUTS!
BUT I'M SCARED WHEN I'M ALONE!
YOU MAY SLEEP IN HELGA'S BUNK ... RIGHT, HELGA?
sniff YES, MAMA.
WHY DO WE HAVE TO GO TO BED SO EARLY?
MAMA CAN HARDLY STOP HERSELF FROM CRYING.
YOU WANT TO GET PLENTY OF SLEEP IN, DON'T YOU, BEFORE WE CATCH THE PLANE?
EVERYONE GETS A KISS, AND THEN WE MUST HAVE QUIET!
WILL HERR KARNAU COME AND SAY GOOD-NIGHT TO US?

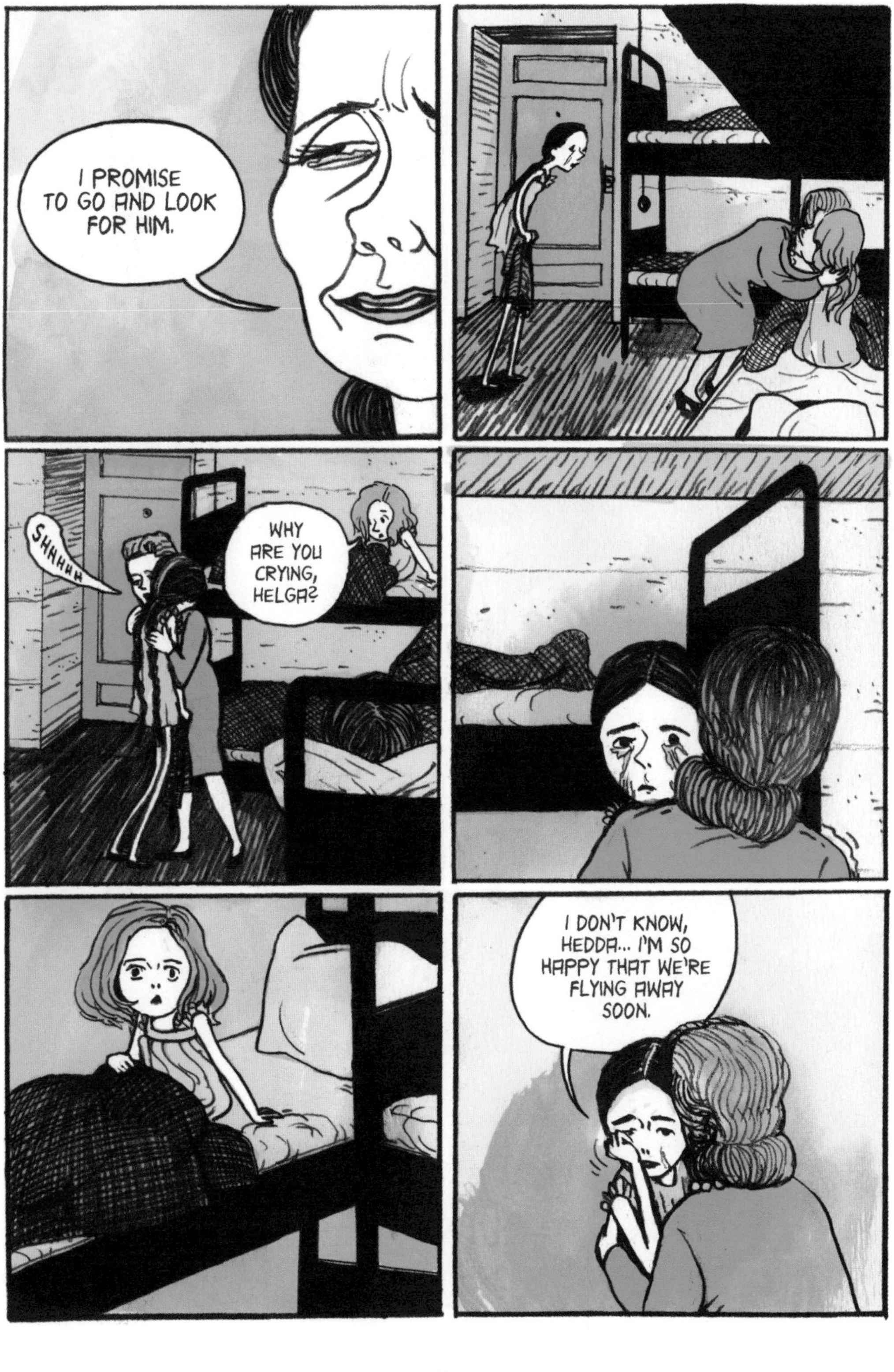
I PROMISE TO GO AND LOOK FOR HIM.
SHHHHH
WHY ARE YOU CRYING, HELGA?
I DON'T KNOW, HEDDA... I'M SO HAPPY THAT WE'RE FLYING AWAY SOON.

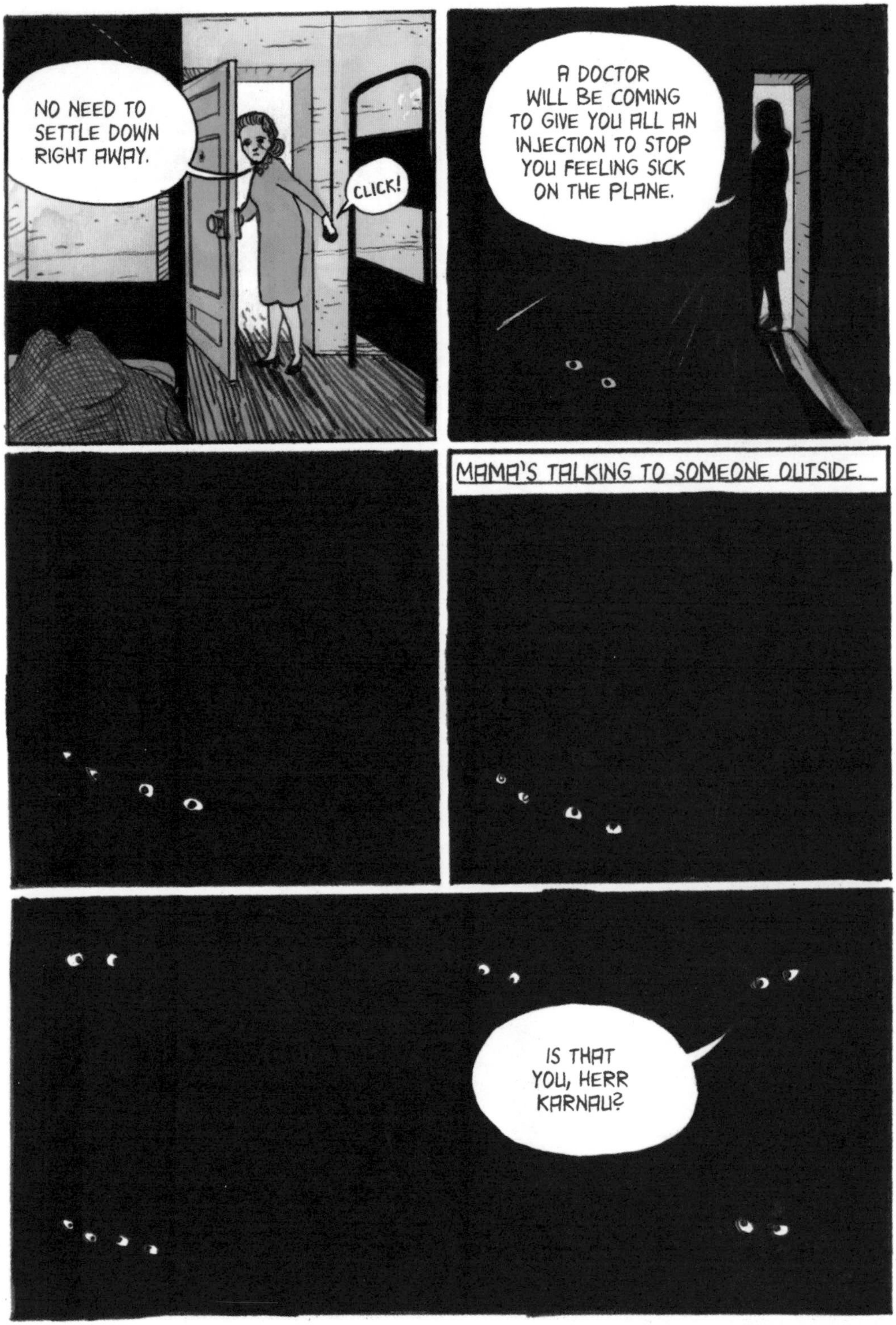
NO NEED TO SETTLE DOWN RIGHT AWAY.
CLICK!
A DOCTOR WILL BE COMING TO GIVE YOU ALL AN INJECTION TO STOP YOU FEELING SICK ON THE PLANE.
MAMA'S TALKING TO SOMEONE OUTSIDE.
IS THAT YOU, HERR KARNAU?

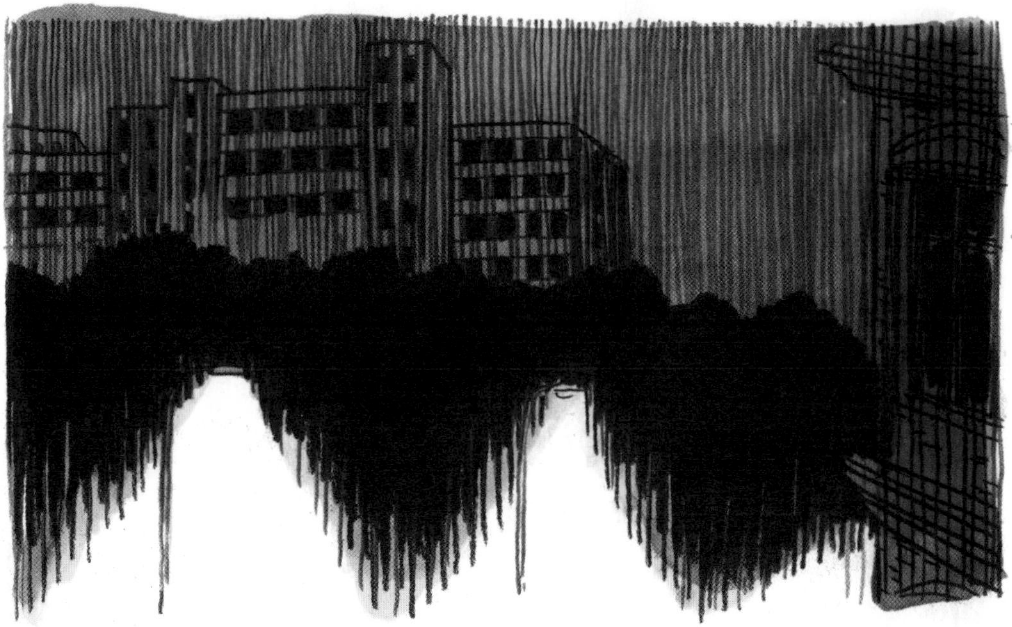

It's still dark.
Silence still reigns. Just the
six children's voices in my head.

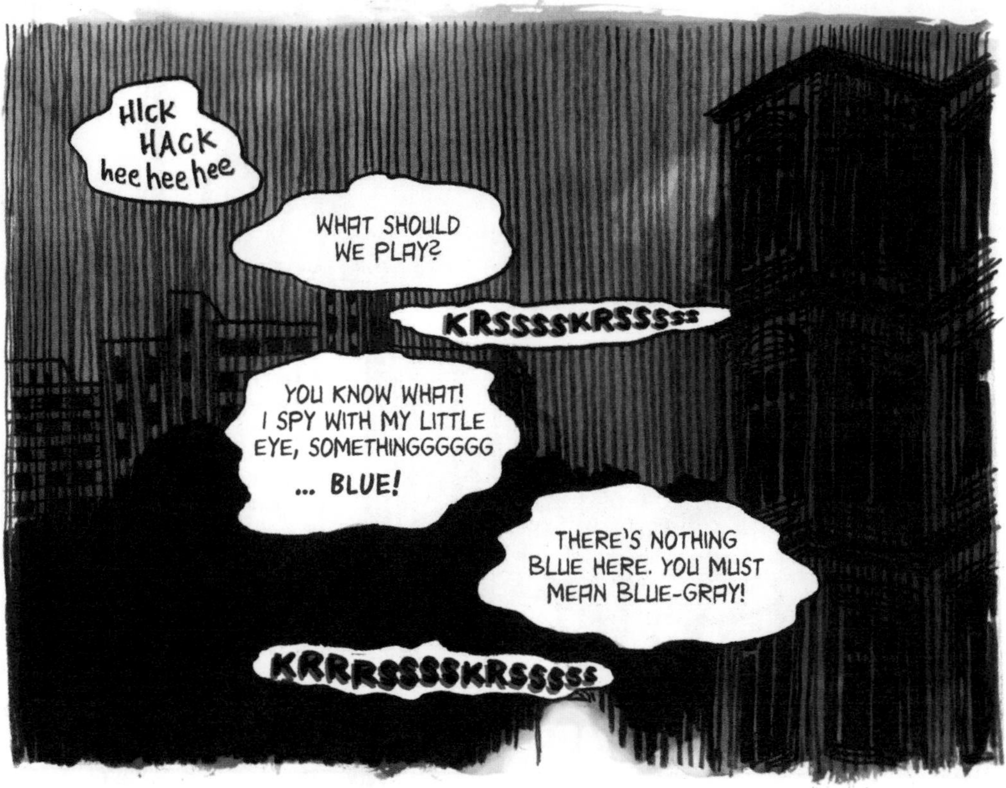

HICK HACK hee hee hee
WHAT SHOULD WE PLAY?
KRSSSSKRSSSss
YOU KNOW WHAT! I SPY WITH MY LITTLE EYE, SOMETHINGGGGGG ... BLUE!
THERE'S NOTHING BLUE HERE. YOU MUST MEAN BLUE-GRAY!
KRRRSSSSKRSSSSS

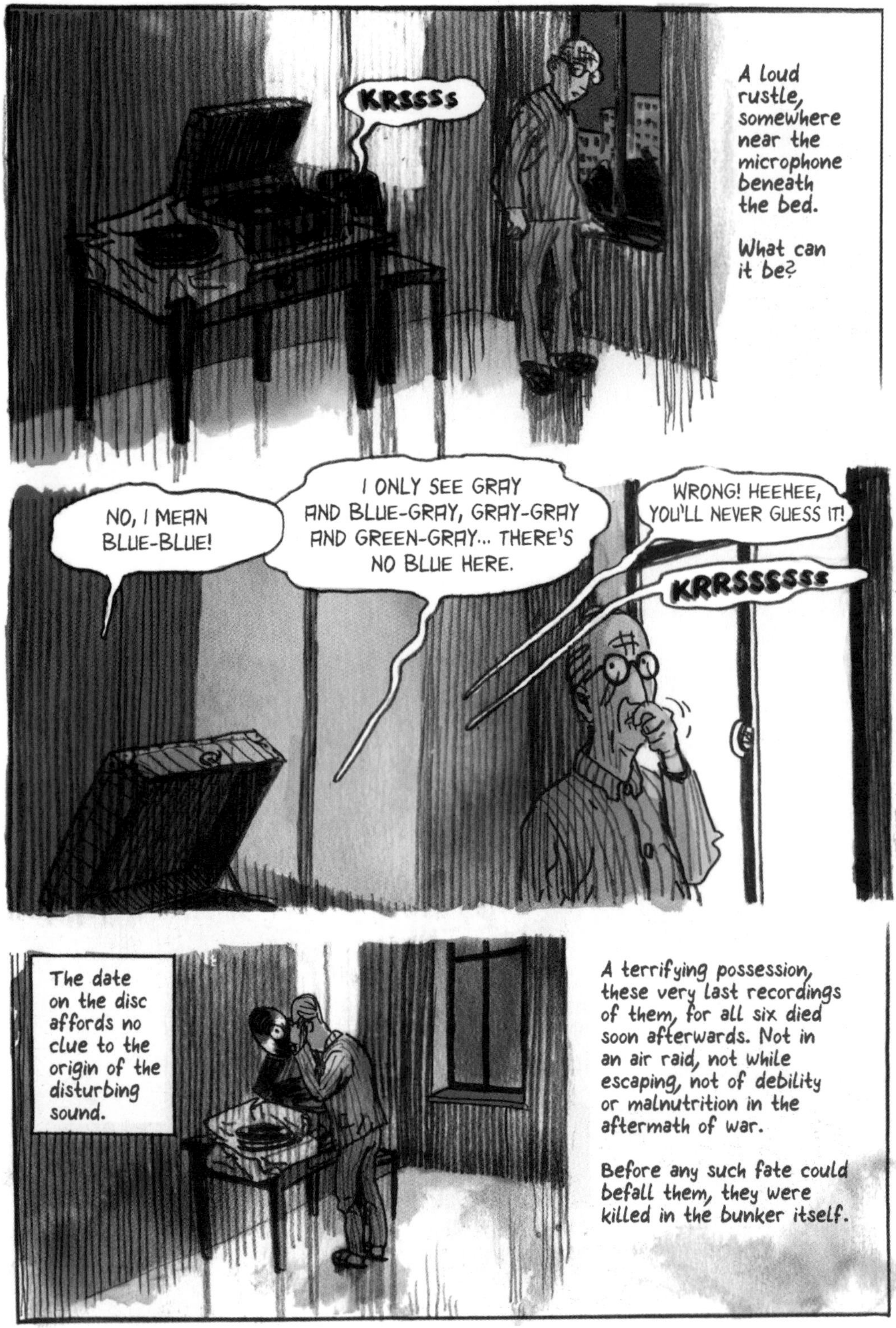
KRSSSS
A loud rustle, somewhere near the microphone beneath the bed.
What can it be?
NO, I MEAN BLUE-BLUE!
I ONLY SEE GRAY AND BLUE-GRAY, GRAY-GRAY AND GREEN-GRAY... THERE'S NO BLUE HERE.
WRONG! HEEHEE, YOU'LL NEVER GUESS IT!
KRRSSSSSS
The date on the disc affords no clue to the origin of the disturbing sound.
A terrifying possession, these very last recordings of them, for all six died soon afterwards. Not in an air raid, not while escaping, not of debility or malnutrition in the aftermath of war.
Before any such fate could befall them, they were killed in the bunker itself.

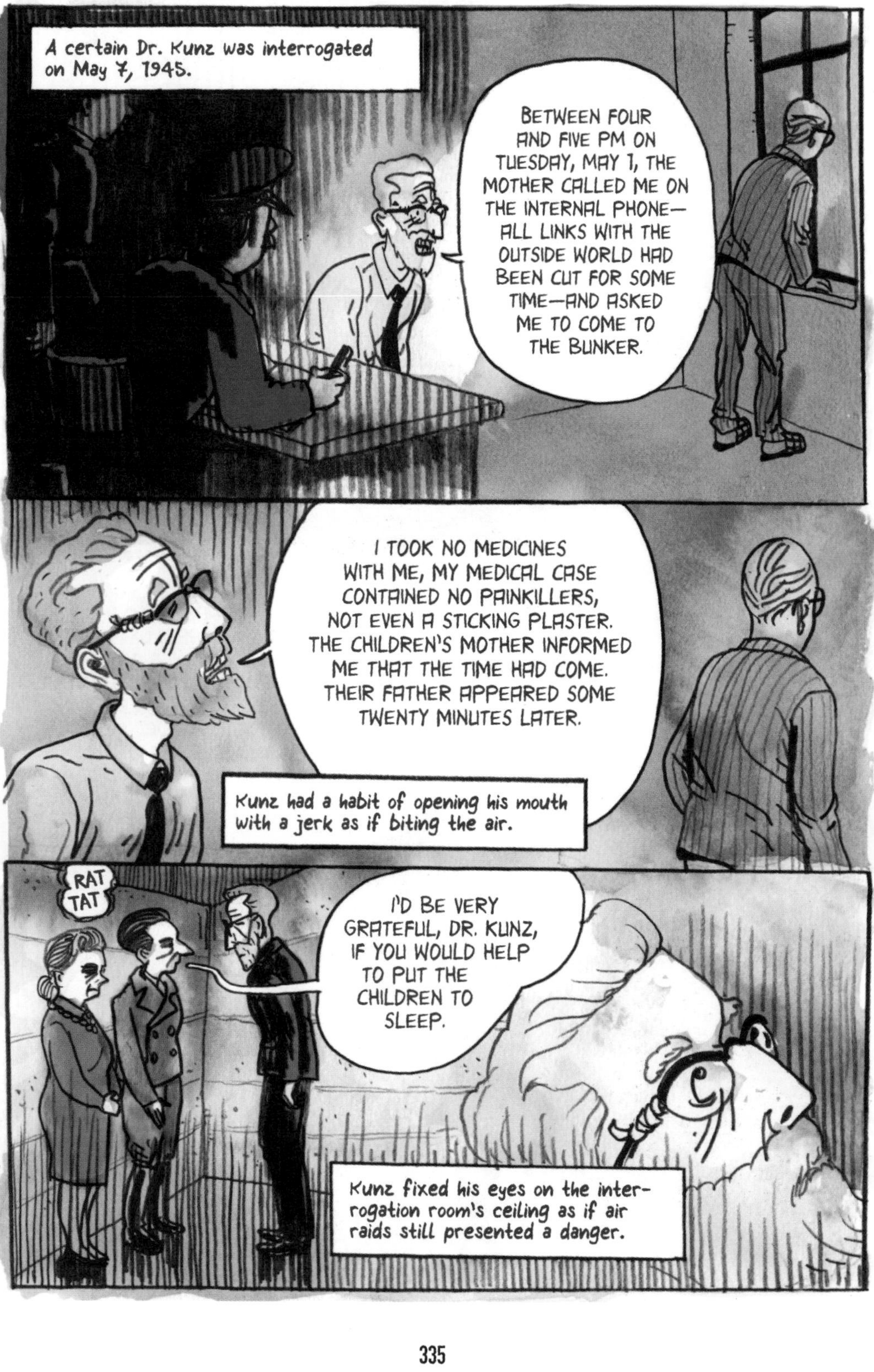
A certain Dr. Kunz was interrogated on May 7, 1945.
BETWEEN FOUR AND FIVE PM ON TUESDAY, MAY 1, THE MOTHER CALLED ME ON THE INTERNAL PHONE—ALL LINKS WITH THE OUTSIDE WORLD HAD BEEN CUT FOR SOME TIME—AND ASKED ME TO COME TO THE BUNKER.
I TOOK NO MEDICINES WITH ME, MY MEDICAL CASE CONTAINED NO PAINKILLERS, NOT EVEN A STICKING PLASTER. THE CHILDREN'S MOTHER INFORMED ME THAT THE TIME HAD COME. THEIR FATHER APPEARED SOME TWENTY MINUTES LATER.
Kunz had a habit of opening his mouth with a jerk as if biting the air.
RAT TAT
I'D BE VERY GRATEFUL, DR. KUNZ, IF YOU WOULD HELP TO PUT THE CHILDREN TO SLEEP.
Kunz fixed his eyes on the interrogation room's ceiling as if air raids still presented a danger.

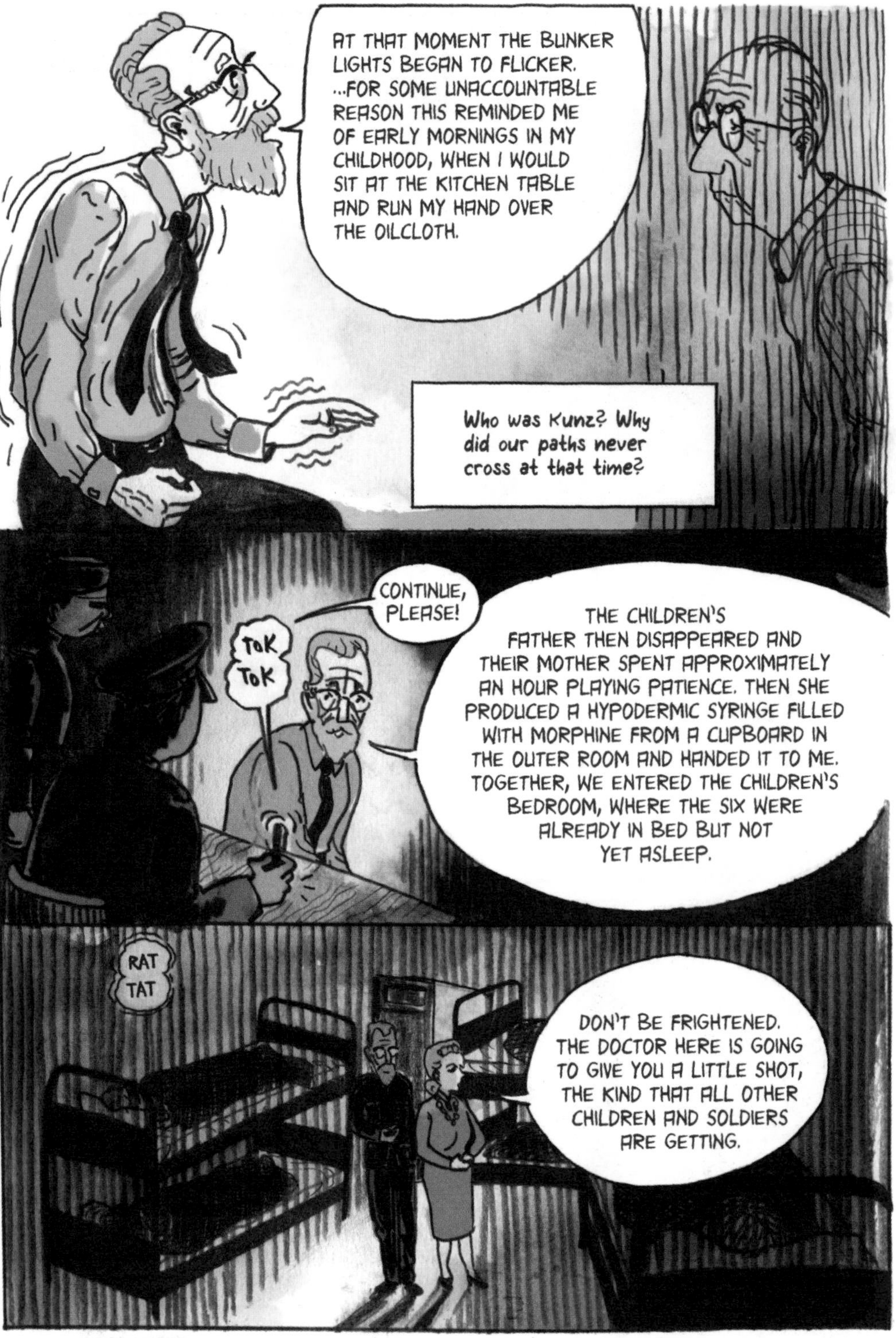
AT THAT MOMENT THE BUNKER LIGHTS BEGAN TO FLICKER. ...FOR SOME UNACCOUNTABLE REASON THIS REMINDED ME OF EARLY MORNINGS IN MY CHILDHOOD, WHEN I WOULD SIT AT THE KITCHEN TABLE AND RUN MY HAND OVER THE OILCLOTH.
Who was Kunz? Why did our paths never cross at that time?
CONTINUE, PLEASE!
TOK TOK
THE CHILDREN'S FATHER THEN DISAPPEARED AND THEIR MOTHER SPENT APPROXIMATELY AN HOUR PLAYING PATIENCE. THEN SHE PRODUCED A HYPODERMIC SYRINGE FILLED WITH MORPHINE FROM A CUPBOARD IN THE OUTER ROOM AND HANDED IT TO ME. TOGETHER, WE ENTERED THE CHILDREN'S BEDROOM, WHERE THE SIX WERE ALREADY IN BED BUT NOT YET ASLEEP.
RAT TAT
DON'T BE FRIGHTENED. THE DOCTOR HERE IS GOING TO GIVE YOU A LITTLE SHOT, THE KIND THAT ALL OTHER CHILDREN AND SOLDIERS ARE GETTING.

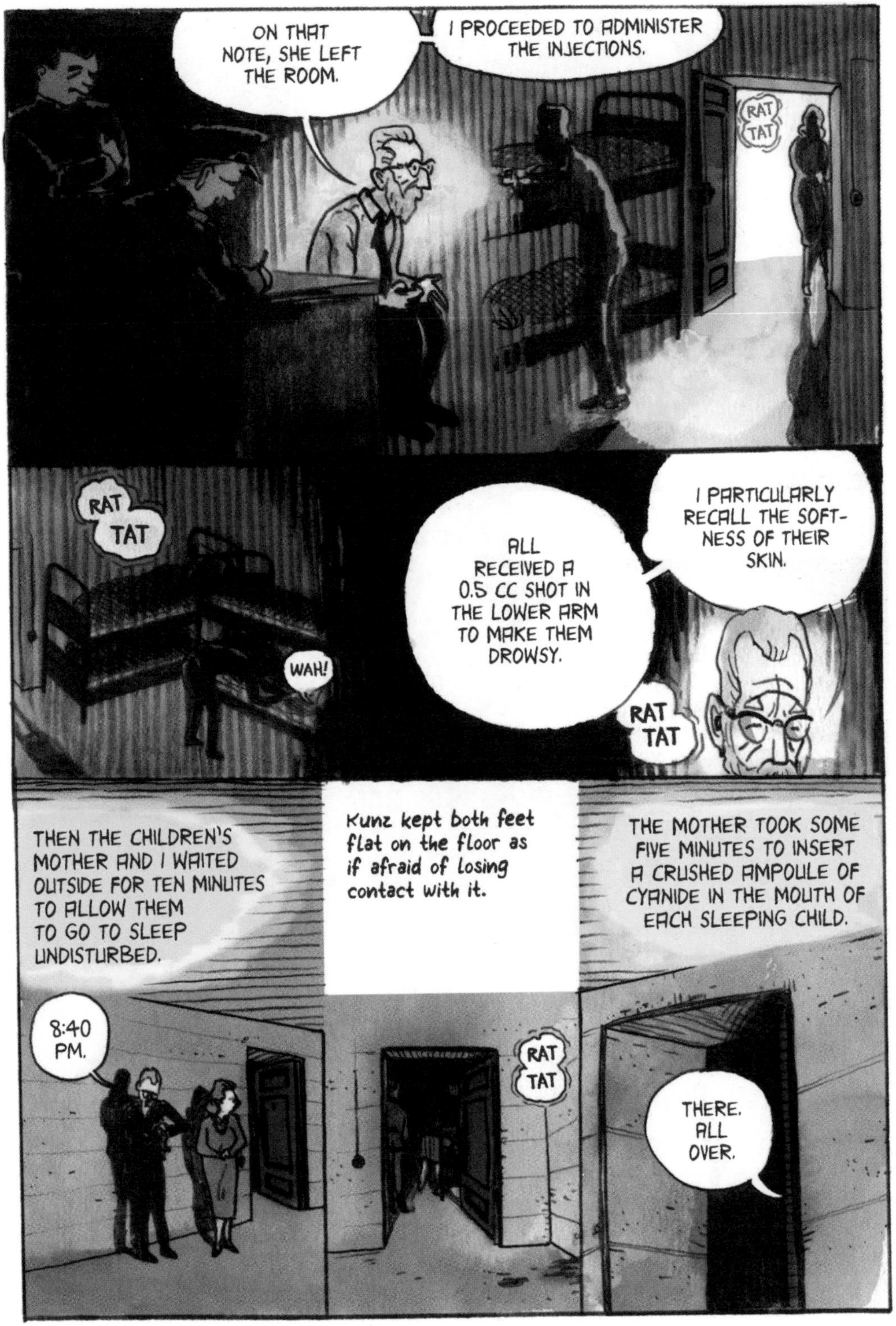
ON THAT NOTE, SHE LEFT THE ROOM.
I PROCEEDED TO ADMINISTER THE INJECTIONS.
RAT TAT
RAT TAT
WAH!
ALL RECEIVED A 0.5 CC SHOT IN THE LOWER ARM TO MAKE THEM DROWSY.
I PARTICULARLY RECALL THE SOFTNESS OF THEIR SKIN.
RAT TAT
THEN THE CHILDREN'S MOTHER AND I WAITED OUTSIDE FOR TEN MINUTES TO ALLOW THEM TO GO TO SLEEP UNDISTURBED.
8:40 PM.
Kunz kept both feet flat on the floor as if afraid of losing contact with it.
RAT TAT
THE MOTHER TOOK SOME FIVE MINUTES TO INSERT A CRUSHED AMPOULE OF CYANIDE IN THE MOUTH OF EACH SLEEPING CHILD.
THERE. ALL OVER.

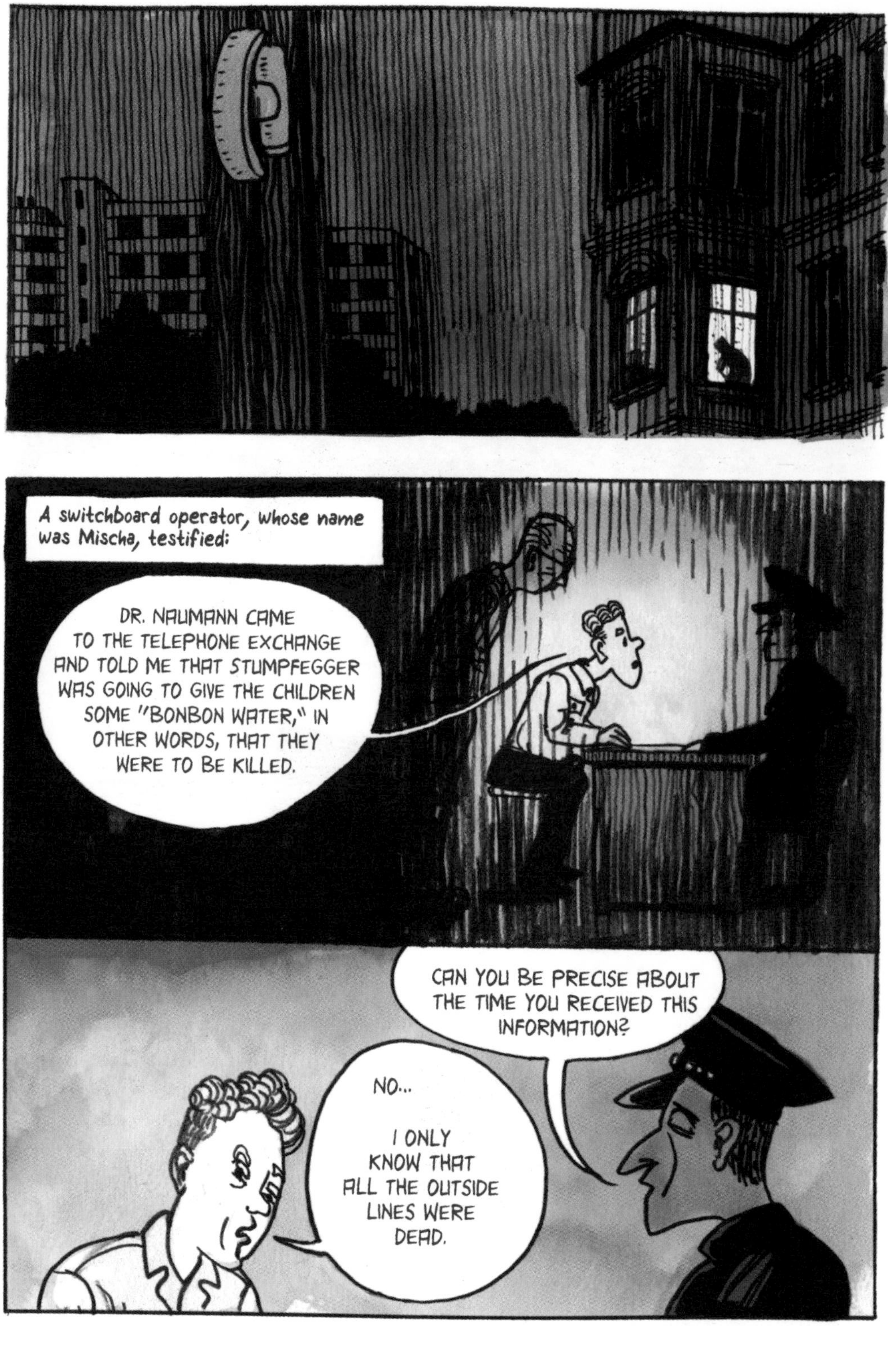
A switchboard operator, whose name was Mischa, testified:
DR. NAUMANN CAME TO THE TELEPHONE EXCHANGE AND TOLD ME THAT STUMPFEGGER WAS GOING TO GIVE THE CHILDREN SOME "BONBON WATER," IN OTHER WORDS, THAT THEY WERE TO BE KILLED.
CAN YOU BE PRECISE ABOUT THE TIME YOU RECEIVED THIS INFORMATION?
NO...
I ONLY KNOW THAT ALL THE OUTSIDE LINES WERE DEAD.

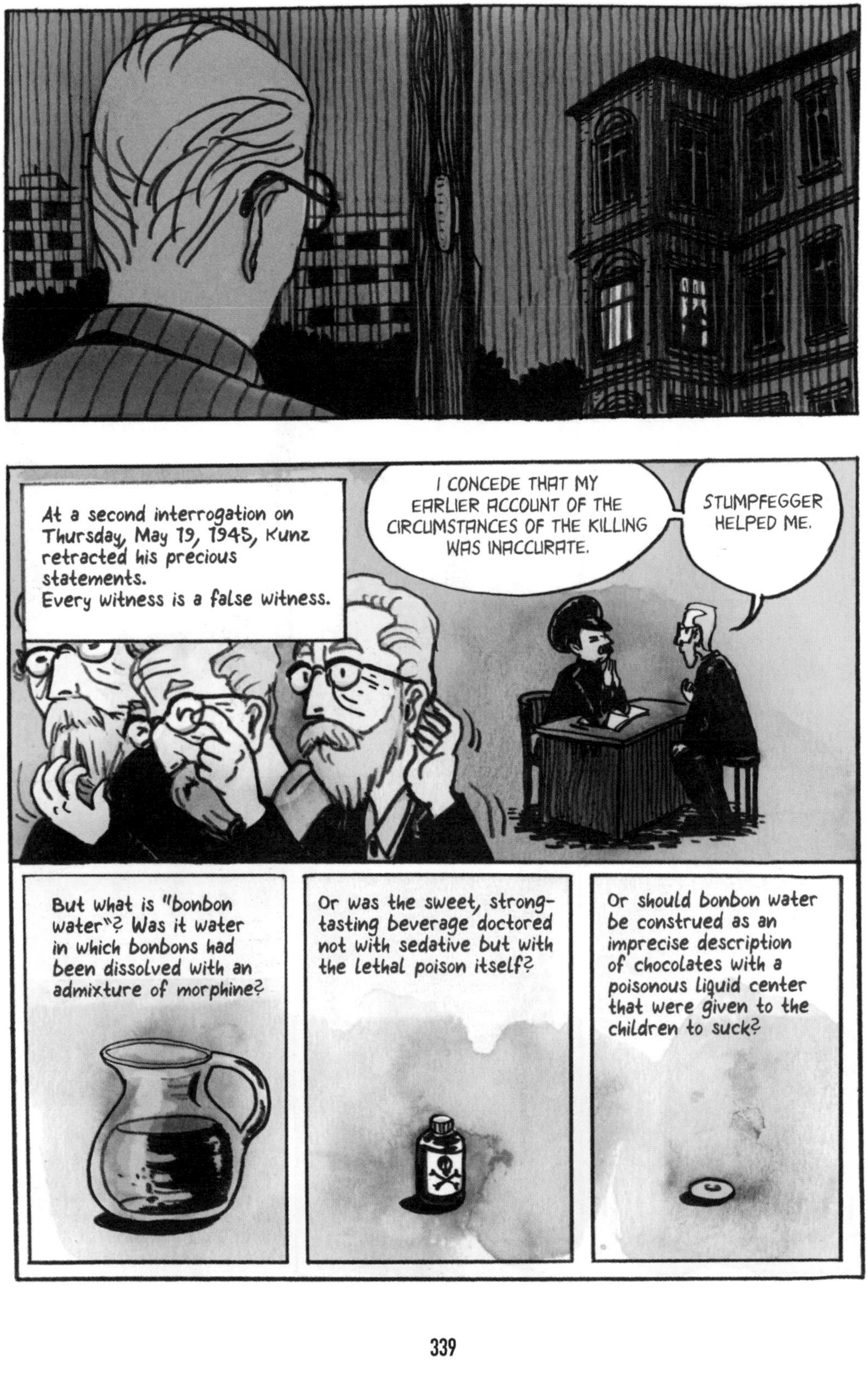
At a second interrogation on Thursday, May 19, 1945, Kunz retracted his precious statements.
Every witness is a false witness.
I CONCEDE THAT MY EARLIER ACCOUNT OF THE CIRCUMSTANCES OF THE KILLING WAS INACCURATE.
STUMPFEGGER HELPED ME.
But what is "bonbon water"? Was it water in which bonbons had been dissolved with an admixture of morphine?
Or was the sweet, strong-tasting beverage doctored not with sedative but with the lethal poison itself?
Or should bonbon water be construed as an imprecise description of chocolates with a poisonous liquid center that were given to the children to suck?

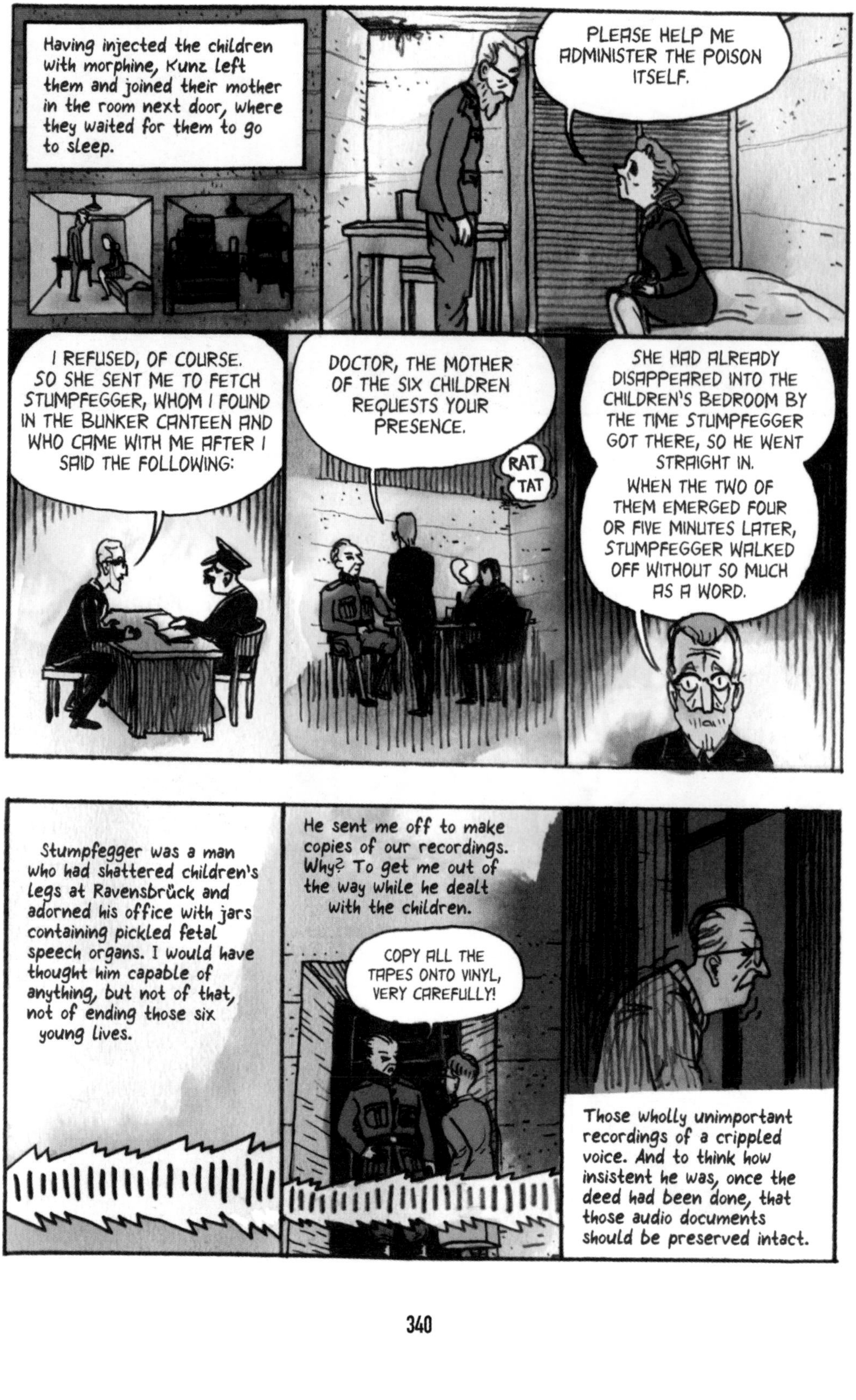
Having injected the children with morphine, Kunz left them and joined their mother in the room next door, where they waited for them to go to sleep.
PLEASE HELP ME ADMINISTER THE POISON ITSELF.
I REFUSED, OF COURSE. SO SHE SENT ME TO FETCH STUMPFEGGER, WHOM I FOUND IN THE BUNKER CANTEEN AND WHO CAME WITH ME AFTER I SAID THE FOLLOWING:
DOCTOR, THE MOTHER OF THE SIX CHILDREN REQUESTS YOUR PRESENCE.
RAT
TAT
SHE HAD ALREADY DISAPPEARED INTO THE CHILDREN'S BEDROOM BY THE TIME STUMPFEGGER GOT THERE, SO HE WENT STRAIGHT IN.
WHEN THE TWO OF THEM EMERGED FOUR OR FIVE MINUTES LATER, STUMPFEGGER WALKED OFF WITHOUT SO MUCH AS A WORD.
Stumpfegger was a man who had shattered children's legs at Ravensbrück and adorned his office with jars containing pickled fetal speech organs. I would have thought him capable of anything, but not of that, not of ending those six young lives.
He sent me off to make copies of our recordings. Why? To get me out of the way while he dealt with the children.
COPY ALL THE TAPES ONTO VINYL, VERY CAREFULLY!
Those wholly unimportant recordings of a crippled voice. And to think how insistent he was, once the deed had been done, that those audio documents should be preserved intact.

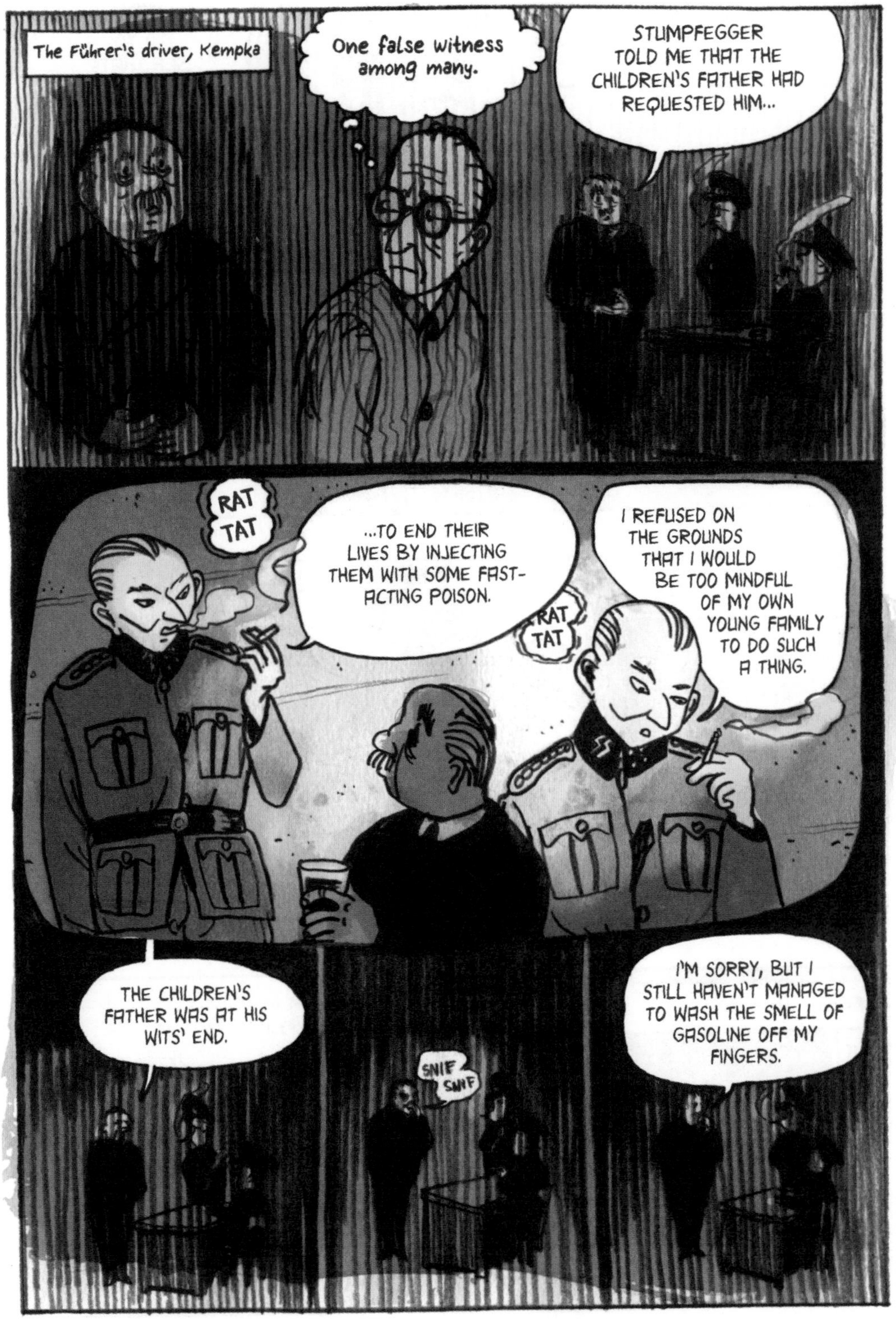
The Führer's driver, Kempka
One false witness among many.
STUMPFEGGER TOLD ME THAT THE CHILDREN'S FATHER HAD REQUESTED HIM...
RAT TAT
...TO END THEIR LIVES BY INJECTING THEM WITH SOME FAST-ACTING POISON.
RAT TAT
I REFUSED ON THE GROUNDS THAT I WOULD BE TOO MINDFUL OF MY OWN YOUNG FAMILY TO DO SUCH A THING.
THE CHILDREN'S FATHER WAS AT HIS WITS' END.
SNIF SNIF
I'M SORRY, BUT I STILL HAVEN'T MANAGED TO WASH THE SMELL OF GASOLINE OFF MY FINGERS.

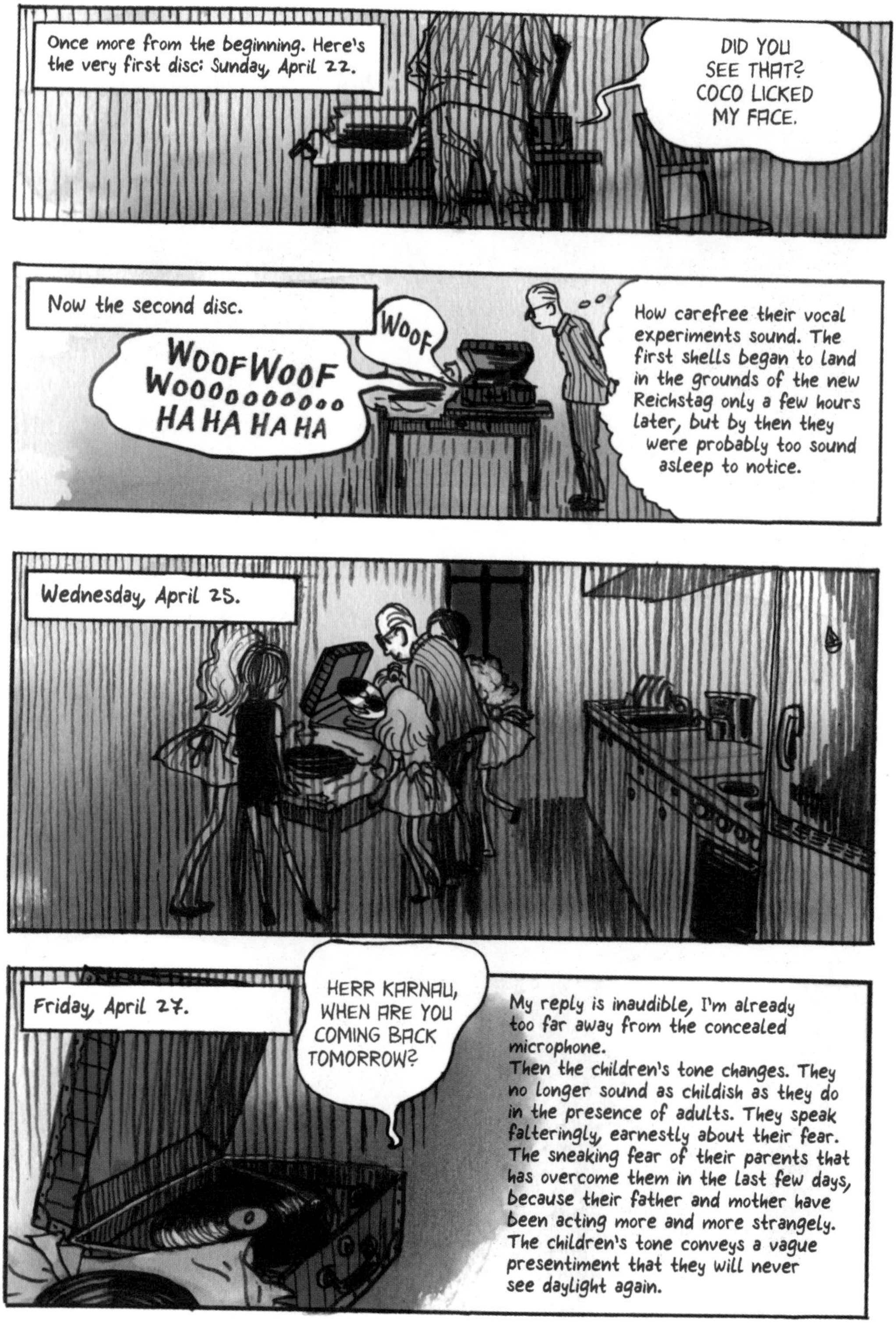

Once more from the beginning. Here's the very first disc: Sunday, April 22.
DID YOU SEE THAT? COCO LICKED MY FACE.
Now the second disc.
WOOF
WOOFWOOF WOOOOOOOOOO HA HA HA HA
How carefree their vocal experiments sound. The first shells began to land in the grounds of the new Reichstag only a few hours later, but by then they were probably too sound asleep to notice.
Wednesday, April 25.
Friday, April 27.
HERR KARNAU, WHEN ARE YOU COMING BACK TOMORROW?
My reply is inaudible, I'm already too far away from the concealed microphone.
Then the children's tone changes. They no longer sound as childish as they do in the presence of adults. They speak falteringly, earnestly about their fear. The sneaking fear of their parents that has overcome them in the last few days, because their father and mother have been acting more and more strangely. The children's tone conveys a vague presentiment that they will never see daylight again.

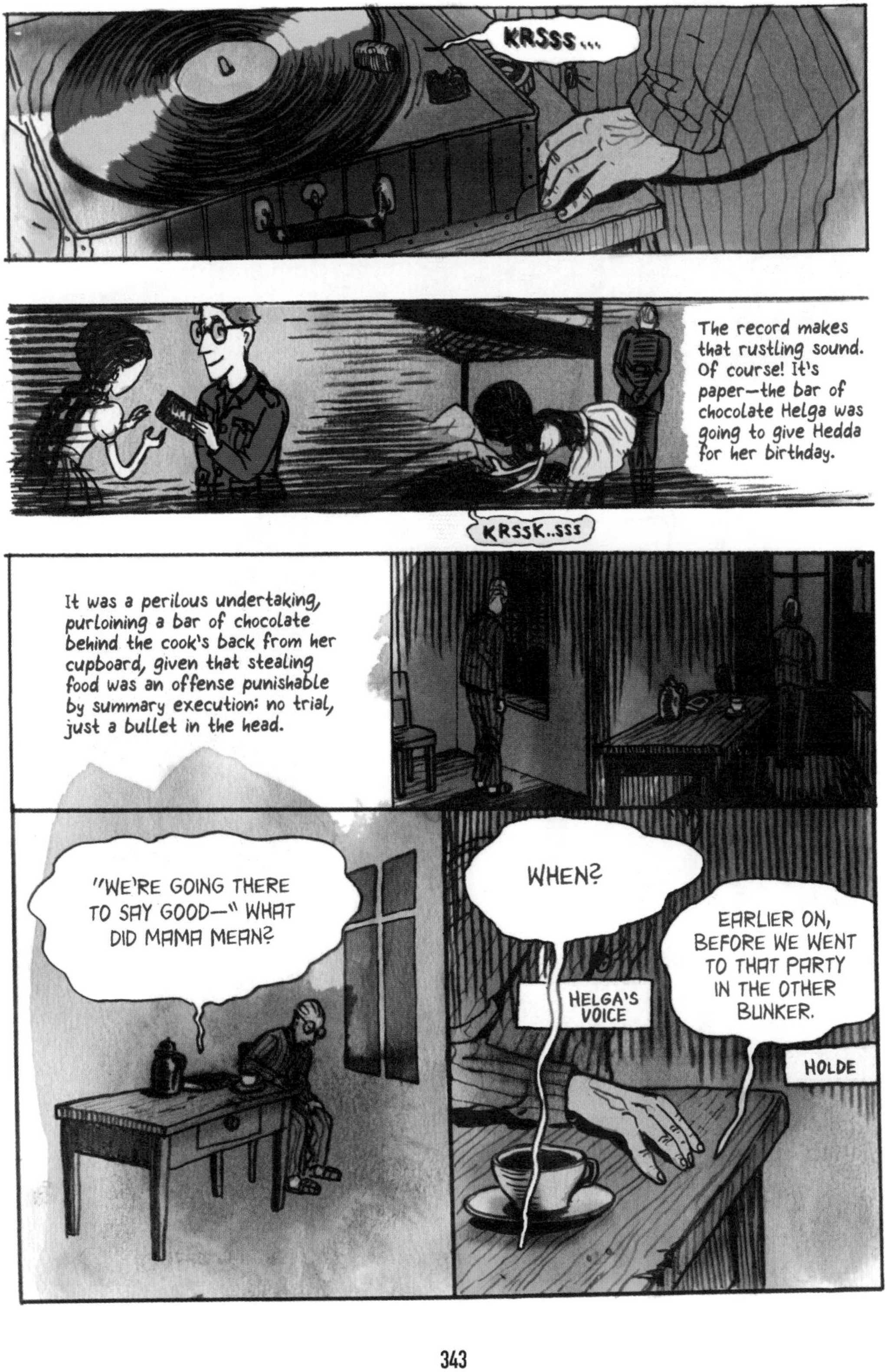
KRSSS...
The record makes that rustling sound. Of course! It's paper—the bar of chocolate Helga was going to give Hedda for her birthday.
KRSSK..SSS
It was a perilous undertaking, purloining a bar of chocolate behind the cook's back from her cupboard, given that stealing food was an offense punishable by summary execution: no trial, just a bullet in the head.
"WE'RE GOING THERE TO SAY GOOD—" WHAT DID MAMA MEAN?
WHEN?
HELGA'S VOICE
EARLIER ON, BEFORE WE WENT TO THAT PARTY IN THE OTHER BUNKER.
HOLDE

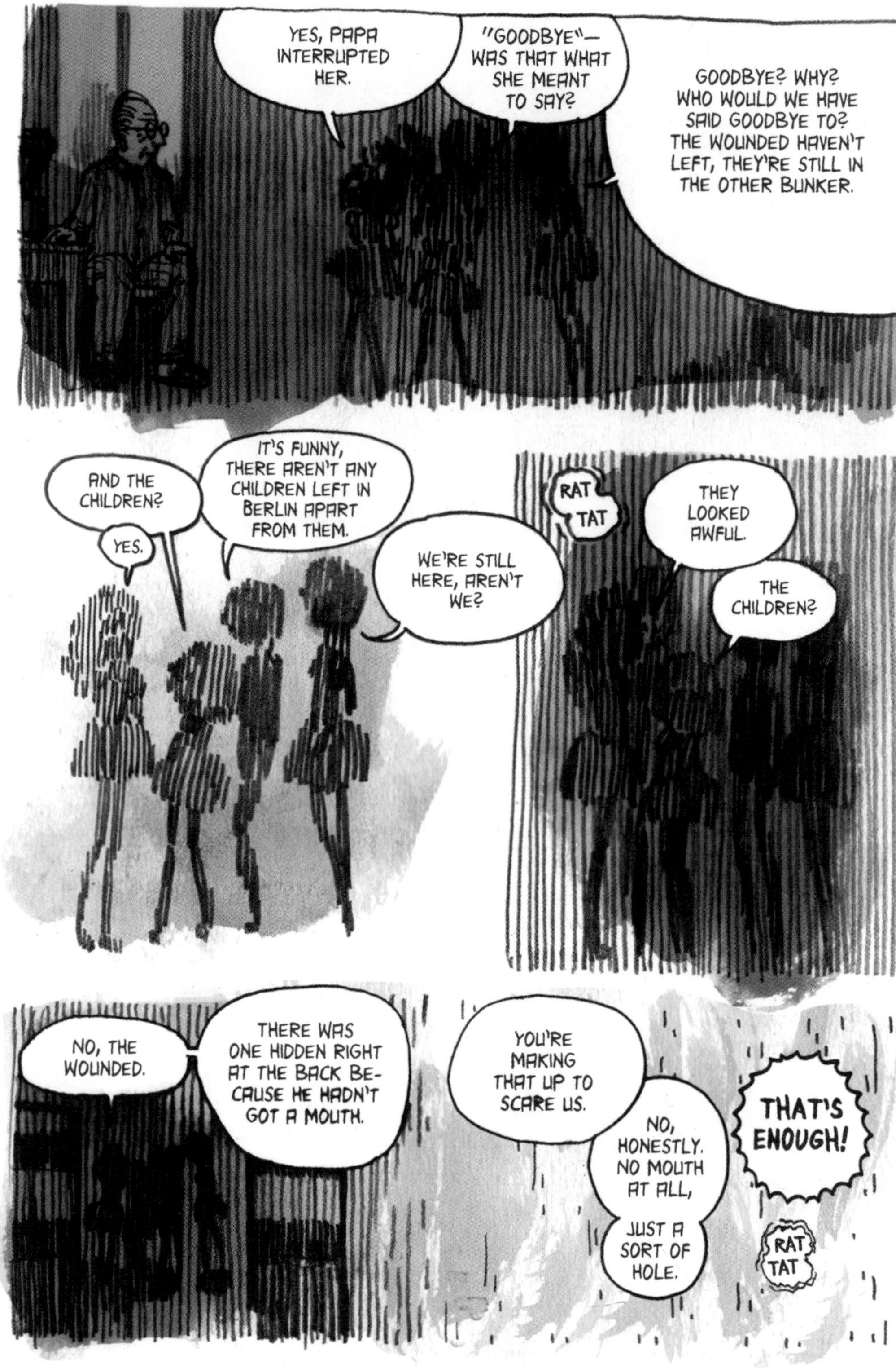
YES, PAPA INTERRUPTED HER.
"GOODBYE"— WAS THAT WHAT SHE MEANT TO SAY?
GOODBYE? WHY? WHO WOULD WE HAVE SAID GOODBYE TO? THE WOUNDED HAVEN'T LEFT, THEY'RE STILL IN THE OTHER BUNKER.
AND THE CHILDREN?
YES.
IT'S FUNNY, THERE AREN'T ANY CHILDREN LEFT IN BERLIN APART FROM THEM.
WE'RE STILL HERE, AREN'T WE?
RAT TAT
THEY LOOKED AWFUL.
THE CHILDREN?
NO, THE WOUNDED.
THERE WAS ONE HIDDEN RIGHT AT THE BACK BE-CAUSE HE HADN'T GOT A MOUTH.
YOU'RE MAKING THAT UP TO SCARE US.
NO, HONESTLY. NO MOUTH AT ALL,
JUST A SORT OF HOLE.
THAT'S ENOUGH!
RAT TAT

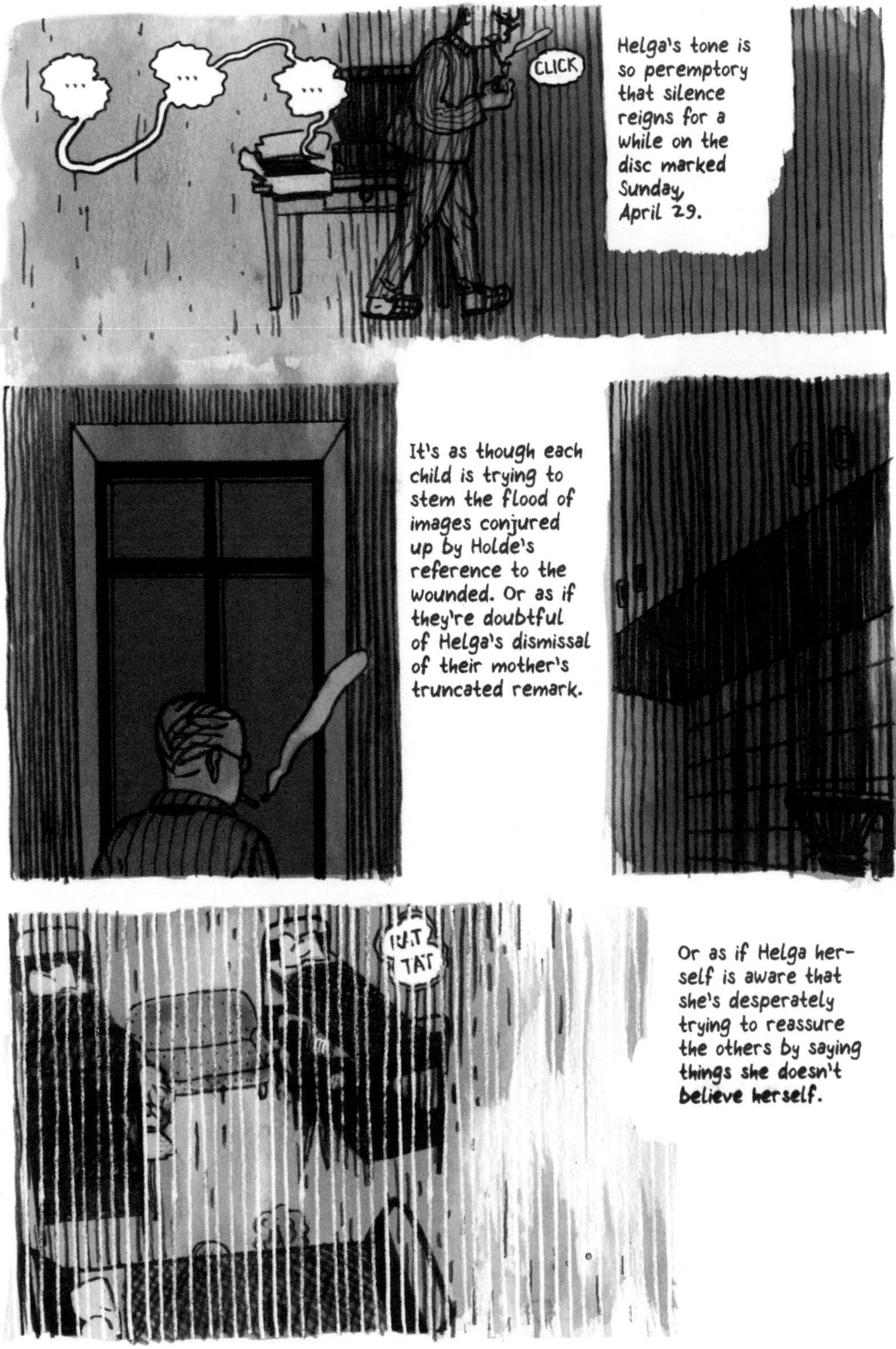
...
...
...
CLICK
Helga's tone is so peremptory that silence reigns for a while on the disc marked Sunday, April 29.
It's as though each child is trying to stem the flood of images conjured up by Holde's reference to the wounded. Or as if they're doubtful of Helga's dismissal of their mother's truncated remark.
TAT TAT
Or as if Helga herself is aware that she's desperately trying to reassure the others by saying things she doesn't believe herself.

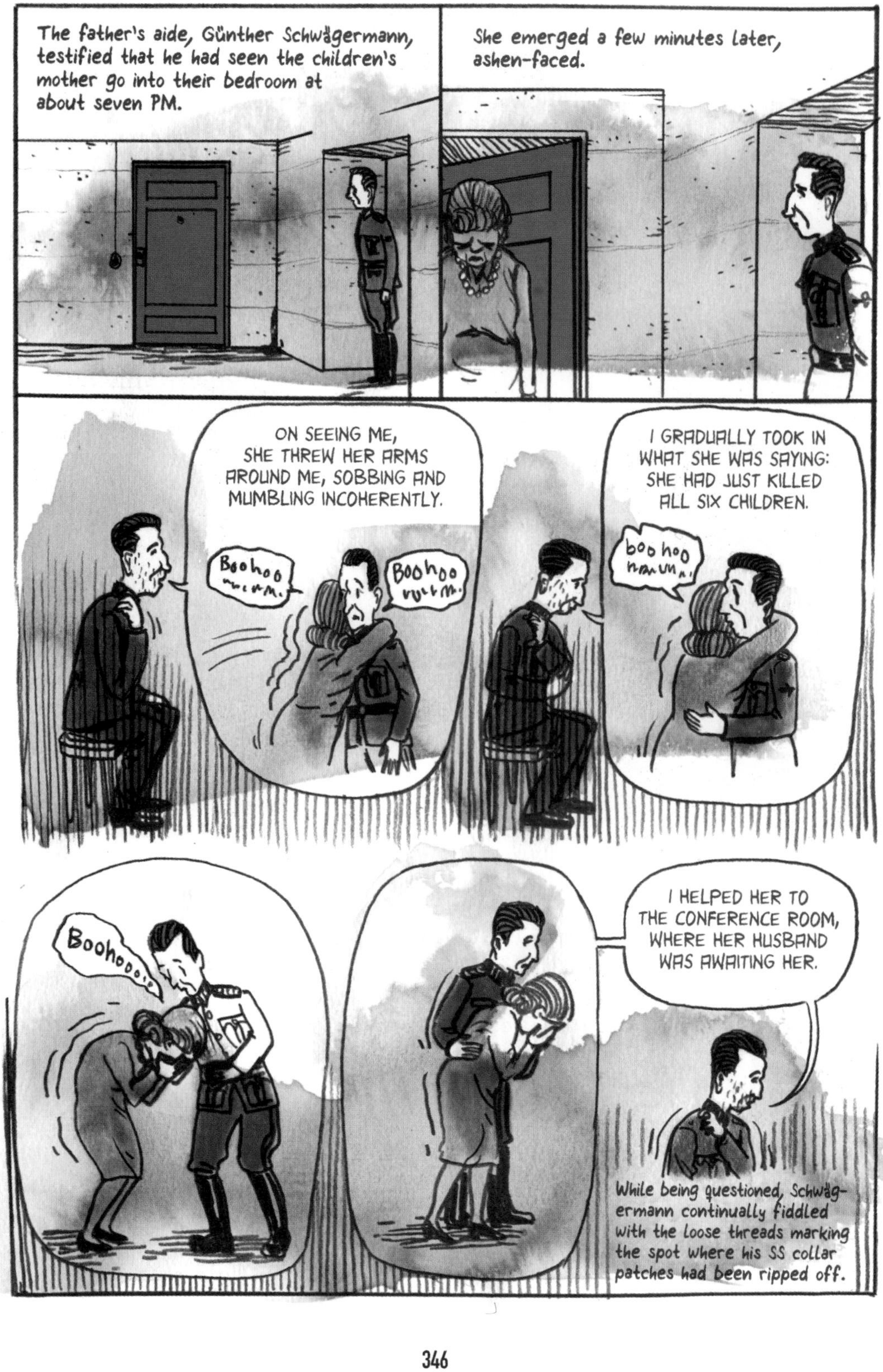
The father's aide, Günther Schwägermann, testified that he had seen the children's mother go into their bedroom at about seven PM.
She emerged a few minutes later, ashen-faced.
ON SEEING ME, SHE THREW HER ARMS AROUND ME, SOBBING AND MUMBLING INCOHERENTLY.
Boohoo
Boohoo
I GRADUALLY TOOK IN WHAT SHE WAS SAYING: SHE HAD JUST KILLED ALL SIX CHILDREN.
boohoo
Boohoooo
I HELPED HER TO THE CONFERENCE ROOM, WHERE HER HUSBAND WAS AWAITING HER.
While being questioned, Schwägermann continually fiddled with the loose threads marking the spot where his SS collar patches had been ripped off.

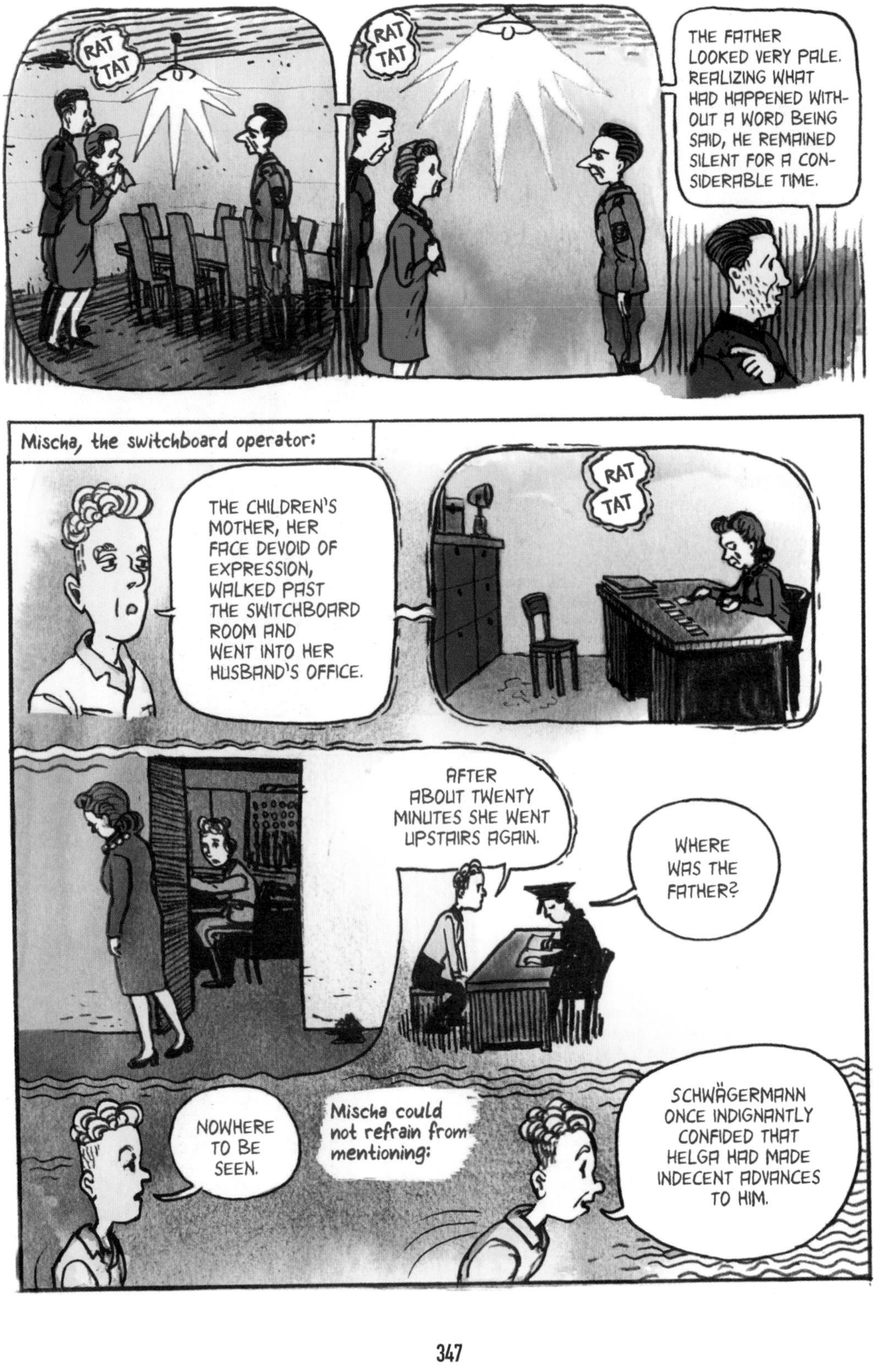

RAT TAT
RAT TAT
THE FATHER LOOKED VERY PALE. REALIZING WHAT HAD HAPPENED WITHOUT A WORD BEING SAID, HE REMAINED SILENT FOR A CONSIDERABLE TIME.
Mischa, the switchboard operator:
THE CHILDREN'S MOTHER, HER FACE DEVOID OF EXPRESSION, WALKED PAST THE SWITCHBOARD ROOM AND WENT INTO HER HUSBAND'S OFFICE.
RAT TAT
AFTER ABOUT TWENTY MINUTES SHE WENT UPSTAIRS AGAIN.
WHERE WAS THE FATHER?
NOWHERE TO BE SEEN.
Mischa could not refrain from mentioning:
SCHWÄGERMANN ONCE INDIGNANTLY CONFIDED THAT HELGA HAD MADE INDECENT ADVANCES TO HIM.

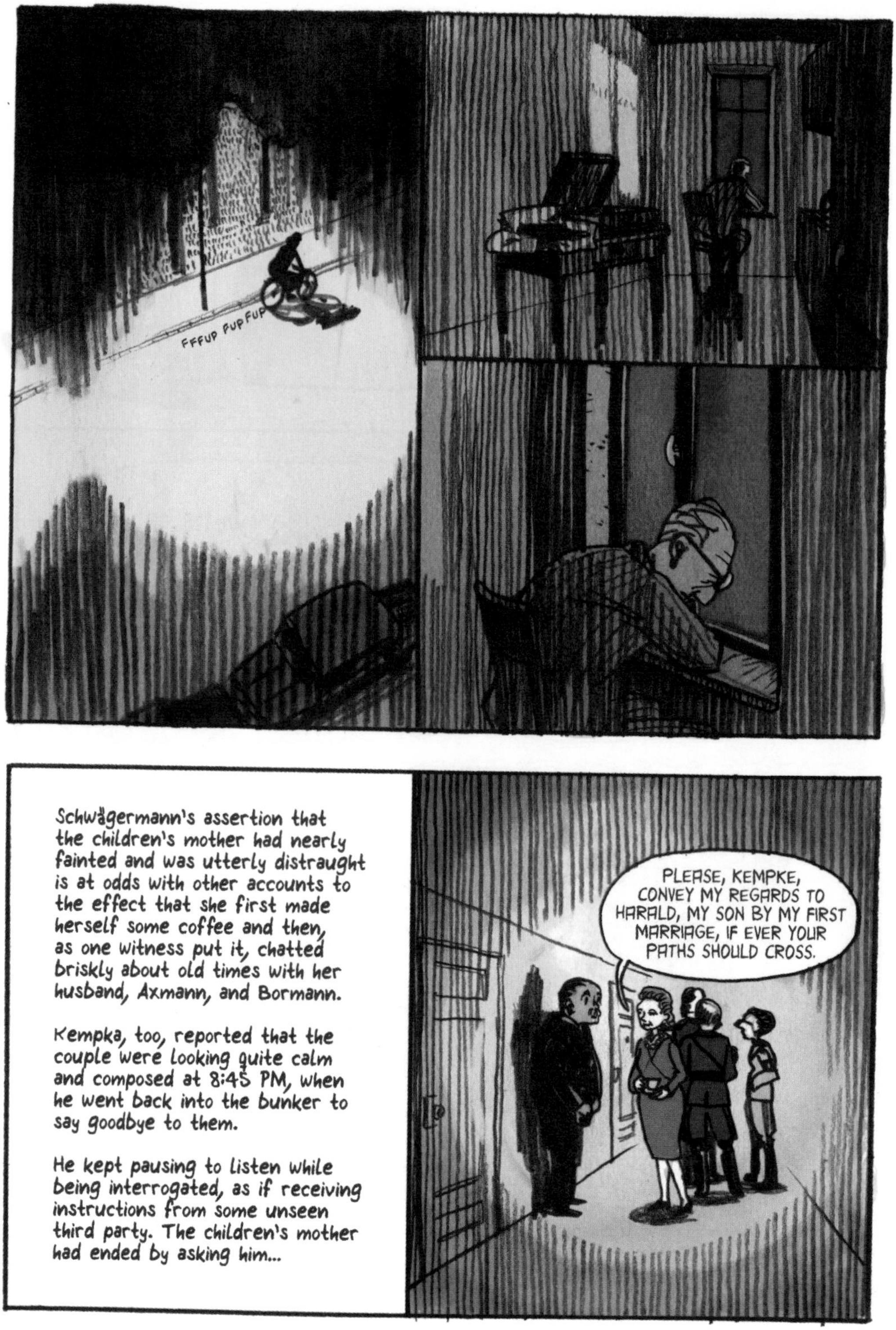
FFFUP FUP FUP
Schwägermann's assertion that the children's mother had nearly fainted and was utterly distraught is at odds with other accounts to the effect that she first made herself some coffee and then, as one witness put it, chatted briskly about old times with her husband, Axmann, and Bormann.
Kempka, too, reported that the couple were looking quite calm and composed at 8:45 PM, when he went back into the bunker to say goodbye to them.
He kept pausing to listen while being interrogated, as if receiving instructions from some unseen third party. The children's mother had ended by asking him...
PLEASE, KEMPKE, CONVEY MY REGARDS TO HARALD, MY SON BY MY FIRST MARRIAGE, IF EVER YOUR PATHS SHOULD CROSS.

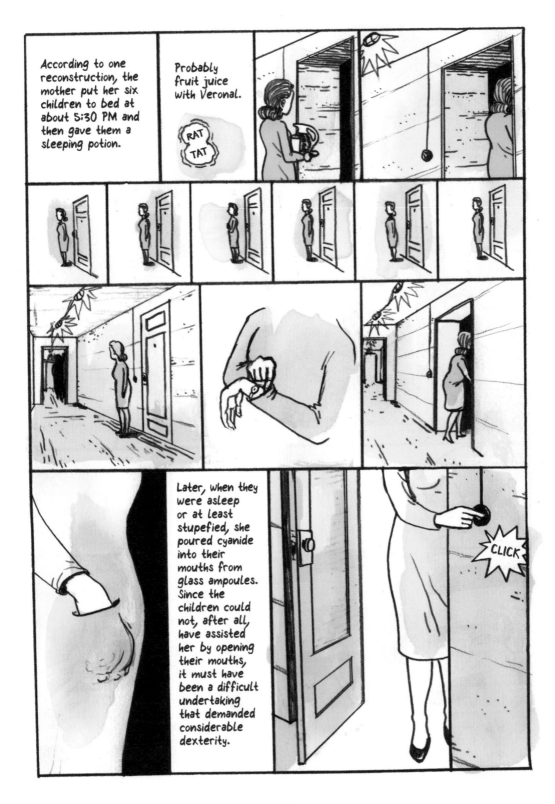

According to one reconstruction, the mother put her six children to bed at about 5:30 PM and then gave them a sleeping potion.

Probably fruit juice with Veronal.

RAT TAT

Later, when they were asleep or at least stupefied, she poured cyanide into their mouths from glass ampoules. Since the children could not, after all, have assisted her by opening their mouths, it must have been a difficult undertaking that demanded considerable dexterity.

CLICK

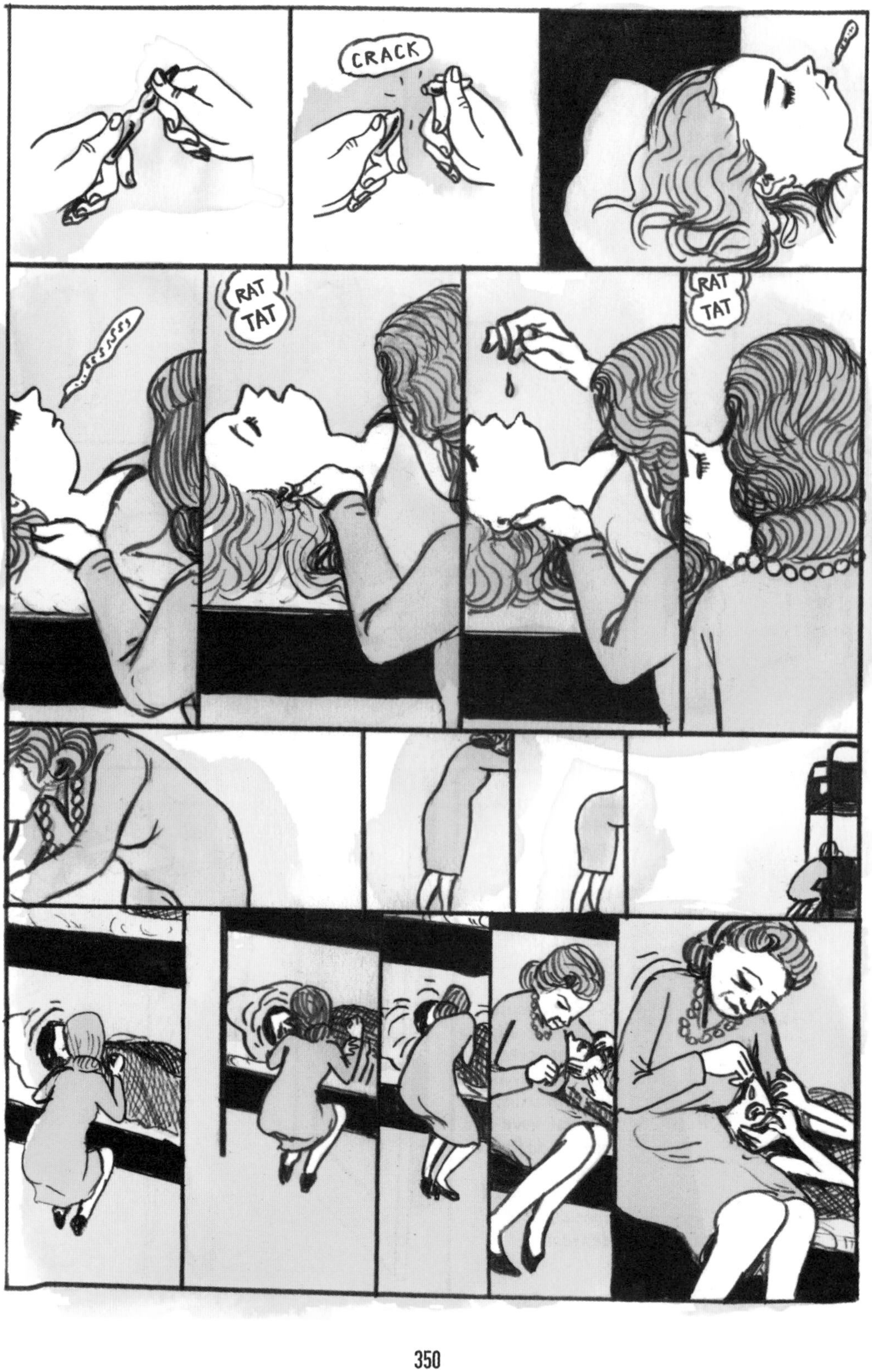
CRACK
RAT TAT
RAT TAT

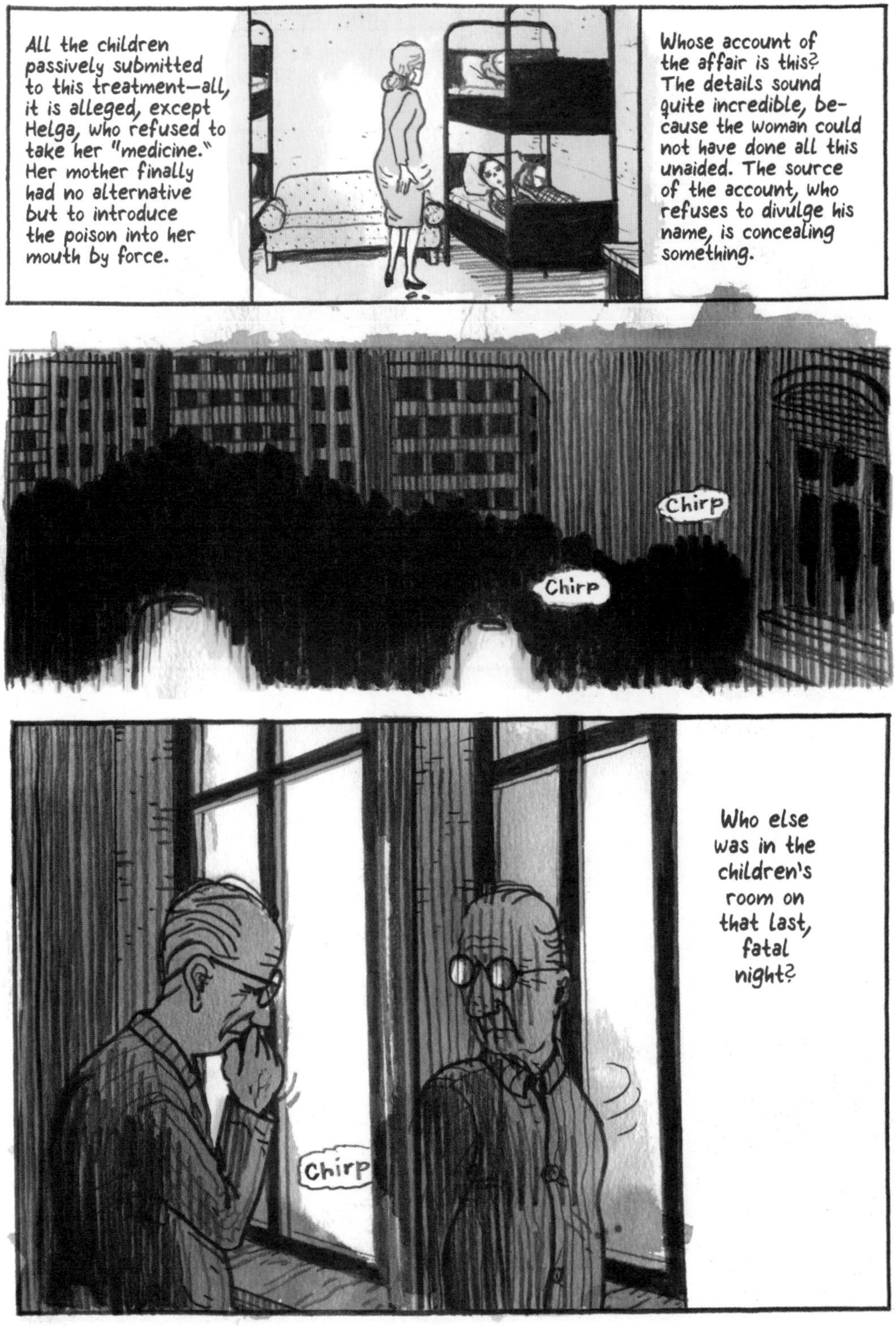
All the children passively submitted to this treatment—all, it is alleged, except Helga, who refused to take her "medicine." Her mother finally had no alternative but to introduce the poison into her mouth by force.
Whose account of the affair is this? The details sound quite incredible, because the woman could not have done all this unaided. The source of the account, who refuses to divulge his name, is concealing something.
Chirp
Chirp
Who else was in the children's room on that last, fatal night?
Chirp

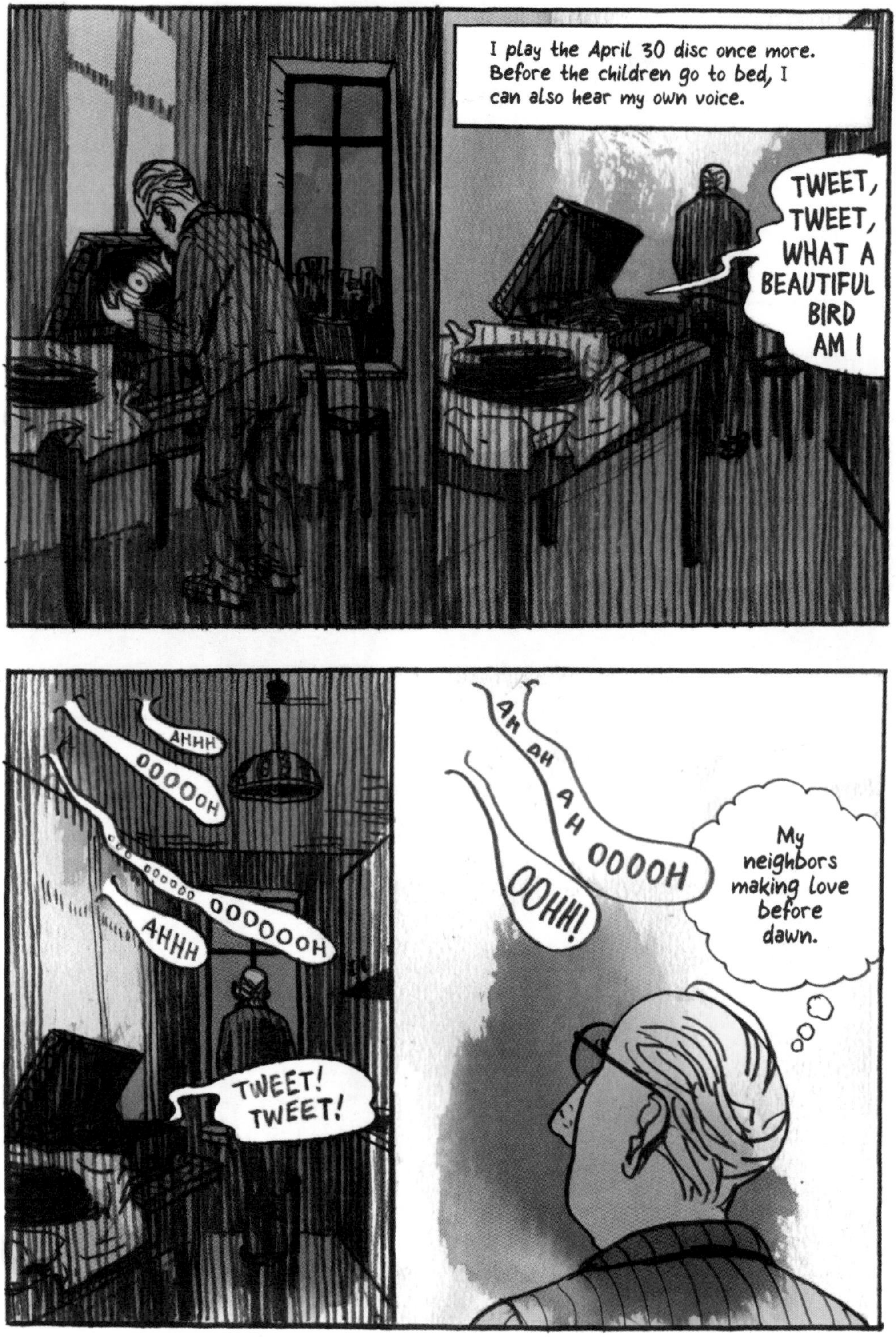
I play the April 30 disc once more. Before the children go to bed, I can also hear my own voice.
TWEET, TWEET, WHAT A BEAUTIFUL BIRD AM I
AHHH
OOOOOH
OOOOOOH
AHHH
TWEET! TWEET!
AH AH AH OOOOH
OOHH!
My neighbors making love before dawn.

The six children, all wearing light night attire, were discovered in their bunks in a separate room in the bunker of the Reich Chancellery, which has since been razed to the ground.

Also buried there, crushed by shattered concrete and mingled with the soil, are the remains of a bar of chocolate.

To enable them to be identified by persons closely acquainted with them, their bodies were removed to the Berlin-Buch headquarters of the Smersh Section of the Red Army's 79th Rifle Corps.

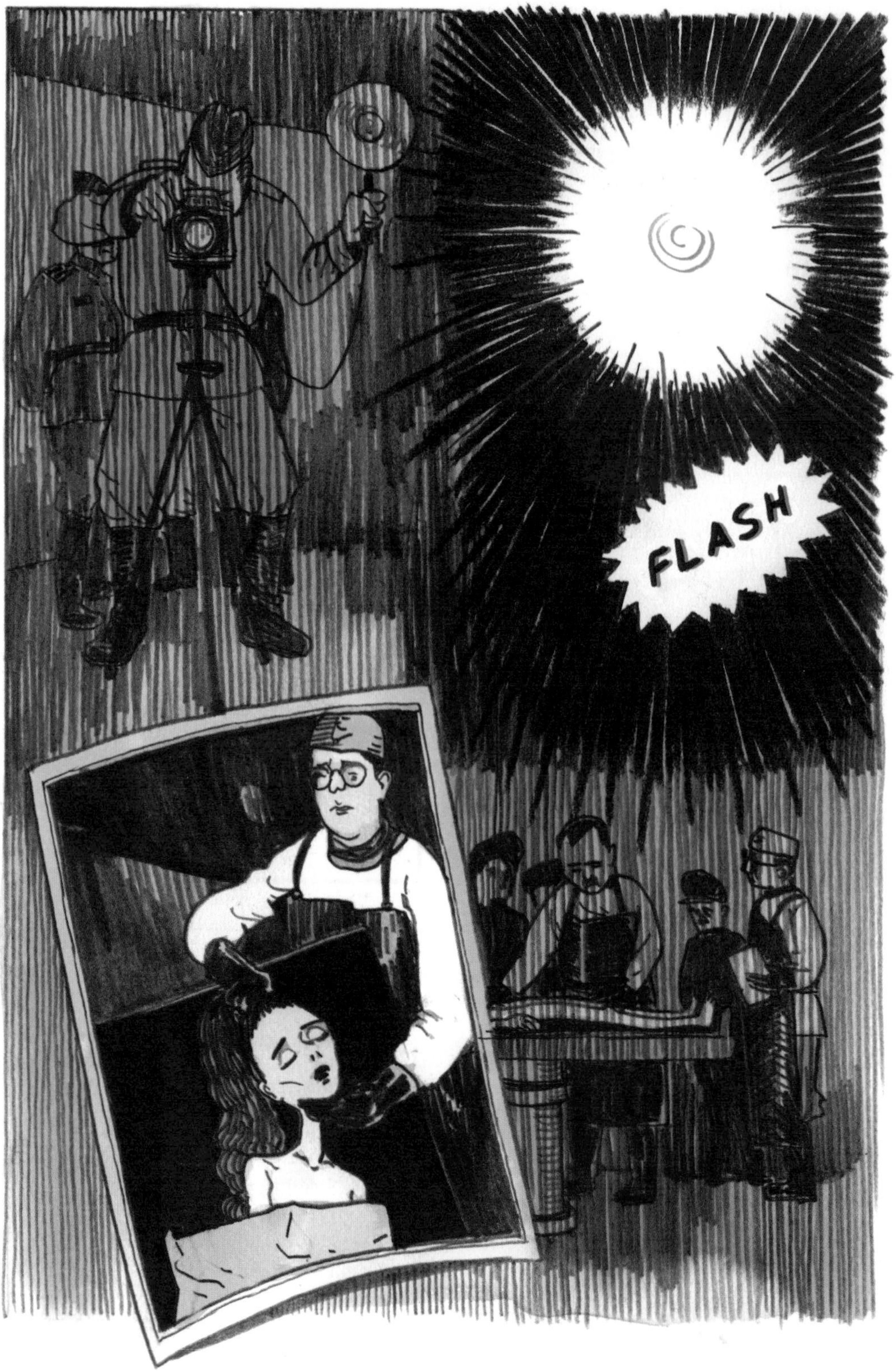
FLASH

The following report was compiled during the autopsy on Helga's corpse:

External examination:
The body is that of a girl about fifteen years old in appearance, well-nourished, and wearing a pale blue nightgown trimmed with lace. Height: one meter fifty-eight. Circumference of chest at nipple level: sixty-five centimeters. Color of skin and visible mucous membranes: pink to cherry-red. Back of the body mottled with red post-mortem lividities that can no longer be dispersed. Fingernails bluish. Skin in the region of the shoulder blades and buttocks noticeably pale owing to pressure. Abdominal skin dull green, discolored by putrefaction. Head macrocephalous with flat temples. Hair long, dark brown, plaited. Face oval, tapering towards the chin. Eyebrows dark brown, eyelashes long, irises blue. Nose straight, regular, small. Eyes and mouth closed. Tip of tongue loosely gripped between the teeth. When the body was turned over and pressure applied to the thorax, serous fluid seeped from the mouth and nose and a very faint smell of bitter almonds could be detected. Rib cage normally developed, nipples small, no hair visible in the armpits, abdomen flat. External sexual organs normally developed. Labia majora and mons veneris hirsute as far as the pubic symphysis.

Internal examination:
Mucous membrane somewhat bluish. Intestinal contents unexceptional. Womb firm, four centimeters long, three centimeters wide and two centimeters thick at the oviduct. Vagina slit-shaped, hymen intact.

Although the autopsy report speaks of plaits, the photograph shows Helga with her hair loose. Who undid the corpse's plaits?

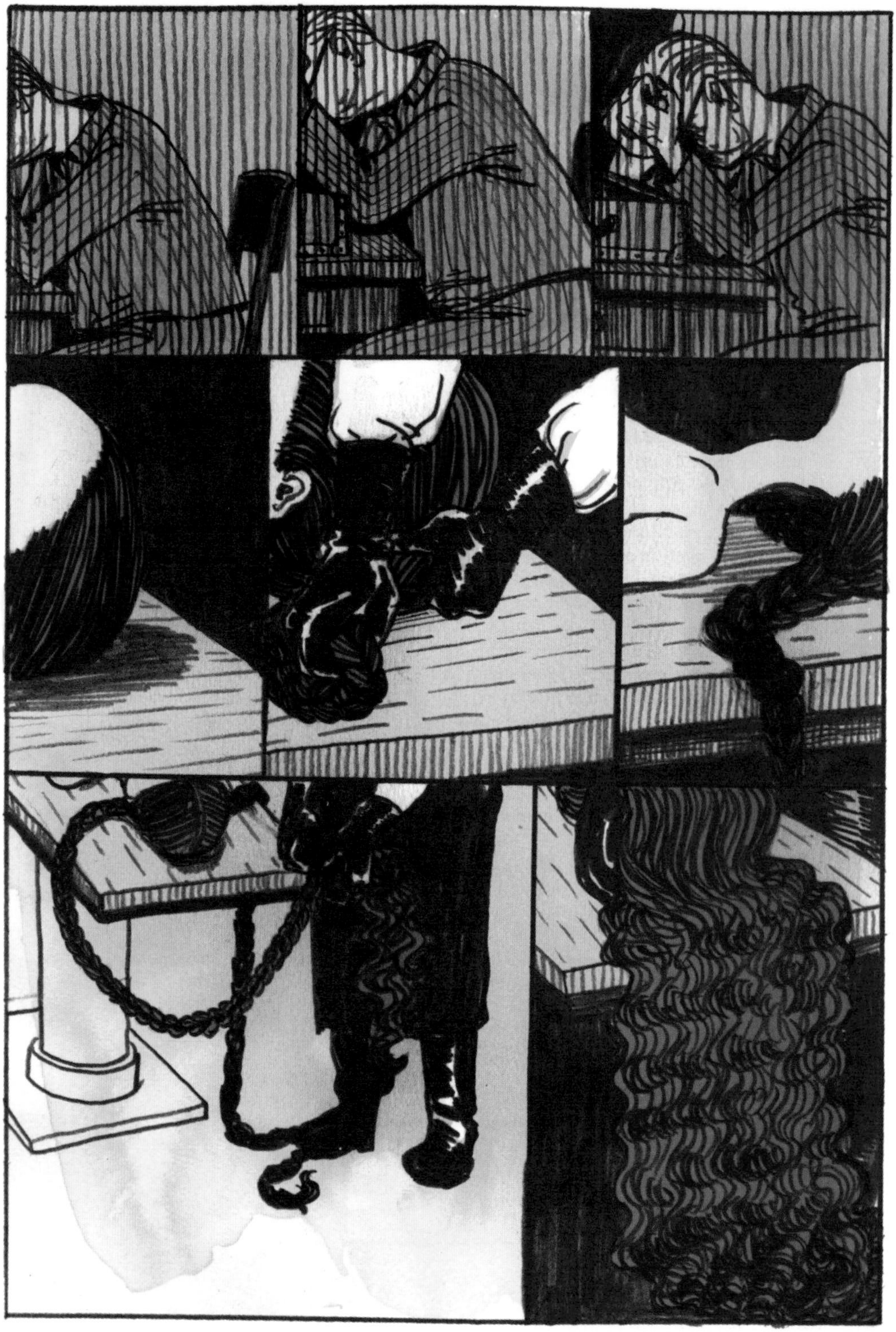

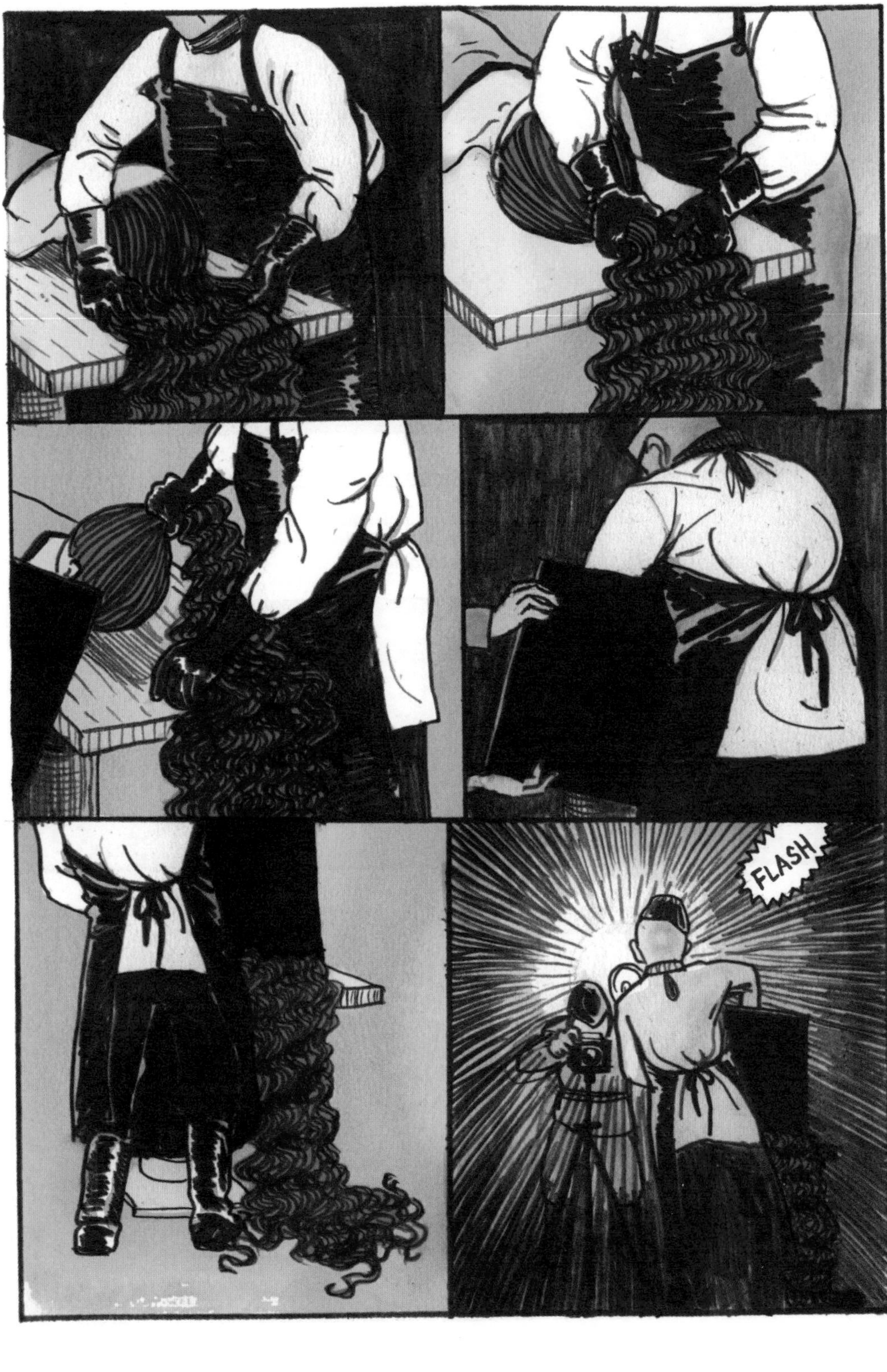
FLASH

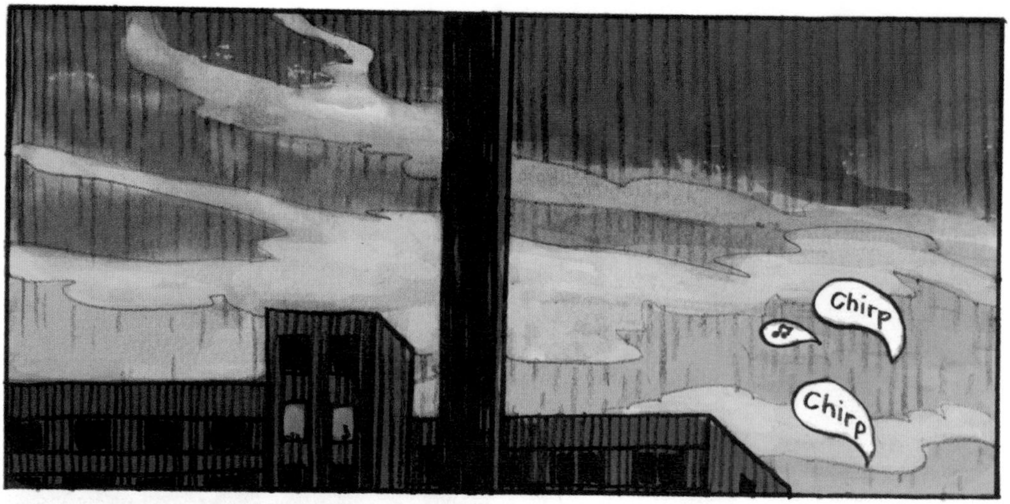
Chirp
Chirp

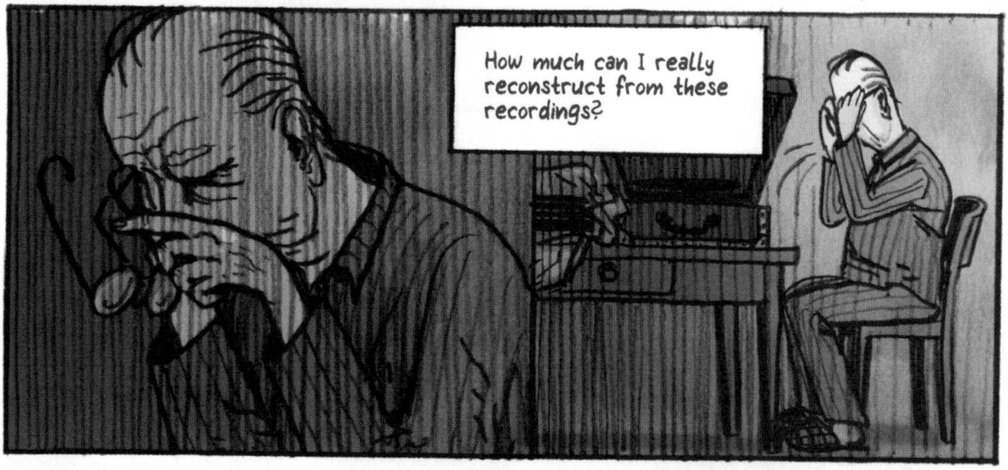
How much can I really reconstruct from these recordings?

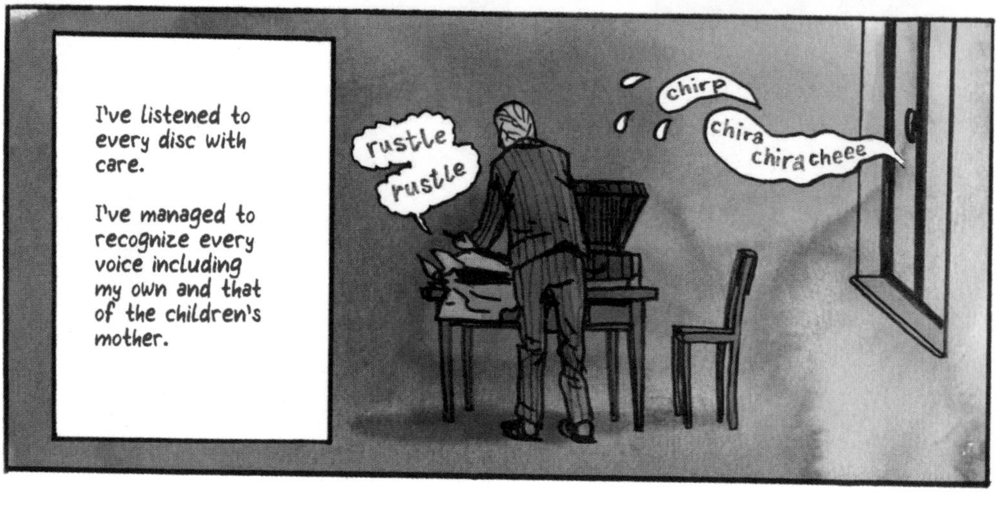
I've listened to every disc with care.
I've managed to recognize every voice including my own and that of the children's mother.
rustle
rustle
chirp
chira
chira cheee

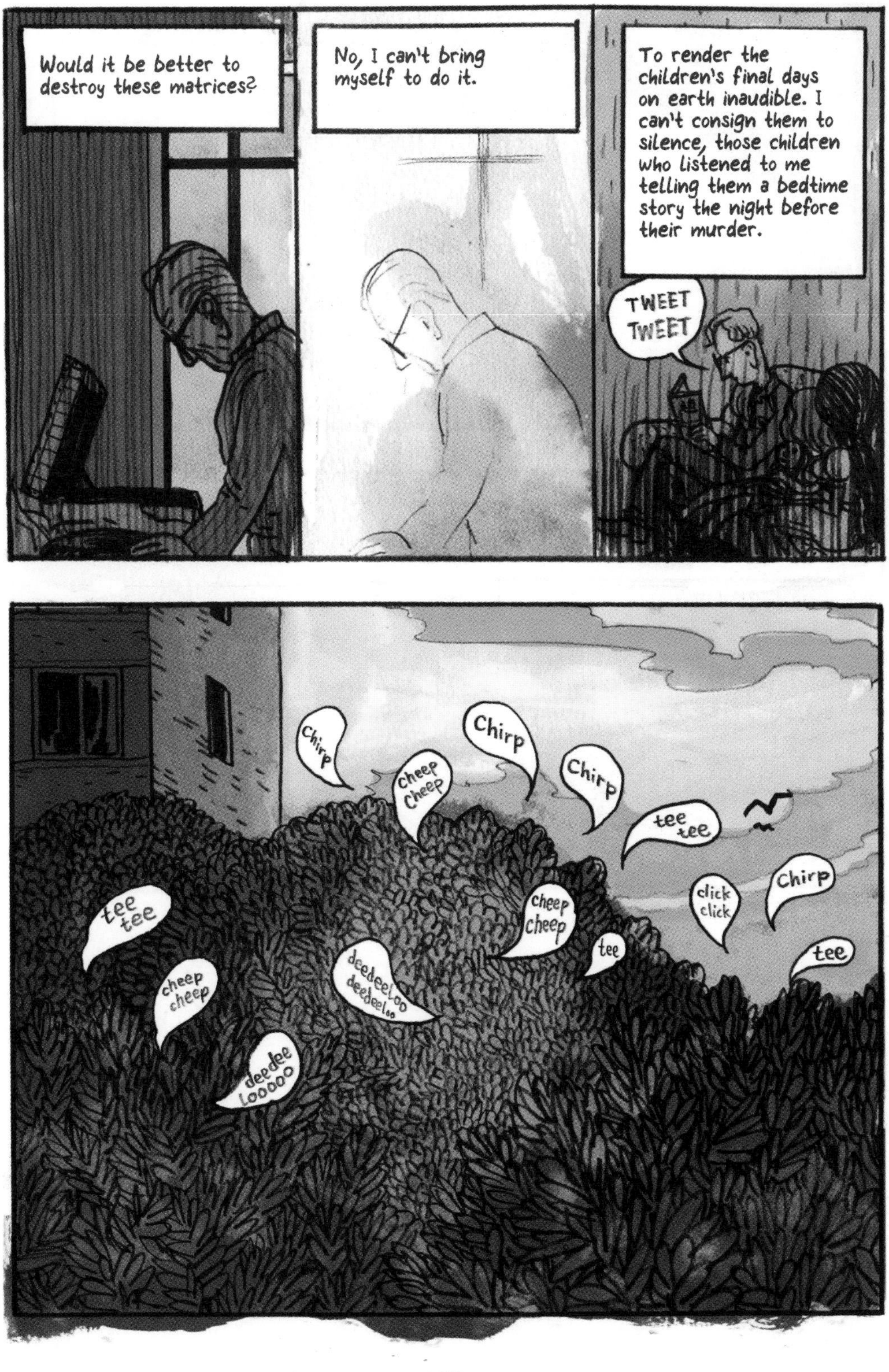
Would it be better to destroy these matrices?
No, I can't bring myself to do it.
To render the children's final days on earth inaudible. I can't consign them to silence, those children who listened to me telling them a bedtime story the night before their murder.
TWEET TWEET
Chirp
Chirp
cheep cheep
Chirp
tee tee
Chirp
click click
tee tee
cheep cheep
tee
tee
cheep cheep
deedeeloo deedeeloo
deedee looooo

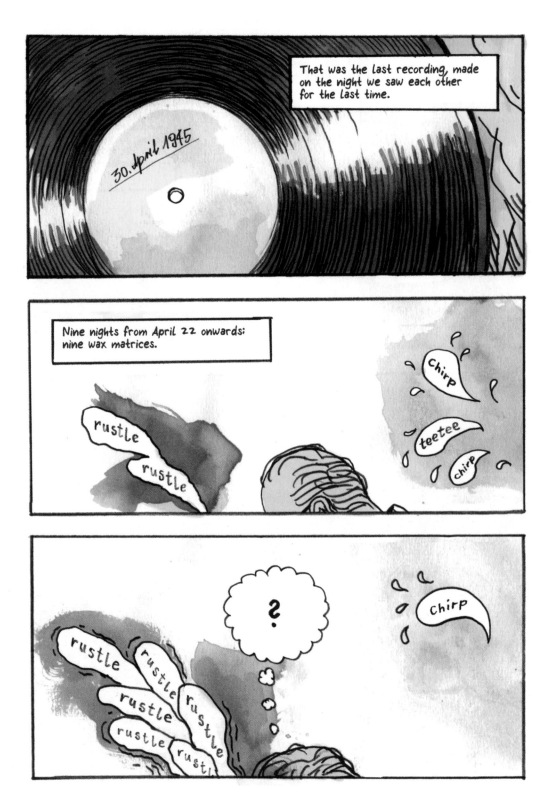

That was the last recording, made on the night we saw each other for the last time.

30. April 1945

Nine nights from April 22 onwards: nine wax matrices.

rustle
rustle

chirp
teetee
chirp

?

rustle
rustle
rustle
rustle
rustle
rustle

Chirp

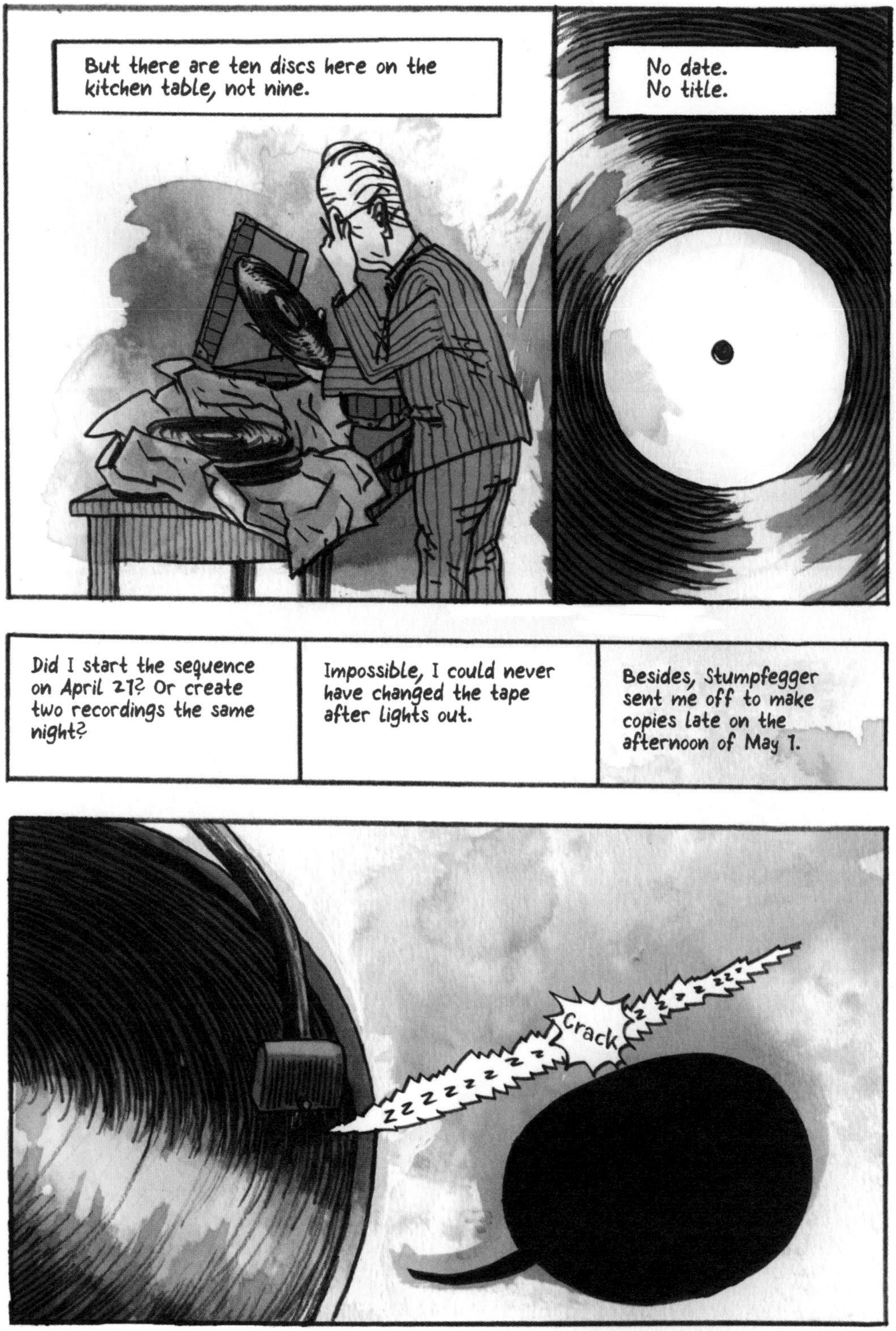
But there are ten discs here on the kitchen table, not nine.
No date.
No title.
Did I start the sequence on April 27? Or create two recordings the same night?
Impossible, I could never have changed the tape after lights out.
Besides, Stumpfegger sent me off to make copies late on the afternoon of May 1.
ZZZZZZZZZ
Crack
ZZZZZZZ

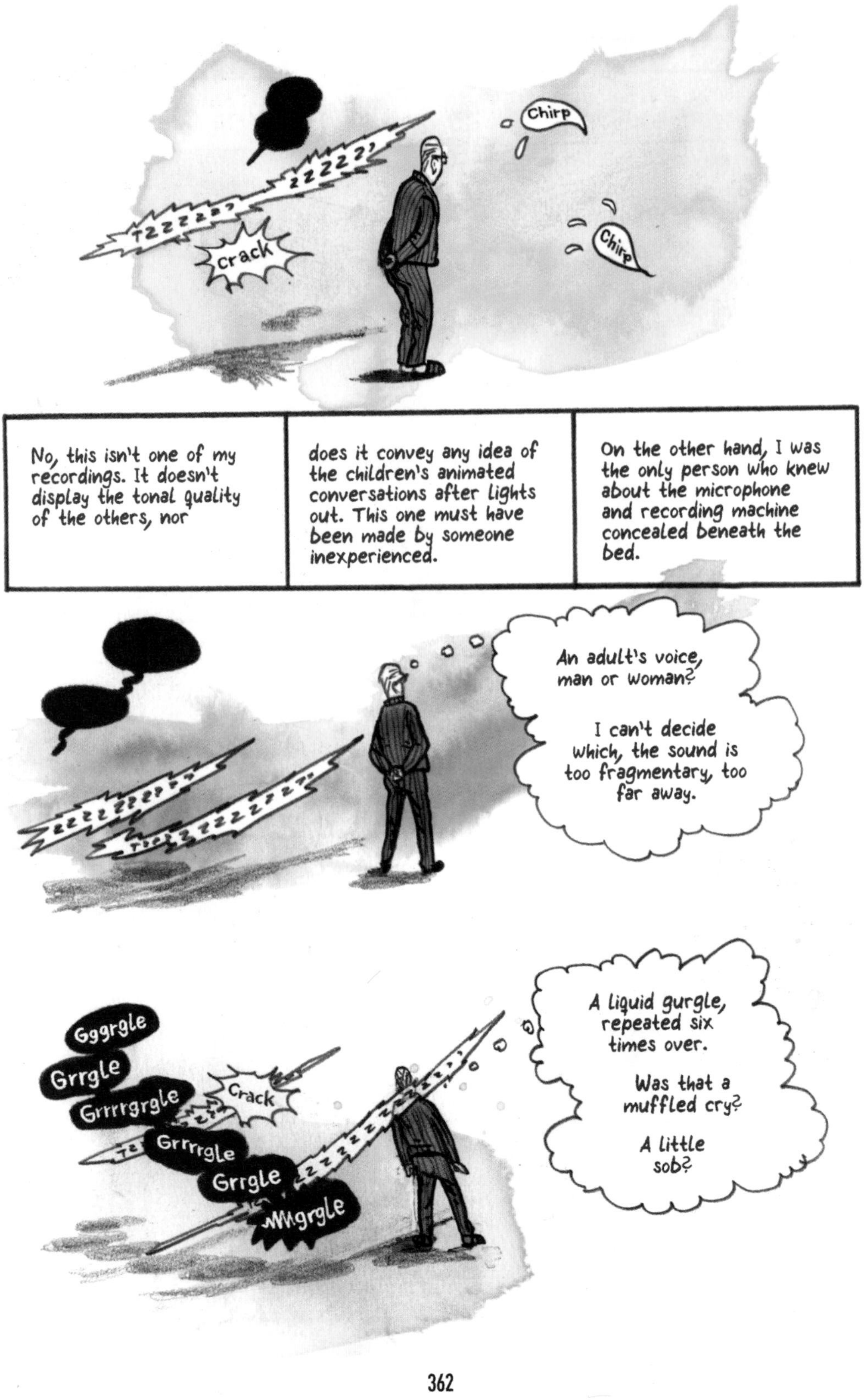
Chirp
Chirp
Crack
No, this isn't one of my recordings. It doesn't display the tonal quality of the others, nor
does it convey any idea of the children's animated conversations after lights out. This one must have been made by someone inexperienced.
On the other hand, I was the only person who knew about the microphone and recording machine concealed beneath the bed.
An adult's voice, man or woman?
I can't decide which, the sound is too fragmentary, too far away.
Gggrgle
Grrgle
Grrrrgrgle
Crack
Grrrrgle
Grrgle
Mmgrgle
A liquid gurgle, repeated six times over.
Was that a muffled cry?
A little sob?